TRAUMA
IN THE AGED

TRAUMA
IN THE AGED

Editor

EDGAR M. BICK, M.D.

Introduction by

ROBERT H. KENNEDY, M.D.

Contributors

Edgar M. Bick, M.D.
Leonard Brand, M.D.
Paul W. Braunstein, M.D.
John F. Daly, M.D.
John W. Draper, M.D.
Alexander Garcia, Jr., M.D.
William J. German, M.D.
Robert H. Kennedy, M.D.
Robert K. Lippmann, M.D.

John L. Madden, M.D.
E. M. Papper, M.D.
Mieczyslaw Peszczynski, M.D.
Walter A. Petryshyn, M.D.
Bernard E. Simon, M.D.
John E. Sullivan, M.D.
Joseph Trueta, M.D.
Preston A. Wade, M.D.
Robert H. Wylie, M.D.

The Blakiston Division–McGRAW-HILL BOOK COMPANY, INC.
New York   Toronto   London

TO MY WIFE

from whom the time was borrowed

Contributors

EDGAR M. BICK, M.A., M.D., F.A.C.S.
> Attending Orthopedic Surgeon, The Mount Sinai Hospital, St. Clare's Hospital; Consulting Orthopedic Surgeon, Brookhaven Hospital, New York.

LEONARD BRAND, M.D., F.A.C.An.
> Assistant Professor of Anesthesiology, Columbia University College of Physicians and Surgeons; Assistant Attending Anesthesiologist in Anesthesiology Service of the Presbyterian Hospital, New York.

PAUL W. BRAUNSTEIN, M.D., F.A.C.S.
> Assistant Professor Clinical Surgery, Cornell University Medical College; Assistant Attending Surgeon, New York Hospital; Senior Attending Surgeon, Good Samaritan Hospital, West Islip, N.Y.

JOHN F. DALY, M.D.
> Professor and Chairman, Department of Otolaryngology, New York University Bellevue Medical Center; Director of Otolaryngology, Bellevue Hospital; Director of Otolaryngology, University Hospital, New York.

JOHN W. DRAPER, M.D.
> Associate Professor Surgery [Urology], Cornell University Medical College, Associate Attending Surgeon [Urology], New York Hospital; Surgeon in Charge Second Division [Urology] Cornell, Bellevue Hospital, New York.

ALEXANDER GARCIA, JR., M.D., F.A.C.S.
> Assistant Professor of Clinical Orthopedic Surgery, Columbia University College of Physicians and Surgeons; Assistant Attending Orthopedic Surgeon, New York Orthopedic Hospital, Columbia-Presbyterian Medical Center; Attending Surgeon, Chief of Orthopedic Surgery Section, North Shore Hospital, Manhasset, New York.

WILLIAM J. GERMAN, M.D.
> Professor of Neurosurgery, Yale University School of Medicine, New Haven, Conn.

ROBERT H. KENNEDY, M.D., F.A.C.S.
> Formerly Professor Clinical Surgery, New York University Post-Graduate

Medical School; Consulting Surgeon, Bellevue, University, and Beekman-Downtown Hospitals, New York.

ROBERT K. LIPPMANN, M.D., F.A.C.S.

Director, Department of Orthopedic Surgery, Mount Sinai Hospital, New York.

JOHN L. MADDEN, M.D., F.A.C.S.

Director, Department of Surgery, St. Clare's Hospital, New York, New York; Associate Clinical Professor of Surgery, New York Medical College, New York.

E. M. PAPPER, M.D.

Professor of Anesthesiology and Chairman of the Department, Columbia University College of Physicians and Surgeons; Director of Anesthesiology Service, The Presbyterian Hospital, New York.

MIECZYSLAW PESZCZYNSKI, M.D.

Associate Professor of Physical Medicine and Rehabilitation, Department of Medicine, Western Reserve University School of Medicine; Chief, Department of Physical Medicine and Rehabilitation, Highland View Hospital, Cleveland, Ohio.

WALTER A. PETRYSHYN, M.D., F.A.C.S.

Assistant Professor Clinical Otolaryngology; New York University Post-Graduate Medical School; Director, Otolaryngology, Hunterdon Medical Center, Flemington, N.J.

BERNARD E. SIMON, M.D.

Assistant Clinical Professor of Surgery, Albert Einstein College of Medicine; Assistant Attending Surgeon for Plastic Surgery, The Mount Sinai Hospital and Bronx Municipal Hospital Center, New York.

JOHN E. SULLIVAN, M.D.

Associate Professor of Clinical Surgery, New York University College of Medicine; Consulting Surgeon, Hospital for Special Surgery; Consulting Surgeon, Bellevue Hospital; Attending Surgeon, St. Vincent's Hospital; Assistant Surgeon, New York Hospital, New York.

JOSEPH TRUETA, M.D.

Nuffield Professor of Orthopedic Surgery, Oxford University, England.

PRESTON A. WADE, M.D., F.A.C.S.

Professor Clinical Surgery, Cornell University Medical College; Attending Surgeon, New York Hospital; Chief Combined Fracture Service, Hospital for Special Surgery, New York Hospital, New York.

ROBERT H. WYLIE, M.D., F.A.C.S.

Clinical Professor of Surgery, Columbia University College of Physicians and Surgeons; Attending Surgeon, The Presbyterian Hospital; Visiting Surgeon and Director of Chest Surgical Service, Bellevue Hospital, New York.

Preface

The recent and rapid increase of "senior citizens" in the world's population has presented contemporary society with urgent new problems in sociology, public economy, and medicine. To a large extent, and particularly in its clinical aspect, it has become a matter of daily concern to medical practice. This book was prepared as an attempt to aid in one facet of the problem. Several of its contributors have already published studies on clinical problems of the aged in their respective specialties. Others, in fields where no previous significant work has been done, have drawn from their personal experience and the observations of their colleagues to extract relevant material.

The preparation of this book would not have been possible but for the serious interest of its contributors in the subject. This volume is a compilation of their experience and their thoughts in a challenging field of surgery. The editor felt privileged to be one of them. I am very grateful for their willingness to accept the challenge and the congenial spirit of collaboration which was maintained throughout the working period.

Miss Helen Kleinwechter, whose sustained efforts in her capacity as assistant to the editor helped so much to bring the work to its completion, has earned his particular gratitude.

EDGAR M. BICK

Contents

Part IV   Injuries to the Aged Somatic Tissues

Part V   Rehabilitation of the Aged

TRAUMA
IN THE AGED

The Special Problem

Robert H. Kennedy

Aged is an indefinite and elastic term. Chronological and biological age commonly have no relation to one another. In fact, the two seldom coincide. The causes of differences in biological age are so many and so varied in character that no common base line is readily determinable. Therefore we must fall back on chronological age as the only referable factor, although this may do an injustice to a great many senior citizens. Sixty-five is a frequent age for compulsory retirement from business, teaching, or other professional work associated with institutions. In recent years there has been a subtle tendency, especially in nonprofit institutions and organizations, to reduce this toward 60. By government directive, however, 65 remains the age when old age assistance commences. By editorial agreement, statistical studies will start in this book at 60, since these years represent a rather fluid borderline biologically.

The presence of large numbers of older people in today's society is without historical precedent. At the time of the Roman Empire, life expectancy at birth was 23 years. In the United States, in 1900, it was 49. Half a century later, in 1956, it rose to 69.6 (67.3 for white males and 73.7 for white females). This rapid increase in the number of the aged, present and continuing, has become a challenging and all but overwhelming problem. Advances in the techniques of civilization, constantly higher physical standards of living, control of infectious diseases of infancy and childhood, improved medical care, and the advent of chemotherapy and antibiotics have all contributed to this changing character of our populations. Between 1900 and 1950 the total population of the United States doubled, but the number of persons over 65 quadrupled. Since 1920, senior citizens have been the most rapidly growing segment of the population. Currently (1958) the expectation of life at age 65 is more than 14 years.

In 1900 persons over 65 made up 4.1 per cent of the population and in 1950, 8.2 per cent. It is estimated that in 1980 this group will constitute

14.4 per cent of a population of between 220 and 225 million people. One out of every twelve United States citizens today is over 65 years of age, making a total of about 14 million. The U.S. Census Bureau has estimated that in 1975 there will be 20.7 million people over 65 years of age, of whom 12 million will be females and 8.7 million males.

Is this steadily increasing unit of the population more or less prone to accident than younger persons? Accidents are the leading cause of death from 1 to 36 years of age, and tie for first place with heart disease from then to 44 years. From 45 to 64 years of age, accidents drop to fourth place behind heart disease, cancer, and vascular lesions affecting the central nervous system. For 65 years and over, general arteriosclerosis is also ahead of accidents, putting the latter in fifth place among causes of death.

However, the relative importance of trauma appears quite different when one considers the number of deaths from accident per 100,000 people in each age group, as follows:

Under one year	96
1–4 years	31
5–14 years	20
15–24 years	63
25–44 years	45
45–64 years	56
65 years and over	184

The high rate of death in this last group is due largely to failure to recover from injuries.

Death resulting from falls occurs 105 times per 100,000 in the group 65 years of age and over, whereas it occurs 9 times in the 45- to 64-year group and considerably less in all the others. Death from motor-vehicle accidents occurs 41 times per 100,000 in the group 65 and over compared with 43 in the group 15 to 24 and much less in all the other groups. Fire burns cause death 12 times in each 100,000 in the 65 years and over group, whereas the next highest death rate from this cause is 7 out of 100,000 in the group under 1 year. Drowning is a less common cause of death in old age than in earlier years. It should be explained that in these statistics death from accident means "an injury which terminates fatally within one year of the date of accident." This includes, for example, deaths which occur days, weeks, or months after nailing a fractured hip. Some of these deaths may be due to the character of initial or aftercare.

Of the 95,000 deaths from accident in the United States in 1957, 27,200 occurred in the 65 and over age group, nearly 29 per cent of the total. The types of accidents in this age group with number of deaths are as follows:

Falls	15,400
Motor-vehicle accidents	5,950
Fire burns	1,800
Drowning	450
Railroad accidents	400
Poison gases	250
Firearms	200
Poisons, solid or liquid	130
All other types	2,800

Seventy-four per cent of all the deaths from falls in 1957 were in the 65 and over age group, and three-fourths of these deaths occurred in the home.

For purposes of medical care, Fox divided the aged as (1) the elderly, (2) the elderly and infirm, (3) the elderly sick, (4) the elderly psychiatric, and (5) special groups: blind, deaf, etc. This classification is important in determining the kind of treatment necessary following injury, since each of these groups may require some modification of an otherwise properly indicated procedure. It emphasizes the principle that an individual has been hurt rather than a bone broken or an abdomen punctured.

The economic factor plays an important role in the community problem of trauma in the aged. The economic consequence is to be found in the fact that in general hospitals, of all admissions at all ages, the average duration of stay is 10.1 days. For the group 65 and over, for all conditions, the average stay is 22.5 days, more than twice as long as the general average. A 1957 survey by the Department of Health, Education and Welfare showed that at least 43 per cent of persons over 65 are covered by Blue Cross or similar plans. As the aged increase in number, more beds will be needed. Paying for these increased facilities will pose a tremendous problem to the general economy. Planning for this must start now and should not be put off until the backlog is overwhelming.

It is easy to say that more injured people must be cared for at home, but too often this forces an otherwise employable member of the family to remain at home to care for the elderly person. Who will assume the financial responsibility for prolonged convalescence or a resulting permanent disability? In spite of age, the patient may have had a certain earning capacity. Will economic independence be lost now? Was there just enough assured income to equal expenses, and no extra cushion with which to pay hospital bills of unknown duration? Is the psychological reaction to posttraumatic disability one of preferring death to becoming a burden to anyone—family, friends, or society?

The pathologic physiology of the traumatized aged individual plays a major role in his initial and definitive care, his later progress, and his chance of living to ultimate recovery. Stieglitz noted that "elderly people often maintain relative homeostasis with a very narrow margin of safety. They appear to enjoy good health by combining a diet deficient in calories, proteins, vitamins, and water with a protected and clocklike life of restricted activity." Anything which upsets this routine may tip the scales and result in tragedy. Elderly people are less flexible in responding to changes in environment, and they convalesce more slowly than do younger adults. Muscle mass and bone matrix, lost during periods of forced inactivity, are restored more slowly and less completely. It has been shown that the average healing period for industrial injuries is longer as age progresses. Among 26,000 workers in four plants the average healing period for the 21- to 24-year group was 23 days, for the 40- to 44-year group it was 30 days, and for 50 years and over, 34 days. On the other hand, the older workers consistently have fewer injuries than the younger ones. In general, the specific treatment of the actual injury varies little among individuals of advanced years and younger persons. However, the problem of the whole management of the aged individual who has suffered an injury includes many important, and even critical, factors not usually stressed in younger persons.

The extent of activity of the person prior to his accident needs emphasis. The majority were up and about doing something of importance to them or they would not have been in a situation where an accident could have occurred. Our aim must be to return them to their earlier condition in the shortest possible time and with the least risk. The minority were mentally incompetent, bedridden, or chair-fast before the accident. They may even have sustained a so-called "spontaneous" fracture from osteoporosis or a pathologic fracture from chronic bone disease. It is not rational to subject them to some treatment which requires early ambulation, either with or without crutches, when they have not walked for months or years. If immobilization is required, this should be instituted in such a manner that nursing care is practical and painless and that deterioration will not result from allowing the patient to lie like a log.

It is important to determine whether the individual was accustomed to physical activity or not, or whether he was mentally and emotionally interested in affairs before the accident. How did he spend his time? Did he have a job? If so, is the nature of the injury likely to prevent him from returning to it? Can he do any part of his regular work while convalescing? Has some hobby kept him alert and stimulated him to go on living? May the injury keep him permanently from continuing to pursue this hobby? Can it be kept up equally well during the period of bed and chair life required for recovery?

Often the confinement following injury forces a person, for the first time in years, to stop to survey the usefulness and future of his life, and he may feel that he has come to a "dead end." Strictly speaking, he is no different immediately after his injury than before except for one or more broken parts, which will usually mend in time. He is no sicker than before the accident, and he must not be allowed to feel that he is. He should not be pampered by family or friends or have to listen to everlasting inquiries as to how he is getting along. He should be treated as a well person and urged to carry on every activity possible within the limits allowed by his broken part.

The attending physician must be aware of all these factors and be prepared to act as an adviser. They are at least equally as important as is the care of the injured part. A well-healed fracture is no asset in a dead person or in one whose chief ambition is to die. Exercise of all uninjured parts should be insisted on from the first day. This does not mean heat, massage, and diathermy. It means the doctor's detailed instructions for active motion of every joint not immediately adjacent to the injured part several times a day, at definite times, and for definite periods. One does not try to make an athlete out of this elderly person but to keep him at least as active as before the accident. Joints and muscles cannot be as easily rehabilitated in an elderly person as in a young person, so deterioration should be prevented at the outset.

If a person is to walk with crutches, his triceps muscles will have to bear a major part of the burden. Lifting his trunk by means of his hands on an overhead bar exercises biceps only. Pushing his trunk up from the bed by arms at his side will develop the triceps. Also, with crutch walking, he will probably bear weight on one foot only. To be able to bear all his weight on one good foot, he must exercise his uninjured leg actively, regularly, and effectively from the day of injury so that it will carry its load promptly at the proper time in his recovery.

In addition to insisting on physical activity the physician must constantly urge the continuation of work, social activities, or hobbies, or introduce new work or new hobbies which really absorb the individual's interest and fill his time within all practical limits. If there is an economic problem or source of worry, it is the physician's duty to explore this and propose possible plans for the future as far as possible in the first few days, otherwise his patient may not recover. If it is probable that there will be permanent crippling or incapacity, this must be faced in the early days and possible solutions made known to the patient. There is everything to be lost by postponing thorough discussion. Probably the patient knows what he is up against fully as well as the surgeon does, and indecision as to the future will delay his recovery much more than being given a definite possible solution to work toward. If even a grain of humor exists in his personality, this should be fostered to the limit.

One must pay attention to what these patients ask for. They have probably learned the easiest way for them to live comfortably; otherwise they would not be alive so long. If the patient has smoked most of his life, he should be allowed to continue. It is not the physician's duty to try to change the patient's lifelong habits unless the physician feels certain that they are harming the patient. At the same time, he should be kept on no more than his usual amount of tobacco since everyone is likely to smoke more when his time is less occupied. If he is accustomed to alcohol, let him imbibe to his usual tolerance. Persuade the dietitian to play up to the patient's idiosyncrasies for food within the limits of hospital diets. It may be childish of him not to like spinach, but there is no reason to try to change him now. An adequate diet will not affect the healing of a fracture in the slightest, although one would like to see him get the calcium in one glass of milk a day unless he is allergic to it. If he is always constipated and takes some medication daily, give him the same thing, even if it is not in the hospital formulary. If he is not usually constipated, do not make him so by continually cleaning out his bowels. If he regularly takes something for sleep, do not try to break him of the habit or to change him to a new drug. In other words, try as nearly as possible to let him live the life he has been used to living for so long.

In the aged, the presence of edema requires even more attention than it does in younger people. Its persistence is more likely to result in joint, tendon, and muscle adhesions. Elevate the injured part early and persistently for this. But remember, particularly in the lower extremities, that elevation even to the horizontal in an arteriosclerotic may result in lack of arterial pulse and therefore local anoxemia. Phlebitis is a more common complication at this age. Change in the walls of the veins is likely to preexist; lack of subcutaneous fat and sluggishness in movement may result in greater pressure on vessels with less filling. Viscosity may be high since many of these patients take little fluid. Observation for phlebitis needs to be carried out daily. Decubitus is too common. I cannot subscribe to the theory that its incidence and treatment is the nurse's responsibility. Certainly good nursing does much to prevent it, but there is no excuse for the surgeon not knowing that redness of the skin is present long before the actual embolic process appears and advising and supporting the nurse in routine care.

Prostatic congestion and hypertrophy will be common in the old men. One often learns that there has never been a suggestion of retention before the present confinement to bed. Catheterization may increase the congestion further. Many will require a prostatectomy as soon as the condition of the injured part allows the movement required for positioning on the operating table. Return of the ability to void normally seems to occur rarely in such cases after serious trauma.

Diabetes and arteriosclerosis seem to make little difference in fracture healing, except for the danger of infection and gangrene in open wounds or secondary infections about the feet.

In any type of injury to an arthritic patient, the process is likely to be activated with resulting increased pain and disability. Recovery is more prolonged, and it is difficult to determine when symptoms are no longer due to injury but to reactivation or increase in the arthritic process. In a back injury the x-ray film may show no abnormality except a minimal arthritis. The pain may be severe and persistent. The ligaments and joint capsule are often much more thickened than is suggested by the amount of ossification or calcium deposit which can be seen. Flexibility has been diminished by the arthritic process and a minor strain of the back may result in torn fibers causing further pain, scarring, and prolonged disability. These persons cannot be brushed off as malingerers or neurotics.

Emergency care of the injured at the scene of accident, in the office, or in the emergency room is in general the same at all ages. This aspect of trauma in the aged has been considered in detail in several of the following chapters. However, certain basic rules must be emphasized. Remember that morphine is for the relief of pain and is contraindicated in older people except when they are in pain. Otherwise, with reestablishment of the circulation on recovering from shock, mobilization of the morphine may result in respiratory depression and perhaps even death. Intravenous fluids, particularly blood, are needed in traumatic shock. These fluids must be administered thoughtfully. In patients of advanced years, this means that they should be given no more rapidly than absolutely required, since the right side of the heart must be protected early and the kidneys later. We must keep in mind the increased danger of a cerebrovascular accident when blood pressure returns to a high level after it has been markedly lowered by shock. There is greater danger of permanent brain, heart, or kidney damage from allowing shock and anoxemia to persist than there is in younger persons. "Oldsters" have less reserve to balance prolonged anoxemia.

There is often much delay in obtaining medical clearance before a required operative procedure. This is particularly true in fractures of the neck of the femur. Except for shock, the patient may never be in better operative condition than he is immediately after an injury. If he has previously been active, he does not need a more thorough checkup preoperatively than does a younger person. If he needs operation and is out of shock, waiting for a report on his blood urea nitrogen or blood sugar is not going to be the factor which saves his life. If an abdominal injury is believed to require operation, this should be performed as soon as shock has been overcome, as in a younger person, without waiting for laboratory reports and arguments as to the condition of vital organs. Otherwise death may result. However, this does not imply undue haste; mandatory examinations cannot be avoided.

Some degree of physiological shock persists even after the patient has gained a degree of consciousness. Coming out of shock must include pulse and blood-pressure return, and fair physiological stability, or further shock may occur following the new trauma of surgery or manipulation.

Burns are particularly serious in older persons. In a recent study by Ziffren of 34 burned elderly people at the University of Iowa Hospitals, there were 15 deaths. Of these, all but one occurred after the initial shock at an average of four days (see Chap. 5). This may signify a tendency to more rapid deterioration after fluid loss, physical inactivity, and periods of negative nitrogen balance. By preference, fluids should be given by mouth whenever possible. The specific gravity of the urine and its output needs to be carefully watched. "Sludging" of blood is more marked and emboli are an ever-present danger.

When a person is found unconscious, the question arises frequently whether a cerebral accident has been spontaneous or the result of external trauma. Even with an x-ray film showing a fracture of the skull the diagnosis is not proved. The patient may have fallen because of a "stroke" and sustained a fracture of the skull in his fall. The presenting unconscious condition may be based on spontaneous cerebral hemorrhage or on extradural or subdural clot or intracerebral damage from the fall. Unless this is kept constantly in mind, tragedy may result from failure to recognize an extradural or subdural clot which might be relieved by craniotomy. Further, negative x-ray findings do not necessarily rule out a *contrecoup* injury which may be fatal if uncared for. On recovery of consciousness, even with paralysis present, we must remember that present-day treatment calls for early mobilization of the patient no matter what was the primary cause of unconsciousness.

In complicated open fractures, early amputation may often be preferable to prolonged care in the presence of sepsis. Attempts to preserve a part by long hospital treatment may be worthwhile in a younger person but foolhardy in the aged, who cannot look forward to a very long future. Pathological fractures, such as through an area of metastatic carcinoma in bone, deserve just as adequate fracture treatment as any other type, since the patient may thereby be made comfortable and the fracture will frequently unite.

We must manage our aged who suffer injury in a way to assure as few useless cripples as possible. For the individual and for society, mental, emotional, or economic crippling following accident is just as much of a loss as physical disablement. We must treat the injured part to the best of our knowledge and at the same time instill in the individual continued hope or expectancy for future recovery.

In the chapters which follow the means of fulfilling these requirements will be discussed in some detail by specialists in their respective fields. The table of contents will indicate the breadth of care which is demanded, ranging from physiological understanding of the special effects of trauma in the aged, clinical procedures which have proven useful, and closing with the important phases of posttraumatic rehabilitation, both physical and psychiatric. The full picture of the aged victim of trauma must always be kept in mind. This is of course true of all patients; it is vital in any elderly person.

BIBLIOGRAPHY

Angel, J. L.: The length of life in ancient Greece. *Jour. Geront.* **2**:18, 1947.

Fox, J.: "The Chronically Ill." New York, Philosophic Library, 1957.

Kennedy, R. H.: Management of injuries in the aged. *Bull. N.Y. Acad. Med.* **32**:487, 1956.

Kirk, D.: Population characteristics and trends and their implications. *Jour. Amer. Med. Ass.* **167**:26, 1958.

Kossaris, M. D.: U.S. Dept. of Labor. *Monthly Labor Review.* Oct., 1940.

National Safety Council: "Accident Facts." Chicago, Ill., 1958.

New York State Legislative Committee on Problems of the Aging: "Making the Years Count," report by Thomas C. Desmond, Chairman. Albany, N.Y., 1955.

Shock, N. W.: "Trends in Gerontology." Stanford, Calif., Stanford University Press, 1957.

Stieglitz, E. J.: "Geriatric Medicine," 3d ed. Philadelphia, Lippincott, 1954.

Waxman, B.: *Population Index.* **23**:210, 1957.

Whittenberger, J. L.: The nature of the response to stress with aging. *Bull. N.Y. Acad. Med.* **32**:487, 1956.

Ziffren, S. E.: Management of the burned patient. *Jour. Amer. Ger. Soc.* **3**:36, 1955.

Part I

Pathologic Physiology of Trauma in the Aged

Chapter 1

Traumatic Shock

John E. Sullivan

In the aged the effect of shock on the individual organs of the body is usually more severe than it is in healthy young adults, and resuscitation is not as easily accomplished. This is due to several factors. There is, of course, an increased incidence of organic disease in elderly people. The autonomic nervous and endocrine systems, even in the intact older person, do not respond as readily to stress. Reduced blood volumes in patients prior to injury are more common because of either debilitating disease or inadequate diet. There is apt to be especially insufficient protein reserve. A disturbed electrolytic balance is characteristic of the chronically ill elderly patient. Many older people have received prolonged rauwolfia or corticosteroid therapy which further affects their response to stress and shock.

The shock state is a complex syndrome, the pathophysiology of which is far from being adequately understood. Its clinical management is even more hazardous when the organs of the body are not normally resilient. It may be difficult in the aged to differentiate the shock of trauma from that caused by coincident coronary thrombosis at the time of injury. Renal suppression may be the consequence of shock, or may be complicated by chronic, intrinsic renal disease. The patient who has had prolonged corticosteroid therapy may have atrophy of the adrenal cortex and may be subject to shock from much less stress than one in good health. Determining the cause and the effects of shock is occasionally difficult in the younger adult, but it is far more frequently a problem in the aged. However, if treatment is timely and proper, older people tolerate shock remarkably well.

Traumatic shock is characterized in most instances by a loss in blood volume. Clinical observations have almost uniformly demonstrated a correlation between the severity of the shock and the extent of its reduction. This reduction may be caused by direct loss of blood as in hemorrhage or by loss of blood or plasma by seepage as in crushing injuries (see Trueta in Chap. 16 on the effects of crush injuries). Massive muscle damage and severe contusions, loss of fluid associated with burns, severe vomiting, diarrhea, intestinal obstruction, and enteric fistulas cause depletion of the active circulation. Certain endocrinological abnormalities, such as an Addisonian crisis, will initiate a similar condition.

There are cardiopulmonary factors which will cause shock. Clinical evidence of this is seen following pulmonary embolism, pericardial tamponade, tension pneumothorax, and myocardial infarction. Reduction of peripheral vascular resistance caused by certain drugs or anesthetics may produce a state of shock. Stresses acting directly upon the central nervous system causing the so-called "vasovagal" or neurogenic shock are often a component of hematogenic shock. Progressive loss of blood from the active circulation may lead to failing cardiac output and anoxia of vital cells with termination in irreversible shock. Renal and hepatic failure may follow sustained hypotension.

Shock of moderate or severe degree develops when the blood volume is reduced by 35 to 40 per cent of its normal value. It has been estimated that when the arterial pressure drops below 100 as a result of blood loss the blood-volume deficit is about 30 per cent. If a reduced blood volume is present prior to trauma, as it often is in elderly people, the patient will be more easily precipitated into shock. Patients who have had a recent weight loss from any of a number of disease states consistently show diminution in blood volume due to both red cell and plasma volume deficits. Bigelow believes that there is a 50 ml deficit in blood volume for every pound of recent weight loss. Therefore, a patient who has had a 20-pound recent weight loss and loses 1,000 ml of blood from hemorrhage may have a deficit of 2,000 ml in total blood volume.

Tissue anoxia is probably the most important physiological alteration which follows decreased blood volume. The reduced volume leads to decreased venous return and to reduction of the cardiac output. In patients with coronary arteriosclerosis, an already limited coronary blood flow may precipitate thrombosis in the diseased coronary vessels or cause myocardial ischemia. Master and Dack have found that electrocardiographic evidence of myocardial ischemia is frequently observed after hemorrhage in elderly patients. Clinical observation of cerebral thrombosis is also not uncommon among older patients who have been in shock following hemorrhage, trauma, or surgery. Thrombosis of the vessels of the kidneys, intestines, lower extremities, and retina is less often described, but does occur.

In order to protect organs which are most vital to existence, such as the central nervous system and the myocardium, there is apparently preferential response to diminished blood volume. This is accomplished by shunt of blood away from the subcutaneous tissues, the skeletal muscles, and the splanchnic area.

Renal blood flow is sharply reduced during shock, and urine formation usually ceases when the arterial pressure falls below 60. After trauma of any type, including surgical trauma, there may be a period of oliguria lasting from 12 to 36 hours, depending upon the severity of the injury. Long periods of shock, major crushing injuries, and severe burns are almost always followed by acute renal failure. In the elderly male with prostatic hypertrophy, difficulty in catheterization or infection of the urinary tract may be further complicating factors.

The liver is particularly vulnerable to damage during shock, and distinct pathological changes in the liver have been described in people dying as a result of shock-producing injury. One probable reason for this is the double blood supply to the liver, furnishing a large venous component to its blood flow and oxygen supply. Impaired liver function has been considered the cause of elevated amino acids, lactic acid, and ammonia found in the blood stream. Regeneration of plasma albumin, prothrombin, and fibrinogen is delayed or ceases during this period. The lowered resistance of the anoxic liver to the bacteria in its tissue and portal system may facilitate irreversibility.

However, in spite of its vulnerability, it is interesting to note how effectively the liver usually responds even in the presence of severe traumatic shock. Hepatic insufficiency is rarely severe enough to cause death after a patient has recovered from the initial phase. There is no direct evidence that the alteration in liver function is of any greater importance in the aged patient than in the young adult.

There is apparently an early and significant increase in the adrenal secretion following trauma. The additional output of adrenal cortical hormones is a defense mechanism of the body, a response to stress, which produces vasoconstriction, cardiac acceleration, and probably splenic contraction. It causes a transient decrease in the urinary volume and excretion of sodium which has a protective effect upon blood volume. Elderly persons with debilitating illness or with dietary deficiencies have a subnormal adrenocortical response to trauma. There is some evidence that the adrenocortical response is diminished in older people, even when they appear to be in good health. A history of prolonged administration of corticosteroids implies probable atrophy of the adrenal cortex. This may become acute if the body is affected by stress, be it trauma, infection, or operation.

Severe infection may produce shock even in the absence of trauma. Sometimes shock is the earliest manifestation of the infection. The mechanism of the production of shock caused by sepsis is not completely understood. It is thought that vasodilatation causes a disparity between the circulating blood volume and the capacity of the vascular bed. Destruction of red cells and exudation of plasma, as in peritonitis or clostridial myositis, may also reduce blood volume. It is also possible that direct action of the bacteria or their toxins upon the peripheral vessels, the medullary vasomotor center, or the adrenal glands precipitates the state of shock. Septic shock is no more likely to occur in the aged than in the young, but it is an easily overlooked cause.

The symptoms and signs of traumatic shock depend upon the degree of reduction of the blood volume and upon the number and character of the complicating factors produced by the injury. The most useful guide to the severity of blood-volume deficiency is the arterial pressure. The pulse rate is usually rapid but may be normal and at times is slow. The pulse volume is always reduced. The facies is pale, white, or ashen, and the skin of the extremities is cold and usually moist. Mottled cyanosis of the skin of the extremities is a sign of severe shock. Pain is ordinarily not prominent in the severely injured patient. Almost all complain of thirst, which is not alleviated until blood loss is restored. Sweating is not common. Consciousness is present until the arterial pressure has been low for some time. Patients in mild or moderate shock are usually restless and apprehensive, but those in deeper shock are apathetic. If coma is present, an accompanying head injury or cerebrovascular accident must be suspected.

Shock produces no demonstrable impairment in pulmonary function although pulmonary ventilation usually is increased by the acidosis and hypotension. There may be some air hunger, but rapid, irregular, and gasping respirations are late manifestations of hemorrhagic shock and are usually an indication of irreversibility. If cardiorespiratory embarrassment is present, the symptoms will vary. Hemothorax and pneumothorax may cause dyspnea, orthopnea, and occasionally cyanosis. With cardiac tamponade the heart sounds are distant or absent, and there is distention of the veins of the neck and upper extremities. With laryngeal obstruction there is pronounced dyspnea.

There are no laboratory guides of practical value in the diagnosis of shock. The hematocrit remains unchanged in hemorrhagic shock until it is reduced by dilution as plasma is recovered from the interstitial fluids. This may take many hours. The hematocrit will rise when the injury produces a large loss of plasma as in burns, crush injuries, peritonitis, and clostridial myositis. When the hematocrit values are high, the rise in peripheral resistance to the increased blood viscosity, along with vasoconstriction, helps to hold up the arterial pressure as the cardiac output drops. This may give a false estimate of the state of the circulation.

DIFFERENTIAL DIAGNOSIS

In the aged, traumatic shock often has to be differentiated from acute cardiac failure. This is rarely difficult when definite evidence of trauma is apparent and when a history can be obtained. Cardiac failure is usually characterized by arrhythmia, increased cardiac dullness, enlargement of the liver, and edema of the extremities. Pulmonary edema and distended systemic veins with dyspnea are signs of cardiac failure and are not found in uncomplicated shock. However, pulmonary edema and dyspnea may be present following some chest wounds. If there is any doubt of the diagnosis a chest roentgenogram is of value.

The fact that elderly people in heart failure occasionally do suffer traumatic shock may at times be diagnostically most disconcerting. To the same degree, shock due to trauma primarily and shock due to myocardial infarction may present an equally difficult problem in differentiation. There remains the fourth possibility of coincident coronary infarction occurring at the time, or soon after, the precipitating trauma. When shock is due to inadequacy of the heart, measures that improve the peripheral circulation may increase the strain upon the heart. This problem in differential diagnosis is rarely encountered in the young.

TREATMENT OF SHOCK

The same principles apply to the aged as to the young in the treatment of traumatic shock. However, in the elderly, more prompt and greater care must be exerted in the application of these principles. Blood replacement and termination of blood loss is the primary measure. An adequate airway must be ensured and oxygen administered. Any neurogenic factors which may be responsible for shock should be eliminated. Infection and toxemia should be prevented by early, well-timed surgery and by the administration of chemotherapeutic and antibiotic agents. Urine flow should be measured and electrolytic blood studies obtained in order to have a guide for proper treatment.

The object of blood replacement is of course to restore the blood volume. In these elderly individuals, however, great restraint must be exercised to prevent overloading the circulation. Strain upon the heart and the production of edema of the lungs must be avoided in the aged as a hazard equal to that of shock. There is no fixed rule for the rate of transfusion. Constant observation for evidence of increased venous pressure is necessary. An early warning of overloading is a fall of arterial pressure after an initial rise, along with distention of the veins of the neck. Dyspnea, orthopnea, and cyanosis, accompanied by rales in the chest, are more serious signs; and delay of but a few minutes in treatment may result in death.

Asthma may on occasion cause similar symptoms, but treatment should be given for overtransfusion unless the differential diagnosis between the two conditions has been definitely established. Prompt application of tourniquets to all four extremities, phlebotomy, and the administration of positive-pressure oxygen may be lifesaving if the patient has been overtransfused.

Greater care of the patient must be exerted when there is a history of recent coronary disease or whenever coexisting coronary thrombosis is suspected. Cardiac failure during rapid intravenous transfusion may be caused by the citrate in the preserved blood. Citrate in such instances produces pulmonary vasoconstriction with consequent failure of the right ventricle. It may also have a toxic effect directly upon the myocardium. Apparently even small doses of citrate are dangerous in some patients with heart disease or severe anemia. The effect of citrate should be counteracted by the administration of calcium gluconate. This should never be given in the same bottle, tubing, or vein carrying the blood, because of the danger of coagulation.

Shock responds better to therapy early than late. This is especially true in the aged patient with preexistent visceral and vascular disease. The response to blood replacement after repeated hemorrhage becomes poorer than the initial response. Whether blood is given by the intravenous or intraarterial route probably makes little difference.

Plasma is useful for sustaining life until whole blood can be given, but plasma given for replacement of major blood loss causes anemia in the patient. Patients resuscitated from shock with plasma tolerate surgical procedures poorly. Serum albumin is also effective as a blood substitute in emergencies. A unit of albumin (25 Gm in a 100-ml vial) is clinically equivalent to 500 ml of fluid plasma.

Plasma expanders, which are colloidal preparations of large molecular weight, may be useful in emergencies when blood or plasma is not available. However, the expanders cause hemodilution and anemia, and in large amounts interfere with the blood-clotting mechanism. They also interfere with blood grouping so that typing must be done before they are administered. The expanders do not contain protein and for this reason should be used only in extreme emergency in the aged patient, who probably has reduced blood proteins to start with. In experimental tourniquet shock there is some evidence that the expanders may be no more effective than normal saline solution.

Control of hemorrhage is as important a principle of treatment as is blood replacement. Application of local pressure dressings, or direct digital pressure when necessary, is usually an efficient method of accomplishing this. Tourniquets are occasionally necessary in order to control major hemorrhage in an extremity but must be controlled most judiciously. Grossly bleeding vessels may be ligated or clamped. However, blind application of a hemostat to bleeding vessels in an extremity may cause such damage to a major artery that it cannot be repaired later. By the same blind maneuver, a previously damaged nerve may be permanently injured. Proper bandaging and immobilization reduce pain, help to control further blood and plasma loss, and are important factors in the prevention of the spread of infection.

An adequate airway must be established and maintained. Encouraging the patient to cough up blood and mucus, manipulation of the head, tongue, and mandible in the semiconscious patient, or suction of the upper respiratory tract may be sufficient to accomplish this. However, a tracheostomy is sometimes necessary and, in the elderly patient, it should be performed whenever there is any doubt of the adequacy of the airway. Suction of the upper respiratory tract and administration of oxygen can often be done more efficiently through a tracheostomy tube.

Many patients in moderate and severe shock do not require medication for the relief of pain. When it is required, 10 mg morphine given intravenously is the most effective drug. Poisoning may result from multiple subcutaneous doses of morphine as the drug may not be absorbed until the blood flow is restored by transfusion. Then the multiple subcutaneous doses are absorbed all at once. Small intravenous doses of short-acting barbiturates have been recommended for the relief of apprehension. However, morphine usually relieves the apprehension as well as the pain.

Antibiotic therapy should be instituted as soon as possible. As noted above, bacterial action may advance shock to the point of irreversibility. Certain experimental work suggests that the mortality rate in dogs subjected to standard hemorrhagic shock procedures is lowered when the bacterial flora of the intestine is reduced. In septic shock, antibiotic therapy is essential since blood replacement is not usually effective until the sepsis is under control.

The value of vasoconstrictor drugs in traumatic shock is questionable. These drugs are not a substitute for blood replacement. In fact, there is some clinical evidence to support the view that once they have been used, there is a poorer response to the transfused blood. Their use in hemorrhagic shock may mask persisting blood-volume deficiency and may delay renal recovery by intensifying renal vasoconstriction. The use of these drugs may be contraindicated in hemorrhagic shock, but there probably is a place for them where shock is not primarily due to blood loss or where blood replacement has failed.

The value of hypothermia in hemorrhagic or traumatic shock is also debatable. Experimental work has produced evidence both for and against its use, but at the present writing there is no clinical evidence of its value. Chlorpromazine has also been advocated in the treatment of traumatic shock, but there is little objective evidence of its value in human beings. In experimental shock in animals, pretreatment with chlorpromazine seems to improve survival rates.

Elderly patients who have had antecedent trauma or debilitating illness may require corticosteroid therapy. These patients usually have a subnormal adrenocortical response to fresh trauma. Whenever a patient has been taking corticosteroids, the administration of extra dosage is imperative at the onset of new stress or of infection. Its use is also advocated by some in the treatment of shock caused by sepsis.

Shock is relatively more easily produced in patients who have been receiving rauwolfia therapy. This is not uncommon in elderly hypertensive patients. Apparently, reserpine depletes the epinephrine and norepinephrine stores of the body. Clinically, this action has been observed in patients during the course of anesthesia where marked hypotension and bradycardia occasionally occur. The use of vagal blocking agents, such as atropine, scopolamine, or oxyphenonium, has been advocated to correct this condition; but Levophed (levarterenol) or Aramine (metaraminol) are probably more effective if such drugs are needed.

An indwelling catheter should be placed gently in the bladder so that the rate of urinary flow can be continuously observed. The formation of urine at the rate of 1 ml per minute is a reliable index of the adequacy of peripheral blood flow. In the aged, it can be assumed that if hypotension lasts over one hour, there will be depression of renal function. The longer the duration of shock, the more time will be required for return to normal renal function.

LABORATORY GUIDES

It was noted previously that laboratory studies will not help in the initial diagnosis of shock. However, since disease of the visceral organs is frequent in the aged and the disturbances from shock are therefore apt to be more complex, laboratory guides may be of considerable assistance in its sustained treatment. Blood-volume studies are helpful, especially in those patients who have lost weight prior to injury. It is of especial value when hypotension exists due to overhydration and in postoperative hypotension where there has been apparently proper blood replacement.

Electrolyte studies of the blood may at times also be valuable guides to treatment and further may be of some assistance in differentiating the cause of shock in a given case. True salt depletion may be present in a traumatized patient if profuse sweating occurs and there has been concomitant administration of electrolyte-free fluids. In those patients requiring intestinal intubation, salt may be removed in excess of water and shock may result. Occasionally it will be necessary to differentiate the cause of a decreased urinary output, whether or not it is due to shock or to intrinsic renal disease. Primary water loss may follow injury, especially if infection is present, and this may only be determined by electrolyte studies. Olmstead and Roth have reported that there are many elderly, chronically ill people who normally have a low serum sodium level and an elevated serum freezing point. This is the so-called "tired cell syndrome." They advocate the combined use of tests for serum sodium levels and serum freezing-point depressions to permit an accurate estimate of the state of water and electrolytic balance.

ELECTRIC SHOCK

So-called "electric shock" is usually incurred in industrial accidents. However it does occasionally occur in household accidents or street contacts. The latter are the obviously more frequent incidences in the aged. The burns from electricity are of two general types, the "arc" and the "contact" burns. In arc burns the injury is very severe as the tissues are heated by a current of 2500 to 3000°C. The affected sites are melted and volatilized. Contact injuries follow contact with a "live" electric wire and the current passes through the victim's body. The effect of the current upon the body depends upon several factors: (1) tension or voltage, (2) intensity or amperage, (3) type of current, (4) resistance at points of contact, (5) the path of the current through the body, and (6) individual susceptibility. Death is due to either cardiac or respiratory failure with ventricular fibrillation as the usual cause.

In patients who survive the original electric trauma, transient hypotension may persist, *but true shock does not occur.* Prolonged muscle contractions may be strong enough to tear muscles, subluxate joints, and fracture bones. Because of sensory-nerve destruction there is usually little or no pain. Coagulation of skin, lymph, and blood vessels prevents loss of plasma, preserves electrolyte balance, and therefore lessens the chance of shock. This coagulation seals off the avenues of bacterial invasion so that infection is usually not a serious hazard.

Cardiac massage, electric defibrillation, and artificial respiration are the measures advocated for emergency treatment. The definitive care of the electric burn is considered in detail by Simon in Chap. 5, and its healing quality is discussed in Chap. 4.

BIBLIOGRAPHY

Shock

Albert, C. A., R. D. Thergaonkar, E. E. Hanley, M. Bain, A. Rafii, and S. N. Albert: The value of blood volume determinations in surgical procedures. *Surg. Gyn. and Obst.* **107**:685, 1958.

Altemeier, W. A., and W. Cole: Septic shock. *Ann. Surg.* **143**:600, 1956.

Anglem, T. J., and M. L. Bradford: Major surgery in the aged. *New Eng. Jour. Med.* **249**:1005, 1953.

Aufranc, O. E.: Care of the patient with multiple injuries. *Jour. Amer. Med. Ass.* **168**:2091, 1958.

Bigelow, W. G., J. F. R. Fleming, and A. G. Gornall: The management of surgical shock in the poor risk patient. *Canad. Med. Ass. Jour.* **65**:37, 1951.

Coakley, C. S., S. Alpert, and J. S. Boling: Circulatory responses during anesthesia of patients on rauwolfia therapy. *Jour. Amer. Med. Ass.* **161**:1143, 1956.

Dack, S., E. Corday, and A. M. Master: Heart in acute hemorrhage: clinical and electrocardiographic study. *Amer. Heart Jour.* **42**:161, 1951.

Davis, H. A., V. J. Parlante, and A. M. Hallsted: Coronary thrombosis and insufficiency resulting from shock. *Arch. Surg.* **62**:698, 1951.

DeBakey, M., and B. N. Carter: Current considerations of war surgery. *Ann. Surg.* **121**:545, 1945.

Downs, J. W.: The problem of overtransfusion in massive hemorrhage. *Ann. Surg.* **148**:73, 1958.

Erskine, J. M.: The relation of the liver to shock. *Internat. Abstr. Surg.* **106**:207, 1958.

Firt, P., and L. Hejhal: Treatment of severe hemorrhage. *Lancet.* **273**:1132, 1957.

Frank, H. A.: Present-day concepts of shock. *New Eng. Jour. Med.* **249**:445, 1953.

Gurd, F. N.: Management of shock and convalescence in the elderly and infirm. *Amer. Jour. Surg.* **83**:379, 1952.

Gurd, F. N., and C. McG. Gardner: Reappraisal of the treatment of hemorrhagic shock. *Amer. Jour. Surg.* **89**:725, 1955.

Hardaway, R. M., and D. G. McKay: Disseminated intravascular coagulation: a cause of shock. *Ann. Surg.* **149**:462, 1951.

Hayes, M. A.: The influence of shock without clinical renal failure on renal function. *Ann. Surg.* **146**:523, 1957.

Horsley, J. S., J. J. DeCosse, M. Hood, N. Sager, H. T. Randall, and K. E. Roberts: Elevation of blood ammonium in hemorrhagic shock. *Ann. Surg.* **146**:949, 1957.

Kajikuri, K., N. B. Shumacker, and A. Riberi: Effect of hypothermia and of chlorpromazine on survival after tourniquet shock. *Ann. Surg.* **146**:799, 1957.

Master, A. M., S. Dack, A. Greshman, L. E. Field, and H. Horn: Acute coronary insufficiency due to acute hemorrhage: analysis of 103 cases. *Circulation.* **1**:1302, 1950.

NATO Handbook: "Emergency War Surgery." U.S. Government Printing Office, 1958.

Nelson, R. M.: Current concepts in the pathophysiology of shock. *Amer. Jour. Surg.* **93**:645, 1957.

Nelson, W., and M. C. Lindem: Studies of blood volume in patients depleted as a result of trauma. *Amer. Jour. Surg.* **80**:737, 1950.

Olmstead, E. G., and D. A. Roth: The use of serum freezing point depressions in evaluating salt and water balance in preoperative and postoperative states. *Surg. Gyn. and Obst.* **106**:41, 1958.

Peterson, C. G., and W. W. Krippaehne: Shock in sepsis. *Amer. Jour. Surg.* **96**:158, 1958.

Postel, A. H., L. C. Reid, and J. W. Hinton: The therapeutic effect of hypothermia in experimental hemorrhagic shock. *Ann. Surg.* **145**:311, 1957.

Rhoads, J. E., W. S. Vaun, W. M. Parkins, M. Ben, and H. M. Vars: Shock. *Surg. Clin. North Amer.* **35**:1585, 1955.

Robb, H. J., D. E. Ingham, H. M. Nelson, and C. G. Johnston: Observations in vascular dynamics during hemorrhagic shock and its therapy. *Amer. Jour. Surg.* **95**:659, 1958.

Savlov, E. D.: Effect of chlorpromazine on renal function and hemodynamics particularly during hemorrhagic hypotension. *Surgery.* **45**:229, 1959.

Serkes, K. D., S. Lang, and M. D. Pareira: Efficiency of plasma and dextran compared to saline for fluid. Replacement following tourniquet shock. *Surgery.* **45**:623, 1959.

Snyder, H. E.: Early recognition and management of shock. *Amer. Jour. Surg.* **83**:382, 1952.

Steenburg, R. W., R. Lennihan, and F. D. Moore: Studies in surgical endocrinology. *Ann. Surg.* **143**:180, 1956.

Ulin, A. W., S. W. Gollub, H. S. Winchell, and E. W. Ehrlich: Hemorrhage and massive transfusion. *Jour. Amer. Med. Ass.* **168**:1971, 1959.

Wise, H. M., A. T. Knecht, D. Pence, and B. S. Ondash: Observations of the function of the liver in experimental traumatic shock. *Surgery.* **45**:274, 1959.

Electric Burns

Baldridge, R. R.: Electric burns. *New Eng. Jour. Med.* **250**:46, 1954.

Levokove, E., and M. H. Morris: Auricular fibrillation after electric shock with complete recovery. *N.Y. Jour. Med.* **54**:807, 1954.

Lewis, G. K.: Burns from electricity. *Ann. Surg.* **131**:80, 1950.

Mackay, R. S., K. E. Mooslin, and S. E. Leeds: The effects of electric currents on the canine heart with particular reference to ventricular fibrillation. *Ann. Surg.* **134**:173, 1951.

McLaughlin, C. W., and J. D. Coe: Management of electrical burns. *A.M.A. Arch. Surg.* **68**:531, 1954.

Chapter 2

Preoperative Care and
Postoperative Supportive Therapy

Preston A. Wade and Paul W. Braunstein

FIRST AID

Most operations performed on injured aged persons are emergency procedures, and the quality of the first-aid care often is a decisive factor in the treatment. It may determine the success or failure of the end result, or even the probability of survival. In the order of their importance, the major steps in first aid are (1) maintenance of an open airway, (2) control of hemorrhage, (3) treatment of shock, (4) splinting of fractures, and (5) careful transportation.

MAINTENANCE OF AN OPEN AIRWAY

The patient with multiple injuries is apt to suffer interference of respiration due to vomitus, blood, or mucus lodged in the trachea or bronchi. In many instances of facial and jaw injuries, the tongue may have dropped backward, obstructing respiration at the pharynx. In these circumstances, the first important step is to remove all foreign material from the mouth and pharynx and to pull the tongue forward. It may be necessary to thrust a safety pin through the tip of the tongue and attach the pin to the clothing by a string to keep the tongue retracted during transportation.

If there is an open, sucking chest wound, it should immediately be covered with whatever material is at hand to prevent the further shifting of the mediastinum by the ingress of air into the pleura.

CONTROL OF HEMORRHAGE

One essential procedure in the control of hemorrhage is the application of a pressure dressing at the bleeding site. A simple circular bandage, composed of a clean handkerchief firmly applied by a tie or strip of clothing, is an excellent temporary pressure dressing. Only the large arteries, e.g., the brachial or the femoral, will not respond temporarily to such applications of pressure. It has long been the custom to apply a tourniquet to any bleeding limb, and it is exceedingly difficult to convince the untrained layman that in most instances this is not only unnecessary, but harmful. It may, in fact, result in the loss of the limb, since the tourniquet cuts off the blood supply to tissues that are already poorly nourished owing to depressed peripheral circulation, advanced arteriosclerotic changes in the major vessels, or both. If the tourniquet is left on for a long period and is then released, the patient is almost certain to succumb to the systemic effect; and if he does survive, the limb will most likely have to be amputated.

TREATMENT OF SHOCK

There is very little that can be done at the site of an accident to treat shock in the elderly person. If an airway is kept open, hemorrhage is controlled by pressure dressings, all fractures are splinted, and the patient is transported carefully, the fundamental steps to prevent further shock have been taken. The patient should be covered and protected from the elements, but no external heat should be applied. For many years it was the routine for many hospital ambulance attendants to give all injured patients an injection of morphine. As was noted by Sullivan in the preceding chapter, this is a dangerous procedure, particularly in elderly patients, and morphine should never be administered unless the patient is in severe pain. If it is necessary to administer the drug, the dosage and time of administration should be recorded in writing and attached to the patient before he is transported to the hospital.

The more extended treatment of shock was discussed in Chap. 1.

THE SPLINTING OF FRACTURES

All fractured limbs and those suspected of being fractured should be splinted in the simplest and least disturbing manner, and the injured patient should be handled as gently as possible. It is unnecessary and sometimes harmful to apply any complicated splinting apparatus.

For the upper extremity, the arm may be bound to the side by means of a sling and swathe or may merely be suspended in a sling. The forearm and wrist can easily be splinted by means of a small piece of wood, a magazine, or a piece of cardboard gently bandaged to the injured extremity. The patient may then be transported with the arm in a sling.

The lower extremity may be secured by a lateral board splint, preferably with the use of a little traction. This is applied by means of a sling in the groin and a bandage attached to the foot over the end of the board, traction being exerted by means of a so-called "Spanish windlass" (Fig. 2-1A). If a Thomas splint is at hand, it is of course preferable to use it for fractures of the hip and of the shaft of the femur (Fig. 2-1B). At times, however, the patient may best be transported on a flat litter or stretcher, simply wrapped in blankets. For the knee and the lower leg, board and pillow splints are the methods of choice (Fig. 2-1C).

Much has been written concerning the absolute necessity of using the Thomas splint in transporting elderly people with fractures of the hip. However, in many instances, the application of the Thomas splint may be more difficult and may be the cause of more pain and manipulation

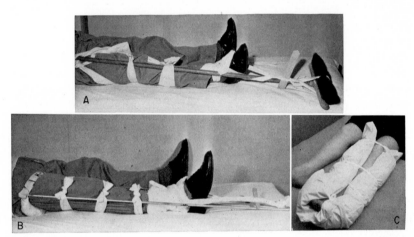

FIG. 2-1. *A*. If no traction or splint is available, any firm structure such as a broom, rod, or tree branch can be employed to provide some degree of limb immobilization. *B*. Thomas splint with traction. *C*. Pillow splint for fractures of leg or ankle.

at the fracture site than simple transportation in blankets on a flat stretcher. Furthermore, the Thomas splint is often applied by amateurs who may do considerable harm. Because the Thomas splint increases the over-all length of the stretcher, it may add unnecessary difficulties in transporting the patient through small passageways and stairways.

TRANSPORTATION

In transportation, the first consideration is gentleness in handling the patient. The second consideration is care and smoothness in carrying. The natural tendency for the layman, and unfortunately for ambulance drivers, is to emphasize speed in transportation. This is not only unnecessary, but extremely dangerous, not only to the patient, but to other occupants of the ambulance and to all unsuspecting individuals in its path. There is rarely any necessity for speed in transportation. Recently many reports have discussed the "speeding ambulance." It has been found that only rarely does the speeding ambulance lead to any change in the ultimate prognosis or outcome in the injured elderly patient, and all too often such speeding leads to additional injury and fatality.

ACCIDENT-ROOM CARE

The modern accident room is assumed to be equipped with the proper materials so that all essential care may be administered promptly and efficiently. The personnel should be adequate in number and well trained, and the surgeon in charge who conducts the preliminary examination and directs the emergency treatment should be an experienced member of the staff. Frequently the care of the seriously and multiply injured patient is relegated to the junior member of the surgical staff. It is here that quick and mature thinking, diagnosis, and decision must be available. It is here that "life is short and art long, occasion instant, experiment perilous, and decision difficult." Often it is of paramount importance that the original regimen of care outlined for the elderly patient be the one most beneficial to him, for frequently later definitive care will be based upon those first acts in the period of emergency. Though accident-room care is not always dramatic, it is always important.

Preliminary Examination

The receiving surgeon should make a rapid but thorough examination of the patient to determine the presence of any injuries which need prompt attention to preserve life. The first consideration is the maintenance of an open airway (Fig. 2-2), and as has been described previously, all retained mucus, vomitus, or blood should be removed from the pharynx. Suction should be at hand for this purpose. The tongue should be pulled and held forward if it interferes with respiration. If there is a respiratory difficulty due to a sucking wound of the chest, it should be promptly covered. In the presence of respiratory difficulty, the chest should be palpated and percussed to determine the presence of blood in the chest or paradoxical respiration. If a tension pneumothorax is present, a needle should be immediately inserted into the second interspace anteriorly where the air can most promptly be removed by aspiration or by the insertion of a catheter with drainage under water. While tension pneumothorax is relatively rare, it is one of the surgical emergencies which can be handled adequately, completely, and easily by the most simple measures. Adequate physical diagnosis and the ability to act quickly once it has been established are of paramount importance. On rare occasions the situation may be too urgent to obtain chest roentgenograms. With a small local injection of procaine three fingerbreadths lateral to the sternal border in the second anterior interspace and through a No. 16 trochar, a No. 16 polyethylene or rubber catheter can be readily introduced into the pleural space to preclude further mediastinal shift. Under absolute emergency conditions, one may insert an open needle or a needle attached to a syringe and three-way stopcock. Simple rubber tubing can connect this to a water seal at the bedside and so gradually empty the pleural space of air. In the presence of paradoxical respiration

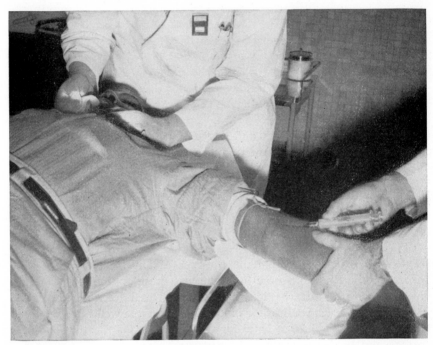

Fig. 2-2. In the seriously injured, immediate attention should be directed toward establishing a patent airway and introducing a large bone needle into a patent vein. As soon as possible, clothes should be cut off if there is any question of aggravating injury by clothing removal in the normal manner.

or accumulation of secretions in the lung, a tracheostomy may be performed in the accident room, but it is usually not necessary to do this as an emergency measure. It is preferable that it be done in the operating room under more advantageous conditions.

The presence of active bleeding makes it necessary to apply a compression dressing as soon as the wound has been inspected. A tourniquet should never be applied in the emergency room, but if one has been applied elsewhere, it is usually necessary to leave it in place until the proper preparations for the treatment of shock can be accomplished. If the tourniquet is removed immediately on admission to the hospital, a sudden drop in blood pressure may send the patient into severe shock;

and if blood is not at hand and being administered, serious consequences may ensue.

TREATMENT OF SHOCK *

As soon as the patient is admitted to the emergency room, a large bore needle (No. 15 to 18) should be inserted into a patent large vein. Blood should be immediately drawn for cross matching and for other pertinent base-line chemical determinations which may prove important at a later date should the patient develop any electrolyte disturbance. Because the elderly patient will not tolerate hypotension as well as a young person with a more elastic extracellular fluid space, the use of extracellular fluid-space expanders becomes quite important. While one awaits blood for correction of the hypovolemic state, plasma and dextran are usually employed. Because the use of pooled plasma involves a real risk of homologous serum jaundice, it is often avoided; and dextran or poly-vinylpyrrolidine (PVP) is substituted. During the earlier days of the use of dextran, it was believed that administration of three or more units of this plasma expander would lead to a bleeding diathesis. However, with the larger molecular weight of the recently produced dextran and with the removal of impurities from the manufactured product, bleeding has seldom occurred following administration of even large doses of this substance. It should be remembered that all blood substitutes are only substitutes, and that none can compare to whole blood, which possesses optimal osmotic properties and oxygen-carrying capacity.

All bleeding may not be external. Concealed hemorrhage, while not as dramatic as external bleeding, may be massive and lead to irreversible shock if not recognized and treated (Figs. 2-3 and 2-4).

It should be stressed that the present conception of the treatment of hemorrhagic shock provides little place for the use of pressor substances such as Levophed. One may well describe the use of a peripheral vaso-constrictor in a patient with already maximal peripheral vasoconstriction as "flogging a dying horse." As noted in Chap. 1, a peripheral vasocon-strictor may occasionally be needed in the management of the traumatic, elderly, hypertensive patient.

SPLINTING OF FRACTURES

If fractured limbs, or those suspected of being fractured, have not been splinted before the patient comes to the hospital, they should be splinted in the accident room. The splinting should be simple and accomplished with as little movement of the injured extremity as possible. Often, fractures of the hip need only be immobilized by means of sandbags or

---

* This has been discussed in detail in Chap. 1.

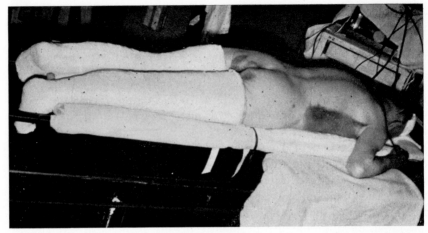

Fig. 2-3. In multiple injury problems, hemorrhage can be totally concealed and yet massive in quantity. Here, following pelvic fracture, retroperitoneal hemorrhage has been marked and has extended well into the flanks. Transfusion requirements are often much higher than originally estimated in such instances.

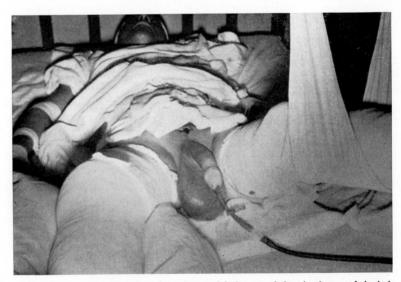

Fig. 2-4. In the seriously injured patient with lower abdominal or pelvic injury, or in those patients with compromised urinary output, indwelling catheter drainage is mandatory. In this patient with ruptured cavernous urethra due to pelvic fracture, note massive scrotal hemorrhage. There was as well extremely large retroperitoneal hemorrhage.

strapping of one limb to the other before proper x-ray examination is performed.

TRANSPORTATION IN THE HOSPITAL

One of the mistakes often made in a hospital is the unnecessary transportation of an injured patient from the accident room, to x-ray department, to ward, and then to operating room. This involves lifting and carrying the patient from the stretcher, to the x-ray table, back to the stretcher, to bed, back again to the stretcher, and finally to the operating table. It may mean moving the patient half a dozen times from the time of admission until the time of operation. These many transferrals of the patient from bed to stretcher to table are actually a serious error, particularly in the handling of the elderly and multiply injured patient, because many soft tissues not involved in the primary impact may be damaged by motion of fracture fragments during these many unnecessary maneuvers. In recent years an adaptable stretcher composed of materials permitting passage of roentgen rays has been developed. This stretcher receives the patient at the emergency room and can be placed over any x-ray table to obtain examinations without moving the patient unduly. It is of course preferable to have adequate radiological equipment in the emergency room, thereby minimizing movements of the patient and loss of valuable time in emergency diagnosis.

During the preliminary examination, the blood pressure and pulse as well as the data from all other examinations should be recorded on the admission note so that the condition of the patient on admission and the preliminary therapy are known to subsequent examiners.

HISTORY TAKING AND GENERAL EXAMINATIONS

After the preliminary examination and after the serious conditions have been evaluated and properly treated, the examiner must proceed to take a detailed history and perform a complete examination. The elderly patient is often in a state of advanced senescence and is unable to remember even major operations he has undergone. Accordingly, all close relatives available should be carefully questioned concerning the patient's past history.

It is essential to investigate and record such details as the time, place, and nature of the accident in which the injuries were sustained. It is also important to know the state of consciousness of the patient at the time of the injury and during the period of transportation to the hospital. Information about medication that was given before admission to the hospital should be ascertained and recorded. This is extremely important in elderly people, particularly in the case of the administration of morphine or other narcotics. If there is any alcohol on the patient's breath, the admitting officer should determine whether an alcoholic stimulant was used before or after the accident and should record this information.

Since much of the treatment of the injuries sustained by an elderly patient consists of the concurrent management of complications, most of which result from the aggravation of preexisting diseases or states of senility and old age, it is exceedingly important that the examiner make careful inquiry as to the patient's past medical history. It is particularly important to know the status of the patient's cardiovascular system, whether or not he had ever had symptoms of cardiac decompensation, and to obtain whatever information is available concerning his blood pressure before the accident. Information about a history of peripheral vascular disorders is also significant, since many injuries to the extremities are made more complicated by preexisting circulatory changes in the limbs.

In investigating the history of the genitourinary system, it is exceedingly important to know whether or not the male patient has had any periods of urinary retention or difficulty that might be the result of hypertrophy of the prostate. Many elderly males are able to get along with a partially emptied bladder but immediately go into acute urinary retention following severe injury. While many systems in the elderly are able to function with a borderline reserve, the added insult of even minor injury may decompensate the function of this organ system. A minor degree of retroperitoneal hemorrhage, for example, may be sufficient to prevent adequate detrusor action of the bladder and so lead to urinary retention. Similarly, paralytic ileus may be precipitated in the face of minor spinal injury or retroperitoneal hemorrhage.

It is essential to know the patient's psychological state before the accident; whether or not he was alert mentally, and whether or not he was subject to depressions. These facts are important in the postoperative period and during the period of rehabilitation. Accordingly, evaluation of the patient's psychological status may often take place following resuscitation and definitive operative procedures. The examiner should also seek information about the extent of the physical activity of the patient; whether he was able to get about well by himself, and what disabilities he may have suffered which might have caused him to be sedentary or bedridden.

The state of consciousness of the patient at the time of injury is important. A careful investigation may be necessary to ascertain whether he became unconscious before the accident or was caused to become unconscious by the violence of the impact. This has some bearing on the patient's future physical condition and on possible medicolegal problems. It is important to find out whether the patient was subject to alcoholism, diabetes or epilepsy, not only because these may have played some role in causing the accident, but because they may be significant in planning for immediate as well as future care.

EXAMINATION

The patient's clothes should be completely removed, and a careful systematic examination from head to toe should be made and recorded. One of the first steps in the examination is to take the blood pressure, the pulse, and the type and rate of respiration.

It is usual to begin the examination at the head and proceed to the neck, chest, abdomen, and extremities. Since the patient is usually in the supine position, it is necessary to turn him gently and to be sure to examine the back for signs of external violence. Not only must the patient be examined for injuries, but his general condition must be evaluated so that his systemic reaction to the treatment required for the injury may be properly estimated.

X-RAY EXAMINATION

As soon as possible x-ray examination should be made of the various areas in which injury is suspected. The preliminary x-ray examination should be done in the accident room and, if at all possible, without removing the patient from the stretcher on which he was originally placed. The removal of a seriously ill patient from the accident room to a relatively distant x-ray department, and hence from the observing eye of the physician, is fraught with hazard. Incipient shock, changes in level of consciousness, changes in respiration and in abdominal findings, recurrent hemorrhage, and similar situations which may vary or develop by the minute cannot and should not be left to discovery by the untrained and frequently uninterested x-ray technician or orderly. Portable x-ray should be available in an accident room to obtain any survey films necessary before initiation of therapy. For the patient who is not seriously injured and who may be transported safely, the stretcher previously described which can be rolled over an ordinary x-ray table is helpful and avoids unnecessary moving of the patient.

The x-ray examination should be complete enough to make a satisfactory diagnosis, but no unnecessary examinations should be made. Diagnosis of most injuries can be made by x-rays taken in the supine position. Although it might be helpful to have the patient in the erect position to secure x-rays of chest and abdomen, it may be decidedly harmful to place him in this position before his condition has been evaluated. It is seldom necessary to take a complete set of x-rays of the skull immediately, and it is rarely necessary to insist upon a lateral x-ray of the hip, since the anteroposterior view will usually make the diagnosis, and the further examination can be made later when the patient is placed either in bed or on the operating table. One of the less important studies in patients with head injury is a complete skull x-ray series. Neurological examination and careful observation for changes in neurological status are much more important than determining the status of the bony skull. When the situation has stabilized, x-rays may assume their proper perspective in the evaluation of definitive care; but it is poor judgment to subject a patient with head injuries and possible upper cervical spine injuries to numerous rotation, flexion, and extension maneuvers to determine the lines of fracture in the skull. The same holds true for an unstable extremity injury where unskilled manipulation during multiple x-ray procedures may lead to serious soft-part damage. In intraabdominal trauma, only occasionally will the gravely injured patient derive much benefit from time-consuming upright abdominal x-rays. Physical examination most often will determine the necessity for laparotomy in the pressing abdominal emergency without the necessity for detailed films.

TREATMENT OF OPEN WOUNDS

Although the ideal situation for the debridement of open wounds is in the operating room under general anesthesia, it is sometimes necessary to compromise and do as complete a debridement as is possible in the accident room if the patient is in a precarious condition or is unconscious and cannot be moved. Sometimes the debridement can be done without anesthesia, or if the patient is conscious, with a local anesthetic. In most instances the wound is left open since the debridement cannot be properly completed under such circumstances and may require further doing in the operating room at a later time. Under most conditions it should be stressed that operating room debridement is the procedure of choice, and only rarely should emergency room debridement be performed. The skin of the elderly patient is atrophic and will tolerate only the most gentle handling by an artful surgeon. The frequent comminution in fractures can lead to overenthusiastic removal of bone chips and resultant delayed union. Any avulsed or operatively produced flaps are precarious owing to the commonly inadequate cutaneous circulation of the aged. It is far wiser to excise flaps where viability is questionable and to apply split grafts primarily rather than await skin slough and consequent infection.

The urine should be examined as soon as possible after the accident and, if the patient can void, the amount of urine voided should be recorded. If the patient cannot void, a catheter should be immediately inserted and residual urine recorded. The catheter is left in place for a considerable period of time since the urinary output and its examination is a most important means of judging the progress of the patient's general condition.

Blood studies should be made immediately to ascertain the patient's condition at admission and to serve as a base line for future observations. Blood should be examined for urea nitrogen, sugar, potassium, and sodium; and a complete blood count, including hematocrit, should be taken. Base line chemistries prove of great value in the immediate postoperative period when electrolyte imbalances often occur. Blood for these determinations is easily obtained at the time of cross matching for transfusion in the accident room, *but it must be stressed that taking material for a barrage of chemistries at this time does not imply any delay in caring for the patient's emergency situation.* While the results of many of these chemistries may not be available prior to surgical care, they may prove of value in the postoperative period following the stress of trauma and surgery.

Before the patient is moved from the emergency room either to his bed or to the operating room, he should be given the proper amount of whole blood to control actual or impending shock. He then may be transported to the operating room if he is to undergo immediate surgery or to his bed if operation may be delayed.

OPTIMUM TIME FOR OPERATION

In many instances, particularly if there are open wounds or if there are intraabdominal injuries, immediate operation is indicated. The patient is taken to the operating room from the accident room. However, in the majority of instances such speed is not necessary. *Under ideal conditions, it is preferable to wait for 6 or 8 or even 12 hours* so that the patient can be evaluated and preliminary treatment instituted. This is particularly valuable in dealing with trauma in the aged. Among the added advantages of a waiting period is the time allowed for assembling a suitable operating team.

PREPARATION FOR OPERATION

In determining the ability of an elderly patient to withstand an operation, the cardiovascular system must first be evaluated. The heart should be examined, blood pressure and pulse taken. Although most elderly people will have some changes in the electrocardiographic record, the important consideration is the condition of the cardiac musculature. Evidence of a recent myocardial infarct may indicate a coronary occlusion which might have occurred at the time of the accident. These findings must be weighed carefully in deciding whether the patient should be operated upon early or whether to risk a delay. If there is clinical evidence of cardiac decompensation, such as edema, dyspnea, or electrocardiographic abnormalities, it is most essential that the decompensation be corrected, if at all possible, before any operative procedure is undertaken. The elderly patient in cardiac decompensation is the worst possible risk, and operation should be delayed unless there is some vital emergency such as hemorrhage or ruptured viscus. Even so, treatment should be instituted immediately and digitalization begun as soon as the condition is discovered.

Patients with marked hypertension do not tolerate sudden drops in blood pressure well, and it is essential that the operative procedure be conducted as smoothly as possible to avoid sending the patient into shock. The use of spinal anesthesia is definitely contraindicated in the presence of marked hypertension.

Fluid-balance and blood-volume studies are important in preparing the patient for operation. If the patient is anemic and has a hematocrit below 35, he should have careful whole blood replacement. It is inadvisable to give whole blood to an elderly person unless the hematocrit is low. Overenthusiastic attempts at correction of a low hematocrit may well lead to pulmonary edema. If blood loss is obvious at the time of injury, careful blood replacement is instituted, trying to "titrate" the amount replaced against the amount lost. Even under such "titratable" situations, it is probably wise to undertransfuse the elderly rather than overtransfuse. Chronic anemia of the elderly is relatively well tolerated, and often it is impossible to correct a hematocrit of 30 to 35. Should there be no obvious blood loss, one may assume that a state of chronic anemia exists and must avoid raising the hematocrit to what is considered a normal level for a young adult. While small drops in red blood-cell volume will be tolerated even during surgery (though hypotension must be avoided), overexpansion of the extracellular fluid space by too vigorous blood replacement may lead to irreversible pulmonary edema and cardiac decompensation.

The blood-volume studies and the electrolyte studies will give evidence as to whether or not the patient needs electrolyte replacement. Because of the dietary fads and indiscretions of the elderly, the increased respiratory inadequacies, and the increased inability to compensate for alterations of blood chemistry caused by trauma, electrolyte imbalance often occurs. Hypoproteinemia is almost the rule in these patients, hence vigorous attempts at correction are unnecessary. A total of 5 to 5.5 Gm per cent with a 1.5 per 1 albumin-globulin ratio is really an excellent level for an elderly individual. Hypochloremia to as low as 90 mEq per liter is acceptable and should be corrected slowly as should any level of hypo-natremia above 130 mEq per liter. Respiratory acidosis will prove re-sistant to most types of therapy. If the carbon dioxide combining power is above 35 mM, the use of any respiratory depressant as medication is contraindicated. If the patient's condition will permit, a rocking bed may be gainfully employed. This promotes diaphragmatic excursion, and hence adequate respiratory exchange in the emphysematous patient. Table 2-1 gives acceptable hematologic and electrolyte values in the aged as related to normal values in the younger adult.

It is very important that any abdominal distention be corrected before operation if at all possible. This may be accomplished by means of enema and removal of fecal impaction if it is present. If there is distention of the upper intestinal tract, a Levine tube should be inserted and left in place during the operation.

In being prepared for operation, the elderly patient in many instances will have been catheterized and the catheter left in place in order to evaluate the urinary output. This is particularly important in the patient with hypertrophy of the prostate who has had a history of difficulty in urination, because the operative procedure may increase the difficulty of emptying the bladder, and a retention catheter will help to control the situation.

Since some elderly patients may have been confined to bed for a con-siderable period before operation, it is essential that there be no pressure on the sacrum or other areas. Any motion of the body allowed the patient while awaiting surgery is of great benefit to the skin overlying bony prominences. Certain types of traction provide this relative freedom of body motion (Fig. 2-5). Extra precautions should be taken to protect the sacrum on the operating table. It is wise to have the patient resting on a well-padded table. Care must also be exercised in placing the elderly patient on the operating table, because he may develop peripheral nerve-pressure symptoms if susceptible areas are not protected. This is particu-larly true of the radial nerve when the arm is extended over an arm board either for blood-pressure determinations or for intravenous fluid administration. Hyperextension of the arm may lead to axillary nerve palsy by simple traction of the humerus against the nerve as it enters the subdeltoid area. Common peroneal palsies may occur from simple external rotation of the leg for a protracted period while the patient is undergoing surgery. This external rotation with pressure on the fibular neck may cause irreversible damage to this important dorsiflexor nerve of the foot. Any metal projection or even a wrinkled sheet or a soft bandage may prove disastrous to the elderly skin already atrophic and inelastic.

TABLE 2-1. COMPARATIVE HEMATOLOGIC AND ELECTROLYTE VALUES

	Normal for adults	Acceptable for preoperative geriatric patient
Clotting time (Lee & White)	5–8 minutes	5–8 minutes
Bleeding time (Duke)	1–3 minutes	1–3 minutes
Prothrombin time	15 seconds	15–20 seconds
Red blood count	Male: 4.5 million	Male: 4 million
	Female: 4 million	Female: 3.5 million
Hemoglobin	Male: 14.5 Gm	Male: 12–13.5 Gm
	Female: 13.5 Gm	Female: 10.5–12 Gm
Hematocrit	Male: 45	Male: 40
	Female: 40	Female: 35
White blood count	5–10,000	5–10,000
Amylase—6 ml	40–110 units	40–100 units
Bilirubin, total—5 ml	0.1–0.8 mg %	1.0 mg %
Bilirubin, direct	0–0.2 mg %	0.2 mg %
Bilirubin, indirect	0.1–0.6 mg %	0.8 mg %
Bromsulphalein—5 ml	0–4.0 mg %	20%
Calcium—6 ml	9–10.5 mg %	9–10.5 mg %
Chlorides (as NaCl)—5 ml	97–106 mEq per liter	90–110 mEq per liter
Cholesterol, total—4 ml	150–250 mg %	150–250 mg %
Cholesterol, esters—6 ml	65–75% of total	50–75% of total
CO_2 c.p.—8 ml	22–27 mM per liter	20–30 mM per liter
Creatinine—6 ml	0.5–1.0 mg %	0.5–1.0 mg %
Phosphorus—4 ml	3–4.5 mg %	2.5–4.5 mg %
Phosphatase, acid—5 ml	0–1.1 units	0–1.1 units
Phosphatase, alk.—5 ml	2–4 units	2–10 units
Protein, total—4 ml	6.0–8.0 Gm %	5–8 Gm %
Protein, total and A/G—5 ml	. . . .	. . . .
Albumin	4.0–5.2%	3.0–5.0%
Globulin	2.0–2.8 %	2.0–3.0%
Potassium—6 ml	3.5–4.7 mEq per liter	2.5–5 mEq per liter
Sodium—6 ml	132–143 mEq per liter	125–140 mEq per liter
Thymol turbidity—3 ml	1–4 units	1–8 units
Uric acid—5 ml	2–4 mg %	2–4 mg %
N. Prot. nitrogen—5 ml	25–35 mg %	25–50 mg %
Sugar—3 ml	70–90 mg %	65–120 mg %
Urea nitrogen—5 ml	8–15 mg %	10–30 mg %

PREOPERATIVE MEDICATION

The use of preanesthesia medication in the elderly is limited to those drugs known to cause minimal adverse effects. Therefore, analgesics which cause respiratory depression are seldom if ever employed. Morphine is

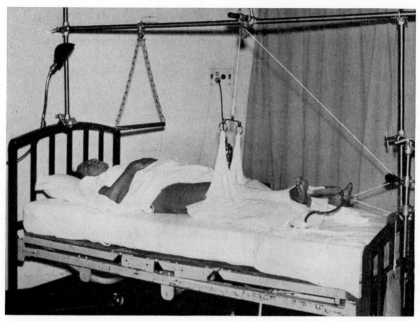

FIG. 2-5. Prior to definitive care of an injury, preoperative examinations must be performed. In this interim period prior to surgery, Russell's traction offers the patient relief from pain and lessens soft-tissue trauma prior to internal fixation of a fractured lower extremity.

rarely necessary or advisable. Sedatives such as the barbiturates are seldom administered because of their not infrequent stimulation of the central nervous system. Scopolamine may also be contraindicated because it is believed by some to cause excitation in the older age groups.

An elderly patient requires less preanesthetic medication per kilogram of body weight than a younger individual. Consultation with a competent anesthesiologist is advisable in any elderly patient.

In many cases the only drug administered preoperatively may be atropine sulphate, 0.2 mg intramuscularly or subcutaneously. The dose may be doubled but is seldom greater than this. If the patient is in extreme pain, a small dose of Demerol may be given in conjunction with atropine. Seldom does the dosage of Demerol exceed 25 mg. Occasionally sedation

12 to 14 hours prior to surgery will consist of 4 to 8 ml of 7.5 per cent chloral hydrate (see Chap. 3, in which Papper and Brand discuss the use of these drugs in relation to anesthesia in the aged).

POSTOPERATIVE SUPPORTIVE THERAPY

IMMEDIATE

General Considerations. Although postoperative supportive therapy often must be directed toward preexisting diseases, there are some important general considerations that apply to all patients.

Medication for sedation in the postnarcotic state is as important as the preoperative medication. Many of these patients, having been under anesthesia for a long period, suffer the postanesthetic depression that makes it necessary to avoid any narcotics that might aggravate this depression. It is usually wise to limit the use of narcotics or any other respiratory depressant in the preoperative and postoperative periods to the barest minimum. Demerol is preferred to morphine because of its lesser effect on the respiratory center, but even this drug should be used sparingly in doses as small as 25 mg every 4 hours. Codeine phosphate by injection (32 mg q. 4 hrs) or codeine sulphate by mouth in similar dosage are preferable to Demerol or morphine. Aspirin in oral doses of 0.3 to 0.6 Gm and rectal dosages of 0.6 to 1.2 Gm is even better. However it must be remembered that the antipyretic effect of aspirin may mask the temperature readings so vital in the postoperative period.

Many elderly people are so childlike in their reaction to pain or possess such a low pain threshold that it is often difficult to determine how much distress they are actually experiencing. On the other hand, one cannot ignore all complaints of pain, for such a course of inaction may cause one to overlook a skin slough under a tight cast or an intraabdominal complication. On occasion, many of these patients develop a postoperative psychosis and it is necessary to use some form of sedative, such as paraldehyde, in doses of 6 to 10 ml per rectum every 4 to 6 hours. In many instances, some of the relaxing drugs, such as the meprobamates, are helpful and are administered in the same clinical dosages as for younger individuals.

Fluid and Blood Replacement. It is exceedingly important that the amount of fluid the patient has received intravenously in the form either of blood or of electrolytes be considered before postoperative fluid is given. Under ordinary circumstances the patient needs 2,000 ml of fluid following the operation, and this should be given in the form of dextrose in water.

The elderly person presents a double problem in care of the extracellular fluid balance. All those extracellular fluid imbalances which occur with specific states such as dehydration, electrolyte fluid loss through the gastrointestinal tract, excessive sweating, etc., are also present in the elderly, but in addition there is the serious and common problem of nutritional deficiencies. The extracellular fluid space of the elderly person is extremely fragile; it will not withstand either overloading or severe restriction of fluid and electrolytes. One may discover most electrolyte disturbances by comparing oral and parenteral fluid intake with urinary output and extrarenal fluid losses, i.e., vomiting, small bowel fistula, etc. Determinations of blood chemistries should include blood urea nitrogen, carbon dioxide combining power, serum sodium, serum potassium, and serum chloride levels. Knowledge of the aforementioned serum chemical levels will lead to more enlightened fluid therapy. Many elderly people fail to eat correctly and some suffer from such disorders as psychic vomiting. These cause marked extracellular fluid disturbances which may be masked behind the senile person's calm or somewhat detached demeanor. It was remarked earlier in this chapter that a careful history of dietary habits or management prior to injury must be ascertained. Should vomiting or marked restriction of intake be noted in the pretrauma history or postoperatively, then emergency studies are in order to determine what electrolyte imbalances exist. A marked azotemia, hypochloremia, or hypoproteinemia may very well preclude surgery for a relatively short period of time while these electrolyte imbalances are corrected. At all times during electrolyte replacement, the lung bases, the periphery, and the sacrum must be carefully observed for signs of fluid retention. The urine specific gravity is extremely helpful in determining the current state of hydration. This, of course, can not be relied upon in the presence of concurrent renal diseases of severe degree.

There are several classical types of electrolyte imbalance which may be present in the elderly person with gastrointestinal or renal disturbances prior to or following treatment of a serious injury.

Hypochloremic Alkalosis. If a patient has lost large amounts of gastric secretions because of paralytic ileus or persistent vomiting, there will be a marked loss of chlorides in relation to the amount of sodium lost. Accordingly, with the drop in chlorides, the patient will have an elevation of the CO_2 combining power (30 to 35 plus mM) and hypochloremic alkalosis. Should this be a pure hypochloremic alkalosis, the usual remedy if the patient has adequate renal reserve is administration of large amounts of sodium chloride. Should the alkalosis remain a problem, 100 mEq of ammonium chloride per day or twice daily can be given, the ammonium chloride being added to the fluids being administered— namely 5 per cent glucose and water or 5 per cent glucose and saline. By providing large amounts of chloride and no sodium, the ammonium chloride will fairly rapidly return the serum pH and CO_2 combining power to a nearly normal level.

Hypokalemic Alkalosis. In those patients with high small bowel fistula, or enteric fluid losses associated with marked vomiting, or gastric suction of such degree that large amounts of small intestinal and gastric contents are lost, there is hypochloremia; but associated with this is a marked potassium deficit. With a potassium deficit, it is impossible to correct the alkalosis by administration of chlorides alone. Before the alkalosis can be corrected, both chlorides and potassium must be administered. Under such circumstances sodium chloride is supplemented with 20 to 40 mEq of potassium chloride per 1,000 ml of fluid for each 1,000 ml of fluid lost by suction or fistula drainage.

Renal Metabolic Acidosis. Patients with renal insufficiency retain phosphates and sulphates and therefore go into metabolic acidosis. Accompanying the acidosis there can frequently be retention of potassium due to poor tubular excretion of this element. By their build-up, the phosphates will cause hypocalcemia; and with this there will appear signs of calcium deficiency, namely, hyperactive reflexes, tetany, respiratory stridor, and then convulsions. Management of renal acidosis is extremely difficult since the only true treatment is an attempt to lessen the acidosis by oral or intravenous administration of sodium lactate or sodium bicarbonate. If it is possible, correction of the renal problem, for example, an acute bacterial pyelonephritis, is probably the most effective action in the care of these patients. Those patients suffering from retention of urinary waste products, as evidenced by high blood urea nitrogen, high phosphorus, and low calcium, can best be managed by attempts at returning the patient to a normal pH with alkalizing agents such as an alkaline ash diet, sodium lactate, and sodium bicarbonate. It is important that the urinary output be kept at an acceptably high level. Should there be loss of body fluids other than through the kidneys, it is of utmost importance that the blood pressure be maintained and that the renal blood flow be stabilized for adequate transfer of as many waste products as possible from the vascular system.

Respiratory Acidosis. This type of acidosis is usually found in those senile patients with marked pulmonary emphysema. Here retention of CO_2 will lead to a respiratory acidosis. The only possible treatment is to place the patient in such a position as to increase his respiratory reserve or respiratory function. A rocking bed, or forced assisted respirations, or both may be necessary. Should the patient become markedly acidotic due to his pulmonary insufficiency, the outlook is extremely poor.

Hypoproteinemia. Should there be a marked drop in the albumin fraction of the total protein determination in a patient suffering from hypoproteinemia, wound healing will be poor, and tissue edema may further interfere with the healing process. Accordingly, if time permits, corrective measures should be carried out by administration of salt-free albumin, intravenous amino acids, or, if possible, a high protein diet. It has been pointed out in this chapter that degrees of hypoproteinemia compatible with the age of the individual cannot be corrected, nor should vigorous attempts at correction be attempted in the elderly.

Blood Pressure and Pulse. Blood pressure and pulse are carefully followed after the operation, and one must be cautious in differentiating between the hypotension which may result from the operation and any evidence of shock which might be the result of hemorrhage. The distinction could be vital.

Renal Function. Arteriosclerotic changes and arteriolar nephrosclerotic changes caused by hypertension are extremely common in the elderly. Diminished renal function will usually have been revealed in the preoperative period by persistent marked albuminuria and casts and cells in the urinary sediment. Suspicion of renal azotemia will be aroused by an elevated blood urea nitrogen, a fixed urinary specific, and a decreased urea clearance. In these instances one must carefully govern or attempt to govern the level of urinary output. Hypotension or decreased oral or parenteral intake may well prove disastrous to already seriously diseased kidneys. Should urinary output decrease in the postoperative period, a relatively vigorous attempt at improving renal blood flow must be made. Hypotension must be corrected rapidly. In some instances even pressor drugs may be used in conjunction with plasma expanders and blood. Where one must accept a fixed urinary specific gravity due to advanced renal disease, adequate fluids must be provided. Here one must balance the danger of pulmonary edema caused by excessive fluid administration against the equally serious danger of oliguria due to inadequate fluid intake.

Respiratory Complications. Since respiratory complications are so common in the elderly person, retention of secretions in the pulmonary tree must be prevented, and consequently the patient should be aspirated during the postoperative period. The patient should be turned frequently and should be made to breathe deeply and to cough in order to remove bronchial obstructions.

Where there is injury to the ribs with multiple fractures or segmental fractures, tracheostomy is extremely helpful and should be done as soon as the respiratory difficulty is noted. Occasionally sternal traction may be employed in conjunction with establishing a tracheostomy (Fig. 2-6). In some instances of injuries about the face, a tracheostomy should be performed preoperatively.

The care of the tracheostomy tube after its insertion is exceedingly important, and the bronchi must be aspirated frequently by means of a low-pressure suction so that no further damage be done to the lung. If the secretions become thick, they may be loosened and liquefied by means of the detergent, Alevaire. In cases of paradoxical respiration, it is often helpful to attach the Bennett or Milch respirator to the tracheostomy tube. This relieves the patient of the need for voluntary chest expansion and helps to aerate the lung completely. It often carries the patient over a very dangerous period, and it is a lifesaving measure in many instances.

COMPLICATIONS

Treatment of Postoperative Shock. The elderly patient is overly susceptible to the trauma of operation and to blood loss. It is, therefore,

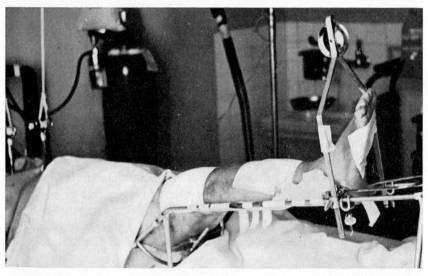

FIG. 2-6. With multiple body-area injuries, concomitant care must be exercised. Here parasternal traction is combined with tibial traction in Braun-Böhler frame. Only by constant care of all injuries and adequate coordination by all members of the medical team can optimal care be provided to the seriously injured.

extremely important that during the operation the surgeon control hemorrhage as quickly and efficiently as possible.

As stressed repeatedly in these chapters, the most important factor in the treatment of shock is blood replacement, and this should be performed carefully and quickly enough to control the symptoms. Some patients have inadequate cardiovascular apparatus, and dangerous overloading of the circulation by too vigorous fluid replacement, either blood or saline, is apt to cause a cardiac failure with dire consequences. The usual hypotension following an operation does not necessarily indicate shock, and only in those cases where the drop in blood pressure is severe and where it is associated with an extremely rapid pulse is blood replacement necessary. During the few hours after the operation is concluded, the patient is in a most dangerous condition, and he should be observed by

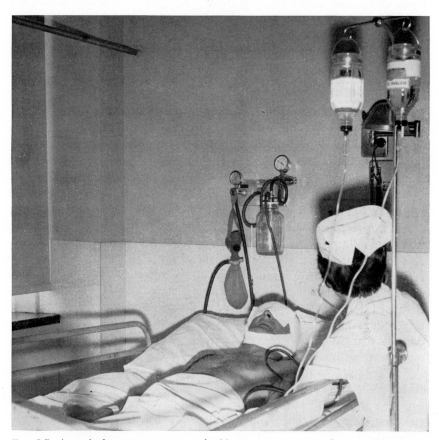

FIG. 2-7. A typical recovery room unit. Note constant care of one nurse to one patient until the patient has reacted. Suction, fluids, observation of vital signs are controlled by this nurse until the patient has reacted. He is then removed to a surgical ward for further postoperative care.

competent nurses in a recovery room where blood, oxygen, and other materials are immediately available for resuscitative measures (Fig. 2-7).

Kidney Shutdown. Following trauma, an elderly patient may show no evidence of renal insufficiency until after an operative procedure. He may then demonstrate evidence of a severe renal shutdown by anuria or decrease in urinary output. Over the last several years advances in the treatment of renal shutdown have added powerful material to the surgeon's armamentarium. Blood dialysis with the artificial kidney and the use of cationic resins are helpful adjuncts in the care of the patient with renal shutdown. Where formerly one treated anuria by alkalinization of the blood and administration of minimal fluids to replace insensible water losses, one may now administer resins per rectum to decrease the serious hyperkalemia. Where hyperkalemia persists and where azotemia becomes more marked, dialysis on the artificial kidney is available. Should these methods prolong the patient's life for approximately fourteen days, very frequently kidney function will resume if the organ has not been irreparably damaged.

Treatment of Urinary Retention—Hypertrophy of the Prostate. Often an elderly male who has been able to empty his bladder satisfactorily up to the time of the accident or operation may suddenly go into urinary retention after the added insult. It is essential that a catheter be kept in place, in some instances until the patient has recovered enough to allow an operative procedure on the prostate. Urinary retention necessitating prostatectomy is an occasional complication following fracture of the hip in the male.

Acute Abdominal Complications. When there is interference with normal metabolic processes in other systems, the superimposed immobilization in bed may incite the development of acute abdominal lesions. One of the most common complications is the occurrence of acute cholecystitis during the postoperative period following a trauma. The elderly patient will develop the signs of pain, tenderness, and rigidity in the right upper quadrant associated with fever and leukocytosis. The diagnosis may be very difficult to make in view of the patient's other signs and symptoms, but it should always be suspected when symptoms point toward the right upper quadrant. In most instances, the best form of treatment is cholecystectomy as soon as possible after the diagnosis is made. If, however, the patient is in a precarious condition, it may be necessary to do a cholecystostomy primarily and defer the removal of the gall bladder to a later date.

Early Ambulation. Early ambulation is probably more necessary in the elderly than in younger individuals. It is essential that the patient be kept erect and moving in order to prevent lung complications. The proper functioning of the bowel and the bladder is greatly aided by ambulation. Furthermore, the patient's stiffened joints and inelastic muscles must be activated so that they may not lose what little function may be left in them. In addition this activity may help to prevent mental and psychic depression.

The patient should be encouraged to move all of his voluntary muscles and should be given definite exercises daily. Being "out of bed" should mean that he is seated in a chair where he is allowed to move his arms and legs and not bundled in blankets and immobilized (Fig. 2-8*A* and *B*). As soon as possible he should be made to walk, if necessary with the assistance of crutches or a walker. Often it is impossible to get the elderly patient to use crutches, and he must be supported by an attendant as he attempts to walk. If the patient has not walked for many years before his operation, it is still necessary that he be exercised even though this be done in a bed or a chair.

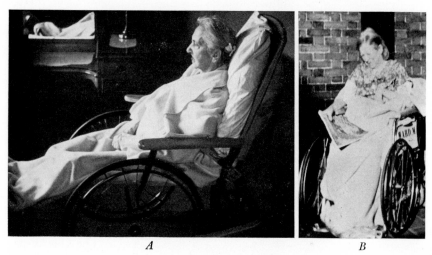

A   *B*

FIG. 2-8. *A*. Incorrect. This is not mobility. *B*. Correct. This permits freedom of motion.

The Prevention and Treatment of Decubiti. One of the most difficult conditions to handle in the elderly is the decubitus which develops over the sacrum, on the heel or lateral surface of the foot of the inactive limb, or in other sites where the weight of the body on the mattress, the cast, or traction apparatus exerts pressure (Fig. 2-9*A*, *B*, and *C*). Although the usual cause of the development of decubitus is often said to be poor nursing, a decubitus can occur despite perfect nursing care. In many instances the decubitus is caused by pressure over the sacrum on the sacral saddle in the operating room; and if this is not recognized, the lesion will appear a few days after operation even though the patient has been properly turned by the nurses. It is therefore important that this area be carefully inspected after operation, and that the patient be turned and not allowed to rest in any single position for any length of time until the region has resumed its normal appearance.

Should a decubitus ulcer develop, ambitious and vigorous therapy must be pursued until the skin returns to its normal state. If necessary, debridement under general anesthesia should be performed down to clean bleeding tissue. Necrotic bone must be excised and local anti-bacterial substances introduced into the area of debridement. Meticulous local care of the wound with frequent sharp dissection to remove necrotic debris must be continued. Exposure of the surrounding healthy skin to a heat lamp will improve its texture. As soon as fresh, healthy, pink-red

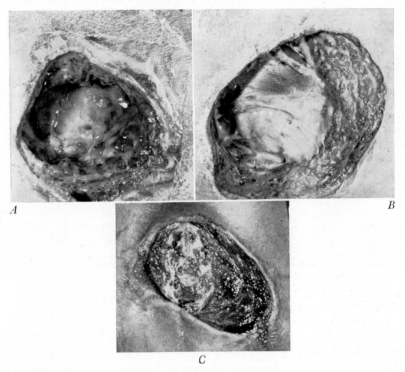

FIG. 2-9. *A.* Sacral decubitus ulcer measuring 8 cm in diameter has exposed the sacral periosteum and gluteal fascia. Chemical and mechanical debridement must be employed to create a rich, clean bed of granulations to accept pedical graft. *B* and *C.* Trochanteric decubitus ulcers in the same patient. These all occurred in a Parkinsonian patient with a hip fracture.

granulations are in evidence over an area of denuded bone, it is necessary to swing full-thickness skin flaps and to apply split-thickness grafts to the residual defects at the donor sites. In most cases simple split-thickness grafting will prove unsuccessful over a bony prominence. Occasionally, excision of the bony prominence will lend itself to simple split-thickness grafting, but this is considered an inferior technique to primary full-thickness flap transfer (Fig. 2-10).

All areas of possible pressure from casts or traction should be carefully watched. A common site of pressure which may result in a foot drop is the area compressed by the sling of the Russell traction. This should be held wide apart by a separator over the patella. The limb may be thin and have little muscle or padding, and only a slight external rotation of the limb will cause pressure against the common peroneal nerve as

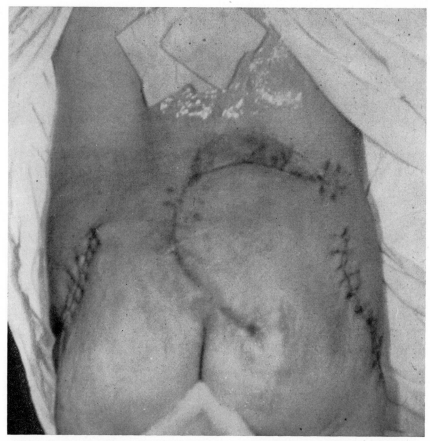

FIG. 2-10. After suitable mechanical and chemical debridement, simple closure of trochanteric decubitus ulcers was performed. Rotation-flap closure was used to close the sacral decubitus.

it curves about the neck of the fibula. Under such circumstances, foot drop can develop in a very few hours. This complication can be avoided if the knee and hip are flexed to at least 45° and the limb elevated on at least two pillows to prevent the external rotation which occurs more easily with the limb in extension.

Treatment of Diabetes. Diabetes in the injured should be under control before the operation. The blood sugar is then followed at frequent intervals after operation, and increasing amounts of insulin are given as are necessary. It may be much more difficult to control the diabetes after the trauma or operation than it had been under the patient's usual circumstances. Trauma or other body stresses may greatly increase insulin requirements and cause great difficulty in attempting to prevent severe diabetic acidosis postoperatively.

Special measures used in caring for the elderly diabetic patient are extremely important. First, continual checks of the patient's diabetic control by spot urines and group urines are necessary. An indwelling catheter is almost mandatory in the seriously ill patient. Should urinary retention remain unnoticed in the diabetic patient, the bladder reservoir of urine containing large amounts of sugar and acetone may mask the degree of correction of the acidosis or glycosuria by producing persistently positive urinary sugar and acetone determinations. Despite the ready control of the normal elderly patient with PZI or NPH insulin, it is most important to control the postoperative patient on a regimen consisting of regular insulin. Following stabilization of his condition by the third or fourth postoperative day, the patient can once again be placed on the required amount of NPH or PZI insulin. Until that time, the status of the patient must be carefully followed by multiple urine determinations and occasional fasting blood sugars and CO_2 determinations. The typical regimen for the elderly diabetic undergoing surgery is as follows:

On the morning of surgery, an indwelling catheter is placed in the urinary bladder. The patient receives no long-acting insulin or intermediate-duration insulin. Infusions are begun whereby each two grams of sugar are covered by one unit of regular insulin added to the infusion so that these are running concomitantly.

If the patient's urinary output or renal function is adequate, saline is administered in amounts of approximately 500 ml a day as a base line dosage. During the procedure, urine specimens are collected and determined. Should this prove to be of long duration, extra amounts of regular insulin are administered, usually intravenously, as necessary to control any marked amount of glycosuria or acetonuria. In the recovery room, another specimen is immediately obtained, and if the patient is acidotic, further care is carried out. The dosage depends upon the urinary determination and acetone.

SUGGESTED INSULIN DOSAGE FOR URINARY SUGAR
DETERMINATIONS EVERY 4 HOURS

Urine Sugar	Dose Regular Insulin
0	None
1	None
2	10 units
3	15 units
4	20 units

Should the patient prove markedly acidotic, i.e., a 4+ acetonuria, it becomes necessary to take hourly urine specimens and to adjust the specific insulin dosages according to them. If the patient receives an amount of glucose insufficient to be metabolized by the administered insulin, it is very possible that he will remain acidotic while the glycosuria may well disappear. Accordingly, it is necessary to supply enough glucose and enough insulin to metabolize this glucose. Thus the patient's stored fat will not be burned off nor will the acidosis and acetonuria so typical of the inadequately controlled diabetic patient be produced. Once the patient is able to carry out normal alimentation, it is possible to try to return him to his preoperative insulin dosage, realizing that the very nature of the procedure may lead to a fairly prolonged increased insulin requirement. Accordingly, a further check of the urine and blood CO_2 combining power and sugar are necessary in the relatively late period of postoperative recovery.

Diet. The nutrition of the elderly patient is particularly important in the immediate postoperative period. During the first few days after operation, the fluid and food intake may have to be given entirely by vein, but as soon as possible the patient should be urged and encouraged to take food by mouth. Many elderly people react in a childlike way to demands that they eat adequately. Here is one of the supreme tests facing the dietetic and nursing staffs of an institution.

Attractively prepared meal trays, pleasant surroundings, and good rapport between patient and bedside staff are all extremely important in this regard. If the aged patient's dietary regimen prior to injury can be determined, this will prove of great benefit in planning the meals following definitive care. Proper balance of protein, fat, and carbohydrate is of course necessary in the elderly patient's diet, the proteins being the most urgent. In the return of the traumatized aged patient to normal activity, diet plays an extremely important part. Because of the insufficiency that may have been present for many years, it is important to realize that protein and carbohydrate are the two more essential items. The fat, while high in calories, is not very useful in counteracting the negative nitrogen balance in the postoperative state. Accordingly, a high protein, high carbohydrate, and moderate fat diet is usually best. Secondly, the administration of large amounts of vitamins is important. Because of dietary indiscretions, the average elderly person is frequently in a state of subclinical or even at times clinical avitaminosis. Because of this, the administration of vitamin supplements, while perhaps unnecessary in a young patient, is extremely important if the elderly person is to continue at normal metabolic levels. A soft diet will be required in the edentulous or poorly dentured patient who cannot sufficiently masticate solid, hard meats or similar foods. It is most important to humor the elderly patient to some degree in handling his dietary difficulties. Should the dietary intake prove inadequate, it then becomes necessary to supplement it by other methods. If oral ingestion of a protein supplement, such as Sustagen or Protinal, prove inadequate in maintaining the patient's serum protein levels, it then becomes necessary to administer intravenous medications. Salt-free albumin can be used for this, but one must remember that by its osmotic properties it may draw a large amount of intracellular fluids into the extracellular system and so lead to some difficulties with overexpansion of this space. Recently fats have been emulsified sufficiently so that they are extremely valuable in the intravenous nutrition of the postoperative patient. It should be remembered that fats contain 9 calories per gram, while proteins and carbohydrates contain only 4 calories per gram. Therefore, though intravenous fats, such as Lipomul or other emulsified solutions, are extremely valuable, reactions can occur. These fats are of limited value because after a certain dosage they must be abandoned. The dietary needs of the postoperative elderly patient remain a very definite problem for several days or weeks following the surgical procedure. One must realize that following a major operative procedure the elderly patient may do very well in the immediate postoperative period, but then slowly lose ground and become either invalided or moribund as a result of poor alimentation associated with one or more of the many other maladies to which he is subject.

BIBLIOGRAPHY

Beal, J. M.: "Manual of Recovery Room Care." New York, Macmillan, 1956.

Gamble, J. L.: "Chemical Anatomy, Physiology and Pathology of Extracellular Fluids." Cambridge, Mass., Harvard University Press, 1954.

Klug, T. J., and R. C. McPherson: Postoperative complications in the elderly patient. *Amer. Jour. Surg.* **97**:713, 1959.

Moore, F. D.: Medical progress articles: common pattern of water and electrolyte change in injury, surgery and disease. *New Eng. Jour. Med.* **258**:227, 325, 427, 1958.

Moyer, C. A.: Acute temporary changes in renal function associated with major surgical procedures. *Surgery.* **27**:198, 1950.

Rhoads, J. E.: Protein nutrition in surgical patients: collective review. *Internat. Abstr. Surg.* **94**:417, 1952.

Roberts, K. E., H. T. Randall, H. L. Sanders, and M. Hood: Effects of potassium in renal tubular reabsorption of bicarbonate. *Jour. Clin. Invest.* **34**:666, 1955.

Scribner, B. H., M. H. Power, and E. H. Rynearson: Bedside management of problems of fluid balance. *Jour. Amer. Med. Ass.* **144**:1167, 1950.

Chapter 3

Anesthesia

E. M. Papper and Leonard Brand

Modern anesthesia makes it possible to provide the benefits of surgical treatment in the aged wherever and whenever it is indicated. The fundamental principles of good anesthesia for young adults can be applied with equal success to elderly patients.

Any attempt to anesthetize the geriatric patient safely must consider not only his physiological disturbances and the pharmacology of the anesthetic drug but also the requirements of the surgeon and the skill and experience of the anesthesiologist. Elderly people who have suffered trauma cannot be grouped as "surgical entities." Nor can generalizations be made about individuals in the same chronological age group since, as has been repeatedly noted in these pages, physiological age is much more meaningful in evaluating these patients. The "old man of 50" and the "young man of 70" are commonly seen.

It is true, in general, that patients in the older age groups have a decreased capacity to adjust to the stress of injury, operation, or anesthesia. This decline in body defenses may be due not only to the degenerative changes of senescence but also to the increased incidence and severity of cardiopulmonary diseases. Aged patients appear to have a diminished ability to detoxify or eliminate potent anesthetic and sedative drugs. They tolerate anesthetic procedures in a more restricted manner than younger patients. This would suggest that the major disturbing effects of anesthesia on aged patients differ only quantitatively from the effects on young subjects.

PRE- AND POSTOPERATIVE CARE

The proper preparation of the elderly patient for anesthesia and operation includes the correction of deficiencies and restoration of function to a status as near normal as possible. These conditions provide maximum insurance for uncomplicated recovery and therefore justify a delay in operative intervention, when possible. Unfortunately, operation on an

injured patient may be necessary before the patient is completely prepared. The problem of determining the optimum time to operate after
improving the patient's general condition is one which requires judgment, experience, and the closest possible collaboration among surgeon,
internist, and anesthesiologist.

The pre- and postoperative care of the patient is discussed more fully
in other chapters, but some of the aspects pertinent to anesthesia will be
considered here.

Cardiovascular. Loss of elasticity in blood vessels and myocardial degeneration prevent normal reflex adjustments to changes in blood flow,
blood pressure, and blood volume. Coronary artery disease, arteriosclerosis, hypertension, arrhythmias, and valvular disease are common.
Clinical or subclinical decompensation with cardiac enlargement, elevated venous pressure, and congestion of lungs and parenchymal organs
may be present. Early, rapid digitalization may be a lifesaving procedure
in these patients, since congestive failure may be precipitated by trauma
and by the stress of surgery and anesthesia. A careful history obtained
from the patient or his family, as emphasized in previous chapters, is
equally important in evaluating the patient's cardiac reserve in reference to anesthesia.

Elderly people normally have a lower blood volume per kilogram of
body weight. They may be anemic or occasionally polycythemic. Whole
blood or packed cells may be necessary to restore an adequate blood
volume.

Respiratory. The respiratory system almost invariably shows signs of
degenerative changes in the aged. Ventilatory function is impaired as
a result of emphysema, increased functional residual capacity, loss of
elasticity of chest wall and bronchioles, and decreased gas exchange across
the alveolar membrane. Tidal volume, vital capacity, and pulmonary
compliance are decreased. Diaphragmatic respiration is increased, and
thoracic respiration is lessened. Tracheobronchial secretions and puru-
lent discharges, as well as pulmonary edema, may impair the exchange of
gases. Arterial oxygen tension may be reduced and the carbon dioxide
level elevated.

The protective cough reflex may be weak and permit aspiration of
vomitus or pharyngeal secretions. Less frequently, the cough, laryngeal,
and bronchial reflexes may be extremely sensitive, making inhalation of
anesthesia difficult. The uncorrected anatomical airway may be poor
because of an edentulous mouth and mandibular atrophy. These patients
are subject to atelectasis and pneumonia from retained secretions, depressed cough reflex, and inactivity. Tracheal suction, frequent turning,
and early ambulation tend to prevent these complications.

Renal and Hepatic. The aging process causes atrophy of cells, an increase in connective tissue, and a generalized arteriosclerosis. The function of these organs may also be affected by chronic passive congestion. Renal function is diminished with decreased plasma flow and glomerular filtration. An indwelling catheter with tidal drainage may be necessary to correct or prevent retention of urine in the bladder. The liver and kidney are less able to detoxify and excrete the various agents used for anesthesia and pain relief.

Other Considerations. Many aged persons have lived on a poor diet and are malnourished. They frequently suffer from vitamin deficiencies and anemia, and have low plasma protein levels. They may be dehydrated and in electrolyte imbalance. The degree of anemia and hypoproteinemia may be hard to estimate until the fluid balance is restored. Endocrine function may be depressed and the use of insulin, estrogens, androgens, ACTH, and cortisone may be necessary. Elderly people are less capable of adjusting to changes in temperature, and care must be taken to help them maintain their normal body temperature.

Although many aged persons have a philosophical attitude and can face their difficulties with serenity, others feel unwanted, unloved, and useless. When they are well they live quite successfully with their physical handicaps and can maintain a healthy mental attitude. When they become ill or the victims of trauma, the multitude of pathological lesions may be overwhelming. In a study of 8,000 aged patients, Monroe found that 69 per cent showed some form of mental or emotional disturbance. Black found mental change in 30 per cent. The common observation that "Grandpa isn't the same since his operation (or trauma)" is, unfortunately, quite true.

The drugs and medications which the patient has been taking must be ascertained from the patient or his family. Digitalis, insulin, ataractic drugs, antihypertensive and hypnotic agents, adrenal cortical hormones, and even opiates and alcohol may be used by some of these patients, and may influence the estimation of risk and choice of agents.

PREMEDICATION

Perhaps the most important means of preparation that an aged, injured person can receive is an unhurried visit from a sympathetic anesthesiologist. It is extremely difficult to dispel with drugs the fear that "I'm too old to survive this operation" or "I'll never wake up from this."

It has been proved amply that the depressant effects of premedicant drugs on the ventilation and circulation of old people require a reduction to one-half or less of the usual therapeutic doses. Unless given intravenously, these agents take longer to act because they are poorly absorbed from tissues or gut. They also tend to last longer because of inefficient detoxification and excretion in liver and kidneys.

It has been our practice to limit the preoperative use of analgesic and narcotic drugs to those elderly patients who are in pain. A confused, irrational patient in pain can be made cooperative and comfortable with 25 to 75 mg of Demerol or its equivalent in opiates. On the other hand, the same treatment of a patient without pain is usually unnecessary and may depress his ventilation and circulation.

The barbiturates are useful for their hypnotic effect. Average doses in elderly patients are 25 to 100 mg of secobarbital or pentobarbital. The barbiturates are not analgesic and, if given to a pained or confused patient, may increase both discomfort and confusion.

Belladonna drugs are given in smaller doses than usual because older people have a decreased power of secretion. There has been controversy as to the relative merits of atropine and scopolamine in geriatric practice. The delirium commonly ascribed to scopolamine is rarely seen in our experience unless it is given to a patient with intense pain. In any event, the dose varies between 0.2 mg and 0.4 mg of either drug.

The type of anesthesia contemplated and the agents to be used have an important bearing upon what premedication should be given. If regional anesthesia is contemplated or if the anesthesiologist will be using potent agents such as cyclopropane, narcotic premedication is rarely necessary. However, if light general anesthesia with nonpotent agents is contemplated, the narcotics may be used.

One has very little leeway with these patients. Even a slight overdose of a depressant drug may result in sudden hypotension or apnea. There may be little warning, and it may be difficult or impossible to reverse these effects. One cannot easily recover these agents once they have been administered but must wait until they have been slowly metabolized or excreted. The use of drug antagonists or stimulants is dangerous and rarely successful.

In general, as few drugs as possible and as little of each drug as possible should be given. It is much easier and safer to supplement with subsequent doses than it is to overcome overdosage.

THE EFFECTS OF ANESTHESIA

In spite of the obvious risks, properly managed anesthesia minimizes the dangers of surgery in aged people. There are several generalizations which can be made in reviewing summaries of anesthetic experiences, including both elective and emergency procedures, in large series of elderly patients.

The mortality rate in surgical patients in the sixth and seventh decades from all causes is about 5 per cent. In the eighth decade and beyond, the mortality is about 15 per cent. When emergency procedures were considered alone, the mortality was considerably higher. These studies were completed over a period of years, and the mortality in the more recent years is lower because of better care. Most of these series included any death that occurred in the postoperative period, regardless of how long after the actual operation it occurred. It is quite difficult to assess the part played by anesthesia in causing or contributing to these deaths. It is doubtful that anesthesia contributed to more than 10 per cent of the total mortality. To put it differently, anesthesia probably caused between 0.4 and 1.0 per cent of all the deaths in these age groups. It should be noted that many different types of anesthesia were used, including spinal anesthesia, thiopental, cyclopropane, ether, various forms of regional and local anesthesia, and even rectal anesthesia. Apparently no one technique or agent appeared best, and one must conclude that in the elderly patient the physiological control of anesthesia is more important than the choice of the specific agent.

TECHNIQUES AND AGENTS OF ANESTHESIA

GENERAL ANESTHESIA

Ether. Ether may be used satisfactorily in the aged. However, it is an extremely potent agent, and the establishment of deep anesthesia with relatively small doses is very easy to accomplish in an elderly person. Profound refractory depression of the circulation is particularly evident with ether overdosage. The first sign of overdosage in the aged may be sudden circulatory collapse. Elderly subjects do not usually develop a preliminary tachycardia or tachypnea as ether anesthesia deepens. Time is apparently telescoped for these subjects, and the effects of profound etherization become evident with much smaller quantities of ether and much earlier in the course of anesthesia. Only the lightest plane of surgical anesthesia, or the stage of analgesia, is utilized. The administration of ether must be skillfully performed, and it should be remembered that very small quantities can achieve relatively profound depths of anesthesia.

Cyclopropane. This agent usually provokes controversy in the field of geriatric anesthesia. Opponents of its use cite the fact that its potential for inciting cardiac irritability makes it unsuitable for elderly patients who may have cardiac arrhythmias. Cyclopropane has the further disadvantage of depressing ventilation easily, thereby making oxygenation of the blood more difficult, despite the high concentration of oxygen in the inhaled atmosphere. More particularly, the excretion of carbon dioxide may be impaired, resulting in respiratory acidosis during anesthesia, postanesthetic hypotension, and ventricular arrhythmias. These defects of the agent may be overcome by the assistance or control of ventilation and the utilization of the lightest planes of general anesthesia.

We have again emphasized the value of light anesthesia for elderly patients. It should also be added that it is usually possible to provide good working conditions for the surgeon, even in the lightest planes of anesthesia, since senescence relaxes tissues. When relaxation is not totally adequate, a satisfactory surgical field can be achieved more safely by the use of a small dose of a relaxant than by deepening the anesthesia.

Other Potent Agents. Trichlorethylene and Fluothane have been used successfully in aged patients. They are extremely potent agents and are best used as supplements to the nonpotent gases. They are nonexplosive. When used in a nonrebreathing system with devices which can deliver known concentrations accurately they have proved safe.

The Nonpotent Gases. Nitrous oxide and ethylene may be considered together since they cannot provide the deepest planes of surgical anesthesia. In aged patients, however, these agents can provide surgical anesthesia of satisfactory depth with surprisingly little supplementation. Ethylene is more potent than nitrous oxide; therefore a somewhat deeper plane of anesthesia can be achieved with it. Ethylene is inflammable and nitrous oxide is not. Neither agent has any known toxic effect upon any organ system in the presence of adequate oxygenation and efficient ventilation.

It is important at this point to lay to rest one of the myths about anesthesia for the elderly patient. It is frequently stated that ethylene and nitrous oxide are unsuitable or dangerous because of the anoxia they produce. If these agents are used for young, robust patients without supplementation, this criticism is valid. In the aged patient, however, these agents are more than satisfactory because anesthesia of satisfactory depth can be achieved with an adequate supply of oxygen and without demonstrable toxicity. *In the modern practice of geriatric anesthesia, ethylene and nitrous oxide should be considered the agents of choice for elderly patients provided that an adequate concentration of oxygen is used (more than 25 per cent).*

Intravenous Anesthesia. Intravenous anesthetic agents produce general anesthesia with all the attendant advantages and disadvantages of general narcosis. There are several drugs in current use. Most of them are barbiturates. In elderly patients doses as small as 50 mg thiopental may produce significant depression of respiration and circulation. These drugs must be given to elderly patients with extreme caution in dilute concentrations which permit the injection of precisely determined doses (.5 to 2.5 per cent). They should be used for basal hypnosis and for the maintenance of anesthesia with nitrous oxide and oxygen or ethylene and oxygen. The barbiturates must not be used in aged patients as the sole anesthetic agent.

It has become fairly common practice to infuse dilute solutions of opiates or synthetic narcotics (morphine, Demerol) to supplement non-potent general anesthesia. Small intermittent doses of these agents have also been used. It should rarely be necessary in aged patients to use these drugs, but if they are found necessary, great care must be used to prevent respiratory and circulatory depression.

Rectal Anesthesia. It is generally advised that Avertin and thiopental by rectum be avoided in elderly patients because, in the doses satisfactory for production of basal narcosis, considerable hypotension may develop. This generalization seems to be a rational and safe one. However, this theoretical objection is not borne out by actual clinical experience, since these agents have been used clinically, and although they increase the incidence of hypotension, they do not appear to increase the mortality or morbidity if the doses used are very small.

Relaxants. The muscle relaxants are not needed as often in the anesthetic management of aged patients as they are in those with greater muscle power and greater "resistance" to the effects of anesthetic agents. However, the employment of relaxants as a substitute for added depth of anesthesia appears to be rational, should this be necessary for elderly patients. It is of particular importance to be certain that prolonged respiratory depression does not ensue with the use of these agents. Conservative dosage is essential, and the preservation of spontaneous breathing or the frequent testing for the return of spontaneous respiration when controlled respiration is used is mandatory. If profound relaxation is needed for only a short time, such as for an exploration of the bowel or the reduction of a fracture, it is better to use a short-acting relaxant such as succinylcholine rather than a longer-acting one.

LOCAL ANESTHETIC AGENTS

If local or regional anesthesia is satisfactory for the surgeon's requirement and for the personality of the patient, it appears to offer maximum safety. A major hazard in the use of these agents is the matter of total dose. In this respect the local anesthetics pose the same problems as the general anesthetics and the narcotics. Elderly patients do not tolerate the doses used for younger patients. Therefore smaller concentrations of local drugs and smaller total doses are safer in the aged.

For lacerations in various parts of the body, local infiltration or field block may be sufficient. For fractures in the hand, forearm, and around the elbow, a brachial block is effective and safe. In this respect we find that approaching the brachial plexus on the medial surface of the upper arm, just under the insertion of pectoralis major and almost in the axilla, gives an excellent block and avoids the possibility of pneumothorax. For work in the foot and ankle, a sciatic femoral block is effective and easily accomplished. Regional anesthesia causes the least interference with the functions of the organism as a whole. Elderly patients tolerate these forms of anesthesia quite well.

SPINAL AND EPIDURAL ANESTHESIA

Spinal anesthesia, segmental epidural anesthesia, and caudal anesthesia have been widely used and advocated by many. Occasionally deformities of the spine caused by arthritis or injuries alter the anatomy sufficiently to make these techniques difficult. The major disadvantage of these methods is the relatively high incidence of hypotension, especially when high levels of anesthesia are reached, and the difficulty of assuring effective correction once it has occurred. Vasopressors are injected prophylactically before establishing spinal or epidural block to help prevent hypotension. Although it appears reasonable to believe that falls in blood pressure are highly undesirable in aged patients, Turville and Dripps found that there were relatively few complications due to the hypotension caused by spinal anesthesia. Hypotension did not appear to be responsible for a significant increase in the incidence of myocardial infarction or renal vascular change.

The continuous caudal or epidural technique, with insertion of a catheter, permits more flexibility in the duration of safe anesthesia. Situations may arise where the basic anesthesia is regional and is supplemented by light general anesthesia. If the patient has a great deal of pain or has an unstable fracture, it is frequently difficult or impossible to secure the proper position for lumbar puncture, and general anesthesia must be used. It is important to make sure that the local or regional technique contemplated will be sufficiently effective to carry out the procedure required. It is much better to start out with a carefully planned and unhurried general anesthesia than to have to supplement an inadequate or unsuccessful regional anesthesia.

PREVENTION OF ASPIRATION

All patients who have suffered trauma and entered the hospital on an emergency basis must be suspected of having a full stomach. Vomiting and regurgitation of the contents of the stomach is a frequent and serious complication with a high mortality and morbidity. A careful history should be taken from the patient and his family to determine what the patient ingested before and since his accident. Different foods leave the stomach at different rates. Fatty foods tend to remain longer. A patient who is emotionally upset or in pain will have a slower emptying time. Gastric lavage and induced emesis may help to remove food from the stomach but they do not always empty the stomach. If the patient receives premedication, or if anesthesia is induced, the cough and gag reflexes may be obtunded and, if he vomits, food may be aspirated. If local or regional anesthesia can be used and the patient remains awake, he is better able to handle any vomiting which may occur.

If general anesthesia is required, the trachea should be protected from the foreign material in the pharynx by the insertion of an endotracheal tube with an inflatable balloon. This must be done with the patient awake, using small sedative doses of thiopental and a topical agent in the Pharynx and trachea. If emesis occurs during the intubation, the patient must be awake enough to cough and adduct his vocal cords. An endotracheal tube can be inserted in older patients with very little difficulty because they are usually edentulous and have very poor jaw-muscle tone. If properly done, this is not an unpleasant experience. The patients usually have complete amnesia for the whole procedure. An equally satisfactory alternative is to insert the tube after inducing general anesthesia in the head-up position, establishing total muscle paralysis with a fast-acting relaxant and quickly inserting the tube and inflating the cuff. On emergence from anesthesia the same problem remains, and the endotracheal tube should not be removed until the patient has recovered sufficiently to cough and protect his airway from foreign material.

It is essential that a good airway be established and maintained during general anesthesia. The use of the endotracheal tube is essential in cases of thoracic injury or where the chest may be entered by the surgeon. An endotracheal tube should be employed, no matter what the site of operation, whenever an airway is difficult to maintain by mask. A good mask fit may be difficult because of mandibular atrophy, or an edentulous mouth, or even because of a beard or mustache. Another important advantage of an endotracheal tube is that it permits effective suctioning of the trachea. This allows better ventilation and helps to prevent postoperative pulmonary difficulties. The complications of using an endotracheal tube are infrequent and minor. The consequences of a poor airway are severe and may be fatal. If at any time during the course of anesthesia a completely satisfactory airway cannot be maintained by mask, an endotracheal tube should be inserted without delay.

Position

Most elderly patients tolerate unusual positions on the operating table poorly. They also tolerate poorly any change from one position to another; therefore all movements should be made slowly, gradually, and gently to minimize the need for circulatory compensation. If the patient must be in the prone position, care must be taken to elevate his abdomen and costal margin from the table by the use of rolls or pads, to facilitate respiration. The use of elastic bandages on the legs may help to maintain the blood pressure if the table must be tilted to a head-up position. It may also help to prevent postoperative phlebitis. These patients are prone to pressure sores and nerve injury so that the table must be well padded and all pressure points carefully protected.

During the operative procedure it may be impossible to reach a site for the insertion of an intravenous needle. Therefore it is essential that preoperatively a good vein be found and a large needle, cannula, or catheter be inserted intravenously and securely protected. The amount of fluids infused should be watched carefully to prevent overloading of the vascular bed with resultant congestive failure. If there is blood loss of consequence, it is important to replace blood as it is lost so as to avoid the twin errors of hypovolemia and overtransfusion.

Postoperative Sedation

In the postoperative period, sedative drugs must be used in small doses or omitted entirely in order to avoid the depressant effects produced by narcotics, since they are apt to be more harmful in the aged than in younger patients. Aspirin, codeine, and phenobarbital (not an analgesic) should be used more often to achieve comfort in the postoperative period. The patient should be gotten out of bed as soon as possible, and if this cannot be done he should be turned frequently and proper tracheobronchial toilet maintained by suction, deep breathing, and encouraging the patient to cough.

BIBLIOGRAPHY

Adriani, J.: Anesthesia for the aged and poor-risk patient. *Amer. Surg.* **22**:1023, 1956.

Beling, C. A., D. T. Bosch, and O. B. Carter, Jr.: Blood volume in geriatric surgery. *Geriatrics.* **7**:179, 1952.

Black, M. G.: Aging—its influence on pre-operative preparation. *Proc. Fourth Cong. Scand. Soc. Anes.* Helsinki, 1956.

Bosch, D. T., A. Islami, C. T. C. Tan, and C. A. Beling: The elderly surgical patient. *A.M.A. Arch. Surg.* **64**:269, 1952.

Burnham, P. J.: Regional block of the great nerves of the upper arm: current comment and case reports. *Anesthesiology.* **19**:281, 1958.

Chope, H. D., and L. Breslow: Nutritional status of the aging. *Hospital Progress.* **37**:46, 1956.

Cole, W. H.: Operability in the young and aged. *Ann. Surg.* **138**:145, 1953.

Davies, D. F., and N. W. Shock: Age changes in glomerular filtration rate, effective renal plasma flow, and tubular excretory capacity in adult males. *Jour. Clin. Invest.* **29**:496, 1950.

dePeyster, F. A., O. Paul, and R. K. Gilchrist: Risk of urgent surgery in presence of myocardial infarction and angina pectoris. *A.M.A. Arch. Surg.* **65**:448, 1952.

Eather, K. F.: Axillary brachial plexus block. *Correspondence.* **19**:683, 1958.

Johnson, N. P., and H. M. Livingston: Anaesthesia in surgery for aged patients with cardiovascular diseases. *Geriatrics.* 7:189, 1952.

LaDue, J. S.: Evaluation and preparation of the patient with degenerative cardio-vascular disease for major surgery. *Bull. N.Y. Acad. Med.* 32:418, 1956.

Landowne, M., M. Brandfonbrener, and N. W. Shock: The relation of age to certain measures of performance of the heart and the circulation. *Circulation.* 12:567, 1955.

McDermott, T. F., and E. M. Papper: Anesthetic management of patients with fractures of the hip. *Surg. Clin. North Amer.* 31:513, 1951.

Oliver, J. R.: "Anatomic Changes of Normal Senescence," in E. J. Stieglitz, "Geriatric Medicine," 3d ed., pp. 44–63. Philadelphia, Lippincott, 1954.

Papper, E. M.: Anesthesia in the aged. *Bull. N.Y. Acad. Med.* 32:635, 1956.

Sadove, M. S., and P. Kahan: Problems related to anesthesia in geriatric surgery. *Jour. Amer. Geriatrics Soc.* 1:123, 1953.

Shock, N. W.: "Age Changes in Renal Function," in A. L. Lansing (ed.), "Cowdry's Problems of Ageing," 3d ed., pp. 614–630. Baltimore, Williams & Wilkins, 1952.

Shock, N. W.: Some physiological aspects of aging in man: Wesley M. Carpenter Lecture. *Bull. N.Y. Acad. Med.* 32:268, 1956.

Shock, N. W., and A. B. Hastings: Studies of the acid-base balance of the blood: variations in the acid-base balance of the blood in normal individuals. *Jour. Biol. Chem.* 104:585, 1934.

Shock, N. W., and M. J. L. Yiengst: Age changes in basal respiratory measurements and metabolism in males. *Jour. Geront.* 10:31, 1955.

Solomon, D. H., and N. W. Shock: Studies of adrenal cortical and anterior pituitary function in elderly men. *Jour. Geront.* 5:302, 1950.

Symposium on biology of aging. American Physiological Society. *Fed. Proc.* 15:938, 1956.

Turville, C. S., and R. D. Dripps: The anesthetic management of the aged. *Penn. Med. Jour.* 51:434, 1948.

Vaughn, A. M., M. S. White, and J. M. Coleman: Problems peculiar to surgery of the aged. *Jour. Amer. Geriatrics Soc.* 4:483, 1956.

Ziffren, S. E.: Reduction in operative mortality in the very aged. *Jour. Amer. Med. Ass.* 152:994, 1953.

Chapter 4

Wound Healing and Reparative Osteogenesis

Edgar M. Bick

WOUND HEALING

The regeneration of viable tissue at the site of injury is a well-observed biologic phenomenon, but its activating forces and its control mechanisms still remain beyond the realms of demonstrable knowledge. Studies in wound healing, among which in modern times that of Arey is classic, describe in detail the histology of the process, and others to some lesser degree have discussed various aspects of its biochemistry. None so far have been able to determine with reasonable certainty the catalyst which conditions the still unknown factors that cause a rapid reproduction of cells and fibers which develop, not aberrantly as in tumors, but with an organized spatial relationship controlled to repair injured tissue. One may consider the trauma as the stimulus. This, at least, is a starting point from which the process of wound healing may be followed descriptively. The phenomenon of repair then becomes a basic process of the vitality of the whole organism. Although the phrase is no longer fashionable, this was once expressed most concisely by Bergson as a manifestation of the *élan vital.*

Because the detailed histology of wound healing may be studied in any textbook on pathology, we shall consider only those aspects of the reaction which are affected by the general process of aging. Furthermore, although by definition a wound may occur in any part of the external surface or in any of the internal tissues and viscera, this section is concerned only with external wounds, that is, wounds penetrating the skin into the tissues lying subcutaneously. The healing of skeletal wounds will be discussed in the second section of this chapter, and wounds of the viscera, vascular tree, and nerves will be considered in following chapters.

A convenient division of the reaction of wound repair into its several more or less distinct phases is helpful not only in understanding this complex process but is most pertinent to its therapeutic management. These phases can be listed in five hypothetical categories. It must be understood, however, that each phase overlaps the other, and the time sequence may vary in different parts of the wound. This of course becomes visibly perceptible in larger wounds. It must be emphasized at this point that wound healing of comparable lesions has been thought to progress with greater rapidity during the growing period of childhood than it does in adult life. Following the published work of Du Noüy in 1916 there was a general belief that the power of healing diminished with age. Further studies by Du Noüy himself, Harvey and Howes, Arey, and others since then have quite contradicted this impression. There is in fact no convincing evidence that, in the absence of certain dietary deficiencies or specific disease states, age per se in an adult has any influence whatsoever in wound healing. In the present writer's clinical experience no such retardation has been observed, even though deliberately looked for.

Phases of Wound Healing

Latent Period. This immediately follows the trauma and ordinarily lasts from 1 to 5 or 6 days depending upon the nature of the wound and the vascularity of its adjacent tissues. It is not otherwise demonstrably influenced by the age of the patient. In the elderly individual it is marked vascular sclerosis rather than chronological age which may retard the onset of repair. The latent period corresponds to the time factor required for the stimulus of trauma to activate the fibroblasts, the cells of the cutis, and capillaries to the point of successfully bridging the spatial defect. During this period there is no significant tensile strength in the wound. If healing *per primam* is anticipated, the wound edges must be held apposed by sutures, clamps, or other extraneous materials.

Secondary Necrosis. Any trauma which causes dissolution of continuity of tissue also causes cellular and interstitial necrosis to a greater or lesser degree. In a fine, clean-cut wound necrosis may be confined to a millimeter or two of both surfaces of the incision. In a rougher laceration, or severe contusion, or in a burn, pressure sore, or crush wound, necrosis may extend considerably beyond the visible area of trauma. Infection is of course a most common cause of secondary necrosis. Moderate or widespread necrosis may remain cryptic during the early phase of wound healing and, often enough, superficial epithelization may cover the surface of the wound temporarily while necrosis of the deeper layers is spreading. It must be recalled that the chemical and enzymatic products of tissue necrosis may in themselves engender further necrosis in adjacent tissues. Eventually the innate tissue reaction to this process does seal it off but too often not before it reaches the epithelium, breaking down old and newly formed skin. The lesion of ulceration then appears with its own modification of wound healing.

Because of the relative frequency of diminished vascularity or because of excessive protein or vitamin C deficiency this retrograde phase of wound healing is a particular threat to the elderly patient. It may not be overlooked with impunity by the surgeon and should be sought for with each dressing. It may subtend the remaining phases of the healing process, both modifying and substantially delaying their completion.

Contraction Phase. During this interim the primary traumatic reaction is subsiding and tensile strength is building up. Interstitial fluids have been or are being absorbed and the fibrin clot has contracted or is in the process of doing so. During this period the age of the adult patient appears to have no perceptible influence.

Epithelization. In uncomplicated healing *per primam* this phase is effectively completed between the sixth and twelfth day. Here the sole controlling factor is the vitality of the adjacent skin. In a histologically normal surface area the chronology of adult age does not appear to exert any influence on its velocity or tensile strength. However, epithelial repair is the most delicate of the histologic proliferations in this complex process. It may go on to completion ahead of the healing reaction in the deeper tissues and often over a deeper area of infection, later to involute or break down with the spread of cryptic necrosis or suppuration. *It is extremely important that the surgeon recognize the simple fact that while epithelization is the most pleasing and most reassuring phase of wound healing it is also the least dependable from the point of view of prognosis.* This observation has become particularly significant since the widespread use of chemotherapeutic drugs and antibiotics.

In the aged, relative avascularity of the subcutaneous structures may permit progressive necrosis of muscle, fascia, or fat within a healing schedule that permits completion of the epithelization. Eventually, however, the necrotic area reaches the newly formed skin and destroys it. It is well for the surgeon to remember that the happy completion of epithelization may be a snare and a delusion and does not necessarily imply satisfactory healing of a deeper wound.

Scar Formation. This, the last phase of wound healing, relates to the complete filling in of the subcutaneous defect by a dense, relatively avascular fibrous tissue. The capillaries no longer needed in quantity for rapid cellular reproduction involute and diminish. The activity of fibroblasts regresses to that of a static connective tissue. The appearance of the scar, level with the skin, elevated, or depressed is established at this time by the quantity of collagen fibers deposited. The velocity with which aging tissues deposit collagen fibers to form the scar, as compared to the younger adult, is still a questionable problem. Experience with elderly patients subject to either traumatic wounds or surgical incision has shown no significant clinical difference in the time factor for comparable lesions. This observation is of course only applicable to otherwise uncomplicated wounds.

TYPES OF WOUNDS

The effect of direct trauma may be highly localized, or it may be extended by a chain reaction of lytic necrosis or by the secondary effect of vascular or neurovascular changes to adjacent tissues. Certain aspects of direct trauma, such as abrasion or laceration, are immediately visible; other aspects, such as the pressure of a crush, or the impact of a dull striking force, may not be perceptible for from 12 hours to several days. Extravasation of blood or pressure necrosis within deeply subcutaneous tissues damaged by the transmitted force of impact takes even longer to become manifest. In the elderly patient, perhaps less sensitive to minor discomforts, perhaps a bit disoriented, these cryptic effects of trauma must be sought for and anticipated rather than awaited.

The management of soft-tissue wounds depends, of course, on the type of lesion. Although for purposes of investigation wounds are all but unlimited in their variety, a working classification may be assumed which will direct a proper therapy.

Abrasions. Simple abrasion is healed by superficial epithelization. However, in the aged patient, it is a really golden rule to hold simple abrasions severely suspect. Too often they represent a spurious visible cover to a deeper injury which is hidden from the examiner by the lessened sensitivity or lessened response to pain of the aged patient. In itself the abrasion is self-curable if kept clean and uncontaminated. It is well to remember that many of the available antiseptics are almost, if not quite, as lethal to new born epithelial cells as they are to septic invaders.

Lacerations. These may be sharply simple or roughly comminuted. Both will heal either *per primam* by direct epithelization or *per secundum* by epithelization over granulation tissue. They may or may not require suture or simple apposition by thin strips of adhesive or metal clips. Treatment of the laceration is no different in the elderly patient than in the younger one but it must be conducted with meticulous attention. The process of healing will proceed normally if the tissues are reasonably normal in their vascularity and if the state of nutrition is not excessively reduced. However, the probably decreased superficial vascular bed even in the minimal or moderately arteriosclerotic patient, or the presence of excessive hypoproteinemia or subclinical avitaminosis is a standing invitation to infection.

Obviously the principal danger of any deep laceration, simple or comminuted, is the threat of damage to blood vessels or nerves. In the aged patient blood vessel damage may be far more dangerous than damage to nerves, and in an arteriosclerotic individual may present the threat of gangrene to a greater degree than in the younger adult. This complication will be discussed by Madden in Chap. 18. It obviously transcends in importance any treatment of the wound itself. It is apparent that the development of a corollary circulation is far less dependable in an arteriosclerotic vascular bed than in a younger, richer network. Laceration of a nerve is a less urgent problem and need not delay emergency treatment of the wound. The prevention of infection is more important than suture of a nerve. This latter problem is discussed by German in Chap. 17.

Avulsion Wounds. These occur not uncommonly in the lower extremities when a person is struck by a moving vehicle. They are always serious wounds. In the elderly patient, especially in the presence of diminished peripheral circulation or extensive varicosities, necrosis of part or all of the avulsed tissue is a constant threat. If the mass is relatively clean, or requires only a small debridement, nothing may be lost by attempting its replacement by suture. Daily dressing is required in the early stages. Anaerobic gangrene is of course the constant danger in this type of wound at all ages. The elderly patient with diminished circulation may be even more susceptible. If the avulsed mass is badly contaminated or obviously and grossly damaged, it is best removed and the underlying surface prepared for early skin grafting.

Crush Wounds. These occur usually as the effect of a falling log or beam or other heavy object striking a surface, but not sufficiently concentrated at the point of contact to lacerate. At least the laceration, if it occurs, is not the chief trauma. In the older person more tissue damage is apt to occur than in the younger adult for several reasons. There is less elasticity or resilience in the fascia and subcutaneous fat; there is less size, firmness, and spring in the muscle masses. Moreover, in the presence of any degree of arteriosclerosis, the damage to a layer of the vascular bed is conducive to widespread failure of recovery by injured cells, and to the spread of the secondary chain reaction of tissue necrosis. In crush injuries, healing takes place through the replacement of necrotic tissue in the affected area by newly formed fibrotic growth. This takes considerable time and, in the elderly, the wound must be constantly observed for involution of the healing process and late stage ulceration which may result in renewed necrosis, anaerobic infection, and ultimate gangrene of the part. In the more extensive cases fatalities may occur due to systemic reaction. The special features of the "crush syndrome" in the aged are discussed separately by Trueta in Chap. 16.

Burns. The local and general effects of thermal trauma have an extensive and active literature of their own. Only those aspects which specially apply to the aged are of interest in this volume. Burn injuries cause a considerably higher mortality rate among the aged than among younger adults with comparable lesions. Local healing proceeds in the aged as it does in younger adults, by replacement of necrotic tissue, granulation tissue, and rather slow epithelization unless supplemented by skin graft. However, the proper care of burns far transcends the problem of wound healing. One of the chief dangers, or at least one of the more serious considerations in the treatment of burns at any age, is the effect of the large loss of serum protein which characteristically occurs by exudation from the exposed surfaces of the thermally denuded skin area. In the aged person already apt to be living at a low protein level, this loss may be catastrophic. The subject therefore merits the fuller consideration given to it by Simon in Chap. 5.

Electric Wounds. Flash wounds and electric contact wounds cause the same degree of severe tissue necrosis in the aged person as they do in the younger adult. The local therapeutic problems are the same in all ages. It must be emphasized, however, that while the flash wound may be solely a local lesion to be treated as such, the electric-contact wound implies the possibility of the systemic shock caused by an electric wave. The aged person is less well able to withstand the effects of such shock and therefore requires more urgent attention even in those instances which would be considered relatively mild in the younger adult. This aspect of electric trauma has been discussed by Sullivan in Chap. 1.

Radioactive Wounds. These are ordinarily due to deep roentgen therapy or treatment by radioactive substances. It is quite likely that the increased civilian uses of atomic energy may introduce this new type of lesion to peacetime practice. Even so, it may become necessary, tragically enough, to recognize and treat such trauma on a fairly large scale in contemporary civilization.

Wounds of this class are notoriously necrotizing and slow to heal. They heal by secondary intention and eventually by contraction of the wound surface. Epithelization is always less than adequate or at best greatly delayed. There is a considerable body of experience of the first two types, and no significant difference can be noted between their sluggish healing in any adult age group. It is always so retarded that any difference in time factor or in the quality of eventual epithelization at any age is not of a magnitude to be clinically differentiated. The healing quality of these wounds is conditioned by the cellular damage caused by the initial trauma. This damage is so often cryptic during the early period of observation that mere surface measurement relative to the influence of age alone is futile. Treatment may best be described as watchful waiting and cleanliness. Skin grafting, often attempted, is more precarious in radiation burns than in ordinary wounds, but may be tried.

Pressure Sores. These are truly the wounds of the aged. Their occurrence is statistically far greater in this group of patients than in younger adults. In the aged, such wounds seem to occur under a variety of circumstances even under the cover of good nursing and careful medical supervision. In some instances they resemble the lesions classified above as crush injuries in that the significant damage lies in the deeper tissues. Because of this, often enough, even the early recognition of local redness or skin abrasion will not prevent the development of the characteristic prolonged ulceration. *Pressure sores in the aged, contrary to the self-induced guilt feelings of many splendid nurses, are not necessarily the result of inadequate nursing care.* Often enough in the aged patient pressure sores occur in multiple areas of skin contact even when such contact is kept at a minimum. They can be seen on many parts of the body where bone is relatively subcutaneous, even under a meticulous bed-turning regimen.

The frequency of pressure sores in the aged has several causes. Among them may be mentioned the often emaciated state which deprives areas such as the sacrum, the heel, the anterosuperior spines of the pelvis, the prominent spinous processes, the olecranon, and the femoral trochanters of the soft covering of subcutaneous fat. A second factor more related to healing than to cause is the commonly diminished vascularity of the peripheral tissues, which conditions a decreased resiliency toward traumatic influences. A third factor lies in the frequent hypoproteinemia and/or subclinical avitaminosis presented by so many in the aged hospital population. Beyond these three there are probably other less apparent physiological elements not as yet properly appreciated but meriting urgent investigation.

In the experience of the present writer, there is no medication, physical modality, or local application which in any measurable way influences the healing of these wounds. Meticulous cleanliness, prophylaxis against local infection (by antiseptic or antibiotic dressings), and every possible nursing technique to avoid hard pressure against susceptible areas (sites of subcutaneous bone wherever they may be) have been the only safeguards and the only therapy. Skin grafting is of course a means of hastening the covering of the denuded area, but should only be attempted after a sound granulation-tissue floor has developed. To graft skin over an area still undergoing necrosis, or where necrotic tissue has not been replaced or debrided, is an invitation to failure.

Frequent reference has been made in this section to the state of hypoproteinemia in the aged individual and its influence on wound healing. It must be conceded that such references are still in the realm of a working hypothesis rather than that of established fact. There is a small but quite provocative reservoir of experimental information on the subject which suggests that up to a certain point, the so-called "hypoproteinemia" of the aged may be a normal response to lesser demand. The problem is complex and cannot be solved by the simple surface measurement of the wounds of laboratory animals on controlled diets. The variables in any given wound, even in a simple, experimental, sharp laceration or measured denudation, are manifold. As it is, the serious reports on the problem have been to some extent contradictory. At times experimental work on laboratory animals has been at such variance with the common experience of practicing surgeons that the need for further investigation is immediately apparent to one who attempts to review the matter.

The problem may not be one of the local protein requirements at the site of the wound. The need for protein in the building of new collagenous tissue, the tissue of the healing process, is obvious. The question is the relationship of the body protein level to the demands of the demarcated local area. When blood needs calcium, it draws on the skeletal reserve, whether the bone has its normal supply or not. When bone minerals are required for fracture healing, they will be drawn from the blood stream whether the body is in a hypocalcemic state or not (see below). If the wound needs protein material for healing, does it draw from the body reserve in the same way? If so, then the state of protein nutrition of the individual is a less urgent matter and it does not concern the immediate needs of wound healing. The same may be said of the vitamin status. However, one is justified in assuming that in the absence of more concrete evidence the care of the body nutrition should be a matter of concern in the general treatment of wounds of any type in the aged individual.

REPARATIVE OSTEOGENESIS IN THE AGED

The distinguishing feature of bone repair in the aged individual is the inevitable presence of a greater or lesser degree of bone atrophy of disuse or of frank osteoporosis. Differentiation between these two is not always a simple matter. In the elderly skeleton the two states may be complementary rather than distinct. In either case, where old bone is so afflicted, no difference in the quality of its healing after trauma can be distinguished. The elderly patient who for reasons unrelated to the presenting trauma had been relatively immobile during the preceding months or years may have suffered a greater degree of generalized bone atrophy than the individual who had been more active. Conversely, even the active older person with moderate or advanced endocrine osteoporosis may present an unfortunate degree of bone loss which has weakened the bones equally. In both instances fracture may follow a quite minor trauma. It may be accepted, at least as a working hypothesis in the management of fractures of the aged, that bone atrophy of disuse and osteoporosis are identical in their effect on the process of reparative osteogenesis.

The metabolic and endocrine problems of bone atrophy and osteoporosis in the aged have their own large literature. Discussions on the atrophy of disuse, senile atrophy of bone, reflex atrophy, and nutritional bone atrophy have been relatively commonplace for several centuries beginning long before such terms entered the language of medical science. In terms of contemporary significance the concept of osteoporosis began with the work of Albright and his colleagues in the 1940s. In the following paragraphs only those aspects of the subject which apply to traumatic lesions in the aged will be considered.

Osteoporosis, for purposes of immediate clarification and allowing for different points of view in detail, may be defined as a decrease in bone substance due to the insufficient formation of bone matrix by the tissue cells (osteoblasts). Bone matrix which is formed is fully mineralized. In the aged, bone mass continues to decrease more rapidly because normal resorption continues as deposition lags. Osteoporosis may start in the middle-aged female at the onset of the menopause because of the deficiency of estrogen which appears with the involution of ovarian function, since that hormone seems to be an essential even though indirect factor in osteoblastic activity. In senile osteoporosis among females this may be a factor added, perhaps, to the bone atrophy of disuse. The relationship of gonadal function to senile osteoporosis in the male is less evident. Vertebral osteoporosis of advanced degree is found much more frequently in females than in males, but osteoporosis of the bones of the extremities seems to occur with more or less equal frequency among the elderly of both sexes. These observations will be further discussed in the following paragraphs dealing with the healing of fractures.

Reparative osteogenesis takes place as the result of two separate processes acting concurrently. The process of ossification, that is, the formation of a histologic structure within a restricted area and in a prescribed lattice form known as trabeculae, depends upon the biochemical synthesis of a complex collagen-type bone protein and upon an as yet unknown biologic factor which conditions this synthesis in a preordained design. The details of this process were excellently described in the extended reports of Urist, McLean, and Johnson in 1941 to 1943. Of the biologic forces concerned in the creation of new bone in adult life, that is, of reparative callus, we know nothing, however much we may know descriptively of the process. Lacroix whose special interest was devoted to the investigation of this phase of osteogenesis designates the initiating biologic force as the "X substance." No specific substance or energy has been isolated, but the X substance concept of a catalytic force in the production of new bone has served to pinpoint the nidus of the problem. This catalyst, be it chemical, hormone, enzyme, or energy factor, seems to appear immediately following fracture.

As the trabecular framework is developed, its complex protein content immediately precipitates an equally complex inorganic bone salt which is composed of minerals otherwise soluble in the blood stream from which they are drawn. This precipitation, the second of the parallel processes which constitute the phenomenon of bone repair, is generally referred to as calcification. In the elderly human body the materials required for calcification of the newly formed bone matrix are ordinarily present in sufficient quantity in the blood stream unless the individual is suffering from a starvation diet, from a disease which seriously inhibits the absorption of calcium from the gastrointestinal tract, or from a physiological dysfunction which provokes too rapid excretion of calcium or phosphate through the kidney.

Leaving the specific subject of histologic and biochemical osteogenesis we come to the secondary factor of its relationship to the structure of the reparative bone. The perpetual deposition and resorption of bone substance is a fundamental characteristic of the animal skeleton throughout its life. The origin, *de novo*, of reparative tissue which heals a dissolution of continuity of bone depends entirely on a local, temporary, intentional change in the normal adult ratio of these two reactions which is due to the unknown stimulation factor discussed above. In reparative bone, the deposition of new trabeculae, locally and in prescribed form, greatly exceeds its resorption until healing has been accomplished. Immediately following this process resorption locally and temporarily exceeds deposition until the unrequired excess is removed. This latter constitutes the so-called "remodelling phase" of bone repair.

The fluctuating ratio of these two processes gives to bone the "biological plasticity" of Weinmann and Sicher required to reform its internal architecture to meet the stress and strain demands of its mass. Such fluctuation of the ratio of bone deposition and resorption is of course not unique to the healing of fractures. A similar long-term fluctuation occurs in the progress of life. During the growth period of childhood the rate of deposition normally exceeds that of resorption. During adult life, under normal circumstances, the two processes are generally in balance. In the aged resorption continues to take place at a normal rate but the synthesis and deposition of bone diminishes because of the involution of glandular activity described as osteoporosis, or owing to the decrease of the stimulus to osteoblastic activity which accompanies the lessened activity of advancing years. The result of this negative balance in the ratio of deposition and resorption of bone in the aged skeleton is the lessened amount of trabecular substance per volume of bone.

Fractures in the aged, as in those of less advanced years, will heal unless prevented from doing so by intrinsic or extrinsic causes. Inadequate or improper treatment is a far more frequent cause of nonunion than are the several intrinsic causes. Atrophic or osteoporotic bone will first

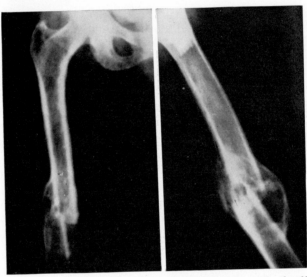

Fig. 4-1. Femur. Osteoporotic callus in osteoporotic bone. The healing callus is no better than the bone from which it is derived.

form primary callus of variable density depending upon its functional need. This is the "uniting callus" of Paget. It is the immediate protective response to trauma by the cells and interstitial substances of bone. It can be seen developing as early as the third day from the periosteal layer on both sides of the fracture line at a distance varying with the degree of displacement of the fragments. It takes the most economic pattern possible to bridge the gap and serves to splint the fragments until the definitive or internal callus has repaired the discontinuity. To form this primary or uniting external callus, the hypothetical force of healing will call on all available sources for its component materials as the soft tissues about a wound call on body reserves, no matter how depleted, for the collagen of scar tissue. However as the definitive, healing intraosseous callus forms, its quality comes to resemble the bone from which it is derived. Osteoporotic bone will form osteoporotic callus in the final state of repair (Fig. 4-1).

The fundamental steps in the healing of fractures were stated by John Hunter in the eighteenth century. These are (1) fracture hematoma, (2) its conversion into a fibrinous granulation tissue, (3) the subsequent transformation of this into fibrous and at times fibrocartilaginous soft callus, and finally (4) the replacement of the last by bone substance following the periosteal and endosteal invasion of osteoblasts and their accompanying vascular network. A further basic formula was added by Paget in the nineteenth century dealing with what may be referred to as the structural aspect of fracture healing. Paget described two forms of callus, each separate in purpose but overlapping in time. The first appearance of bone callus develops at or under the periosteum of both fragments some distance from the fracture site. Whether this is derived from periosteum or a hypothetical "cambium layer" remains still an unresolved problem of osteology in spite of a library of controversial papers and monographs on the subject. Nevertheless, whatever its origin, it represents the primary callus of bone repair. This is Paget's "uniting callus," referred to in more recent parlance as primary callus. It soon bridges the gap and tends to hold the fragments in their position of interfascial balance whether this be in good alignment or poor. Paget's "healing callus" appears later and is the definitive callus which effectively accomplishes solid union. It derives partly from the primary callus and partly from endosteum.

The recognition of a third aspect of fracture healing is a development of the mid-twentieth century. The structural pattern of the callus mass expresses the most economic expenditure of materials possible with which to complete bone union (Fig. 4-2A). Where larger amounts of primary callus are required to hold the fragments in their found positions, or to bridge lateral gaps or gaps due to loss of substance as in gunshot wounds, nature attempts to produce a sufficient quantity to accomplish its end. When there is little or no displacement, or where no muscular or weight-bearing force is distracting the fracture surfaces, primary callus will be minimal. A well-placed bone plate or intramedullary nail may all but eliminate the need for primary or "uniting callus" since the metallic appliance accomplished the purpose for which this early callus is intended (Fig. 4-2B). Too often x-ray films in such instances are falsely interpreted as showing no callus. What is meant is that no primary or external callus is visible.

Where unwarranted preconceived notions anticipate retarded union in aged bone, such interpretations must be reconsidered in the light of the normal structural pattern of the callus expected in the given circumstance. A lack of x-ray evidence of primary (external or periosteal) callus in a non-weight-bearing and nonmuscular area, such as undisplaced styloid processes, carpal navicular, or an impacted or properly nailed femoral neck without displacement, is to be expected and does not imply nonunion or delayed union. If internal fixation is not excessive, primary callus will be produced of an irregular form, since natural forces have been interfered with but not supplanted (Fig. 4-2C).

The stimulus of trauma and the basic steps toward fracture healing are identical in time and in form in the aged person and in the younger adult. The healing processes are balefully influenced by the same interceptors that retard or prevent their completion at any age. Their one

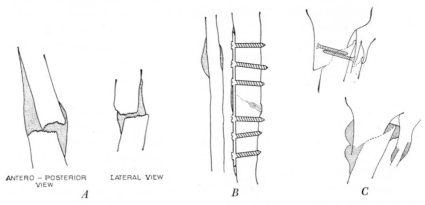

ANTERO – POSTERIOR   LATERAL VIEW
VIEW
A   B   C

FIG. 4-2. *A*. Normal economic pattern of primary callus. *B*. Minimal callus in the presence of a well-set plate. *C*. Excessive and irregular callus from inefficient fixation. (*From E. M. Bick: Structural patterns of callus in fractures of the long bones. Journal of Bone and Joint Surgery. 30A:141, 1948.*)

difference is qualitative, the quality of the end product. *The healing callus is no better, no stronger, no more resistant to strain than is the aging bone from which it is derived.*

It must be emphasized that bone healing, as far as present clinical and experimental experience discloses, is an entirely local reaction confined to the immediate vicinity of the fracture. In spite of much deductive reasoning to the contrary, years of intensive investigation have failed to show that systemic processes have any consistent effect upon the local phenomenon of reparative osteogenesis. Old age furnishes no exception. The local tissue reaction proceeds inexorably unless fortuitously impeded, regardless of, and if necessary at the expense of, other bodily needs. The large and persistent loss of body nitrogen following fractures, noted by Howard and Parson, may cause a degree of general debility in the patient but does not clinically influence the local progress of union. In the aged individual the worsened hypoproteinemia may provoke a serious deficiency in bodily metabolism, but the fracture will heal. The density of the trabeculae may be less per volume according to the degree of osteoporosis or bone atrophy, but those that are formed will be fully mineralized. The component inorganic salts may be drawn from other tissues, but will be found, unless the patient suffers from a too severe starvation or advanced pathological osteomalacia which decreases the mineral content of the body to an extent of extreme general debility. In very elderly and debilitated patients, the extremes at which fracture healing will take place in a normal time period is one of the amazing observations of fractures in the aged.

The term *fracture healing* has been used rather freely in this and most other discussions of reparative osteogenesis. In the sense that it signifies an active process, the term is clear enough. When it is used as a past participle, *the fracture is healed,* a less clear concept is revealed. The point in time at which a fracture is healed is not as yet measurable by any known method even within a reasonable margin of error. The healing point of a fracture has been defined as that moment during the process of reparative osteogenesis at which callus has been formed in sufficient strength to enable the bone to withstand the stresses and strains which it is accustomed to bear in its sound state. The definition of this moment is subject to several interpretations. It is not at the end of the reparative process, since a phase of that process continues past this point and is concerned with the absorption of excess primary callus and the reformation of intraosseous lines of stress and strain, the so-called "remodelling phase." Clinical experience has taught that functional healing in respect to the ordinary activities of life occurs long before the normal intraosseous architecture has been restored and perhaps before maximum strength has been attained.

This concept of a healing point in bone repair is of particular importance in relation to fractures in the aged, since the need for early freedom of the limbs from restraint is more urgent. However, the determination of this point is even more difficult than it is in the younger age group. It was noted above that the definitive callus produced by atrophic or osteoporotic bone in the aged skeleton shows as little relative density on the roentgenogram as does the parent bone. This density is often wrongfully interpreted as being inadequate for its functional purpose. On the other hand the demand on the strength of the new bone may be considerably less in the elderly individual than it would be in the more muscular and probably more active younger adult. The lesser roentgenologic density of the definitive callus may give an impression of delayed healing when in fact a competent union has been established by a less mineralized skeleton.

A useful test of the degree of healing in the aged long bone is Lippmann's auscultatory percussion, a valuable and too often neglected method. This test depends upon the observation that the pitch of sound transmitted through any substance varies directly with the density of the transmitting material. A stethoscope is placed on a subcutaneous surface near one end of a long bone, and the auditor's finger taps another sub-cutaneous surface of the bone or limb beyond the fracture line (Fig. 4-3). If the healing point has been reached, the pitch of the transmitted sound will equal that transmitted between similar points on the normal limb. The patellae and malleoli serve well for fractures of the leg; the pubis

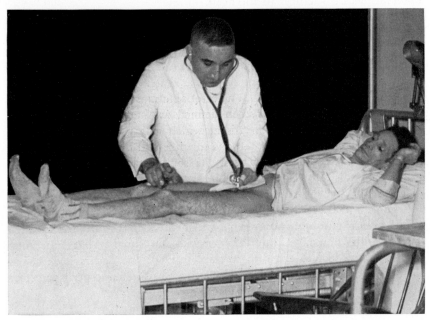

FIG. 4-3. Auscultatory percussion for painless clinical diagnosis of fracture of the long bones.

or trochanter and patella serve well for the hip or femoral shaft. The sternum or acromion process and olecranon are useful joints for the humerus. Other sites should be apparent from these examples. The test is not valid after a metallic device has been inserted into or along the fracture since the metal will transmit the sound at a pitch different from bone, and, bypassing the fracture, it will give a false observation.

McMurray of Liverpool somewhere remarked that "figures collected by different surgeons with respect to the normal rate of union of any particular fracture are of comparatively little value because the standard varies so greatly as to what clinical and x-ray evidence constitutes union." One cannot with impunity contradict this statement. With it in mind, a study of any significant case series of fractures in elderly patients leads to the clinical conviction that *bone repair proceeds in the aged skeleton with a velocity not in any measurable or perceptible degree less than is found in other adult age groups* (Fig. 4-4). This statement, quite contrary to the well-worn tradition concerning "old bones," is based on observation made specifically for that purpose during the past decade. Unfortunately, because of the difficulty of determining a precise healing point, the statement is not subject to either measurable or experimental proof

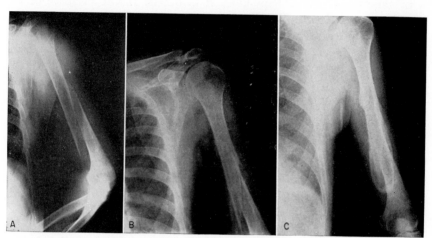

FIG. 4-4. Fracture of the humerus, male, age 77. *A.* Time of fracture. *B.* Six weeks later. Uniting callus quite visible. *C.* Twelve weeks, solid union. Treated by swathe and sling.

and remains therefore a matter of clinical impression. *That "old bones" heal as rapidly as those of younger adults is the chief lesson which has been learned from contemporary studies of fractures in the aged.*

PATHOLOGIC FRACTURES

Pathologic fractures are relatively far more common in the aged than in childhood or in the younger adult group. By pathologic fractures are meant those occurring through a locally diseased area. The term in its present connotation does not apply to fractures in the aged skeleton marked by generalized atrophy or osteoporosis. In the aged, pathologic fractures occur most commonly in (1) metastatic carcinoma, (2) multiple myeloma, (3) Paget's disease, (4) old or chronic osteomyelitis, and (5) radiation necrosis. Other less common lesions do occur; a list would include most of the diseases and neoplasms of bone through which fracture occurs in any adult period.

A primary rule of reparative osteogenesis in the presence of a destructive lesion is that callus will be derived from the remaining normal or at least viable bone trabeculae and subperiosteal layers, and obviously cannot be expected from the cells or fibers of the adventitious pathologic invader or replacement. Therefore the structural pattern of the callus will depend on the structure of the residual normal bone and the form, size, and location of the lesion. In Paget's disease, or in the burned-out osteomyelitic area without residual hiatuses, the callus will appear in somewhat the usual pattern except in so far as sclerotic areas will retard it in some parts and perhaps block it in others. In the presence of an invading osteolytic neoplasm, such as metastatic carcinoma, myeloma or the lipoidoses, callus will come from only those areas in which viable bone remains. The subperiosteal primary callus appears at its usual time some distance away from the fracture line and will cross it unless a tumor mass protrudes from the area and blocks it at that surface. The definitive callus will appear across that part of the fracture surface not invaded by the foreign cells. It is theoretically possible, though rarely observed, that new trabeculae may grow with sufficient force to reinvade a small cancerous area, but more commonly an x-ray film suggesting this may be interpreted as overlapping shadows of trabeculae transversing a part of the fracture area behind or before the nonosseous substance.

Progressive lesions will of course in time destroy the newly formed bone. A benign localized lesion may be sufficiently reinforced by the healing of part of the fracture line so as to permit some degree of function. However, in the elderly, the type of benign, self-correcting lesion which goes on to normal repair, such as the eosinophilic granuloma or the simple bone cyst of childhood, is a rare occurrence.

Reparative osteogenesis in the pathologic fractures of the aged skeleton requires for its estimation no more than the understanding of bone repair in that age group, and the structural effect of the invader or alteration on the bone from which the callus is to be derived. The fracture will heal if normal or even viable bone lies along the line of dissolution. The amount of new bone uniting the fracture will be measured by the surface area available for contact of bone tissue to bone tissue, or more rarely by the volume of the invading tissue, if this be small enough to permit new bone growth to traverse it. Prognosis depends on the diagnosis of the invading lesion. Treatment cannot be properly planned until that diagnosis is established. The risk of biopsy is often far less than other risks involved in treating a pathologic fracture blindly.

BIBLIOGRAPHY

Wound Healing

Absoe-Hanson, G.: "Connective Tissue in Health and Disease." Copenhagen, Ejnar Munksgaard, 1954.

Arey, L. B.: Wound healing. *Physiol. Rev.* **16**:327, 1936.

Bick, E. M.: Histologic observations on aging of the human connective tissues. *Jour. Mt. Sinai Hosp.* **26**:501, 1959.

Calloway, D. H., M. I. Grossman, J. Bowman, and W. K. Calhoun: Effect of previous level of protein feeding on wound healing and in metabolic response to injury. *Surgery.* **37**:935, 1955.

Dibble, J. H.: Inflammation and repair. *Ann. Roy. Coll. Surg. Eng.* **6**:120, 1950.

Du Noüy, P. L.: Cicatrization of wounds. *Jour. Exp. Med.* **24**:461, 1916; also *Compt. rend. Soc. Biol.* **109**:1227, 1932.

Harvey, S. C., and E. L. Howes: Effect of high protein diet in the velocity of growth of fibroblasts in the healing wound. *Ann. Surg.* **91**:641, 1930.

Howes, E. L., and S. C. Harvey: The age factor in the velocity of growth of fibroblasts in the healing wound. *Jour. Exp. Med.* **55**:577, 1932.

Lansing, A. I.: "Cowdry's Problems of Ageing." 3d ed. Baltimore, Williams & Wilkins, 1952, chap. 18 (N. W. Shock), chap. 31 (R. Elman).

Ravdin, I. S.: Hypoproteinemia and its relation to surgical problems. *Ann. Surg.* **112**:576, 1940.

Thompson, W. D., I. S. Ravdin, and I. L. Frank: Effect of hypoproteinemia on wound disruption. *Arch. Surg.* **36**:500, 1938.

Ziffren, S. E.: Management of burned patient. *Jour. Amer. Geriatric Soc.* **3**:36, 1955.

Reparative Osteogenesis

Albright, F.: Osteoporosis. *Ann. Int. Med.* **27**:861, 1947.

Albright, F., and E. C. Reifenstein: Metabolic effects of steroid hormones in osteoporosis. *Jour. Clin. Invest.* **26**:24, 1947.

Bick, E. M.: "Source Book of Orthopaedic Surgery," 2d ed., chap. 6. Baltimore, Williams & Wilkins, 1948.

Bick, E. M.: Structural patterns of callus in fractures of the long bones. *Jour. Bone and Joint Surg.* **30***A*:141, 1948.

Bick, E. M.: Healing of fractures. *Amer. Jour. Surg.* **80**:843, 1950.

Bick, E. M.: Physiology of the aging process in the musculoskeletal system. *Geriatrics.* **10**:274, 1955.

Bick, E. M.: Clinical aspects of aging connective tissues. *Bull. N.Y. Acad. Med.* **35**:547, 1959.

Bick, E. M., and J. W. Copel: The senescent human vertebra. *Jour. Bone and Joint Surg.* **34***A*:110, 1952.

Howard, J. E., and W. Parson: Studies in fracture convalescence: part 1. *Bull. Johns Hopkins Hosp.* **75**:156, 1944; with K. Stein, H. Eisenberg, and V. Reidt, part 2, *ibid.* **75**:209, 1944; with R. S. Bigham, part 3, *ibid.* **77**:291, 1945.

Lacroix, P.: "The Organization of Bones." Eng. trans. by S. Gilder. London, J. and A. Churchill, 1951.

Lippmann, R. K.: The use of auscultatory percussion for the examination of fractures. *Jour. Bone and Joint Surg.* **14**:118, 1932.

Urist, M. R., and F. C. McLean: Calcification and ossification. *Jour. Bone and Joint Surg.* **23**:1, 283, 1941; **24**:47, 1942.

Urist, M. R., and R. W. Johnson: *Jour. Bone and Joint Surg.* **25**:375, 1943.

Waller, A.: in Philip D. Wilson, "Management of Fractures and Dislocations." Philadelphia, Lippincott, 1938.

Weinmann, J. P., and H. Sicher: "Bone and Bones: Fundamentals of Bone Biology." 2d ed. St. Louis, Mosby, 1955.

Chapter 5

Treatment of Burns

Bernard E. Simon

SCOPE OF THE PROBLEM

In his introduction, Kennedy has pointed out that in the United States in 1957 there were 95,000 fatal accidents. Of these, 27,200 occurred in individuals aged 65 or over. Third in frequency in this latter group were burns, which accounted for 1,800 deaths. Only two categories, namely, falls accounting for 15,500 and motor-vehicle injuries accounting for 5,950, caused more fatalities. Burns in the elderly, therefore, account for almost 2 per cent of all fatal accidents in any one year in the United States, and account for 6 per cent of fatal accidents to individuals 65 years of age or older.

Even more serious are the high mortality rates resulting from burn trauma in the elderly. Bull and Fisher, whose mortality probability tables are included for use in prognosis by those who treat burns in the elderly, give the following statistics for the 65 and older age group (Table 5-1). The mortality is 18 per cent when 0 to 4 per cent of body surface is burned, 41 per cent mortality for the 5 to 14 per cent group, 80 per cent for the 15 to 24 per cent group and the frightful mortality of 100 per cent for all patients aged 65 or older with burns covering more than 25 per cent of the body surface. Studies from other clinics are in entire accord. Moyer has demonstrated that a burn of 13 per cent carries a 50 per cent mortality rate in an individual over 61 years of age. In Blocker's series not a single patient in the older age group survived burns of 30 per cent or more. Ziffren studied 34 burned patients aged 60 or older and reported 15 deaths, a mortality rate of 41 per cent. This series is unusual in that post-mortem studies were obtained in all but three of the patients. The results are appended in Table 5-2.

The striking finding which runs consistently through the series is the high incidence of infarction of one or several organs. Including the presumptive diagnosis of pulmonary embolism with infarction in two of these patients in whom no autopsy was obtained, the incidence reaches 93 per cent. By contrast, only 40 per cent of patients over 60 dying of

TABLE 5-1. GRID OF APPROXIMATE MORTALITY PROBABILITIES FOR VARIOUS COMBINATIONS OF AGE AND AREA

% body area burned	Age—Years																
	0–4	5–9	10–14	15–19	20–24	25–29	30–34	35–39	40–44	45–49	50–54	55–59	60–64	65–69	70–74	75–79	80–84
78 or more	1	1	1	1	1	1	1	1	1	1	1	1	1	1	1	1	1
73–77	.9	.9	.9	.9	.9	1	1	1	1	1	1	1	1	1	1	1	1
68–72	.9	.9	.9	.9	.9	.9	.9	1	1	1	1	1	1	1	1	1	1
63–67	.8	.8	.8	.8	.9	.9	.9	.9	1	1	1	1	1	1	1	1	1
58–62	.7	.7	.7	.7	.8	.8	.8	.9	1	1	1	1	1	1	1	1	1
53–57	.6	.6	.6	.6	.7	.7	.8	.8	.9	1	1	1	1	1	1	1	1
48–52	.5	.5	.5	.5	.6	.6	.7	.7	.8	.9	1	1	1	1	1	1	1
43–47	.4	.4	.4	.4	.4	.5	.5	.6	.7	.8	.9	1	1	1	1	1	1
38–42	.3	.3	.3	.3	.3	.4	.4	.5	.6	.7	.8	.9	1	1	1	1	1
33–37	.2	.2	.2	.2	.2	.3	.3	.4	.5	.6	.7	.8	.9	1	1	1	1
28–32	.1	.1	.1	.1	.2	.2	.2	.3	.4	.5	.6	.8	.9	1	1	1	1
23–27	.1	.1	.1	.1	.1	.1	.1	.2	.2	.3	.4	.6	.8	.9	1	1	1
18–22	0	0	0	0	0	0	.1	.1	.1	.2	.3	.4	.6	.8	.9	1	1
13–17	0	0	0	0	0	0	0	0	.1	.1	.2	.3	.4	.6	.7	.8	.9
8–12	0	0	0	0	0	0	0	0	0	0	.1	.1	.2	.4	.5	.6	.7
3–7	0	0	0	0	0	0	0	0	0	0	0	0	.1	.2	.3	.4	.5
0–2	0	0	0	0	0	0	0	0	0	0	0	0	0	.1	.1	.2	.3

SOURCE: J. P. Bull and A. J. Fisher: A study of mortality in a burns unit: a revised estimate. *Ann. Surg.* **139:**269, 1954.

TABLE 5-2. SUMMARY OF FATAL CASES

Causes of death	% body surface with 3d degree burn	No. days after burn until death	Age (yrs)	Autopsy
Pulmonary embolus......................	20	27	79	*
Pulmonary embolus (clinical diagnosis only)...	6	65	82	no
Myocardial infarct; thrombosis circumflex branch left coronary artery; acute pericarditis; renal tubular damage with regeneration............................	25	33	78	*
Multiple infarcts of lungs; bilateral suppurative bronchopneumonia...........	15	47	89	*
Pulmonary embolus (clinical diagnosis only)...	14	126	84	no
Pneumonia (clinical diagnosis only).........	18	25	82	no
Splenic infarct; lobular necrotizing pneumonia.	20	26	74	*
Infarcts of lung; suppurative pneumonitis with abscesses; pyelonephritis; decubiti........	15	90	82	*
Acute dilatation of stomach; bronchopneumonia............................	20	58	65	*
Infarct of lung; pulmonary edema and pneumonia; fractured neck of femur; azotemia............................	15	9	76	*
Massive myocardial infarct; thrombosis left descending coronary artery..............	18	7	73	*
Pulmonary edema; nectrotizing pneumonia; renal tubular damage..................	50	11	60	*
Multiple infarcts of spleen, lungs, kidneys; Curling's ulcer, multiple; bilateral acute bronchopneumonia.....................	80	4	66	*
Thrombosis lateral sinus and confluence; thrombosis both iliac veins; splenic infarct; adrenal cortex exhaustion................	20	44	80	*
Pulmonary emboli; lobular pneumonia; atrophy adrenal cortex..................	15	30	77	*

* Autopsy performed.
SOURCE: S. E. Ziffren: Management of the burned patient. *Jour. Amer. Geriatric Soc.* **3**:36, 1955.

other causes in the same institution showed infarcts. The surprising finding of infarction occurring almost universally in these patients opens up several avenues of approach. Why the burn in its later course should set the stage for vascular thromboses is not clear. In the early stages, sludging, slow circulation, hemoconcentration and other factors would favor intravascular clotting. However, many of the deaths occurred long after the initial period in which thrombosis would seem likely to occur. In these later stages, the presence of large granulating areas, with consequent diffuse, acute, and chronic infection and massive depletion of protein resources, throws an intolerable burden on a worn out organism which is just able to get by under normal circumstances. Chronic anemia, reduced plasma protein levels, and a contracted blood volume appear quite characteristically in the aged, even in the presence of relatively small granulating areas. Moyer has likened a granulating area to a hole in a bucket. It leaks everything—red cells, protein, sodium, potassium, and calcium. This exhausting depletion can be withstood by the younger individuals but is simply not compatible with life in the elderly despite what appears to be adequate replacement therapy. There are many facets of the problem of high mortality in the aged which are not understood. The two lines of investigation which might be pursued with profit are study of the problems of thrombosis and infarction, and inquiry into the properties and physiology of granulation tissue.

Special Problems in Treatment of Burns in the Aged

Before discussing details in treatment, it might be well to ask what makes burns in the aged differ from burns in younger individuals. In the first place, the accident itself is often conditioned by the senility of the patient. Older people who become forgetful or confused are frequently victims of burns through the careless or inept handling of such household objects as pots, pans, coffee makers, electric irons, etc. Major burns are sustained as the result of transient attacks of syncope due to either temporary loss of consciousness associated with vascular spasm or even cerebral accidents of a somewhat more severe variety. Blocker has emphasized the fact that many elderly people live alone or in the company of others who may be likewise less competent to deal with major accidents occurring in the home.

A second factor is the relative fragility of the entire organism of the older person, emphasized in the introduction to this chapter. From the pathologic findings of Ziffren's series one may note how often a mild pneumonic process, ordinarily easily tolerated by a younger individual, led to the patient's death. This observation has been confirmed by our own experiences and those of Blocker.

This fragility of the various major organ systems of the body carries over to the heart and vessels. The strain of great fluctuations in blood volume and transient periods of shock and hypovolemia in the early stages followed by the effort to cope with the "high tide" of fluid re-entering the circulation after the initial phase places an intolerable burden on the senile heart. The elderly patient is always between the Scylla and Charybdis of undertreatment and pulmonary edema. The same factors which have thrown this considerable strain on the heart make demands on the senile kidney to which the latter may not be equal. There are the same massive fluctuations in blood volume which necessitate changing rates of filtration, and the same periods of shock during which blood flow through the kidney and therefore oxygenation of the tubular cells may be quite deficient and during which the kidney must selectively absorb and reabsorb water and various other constituents of the urine.

Cerebral arteriosclerosis and various other senile degenerations of the brain profoundly affect the course of treatment in the elderly. Personality patterns may range from depression and apathy to agitation and combativeness. Generalized weakness and/or an inability to cooperate may require increased nursing care without which hypostatic pneumonic complications and decubiti may easily occur. The newer tranquilizing drugs have not been completely successful in the management of these states since they often lead to depression or even hypotension in therapeutic doses. Confinement in bed, inactivity, anorexia due to febrile illness, and apathy on a psychologic basis make for feeding problems in the elderly which can be difficult to manage.

Lastly, the thin, atrophic skin of the senile patient creates specific problems. Such skin is easily burned through and through, creating third-degree burns in areas which in younger patients would probably result in partial-thickness skin loss. The paper-thin skin is extremely difficult to use for donor sites and so-called "second drops" of skin are very hard to obtain without creating full-thickness donor defects which become problems in themselves. Blocker has pointed out that not only is the "take" of such grafts precarious but that postoperative care is more difficult in these patients because of the extreme restlessness often associated with periods of confusion. Added to these difficulties are the problems of associated degenerative diseases, such as diabetes, arthritis, prostatic hypertrophy, hypertension, and others.

A word about the treatment of burns in general. Even excepting the elderly, no traumatic lesion taxes the skill and patience of the physician as does the major burn. Affecting almost every organ system, a major burn requires a broad knowledge of general medicine and physiology. In addition, special knowledge of fluid and electrolyte balance, management of acute and chronic infection, correction of nutritional deficiency, management of large sloughing and granulating areas and their resurfacing, and finally of rehabilitation is necessary. All of this is difficult enough in a patient who before injury was young and healthy. If to the above are added the special problems of old age, the attending physician has, indeed, a formidable task in prospect if he is to carry the patient through his ordeal successfully.

PATHOLOGIC PHYSIOLOGY OF THE BURN WOUND

Modern concepts of fluid replacement therapy in the burned patient in the early stages following injury are based on the changes which take place in the burn wound. The sweeping nature of these local changes is such as to produce effects on the rest of the organism almost immediately. Following thermal trauma, and parenthetically it may be noted that this applies as well to frostbite and other forms of cold injury, there is rapid and unremitting swelling of the burn wound. The nature and extent of this swelling is poorly appreciated because only a small increase in the diameter of an injured part represents a relatively huge increase in its fluid content. Artz has shown mathematically that in the lower extremity of an adult a change of only 1 inch in the circumference above the ankle and 3 inches in the circumference of the thigh results in a volume increase in the limb of 2.4 liters. Therefore, from a clinical point of view, it is extremely difficult to achieve a correlation between the amount of fluid lost into an injured area and the visible formation of edema. The greatest improvement in the mortality of burns has been the salvage of patients during the first critical 48 to 72 hours. This improvement was accomplished by a clearer understanding of the events which take place in the burn wound in particular and the body in general during this period.

Let us assume a normal capillary circulation in an unburned area of skin and subcutaneous tissue. Blood with a serum protein of about 7 Gm per 100 ml is entering the arterial end of the capillary bed under a head of pressure sufficient to force a certain amount of electrolyte-containing fluid through the capillary wall into the extracellular tissue spaces. The protein content of the extracellular fluid surrounding the relatively impermeable capillary wall is approximately 1.0 to 1.5 Gm per 100 ml. As the pressure gradient falls at the venous end of the capillary, the much greater osmotic pressure of the protein-rich plasma tends to pull back some of the fluid which was filtered through at the arterial end. A certain amount of excess fluid is brought back into the circulation via the lymphatics of the area.

Let us now assume that the normal area described in the preceding paragraph is subjected to thermal trauma. Immediate swelling of the area occurs, this swelling being in proportion to the extent and serious-ness of the thermal trauma. Two factors are responsible for this rapid formation of edema. There is an immediate and rapid change of capillary permeability which permits a protein-rich plasma filtrate to flow through the capillary wall almost as if its normal barrier had disappeared. The nature of the change in the capillary wall which permits this to happen is not as yet understood, but the protein content of the fluid in the extracellular spaces rises from its normal of between 1.0 and 1.5 to values as high as 4.5 Gm per 100 ml. The second factor producing edema is the reflex increase in blood flow to the injured part by release of the normal vasoconstricting mechanisms. This action is, of course, the common re-sponse to all types of trauma. The increase in both flow and pressure at the arteriolar end of the capillary markedly increases the filtration. With the absence of the normal restraint of the now permeable capillary wall, the increase in fluid on the outside of the vessel can reach enormous proportions. The loss of fluid is at the expense of the circulating plasma. Continuing loss, as in a severe and extensive burn, can cripple the general circulation badly owing to severe contraction of the circulating blood volume and extreme hemoconcentration of the retained and partially intact red blood-cell content of the blood. In recent years, the loss has been shown to be roughly proportional to the extent of the burn and to the size of the patient. As a result, several replacement formulas have been devised, which have somewhat lessened the confusion surrounding the problem of fluid replacement in extensive thermal burns.

Most of the increase in swelling and edema of the burned part occurs within the first few hours after the burn. Rising tissue pressure soon begins to counteract the factors producing edema and, in part, limits them. Later, during the healing phase, the return of normal capillary permeability begins to permit resorption of edema directly through the capillary wall but principally via the lymphatics. Great increase in local edema and tissue pressure leads to a remarkable increase in the lymphatic flow from the burned area. This often increases as much as sevenfold, according to Drinker. But Master has shown that there is an increase in the permeability of the collecting lymphatics which additionally permits transfer of large amounts of protein-rich extracellular fluid to enter these vessels, thus contributing to the increased lymphatic flow. Meanwhile, the remainder of the extracellular space of the body, whose fluid reserves are called upon to sustain the failing circulation, suffers an almost complete cessation of lymphatic flow.

The edema, as was noted, reaches its peak somewhere between the thirty-sixth and forty-eighth hour. In untreated cases, this sometimes continues even until the seventy-second hour after burn. At this point there is noted healing of the previously quite permeable capillary membrane and a diminution of the heretofore voluminous blood flow to the burned area with consequent rapid resorption of edema. This resorption may be almost as strikingly rapid as its formation. The return of the large quantities of edema fluid into the circulation throws a marked burden on the kidneys and cardiovascular apparatus, this being a hazard which is particularly noteworthy in the elderly. Cope and others have studied the protein contents of the extracellular fluids following burns by examination of the fluid contained in the blebs resulting from second-degree burns. This protein content can be shown to be proportional to the intensity of the burn, but it is never as high as that of the plasma. In mild burns it is about 3 Gm per 100 ml. In moderate burns it may reach as much as 4 Gm per 100 ml. Severe burns rarely give rise to protein concentrations over 4.5 Gm per 100 ml. The rises noted in bleb fluid are comparable to the rises in the protein content of the lymphatic fluid draining from the limbs of burned animals. During the period of healing and resorption of wound edema, the protein content falls, and Cope has shown that at 7 days the concentration may be 2 Gm or less, these figures not being much higher than those of the normal extracellular fluid of skin and subcutaneous tissue.

It must not be thought that the burn exudate is a static body of protein-rich edema fluid undergoing little or no change. It must be thought of as a dynamic unit continually undergoing change in composition and turnover of its constituents. Observations using albumin labeled with radioactive iodine (I^{131}) show large increases in the transfer of the fluids in the damaged tissues with increase in local blood flow being accompanied by increase in the rate and volume of transfer of fluid from the vessels to and from the interstitial fluid and from the draining lymphatics.

It was noted before that the most important restraining influence during the early phase after burn is the increase in tissue pressure. This varies in accordance with at least two factors. In areas where the body tissues are extremely loose, relatively huge swelling can occur. This is particularly noteworthy in the genital region and in the head and neck where, within 24 hours of severe burn, enormous and startling edema is frequently seen. Contrariwise, when there is full-thickness loss of skin in certain areas of the body, the rigid, leather eschar, contracted and inelastic as it is, may sharply limit edema formation, particularly in the extremities. Indeed, in such an area there may be local ischemic effects due to the tourniquet-like constriction of such eschars. The limitation of swelling by the inelastic eschars of full-thickness burns may lead to a paradoxical situation in which swelling and fluid loss into the tissue

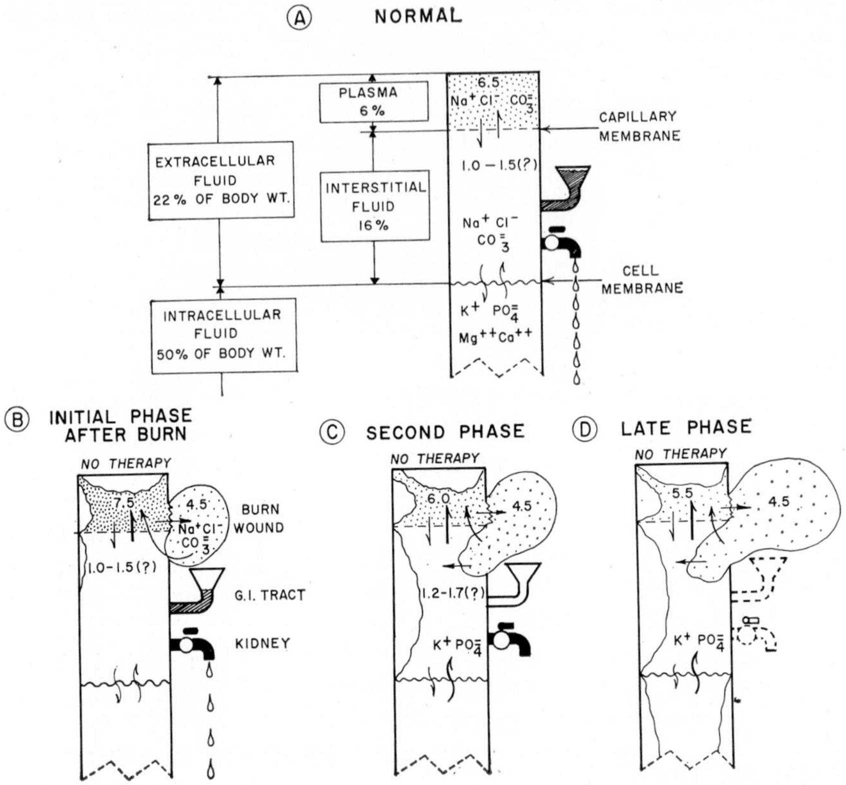

FIG. 5-1. *A.* Normal distribution of fluid, protein, and electrolytes in circulating blood, interstitial fluid, and within the cells. *B.* Initial phase after burn. Although protein is lost into the burn wound, it does not match the loss of fluid. The protein remaining dissolved in the residual circulating plasma causes a rise in concentration to 7.5 Gm per 100 ml. The elevated osmotic pressure of the concentrated plasma protein has a dehydrating effect on the unburned tissues, causing movement of fluid from the interstitial spaces. The volume of interstitial fluid is not as yet compromised, but urinary flow is slowed considerably. The concentrated plasma is unable to effect resorption of fluid from the burn wound owing to damage to the capillary membrane. *C.* In the second phase, there has been further movement of fluid into the circulation with fall of the plasma protein concentration, in contrast to the rise of the first phase. The depletion of the extracellular water resources is now considerable, and water is beginning to move from the cells. Necessarily there is concomitant loss of electrolytes characteristic of the cell, such as potassium and phosphate. Kidney function has ceased. *D.* In the final phase of an untreated burn in which spontaneous recovery does not take place, there is further swelling of the wound and profound loss of fluids from the interstitial and cellular components. Permanent and fatal damage to kidney, liver, and brain ensues, partly from dehydration and partly from anoxia due to inadequate blood flow. (*Modified from Cope, 1951.*)

may be distinctly greater in second-degree or partial-thickness burns than in full-thickness burns because the distensibility of the local tissue has not been curtailed by coagulation necrosis of the dermis.

In the untreated burn, the remaining concentrated plasma creates an elevated colloid osmotic pressure. Circulation in the unburned tissues of the body is therefore dehydrating, and fluid from the unharmed extracellular spaces of the body is drawn into the circulation in an effort to maintain it. There is further redistribution of the remaining blood by selective vasoconstriction, which helps to maintain flow of blood and an adequate supply of oxygen to the parenchymatous organs, such as the heart, brain, liver, and kidneys, on whose integrity life itself depends. If circulation can be maintained in the face of the tremendous drain by the burn wound until the spontaneous reversal of flow into the burned tissues results, the organism will survive. If, on the other hand, the flow into the wound is great and the compensatory mechanisms outlined are insufficient, death in shock and dehydration occurs. During the last stages of the latter train of events, the body, in an effort to maintain the failing circulation, draws fluid from its ultimate reserve, the water contained within the cells, thus dehydrating them and destroying the integrity of vital organs. With this flow there is a release into the circulating fluids of the electrolytes characteristic of the cell itself, including both potassium and phosphate.

It must not be thought that all burned patients die without treatment. Oddly enough, the tremendous burn mortality in the elderly has not been much changed by treatment. It should be very clearly understood that in the eons of development of the various forms of life, including both animals and plants, certain protective mechanisms for the preservation of life after severe trauma and infection have become highly developed. It is of interest to note that these survival mechanisms, all part and parcel of the stress reaction of Selye, are only modified by treatment and are not completely lost. For example, the large urinary excretion of nitrogen during the first 4 to 7 days after operation or injury may be reduced, but it is not entirely abolished by the administration of amino acids and fat emulsions, as Abbott and his coworkers have shown. It must further be remembered at all times that urinary changes can only be accomplished in conjunction with a normal urinary tubular system and relatively normal urinary blood flow. The changes in the senile kidney are such as to make this urinary response one of the weakest links in survival after severe thermal trauma, and may account for some of the high mortality seen after burns in the aged.

Normal survival mechanisms in the untreated patient have been stressed because modern treatment depends upon replacement, unit for unit, of the fluid, protein, and electrolyte into the burn wound. This has the obvious effect of stuffing the extracellular space. Although this type of treatment is excellent for children and most adults with normal cardiovascular-renal mechanisms, it may easily lead to unnecessary overloading of the circulation and death in pulmonary edema in the aged patient. Indeed, vascular overload may be one of the chief causes of the extremely high mortality in burns in the aged. Accordingly, it must be clearly realized that there are a series of important measures put into play by the body itself, without the aid of the physician, in an effort to conserve life during the critical period following injury. The physician must constantly attempt to follow a somewhat modified pattern in treating the aged as regards fluid, electrolyte, and protein replacement so as to avoid death in shock and dehydration, as well as vascular overload and pulmonary edema.

INITIAL EXAMINATION AND ASSESSMENT

The assessment of the burned patient begins with the taking of a brief history. This can be accomplished while preparations for treatment are carried out. In a major burn (over 10 per cent) a needle or cannula is immediately placed in an accessible vein, and specimens for initial blood chemistries, blood typing, and cross match are taken. Simultaneously a brief history of the present illness is obtained from the patient, if possible, or from a relative or friend, if present. Particular attention is paid to a history indicating or suggesting such complicating diseases as diabetes, hypertension, cardiovascular-renal disease, cerebral arteriosclerosis, etc., all of which may seriously complicate or affect the subsequent treatment of the patient. In taking the history, the circumstances of the burn and agent which caused it are of clinical significance. Flame, with its temperatures of over 750°F, characteristically causes deep burns; whereas hot water and scalds may burn not quite as deeply, more often producing partial-thickness burns. Sharply circumscribed burns accompanied by a history of loss of consciousness may hint at the presence of a convulsive state, Stokes-Adams syndrome, or other serious organic disease.

Assessment of the burn wound itself may be made in a somewhat more leisurely fashion after attention has been directed to the patient's general physical condition. In general, partial-thickness burn areas with characteristic simple erythema or superficial blistering and full-thickness burned areas with dense eschar formation or even charring are easy to identify in terms of depth. Evaluation is often not as easy as this and in many instances must be deferred until a period of 10 to 14 days has elapsed. Examination using a sterile pin may be of value in demonstrating the classic insensitivity of the full-thickness burn. This, however, may be misleading, particularly in the thick skin of the back where it is possible to have a very thick eschar and still have viable dermis with epidermal elements beneath from which regeneration may occur. In Allen's work, "10 days has been taken as the time when demarcation between incomplete and whole-thickness skin loss is very apparent." From the practical standpoint, however, it may be assumed that wherever the appearance of a burn is such that the differentiation between a full-thickness loss and partial-thickness loss cannot be made at the time of initial examination, the patient should be treated as if this area were completely nonviable, since treatment in the early stages is the same.

At the time of admission, the question of whether a particular area is second- or third-degree is of less importance than is the total extent of the burn in terms of surface area. The treatment for a 20 per cent third-degree burn in a 65-year-old patient is almost the same as that for a second-degree burn of a similar extent.

The modern formulas for the administration of fluids to a burned patient depend on knowledge of the percentile extent of the burn and of the patient's weight. Accordingly, a reasonably accurate knowledge of the per cent of the total body area constituted by each portion of the body is essential to the surgeon who treats an acute burn. Berkow, in 1924, presented data concerning the percentage of surface area of various parts of the body. These were modified in 1944 by Lund and Browder, who emphasized the striking difference in surface area distribution noted in children. The precise estimation of the extent to which the body is burned is difficult. The rather rough and ready rule of nines is ordinarily sufficiently accurate for practical purposes. According to Artz, this rather simple formula was first used by Pulaski and Tennyson. In this form of notation, the body is divided into areas representing 9 per cent of the body surface or multiples thereof. The entire head and neck is 9 per cent, each upper extremity represents 9 per cent, the entire front of the trunk is 18 per cent, the entire posterior trunk is 18 per cent and each lower extremity represents 18 per cent. These add up to 99 per cent, and the genital area measuring about 1 per cent completes the surface distribution.

PATTERNS IN BURNS

To the surgeon experienced in the treatment of burns, certain patterns of distribution are characteristic and often tell a story in themselves. The burn of one or the other upper extremities, the axilla, and the corresponding side of the chest wall, for example, is quite typical of the smoker who falls asleep in bed holding a lighted cigarette in his hand. The extremely deep, circumscribed burn sustained by a patient falling unconscious against a hot object and remaining there for a relatively long period of time is characteristic of preceding loss of consciousness. It is seen most often in convulsive patients, usually with idiopathic epilepsy, although in older people it occurs in the course of syncope from other causes. Burns localized to the hands and face, sparing those portions of the body covered with clothing, are quite characteristic of the so-called "flash" burn. This is a thermal burn due to the action, for a short period of time, of intense heat, particularly within a closed space. These are seen in industrial explosions or in flash fires within a closed space, such as a burning aircraft. In military circumstances they were noted also in fires within tanks and in explosions within the gun turrets of naval vessels. The atomic explosions at Hiroshima and Nagasaki produced typical flash burns.

Of extreme importance in the initial assessment and evaluation of a burned patient is the recognition and appreciation of those burn patterns which indicate possible damage to the respiratory tract. Such damage may be present in patients with a history of having been burned while in a closed space, such as in the hallway of a burning house, and with visible burns of the head and neck, particularly about the mouth and within the oral cavity and associated with the presence of singed nasal vibrissae. If, by the time the patient has reached the accident room or hospital, a slight, irritative type of cough is heard, the index of the examiner's suspicion should rise precipitously. The diagnosis can be made with assurance when such obvious symptoms as cyanosis and cough with production of frothy sputum, denoting established pulmonary edema, have appeared.

The Steps in Treatment of the Early Phase

It is quite evident that the evaluation described in the preceding paragraph need not take an inordinate length of time. It is just as obvious that in the more severe burns the preparations for treatment can be carried out while information is being gathered. The patient's clothing is removed and if possible he is weighed. He may be placed on clean sheets while the decision is made as to what method of local treatment for the wound will be employed. Areas which are small, open, and weeping can be placed on sterile towels if they are not too extensive. It is also wise, in the presence of moist, weeping areas, to have the personnel handling the burned patient at least masked and gloved to prevent gross contamination of the fresh, open wounds. In the presence of thick, dry burn eschar, where it is probable that the decision will be made to expose the area, such precautions may be dispensed with.

The need for sedation varies. Superficial burns are, oddly enough, more apt to be the source of severe pain than deep burns in which the nerve endings have been destroyed. In extensive burns, particularly where shock is present or impending, narcotic drugs such as morphine should only be given intravenously so that their effect can be obtained and evaluated at once. In old people, large doses of narcotics are unnecessary and even dangerous. As noted in preceding chapters the administration of drugs by the subcutaneous route, where they may remain unabsorbed to exert a later cumulative effect, is strictly contraindicated. Barbiturates in older people with cerebral arteriosclerosis will frequently lead to disorientation and combativeness. Tranquilizer drugs, such as Compazine and Sparine, are distinctly superior but must be carefully administered for fear of their hypotensive effect. Restlessness and disorientation early in the course of a burn may be due to impending shock because of hypovolemia and cerebral anoxia. Administration of fluids may cause clearing of the sensorium, whereas additional sedation would have resulted in further increase of cerebral difficulties.

It is to be expected that, either at the time of admission or shortly thereafter, preparations will have been made for the insertion of what Artz has called "the intravenous life line." It must be anticipated, especially in the more severe burns, that intravenous therapy will be prolonged. There will be further need of intravenous portals if the patient survives the initial period of burn and separation of burn slough and eschar, and requires repeated skin grafting and reconstructive procedures. There are not very many superficial veins available, and these patients are apt to be restless and thus to displace needles. Therefore the intravenous portal must be a fairly secure one. A cut down with a fairly large-bore polyethylene tube, well anchored in place, is highly desirable. In the elderly, the lower extremity should be assiduously avoided unless no other veins are available, since the incidence of thrombophlebitis and thromboembolism is inordinately high. The author has for many years taught his house staff that in performance of the cut-down intravenous it is usually not necessary to tie off and, in so doing, to destroy a perfectly good vein. Veins which are exposed can often be cannulated, using one of the newer Rochester-type needles. These consist of a plastic outer jacket and an inner sharp, pointed needle-stylet so that the advantages of ordinary venipuncture and of a soft cannula are both enjoyed. By anchoring the hub of the needle securely to the skin below the point of puncture, a secure life line is obtained without the necessity of ligating and destroying a vein which in time will recanalize or possibly not thrombose in the first instance. Injection of 1 ml of 1 per cent aqueous heparin solution into the catheter at intervals of 4 to 6 hours is useful to prevent thrombosis and plugging of the tip.

At the time the vein is exposed and the cannula inserted, blood samples should be withdrawn for blood grouping, cross match, hematocrit determination and any blood chemistry determination which may be indicated. In an elderly person whose medical history is not known, a blood urea nitrogen and sugar are the least which should be done in terms of chemical examination. After the samples have been obtained, a slow intravenous of 5 per cent dextrose in saline is begun until the plans for intravenous therapy, according to the needs of the patient, have been worked out. If the burn is obviously of major proportions and shock is imminent, plasma or a plasma expander can be commenced as the first fluid until the blood grouping has been completed.

Tetanus Prophylaxis

The occurrence of tetanus in burned patients has been reported on numerous occasions. Anaerobic conditions exist beneath the thick and impervious burn eschar. These conditions plus the presence of devitalized or dead tissue explain the high incidence of the disease. Accordingly, all burn patients should receive a booster dose of tetanus toxoid if they have been previously immunized, or a large dose (at least 3,000 units) of tetanus antitoxin after appropriate skin tests. If there is any question about the adequacy of previous immunization, both the booster dose and the antitoxin may be administered.

Inlying Urethral Catheter

During the critical first 48 to 72 hours, the urinary output is one of the most important and sensitive guides to therapy. During the first 24 hours an absent or falling urinary output denotes inadequacy of treatment, and in the second and third 24-hour period a rapidly rising urinary output is warning of overtreatment, hypervolemia, and the danger of possibly fatal pulmonary edema. Since many of these elderly patients, particularly the aged male with prostatic hypertrophy, will have difficulty in voiding, the presence of an inlying catheter is a necessary piece of diagnostic and therapeutic equipment. The modern Foley catheter, which does not require the messy adhesive-plaster fixation of earlier days, serves admirably for this purpose. In addition, the smaller sizes permit proper urethral drainage alongside the catheter and the incidence of difficulties during the first week is very slight, particularly since the patients are apt to be on high doses of antibiotics. During this period, it is not necessary to have the catheter connected to a bedside bottle. It may be plugged by a sterile medicine dropper and opened at hourly intervals at which time the content of the urinary bladder is emptied, measured, and recorded on a special hourly urine chart. It is important to instruct the nursing staff to be on the alert for the excretion of urine of unusual color and, in particular, the port wine-colored urine associated with the presence of free hemoglobin. During the first 24 hours, hourly increments below 25 ml should be reported at once. During the second and third 24-hour periods, the nurse must report at once any urinary output rising over 100 ml per hour.

ANTIBIOTIC THERAPY

The burned patient, faced as he is with a massive bacterial assault on the wide expanse of burn wound, should be protected by the administration of one or another of the antibiotic drugs. During the phase of intravenous therapy, penicillin and streptomycin are convenient and effective. Penicillin can be given in doses ranging from 1,000,000 to 2,000,000 units, and 0.5 Gm of streptomycin can be given twice a day. This can be continued until such time as the patient is tolerating fluids by mouth, at which time the penicillin and streptomycin can be more conveniently given intramuscularly. Antibiotics can be used either in conjunction with or supplanting the first two drugs according to the patient's needs, as determined by appropriate cultures and sensitivity tests. No matter how severely burned a patient may be, a history of sensitivity must be inquired into lest a severely burned patient be subjected to the added burden of a severe drug reaction.

MANAGEMENT OF FLUID THERAPY

While some of the previous therapeutic measures are being carried out, often by nursing and house staff, it behooves the attending physician or surgeon to retire to some quiet corner and carefully plan the fluid therapy for the first 48 hours, including the types and amounts of fluid to be given and the rate of administration. This plan is more or less like that of a battlefield commander who has a mission to carry out and a plan by which he hopes to achieve his objective. He realizes that if all does not go well or if there is a change in anticipated conditions, he will, of course, at any time modify his plan to the changes. Nevertheless, he must start with a plan, necessarily on paper, by which he hopes to reach his objective. In this instance, the mission is prevention of burn shock by replacement in the blood stream of fluid, protein, and electrolyte lost into the burned tissue. The plan must anticipate the return of much of this material into the blood stream after the thirty-sixth hour and the tapering off of fluid therapy to adjust to this spontaneous return.

The recognition that the loss of plasma and electrolyte from the burn patient is proportional to both the extent of burn and the weight of the patient is the basis for the modern, successful fluid replacement formulas. The formula of Cope and Moore, published in 1947, was the first one which was based on surface area. It did not take the weight of the patient into account and, accordingly, led to difficulties of over- and undertreatment. In 1951, Dr. James Brooke, working in Evans's laboratory, showed that in the dog, by the sixth hour, approximately 1 ml of plasma per kilogram of body weight was lost for each per cent of body-surface burn. The same proportionate loss was observed in human burns involving 20 per cent of the body surface. Accordingly, a new formula taking into account both the surface area and the weight was published by Evans in 1952. The Evans formula with varying modifications has become a fairly reliable standard guide in the fluid treatment of burns. Basically, it is very simple and consists of replacement of 1 ml of colloid (blood, plasma, or plasma substitute) per kilogram of body weight per 1 per cent of surface area burned. This amount is matched by the same amount of electrolyte solution, usually physiological saline, the ratio again being 1 ml per kilogram per each per cent of burn. The requirements during the second 24 hours are considered to be half of those during the first 24-hour period. There is, of course, a limit to the amounts of fluid which may be introduced into the body. In burns of over 50 per cent of the body area, only those amounts of colloid and salt are given which would be calculated for a 50 per cent burn. Evans himself clearly pointed out that all fluid formulas are merely guides to therapy and stated that "it is to be emphasized strongly that the simple formula presented here for calculation of fluid and salt requirements is only a guide to therapy and not to be considered an infallible rule." The most important guide is the clinical response of the patient, and no formula exists to date which has resulted in freeing the attending physician, house staff, and nursing staff from close observation of the patient. Those attending a burned patient must be guided by the pulse rate, blood pressure, peripheral circulation as evidenced by color and capillary return in the nail bed, the hourly urinary output, and such responses as pallor, thirst, restlessness, etc. Two examples are given below to illustrate the calculations for a 25 per cent burn.

The laboratory examinations necessary in the care of even a severe burn need not be elaborate. Most complex chemical examinations, particularly those relating to electrolyte balance, are usually reported much too late to be of value. Even the hematocrit examination so widely urged by many authors takes at least one-half to three-quarters of an hour to spin down properly. In a sick patient on whom urgent information is necessary, such a delay at 2 o'clock in the morning is tedious and unnecessary. A hemoglobin determination, which can be taken every 4 hours, even at the bedside, suffices for following the patient during the first 48 hours. Evans found this to be sufficient even in a research unit in which any conceivable type of elaborate examination was available. The clinical observations mentioned above, including especially the hourly urinary output, together with the 4-hourly hemoglobin determination, should give sufficient information to evaluate and manage most severe burns during the early stages. Later in the course of the burn, particularly on the third and fourth days, there may be occasional puzzling changes in hydration and electrolyte balance which may make a determination of plasma sodium or other electrolytes helpful or desirable. Again, such a determination is useless if it cannot be reported within an hour of the time at which the specimen was drawn.

The most recent modification of the Evans formula is that reported from the surgical research unit at the Brooke Army Hospital, Brooke Army Medical Center, located at Fort Sam Houston in Texas. The Brooke formula differs from the Evans formula in that an electrolyte-colloid ratio of 3:1 is proposed in contrast to Evans's 1:1 ratio. The formulas are identical as regards recommendation of total fluid volume. The Brooke formula was developed in response to work demonstrating the importance of sodium salts in the treatment of shock in animals and partly by the fact that electrolyte solutions are much cheaper than colloid solutions and might be secured in larger quantities in case of disaster. The experiences at Brooke Army Hospital showed that, indeed, the patients did as well as those on the straight Evans formula and had remarkably smooth clinical courses during the period of fluid replacement.

According to the Brooke formula, as described by Artz, the electrolyte requirements during the first 24-hour period are, (1) colloids, 0.5 ml per kilogram of body weight for each per cent of body surface burned, (2) electrolytes, 1.5 ml per kilogram for each per cent of body surface burned, and (3) 2,000 ml of glucose in water. The second 24-hour-period requirements for colloids and electrolytes are about one-half those for the first 24 hours. Again, as with the Evans formula, in applying the treatment to burns involving more than 50 per cent of the body surface, the fluid requirement should be calculated as though only 50 per cent of the body surface had been burned.

Rate of Administration. If the rate of administration of the calculated amount of fluid is distributed evenly during the first 24 hours, it will usually not keep up with the losses into the burned tissue. This is because most of the loss has occurred within the first 6 to 8 hours. Accordingly, it is well to time the rate of administration so that half of the calculated 24-hour total is given during the first 8 hours, one-quarter during the second 8-hour period, and one-quarter during the remaining 8 hours of the first day following burn.

Choice of Colloids. There is still controversy regarding the types and amounts of colloids to be administered to the burned patient. Evans, Moyer, et al. have emphasized the use of whole blood in large amounts, and Moyer has even taken the position that perhaps no other colloids are needed. Quinby and Cope, however, have pointed out that in some instances, extra erythrocytes may be added unnecessarily to an already concentrated circulating blood volume resulting in marked increase in viscosity, thereby increasing the work load on the heart. As with many such controversies, there seems to be a sensible middle ground, based on rational considerations. There is a close correlation between the need for additional circulating hemoglobin and the depth of the burn. It has been repeatedly pointed out that a burn is a three-dimensional wound involving depth as well as surface area. In deep burns with destruction of the entire thickness of the dermis and of deeper tissue, there is actual destruction of a portion of the circulating red-cell mass. Some authors have placed this as high as 30 per cent. This is due to the fact that the skin itself contains great quantities of blood and that these trapped erythrocytes are coagulated and destroyed by the same thermal trauma which renders the burned tissue nonvital. In addition, the blood in those vessels which have not actually been coagulated has been heated to temperatures which have so damaged the contained red cells that the latter disintegrate upon reaching the systemic circulation. This action of heat in causing osmotic and mechanical fragilities and hemolysis of erythrocytes has been thoroughly discussed by Ham and his associates. In these cases, there can be little doubt that a much greater proportion, if not all, of the colloid replacement should be in the form of whole blood. Somewhat less extensive full-thickness burns should have a proportionate share of the colloid in the form of whole blood as well.

In the case of the more superficially burned patient whose surface area of burn is just as extensive, a somewhat different state of affairs exists. The over-all leakage of fluid and loss of circulating blood volume is just as great and in some ways greater than that of the patient with deeper but equally extensive burns. This leakage occurs because the circulation continues in the burned vessels whose highly permeable walls permit the loss of large amounts of fluid into the distensible extracellular tissue. In these cases, shock may be as great and hemoconcentration even greater than in the patient with deeper burns. The total amount of fluid necessary to replace the failing circulation is just as large. However, since there is not the enormous destruction of circulating red-cell mass that exists in the deep burn, it is possible to rely to a much greater extent on plasma and plasma volume expanders, such as dextran and polyvinyl-pyrrolidine (PVP). As always, one must not fall into the trap of slavishly following even the advice given above. For example, it might be wise to give a patient with a 60 per cent partial-thickness burn but one unit of blood and certainly one would not necessarily need to give a patient with a 5 per cent deep burn whole blood except under unusual circumstances.

Choice of Electrolyte; Route of Administration. The principal electrolyte in the fluid which is lost into the burned area is sodium, accompanied by amounts of chloride and bicarbonate proportional to the amounts found in normal blood plasma. It is wise to replace the deficiency with fluid of somewhat the same chemical composition. There are two simple solutions available. The first is lactated Ringer's (Hartmann's) solution. The second solution, which can be easily made up, is a mixture of two volumes of physiologic saline to one volume of $\frac{1}{6}$ M sodium lactate. Ordinary physiologic saline has been used extensively but is far from ideal, especially in the elderly where renal function cannot be securely counted upon to balance the excess of chloride ion. The mixture of two volumes of saline to one volume of $\frac{1}{6}$ M lactate contains 159 mEq of sodium and 103 mEq of chloride per liter. Hartmann's solution contains 131 mEq of sodium and 110 mEq of chloride per liter. It will be noted that the combination solution is slightly hypertonic to the plasma in its concentration of sodium and that Hartmann's solution is somewhat hypotonic. These differences are not significant and do not have to be taken into account in therapy.

In discussion of the fluid formulas for treatment, it will be evident that the intravenous route is mandatory for the colloid fraction of the replacement therapy. In recent years, administration of the electrolyte and water portion of the fluid requirements has been accomplished successfully in many cases by mouth. When so administered, it must be remembered that concentrations must be reduced lest nausea and vomiting result. A solution of 3 to 4 Gm of sodium chloride (1 teaspoonful) and from 1.5 to 2 Gm of sodium bicarbonate or sodium citrate ($\frac{2}{3}$ teaspoonful) to each quart of water is reasonably palatable and is tolerated well enough in many instances to form the entire basis for the fluid and electrolyte requirement. Intolerance, however, must be carefully watched for, and at the first sign of vomiting or of gastric dilatation, treatment must be discontinued and reliance placed on intravenous therapy. This type of treatment is particularly useful in the elderly individual who cannot tolerate large increases in blood volume owing to the impaired circulatory efficiency and danger of overloading.

Water Intoxication. Before the need for electrolyte replacement was as widely understood as it is now, water intoxication was common and probably accounted for a great many instances of the so-called "early burn toxemia." This toxemia is due to the unrestricted drinking of water by the burned individual without the addition of sodium either orally or by vein. The fate of this ingested water is as follows. Either it is absorbed, thus diluting the remaining salt concentration of the intra- and extracellular fluids, or it remains in the stomach where sodium salts diffuse into it, thus further decreasing sodium concentration in the circulating plasma. In both instances, with the cells of the body bathed in a markedly sodium-deficient medium, water enters the cells, thus seriously interfering with their function. The disturbance occasioned by water intoxication is manifested by headache, tremors, twitching, blurring of vision, vomiting, diarrhea, disorientation, salivation and mania. Later convulsions, coma, and death supervene. Prevention is simple: salt must be given with water when the latter is administered by mouth or as glucose and water by vein. When the clinical picture is confused, sodium determinations are essential for clarification.

EARLY PHASE OF BURN THERAPY

PRINCIPLES OF LOCAL CARE

The principles governing the local care of a burn wound have evolved slowly but surely over many decades of study. From the mass of conflicting data and diametrically opposed "fashions" in therapy, there has evolved a rather clear understanding of the basic principles of local treatment. They are as follows:

1. Clean the burn wound if grossly soiled.

2. Prevent further loss of viable elements by gentleness in handling and by avoiding local use of irritating or toxic chemicals.

3. Prevent infection by creating a local environment which is unfavorable to the multiplication of microorganisms. This is accomplished by keeping the burn wound dry and cool, and, where practicable, exposed to the light.

4. Rest injured parts and elevate burned extremities to prevent edema.

CLEANSING AND DEBRIDEMENT

This phase of burn treatment can often be omitted. Local cleansing of a clean, full-thickness burn wound in an individual who habitually maintains a reasonable state of personal cleanliness is wholly unnecessary. Burns covered with dirt or grease and those burns in which large amounts of devitalized strips and tags of epithelium are present are probably best cleansed and debrided. In elderly patients, particularly in cases where the evaluation of general factors is uncertain, general anesthesia is to be avoided at all costs. The most gentle of scrubbing and debridement, if done slowly, carefully and skillfully, can be accomplished either with no anesthesia or with sedation achieved by a small dose of intravenous morphine. In severe burns, this procedure must await the commencement of fluid therapy. In burns of lesser extent and depth, i.e., below 10 per cent of the body surface, the local treatment can often be accomplished before fluid therapy is begun. Oil and grease are gently scrubbed, using a detergent such as pHisoHex, and flushed away with copious quantities of normal saline. Partly detached tags of burned epithelium are cut away and blisters are opened and the contents evacuated. The tops of the blisters can be removed since they represent dead epidermis. An exception should be made in the case of the hand where blisters often will remain sterile beneath a pressure dressing and epithelization take place despite the presence of overlying fluid. Further treatment at this point depends on whether the burn is to be treated by exposure, by an occlusive pressure dressing, or by a combination of both.

THE OCCLUSIVE PRESSURE DRESSING

This is begun either by laying onto the wound strips of dry, fine-mesh gauze or by the use of fine-mesh gauze strips lightly impregnated with either petroleum jelly or, in some cases, Furacin Soluble Dressing. It is of great importance to lay on the strips either longitudinally or spirally, since, with the swelling of the burned part, circular dressings will become a series of firm, constricting bands, exercising a tourniquet-like effect. The basic layer of fine-mesh gauze is followed by a variety of dressings which should have one basic quality in common; they should be highly absorptive. It is to be noted, at this point, that the pressure dressing, although occlusive, should be designed to keep the wound surface dry by permitting drainage of exudate away from the wound and by encouraging its diffusion and absorption into the bulky mass of peripheral dressing.

Any dressing which macerates the wound or prevents the escape of fluid exudate from the wound surface is therefore contraindicated. This includes such materials as fine-mesh gauze *heavily* impregnated with petroleum jelly–based ointments and some of the newer plasticized dressings whose virtue is that they can be removed painlessly. Nylon and other synthetic materials of extremely fine weave are also probably unsuitable due to the fact that dried serum occludes the tiny interstices of the fabric, thereby rendering it completely impervious. The composition of the outer dressing is unimportant provided it is highly absorptive. The Universal Protective Dressing developed under the auspices of Subcommittee on Burns of the National Research Council serves very well. It consists of an inner surface of dry fine-mesh gauze with an intermediate layer composed of absorbent cotton and layers of absorbent cellulose. An outer, water-repellent layer of cotton fabric serves to prevent fluid reaching the outside and thereby forming an avenue for bacterial growth. The outer, nonabsorbable layer serves to ensure the diffusion of the exudates throughout the bulk of the absorbent material, thereby ensuring a relatively dry wound surface. A similar dressing can be improvised in any hospital, the Brooke Burn Dressing being an example. It is composed of an inner layer of absorbent cotton backed by an absorptive bulky layer of fluffed gauze with an additional pad of cotton encased in a single layer of bolt gauze. This dressing has the advantage of being thick, absorptive, and quite pliable. The entire dressing is now carefully bandaged into place, taking care to make the turns of outer bandage smooth and even, with exertion of constant pressure. Several of the newer, somewhat elastic gauze rolls, such as Kerlix, serve admirably for this purpose. Additional pressure can be built up (but great care must be exercised) by adding a layer of cotton elastic bandage.

Where possible, the original pressure dressing is not disturbed for a period as long as 10 to 14 days. The dressing is usually well tolerated and pain is strikingly absent. There is always a great temptation, to say nothing of pressure from both the patient and his relatives, to change the dressing in order to "see what is going on." As long as there is no evidence of toxicity and temperature is minimal, this temptation should be resisted. In the more superficial burns, epithelization is often going on without infection, and the early dressing will not only be extremely painful but will result in the tearing away of large sheets of fresh, young, fragile epithelium.

However, in the presence of rising temperature, pain, and exudate, particularly greenish in color, suggesting infection by *Pseudomonas aeruginosa,* the wound must be investigated. Again, as suggested before, general anesthesia is undesirable if it can be dispensed with. Many patients can be managed by small doses of intravenous morphine, accompanied by a very gentle technique in handling the burn wound. In the case of superficial burns in which nerve endings have not been destroyed, this may be impossible, and a very light general anesthesia may be necessary. In the absence of infection, the same type of dressing may be replaced. If the area is found to be infected, wet dressings are indicated. These will be discussed later under the problem of the infected burn wound.

Exposure Treatment: Principles and Technique

In a now classic paper published in 1948, Wallace reintroduced the exposure treatment of burns. The tannic-acid and triple-dye methods of the late twenties and thirties involved exposure of a sort. They were, however, unphysiologic in the sense that they did not permit the second-degree burn to form its own plasma pellicle; and in the case of third-degree burns, they actually resulted in tanning of the leathery eschar. Wallace pointed out that he had used the occlusive pressure method of Allen and Koch quite successfully but had begun within the past year to expose burns of the head and neck. The striking simplicity of this method and excellent results obtained by it led him to extend its use to other areas of the body. Equally good results were noted. Wallace stated that this was merely a reintroduction of an old method, Sneve of St. Paul having described it in some detail in 1905. The latter author remarked that "in spite of all our pastes and powders, salves and solutions, the mortality in burns involving more than one third of the body surface is nearly 100 per cent." As noted above, the basis of effectiveness for the exposure technique lies in the creation of a dry, cool environment with the elimination, during part of the day at least, of darkness. Thus conditions unfavorable to the growth and multiplication of microorganisms are created. Cultures taken from an oozing burn surface will frequently show the presence of bacteria which disappear a few days after the wound has become hard and dry.

Technique of Exposure. As with the pressure method, local care commences with a meticulous cleansing and debridement of the burn wound after blood pressure has been stabilized. A clean wound, however, without epithelial tags, does not require washing just for the sake of carrying out a surgical routine. The patient is then returned to his room and the involved areas are exposed to the air. A certain amount of contamination must be anticipated where burns are exposed. Accordingly, laundry-clean linen can be accepted as proper preparation of the bed. Where exposure is used in the treatment of circumferential areas, the patient must be placed on absorptive, disposable dressings and turned every 6 hours to permit drying of the entire burn. Certain areas lend themselves better to exposure than others, for example, the face, the anogenital region, and either the anterior or posterior surface of the trunk or of a single extremity. Great ingenuity is sometimes necessary to arrange a patient in bed or out of bed so that the burned area is not in contact with the bedclothes. If this is neglected, maceration and weeping of the wound and hence failure of the method can be anticipated. It must be remembered that *exposure is a surgical technique and not a policy of abandonment.* Too often, exposure of burns becomes equated with neglect. Occasionally, foul, infected wounds, discharging highly contagious material, are seen in surgical wards. Questioning of the nursing and house staff sometimes elicits the comment, "Oh, he's being treated by exposure." Wallace's description is classic and should be read by all surgeons whose work does or may demand the care of burn cases.

After about 48 hours, the plasma which has exuded from partial-thickness burns has formed a coagulum which is called a "plasma pellicle." This relatively tough but pliable layer has now served to close what has been hitherto an open surgical wound. In the case of full-thickness burns, the problem is simplified because of the tight, dry, sterile, leathery eschar which effectively closes the wound in a way somewhat similar to the plasma pellicle of the partial-thickness burn.

Exposure versus Pressure Dressing. In burns more than in any other form of trauma there has been a tendency to seize on the latest fashion in treatment and to discard out-of-hand all that has gone before. In the author's surgical experience, he has seen the tannic-acid treatment introduced by Davidson give way to the triple-dye treatment of Aldrich, following which all the tanning methods were discarded in favor of the pressure-dressing technique of Allen and Koch. In turn, the pendulum has swung back again and all burns are now exposed. This method is now applied indiscriminately to all sizes and shapes of burns, deep or superficial, circumscribed or diffuse. As with most controversial areas in medicine and surgery, there is usually a solid and sensible middle ground. Certainly, the pressure dressings used to cover the entire head of a burned patient suffering from some mild second-degree burns of the face (usually in the summer with the environmental temperature reaching about 90°) and with four inadequate holes for the eyes, nose and mouth was indeed "cruel and unusual punishment." It is almost as foolish to see a healthy patient with a circumscribed burn of part of one upper extremity confined to bed with the arm carefully exposed on a pillow, when with a good pressure dressing he might be not only up and about but out of the hospital and attending to his or her affairs.

Certain areas should categorically be exposed. The head, face and neck, and the anogenital region are the most obvious. Although Metcalf and others have shown that burned hands can be exposed with excellent results, nevertheless, in the absence of other large areas of burn confining the patient to bed, an adequate pressure dressing with elevation seems to give the patient more comfort and certainly more mobility. Ross, reporting on 269 freshly burned hands from the Birmingham Accident Hospital, reported excellent results using massive pressure dressings with elevation. In summary, it must be remembered that exposure is not a panacea, but a method of treatment which, according to the particular situation of the patient, can be modified, used in part, or it can be discarded altogether. In general, elderly patients do well with exposure, possibly because of its restraining effects on bacterial growth.

THE INTERMEDIATE PHASE OF BURN THERAPY

INTRODUCTION

The initial phase of fluid and electrolyte imbalance is usually over after about 48 to 72 hours. At this time, if the patient is to survive, he has usually had a striking diuresis due to the return of extravasated plasma from the interstitial spaces back into the blood stream. During these next few days, several additional forms of fluid imbalance may become manifest and require treatment.

PULMONARY EDEMA

The greatest danger to the elderly burn patient occurs toward the end of the second day when his cardiovascular apparatus, already burdened by the stress of an acute injury and possibly damaged by previous cardiovascular disease, is called upon to accept the additional load of a large amount of fluid pouring back through the capillary walls and via lymphatics into the blood stream. To these factors may be added the additional insult of a certain degree of respiratory-tract burn due to the inhalation of smoke or superheated gases. The treatment for this type of pulmonary edema is largely preventive and anticipatory. Older people should receive the minimal amount of fluid consistent with calculated fluid requirements. It is always possible to vary the estimates of the initial burn, keeping to the low side to avoid overloading. During the second 24 hours, a rising hourly urinary output reaching levels of 75 to 100 ml should indicate that the tide has turned. Fluid by vein should immediately be cut back to a flow just sufficient to keep the polyethylene tube or cannula open, and fluids by mouth should be restricted markedly.

Treatment of pulmonary edema may require urgent phlebotomy, administration of oxygen, and rapid digitalization.

INFECTION IN BURNS

There seems little doubt that the major cause of death in patients who have survived the period of fluid imbalance is infection. Early observers noted that those patients who survived the initial insult often suffered an illness of more or less gravity which usually reached its peak during the first 10 days and continued thereafter for several weeks. The symptoms during this critical period included high fever, tachycardia, tachypnea, marked prostration, and in some cases disorientation, delirium, and death. These observers, noting the presence of large amounts of burned tissue and further noting that the greater the extent of burned tissue the more severe the symptoms, postulated the presence of a toxin which, being absorbed from the underlying viable tissue, overwhelmed the organism. Underhill et al. performed careful experimental work casting doubt on the presence of an active toxin from burned tissues. Aldrich suggested that all the previously described symptoms could be reproduced by overwhelming infection. There now seems little doubt that susceptibility to massive infection dominates the intermediate phase of burn treatment and is the leading cause of death after the first few days. In the elderly, whose fragile cardiovascular-renal systems are serving their aged owners in a modest way, the added strain of invasive infection and sepsis arising in large burned areas is intolerable. The anatomical causes of death noted by Ziffren and mentioned in the introduction are entirely compatible with death by infection and sepsis.

Types of Infection. The mildest of these is mere contamination and colonization of the burn wound. In ascending order of severity there is noted *local* invasive infection with suppuration, *regional* invasive infection with cellulitis, lymphangitis and regional adenopathy, and finally blood-stream infection with massive septicemia and distant infectious metastasis. The principal source of offending organisms includes the burned skin itself, which has been shown to harbor viable bacteria surviving even the thermal death of the skin. The second most important source includes the nose, throat, and hands of attendant personnel, and the patient's intimate environment consisting of dressings and bed linen. The nasopharynx, anogenital region, and the patient's own surrounding normal skin must, of course, be included in the list of contaminating agencies. The occlusive pressure dressing was devised in part to cut down on some of these sources of contamination and in many instances was successful in doing so. In the case of exposure treatment, it is postulated that the contaminating bacteria falling on a dry, cool surface do not find conditions suitable for multiplication and are thereby rendered more or less impotent.

Factors Affecting Severity and Mortality. It will be recalled that in terms of fluid imbalance a partial-thickness burn may cause even more initial disturbance than a full-thickness burn of similar extent. In relation to the problem of infection, however, there seems little doubt that infectious complications in the second-degree burn are not only less frequent but less severe than in the third-degree burn. The deeper layers of unburned skin, comprising dermis with an extremely rich blood supply, seem to form an effective barrier against the contaminating organisms multiplying in the more superficial burned tissue. Not only does the totally burned skin seem to lack such a barrier to infection, but the extent of infection seems to be mathematically proportional to the extent of full-thickness loss. Artz and his coworkers at Brooke Army Medical Center, in an as yet unpublished study of septicemia, have pointed this out. In reporting on 31 fatal burns associated with clinically proved septicemia, they showed that the fatal outcome was associated with the larger extents of burn. This group plotted the cumulative case fatality rate against the extent of burn and obtained an S-shaped curve, similar to the S-shaped fatality curves of the Brooke Army Hospital. In other words, a small increase in extent of full-thickness burn beyond a certain point results in a great increase in mortality. This, to the author, is probably the most logical explanation for the enormous increase in mortality in aged patients relative to increasing extent of full-thickness burns, as is noted in the mortality probability tables quoted in the introduction to this chapter. Artz feels that this is a dosage phenomenon related to the number of pathogenic microorganisms gaining access to the circulation. Given a large enough area for such entry, the larger dosage of pathogenic microorganisms will overwhelm the host.

Types of Organisms. A wide variety of pathogenic and nonpathogenic organisms can be cultured from a burn surface. The most important pathogens encountered are the beta-hemolytic streptococci, the hemolytic *Staphylococcus aureus A, Pseudomonas aeruginosa (Bacillus pyocyaneus), Proteus vulgaris,* and a variety of diphtheroids and even clostridia. Tetanus spores have been found and have developed, with consequent clinical appearance of the disease. In burns near body orifices, particularly on the thighs or buttocks, intestinal bacteria, such as members of the coliform group, enterococci and *Aerobacter aerogenes,* have been found. The mere presence of a particular organism does not mean that it is invading or acting as a pathogen. Studies of Langohr and Cope have demonstrated that the presence of slough and eschar on a burn wound ensures the viability of bacteria since the defensive fluids and cells of the body cannot get at them. Accordingly, it can be assumed that every burn on which slough is still present contains bacteria. Whether they are acting as invasive pathogens is a matter of clinical evaluation. In a patient who is doing well, holding his own, with virtually no alteration of temperature or pulse, the presence of most organisms can virtually be disregarded. On the other hand, with high fever, rapid pulse and mounting toxicity, not only should the presence of a pathogen on the burn wound be suspected, but frequent blood cultures should be taken to establish the diagnosis of blood-stream invasion.

Because of destructive action on skin grafts, the finding of either hemolytic streptococci or staphylococci on the burn surface is real reason for concern. Proper *in vitro* sensitivity tests should be performed so that the appropriate antibiotic may be administered. In general, hemolytic streptococci are rarely seen since this is a fragile organism which has not become resistant to the antibiotics in common use in our hospitals. The staphylococcus, however, presents a serious problem. It has become progressively resistant to most of the common antibiotics. Occasionally the physician will be hard pressed to find a preparation to which this tough and wily organism is sensitive. *P. aeruginosa* may or may not be a pathogen. When it is, it can be very vicious and is probably responsible for many deaths in the early stages of slough separation. When it is not invasive, it can almost be disregarded and, oddly enough, skin grafts will often take well in its presence. The matter of whether or not an organism is acting as a pathogen is a combined bacteriologic and clinical decision.

Treatment of Infection. This is one of the few areas in which the aid of the laboratory is a necessity. Careful bacteriologic study of the local wound, carefully conducted sensitivity tests and blood cultures when indicated, form the basis for treatment. When invasive infection occurs it is reasonable to change empirically the antibiotic which is being currently administered since it is obvious that it is of no value. Occasionally, dramatic relief of symptoms, such as fever, will occur when this is done. It must again be pointed out that it is always hard to control infection during the phase in which there is still dead tissue on the burn surface since even the parenterally administered antibiotics cannot reach the organisms. Occasionally, the systemically introduced antibiotics can be supplemented by local applications. This is particularly pertinent where the offending organism is known and its sensitivities have been determined.

Soluble antibiotics, such as Chloromycetin, can be dissolved using 1.0 Gm of drug to 1,000 ml of saline. The solution is applied locally as a wet dressing. The nitrofurans are highly effective against many organisms, especially the members of the staphylococcus group. The proprietary ointment Furacin Soluble Dressing is applied liberally to fine-mesh gauze and placed over the wound. Local applications should be changed at least every 48 hours since they become ineffective after that time. Lastly, in evaluating local infection, the gross appearance of the wound is important. Gross suppuration with production of large amounts of pus between dressing changes obviously denotes uncontrolled infection. Granulations which are edematous, pink, and dirty are usually infected, whereas tight, flat, deep-red granulations with evidence of epithelial ingrowth at the edges usually denote a wound sufficiently free of infection as to be able to accept the grafts readily. The final evaluation of such areas is a matter of clinical judgment, although occasionally the experienced observer can be badly misled.

REPARATIVE PHASE

PREPARATION FOR SKIN GRAFTING

Preparation of the burn wound begins with removal of slough and eschar. Despite claims to the contrary, this continues to be one of the most difficult phases of treatment. The spontaneous separation of the burn eschar is a biologic process dependent on enzymatic action at the interface of burned and viable tissue. In recent years, a host of substances has been tried in an effort to secure more rapid separation of slough and eschar. Among them are such chemicals as pyruvic and phosphoric acids, and such enzymes as streptokinase-streptodornase and trypsin. These have been found to have the disadvantage of requiring elaborate methods of application. They are quite expensive, and do not significantly hasten the process of separation compared with the more humble methods of debridement, application of saline wet dressings, or frequent change of dry dressings. Unless these agents are applied to the interface, they are ineffective. Accordingly, they require introduction beneath the burn eschar or an elaborate cross-hatching procedure which is not particularly advantageous as compared with surgical intervention.

There are three presently accepted methods for removal of slough and eschar. The first is spontaneous separation. This will be found to proceed rather rapidly, in a matter of 7 to 12 days, in areas where the skin is notably thin, such as on certain portions of the face, particularly the eyelids, and on the back of the hand. In areas where the skin is unusually thick and tough, such as the scalp, back, shoulders, and posterior aspects of the thigh, spontaneous separation of eschar and slough will seem almost interminable and may last up to 6 weeks.

Surgical removal and debridement is the second method and in many instances is the method of choice. This may vary from a formal procedure in which, by sharp dissection, the eschar is actually dissected away from what is taken to be the interface, to a mere lifting away of dead tissue. This procedure is not to be confused with actual surgical excision of a burn in which a block dissection of the entire burned area is performed, the plane of cleavage actually being through presumably viable tissue in the same sense as one might cut out a superficial tumor or perform excision and primary closure of a traumatic wound. In the case of debridement at the interface, there are presumed to be tiny tags of dead tissue still remaining which necessitate delay of skin grafting for a few days. The advantage of debridement is that it eliminates the dead tissue almost at once. The disadvantage is that the procedure is often accompanied by brisk bleeding to the point of shock if adequate replacement is not made at the same time. The procedure may also be followed by massive invasive infection due to the large areas opened up to the contamination residual in the slough before a protective barrier of granulation tissue has been formed.

The third method consists of systematic change of dressings. The dressings are usually saturated with physiologic saline which seems to hasten separation strikingly. The effect of this treatment is probably twofold. It aids drainage from the burn area by preventing crust formation, and it softens the stiff, leathery eschar, permitting spontaneous bacterial and enzymatic action to take place. Acetic acid 1 per cent may be substituted with advantage for the saline. It seems to inhibit effectively certain bacteria. In the case of *P. aeruginosa* it decolorizes the greenish discharge, although it does not have too much effect on the growth of the organism. There is no doubt that wounds clear up very rapidly on this regime although the exact mechanism is not clearly known. Blocker uses a combination of acetic acid ¼ per cent in Zephiran chloride 1 to 4,000. In using acetic acid, patients may at times complain of slight burning, in which case the concentration can be cut down from 1 to ½ per cent. The use of a wet-dressing technique does not of course preclude debridement, which is carried out almost painlessly at the time of the dressing by lifting up by means of a forceps all tissue which is distinctly separated and gently cutting it away with scalpel or sharp scissors. The disadvantage of this method lies in the fact that dressings must be changed as often as daily or every other day. Despite all care in removing dressings, there may be pain of varying degrees. It is often not a factor but sometimes may be complained of so severely as to make dressings impossible without anesthesia.

The second objection is the fact that this period may be quite prolonged, during which time the patient may lose ground due to the combination of protein loss, anemia, and infection. During this phase, replacement therapy and supportive therapy must be meticulous. Repeated blood transfusion is necessary to maintain hemoglobin at normal levels. A high-protein diet is essential. At least double to triple the normal requirement of 1 Gm of protein per kilogram of body weight daily must be administered.

SELECTION OF METHOD OF SLOUGH REMOVAL

There are several considerations which can be used as guides in selecting the appropriate method of slough removal. True excision should be limited to small, deep, circumscribed burns which do not affect the general condition of the patient and which are situated in certain strategic areas in which rapidity of return of function is important. A prime example would be the dorsum of the hand or of the foot. This procedure is rarely indicated and the opportunities to employ it are few. Ordinary surgical debridement should be restricted to those areas in which there is no question of the full-thickness nature of the injury. It is contraindicated in very extensive burns (over 15 to 20 per cent) since in these instances the general condition of the patient is somewhat precarious (note the mortality rates in the elderly), and since it is deemed necessary to avoid damaging any area in which spontaneous healing from second-degree burns may take place. This is especially true in deep burns of the thick skin of the back where a deep partial-thickness burn may simulate full-thickness loss. In these cases, spontaneous epithelization has been noted beneath the separating eschar as late as 4 to 5 weeks after injury. It is sometimes possible to combine methods, for example, burns of face, neck, and arms may be treated by early debridement and skin grafting, while areas on the trunk may be permitted to separate spontaneously. It is important to fit the method to the particular needs of the patient rather than to subject him to a course of action based on slavish devotion to a particular routine.

Planning the Reconstruction

Long before the patient is brought to the operating room for definitive skin grafting, careful thought must be given to the plan of action. Many questions must be asked. How extensive is the burn? What is the extent of the donor sites? Can enough skin be removed from the latter to resurface the former? Must thin grafts be taken to permit regeneration of skin for a so-called "second crop" of donor skin to develop? Should the skin be applied as full sheets of skin or divided into grafts of postage-stamp size, leaving areas between for spontaneous epithelization? Are the available donor sites so situated, for example, on the back, that plans must be made to take the skin with the patient in the prone position and to turn him on his back for application of the grafts? It is apparent that in the elderly, often in poor condition, in whom surgery must be as expeditious as possible, these details must be worked out in advance. It is possible to estimate easily the extent of surface to be covered, in square inches or square centimeters, and similarly to estimate the available donor skin. A sterile ruler should be available at every dressing change and the burned area and donor sites can then be measured to avoid such common errors as using much or all of the available donor skin to cover a small portion of the burn, only to find large areas for which little or no donor skin is available.

It must be remembered that not only are donor sites limited because of technical considerations, but that it is extremely difficult to cut second crops from senile skin. In cases where a shift in position during surgery will be necessary because of the location of donor sites in relation to burns, the question of anesthesia should be considered in advance. Removal of skin grafts from the back under general anesthesia usually necessitates endotracheal intubation since the patient must be turned. Such considerations as the most efficient method of draping and redraping involved in such a maneuver, to say nothing of the position and security of the intravenous portal used during the procedure, must be worked out in advance.

The Skin Grafting of Burns

Skin grafting is begun at such time as it is felt that the open granulating areas are sufficiently free of slough, eschar, and infection to accept transfer of donor skin. The patient must be in at least good enough condition to withstand a brief general anesthesia and the trauma of skin removal. If even these minimal requirements cannot be satisfied, the patient is in a sorry state indeed, and homografting, using live donor skin or cadaver homografts, must be considered. Discussion of the types and uses of instruments designed to remove donor skin, ranging from the freehand knife to the more elaborate electric dermatomes, is out of place in this chapter. Excellent discussions of the use of these instruments can be obtained from the standard textbooks on plastic surgery, from the two excellent monographs of Brown and McDowell on skin grafting, and from Artz's monograph on burns. The choice of method to remove the donor skin will rest on the skill and experience of the operator and occasionally on the particular instrument available to him. It must always be remembered that the value of a skin graft knife or dermatome depends upon the sharpness of its blade.

The ideal material for resurfacing is the large sheet of skin cut as thick as is compatible with the uncomplicated healing of the donor site. Depending on the area used (the skin of the back is much thicker than the skin of the anterior thighs, for example), this thickness will be found to range between 0.012 and 0.018 inch. The grafts are cut and immediately placed in laparotomy pads which are wet with cool physiologic saline. The grafts are carefully placed in a suitable container in the center of the nurse's back table so that there is no possibility of accidentally upsetting them. Grafts wrapped in sponges and placed on the Mayo table can easily be thrown into the nearest waste receptacle. Grafts should not be placed into a bowl of saline since the various thromboplastic substances contained in the interstices of the collagen network are easily leached out into the fluid medium. It must be remembered that if at any time the operation must be interrupted, grafts can be wrapped in saline sponges, placed in a sterile jar, and stored at blood bank temperature for as long as two weeks. Extra skin, available after covering the recipient sites, can be banked in a similar manner.

The sheets of skin can be applied with or without suturing. In certain areas, notably the extremities, it is entirely possible to spread the skin over the granulating area and to secure it with a circular dressing. Petroleum jelly–impregnated gauze bandage rolls are useful for this purpose. In other locations, such as the trunk, it is much more difficult to obtain adequate fixation of grafts in this manner and it may be necessary to secure them with sutures around the periphery. So-called "basting sutures" as used by Brown are extremely useful in certain locations where displacement is likely to occur, as on the neck. Drainage holes or "pie-crusting" of grafts is rarely necessary and has not been used by the author for many years.

In those instances where donor sites are insufficient and where the granulating area is extensive, another method must be used to effect coverage. By dividing the available donor skin into patches or postage stamps, ranging in size from ½ to 1 inch, and by placing them on the recipient site ¼ to ½ inch apart, it is possible to cover quite large areas with relatively small amounts of skin. The intervening granulating area is shortly covered by the outgrowth of epithelium from the edges of the adjacent patches, leaving a checkerboard effect but effectively closing the open wound. Other variations involve the use of the donor skin in long strips. This, however, is a minor variation. It must always be remembered that the smaller the patch graft, the larger the available edge of skin from which epithelium can sprout. For example, a 1-inch square of skin measures 4 inches around its periphery. If one divides this 1-inch square of skin into sixteen ¼-inch squares, it will be found that there are now 16 inches of skin edge available for epithelization. It is not practical, however, to use squares much smaller than ½ inch along each edge because of the technical difficulties involved in handling them.

Technique of Patch or Postage-stamp Grafting

Since this is one of the most important methods of skin grafting employed in the elderly, it will be described in some detail. Many burns in old people will be found to be minor in extent and yet require grafting. The patch or stamp graft is extremely simple, requiring no elaborate instrumentarium, and can often be performed under local anesthesia. It has supplanted the old pinch-graft technique which, although technically easy, has no real advantage over the patch graft. It has several disadvantages, however, the most important being deep and bizarre scarring of the donor area. The technique of patch grafting begins with the removal of an amount of skin adequate for the purpose at hand. The instrument used to take the skin can be varied according to the operator's preference. In general, and especially when the resurfacing of small areas is involved, a freehand knife or disposable straight-razor blade, such as the Weck, is preferable since long thin strips can easily be cut with a small amount of practice. A rather light general anesthesia is sufficient. In areas measuring not much more than 4 by 6 inches, local field block may be easily accomplished using solutions of procaine—as dilute as ¼ per cent—large amounts of which can be administered without fear of intoxication. A very small amount of epinephrine, 1 to 250,-000, can be used to potentiate the local anesthetic effect unless marked hypertension or cardiac failure is present. A series of wheals is made around the area to be blocked and they are connected by subcutaneous infiltration of local anesthetic solution.

The area is now covered by "crossfire injections" from the various wheals on either side. A delay of about 5 to 8 minutes is essential if grafts are to be cut from the area without causing pain. The grafts obtained are placed in a cool saline sponge until ready for use. They are then laid out onto sheets of Xeroform ointment or petroleum jelly gauze, with their external surfaces downwards. By gently teasing them out with a plain thumb forceps, the grafts are stretched out smoothly to approximate normal skin tension. They are then cut into strips ½ to 1 inch in width, using a sharp, straight scissors, after which each strip is cross cut into squares of the proper size. The patches are placed on a folded towel which is used to carry them from the work table to the patient, where another member of the surgical team applies them to the granulating area. Whether they are placed close together or as much as 1 cm apart depends on the size of the area to be covered and the amount of skin available. If possible, the grafts are placed almost edge to edge so that the area which must necessarily heal by scar epithelium is reduced to the minimum. In skin grafting contaminated areas it is sometimes advantageous to moisten the grafts in a dilute solution of penicillin in saline or to dust them lightly with one of the soluble sulfonamides, such as sodium sulfadiazine. One must also be careful to alternate the position of the various rows of patches much as a mason alternates the position of bricks in the various courses of masonry. This prevents straight-line contractures of the intervening scars. Any patches which are left over can be banked in a fashion similar to that described above for skin grafts.

The Care of Donor Sites. The care of the donor site is just as important as the care of the burn since it actually represents a partial-thickness skin loss. Oddly enough, the patients often complain much more bitterly of pain and difficulty with donor sites than they do of the original burn area. The same principles hold for the physiology of donor sites as hold for burns. They may be treated by exposure or occlusive dressings. They may become infected and be transformed from partial-thickness areas to areas of full-thickness loss, and in rare instances may even require resurfacing. The problem is compounded in the case of the elderly because of the extreme thinness of the senile skin which makes it very easy to produce full-thickness loss by careless use of a dermatome or the skin grafting knife.

After experimenting with a wide variety of methods of handling donor sites, the author and his associates have found that a modified form of exposure gives far and away the best results. As soon as the skin graft is cut, the donor area is covered with a thin layer of fine-mesh gauze, usually taken from a roll of sterile bandage of relatively high mesh count. The blood oozing from the donor site saturates the layer of gauze which is not covered further during the course of the operation. At the termination of the procedure, the blood will be found to have clotted but the surface of the bandage will still be moist. In cases where the donor site is on the anterior aspect of the body, particularly of the thighs, no further dressing is employed. A cradle is placed over the patient to keep the bedclothes from touching the as yet moist donor area, and it will be found that it becomes quite dry and relatively comfortable in about 48 hours. The patient may at that time even be allowed to be up and about with a thin nightgown or pair of pajamas over the freshly dried gauze. The gauze is never removed except under the most unusual circumstances. Any attempt to pull it loose will result in pain, bleeding, and the tearing away of young, sprouting epithelium. It is allowed to separate spontaneously, which it does in from 10 to 20 days, depending on the thickness of the skin graft taken from the area. As the gauze separates from the wound, it is trimmed until total healing has taken place.

Occasionally, despite all efforts, donor sites become infected and are then treated in a variety of ways. Saline or acetic acid wet dressings can be employed or solutions containing an appropriate antibiotic. Furacin Soluble Dressing is very useful against most organisms. Its only disadvantage is the appearance of skin sensitivity which may be very severe. It is wise not to use Furacin longer than two weeks. Scarlet Red 5 per cent Ointment, a very old treatment for donor sites, is still extremely useful. It was once thought that the dye promoted epithelization; it is more likely that it acts as an antimicrobial agent. Recently, in the case of a depleted elderly patient with neglected burns whose donor sites failed to heal despite all treatment applied, the use of Scarlet Red Ointment turned the tide quite dramatically. One must not hesitate to change treatment, however, if any particular agent applied does not show results within only a few days.

BIBLIOGRAPHY

Aldrich, R. H.: The role of infection in burns: the theory and management with special reference to gentian violet. *New Eng. Jour. Med.* **208**:299, 1933.

Allen, H. S., and S. L. Koch: The treatment of patients with severe burns. *Surg. Gynec. & Obst.* **74**:914, 1942.

Artz, C. P., and E. Reiss: "The Treatment of Burns." Philadelphia and London, Saunders, 1957.

Berkow, S. G.: A method for estimating the extensiveness of lesions (burns and scalds) based on surface area proportions. *Arch. Surg.* **8**:138, 1924.

Blocket, T. G., Jr.: Newer concepts in the treatment of severe extensive burns. *Surgery.* **29**:154, 1951.

Braithwaite, F.: Plasma and blood transfusion in the treatment of burned patients. *Brit. Jour. Plastic Surg.* **2**:95, 1949.

Brooks, F., L. R. Dragstedt, L. Warner, and M. H. Knisley: Sludged blood following severe thermal burns. *Arch. Surg.* **61**:387, 1950.

Brown, J. B., and F. McDowell: "Skin Grafting," 3d ed. Philadelphia, Lippincott, 1958.

Bull, J. P., and A. J. Fisher: A study of mortality in a burns victim: a revised estimate. *Ann. Surg.* **139**:269, 1954.

Cope, O.: Fluid and electrolyte requirements in burns: symposium on burns. Washington, D.C., The National Research Council. **47**:33, 1951.

Cope, O., and F. D. Moore: The redistribution of body water and the fluid therapy of the burned patient. *Ann. Surg.* **126**:1010, 1947.

Dallas Ross, W. P.: The treatment of recent burns of the hand. *Brit. Jour. Plastic Surg.* **2**:233, 1950.

Davidson, E. C.: Tannic acid in the treatment of burns. *Surg. Gynec. & Obst.* **41**:202, 1925.

Davidson, E. C.: The prevention of toxemia in burns: treatment by tannic acid solution. *Am. Jour. Surg.* **40**:114, 1926.

Davidson, E. C.: Sodium chloride metabolism in cutaneous burns and its possible significance for a rational therapy. *Arch. Surg.* **13**:262, 1926.

Evans, E. I., and I. A. Bigger: The rationale of whole blood therapy in severe burns: a clinical study. *Ann. Surg.* **122**:693, 1945.

Evans, E. I., and W. J. H. Butterfield: The stress response in the severely burned. *Ann. Surg.* **134**:588, 1951.

Evans, E. I.: The early treatment of severely burned patients. *Surg. Gynec. & Obst.* **94**:272, 1952.

Evans, E. I., et al.: Fluid and electrolyte requirements in severe burns. *Ann. Surg.* **135**:804, 1952.

Ham, T. H., S. C. Shen, F. M. Fleming, and W. B. Castle: Studies on the destruction of red blood cells. IV thermal injury: action of host in causing increased spheroidicity, osmotic and mechanical fragilities and hemolysis of erythrocytes; observations on the mechanisms and of destruction of such erythrocytes in dogs and in a patient with a fatal thermal burn. *Blood.* **3**:373, 1948.

Harkins, H. N.: "The Treatment of Burns." Springfield, Ill., Charles C Thomas, 1942.

Langohr, J. L., C. R. Owen, and O. Cope: Bacteriologic studies of burn wounds. *Ann. Surg.* **125**:452, 1947.

Lund, C. C., and N. C. Browder: The estimation of areas of burns. *Surg. Gynec. & Obst.* **79**:352, 1944.

Moore, T. D., et al.: The role of exudate loss in the protein and electrolyte imbalance of burn patients. *Ann. Surg.* **132**:1, 1950.

Moyer, C. A.: Recent advances in the chemical supportive therapy of thermal injury. *Texas State Jour. Med.* **45**:635, 1949.

Moyer, C. A.: An assessment of the therapy of burns. *Ann. Surg.* **137**:628, 1953.

Muir, I. F. K.: The treatment of electrical burns. *Brit. Jour. Plastic Surg.* **10**:292, 1958.

Quinby, W. C., Jr., and O. Cope: Blood viscosity and the whole blood therapy of burns. *Surgery.* **32**:316, 1952.

Robertson, D. C.: The management of the burned hand. *Jour. Bone and Joint Surg.* **40A**:625, 1958.

Sneve, H.: The treatment of burns and skin grafting. *Jour. Amer. Med. Ass.* **45**:1, 1905.

Wallace, A. B.: Treatment of burns: a return to basic principles. *Brit. Jour. Plastic Surg.* **1**:232, 1948–49.

Wallace, A. B.: The exposure treatment of burns. *Lancet.* **250**:500, 1951.

Wallace, A. B.: A present (1957) outlook on burns. *Plast. and Reconst. Surg.* **21**:243, 1958.

Wight, A., J. W. Raker, W. R. Merrington, and O. Cope: The ebb and flow of the eosinophiles in the burned patient and their use in the clinical management. *Ann. Surg.* **137**:175, 1953.

Wilkinson, A. W.: The early treatment of burns. *Brit. Jour. Plastic Surg.* **10**:275–291, 1958.

Ziffren, S. E.: Management of the burned patient. *Jour. Amer. Geriatric Soc.* **3**:36, 1955.

Part II

Musculoskeletal Trauma in the Aged

Chapter 6

Fractures of the Extremities

Edgar M. Bick

In a study of 600 cases of fracture in persons over 60 years of age, it was observed that except for three categories their distribution approximated that of any adult listing (Table 6-1). Together, fractures of the hip, the vertebrae, and the shoulder represent about 60 per cent of all fractures occurring in the elderly population. Fractures at the wrist, equally high in any age group, add another 14 per cent. All together, these four—hip, wrist, vertebrae, and shoulder—constitute about 75 per cent of all fractures in the aged. Reference to the Table of Distribution will disclose the relative numerical order of the fractures. Reference to the table will also demonstrate that fractures occur more frequently in elderly females than in males of equivalent ages. Between the ages of 60 and 75, the ratio of fractures in the female to those in the male is about 3:1. In the older group, persons over 75 years of age, the ratio is 11:1. This is far in excess of the ratio of elderly females to males in the general population. In 1956 the aged population of New York City showed an over-all ratio of 1.2 females to 1 male. In New York State the ratio was 1.1:1.

The elderly female therefore appears to be far more susceptible to fracture than is her contemporary male. This may be due to one or more of several factors. The aged female skeleton is said to be relatively more osteoporotic than is that of the aged male. It is difficult to demonstrate this. Osteoporosis does appear earlier in the female and may be more advanced in the lower age span of this group. The spine of the female between 60 and 65 is more apt to show signs of vertebral atrophy or osteoporosis than is that of the male, but as the years go on, the difference becomes very much less perceptible. In the later decades both sexes show more or less the same degree of brittleness. This brittleness in the elderly skeleton cannot be the sole factor in the large difference of frequency of fracture, since at the period of greatest difference of frequency the skeletons most closely resemble each other.

It has been suggested that among the aged the female is apt to be

TABLE 6-1. DISTRIBUTION OF 600 CASES OF FRACTURES AND DISLOCATIONS IN PATIENTS OVER 60 YEARS OF AGE

Tabulated in order of frequency of age and sex (excluding pathologic fractures)

Fracture site	60–64		65–69		70–74		75–79		80–84		85–89		90–94		95–99				Total
	M	F	M	F	M	F	M	F	M	F	M	F	M	F	M	F	M	F	
Hip: intracapsular	2	14	5	12	3	20	1	23	3	22		14		3			14	108	}191
intertrochanteric	2	4	4	2	1	8	1	15	1	14		13		2		2	9	60	
Radius-ulna (wrist)	3	26	8	15	1	9		8	1	11		4					13	73	86
Vertebra	7	18	7	17	3	14	5	7	2	3		1					24	60	84
Humerus (shoulder)	2	9	5	18	4	4	2	9	1	3		3					14	46	60
Foot and toes	6	11	2	9	1	8	1	4		6							10	38	48
Tibia-fibula (ankle)	3	9		5		3		4		1		1			1		4	23	27
Hand and fingers	1	4	1	3	7	1		3		2		1					9	14	23
Femur (shaft and lower end)	1		1	1		2		4		7							2	14	16
Pelvis		4	1		1	3			1	2							3	9	12
Ribs			3	4		2			1	1							4	7	11
Shoulder (dislocation)	1	1	1		1	3		1						2			3	7	10
Clavicle		1		1		3		2			1						1	7	8
Humerus (shaft)	1	3						2		1							1	6	7
Tibia-fibula (shaft)	3	1			1												4	1	5
Patella	1			2		2											1	4	5
Elbow (dislocation)		1	1					1									1	2	3
Radius-ulna (shaft)		1	1			1											1	2	3
Scapula								1										1	1

122

more active than the male; that in lower economic levels especially she is still keeping house, cleaning, cooking, marketing, and "straightening things out," at a period of life when the man is more apt to be relaxing and living quietly on his pension or social security check. Besides these physically and socially demonstrable factors there is a well-established, though intangible, principle, important to the actuaries of casualty companies but difficult to define, that is, the concept of accident-proneness. This is a concept based on factors which are predominantly psychological, but apparently effective statistically. We must content ourselves here with the observation that the elderly female is more accident-prone than is the elderly male. The explanation of this phenomenon must be left for future study.

In the treatment of fractures of the aged there are as yet no special methods or technical procedures beyond those in the accepted armamentarium of fracture therapy. The factors which merit supplementary concern in this group of cases are those conditioned by the limitations inherent in the structure and chemistry of aging tissues. Among these limitations are the reduced strength and decreased tensions of aged bone, the lessened elasticity of aged connective tissue, and the often precarious state of the peripheral vascular network (see Chap. 4). Perhaps most important is the decreased physiological resiliency of the older person from the systemic effects of trauma whether that trauma be accidental or surgical. *The primary trauma, the accident, cannot be controlled by the surgeon; the secondary trauma is controllable, often to a large extent by the choice of method and the gentleness with which it is applied.*

Aging bone will not withstand the internal pressures or tensions of screws, plates, or nails as readily as does younger adult bone. Local erosion may loosen the screws, or cause nails and pins to work their way through the cortex outside the bone whenever subject to angular or direct pressures. Osteoporotic bone does not produce reactive intraosseous trabeculae of the same density as does normal bone and therefore does not develop the same grasp on the inserted metal. This of course varies with the type of fracture, type of device, and the relative strength of the bone involved. Methods of metallic internal fixation are not necessarily contraindicated in the elderly patient, but their usefulness must be gauged with caution and with recognition of the probable softness and lack of potential grasp of aging bone. It must be understood that the effectiveness of metallic devices for internal fixation is less dependable in the aged skeleton than in the younger.

Forceful manipulation of displaced fracture fragments may in many situations destroy fracture surfaces to a degree more deforming in the end result than would have occurred had a less perfectly aligned but adequate position of reduction been accepted. This is particularly true, for instance, in the common fractures of the wrist joint (see below). In the fractured tibia of the elderly patient, as another example, the acceptance of ½ inch of shortening, or not overly conspicuous angulation, may save a more useful leg than repeated manipulation, traction, or surgical intervention in an area conspicuous for its slow healing or high percentage of nonunion.

The vascular network serving the extremities of the aged person is inevitably impaired to a greater or lesser degree by the degenerative factors inherent in the aging processes. This impairment involves all of the tissues of the extremities from skin to bone. Circular traction devices, pressure splints, so-called "three-point pressure plasters" and similar apparatus which may be controllable in younger and more wholesome tissues are often intolerable in the less vascularized and less elastic tissues of the older patient. Gentle manipulation of an oblique fragment lying near a major vessel may safely displace a normally elastic artery, but may far more easily rupture or lacerate the brittle coat of a sclerotic artery.

The effect of a major fracture on the organism may be no greater in an aged individual than in a younger one, but recoil from the shock of trauma is certainly less virile. This response becomes a very important element in the choice of therapy and particularly in the choice of time of its employment. Certain procedures applicable to the reduction of fractures bear in themselves an element of trauma. They may not with impunity be used on any patient not yet out of the state of primary shock. In the aged individual this state may last beyond the period of usefulness of a procedure which under other circumstances would be the method of choice.

In the aged, the chief limitation in restoring function to a part is the relative inelasticity of the periarticular and perimuscular connective tissues. This histologic factor was discussed in an earlier chapter and need only be mentioned here. Because of this factor, postfractural rehabilitation must be often of a quite different order than is possible in the younger adult. At times it may be advisable to temper the urge for early and rapid mobilization. Many of the currently fashionable methods of mobilization serve merely to cause strains and damage to the fibers of ligaments, capsules, and fascial planes of the less resilient tissues. Overly enthusiastic attempts to increase motion by certain prescribed exercises or apparatus are often apt to result, if not in tissue damage, at least in a sequence of pain-muscle spasms which retard recovery.

Above all, and this warning is not at all as obvious in practice as it seems to be in the reading, it must be remembered that most aged patients were the victims of a variety of limitations in locomotion and physical activity before they sustained the presenting fracture. It is seldom indeed that those preexisting limitations can be lessened by any improved management of the recent trauma. *The object of treatment in fractures of the extremities in elderly persons is to attain the quickest possible return to the status of life enjoyed at the time immediately preceding the fracture. The expectancy of some inconspicuous or modest cosmetic defect should not interfere with this objective. This not to condone poor reduction; it is to urge the use of surgical judgment in respect to the elderly person's needs. One can walk well with a small angulation of the tibia, and one can garden very nicely with moderate limitation of wrist motion. The risk of failure or infection always present in the operative care of fractures is even greater in the less resistant, atrophic bone of the aged. The use of such measures must be very carefully weighed against the risk; there is so little time left for a second attempt.*

FRACTURES OF THE UPPER EXTREMITY

CLAVICLE

Incidence. Of 600 fractures in persons over 60 years of age recorded earlier in this chapter, 7, or about 1 per cent, occurred in the clavicle. Of these, 6 occurred in females, and only 1 in a male patient.

Common Sources of Trauma. The most frequent cause of fracture of the clavicle in the elderly is the same as in other age groups, a fall in which the individual lands directly on the outer surface of the shoulder, or on the outstretched arm. A rare cause is a direct blow on the clavicle with a weighted object such as pipe, rod, or baseball bat.

Clinical Diagnosis. A diagnosis of fracture in the clavicle is often missed on clinical examination since pain and disability seem to be directed more to the shoulder than to the collarbone. Only when fracture of the clavicle is kept in mind in the presence of shoulder trauma and the clavicle is deliberately palpated for local tenderness and deformity will all such lesions become clinically apparent. Local tenderness and the presence of a palpable deformity due to either angulation or overriding are the diagnostic marks.

Fractures of the clavicle in the aged are more apt to occur in the outer third than in the mid-shaft as in younger adults. The junction of the shaft and the expanding acromial extremity appear to be particularly susceptible. This is one of the common causes of error in clinical diagnosis since the proximity of this junction to the shoulder rather suggests the far more common fracture of the humeral head. Fractures of the shaft of the clavicle in the elderly are apt to exhibit considerable displacement or overriding since the retaining ligaments are less powerful than in the younger adult. To one unacquainted with the felicitous outcome of most of these shaft fractures the appearance of the x-ray film can be quite frightening. Fracture of the clavicle near the sternoclavicular end is rare in this age group, though such have been noted. The distinctions between the sites of fractures of the clavicle in the elderly are actually of academic interest, since therapy and outcome differ but slightly, if at all.

X-ray. Simple anteroposterior views are ordinarily sufficient to disclose the fracture when it is suspected. Occasionally, in a case clinically suspect where a single view fails to reveal a break in the cortical line, oblique views from a cephalic or caudal angle may disclose an oblique undisplaced example of such a break. At a later stage the primary callus is clear enough on the anteroposterior film. Fractures of the clavicle are among those often misinterpreted in their healing stage. They are not weight-bearing bones and, in the elderly at least, they are not subject to great muscle tensions. They may be clinically healed, in the sense discussed in Chap. 4, long before roentgenologic evidence of obliteration of the fracture line is apparent. In these fractures, auscultatory percussion is often a more accurate gauge of the progress of union than is the x-ray film.

FIG. 6-1. "Swathe and sling."

Treatment. In the treatment of fractures of the clavicle in the aged, at whatever sector of the bone the fracture may be, the commanding principle is to use no more restraint than is necessary for the relief of pain. Except for the most unusual circumstances, fractures of the clavicle will unite and heal with sufficient strength to withstand the ordinary demands of the elderly patient in about five weeks. A simple swathe applied comfortably but not tightly about the upper arm and chest, with the forearm resting freely in a loose sling, offers adequate mobilization (Fig. 6-1). A soft cotton pad placed in the axilla will add to the patient's comfort and prevent irritation of the skin. A few days of rest with proper analgesic medication is usually enough to carry the patient over the stage of severe pain. By the end of the first week, discomfort is not ordinarily unbearable though it may still cause some disturbance.

The patient is encouraged from the beginning to move the hand and fingers, and, as far as tolerable, to move the forearm within the range permitted by the sling. This is a particularly important aspect of management. Watson-Jones has correctly pointed out that an upper extremity may suffer a severe, permanent disability from a fractured clavicle although the fracture itself may be one of the simplest to treat. The disability arises from tight restraints applied too long to the arm, hand, and fingers. A frozen shoulder or a restriction of finger function is not an infrequent sequel to this fracture in the aged. Certainly at the elbow, wrist, and phalangeal joints there should be no excuse for such restriction of function because these joints can be exercised with comfort a few days after trauma.

The swathe may be removed between the fourth and fifth week. The swathe may often be removed even earlier by surgeons experienced in the auscultation of bone. The sling is best worn alone to the sixth week to protect the shoulder girdle from excessive strain or casual outside pressures. Evidence of final union is best demonstrated by the equality of transmission of percussion sounds between the sternum and the acromion processes of both clavicles. When these are equal, all restraint may be lifted from the shoulder girdle even though x-ray films still show apparent fracture-line translucencies.

In the aged, so-called "figure of eight bandages" or clavicular splints are uncomfortable and present the risk of interference with the vessels and nerves passing through the axilla. Furthermore, they seldom are tolerable when applied with effective firmness, and when they are used require almost constant adjustment.

Surgical intervention to secure more cosmetic reduction is inexcusable in fractures of the clavicle in the aged. It is even inexcusable as an attempt to assure union before true nonunion is established, since such an event occurs so infrequently. When and if true nonunion is discovered, and such cases have not been reported in the aged often enough to establish any standard of treatment, it is a valid suggestion that a partial resection would be preferable to any internal fixation. Resection would certainly allow much earlier mobilization of the extremity than would any method of osteosynthesis in so thin and delicate a structure.

Common Complications. The most common complication of fracture of the clavicle in the aged patient is a disabling and painful limitation of motion at the adjacent shoulder joint. With occasional exceptions due to unrelated factors such as general weakness, mental deterioration, or other marks of advanced senility, this complication should not occur. A second frequent disability is that of limitation of motion of the fingers. This complication will inevitably occur if attention is not constantly directed to the necessity of exercising them through a complete range of motion. The patient should be instructed to carry an ordinary hand sponge to be constantly squeezed within the palm of the hand. This will ensure proper use of the metacarpophalangeal and interphalangeal joints and avoid the frequent error of simulating movement by fluttering the fingers. Since one can not properly squeeze an object in his hand without extending the wrist, this "game" also ensures wrist motion.

In a broad definition, injury to the brachial plexus or its trunks may be considered a complication of fracture of the clavicle. This however indicates an injury far more extensive than mere fracture. In effect it becomes a primary neurologic lesion from which the fracture recedes as an incident of the greater trauma. A tear of the subclavian artery which runs close to the clavicle is an age-old fear in all considerations of these fractures. One would expect it to occur often; in fact the artery is rarely damaged. The threat is, of course, theoretically greater in the elderly person since a sclerotic vessel is potentially more susceptible to damage. This artery is a large and vital vessel, the damage of which would be a major catastrophe. When rupture of this artery occurs it becomes an emergency of vascular surgery.

Aftercare. By the time the swathe and sling are removed, the extremity from the elbow down should be fairly mobile. Motion at the shoulder joint will ordinarily be restricted to a greater or lesser degree, and it is at this area that rehabilitative measures should be concentrated. Mild circumduction exercises prove useful. "Wall climbing," performed with moderation, is also effective. An invitation to "keep using the arm and reach up for things," i.e., the use of purposeful activity, has often proved the best of aftercare.

Prognosis. The end result of fracture of the clavicle in the aged is likely to be a good one. Because of the structural limitations of the periarticular connective tissues there may remain some measurable degree of limitation of motion at the shoulder, or even a few degrees less than 180° extension at the elbow. Neither of these limitations should be sufficient to interfere with any of the activities normal to the elderly individual. However, more often than not, a residual discomfort remains about the shoulder girdle due to the incidental scars of the periosteal and adjacent peri-articular connective tissues. At times the discomfort may be aggravated by added activities, weather changes, or perhaps a temporary drop in the pain threshold. Such exacerbations may from time to time be relieved by the local application of warmth provided by any available means.

A bony prominence may remain at the site of fracture. Its size will of course be conditioned by the original displacement of the fracture frag-ments. In the elderly this will ordinarily be a minor consideration. To the fastidious "lady of years" such a cosmetic asymmetry may with justi-fication be actively resented. However, its presence is at times unavoidable since measures which might be used to prevent or correct it are inadmissible in the aged.

SCAPULA

Incidence. Isolated fracture of the scapula is uncommon among the aged. Occasionally in severe multiple-injury cases, it appears as an incidental finding among more consequential lesions. Fractures about the neck and acromion are less frequent effects of the forces which ordinarily cause fracture of the upper end of the humerus.

Common Sources of Trauma. Isolated fracture of the body or spine of the scapula is the result of direct trauma to that area. Fracture of the neck and glenoid may be due to the thrust of an outstretched humerus that resisted fracture to itself and transmitted the impact to the glenoid (Fig. 6-2). Fracture of the acromion is due either to a direct blow on top of the shoulder or to shearing stresses transmitted through a resistant humeral head. Fracture of the coracoid may occur as a muscle avulsion due to the pull of the conjoined coracobrachial muscle and short head of the biceps. This would indeed be a rarity in an elderly person.

Clinical Diagnosis. The first impression when examining any person who has suffered a fracture of the scapula is that of a shoulder injury, since the chief pain and disability is referred to that area. Local pain over the shoulder blade, direct tenderness, and the aggravation of such pain with movement of the humeroscapular articulation invite suspicion of fracture. The history of a direct trauma to that area adds to the suspicion. Because of the rather massive muscle attachments about the scapular body, severe displacement of the fragments at any age is unusual. Pain about the shoulder and limitation of its motion invite a roentgenographic distinction between the far more common fracture about the head and neck of the humerus and fracture of the scapular neck or acromion process. Only an x-ray film can truly distinguish them. Sharp pain and local tenderness over the coracoid process following a particularly noted strain on the arm, especially an attempt to lift a weight with the forearm supine, suggest a possible avulsion fracture of its prominences.

Clinically any severe trauma about the shoulder may include injury to the scapular neck and glenoid fossa or to the coracoid and acromion processes. A direct blow on the upper back over the shoulder blade may fracture the scapula, but a blow severe enough to do so in an aged person would be more likely to damage the underlying rib cage and lungs.

X-rays. The same exposure which exhibits the upper end of the humerus should include the scapula, at least on one film. Because of its massive muscle attachments, fractures of the scapula seldom show marked deformity or displacement, except perhaps those of the neck. Fractures of the body of the scapula may not be obvious to a casual examination of the shoulder film and will only be seen when deliberately looked for.

Treatment. In the aged person, fractures of the glenoid and the neck of the scapula are apt to be seriously disabling injuries, not perhaps so much because of the osseous damage as to the inevitable incidental injury

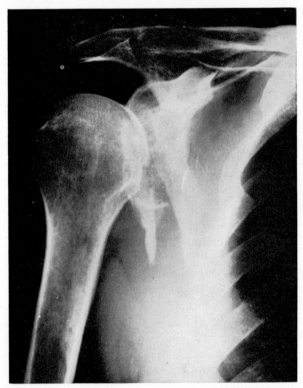

FIG. 6-2. Fracture of scapula. Male, age 69. Uneventful recovery. Three weeks in swathe and sling, followed by graded daily movement.

to the articular and periarticular soft tissues of the shoulder joint. This area is so protected by a complex of capsule, ligaments, tendons, aponeuroses, and fascial tunnels that any serious injury in the aged individual must of necessity produce fibrotic changes and contractions in the aged, inelastic connective tissues. Except in the most unusual and unforeseen circumstances, open reduction of displacement would be most injudicious and probably invite further soft-tissue contractions. Surgical intervention in this area is always a threat to the nearby blood vessels and nerve trunks; in the aged shoulder with its probably sclerotic vessels, the threat is immeasurably greater.

In fractures of the neck and glenoid, surgical intervention is only justified in the aged person when the vascular integrity of the limb is threatened. The incision aims toward the artery first, toward the fracture only when its displacement threatens the blood vessel. The scapulo-humeral joint is of the universal type, and since weight bearing is not one of its normal functions, a fair degree of motion may be recovered in spite of serious displacement. There is perhaps one exception to the plea against surgical intervention. A badly displaced fracture of the outer half or so of the acromion may be easily excised without serious involvement of the joint capsule. Its excision at times permits greater freedom of motion at the scapulohumeral joint.

Treatment of fractures of any part of the scapula in the aged is best conducted with a light and not too firm swathe and sling. This is removed as soon as symptoms permit, usually in 3 to 5 weeks. In the aged, one does not anticipate an early return to full use of the extremity, so that the union of early callus or even fibrous tissue is sufficient to maintain the position of the fragments.

Early, graded, purposeful activity is encouraged, especially actions inviting abduction and elevation of the arm. Circumduction exercises may be used, but with restraint. It should be emphasized to the aged person that some degree of discomfort will persist for many weeks or months. Ordinarily its intensity will lessen as time passes. Local therapy in the form of warm applications, light massage, or analgesic balms is often palliative and should not be withheld from the older patient. Comfort is far more important to the relatively inactive elderly individual than it is to the younger person whose work is more apt to divert his attention from his residual ache.

Complications. Three complications are serious threats in fractures of the scapula. The first is the possibility of damage to the axillary artery or its branches when the glenoid and neck are involved. This threat is particularly important among the aged because of the possible brittleness of the arterial wall. Any valid suspicion of damage demands immediate exploration of the artery. The second threat is that of damage to the major brachial nerves. A third complication to be sought in the presence of fracture of the scapular body is that of serious injury to the posterior thoracic wall and to the underlying pleura or lung. Each of these three may be catastrophic and require the special procedures described elsewhere in this book.

Aftercare. The early and continued encouragement of purposeful activity, carefully guarded against overenthusiastic strain, with the palliative effect of local warmth and analgesic medication constitutes the aftercare of these fractures.

Prognosis. Restoration of normal, painless function in serious fractures of the neck of the scapula and the glenoid fossa is probably not possible in the aged. Some degree of restriction of motion at the shoulder joint is inevitable.

If it is no more than a split or crack, a fracture of the body of the scapula may be forgotten; but the associated injuries to the underlying rib cage and thorax present a matter of prognosis in themselves. A more severe fracture of the scapular body with some displacement may cause permanent discomfort in the function of the shoulder joint. In considering fracture in any part of the scapula, it must be remembered that the bone contributes to all motions and functions of the shoulder girdle, and its integrity is therefore important to upper extremity activity.

HUMERUS

Incidence. Fractures of the humerus are among the most common fractures of the aging skeleton. They represent about 14 per cent of all fractures in this age group and are exceeded in incidence only by those of the hip, wrist, and vertebrae. By far the greater number occur about the head and neck of the humerus. Fractures of the shaft are far less frequent among elderly persons, and at the condyles are quite unusual.

Common Sources of Trauma. Fractures of the shoulder or shaft of the humerus occur most commonly as the result of a fall. The impact may be directly on the side of the shoulder or arm or may be indirect as a result of an attempt to break a fall on the outstretched arm. Occasionally the shaft may be fractured by a direct hit on the upper arm.

Clinical Diagnosis. Fractures of the humerus are usually classified into a number of separate categories, some of which are chiefly of anatomic or instructional interest. For purposes of clinical distinction and therapy in the aged, they are best grouped into a more simple classification.

1. Fractures of the head and neck of the humerus
   a. Fracture of the head and/or neck without dislocation of the shoulder joint
   b. Fracture of the head and/or neck with dislocation
   c. Fracture of the tuberosity
   d. Fracture of the tuberosity with dislocation
2. Fractures of the shaft of the humerus
   a. Transverse
   b. Oblique
3. Fractures of the lower end of the humerus
   a. Supracondylar
   b. Intercondylar

Distinction between fractures of the head and those of the surgical or anatomical neck of the humerus in the aged is of anatomical interest only. Clinically they represent the same therapeutic problem and are diagnosed by the presence of pain, swelling, and disability of the shoulder joint following a sufficient trauma. In less severe injuries its symptoms may be simulated by strain of the periarticular capsule or tears of the tendons of the rotator cuff, principally that of the supraspinatus tendon. Fracture of the outer third of the clavicle or acromion process may also suggest fracture of the humeral head. Fracture of the upper end of the humerus is often part of a fracture dislocation. If the conformation of the shoulder suggests dislocation, x-ray investigation is urgent, since a manual reduction which in an elderly person may be simple during the first few hours posttrauma may be quite difficult or at times impossible 24 hours later.

Fracture at the shaft of the humerus occurs far less frequently than at its upper extremity. Whether it is transverse or oblique will be determined by x-ray. The presence of localized pain and tenderness, disability of the extremity, especially the inability to abduct, and the history of the trauma should simplify diagnosis. Diagnostic auscultatory percussion of the humerus is quite simple between the acromion process and olecranon. The marked variation of its pitch compared with the normal arm is pathognomonic in fracture of the shaft.

Fracture of the lower extremity of the humerus is quite unusual in the aged and is difficult to distinguish from other fractures about the elbow. Such injuries are manifested by pain, swelling, local tenderness, and disability of the elbow joint. They demand x-ray diagnosis at the earliest moment possible since here the time factor may control the prognosis. Early recognition of a condylar or supracondylar fracture may permit a simple manipulative reduction. Conversely, loss of time may provoke an irreversible ischemic paralysis of the forearm and hand.

X-ray. In any x-ray study of fracture of the shoulder joint, it is not sufficient to establish the type of fracture of the upper end of the humerus. The acromion process, coracoid process, glenoid fossa, neck of the scapula, and the outer end of the clavicle must be deliberately studied, on the film, whether the humeral head is fractured or not. In the aged, where osteoporotic and arthrotic changes are common, fracture lines are not always as obvious in these adjacent areas as they might be in the more clearly defined cortices of the younger skeleton.

Oblique fractures of the humeral shaft may require two views. In undisplaced fractures of the oblique type in the osteoporotic, aged humerus, the fine line of a torsion fracture may be missed. In old patients with high thresholds of pain or senile personality changes, such injuries have

been passed off as contusions. Often enough an apparently undisplaced
fracture in an anteroposterior view becomes a dangerously displaced,
sharp fragment in a lateral view.

At the lower end of the humerus, that is, in fractures about the elbow,
the x-ray definition of the type of fracture and degree of displacement
conditions to a large extent the nature of the treatment. In study of the
film, additional fracture lines should be sought in the radial head, and
coronoid and olecranon processes.

The search for additional fracture lines in adjacent structures is of
course demanded in the x-ray films of fractures in all age groups. In the
elderly patient an even more careful scrutiny is necessary since a generalized osteoporosis, always more evident about the joints, or the cystic
degenerations of advanced osteoarthrosis serve to dissemble simple fracture lines and put the observer off guard.

HEAD AND NECK OF THE HUMERUS

Treatment. Uncomplicated fractures of the head and neck of the
humerus in the elderly patient may be treated with a light rein. The
scapulohumeral joint is a universal joint; it does not bear weight and
even in the presence of considerable deformity is capable of a very
satisfactory range of motion. Except for complete displacement, there is
ordinarily no need for any attempt at reduction of these fractures be
they of the head, neck, or tuberosity. A simple swathe holding the upper
arm to the chest with a pad of absorbent material such as gauze, sheet
wadding, or cotton between the arm and chest is sufficient immobilization
to prevent the pain of motion. The forearm rests lightly in a sling. In
10 days or so the swathe may be removed and the sling used alone. During
this period, both may be removed for cleansing purposes and the restrained motion of the shoulder needed for cleansing will do no harm.
After the tenth day when the swathe is removed, whatever motion is
tolerated in the sling is to be encouraged. By the third week, or if pain
is more persistent than ordinarily by the fourth week, the sling is
removed and motion encouraged.

If the lesion is a fracture dislocation of the head, the problem may
be far more complicated. It requires immediate care since the ease with
which the dislocation may be reduced is conditioned to a great extent
by the time that elapses postfracture before it is attempted. An experienced surgeon may sometimes be able to reduce the dislocation of such
lesions manually without significantly disturbing the relationship of the
fracture fragments. This is particularly true if the fracture is an impacted
one. However, if the combined lesion is such that manipulation of the
arm distracts the shaft from the head, immediate arthrotomy must be
performed to reduce the dislocation.

Late-stage open reduction of the shoulder, after the capsule has contracted, is a difficult procedure at any age; in the elderly it is far more so. When open reduction is delayed excising the head of the humerus is less traumatic and less deforming in its final result than an attempt to force it back into place against a tight capsule and contracted periarticular ligaments. It is in such attempts that the friability of the adjacent sclerotic arteries becomes apparent. After complete excision, restoration of function of the shoulder is much more rapid and is more than adequate for the ordinary demands of the elderly person.

In fractures of the tuberosity, often enough the outer fragment is still sufficiently attached to the shaft by periosteum or muscle fascia to maintain its position during the manual reduction of the fracture dislocation. Following a successful, early manipulative reduction, treatment is continued as for closed fractures of the humeral head or neck. The care of the reduced dislocation does not differ from that of the fracture in the aged individual, and the time factor overlaps. A disregard for the finesse of realignment of the fracture fragments is important in treating the elderly patient. The future demands on the shoulder joint will not require the last 20° or 30° of abduction nor the ultimate in normal rotation. On the contrary, attempts at fine replacement of the fracture fragments are an invitation to further trauma to the surrounding soft tissues, and as will be discussed below, the soft-tissue trauma ordinarily presents a far greater hazard to future function than the fracture itself.

Two types of injury to the upper end of the humerus demand the utmost in surgical judgment and experience, and both require immediate decision if the optimum result is to be obtained in the elderly hypoelastic joint. One is the fracture dislocation which is not reducible by closed manipulation either because of the wide detachment of the fragments or because of the loss of time posttrauma has been such as to permit contraction of the muscles or connective tissue. This may be a matter of 24 to 48 hours. The second is the complete displacement of the humeral head which not uncommonly rests alongside the lateral or medial shaft.

In both these lesions the threat of a disabling stiff shoulder is even more serious in the elderly patient than in the younger adult since contraction of the soft tissues is far more difficult to overcome. Both require early surgical intervention and the earlier the better. The fresh dislocation is approachable through the usual deltopectoral incision or through the anterior half of the saber incision. The operation should be performed quickly with a minimum of exposure and a minimum of dissection. Only major tendons or tissues need be repaired after reduction is accomplished since in the elderly patient recurrent dislocation is far less probable than in the younger adult. This is true because of two factors: first, the decreased functional demand on its supportive structures, and second, the greater degree of postoperative fibrosis and the normal relative inelasticity of its capsules and associated ligaments.

If the fracture line of a fracture dislocation is visible through the operative field the existent displacements may of course be corrected. Unless they are quite extreme, however, correction is not worth any extension of the exposure or further dissection of the soft tissues. It must always be emphasized with regard to fractures about the shoulder in the elderly, that avoiding additional soft-tissue trauma is the principal guide to therapy. Following open reduction, treatment remains the same as for any such fracture dislocation. (Note: This applies to early open reduction. As stated previously a late-stage open reduction is best carried out by excision of the head rather than an attempt at replacement.)

The second situation requiring surgical intervention is that of complete displacement of the humeral head. Here too decision must be immediate and action follow at the earliest feasible instant. Regardless of the controversial views which apply to reduction of these heads in younger adult groups, in the elderly their removal through a minimal exposure does not allow argument. The threat of avascular necrosis and/or secondary arthrotic degenerations is inexorable in the aged shoulder joint. The only factor which mitigates against the removal of the completely displaced humeral head in the younger adult group is the consequent relative weakness of the shoulder mechanism. Even in the younger group, however, residual function following excision is excellent provided the patient is not required to exert maximum stress or strain on the extremity. In the elderly patient no such excessive strain is demanded. He will not have to push heavy furniture or use heavy picks, axes, or shovels. The elderly lady will probably not be required to carry heavy trays or lift heavy packages.

The anterior deltopectoral incision easily approaches the displaced head resting along the medial or anterior surface of the shaft. A simple incision longitudinally through the deltoid fibers reaching no more than an inch and a half below the acromion process often will allow removal of the head resting on the lateral surface. The incision must not be carried more distally or the circumferential axial nerve may be compromised. Rarely is the head lower than this, and when it is, it is usually possible to reach it under the deltoid, or to "milk it" up to the exposure. If this is not possible, or if, as on occasion occurs, the head has been forced into a lower position, the incision can be made through the more distal fibers of the deltoid. Sufficient postoperative comfort is provided by a simple sling which may be removed in 10 days to 2 weeks. Motion of the shoulder joint is encouraged.

Only under the most extraordinary circumstances, if indeed ever, is surgical intervention required for fractures of the humeral tuberosity.

Regardless of the size of the fragment or its degree of displacement, the periosseous soft tissues will prevent the fragment from becoming distracted to a degree that might significantly interfere with the function demanded of the aged shoulder. Fibrous union, if it occurs, will serve such shoulders well enough, and allow sufficient mobility.

Complications. There are two serious complications of fracture or fracture dislocation of the upper end of the humerus which must be anticipated in the examination and management of every such case. They appear to occur more frequently in the aged than in younger adults although no statistical study has as yet appeared to confirm this. The first is injury to one or more of the nerves passing into the arm through the neurovascular bundle along the medial side of the upper end of the humerus; the second is injury to the brachial artery at this level. Both portend permanent loss of function of the extremity; the latter may even threaten loss of the extremity. Damage to the nerves is more frequent, damage to the artery is more dangerous.

The mechanism of both of these lesions is similar, that is, the thrust of the upper end of the humeral shaft or thrust of the displaced head medialward against the neurovascular bundle or its vicinity. This is a particularly dangerous event if the fracture of the neck produces a sharp angle of bone at the medial or anteromedial end of the fracture line. In such instances, not only must the neurovascular structures resist the pressure of the displaced bone, but they are exposed to the thrust of a sharp edge or a point sharp enough to cut the finger of the surgeon. In one such case the sharp protruding point of bone had fortunately not penetrated the artery but slipped over its anterior surface and settled into its displaced position with the point sharply kinking the artery posteriorly (Fig. 6-3). This position effectively stopped the blood flow and required surgical intervention to release the vessel.

Both of these complications require early surgical intervention. Both may be exposed through all or part of an incision extending from the anterior axillary border distally along the medial surface of the abducted arm. In cases of suspected injury of the axillary artery the incision may be curved upward and medially along the outer third of the clavicle. In the aged person this exposure must be employed with consummate caution, as in all vascular surgery in the aged (see Chap. 18), because of the friability of the vessels. While investigating the brachial and axillary arteries in the aged person one must accept the added trauma of extensive exploration unless a fortuitous incision brings one to the lesion directly.

Damage to the nerves about the shoulder is a complication of serious importance but of a different order of urgency than that of injury to a major vessel. The aged individual can live, and under certain circumstances can live with not much less enjoyment, even with partial paresis of an upper extremity. Nerve damage may involve any one or all of the major nerves, radial, ulnar, or median, partially or completely. Therefore dysfunction may be highly variable.

Nerve involvement in fractures or fracture dislocations about the shoulder is not in itself an invitation to surgery. In most cases the nerves have been temporarily compressed and freed by the recoil of the bone

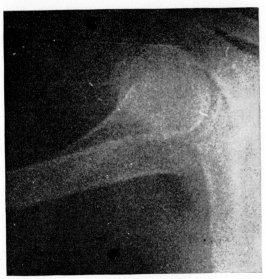

FIG. 6-3. Fracture—upper end of humerus—requiring open exploration of brachial artery. Male, age 81.

fragments. In these cases much if not all of the paresis will disappear with time. In the aged, refined neurological testing of the sensorium to determine the extent or intensity of the lesion is unfortunately not as facile as in younger, more sensitive patients. A careful balance between the estimated residual function of the extremity and the anticipated functional demand of the patient by circumstance and environment should determine the decision for or against surgical intervention. In this decision the neurosurgeon, if available, should take some responsibility. However, the results of resuture of a completely separated nerve at this level have not heretofore been satisfactory even in younger adults. The more consequential accomplishments in exploring the area have occurred in those cases in which the nerves have been found intact, but a pressing bone fragment has been released. The techniques of surgical procedures on the nerves, as well as those for the artery, will be discussed in their respective chapters.

A third complication seen in the aged individual occurs in cases of unreduced fracture dislocation, where the fracture itself is apt to heal even in the luxated position. The problem then becomes one of un-reduced dislocation of the shoulder. This is a difficult surgical matter even in younger adults. In the aged it is even more so. Its treatment is properly the concern of Garcia in Chap. 11. However, it may be stated here as a matter of experience that several such unreduced dislocations seen in quite elderly people have not greatly interfered with their pre-traumatic way of life. Unlike unreduced fracture dislocations of weight-bearing joints, those at the shoulder may be borne with little discomfort by the aged individual, and although restriction of motion is obvious to the examiner, to the victim the disability may not seem great if the physical demands are not exceptional. When disability is quite real, the present writer prefers a simple excision of the head to the large exposure required for open reduction.

Aftercare. The aftercare of the uncomplicated fracture or fracture dis-location of the head and neck of the humerus requires modification when adapted to the elderly patient. It is here particularly that enthusiastic encouragement of wall climbing, active circumduction exercises, and the other rehabilitative measures which are so effective in the younger adult group will more often than not retard progress and create prolonged and unnecessary pain. The periarticular tissues of the shoulder joint freeze quickly, the soft-tissue scarification about the fracture is a major concomi-tant of the trauma and strenuous exercise is more apt to cause strain of the relatively inelastic soft-tissue structures than it is to stretch them.

In the elderly patient it is better to encourage daily purposeful activity. The patient will be more responsive, and although daily progress may seem slower, optimum motion will appear at its proper time with far less pain to the patient. The time required for the attainment of opti-mum functional return cannot be estimated at the onset of aftercare since the extent of articular and periarticular damage varies greatly from case to case. In some instances the optimum is reached in 3 to 6 weeks, in others months pass before it is attained. Patient encouragement and restraint from overexertion are the most effective rehabilitation technique in these cases. If it takes somewhat longer than average, let it. The elderly patient will mind this less than the pain associated with the daily strenuous exercise.

Prognosis. Fracture and fracture dislocation of the head or neck of the humerus in the aged must be expected to leave some degree of permanent restriction of motion. In a successful or better to say fortuitous case, the limitation of motion may be about 10° to 15° from the full range of abduction and rotation. In most cases the limitation is somewhat greater. Occasionally in the simpler fractures in physiologically under-average aging, the end result may approach normalcy. This however is not to be anticipated in most instances. Nevertheless, in consideration of the demands placed upon the shoulder joint or upper extremities, such fractures in the elderly, when properly treated, will heal to a functionally satisfactory degree.

SHAFT OF THE HUMERUS

Incidence. Fractures of the shaft of the humerus occurred in only 1.2 per cent of 600 cases of fractures in the aged. In a younger adult group, the ratio of shaft to head and neck fractures is considerably higher.

Common Sources of Trauma. The most common injury causing fracture of the shaft of the humerus is a fall in which an attempt has been made to break the impact by a partially outstretched arm. The weight of the body falling at a particular angle will snap the shaft either transversely or with a twisting motion causing an oblique torsion fracture. Describing the particular mechanics whereby different types of fractures were caused was a favorite diagnostic study in an older generation, but it would seem to be a futile occupation in an era of easily available x-ray. A second common cause of fracture is of course direct impact to the arm, such as from a club or a rail struck in falling.

Clinical Diagnosis. The clinical diagnosis of fracture of the shaft of the humerus is ordinarily not difficult. Local pain, pseudoparalysis of the extremity, and deformity are usually present and obvious. If there is doubt, auscultatory percussion from the acromion to the olecranon process will easily confirm the presence of fracture.

X-ray. X-ray evidence of fracture of the shaft presents no problem. Even in the presence of generalized osteoporosis breaks in the cortex are self-evident. In healing, the auscultatory method of testing union is more reliable than x-ray since here particularly the fracture line appears visible for some time after the healing point has been passed (see Chap. 4).

Treatment. In the uncomminuted fracture of the shaft of the humerus in the elderly, closed reduction means simply alignment of the long axis of the bone. In oblique fractures a small amount of overriding is inconsequential, and more than this is seldom found. A splint held to the lateral surface of the arm, not tightly, and the arm and splint held to the chest by a swathe, the whole resting in a sling, is usually adequate treatment after reduction. A plaster splint may be more comfortable if it is extended at a right angle along the forearm. This restraint is required from 6 to 8 weeks, rarely more. The apparatus may be removed at intervals for skin cleansing.

Open reduction and internal fixation is rarely necessary in the elderly patient. The usually atrophic humerus is relatively soft and will not retain screws as well as younger bone. Intramedullary nailing of the humerus in the aged individual is a certain invitation to compromised shoulder function and if it does not actually retard union it will at least not hasten it. If in an exceptional case open reduction and fixation are necessary, a well-placed plate with screws passing through both cortices is still probably a more dependable procedure.

Possibly because of lessened activity or lessened muscle tensions, or perhaps lack of a gravity pull on the lighter extremity, nonunion of the shaft of the humerus in the aged is an uncommon event. If it does occur, the usual bone-grafting procedures are indicated. However, a quite elderly individual who has no significant physical demands made upon him can live quite painlessly with nonunion of the humeral shaft, and it may be amazing to see the extent of function still possible in its presence. Cases have been observed in which octogenarians were quite unaware of an existing nonunion of the humeral shaft.

Common Complications. The most frequent complication of fracture of the shaft of the humerus in the aged, as in younger groups, is injury to the radial nerve as it passes behind the midshaft. If the injury is partial, a fair amount of recovery will occur spontaneously. Aside from a hand and finger splint to prevent contraction due to the uninhibited flexor activity, and daily movements with the hand splint removed to prevent stiffness of the fingers, little else in the way of therapy is necessary. If it can be conveniently arranged, simple massage of the forearm and hand will preserve muscular and vascular tone in the elderly limb, but active and passive motion of the parts will be better.

The less frequent but more dangerous complication is laceration of the brachial artery by the movement of the sharp point of an oblique fragment at the time of fracture. This will be recognized by the usual signs of interruption of a major vessel and of course demands immediate surgical intervention. Suture of a laceration or the use of an arterial graft is determined by the lesion presented by the exposed vessel.

Aftercare. The aftercare of a united fracture of the shaft of the humerus in the elderly patient follows the pattern set for that of fractures of the head and neck. In shaft fractures limitations of motion affect both the shoulder and elbow joints but perhaps not to the same extent as fractures involving the joint structures. Limitation of joint function is due to the unavoidable period of immobilization rather than to periarticular tissue damage and is sooner overcome.

Prognosis. Fractures of the shaft of the humerus in the aged heal as quickly as do those of a younger adult group (see Fig. 4-4). Actually, owing to the lesser demand and lesser muscle pull, these fractures may be released from restraint at a somewhat earlier date. Nonunion is quite infrequent. In uncomplicated cases a satisfactory return of function may usually be anticipated.

LOWER END OF THE HUMERUS

Treatment. Fractures of the lower end of the humerus in the aged present a greater challenge to the surgeon's judgment than do fractures of head, neck, or shaft. The disability of a stiff elbow is a greater detriment to self-care in the elderly person than either a stiff shoulder or pseudoarthrosis of the shaft. It interferes with eating, ablutions about the face, and the other necessary upper-extremity motions of daily life. Fortunately such fractures are not as common among the aged as in younger adults, but when they occur treatment must be meticulous. In this lesion there can be little compromise with age as far as reduction is concerned. The challenge in the aged patient is the choice of method.

Closed reduction when feasible is of course attempted. The techniques are those customarily used for similar fractures in the young adult and when successful are apt to leave a satisfactory range of motion. There will perhaps be less range of extension and flexion than one might expect in the younger adult, but in the simpler types of fracture without great displacement, closed reduction is often quite satisfactory. A displaced medial or lateral epicondyle which does not slip into the space of the elbow joint is best left alone in the elderly person. It will not interfere to any significant extent with the anticipated range of motion and the fibrous union or fibrous attachments which eventually develop are sufficient to support the muscle strains necessary to serve the needs of the elderly individual.

Following closed reduction, immobilization should be absolute for about 4 weeks, after which gently active and passive motion is undertaken daily. By the sixth week, union is sufficient to permit the removal of splints and purposeful activity is permitted. The muscle pulls and demands of activity will not ordinarily cause displacement in the aged person.

The severely comminuted fracture, such as the T fracture with marked displacement, is a problem in surgical judgment. Open reduction must not be withheld because of age in an otherwise healthy person. Although the same degree of motion may not be anticipated as in the younger adult following open reduction, the degree of restriction which will occur if the traumatized elbow is not fairly aligned will jeopardize function to an even more unacceptable extent. In open procedures about the aged elbow, minimal exposure and mechanical simplicity must be the controlling surgical principle. Perfection of alignment is less important since the ease with which the elderly person forms tough and relatively inelastic adhesions and the speed with which periarticular structures about this joint contract will mitigate against the otherwise salubrious effect of a perfect reduction gained by greater tissue dissection and numerous metallic implants. Often one or two simple screws will suffice in the elderly patient although such a procedure might prove inadequate against the tonic muscle strains of the more powerful, younger brachial muscles.

In the presence of multiple fragments, the so-called "smashed elbow," the classic procedure of resection of the elbow is by far the procedure of choice. A good thesis might be developed for resection in all severe fractures about the elbow in the aged. In the older nonlaboring arm, agility is infinitely more important than resistance, and resection is apt to ensure the former even though at some expense of the latter. Among the several advantages of this procedure in the elderly is the resultant almost immediate postoperative mobility. Although the relative weakness of the resected elbow as compared to the normal is always conceded, experience with the method during the wars demonstrated the amazing retention of function in the joints except when they were exposed to major efforts. In the elderly patient resection must be performed before the development of periarticular ankylosis or contractions spoil its potential value.

Common Complications. Fractures about the elbow are the classic instigators of Volkmann's paralysis. Bleeding into the tight fascial compartments of the fascial planes about the elbow causes pressures which interrupt the blood flow to all the tissues of the forearm, especially to the muscles and nerves. The pathology and dysfunction of Volkmann's paralysis in the aged are the same as in the younger adult. At this time there is no existent published evidence to indicate that it occurs with any greater or lesser frequency in the aged. The treatment must be immediate and the usual fascial incisions made as are indicated in similar lesions at any age.

A further complication, less serious in terms of survival of the limb or ultimate degree of disability, is injury to the radial, medial, or ulnar nerve by the displaced fracture fragments. Fortunately these are only seldom complete dissolutions of continuity and in most cases a fair degree of recovery of neuromuscular function may be anticipated. The principal object of therapy is to preserve the fingers and wrists from flexion contraction by the use of proper splints. Here too there is no evidence to indicate that the aged are more susceptible than are younger adults.

Aftercare. In fractures about the elbow, even more than in other joint fractures, motion at the earliest possible moment is a matter of urgency as great as the surgical intervention itself. In open reduction this ordinarily is possible during the fourth postoperative week, and free motion may be permitted about the sixth week. In expert hands, and with recognition of the risk of some displacement, controlled motion can be started at an earlier date. Following joint resection, with the arm merely in a sling and no rigid support, motion is encouraged immediately.

Prognosis. Fractures about the lower end of the humerus in the aged inevitably lead to some degree of permanent limitation of motion. Speedy "freezing" of the elbow joint is commonly observed at all ages. In the elderly it is far more difficult to overcome. In severely comminuted cases, a considerable degree of restriction occurs unless the case has been expertly handled.

FOREARM

Incidence. Fractures of the lower ends of the radius and/or ulna are as common in the aged as they are in younger adult groups. They stand second in numerical order among 600 consecutive cases and represent 14 per cent of the total. Fractures of the shafts of these bones are less frequent in the aged (0.5 per cent). Fractures of the radial head are no more frequent in the aged than are those of the shaft. Fracture of the olecranon is somewhat more common than that of the radial head.

Common Sources of Trauma. Falls broken by the outstretched hand of an elderly person either are apt to cause a fracture near the wrist joint or are transmitted through the radius and ulna to the humerus. Fractures of the shafts of the radius or ulna may occasionally be caused by the same type of fall, but may also be the effect of a direct blow on the forearm.

Clinical Diagnosis. Fractures of the radial head are to be suspected in the presence of pain near the elbow, local tenderness at the radial head, and limitation of supination and pronation. Fractures of the shafts are easily recognized when the fracture fragments are displaced or angulated, but must be suspected with local pain and tenderness even in the absence of deformity. So-called "greenstick fractures" are not ordinarily found in the aged.

Fractures of the lower ends of the radius and ulna in the aged are ordinarily easily recognized. Deformity may be due to dorsal or to volar displacement, to angulation of the distal fragment, or to radial or ulnar deviation with or without much displacement. Impaction with compression of the cancellous and osteoporotic distal fragment may prevent marked displacement. With compression of the radial expansion the ulnar styloid becomes quite prominent.

X-ray. In the elderly patient with some degree of osteoporosis, fracture of the radial head without displacement may be difficult to detect in x-rays taken shortly after fracture. The telltale sign may be a minute crack in the cortex of the proximal joint line. As in younger adults this indicates far greater damage to the radiohumeral articular surface than x-ray evidence would suggest. With displacement of the head x-ray inter-pretation is not difficult. Fracture of the olecranon is self-evident since there is always some degree of distraction due to the pull of the triceps muscle. An interesting fracture which fortunately occurs but seldom in the aged is that of the coronoid process of the semilunar notch. In an osteoporotic elbow, or in an aged elbow in which multiple small osteo-phytes emanate from sites of musculotendon insertions, it may be quite difficult to detect a fracture at this area. However, when it is missed and

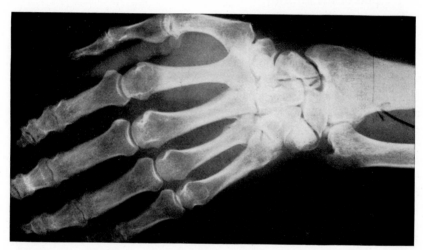

FIG. 6-4. Undisplaced fracture—lower end of radius—involving articular surface. This fracture is easily missed. Prognosis must be guarded in view of probable arthrotic involvement of wrist joint.

a false negative report rendered, a serious prolongation of disability of the elbow and forearm is likely to ensue. Fractures of the shafts do not ordinarily present any x-ray diagnostic problem in the aged person.

Fractures of the lower end of the radius may be obvious when displace-ment or angulation occurs. However, osteoporosis or bone atrophy about the aged wrist joint is a common occurrence and causes considerable roentgenologic irregularity in the broad cancellous carpal bones. Because of this, an undisplaced transverse or longitudinal fracture may easily be missed unless the film is carefully examined. Small longitudinal cracks leading across the radiocarpal joint surface are not uncommon in the atrophic wrists of the elderly and in fact are often enough unrecognized (Fig. 6-4).

An excellent rule to follow in injuries to the wrist in elderly patients when local tenderness persists in spite of an originally negative x-ray film is to retake an x-ray one week after injury. It is not uncommon to find the evidence of fracture at that time. As in the navicular, a lesion which had only been suspected immediately following the trauma may be obvious after a week of traumatic bone cell necrosis. This rule is emphasized in the aged to a greater degree than in the younger adult because it is frequently difficult to distinguish undisplaced fractures in the presence of atrophic or porotic cancellous bone.

Fracture of the ulnar styloid is not uncommon in the aged and is usually apparent on x-ray, since the distal fragment is apt to be distracted by the pull of the ulnacarpal ligaments.

Treatment. Treatment of fracture of the radial head in the aged depends on the degree of damage done to the part. Simple fractures without 50 per cent or more of displacement are best treated lightly in a sling without other immobilization. Movement is encouraged as tolerated and is often possible in a week or so. After 2 or 3 weeks, the arm is freed from the sling for increasing lengths of time and light, purposeful motions are encouraged. Until sufficient improvement occurs, the arm may be rested in the sling between periods of light activity.

Fracture of the olecranon in the aged is not a seriously disabling injury. Often the distraction of the proximal fragment does not exceed a few millimeters. Unless the separation is marked, these fractures in the aged do not require surgical reduction or fixation as would similar fractures in a younger adult group. If surgical intervention is avoided, less scarification occurs about the elbow joint, and although some degree of relative weakness may occur it will probably not interfere with daily activity.

Little in the way of immobilization is required. A posterior splint with the elbow bent to an angle of 140° to 150° will relieve early discomfort and should be removed in 10 days or so, as the pain subsides. After this, a simple "low" sling should suffice. Fibrous union is acceptable and it will be found that the usefulness of the arm early freed from restraint will far exceed that anticipated from the appearance of the x-ray film.

Fracture of the shafts of the radius and/or ulna in the aged require the same meticulous reduction, by either closed or open procedures, as is required in any adult age group. In these fractures the problem is not one of simple positioning of the fragments; the problem is that of union. In the elderly person nonunion of the bones of the forearm is disabling beyond the point of acceptance and any technique which will ensure union must be attempted. Sufficient evidence has not as yet been collected to establish the relative merits of bone plating and intramedullary fixation in the atrophic shafts of the radius and the ulna. Until such evidence is gathered choice of the method to be used is the responsibility of the surgeon. With closed reduction the error of too early removal of plaster must be avoided even at the possible cost of elbow stiffness. The plaster molds must include the elbow in the aged as in all such cases. Less than 6 weeks will not suffice, and recheck x-ray films will more often than not suggest 8 to 10 weeks of immobilization whether closed or open reduction has been performed.

Fractures of the lower end of the radius with or without involvement of the ulna in the aged require rather special consideration. It must be recalled from Chap. 4 that the bone tissues at a healing fracture line pass through a stage of atrophy and surface necrosis. It must be further recalled that as the cortex of the radial shaft approaches its lower expansion, it thins out to a marked degree leaving a volume of cancellous bone that is often markedly atrophic in the aged and is actually in a state making it quite susceptible to collapse, compression, or splintering. These fractures at any age appear more damaged when seen surgically than they do on x-ray films.

In the treatment of fractures of the lower end of the radius in the aged, manipulation must be more gentle than usual. Force exerted in manipulating these older wrists will crush trabeculae and cause further surface atrophy at the fracture site. The resultant deformity and dysfunction are often greater than they would have been had an adequate though less perfect reduction been accepted in the first place.

However, the term *adequate reduction* requires some delineation. It must not be used as an excuse for no reduction at all or as a justification for a state of displacement or deformity which would seriously interfere with the expected function of the wrist and hand. If the distal fragment is angulated to the extent that the radiocarpal articular surface is dorsally tilted more than 30° from the axial line, it will too seriously interfere with function and must be reduced. If displacement of the fragment is 30 per cent or more of the fracture surface area it may not be left unreduced. However, an angulation of less than 30° or a displacement of less than 30 per cent in the atrophic elderly wrist may better be left alone if it does not reduce easily than incur the further damage of forcible reduction. There will be of course permanent limitations, but these will probably be less extensive than they would be if further damage were done to the bone structure.

The reduction of these fractures requires anesthesia. It would be a simple matter to recommend reduction under local Novocain, procaine, or Xylocaine anesthesia. It is often used very successfully if the principle of its technique is observed, that is, *if the needle enters the fracture hematoma*. This was originally emphasized by Böhler who popularized the technique in the 1930s, but is too often forgotten. Unless the anesthesia is complete and its effect absolute, it is more harmful than useful. If it is only partly effective, the reduction will be accomplished against the resistance of muscle spasm and pain, and further tissue and cellular trauma will occur at the fracture plane. Furthermore, the infiltration of Novocain or procaine anesthesia about these fractures in the elderly has provoked painful osteodystrophy in a number of cases. When the hematoma cannot be entered it seems at this writing that reduction under general anesthesia, either parenteral or inhalation, appears to be a safer procedure insofar as avoiding traumatic osteodystrophy of the wrist and carpus is concerned.

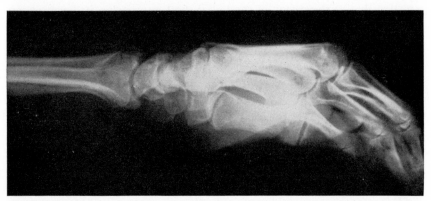

FIG. 6-5. Moderately displaced fracture—lower end of radius. Radial articular surface not angulated. Simple splint is sufficient immobilization of this fracture in the elderly and permits earlier return of function than would complete plaster of paris cast.

In the elderly patient a wrapped plaster cast is apt to be uncomfortable, heavy, and in general a burden. The use of anterior and posterior slabs held in place by gauze or preferably flannel bandage has several advantages. It is lighter. It is easily loosened by release of the bandage if swelling is excessive. It is removable in part or entirely for observation, and in a properly reduced fracture it is sufficiently strong to maintain reduction. The plaster slabs reach only to behind the heads of the metacarpals and motion of the fingers is encouraged immediately. The average time of plaster immobilization is 30 to 35 days.

If the fracture is not severe, or if it is somewhat impacted and does not present enough displacement or angulation to warrant reduction (Fig. 6-5), a simple volar cock-up splint is often enough immobilization. The lightweight plastic splint is an appreciated comfort to the elderly person when used in place of the heavier plaster slab. It does not of course mold itself to the part as well but its use in an impacted fracture is sufficient to relieve pain and hold the relative position of hand and forearm during the healing stage.

Common Complications. There are two complications which occur with much greater frequency in the elderly fractured wrist than in similar cases in the younger adult group. One has been known by a variety of names including Sudeck's atrophy, spotty atrophy, traumatic osteoporosis, traumatic neurovascular osteodystrophy, and traumatic osteodystrophy. The last may be used as descriptive of its pathology without assuming an as yet unknown pathogenesis. This lesion is well known descriptively. In a fully developed case, the wrist, hand, and fingers are swollen, the skin takes on a glassy surface appearance, and the x-ray film discloses irregular or spotty areas of atrophy in the lower end of the radius, ulna, and carpus. Perhaps of greatest clinical significance is the fact that the motion of the finger joints becomes greatly restricted. The syndrome is unfortunately accompanied by severe, protracted pain.

While traumatic osteodystrophy does not occur exclusively in the aged, it does occur with greater frequency in this group and its effect on finger motion is more difficult to overcome. Not all cases develop to an advanced state. Mild or abortive forms appear more frequently. When the syndrome is fully developed, however, the suffering it causes can be quite tragic. In spite of much experimental use of stellate ganglion block, brachial anesthesia, vasodilation medication and local therapy of almost every conceivable type, there is no convincing evidence that any therapy significantly influences the course of recovery. Analgesic medication and constant encouragement of finger motion must be given as long as the lesion remains. The symptoms of this complication begin to abate after 2 or 3 months of seemingly static existence, and improvement progresses slowly as the months pass.

A second common complication of fractures of the wrist in the elderly is prolonged stiffness of the fingers even in the absence of traumatic osteodystrophy. This is ordinarily preventable. The patient must be encouraged to move the fingers constantly. In the younger age group this order is more easily obeyed, since with the fingers free there is more incentive to their use in daily activities. In the elderly person no longer required to be active in employment, business, housework or social activities, there is a great tendency to just rest the hand. When merely told to move the fingers, with the forearm and hand bound in plaster slabs, the usual response is to wiggle the fingers at the knuckle joints. Unless specifically instructed and supervised, the elderly patient is apt not to move the interphalangeal joints to any significant extent during this period.

Other complications of this fracture are not peculiar to the aged. They occur infrequently and demand the same care as they do when found in any adult group. Late-stage rupture of an attenuated tendon crossing an angular surface of a displaced bone, closure of an artery by damage at the time of fracture or later thrombus, and nerve damage by compressing callus or fibrous tissue do occur and must be anticipated in large consecutive series of cases. The last includes the so-called "carpal tunnel syndrome."

This complication, due to the pressure of fibrous tissue or bone on the median nerve as it passes through the tunnel of the carpus and carpal and volar ligaments, causes a characteristic clinical picture. Persistent pain occurs in the hand and fingers with atrophy of the thenar eminence and palmar space. This complication is not self-limited and when discovered requires surgical exposure of the carpal tunnel and freeing of the median nerve from its constriction or pressure. Age should not be permitted to deprive the patient of this relief. The carpal tunnel syndrome may at times be as disablingly painful as traumatic osteodystrophy with which it is too often clinically confused. Above all, *the surgeon must avoid passing off all postfracture pains of the wrist and hand in the elderly patient as "arthritis"; they are more apt not to be.*

Aftercare. The aftercare of an uncomplicated fracture of the lower end of the radius and ulna in the aged is as important to its end result as the primary care. After a fracture has been properly reduced in the younger adult, even though it may take time, adequate if not normal motion of the wrist and hand will eventually return with the gradual resumption of normal daily chores. In the elderly wrist spontaneous recovery of function cannot be depended upon except under circumstances unusual to elderly life. These patients are often indifferent when told about the necessity for movement. In the absence of pain many of the older age group are apt to settle into contentment and ease, happy that the plaster or splint is off and giving no attention to the recovery of function. Too often this early posttraumatic attitude is regretted when some activity or event emphasizes the loss of manual agility. Hence the importance of giving repeated emphasis to the urgency of such gestures as sponge squeezing, and, above all, encouraging optimum purposeful manual activity.

Prognosis. Fracture of the lower end of the radius, with or without concurrent fracture of the ulna, in an aged individual inevitably leaves some degree of permanent disability. This is caused either by the residual bone deformity or by the scarification, fibrosis, or contractions of the ligaments and fasciae about the wrist joint. Even a well-reduced Colles' fracture, with no apparent deformity during the first few weeks in plaster, often, and more often than not in the aged, will show some radial deviation of the hand or some prominence of the ulnar styloid due to atrophy of trabeculae along the fracture surface of the radius during the healing process. The degree of deformity or dysfunction in the aged wrist does not necessarily depend upon the acumen or technical ability of the surgeon. To some extent it depends upon the degree of senility of the bone, the articular soft tissues, and the resiliency of the periarticular ligaments and fasciae. Some measurable weakness in the hand grip remains as the result of restrictions of motion or deformity of the articular surface. Adequate function should be restored by proper management of these fractures, but except for very simple cases, completely normal restitution of function should not ordinarily be anticipated.

HAND AND FINGERS

Incidence. In the list of 600 fractures of the aged noted in the introduction of this chapter, fractures of the hand and fingers occurred in 3.8 per cent of the cases. This places such injuries among the more common of those listed. In actual practice such fractures in the aged are usually found in the phalanges, less often in the metacarpals, and quite seldom in the carpus.

Common Sources of Trauma. Fractures of the phalanges in the aged are associated with a crushing injury such as may occur when a door is closed on the hand or a heavy object falls on it. Such injuries may be more common in the aged because of the lessened speed of what may be referred to as the "pull-away reflex." These injuries are therefore often associated with soft-tissue contusion and laceration which may demand more careful attention than the bone trauma.

Clinical Diagnosis. Fractures of the phalanx in the aged are very apt to be unrecognized under the evil appearance of an ecchymotic and swollen or lacerated finger. If marked angulation deformity occurs the fracture is evident, but this is not often present. Fracture of the metacarpal is of course more easily recognized by the classic signs of dorsal prominence in most shaft fractures or the apparent loss of the knuckle in the more common fracture of the neck of the bone with its characteristic anterior angulation.

Fracture of the carpus in the elderly is unusual and may only be suspected on the basis of local tenderness. As in the younger adult a sprain of the wrist remains suspect until the possibility of fracture of the navicular is eliminated. In general, diagnosis of such fractures in the aged does not differ from that in younger groups.

X-ray. The ultimate measure of diagnosis in hand injuries is of course the x-ray film. Fractures of the metacarpals and phalanges present no special difficulty in x-ray interpretation. Fractures in the carpal bones, uncommon as they are, do present a special problem in that such fractures are often unrecognized even in younger age groups, and in the elderly may be more difficult to recognize in this frequently osteoporotic area. It has been noted that the areas about the wrist joint, both at the lower end of the radius and at the carpal bones, are among the earliest parts of the skeleton to show osteoporosis and bone atrophy.

Treatment. The function of the fingers is far more important to the aged individual than is their cosmetic appearance. Fingers will stiffen more quickly in the aged than in the younger adult and once stiffened will seldom regain their normal motion. *In the treatment of fracture of the metacarpals and fingers in the aged, everything, including appearance, must be sacrificed to the maintenance of as much mobility as can be saved.* Fingers will not ordinarily accept the traction methods used in the younger age groups. The peripheral circulation will not accept the pull of the circumferential glove-type traction, and it will hardly tolerate adhesive traction for any sustained period. The fibrous reaction to wires inserted through the phalanges is apt to decrease later mobility to a greater degree than would be caused by moderate deformity.

Severe deformity may be overcome by simple manual traction which if applied shortly after fracture and applied with gentle pull rather than a sharp jerk can often be accomplished without anesthesia. Under the analgesia effected by an ethyl chloride spray, manual reduction of finger fractures may be greatly simplified. If necessary, of course, in metacarpal fractures a small local injection of 1 or 2 ml of 1 per cent Novocain can be used. When the major deformity has been corrected a small anterior finger splint reaching from the tip of the finger to the thenar or hypothenar space is bandaged into place and kept on for 10 to 15 days depending upon the severity of the fracture. The greater time interval is used for fractures through the shaft of the phalanx or metacarpal, the lesser time for the impacted fracture of either end of the bone. Certainly this may permit some retrogression of the angulation or shortening of the shaft in oblique fractures. But early release from immobilization will help to prevent soft-tissue reaction to inserted wires, and any minor residual deformity will ordinarily be compensated for by return of function.

In fracture of the neck of the metacarpal with its customary anterior angulation and loss of knuckle, no reduction is necessary beyond a simple attempt to improve the angle. This may be aided by the injection of 1 or 2 ml of Novocain. The unsupported correction is seldom maintained, however. A simple, firm bandage is used to hold the metacarpal and finger over a rolled bandage in the palm only until acute pain has subsided. It may be released in 10 days or so, and except for protecting the hand against being struck at its tender area, no further restraint need be used. Motion of the fingers is encouraged to the point of toleration.

Fractures of the carpal bones other than the navicular, or displacement of the lunate, may be ignored in the elderly. In fractures of the other bones of the carpus, which are never seriously displaced, a simple anterior forearm splint will suffice for comfort for a week or so or until severe pain subsides. After the splint is removed, the wrist and hand may be used as tolerance permits, but the patient will probably be unable to exert manual force against weighted objects or resistant surfaces for a while. Active motion of the fingers is particularly encouraged. Fortunately fractures of the carpus are rare in the elderly.

The navicular may be treated as at any age, but particular attention must be directed to ensuring freedom of motion of the fingers not included in the plaster. The distal phalanx of the thumb must also be free, and its movement must be encouraged. Six weeks of plaster immobilization under these conditions should suffice to attain union in those fractures of the aged navicular which will unite. Fibrous union will suffice for a number of the others. A certain number may remain unavoidably symptomatic when the hand is used against resistance. In these, avascular necrosis or cystic degeneration will be found on later x-rays.

Traumatic dislocation of the lunate is almost unheard of in the aged. If it can be reduced by simple manipulation under anesthesia, such would be the treatment of choice. If it is not reducible manually, excision of the bone would be perhaps less traumatizing to the elderly radiocarpal complex than the dissection needed for surgical replacement. Avascular necrosis of the bone and the damaging effect of this on joint function would be all but inevitable.

Operative intervention in closed fractures of the hand or the insertion of nails or wires should only be attempted under very special circumstances, and the surgeon must hold himself responsible for that choice. The high probability of inelastic periarticular and peritendinous fibrosis in the aged hand must always be measured against the probable functional profit of any contemplated intervention.

Common Complications. There are two complications of fractures of the hand and fingers which are peculiar to the aged. One is that of traumatic osteodystrophy of the bones adjacent to the radiocarpal joint. This was mentioned in the discussion of complications in fractures of the lower end of the radius. In fractures of the carpus and metacarpus, the same lesion is apt to appear, and when it does, the dysfunction and discomfort of the hand persist for weeks and even months beyond that anticipated from the relatively simple fracture. As noted in the previous discussion, no known therapeutic measures seem to influence either the onset or the course of traumatic osteodystrophy. One thing is important in its management: the fingers must be kept constantly mobile no matter how limited the range, and finger splints are therefore to be removed at the earliest possible moment. A cock-up wrist splint is often a means of relief and may be necessary.

A second complication more common in the elderly than in younger age groups is the early appearance of stiffness, not only in the fingers related to the fractured phalanx or metacarpal but in the other fingers as well. Encouragement in the daily use of the unsplinted fingers must be even more urgent in the aged. The natural reluctance of the older person to cause himself discomfort, or possibly the lack of incentive or the natural indolence of age in most persons, is apt to cause some disregard of instructions about moving the fingers. The necessity for correcting this attitude cannot be overemphasized.

Of course, the other complications of infection, vascular, or nerve trauma also occur, but in these the management does not significantly differ from that of the younger age group.

Aftercare. When splints are removed, the continued emphasis on mobility of the fingers must be maintained and even increased. The aged person is too pleased that "treatment" is over and is more than willing to "forget the whole thing," often to his later regret. At this time, mild heat and massage, which may be given by nurse, relative, or attendant at home, is helpful. It does not require the expert facilities of a masseur or therapist. The simple stroking or moving of fingers at this stage of recovery may be taught to any one of average intelligence.

Prognosis. At best, fractures of the phalanges in the aged are more apt than not to leave some residual restriction of motion even in well-aligned cases. The degree of restriction varies widely from 20 to 50 per cent of the normal range. This may not greatly interfere with activity demanded of the aged individual unless he or she habitually uses the hand in several of those activities common to elderly persons, such as knitting or sewing among women or various hobbies among men. At times of course a 50 per cent restriction of motion in the fingers may be a serious disability in the elderly craftsman still engaged in engraving, watchmaking, or other trades in which older individuals may remain gainfully employed. At best the prognosis of fractures in the aged hand must be guarded.

FRACTURES OF THE LOWER EXTREMITY

FEMUR*

Incidence. Fractures of the shaft and lower end of the femur are not at all uncommon in the aged, occurring in about 2.5 per cent of these cases. They appear to be more or less equally divided between the three thirds of the femur below the trochanters.

---

* (*Fractures of the neck and head of the femur are not discussed in this chapter since the special problem of fractures of the hip in the elderly merits its extended consideration by Dr. Lippmann in Chap. 8.*)

Common Sources of Trauma. The usual cause of fracture of the shaft is of course a fall. However, with the atrophic skeleton of the elderly individual even a simple fall to the ground may suffice to cause fracture of the shaft. The lower extremities of the aged are often seriously affected by injuries which in the younger adult would be relatively insignificant. There are several reasons for this. One factor concerns the weight of the body and the force of its angled momentum on atrophic bone during the fall. A second factor is the lessened reactivity in the older person of the postural reflex which tends to help the younger individual to resist the fall. A third element is the unstable knee joint frequently found in the elderly. The highly frequent advanced osteoarthrotic changes in the knees, with accompanying periarticular adhesions, hypertrophic synovia, and narrowed intraarticular space, restrict the motions of the joint and prevent its normal "give" and recovery during sudden slips or trips on irregular ground or steps. During the fall the impact concentrates considerable stress at the lower end of the femur and is quite apt to fracture the condyles or the shaft at the supracondylar level.

Clinical Signs. Fracture of the shaft of the femur is recognized quite easily and by the same signs in the elderly as in the younger adult, i.e., complete disability of the limb, outward rotation, sagging of the mid-thigh, or angulation, local pain, and tenderness. Shortening may and usually does occur from overlapping of the fragments of a transverse fracture of the shaft, or the shearing of the oblique. However, fracture of the lower end of the bone may confuse the examiner if it has occurred near the swollen edematous knee of an advanced osteoarthrosis. The pain and local tenderness of a wrenched osteoarthrotic knee may present a disability of the same order as does fracture of the lower end of the femur.

In fractures of both the shaft and the lower end of the femur, before x-rays are taken, the surgeon experienced in the method of auscultatory percussion can easily ascertain whether dissolution of continuity of bone has occurred (see Chap. 4). The diaphragm of the stethoscope may be placed over the pubic symphysis and comparative densities ascertained by tapping the patellae of both sides. If this is impracticable because of local pain, a practiced ear can determine relative pitch of transmitted sound by tapping the malleoli of both ankles.

X-ray. Roentgenologic examination of fractures of the shaft and lower end of the femur presents no special difficulty in the elderly. The expanse of the lower end is great enough that even in the presence of osteoporotic or osteoarthrotic changes, fracture lines are easily discernible. Furthermore, fractures of either of these sites are almost invariably displaced to some perceptible degree.

Treatment. Treatment of the middle or upper thirds of the femoral shaft in the aged always presents a difficult decision. In the younger adult, intramedullary nailing or bone plating are the obvious methods of choice if traction is to be avoided. This choice is not quite as simple in the elderly. If the bone tissues are not in a state of advanced atrophy or osteoporosis, intramedullary nailing is the preferred procedure in fractures of the middle and lower thirds of the shaft and allows early mobilization. In the upper third, a blade plate such as the Jewett, Neufeld, or Blount, with the plate a long one, is an effective method. However, femora with even moderate atrophy or osteoporosis will not hold cortical metal attachments well without adequate external assistance. The screws of a plate loosen easily unless some form of protection by plaster, brace, or traction is used. The risk nevertheless must be taken with as much protection as can be devised. Often a long leg brace will afford enough protection even though some angulation from muscle pull may be expected. The traction-countertraction devices such as that of Roger Anderson have at times worked satisfactorily but require painstaking care to avoid pressure sores.

In the quite elderly who have been more or less bedridden or chair ridden for months, simple traction suspension may give greater comfort, lead to earlier healing, and subject the patient to no more immobilization than he has been accustomed to. Felt or foam-rubber traction strips held in place by elastic bandages are used in place of adhesive. Skeletal traction devices may be suitable at times but in advanced bone atrophy are apt to pull through the bone.

Fracture of the femoral shaft in the elderly at or near the supracondylar area is seldom marked by great displacement, but the distal fragment is apt to be angulated anteriorly. In the aged, this presents a special problem distinct from the same fracture in the younger adult. In the "younger and active" or borderline aging person in the early 60s, in good preservation, with normal contours of the knee joint, the treatment used in the younger adult may be employed and perfect alignment sought. This ordinarily takes the form of open reduction with the insertion of a right-angled blade plate. In the aged person with osteoporotic bone and advanced osteoarthrosis of the knee joint, the use of bone plates, nail plates, intramedullary nails, and other metallic devices may be precarious. Soft bone may be further destroyed, and periarticular adhesions may be increased. A long leg brace, or even a long elastic knee cage with rigid lateral bars equipped with a lock-stop knee joint, will often prove an effective restraint. If the angulation is marked, it may be manually corrected under anesthesia and temporarily held in a long leg plaster with the knee bent at 150° for a few weeks, followed by the application of a brace or knee cage. The latter permits greater comfort than the plaster, cleansing of the limb, and after an adequate degree of primary union, restrained early mobility. In the brace, knee motion may be started in

4 to 6 weeks, depending upon the nature of the fracture (Figs. 6-6 and 6-8*C*).

Common Complications. There are ordinarily few cases of fractures of the upper or midfemoral shaft in which serious complications occur unless one is dealing with open fractures. Then, of course, traumatic

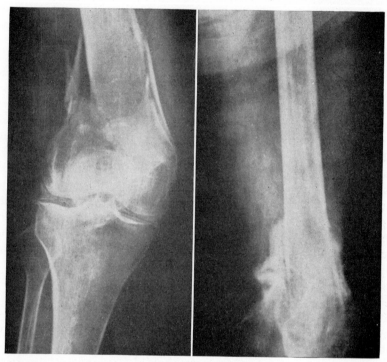

FIG. 6-6. Comminuted fracture—lower end of femur—treated by long elastic knee cage with rigid lateral bars. Healed with 60 to 70° residual motion at knee joint. Female, age 86.

osteomyelitis remains a threat usually controlled by the proper use of chemotherapy or the antibiotics. Vascular or neural damage in the soft fleshy thigh is most uncommon.

In fractures of the lower third at or near the supracondylar area or involving the condyles, the threat of major limitation of knee motion is indeed considerable. Lower-third and supracondylar fractures involve the under surface of the quadriceps muscle and tendon and the suprapatellar pouch of the synovial cavity. These may too easily become adherent to the damaged periosteum or the early callus of the femur and eventually prevent flexion of the knee. Fractures involving the condyles adjacent to a knee joint already damaged by degenerative arthrotic changes may cause severe intraarticular adhesions and fibrous ankylosis. That is why, in the treatment of these lower-third and lower-end fractures, much must be sacrificed to early mobility and the avoidance where ever possible of prolonged immobilization.

Aftercare. Aftercare in fractures of the shaft and lower end of the femur begins when healing has progressed to the point where partial weight bearing with crutches or canes is permitted. In the elderly rehabilitation may not be conducted with the same urgency as is valid in the younger adult group. It must be gentler or else fibrotic tissue will be painfully strained, and weakened ankles and feet will become temporarily disabled by edema and slow up the rehabilitation so anxiously sought. So-called "resistance exercises" for quadriceps muscles in the elderly, while perhaps theoretically sound, have generally proved to be a waste of time.

Motion at the knee is best and most rapidly attained by permitting the knee to bend over the side of a bed or table, aided only by gravity. Flexion will increase day by day, and optimum if not complete flexion will be attained after 1 to 3 weeks. Strength of the limb is attained by walking more each day with two canes or a single cane used preferably in the hand opposite the fracture. In general, one depends on the daily increase in purposeful activity rather than formal exercises. Given proper incentive, the elderly person will do best when simply encouraged to walk, since careful instructions may only confuse him. Massage of the limbs may improve the muscular tone and peripheral circulation and may at times hasten recovery. It is not essential nor is it nearly as important as the effect of sympathetic encouragement.

Prognosis. Nonunion is always uncommon in fractures of the shaft of the femur unless it is provoked by inauspicious surgery or overly enthusiastic traction techniques. Left alone in simple immobilization or gentle traction suspension, the femoral shaft almost always unites. It will do so at any age, in the elderly as well as in the younger adult. In the relatively broad thigh slight or even moderate angulation or displacement presents no significant cosmetic problem in the aged person and is acceptable if the bone will thus be enabled to bear weight sooner.

In the lower-third or lower-end fracture, prognosis must always be guarded and is rarely classifiable as better than fair. Bone union occurs with equal alacrity, but it is unusual to regain full knee motion or a painless knee. Some degree of limitation of knee function and some degree of persistent articular pain is almost inevitable.

A small amount of shortening of the limb is anticipated in most cases of fracture of the femur due either to the shearing of an oblique fracture or to some degree of angulation in the transverse type. It should be kept within 1 cm more or less; at times it may be rather more. Often enough, the technical pride of the surgeon is hurt since he knows of procedures which will overcome this shortening. True, too much shortening is unwarranted, but the threat of nonunion from distraction, or excessive loss of knee-joint function to which the aged limb is far more susceptible than is that of the younger adult, must not be risked for the sake of the surgeon's sense of technical excellence as measured by x-ray film or the measuring tape. A half- or three-quarter-inch raised heel is not too great a price for the aged individual to pay for a safe and speedy return to the activities of life.

Tibia and Fibula

Incidence. Fracture of the tibia with or without coincident fracture of the fibula and fracture of the fibula alone occur in 5½ per cent of fractures of the aged. However, of these only 10 per cent involve the shafts or upper ends, and 90 per cent the lower end, i.e., fractures about the ankle joint. Presented another way, about 5 per cent of fractures of the aged occur adjacent to the ankle joint in the lower end of the tibia and/or fibula.

Common Sources of Trauma. Fracture of the upper end or shaft of the tibia usually follows a fall or the impact of an automobile or other vehicle, as in the younger adult. The ease with which even a minor misstep may cause fractures of the lower end of either or both of the bones, however, is exceptional in the aged.

Clinical Diagnosis. Fractures of the leg bones are classifiable into several categories, each requiring different care and each offering a different prognosis.

1. Fracture of the tibial condyles with or without fracture of the head of the fibula
   a. Fractures of the fibular head alone
2. Fracture of the tibial shaft with or without fracture of the fibula
   a. Transverse fracture of the tibial shaft
   b. Oblique fracture of the tibial shaft
3. Fracture of the lower end of the tibia with or without fracture of the fibula
   a. Fracture of the lower end of the fibula alone

Clinically all of these are associated with pain localized to the injured part. The fractures occurring near the joints are too often passed off as sprains, and an x-ray is not taken until a period of unnecessary suffering is past. *Although it will be painful, it is quite possible to bear weight on a fractured tibial condyle or even on certain fractures about the ankle at any age; but in the elderly where the threshold of pain is often higher than in the younger adult, this ability to bear weight on a fracture of either end of the tibia may be quite amazing.* Because of this, such fractures are "missed" more often in elderly patients whose activities are normally restricted.

In the elderly, perhaps even more than in younger groups, it is inexcusable to diagnose a sprain of the knee or ankle without an x-ray film. A common experience in orthopedic or traumatic practice is the reception of an elderly female with a preexisting swollen osteoarthritic knee upon which she has recently fallen and suffered aggravation of her customary pain. A diagnosis of arthritis of the knee aggravated by trauma is taken for granted until pain persists in spite of rest or local palliation. An x-ray film taken later on may well show a fracture about the tibial condyles, too often beyond repair by simple manual reduction. A second common type of patient is the elderly gentleman who twisted or turned his ankle in what appeared to be a minor misstep, but kept hobbling about a bit with not too much pain. He is treated for several weeks for a sprained ankle before an x-ray film changes the recorded diagnosis. It must be admitted that often enough this neglect is due to the patient's self-diagnosis and disinclination to spend his or her remaining capital on doctors. That this is a serious consideration is too often demonstrated in practice. The layman's belief that one cannot walk on a broken bone is deeply ingrained, especially in our older population.

X-ray. The tibial condyle may suffer a serious comminuted spreading fracture, but this is not common in the elderly. Ordinarily one may have to look carefully in the early films for the longitudinal crack running from the articular surface distally into the condyle with but little apparent displacement. The more common type of fracture of the upper tibia is the moderate compression fracture of either condyle.

Fractures of the shaft of the tibia present no x-ray problem unique to the elderly age group. Transverse or oblique fractures with or without fibular involvement occur in about the same relative percentages.

At the ankle, fractures of the lower end of the tibia with or without fibular involvement are ordinarily easily visualized. There are several types of fracture however which require more careful observation. One is the longitudinal or long oblique fracture of the lower end of an osteoporotic tibia which in its early stage is either not displaced or the position of which is not clearly shown in the ordinary anteroposterior or lateral views (Fig. 6-7). In the younger adult bone with a clear roentgenogram, a fracture line may be visible or at least suggested through the more or less homogeneous density of the tibia; in the elderly a simple "hidden" line may be less obvious in the irregular trabecular network of osteoporotic bone near the ankle. When fracture is clinically suspected several views of this area may be necessary.

Treatment. *Fractures of the tibial condyles* at all ages represent a challenge in choice of treatment. The decision depends upon the surgeon's judgment as to the relative degree of compression or displacement of the articulating surface (tibial plateau) of the condyle. The object of course is to restore the articulating surface to a degree sufficient to permit good function of the knee joint. Absolute restoration of the tibial surface demands operative intervention. Unfortunately even with the most ingenious of such procedures complete correction is seldom fully maintained in the compression type of fracture. In designing such surgical procedures the postfracture necrosis of the traumatized bone tissue at the fracture

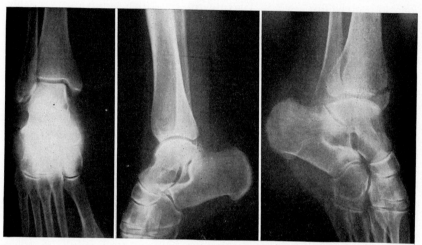

FIG. 6-7. Fracture at the ankle not disclosed by ordinary anteroposterior or lateral views, but obvious on the oblique view. This fracture is not uncommon in the aged.

site must be taken into account, and the later compression due to this will invalidate some part of the original correction.

In 1941 a series of 61 compression fractures was studied from the point of view of end results a year or more after fracture. Many of these occurred in persons of late middle age or older. It was observed that except for the very serious depressions of the condyle, early and good functional recovery was possible without absolute restoration of articular integrity. The instability noted in the knee joint during the earlier posttreatment months had all but disappeared by the end of a year of weight bearing and indeed greater freedom of flexion or extension was attained than in those cases in this series which had been operated upon. Of course severe compressions of the condyles are treated surgically and the reduction is maintained by internal fixation with screws or bolts. The final conformation of the joint is seldom as satisfactory as it appears to be on the operating table.

In the aged the most common fracture about the upper end of the tibia is the compression fracture of the outer table, the result of an automobile or hand-truck impact along the outer surface of the leg causing a forced valgus position of the knee. In most of these cases a simple long-legged plaster or rigid knee cage worn for about 6 to 7 weeks is sufficient. During that period, if the elderly patient's agility permits it, crutch walking without weight bearing is permitted. Afterwards increasing weight bearing is allowed as tolerated until cane walking can be accepted. For the less frequent compression fracture of the inner table, or for the not too widely displaced T fractures of the tibial condyles, this same treatment will suffice in treatment of the elderly.

In the aged one does not see isolated fractures of the upper end of the fibula as frequently as one does in the younger adult simply because the elderly patient is not as frequently exposed to the type of direct impact which is most apt to cause this lesion. When fracture of the upper end of the fibula is present with fracture of the tibial condyle, it may be all but ignored. It will ordinarily heal regardless of its position before the final care of the tibial fracture is accomplished. When present alone it requires no particular care beyond simple splinting until pain subsides enough to permit walking. The fibula is not a weight-bearing bone and its upper end, unlike the lower, does not form part of a major articulation.

In the aged person who is not active and who spends the greater part of his or her day in a chair, one may sometimes treat fractures of the tibial condyles successfully without plaster or brace. A few days to a week after the application of a simple restraining bandage over cotton or sheet wadding, gentle motion within the limitations of the bandage may be permitted. Gradually, within 3 or 4 weeks, the pressure bandage may be released and further motion allowed. Even partial weight bearing, however, is not permitted for the full 6 or 7 weeks.

The operative treatment of fractures of the tibial condyles in the elderly merits the controversy it causes. Certainly, in the aged, there are a few fractures in this area in which compression or comminution is so marked that surgery must be considered. This must remain the decision of the responsible surgeon. When surgery is indicated several of the special characteristics of aging bone must be carefully considered. It is unfair to undertake a surgical procedure designed to recover the integrity of the articular surface of the tibia if such a procedure (for example, a strut graft) requires 6 to 12 months of serious disability. The elderly person will himself remind the surgeon that he cannot afford to waste so much time for an improved knee if a less time-consuming procedure will permit earlier ambulation even at the cost of less efficient articulation. In all fairness to the aged patient, the surgeon must bear in mind that even with an operative procedure which may greatly improve the efficiency of the joint in an active younger adult, a perfect restoration rarely if ever persists in follow-up studies of aged patients. In the aged person a good part of the anatomic gain will be lost in the atrophic or osteoporotic bone by secondary necrosis and compression, and some degree of osteoarthritic degeneration will take place in the knee joint regardless of the temporary excellence of the alignment.

The one procedure which may be justified in the aged is the use of screws or bolts to hold together the spreading T fracture of the condyle if the displacement is marked. This permits earlier reparative osteogenesis and earlier ambulation and at least affords a weight-bearing plateau. Severely comminuted condyles, unusual though they are in the elderly, are best left alone except for some manual modeling. The large area of the fracture surfaces encourages relatively rapid union, and no surgery will lessen the extent of articular tissue disruption.

In brief, in the treatment of fractures of the upper end of the tibia in the elderly, certain consideration must be borne in mind. Early weight bearing with a "pretty good knee" is more valuable to the patient than prolonged disability with a better x-ray picture. The knee joint in any adult group adapts itself well to a small or even moderate degree of condylar compression. With the lesser demands of elderly life, the knee in the aged will adapt itself to even further compression. Knee function following fracture of the tibial condyles is always impaired to some degree in the aged. Prolonged splinting or a prolonged period of nonweight bearing defeats the purpose of many procedures which are of value in the younger adult because it permits further atrophy and softening of the bone during the protracted healing period.

Fractures of the shafts of the tibia or of the fibula are less frequent in the elderly than upper-end fractures. Their treatment is always as time consuming as it is in the younger adult and the fact of age in this fracture adds or subtracts very little in the choice of therapy. For the most part such fractures are best treated by simple plaster cast immobilization. For those instances in which widely separated fragments cannot be held in reasonable apposition, surgical measures may be necessary. It is not as yet quite certain that intramedullary nailing of the tibia at any age does not retard union and its failure is costly to the elderly patient. There is even now a strong opinion that, when necessary, internal fixation of this bone by plates and screws, or by screws alone to effect surface to surface apposition, supplemented by plaster cast and early wheel chair or crutch mobility might not in the end be a more dependable method than intramedullary nailing and less subject to delays in healing.

One special factor may be kept in mind in managing such fractures in the aged. In an oblique fracture, a shortening up to $\frac{1}{2}$ inch is less of a handicap than in the younger adult and is not worth surgical procedures or extended skeletal traction to overcome. Early walking with a limb shortened only to this extent, with possibly a raised heel, is more acceptable than perfect length at the expense of extra months of invalidism.

Metallic fixation must be used cautiously in the presence of bone atrophy or osteoporosis. Soft bone will not hold attached metals or skeletal-pin traction as well as more solid bone, and conservative management may in the end effect a better result. Furthermore, the presence of advanced vascular sclerosis or vascular insufficiency adds considerably to the risk in many elderly cases which otherwise would be considered suitable for surgical intervention.

Fractures of the lower end of the tibia with or without fracture of the fibula also call for special consideration in the elderly to a greater degree than do fractures of these bones at other levels. The "fractured ankle" is among the common injuries in this age group, and many occur as the result of apparently minor injuries. An unguarded step from the curb may cause a most severely displaced comminuted fracture of both bones with considerable luxation of the ankle joint. Furthermore, the lower end of the tibia, like the lower end of the radius being predominantly cancellous bone, is far more affected by the bone atrophy or porosis of age than is the cortical bone of the shaft and it is therefore more subject to intraosseous compressions and necrosis.

In the treatment of such fractures in the aged, one factor must be kept dominantly in mind, the alignment of the tibiotalar axis. In effect this means the restoration of as nearly horizontal a line along the articular margin of the lower end of the tibia as method can effect. In the aged this is far more important than other elements of reduction. A slight widening of the mortise of the ankle, or some lateral displacement of the fibular malleolus may, if necessary, be permitted if their correction involves more prolonged disability. The horizontality of the tibial surface and its tibiotalar axis, however, must be preserved at almost any cost of time to any aged person who is still at all active.

In fractures at this level in the aged, a short-legged plaster with walking heel or iron is required. A lightweight old person, assisted by a cane in the opposite hand, may be permitted as much partial weight bearing in the walking plaster as is tolerated. In the heavier or more active elderly person, ambulation with crutches and without significant weight bearing in the plaster may be started early and a single cane permitted in 6 weeks or as soon after that as tolerated. In most cases of fracture of the lower end of the tibia, with or without fibula involvement, the plaster may be removed after 10 to 12 weeks. In uncomplicated malleolar fractures, 6 to 8 weeks may suffice.

There are several rather simple fractures of these bones about the ankle which do not require the major treatments described above. Fracture of a single malleolus, be it fibular or tibial, when it occurs below the line of the ankle joint and does not enter into weight bearing, requires little or no immobilization. Simple strapping with the use of crutches or even a cane after a few days to a week of relative rest often suffices. Fractures of the lower end of the fibula above the ankle joint require no immobilization in view of the restricted activities of the elderly since this bone takes no part in weight bearing. Walking may be permitted as tolerated. In such fractures of the malleoli, during the early acute days, elevation of the foot, cold compresses, and elastic bandages furnish considerable relief. A local injection of Novocain (3 to 4 ml of 1 per cent) into the fracture area, with or without hyaluronidase, will often give dramatic relief of pain.

Fractures of the malleoli at the level of the ankle-joint line are not comparable to those occurring at a lower level since the integrity of the joint is involved. In the elderly, a light plaster should be applied and full weight bearing restricted at least 6 weeks or until x-ray evidence demonstrates good union of the fragments.

Finally there is a special lesion which technically must be considered a fracture but which in effect is a severe sprain of the medial or lateral ligaments of the ankle joint with avulsion of a small piece or even a mere fleck of bone from the tip of the malleolus. These are best treated as sprains. Actually they are quite uncommon in the elderly. The type of injury which is apt to cause so severe a sprain in the younger adult more often than not causes a real fracture about the ankle in the elderly.

Common Complications. At the upper end of the tibia an occasional complication is secondary collapse of the fractured condyle after apparent healing. This is not particularly characteristic of such fractures in the aged but may occur at any age. It is perhaps a less serious matter in the elderly since in fact the knee will function quite acceptably if the deformity of the tibial plateau is not too great.

The most serious complication of fractures of the tibia, which occurs in those fractures involving the upper third of the shaft, is rupture of the popliteal artery or its posterior tibial division. When this occurs one is faced with an urgent vascular emergency. The event may and often does lead to gangrene of the extremity unless early surgical intervention is employed. Neither diagnosis nor treatment of this complication in the aged differs from that in the younger adult. Because of the greater friability of the blood vessels, this accident is more to be feared in the aged, and when it occurs it presents a greater potential danger. Treatment of course demands immediate exposure of the torn vessel. If possible, continuity of the blood vessels is restored; or in a laceration of the wall, the opening is closed. Unfortunately it is not always possible to restore continuity under the emergency circumstances in which this lesion is found, and ligation of the bleeding vessel becomes necessary. This leaves the leg dependent upon the physiological efficacy of the anastomotic circulation. Herein lies the added danger to the aged patient. The circulatory apparatus of sclerotic extremities does not easily substitute for a damaged major vessel.

There are two common complications which are far more associated with fractures of the lower end of the tibia in the aged than with comparable fractures in the younger adult. The first is posttraumatic osteodystrophy of the tarsus (see Chap. 4). This painful atrophy involves the lower ends of the tibia and fibula and all the bones of the tarsus, and in severe cases, even the metatarsus. This event causes protracted pain in the extremity which at times may warrant the term *excruciating* and greatly prolongs the disability.

Treatment of posttraumatic osteodystrophy has acquired an extended bibliography during the past two decades. It is a problem in neurovascular physiology. In common experience the efficacy of the inhibiting and dilating procedures employed, from nerve block to major ganglionectomy or Leriche's periarterial sympathectomy, has not been dependable at any age. In the elderly, where the more extensive methods have been less often tried, they are apparently of no greater usefulness. Physiotherapeutic modalities of all types were in use even before the pathology was recognized, usually to no significant avail. Time and gradually increased use have been so far the only treatment, if treatment it is, that has proved effective. Even at the cost of some compression of the talus, which in the elderly is not too great a handicap, function must be encouraged. Purely empiric experience indicates that hot foot soaks used for periods of 15 to 20 minutes during the day or night have afforded some temporary relief during the more painful episodes.

The second common complication of these fractures more frequently found in the aged than in younger adult groups is a secondary compression of the bone at the fracture site when weight bearing has begun. When a fracture of the lower end of the tibia has healed, judgment may rest between Scylla and Charybdis. Weight bearing on the porotic bone invites secondary trabecular compression with consequent deformity of the joint surfaces. Postponing such weight bearing invites further atrophy and merely puts off the evil day. The aged person with his more limited potential demands is better off starting to walk even at the expense of some ankle deformity. However, to the best of one's judgment, the decision must mark a careful compromise between the necessity for a proper tibiotalar axis and the avoidance of progressive bone atrophy.

Prognosis. All fractures of the tibia and/or fibula in the aged individual merit a guarded prognosis no matter how promising they may appear to be at first. Periarticular fibrosis, disruption of knee and ankle joint either directly due to fractures involving the articular surfaces or indirectly due to imbalance in the recovery period, inexorably take their toll, and in the elderly more so than in the younger adult. The only saving grace that experience has demonstrated is that the lesser functional demand in the aged makes the disability relatively less important than it would be in the younger adult.

PATELLA

Incidence. Fracture of the patella occurred in about 0.8 per cent of a series of 600 consecutive fractures in the aged. Most of these were transverse fractures across the middle or lower half of the bone.

Common Sources of Trauma. In most cases the fracture occurred as the result of a fall after the foot was caught (tripping) on some rise on the floor of a house or pavement outdoors. It has been suggested that fracture of an aged patella might occur as an avulsion fracture because of the pull of a tightened quadriceps against the patellar ligament. This assumes that the atrophic bone of the elderly individual will part sooner than will ligament, tendon, or muscle. This must be admitted as a possibility and such cases have been reported. However, they are at best unusual, and in most cases the patella has received a direct impact on the floor or ground.

Clinical Diagnosis. Fractures of the patella in the aged may be transverse through the body, may be a separation of a small fragment of the lower end, or as in any age group, may be severely comminuted. The transverse fracture through the body is the most common. Its diagnosis should be palpably apparent even before x-ray is available.

The clinically important element in fracture of the patella is the extent of the tear along the adjacent fibers of the quadriceps tendon and capsule. This is ordinarily manifested by the palpable diastasis between the fractured fragments. It is this separation of the anterior capsule and tendon which causes the subsequent relative weakness in the knee when it is extreme and when it is left untreated.

At times, especially if the patient is examined some hours after the trauma, the swelling of the area due to intra- and extraarticular hemarthrosis may make the separated fragments somewhat less perceptible by clinical palpation. Nevertheless, except for undisplaced comminuted fractures or those occurring at the lowest portion, most such lesions can be clinically recognized.

X-ray. There should be no excusable difficulty in the interpretation of these films even in the aged. Atrophy or osteoporosis should not occlude fracture lines involving the sharper edges of this bone with its simple contours. The chief contribution made by the film is in helping to determine whether or not in the transverse fracture or in the comminuted fracture separation of the fragments is great enough to warrant surgical intervention.

Treatment. It is in the treatment of fractures of the patella that the factor of aging becomes important. The necessity for restoring quadri-

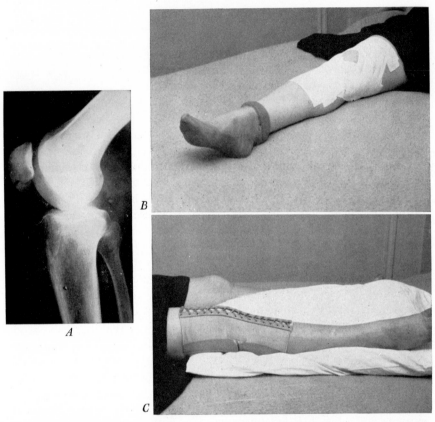

FIG. 6-8. *A.* Common type of fracture of patella in elderly not requiring rigid support or surgery. *B.* Adhesive support for undisplaced or slightly fractured displaced patella. *C.* Elastic and laced knee cage with hinged side bars. May be used for fractures about the knee in several circumstances. Lock-stop hinges control the range of flexion.

ceps power as near to normal as is possible, regardless of time, whether by surgical apposition of the fragments or prolonged immobilization, is unquestioned in the child or younger adult. In the elderly individual, restoration of strength in the limb may well be hindered by the very measures which would accomplish this purpose in the younger.

Cases in which fracture fragments, either transversely sectioned or comminuted, are not widely separated may not require rigid plaster immobilization in the elderly (Fig. 6-8*A*). A simple adhesive support (see illustration) used for 4 to 6 weeks is often sufficient to maintain the relative position of the fragments and still allow some freedom to the knee joint and to the muscles of the extremity (Fig. 6-8*B*). Where available, a laced elastic knee cage with lock-stopped lateral bars may be equally effective (Fig. 6-8*C*). The fibrous union which occurs is quite sufficient to allow satisfactory function in the aged person. Unlike the effect of the rigid long-leg plaster cylinder, the knee cage does not provoke marked muscle atrophy nor does it aggravate an existing bone atrophy or osteoporosis during treatment. The restricted muscle function which is permitted by the adhesive or the knee cage does not interfere with fibrous union, but allows enough movement to prevent the baneful effects of complete disuse.

In the early stages of this treatment, crutches or a walker may be used until canes can be tolerated. Weight bearing is never a problem. After three weeks, sufficient fibrous union is present to permit walking rather easily as long as the patient is warned against, or protected from, sharp flexions. Seldom in these cases is a plaster cast or other rigid support necessary. It might even be said categorically that plaster casts should not be used in such cases.

When diastasis between the fragments of a transverse or markedly comminuted fracture is too wide to anticipate satisfactory fibrous union (Fig. 6-9), surgical removal of the lesser fragment and suture of the aponeurotic tear will permit motion of the joint in 3 weeks. Walking with canes is allowed even before motion is permitted with protective pressure dressings of gauze, flannel, or elastic bandage over cotton reaching from the upper thigh to lower calf. Suturing the fragments together is inadvisable in this type of case since the period of immobilization required for bone union is not warranted by the benefit such suturing lends to an aged knee joint. The relative weakness which allegedly follows excision of a fragment is of slight concern to the elderly person compared to the advantage of early mobility.

Common Complications. There should be no common complications in the treatment of fracture of the patella in the aged if early restoration of motion and walking is made a paramount consideration. Phlebitis of the neighboring saphenous vein or its branches, or of the deeper veins, is of course always a threat. Recurrence of a primary hemarthrosis due to spontaneous rupture of a blood vessel near the articular cavity may occur and requires early aspiration if it threatens to disrupt the sutured capsule. Otherwise hemarthrosis in its milder manifestations may be treated with a few days' rest and a pressure dressing of elastic bandage over sheet wadding which should suffice to permit a resumption of assisted walking.

Aftercare. The aftercare of a fracture of the patella and its consequently torn aponeurosis in the aged patient requires gentle handling. The objective of this aftercare is to restore the ability to walk without a limp, to sit with the knee comfortably flexed, to gain enough flexion to permit putting on socks, stockings, and shoes. Full flexion in the aged

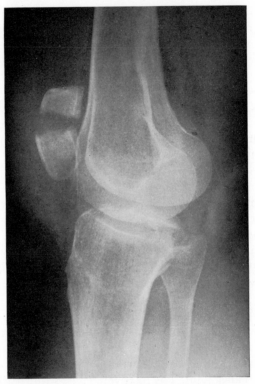

FIG. 6-9. This fracture in the elderly, with its wide diastasis between the fragments, is best treated by partial patellectomy, suture of the quadriceps tears, and early mobilization.

is seldom necessary and need not be forced. Flexion to a little more than 90° suffices for all the activities of the elderly person leading the life natural to his or her age. Extension is usually easily maintained if a severe osteoarthrosis with hypertrophic synovitis is not an accompanying lesion.

The attainment of this optimum may be assisted by light massage of the knee and leg. Flexion is encouraged by the force of gravity from a sitting position on a chair or table. Finally a graded degree of daily walking is to be urged, with constant encouragement to regain confidence in the stability of the fractured limb.

Prognosis. Prognosis following fracture of the patella in an aged person must be guarded. This trauma, even in its mildest form, involves joint surfaces and opens the synovial space to blood, pathologic fluid, and abnormal tissue reactions. Since a greater or lesser degree of degeneration is normally present in the articular cartilage of the aged skeleton, this traumatic lesion must of necessity aggravate the degenerative process in one way or another. The degree to which this takes place, or the post-trauma time at which this inexorably disabling tissue reaction becomes manifest, varies in each case. Unfortunately, except for a proper balance between rest and activity, nothing known will influence its progress. Eventually, if the elderly patient remains active long enough, treatment for this secondary reaction will be sought.

FEET

Incidence. Fractures of the feet occurred in only 0.7 per cent of a large series of fractures of the aged. Except as part of a major crushing injury of the foot, the bones of the tarsus in the aged are not particularly susceptible to fracture. The metatarsals and phalanges seem to divide the lesion rather equally.

Common Sources of Trauma. The two most common causes of this trauma among the aged are striking the toe against a piece of furniture, or an unguarded step from a curb or stair. Major falls will sooner fracture the ankle or tibial shafts in this age group. In the tarsus, fracture of the calcaneus is as usual the most common.

Clinical Diagnosis. Injury due to direct impact of the foot against a fixed or weighted object or incurred indirectly by the weight of the body on an unbalanced foot, with localized pain and tenderness, demands x-ray investigation before the diagnosis of sprain, contusion, or "phlebitis" can be validly entertained. It is quite possible to walk with pain on a foot in which one or several bones are fractured. It is unusual except in major crush fractures for any deformity other than diffuse swelling and often ecchymosis to be visible. This is particularly true in the aged where activity is normally restricted and where the body weight has become lessened. Ordinarily it is only by the location of the point of maximum tenderness that the site of fracture may be suspected.

One fracture too often missed because not commonly sought for in the x-ray film is that of the anterosuperior beak of the calcaneus. It is quite uncommon in the aged but does occur on occasion, and must be suspected particularly when tenderness is maximum over the common areas of sprain, the lateral and medial ligaments of the ankle joint. Just as fracture of the navicular must be sought in special views in protracted cases of suspected sprain of the wrist, fractures of the calcaneal beak must be sought by special views when "sprains" remain severely symptomatic in an aged person beyond the first week or so.

X-ray. If a fracture is present, it will ordinarily be self-evident in x-ray films of the foot taken from the dorsoplantar, oblique, and lateral views. However, unless one keeps fracture of the calcaneus or calcaneal beak especially in mind, this lesion may be missed in a casual inspection of the metatarsus and tarsus. A linear fracture through the atrophic body of the calcaneus in the aged may occur with little displacement in its early stage, but if ignored may present a considerable increase in osteoporosis and deformity after a period of painful weight bearing urged by the surgeon.

Treatment. *Tarsus.* Serious fractures of one or several bones of the tarsus at any age tend to develop some degree of permanent restriction of motion, from minor rigidity to complete ankylosis. Unless the fracture is an almost insignificant linear crack it will leave some degree of permanent pain or discomfort. The natural prevention of this is a periosseus ankylosis to the neighboring bones. Hence attempts at reduction which distract the fracture surfaces are more apt to cause greater and more prolonged disability even though the x-ray appearance is more gratifying to the surgeon. However, a lateral manual compression of a spread comminuted fracture of the calcaneus is quite in order both for its better and earlier healing and for its ability to fit more easily into an ordinary shoe.

Immobilization in a light plaster and the use of crutches or canes as early as tolerated with increased weight bearing as local sensitivity allows offer the best possibility for rapid recovery of function. Any compression of the talus or calcaneus during the process of ankylosis is immaterial to the functional end result for an aged person who only wishes to return to his or her customary way of life as soon as possible. When a plaster boot is used, a lightweight heel of the Stryker type serves to distribute the line of weight bearing and saves the plaster from contact with soiled and damp surfaces. The plaster may be required from 6 to 12 weeks, the time factor in an aged person resting entirely with the degree of pain on weight bearing.

In fractures of tarsal bones in the elderly individual, plaster immobilization is in fact a comfort rather than a necessity. Most of these fractures will not displace further after the initial trauma. If the elderly individual is still sufficiently agile to use crutches, plaster may be avoided altogether. A few days to a week of rest, with the foot elevated and analgesic local therapy such as cold packs, superficial massage, or restraining bandage until the acute phase of the trauma has subsided, will allow crutch walking at first without weight bearing and after 3 or 4 weeks with partial weight bearing. Weight bearing is to be encouraged as soon as it is tolerable. A cane used in the opposite hand may ease up to 50 per cent of the stress of weight bearing and should replace the crutches in 4 to 6 weeks.

Fractures of the metatarsus in the aged are ordinarily, except for pain, not major incidents. However, pain may be severe for a week or two. Simple adhesive strapping of the metatarsus, not circular, but leaving a slight opening between the ends of the strips, gives sufficient support to the metatarsal and associated ligaments during the early days (Fig. 6-10). This and either crutches or a cane for a short period will prove sufficient treatment for most cases. In 2 to 3 weeks, the patient should be walking fairly easily with a cane. At that time a simple leather foot support to maintain the weakened plantar ligaments often affords considerable comfort and may be procured inexpensively by size of footprint from any reputable surgical supply house. Unless there has been serious deformity from a crush fracture (see below) custom-made plates are not ordinarily required.

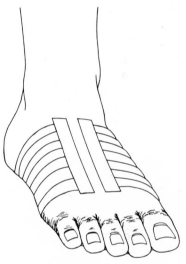

FIG. 6-10. Adhesive strapping for fractures of metatarsal bone.

Fractures of the *toes* in the aged when present as a single injury are treated lightly by taping the toe to its neighbor, with intervening cotton or other protection against skin maceration. The use of a large slipper or a shoe with the toecap cut out suffices for comfort. Usually the disabling pain lasts a few days, but the minor discomfort may last for some weeks.

Crush injuries of the foot (multiple injuries) vary as greatly in their seriousness in the elderly as they do in younger adults. In some cases the problem is chiefly the management of soft-tissue damage which may become a problem of impending gangrene when it includes the blood vessels. In other cases avulsion of the skin and subcutaneous tissues may require skin grafting.

The fracture element in these multiple foot injury cases is apt to be of secondary importance. When multiple fractures are present the special feature to be kept in mind in the aged is that early resumption of activity is relatively more important than is the restoration of the finer function or contours of the foot. Deformity of the foot immediately following a multiple fracture injury may often be sufficiently reduced by manual molding of the tarsus and arch, and if maintained adequately in a plaster boot will heal in a position satisfactory for weight bearing in 5 to 6 weeks.

In the elderly a degree of fibrous ankylosis between the bones of the tarsus and metatarsus is not always the disadvantage it might be to the more agile younger person. Widening of the heel or a prominence over the dorsum of the foot is not ordinarily conspicuous, and even if cosmetically annoying to the elderly lady, may be a lesser cause of complaint than a more prolonged period of disability. Walking plaster boots may sometimes be used as early as the third week, and their use if tolerated should be encouraged.

The chief complication of fractures of the foot in the aged is that of pressure sores due to a well-intentioned attempt to mold the plaster properly to the reduced fracture of the tarsus. Serious attention must be paid to early complaints of pain in the heel, over the lateral surface of the dorsum of the foot, or over the malleoli at the ankle. These are frequently the sites of pressure sores. If symptoms are relieved early, prolonged disability and even possible difficult plastic surgery may be avoided. In the event of pressure sores a new plaster boot is required, nothing less will do, since cutting a window is apt to permit local edema and further difficulty.

Posttraumatic osteodystrophy or osteoporosis does not seem to occur as often in fractures of the feet as it does in fractures about the ankle and wrist. When it does, it is a most unfortunate complication. Little may be done to influence its course, and disability may be truly prolonged (see above).

A complication of slight anatomic importance but of distressing symptomatic consequence occurs in the simple fracture of a phalanx. A slight displacement, especially near the base of a proximal fragment, may provoke a persistent disabling pain when the elderly person attempts to walk in a shoe. This is comparable to the small osteophyte often found at this site underlying the common so-called "soft corn." As minor as the matter may seem, leveling off this protuberance through a small lateral incision on the toe under local anesthesia may make all the difference between comfort in walking and a truly painful permanent disability in the elderly individual.

A further complication rather special in the elderly is worsening of the arterial circulation of the foot, and increase of the symptoms incident to angiosclerotic disease. In most elderly feet progressive peripheral hypovascularity is normal even though often quite asymptomatic. Even after a simple fracture, and particularly after a more severe one, the circulation, already below par, may be further embarrassed to the point of claudication or even persistent rest pain.

Aftercare. Healing of most fractures of the tarsus and metatarsus takes place in about 5 or 6 weeks. However, the extent to which each bone takes part in the axis of weight bearing varies, and therefore the time factor for complete nonweight bearing differs. Fracture of the calcaneus will require a longer period of protection than that of the metatarsus, and these in turn will require more than the phalanges.

In any case the healed fractured foot, because of the strain of weight bearing on the many weakened ligaments, will remain to some degree uncomfortable for weeks after bone healing is effected. The discomfort may become actual pain and be referred to the long plantar ligament, the heel, or the metatarsus. In the elderly person, following any fracture of the foot, the removal of plaster or adhesive strapping should be followed by the use of a leather insole containing a scaphoid pad and metatarsal pad. This often offers sufficient support and is more easily worn by the aged person than is a metal or other rigid support.

Prognosis. The simpler fractures of the metatarsals and phalanges and some of the less consequential cortical fractures of the tarsal bones may pass off after a few months without any permanent effects. Serious fractures of the tarsal bones and multiple fractures of the metatarsals may leave a variable degree of permanent pain or discomfort which may be only partly relieved by foot supports. The degree of final deformity cannot be related to the degree of disability in the elderly foot as it is in that of the younger adult, partly because of the fact that the aged foot is naturally less mobile and therefore its function is already adapted to a lesser range of motion. Deformity may also be a lesser disability in the aged because the elderly person is not required to be active and agile. These observations must be considered in estimating the disability of the aged foot and may be of a different order than such estimates in the younger adult.

RIBS

Incidence. Two per cent of fractures in the aged involve the ribs.

Common Sources of Trauma. In elderly patients ribs are fractured more easily than they are in the more elastic thoracic cage of younger adults. Many occurred as the result of relatively minor traumata, such as striking the chest against a dresser top or falling against a chair. Often enough, however, fractures of the rib are concurrent with severe injuries elsewhere. This fact is too frequently unappreciated and may work to the serious detriment of the victim.

Clinical Diagnosis. Fracture of the rib cage should rarely go unrecognized. Pain in any part of the thorax of an aged person following trauma must be considered a sign of a fractured rib until proved otherwise by painstaking x-ray studies. Pain in the chest with hemoptysis, bloody mucus with cough, or any difficulty in breathing following trauma strongly suggests fracture of the rib with injury to the pleura or lungs. Sullivan in Chap. 13 notes that if a patient goes into shock following trauma to the right lower thorax, with peritoneal spasm over the right upper quadrant, he may well have a fracture of the lower thoracic cage with rib puncture of the liver.

In the less severe injuries, the elderly person simply complains of localized pain and tenderness over the injured portion of the chest wall. Pain is increased by deep breathing, may be quite excruciating with coughing, and aggravated to some extent by any motion of the trunk. Local tenderness points to the site of injury. Classically, hand pressure bilaterally to the sides of the chest will indirectly provoke pain at the fracture site.

X-ray. Even in the virile young adult diagnosis of fracture of the rib may be difficult enough to strain the perspicacity of a keen observer. Unless there is gross displacement of the fragments, and this is quite uncommon, a simple fracture line somewhere between the vertebral articulation and the sternal or free end may be quite obscure among the many unrelated shadows of an adult chest. In the aged, x-ray diagnosis is far more difficult. The fracture line may be hidden among the ligamentous, periosteal, and intercostal calcifications of the elderly rib cage, behind the pulmonary, bronchial, or lymphatic calcific deposits, or confused by the irregularities of atrophy or osteoporosis of the bony thorax.

When clinical diagnosis suggests fracture of a rib, the ordinary anteroposterior view cannot be accepted as establishing a negative observation. Oblique views taken from the right and left must be examined. If all are negative but local signs persist, x-ray studies should be repeated in 5 or 6 days. Not infrequently a negative diagnosis made from a film taken at the time of injury becomes positive on the basis of later x-rays.

Treatment. When discussing the treatment of fractures of the rib in the aged a vital distinction must be made at the outset. Treatment of simple fracture without involvement of the pulmonary system, or more rarely puncture of the liver, is not a major procedure. In the presence of either of these complications on the other hand, a truly major catastrophe may be impending compared to which treatment of the fracture itself is a small consideration.

Uncomplicated fracture of the rib in the aged demands the treatment of local pain. This pain is important not only because of the discomfort it causes to the elderly victim, but because it is apt to decrease the depth of his inspiration for a number of days. In the aged this in itself is an invitation to hypostatic pneumonia, bronchitis, decreased oxygenation, and circulatory difficulty.

It is ordinarily unwise to apply adhesive strapping to the aged skin. Strapping must be maintained for 10 days to 2 weeks if it is to furnish effective comfort during the early stage of treatment. On the elderly patient a firm elastic rib belt will be far more comfortable, may be removed for purposes of cleanliness, and will give quite some support while allowing sufficient chest expansion for breathing (Fig. 6-11).

During the early acute stage, the injection of 1 or 2 ml of 1 per cent Novocain (*without epinephrine*) into or about the fracture site will often provide relief of pain for a period of time far greater than is accounted for by its anesthetic action, just as it does when used in sprains of the ligaments elsewhere. Sometimes in thin aged persons similar relief has been obtained by the silver-dollar technique of the ethyl chloride spray.

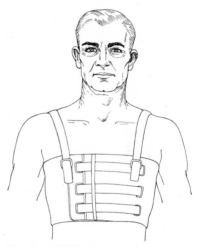

FIG. 6-11. Rib belt—canvas, linen, or elastic.

The patient must be kept as ambulatory as his physical circumstances permit. He must be made aware of the need for normal breathing, rather than permitted to cater to the local discomfort by persistent shallow breathing. Supportive therapy, proper food, and the stimulation of time spent in the open air are important adjuncts to his management.

The acute or severely painful stage ordinarily passes over between 5 and 15 days postfracture. As soon as possible the rib belt is removed, at first for short intervals of an hour or two. These intervals are increased as his tolerance permits. It is well to warn the patient that although his severe pain will abate shortly, a period of local discomfort is apt to last 5 to 6 weeks or more. Such advance warning serves as assurance against the fear of lasting symptoms. During this period simple analgesics such as the salicylates and their nonnarcotic compounds are most useful. The rib belt still may be worn during the more troublesome hours.

Complications. Complicated fractures of the ribs call for the major consideration of the thoracic surgeon (see Chap. 14), the abdominal surgeon (Chap. 13), or in the event of multiple injuries, a surgical team prepared for impending human catastrophe. Pulmonary involvement varies in severity from a persistent, annoying pleurodynia to massive laceration of the lung.

Aftercare. In the uncomplicated fracture of the rib aftercare entails merely the use of proper analgesics and, above all, reassurance.

OPEN (COMPOUND) FRACTURES

Open fractures in the aged present a problem of serious consequence above that of similar trauma in the younger age group. There is no evidence to substantiate an impression that the aged are more susceptible to infection following trauma than are individuals of a younger age group, but all experience is evidence of the fact that when infection does appear it is far more difficult for the aging body to counteract it. For this reason above all others open fractures in the aged require the utmost in meticulous care.

It is not enough to depend on the general cover of a broad-spectrum antibiotic at the onset. The wound must be most carefully attended to, dressed, debrided if there is any question of contamination, and watched assiduously. If any infection appears, sensitivity tests should direct the proper antibiotic.

It has been emphasized in previous sections of this chapter that treatment with a light rein, even at the cost of some sacrifice of anatomic perfection, leading to the earliest possible resumption of function is the primary rule in all fractures in the aged. Insofar as anatomic perfection is concerned this is equally valid in open fractures. However, infection or the threat of infection requires the tightest rein and may not be neglected with impunity. The decreased vascularity of peripheral aged bone and the generality of some degree of venous stasis materially decrease the power of resistance to bone infection. Peripheral infection in the aged is a permanent invitation to further vascular impairment, and presents the awful threat of gangrene. In spite of a disinclination to immobilize the elderly individual, this risk is the lesser evil in the presence of an open fracture until the wound is healed and the threat of infection has passed.

Delayed primary closure, used by Blake and his colleagues in World War I, completely forgotten for 25 years and redeveloped in the second half of World War II, is most applicable to the wounds of open fractures in the aged. Following debridement, the wound may be left open for 3 to 6 days under intensive antibiotic treatment until it is reasonably certain that infection has been controlled. At that time, under meticulous surgical technique, the wound may be sutured and the fracture treated as a closed one.

If the wound of the open fracture is an avulsed or denuded one, a few days of intensive antibiotic control should be followed by an early "dressing" with a split-thickness graft. This is what was meant by the once popular phrase of "making a closed fracture out of an open one." The fact that secondary skin grafting may be required at a later date to cover the areas of no-take is inconsequential compared to the advantages of early covering.

There is but one principle in the care of open fractures in any age group: avoid infection and thereafter close the wound at the earliest opportunity in order to prevent later infection or reinfection. In the younger adult this may be done after allowing for some freedom of action in reducing the fracture by surgical means. In the aged, less freedom of action is permissible because the risk is greater. Infection of soft tissues and especially of bone in the aged is not only more difficult to control, but persists for a longer period and invites vascular complications which may be irreversible.

A radical approach to open fractures of the aged puts the burden of defense on the surgeon. There is not so much time left for the elderly to recover from the prolonged effects of infection protracted or induced by metallic fixation. As in so many other surgical situations an occassional brilliant success may follow a *tour de force,* but does not excuse the tragedies which unfortunately usually remain unreported. A conservative approach, even at the expense of time, will more often prove the shorter path to recovery in open fractures in the aged.

PATHOLOGIC FRACTURES

A fairly large variety of pathologic lesions may invade the skeletal apparatus and, with a few exceptions confined to early childhood, most may be found in the aged. Their study belongs to the realm of bone pathology. In exceptional cases any of these lesions may be found to be the site of fracture. The problem of pathologic fractures in the aged resolves itself into two general categories, (1) fractures through any part of a bone in an osteoporotic or atrophic state, and (2) fracture through a local lesion which by its presence weakens the bone at that site. The latter category in the aged refers in over 90 per cent of the cases to metastatic carcinoma, myeloma, or Paget's disease. Other pathologic lesions are quite uncommon, but the problem of their management does not differ from those listed.

The literature on pathologic fractures is not rich at best and is particularly poor in case studies of the rate of healing. Of the several reports published, none are specifically concerned with the aged, and few even discuss them. However pathologic fractures through sites of metastatic carcinoma and multiple myeloma occur often enough in this present decade of an increasing older population to warrant greater attention than has been given to the subject.

1. Fracture through osteoporotic or atrophic bone is only pathologic by definition of fracture occurring in weakened bone. It was noted in

Chap. 4 that the healing point of these fractures is not perceptibly re-tarded but remains within the range of normal healing. However, the healing callus is composed of the same type of faulty trabeculae as are present in the rest of the bone. Treatment of these fractures requires no procedures or judgments other than those discussed in previous sections of this chapter for the respective individual fractures. In fact, since it has been stated that all aged bone is to some extent atrophic or porotic, the inclusion of this subject again under the heading of pathologic frac-tures is merely a matter of recognition.

2. Paget's disease. Fractures in Paget's disease are of two kinds. The first, which may not be uncommon if searched for, is the partial fracture through thickened, friable cortex in the early stages of the disease. Such fractures, due to intraosseous trabecular weakness, are comparable if not similar to the fatigue fractures of other syndromes. These cause local pain, and will heal without special treatment. However, moderate protection must be given the limb to prevent extension, and the possibility of similar cracks elsewhere in the bone must be kept in mind. A few weeks of bracing or plaster cast will usually suffice, and weight bearing in the ap-paratus may be permitted. It is even possible, though as yet not demon-strable, that weight bearing in these cases should be encouraged.

The second type of fracture occurring in Paget's disease is complete, and more often than not, transversely through a shaft. Oblique fractures through the neck or trochanteric region of the femur are also not un-common. These fractures all heal, and heal in normal time. Bloodgood many years ago remarked that nonunion of a fracture in Paget's disease suggests sarcoma. However, again the reparative bone is Paget's bone and the healed bone will not be stronger than the original one.

Treatment of fractures through Paget's osteitis should be nonoperative in the early stages of the disease when the bone is hemorrhagic and rela-tively friable. In later stages, it is frequently found to be all but impos-sible to introduce screws through the hard bone. Before attempting to insert an intramedullary nail, the encroachment of the disease on the medullary canal must be considered. If it is feasible to insert an intra-medullary nail in the femoral canal, this is more effective than it would be in the softened atrophic bone normally found in the aged; but one must proceed with caution. For the most part all fractures in Paget's disease are most dependably treated by closed methods.

3. Pathologic fractures through the two common localized lesions of the aged skeleton, metastatic carcinoma and multiple myeloma, present similar problems in therapy. Healing in these fractures is quite unde-pendable. Reparative osteogenesis can only come from the residual viable bone about these osteolytic lesions and what is produced is subject to destruction by the progressing neoplastic lesion.

It is in these and the other less frequent osteolytic lesions of aged bone that fracture is most suitably treated by the intramedullary nail. If the nail had no other use, its invention would be a major contribution to bone surgery for this application alone. A limb can be made reasonably useful after fracture through a neoplastic area by the stabilizing intramedullary nail, even in the absence of healing. The elderly patient can walk at least to some degree on an ununited femur or tibia maintained by the nail. It is true that eventually, in the state of nonunion, the nail will meander, due to torsion or a "pumping" movement at the fracture site, or may itself break at the point of maximum strain. But this takes time, and in the presence of metastatic carcinoma, hypernephroma, myeloma, or similar diseases, especially in the aged, often the nail outlasts the prognosis.

It is of course self-evident that aside from the treatment of the fracture the local lesion may receive whatever palliative treatment is otherwise deemed most suitable.

BIBLIOGRAPHY

Bick, E. M.: General principles of fracture management in the aged. *Surg. Gyn. and Obst.* **106**:343, 1958.

Bick, E. M.: Clinical aspects of aging connective tissues. *Bull. N.Y. Acad. Med.* **35**:547, 1959.

Bick, E. M.: Fractures of the tibial condyles. *Jour. Bone and Joint Surg.* **23**:102, 1941.

Bick, E. M.: Healing of fractures. *Amer. Jour. Surg.* **80**:843, 1950.

Bick, E. M.: Structural patterns of callus in fractures of the long bones. *Jour. Bone and Joint Surg.* **30A**:141, 1948.

Böhler, L.: "Technic der Knochenbruchen Behandlung." Engl. transl. 13th German ed. by O. Russe and R. B. G. Bjornson. Bristol, England, John Wright and Sons, Ltd., 1957.

Cave, E. F.: "Fractures and Other Injuries." Chicago, Year Book Publishers, 1958.

Key, J. A., and L. T. Ford: Compression and extension fractures at the wrist. *Geriatrics.* **10**:17, 1955.

Key, J. A., and H. E. Conwell: "Management of Fractures, Dislocations and Sprains," 6th ed., St. Louis, Mosby, 1956.

Lippmann, R. K.: The use of auscultatory percussion for the examination of fractures. *Jour. Bone and Joint Surg.* **14**:118, 1932.

Nicholson, J. T.: Compound comminuted fractures involving the elbow joint. Treatment by resection of the fragments. *Jour. Bone and Joint Surg.* **28**:565, 1946.

O'Brien, R. M.: Treatment of fractures of the surgical neck of the humerus. *Geriatrics.* **9**:406, 1954.

Rowe, C. R., and R. C. Detwiler: Fractures of the aged. *Jour. Amer. Med. Ass.* **162**:1517, 1956.

Wade, P. A.: "Trauma in Orthopaedic Surgery." New York, Grune & Stratton, 1960.

Wade, P. A., and A. J. Okinaka: The problem of the supracondylar fracture of the femur in the aged person. *Amer. Jour. Surg.* **97**:499, 1959.

Watson-Jones, R.: "Fractures and Joint Injuries," 4th ed. Baltimore, Williams & Wilkins, 1952.

Pathologic Fractures

Altman, H.: Intramedullary nailing for pathological impending and actual fractures of the long bones. *Bull. Hosp. Joint Dis.* **13**:239, 1952.

Bick, E. M.: Management of pathologic fractures. *Surg. Gyn. and Obs.* **69**:524, 1939.

Bloodgood, J. C.: In Scudder's "Treatment of Fractures." Philadelphia, Saunders, 1926.

Cave, E. F.: Medullary nails in pathological conditions of the femur. *Amer. Acad. Orth. Surg. Instructional Course Lectures.* **8**:46, 1951.

Fitts, W. T., Jr., B. Roberts, and I. S. Ravdin: Fractures in metastatic carcinoma. *Amer. Jour. Surg.* **85**:282, 1953.

Geschichter, C. F., and M. M. Copeland: Tumors of bone. *N.Y. Amer. Jour. Cancer.* 3d ed. 1949.

Goisman, J., and E. L. Compere: Healing of fractures of atrophic bone. *Jour. Bone and Joint Surg.* **20**:587, 1938.

Jaffe, H., and L. Lichtenstein: "Bone Tumors." St. Louis, Mosby, 1952.

Rogers, M. H., and R. Ulin: Fractures in Paget's disease. *Jour. Bone and Joint Surg.* **18**:914, 1936.

Chapter 7

Fractures of the Vertebrae

Edgar M. Bick

Fractures of the vertebrae represent a group of traumatic lesions which have in common only their anatomic location in the spinal column. Under this heading are some cases so inconsequential that the aged patient would be better off emotionally and physically if he were not aware of the diagnosis. Other cases are all but irreversibly fatal. Between these two extremes there exists the very much larger group of fractures that are not fatal but do condition in the elderly patient persistent discomfort of variable degree, due in part to the direct effect of the fracture and in part to the decompensation of the balances which nature often has effected in the aged spine beset with osteoarthritic, osteoporotic, osteophytic, and disc degenerations.

In discussing the care of fractures of the vertebrae several distinctions must be made immediately since prognosis and treatment differ greatly in different circumstances.

1. Type of fracture (Fig. 7-1)
   a. Fractures of the vertebral body: wedge, central, anterosuperior margin, fracture dislocation
   b. Fractures of the neural arch
   c. Fractures of the vertebral appendages: transverse and spinous processes
2. Location of fracture
   a. Cervical: with special reference to atlas and odontoid process
   b. Dorsolumbar
   c. Sacrococcygeal
3. Lesion
   a. Traumatic
   b. Spontaneous osteoporotic compression (common in the aged spine)
   c. Pathologic: chiefly metastatic carcinoma or multiple myeloma

It was remarked in Chap. 6 that there were no special techniques in the therapy of fractures in the aged, but there were limitations of treatment tolerance and limitations of response to the lesion and to its treat-

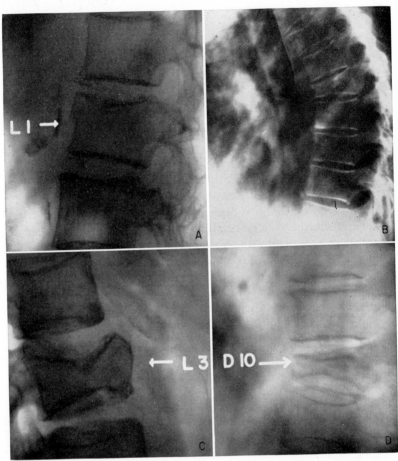

FIG. 7-1. Common types of fractures of the vertebrae in the aged. *A*. Anterior superior rim. *B*. Wedge compression. Degree of final compression probably not influenced by treatment. *C*. Central fracture. Relatively unstable. Requires at least moderate back support and is apt to lead to *D*, vertebra plana, the result of avascular necrosis.

ment (Fig. 7-2). In dealing with fractures of the spine in the elderly patient these limitations must be kept in mind if the surgeon wishes to do his best for the patient rather than merely to exhibit a *tour de force*. Between 1930 and 1950, many unfortunate elderly victims suffered unnecessarily from the extreme discomfort of the hyperextension maneuvers and plasters which were fashionable before it was realized that the more or less rigid aged vertebral column with its softened bone and inelastic ligaments could not properly withstand the strain of these procedures. Furthermore, in view of the usually concurrent degenerative changes, more of the adjacent vertebral areas were painfully deranged than the expected correction of the compression could possibly compensate for.

It is therefore necessary to bear in mind certain general limitations when undertaking treatment of fractures in the aging spine. These of course supplement rather than replace the precautions ordinarily recognized in vertebral fractures of all ages. First, the lack of resiliency in the aged vertebral column must be recalled. Because of their relative inelasticity, the vertebral and paravertebral ligaments resist much of the manipulative correction possible in the younger adult. In the presence of any degree of osteoporosis, manipulation may cause painful damage to adjacent or even distant vertebral bodies. Secondly, prolonged bed rest or plaster immobilization is contraindicated in these cases, since either increases the degree of bone atrophy or osteoporosis and so in itself invites spontaneous compression of other vertebrae.

FIG. 7-2. Apertures for cortical (subperiosteal) vascular network—concentrated at upper half of vertebral body. Compression damage here leads inevitably to postfracture necrosis and vertebral wedging or collapse.

TRAUMATIC FRACTURES OF THE CERVICAL SPINE

Incidence. Fractures are found much less commonly in the cervical than in the dorsolumbar spine of the elderly patient. Occasionally compression of the vertebral bodies appears adjacent to obviously atrophied disc substance. Often enough a small degree of forward displacement of a midcervical vertebra over its inferior neighbor suggests a fracture dislocation with dissolution of the neural arch. Such x-ray appearances will be found far more often to be residual deformities of old compressions, related to atrophy of the intervertebral disc and its annulus and associated with symptoms of strain of the posterior interspinous ligaments. In the aged cervical spine, only the passage of time will distinguish evidence of its progressive compression over a period of several weeks. In one series of 50 specifically traumatic lesions of the spine in patients over 60, no demonstrable instance of compression fracture of the vertebral bodies or fractures of the neural arch occurred in the cervical spine. Two cases of fatal fracture dislocation were recorded aside from this series in instances of severe multiple lesions. However Grogono reported eight cases of atlanto-axial injuries of which two occurred in females aged 69 and 79. In his experience it was usually not fatal and a simple cervical collar sufficed for treatment. Fractures of the spinous processes have not been observed, probably because the type of activity which leads to so-called "shoveler's fracture" is not ordinarily practiced in this period of life. Furthermore even if such activity were practiced the spinal musculature would hardly be powerful enough to avulse the spinous process.

Common Sources of Trauma. The two types of trauma most related to fractures of the cervical spine in the elderly patient are the so-called "whip-lash injuries" of automobile or other vehicular accidents, and falls from rather high places. (A third common trauma causing such fractures in a younger group arises from diving into relatively shallow water. This is not a sport generally indulged in by elderly ladies or gentlemen.) In the vehicular collision or short stop, the fracture, if it occurs, is to be looked for in the vertebral body, in the odontoid process, or as a fracture dislocation with the fracture site near the intervertebral articulation or in the posterior neural arch. In a suspected case, multiple x-rays may be required to confirm the diagnosis.

To refer to these fractures as extension or flexion fractures is of interest in the study of their mechanism, but is a rather futile exercise in the actual case. In any given instance both acute flexion and extension are apt to occur, one by direct reaction to the force of impact and the other by recoil. Of course in the unusual circumstances of an elderly person having been punched in the chin, an extension fracture may be recorded. The distinction between flexion and extension fractures may be said to be of academic interest in the aged.

Clinical Diagnosis. Injury to the cervical spine is manifested chiefly by pain. The pain at the onset may be in the neck, but often is felt more severely as a radiation over the shoulder girdle or down the upper extremities along the nerves of the brachial plexus. In other instances the predominant pain may be occipital due to involvement of the upper roots of the cervical plexus. Often enough an incipient pain in the neck subsides leaving the radiating pain as the residual symptom. Occasionally, if the lower elements of the brachial plexus are involved, the pain may be felt in the upper thorax, at times even simulating anginal symptoms.

At the onset, a reflex protective muscle spasm may cause some degree of rigidity of the neck. This symptom is apt to subside in a few days to the point where partial mobility of the neck is possible before pain provokes its resistance. Local tenderness is all but invariable in the presence of fracture when the back of the neck is subject to the examiner's finger pressure. At times a unilateral diminution of the biceps tendon reflex may be found.

A week or so after the injury, a false lead is often suggested by the presenting complaint of pain and stiffening in the shoulder, usually but not invariably unilateral. It may appear to be the result of an incidental injury to this joint unrecognized at the time of accident. This of course may be so. However, it is quite apt to be the result of a secondary "freezing" of the shoulder due to the recent painful immobility of the tight muscles of the shoulder girdle. As local symptoms at the neck lessen, those at the shoulder often increase.

All of the above clinical manifestations are equally apt to appear without fracture in an aged cervical spine already subject to preceding degenerative processes. Osteoarthrosis, disc collapse, or osteophytosis aggravated by simple traumatic sprain of its interspinous or paravertebral ligaments, may easily simulate the symptoms of fracture. The distinction between sprains and fractures in these senile vertebrae may be most difficult. In a courtroom, evidence of osteoporotic compression, compression of soft vertebral bone adjacent to atrophic discs, and traumatic compression fracture may be most difficult to differentiate factually. The evidence is often, and with complete integrity, based on one's interpretation of the medical and traumatic history of the case.

A major fracture dislocation of the cervical spine in the aged patient may of course be a most serious injury. If it occurs without cord damage, the symptoms do not differ materially from the simpler fractures. If the spinal cord has been damaged, the paralysis is clinically identical to that found in younger age groups.

X-ray Diagnosis. Injury of any type to the cervical spine or its paravertebral tissues is apt to be manifested on the x-ray film as a loss of its normal anteroposterior curve. This is an effect of the reflex protective muscle spasm with the flexor group acting more forcefully than the extensor. In itself it indicates only a reaction to trauma or other irritating stimulus. The difference between previous spontaneous anterior wedging in osteoporotic vertebrae adjacent to the unequal intervertebral spaces of collapse or atrophy of disc material and a recent compression wedge due to a flexion injury or a flexion recoil from an extension injury is far more often than not a matter of medical opinion than of diagnostic fact. Of course, the existence of a recent pretraumatic x-ray film showing normal structure is the perfect evidence, but this is not ordinarily available. A minor "spondylolisthesis" in an aged cervical spine is more apt to be an anteroposterior displacement of a vertebra adjusting to the imbalance of a disc lesion than to an intervertebral traumatic luxation. The normal degenerative processes associated with the articulation of aged vertebrae make fine distinction difficult. In the case of vertebral body compression, it is often possible to determine the difference between the effect of recent trauma and preceding spontaneous compression by successive x-rays over a period of weeks. A recent traumatic lesion is far more apt to show progressive collapse of the body than is the older lesion. Another mark of duration in a vertebral compression in the elderly cervical spine, as compared to a recent and possibly traumatic compression, is the visible presence of fully developed osteophytes emanating from the adjacent longitudinal ligaments at their insertions into the

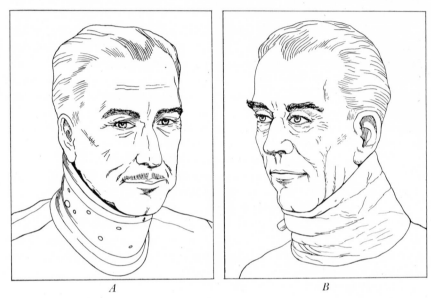

A B

Fig. 7-3. *A*. Plastic-type Thomas collar. *B*. Soft Lewin collar.

vertebral rims. Although minimal osteophytosis may appear in a matter of weeks, fully developed specimens require months to develop.

Treatment. In the cervical spine the common fracture involves the vertebral body, and more often than not, includes compression injury of the intervertebral disc tissues. In the early treatment of such cases in the elderly patient, a cervical collar of the Thomas type often gives considerable comfort, aided by properly prescribed analgesics. With these the patient can be kept ambulatory as soon as the immediate reaction to trauma is over. Adequate cervical collars of leather or plastics are easily available from surgical supply agencies (Fig. 7-3*A*). They are sold in several sizes and rarely need to be made to measure. The aged patient seldom, if ever, needs the four-poster cervical brace, and ordinarily is unable to tolerate its pressure on the sternoclavicular or occipital areas.

If pain persists in spite of the protective collar and analgesic medication, traction devices may be used, though here too the elderly patient may find even the least effective weight intolerable for any significant period of time. However, the type of simple portable traction apparatus distributed by surgical equipment dealers for use in the home is often helpful when employed as "intermittent" traction. This may be applied from a sitting position for periods of 15 to 30 minutes three or four times daily for relief of pain, along with the collar. With this apparatus, weights of 10 to 20 lb are found most acceptable. Traction used in this way is of course palliative and is not intended as a reduction method.

The inelasticity of the paravertebral ligaments and the frequent partial rigidity of osteoarthritic intervertebral joints tend to make these vertebral body fractures of the cervical spine less troublesome and less threatening in the elderly patient than in the. younger adult. It is difficult to estimate how long the collar should be worn. In some cases 4 to 6 weeks of constant use is adequate, allowing for the development of intervertebral fixation to a point where the lighter Lewin padded linen collar is sufficient (Fig. 7-3B). In other instances, the Thomas collar must be worn for a much longer period, even up to 3 or 6 months, more for the comfort it allows than for any effect on the healing of the fracture.

In most cases of vertebral body fractures in the elderly patient the compression will heal itself; nothing that one can do will influence the developing atrophy of the disc tissues or the final degree of avascular necrosis about the fracture lines in the vertebral body. Therefore, treatment is above all palliative. Collars, intermittent traction, analgesic medication, and perhaps the soothing effect of local physical therapy form the therapeutic armamentarium from which the surgeon must choose at his discretion.

A severe fracture dislocation of the cervical spine in the aged individual carries the same threat to life and neuromotive power that such an injury would at any age. The danger is greater in the aged since the tissues of the older patient may not tolerate or respond to the manipulations or powerful skeletal tractions required for reduction. Manual reduction under anesthesia, skeletal traction in bed, or even open reduction of the fracture may of course be attempted as daring measures to be justified only by the belief that they will be lifesaving. On the other hand cases have been seen some time after injury, in which, with rather amazing alacrity and without attempts at reduction, the local osseous tissues have thrown out protective osteophytes which stabilized the displaced fragments in positions which, though quite frightening when viewed on x-ray films, were adequate enough to relieve symptoms and restore an effective stability to the cervical spine (Fig. 7-4A).

If the fracture dislocation is severe enough to have caused cord paralysis in an elderly individual, reduction must of course be attempted. However if the possibility of restoration of function in such cases is questionable in the younger adult it is even less promising in the elderly. Whether sur-

gical intervention is justified or not must remain the decision of the responsible surgeon and must depend solely on his interpretation of the
pathology of the lesion. If he has reason to believe that the paralysis
is due to the pressure of a fracture fragment of the neural arch, or to
angulation of the cord over the posterior surface of the vertebral body,
laminectomy and decompression is of course indicated as a calculated risk.

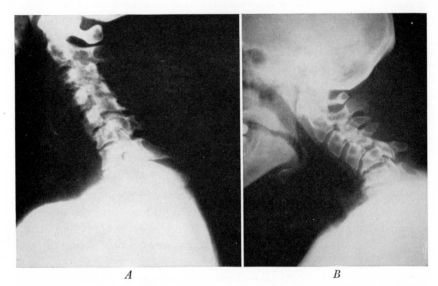

A   *B*

FIG. 7-4. *A*. Female, age 61. Spontaneous stability by osteophytes 3 months following fracture dislocation cervical spine. Mildly symptomatic recurrently 9 years
later. *B*. Male, age 62. Fracture dislocation—cervical spine. Paresis appeared first
10 months after injury. Laminectomy and fusion at 11 months with relief. This
was exceptional among the aged. Ordinarily spontaneous stability of osteophytes
suffices.

The question of intervertebral fusion after cervical fractures in the
elderly is again a question of life expectancy. In the physiologically
younger old person, whose tissues are still resilient to a significant degree,
fusion may be attempted if pain has persisted unrelieved by nonoperative
procedures. However, since most aged spines are characterized by decreased intervertebral mobility, instances in which fusion may be justified
must be rare indeed.

Isolated single or multiple fracture of the spinous processes of the
cervical vertebrae in the elderly is rare, and when present should be
treated with reassurance, a light Lewin or Schanz type collar, local physical therapy, analgesics, rest, and patience. It is in fact a quite inconsequential injury to be treated with palliation. However, because such injuries must of necessity involve the vertebral ligaments, the prognosis in

the aged as far as pain is concerned must be guarded. Persistent sprain of these ligaments may be in itself cause for all but permanent discomfort.

Common Complications. Persistent pain emanating from adjacent segments of the cervicodorsal and even dorsolumbar spine is the most frequent complication of fractures of the cervical spine in the elderly patient. If the aged vertebral column had been asymptomatic before the accident it may be considered to have been in a state of "pathologic balance." A certain degree of rigidity had been occasioned by osteophytic outgrowth in the paravertebral ligaments, and perhaps by ankylosis in the intervertebral articulation as the result of osteoarthrotic degeneration. In a significant percentage of cases pretraumatic spontaneous compression of one or more vertebrae of the dorsolumbar spine have come into functional balance and have been quite unnoticed. The trauma which caused the fracture of the cervical spine also jolted, or at least put stresses on, the rest of the column, particularly the upper dorsal and lower lumbar area, and long after the cervical vertebra is "healed," the disruption of the other parts of the spine may remain as the cause of constant or recurrent symptoms.

The complication of late paresis following fracture or fracture dislocation of the cervical spine, not unusual in the younger adult, is seldom met with in the elder. This may be partly because of the inelastic supportive connective tissues, the decreased spring of the intervertebral discs, or the lessened physical activity and muscle pull of the older age group. When such progressive weakness does occur, renewed use of the supportive collar and palliative physical measures are again called upon. In the rare instances of progressive paresis in spite of supportive apparatus, surgical intervention must of course be considered (Fig. 7-4*B*).

Headache, usually occipital, remains, in the aged patient as it does in the younger, one of the most intransigent of symptoms or complications. It is a common experience to enjoy the pleasure of having an elderly patient quite recovered from fracture of the cervical spine in all respects and then to be dismayed by the uncontrollable persistence of occipital and/or temporal pain. This complication seldom if ever responds to therapy when it persists beyond the first few weeks, and only time, in terms of months or even several years, assisted by analgesic medication, seems to have any influence. Headache of this type must not be confused with pain involving the frontal portion of the skull, which is more apt to be the result of a concurrent concussion.

Aftercare. The aftercare of the simple compression fractures of the cervical spine in the aged is almost indistinguishable from its early care. As time allows for compensatory adjustments, simple analgesic medication is often sufficient. When symptoms reappear, the collar or therapeutic measures are resumed for a while until relief is obtained. Home therapeutic measures ordinarily suffice, and the elderly patient or his family should be instructed in the proper use of the collar and traction, and in the application of local heat.

Prognosis. The prognosis of a severe fracture or fracture dislocation of the cervical spine causing paralysis by cord pressure or cord rupture is all but fatal in the aged, though life may be protracted for a while. The elderly individual, with his decreased physiological resiliency, is not apt to withstand this type of catastrophic lesion. In fractures not involving the cord, prognosis as to life is of course very much better. However, considering the pathology of the aged spine, some variable degree of persistent or recurrent pain will most likely be permanent. Its intensity will vary from time to time. It may be local about the neck, or radiate into any of the nerve distributions emanating from the cervical or brachial plexus. Pain in or from other parts of the vertebral column may persist as a result of the accompanying indirect damage at those levels (see below). The elderly patient who makes a completely asymptomatic recovery from fracture of the cervical spine either possesses an unusually high threshold of pain or is a very brave and uncomplaining individual.

Fracture of the Atlas and Axis (C1 and C2)

Fractures of the atlas or axis in the elderly patient are apt either to go unrecognized or to be catastrophic. In several large institutions consulted, none were recorded in the age group over 60. Their rarity is due to the fact that individuals of this group do not ordinarily engage in activities which lead to falling from great heights. However, Watson-Jones speaks of a hyperextension fracture dislocation of the atlas and odontoid in which reduction was effected and a plaster cast applied, "but the patient was elderly and querulous" and within a few days the plaster was removed and a collar applied. It is to be assumed that the querulousness subsided with his lessened discomfort after the plaster was removed.

Fractures of the atlas and axis not involving the cord are treated as are other cervical fractures in the aged, with the rest and immobilization afforded by a collar or intermittent traction. The patient need not be bedridden after recovering from the reaction to the trauma. When the dislocated atlas carries the odontoid, union will usually occur in the displaced position if the fracture is not immediately catastrophic. The late stage secondary effects which one might anticipate in the younger adult either will not appear in the elderly or, if they do, will appear as one of the discomforts attending the aging posttraumatic spine. In these cases, collar protection should be urged, if tolerated, for 10 to 12 weeks. The few cases of this lesion on record were either catastrophic or, if not immediately so, seem to have done well with simple protection. No case is known to the writer either by personal experience or by reference in which a secondary or late stage paresis developed following primary escape of the cord.

Fracture of the Dorsolumbar Spine

Incidence. Traumatic fracture of the vertebral bodies of the dorsolumbar spine is a common injury in persons over 60 years of age. It will be noted in the table of fractures in Chap. 6 that such an injury is the third most common of all fractures in this elderly group. If one includes pathologic fractures, vertebral fractures might well lead the list. This frequency of traumatic fracture of the vertebral body is of course related to the fact that bone atrophy or osteoporosis is generally found to be more advanced in the spinal column than elsewhere in the aging skeleton.

In a published series of traumatic fractures in this age group, more than half occurred between the eleventh thoracic and second lumbar vertebrae inclusive, and more than half of the remainder within a vertebra or so of these. It is evident that in the aged, the spinal segment most subject to fracture (as in the lower adult age groups) is at or near the lumbo-dorsal junction where a relatively rigid column joins a rather freely movable one.

Common Sources of Trauma. By far the most common cause of fracture in the vertebral bodies of aging spines is a simple fall to the ground, either at home or on a paved street. Next in order is the strain of attempting to lift a weighted object from the flexed position (more often a causative factor in the elderly than in the younger adult). Shock therapy seems to account for an increasing percentage of these cases. Accidents occurring while riding in moving vehicles, automobiles, trains, etc., also account for a significant number of these lesions.

It must be emphasized that relatively minor impacts are far more apt to cause fracture in the vertebral body of an aged person than in a younger person. No elderly individual subject to such trauma, no matter how insignificant it may seem to be, should be permitted to leave medical supervision without an x-ray of the painful segment of the vertebral column.

Clinical Diagnosis. The clinical diagnosis of a simple fracture of the vertebral body is suggested by pain and local tenderness. Both of these may vary in intensity in the beginning from slight and transient to very severe. If the cord is involved, the usual neurological evidence will be manifest. At times a minor transient paresis, which may be due to a slight contusion or impact of the cord on the walls of the canal, appears immediately following the injury. A minor fracture may give such slight local evidence as to tempt the examiner to pass the case off as a "strain of the back." A severe fracture dislocation may produce permanent damage to the cord, usually fatal in the elderly, or a transient paresis which subsides with rest, whether or not the dislocation has been reduced.

Fractures of the neural arch cannot be clinically distinguished from those of the vertebral body. They present the same greater or lesser degree of pain and local tenderness and appear with or without neurological manifestations. Fractures of the transverse processes may be suspected by the usually highly localized site of tenderness, but one may not with impunity depend on this clinical finding without x-ray investigation.

In each of the above fracture types a variable degree of lumbodorsal protective muscle spasm will be noticed by the examiner. The degree of muscle spasm in the elderly patient is not ordinarily an indication of the extent of trauma since the intensity of the so-called "protective spasm" will be conditioned by the underlying freedom or rigidity of the aged spine itself. A fairly rigid spine produced by years of osteoarthrosis, osteophytosis, and disc-space collapse requires little in the way of protective muscle spasm to maintain itself against painful motion.

The chief considerations in making a clinical diagnosis of fracture of the vertebral body in the aged, are the nature of the injury, the presence of pain in some part of the back following the accident, and the susceptibility of the aged spine to such fracture as the result of even minor trauma.

X-ray. The x-ray film, anteroposterior and lateral, is of course the deciding source of diagnosis in these cases, but may at times be difficult to interpret. The film will disclose three common characteristic types of fracture of the vertebral body.

1. The "wedge" type follows a flexion injury in which there has been compression of the anterior portion of the vertebral body, causing the formation of a rhomboid appearance in the lateral view rather than the normal rectangular.

2. In the anterosuperior "flush" type a portion of this area of the vertebral body has been broken off from the main mass and usually remains slightly displaced.

3. The central compression fracture occurs when the force has been exerted in the center of the superior surface of the body causing a greater or lesser degree of comminution. This type is most apt to lead to the severe flattening or avascular necrosis of the Kümmell lesion of the older literature.

Treatment. No mention has been made so far of the distinction between stable and unstable fractures of the vertebrae in the aged. In the youthful or young adult spine, treatment is controlled to a considerable extent by this factor. In the aging spine this factor is less often of consequence for several reasons. The relative inelasticity of the paravertebral ligaments, the lessened mobility of the intervertebral articulations, and the frequent occurrence of osteophytic stabilization between several or more intervertebral bodies offer a degree of stability not found in the younger adult group. However in occasional severe cases such instability is found and must be cared for.

The so-called "unstable" fracture of the vertebral body is one that permits immediate or latent injury to the cord by displacement of one vertebral segment across the other. This implies dissolution of the continuity of some portion of the intervertebral articulations, or the pedicles upon which their surfaces rest, or a serious tear of the otherwise powerful paravertebral ligaments which, along with the articulations, hold the bodies in their proper positions. More often than not, such instances are associated with severe comminution and the central type of fracture described. Of course a complete fracture dislocation is the unstable fracture having the most dreaded consequences. Whether the patient is young or old, such unstable fractures require external immobilization by plaster casts or braces, and in extreme cases by surgical reduction. Spine fusion may sometimes be necessary. Fortunately such instability following fracture is relatively infrequent at all ages compared to the occurrence of the stable fracture; in the aged they are quite rare.

The common fracture of the vertebral body in the elderly person is a stable fracture which may and should be treated with a "light rein." A few days to a week of unrestrained bed rest is ordinarily sufficient to permit the patient to recover from whatever systemic reaction the trauma has provoked. During that period the head of the bed is best not raised beyond 30° since a greater rise is apt to put a painful strain on the associated ligaments and musculature of the paravertebral areas. During this brief rest period the patient is permitted to turn in bed, or even urged to turn from side to side as pain lessens. Also during this period other injuries incident to that of the vertebral column may be sought, the symptoms or signs of which had been minimized by the pain and disability of the vertebral fracture (Fig. 7-5).

At the end of this period, pain, whether osseous or due to concurrent strain of paravertebral ligaments, should have subsided sufficiently to permit the patient to be out of bed and taking a few steps around the room. A lightweight corset, ordered shortly after the injury, should be ready at this time to serve as a support to the paravertebral ligaments and muscles maintaining the spine upright. Though it is probably true that such corsets have no influence on the position of the fracture, it does give considerable relief to the associated paravertebral soft-tissue strains incident to the fracture.

In the stable fracture uncomplicated by neurological signs and in lesions of the vertebral body or those of the neural arch this regimen is equally suitable. Late-stage instability is recognized of course by the appearance of developing weakness in the lower extremities or in bladder

control, or other increasing signs of paresis. Such symptoms demand
immediate return to bed rest and roentgenologic reevaluation of the
fracture with a view to immobilization procedures.

Fractures of the transverse processes in the aged, or more rarely of
the spinous process, are of minor consequence. The transverse-process
fracture is apt to be an avulsion fracture, since in the human this area
of bone appears to have the sole function of being a point of attachment

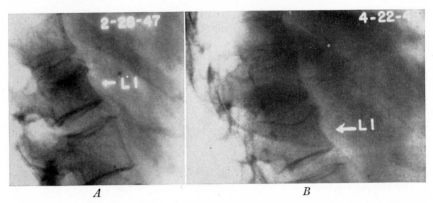

A   B

FIG. 7-5. Compression fracture upper third vertebral body. Female, age 65. Bed
rest 2 weeks, partial bed rest 2 weeks, light corset. *A.* Time of fracture. *B.* Two
years later. No significant further compression.

of the powerful erector spinae muscle group. Therefore, fractures of these
processes imply, without exception, painful tears of a lesser or greater
number of muscle fibers. As the muscle fibers heal, symptoms abate. The
acute pain should be over in a week or so. Less severe but aggravating
pain should subside 2 or 3 weeks later. During these weeks the patient
is advised to rest, to avoid activity beyond that necessary for his personal
needs, but not necessarily to remain in bed beyond the period of acute
severity.

The patient is encouraged to "move about a bit" as soon as such light
activity is tolerated. If it were not for the legal implications involved,
diagnosis of fracture of the transverse processes would be best withheld
from the elderly patient and the injury explained as a sprained back.
The idea of a "broken spine" cannot be ordinarily minimized to the
elderly patient by any simplification or explanation whatever, unless one
is indeed dealing with a very superior personality. Withholding diagnosis
in such cases, or if you will, telling a minor "fib," can actually be an
important contribution to therapy. But unfortunately in contemporary
life the legal implications of trauma or of withholding diagnosis from
the patient too often outweigh other considerations.

Common Complications. The most common early complication of fracture of the spine in the aged is paralytic ileus. This seems to appear as an incidental effect of trauma to the spine since experience has shown no relationship between its appearance and the type, degree, or severity of the vertebral fracture. It appears usually within the first few hours of trauma and may be of any degree of severity from a mild abdominal discomfort to an acute emergency. In the latter instance, gastric dilatation may accompany the intestinal ileus.

Ileus marks its appearance by abdominal distress, distention of the abdomen, increasing pulse rate, perspiration, and subjective apprehensions of impending calamity. At times a distressing desire to defecate without being able to do so becomes a chief and agonizing complaint. At other times symptoms include a distended bladder and an inability to empty it spontaneously.

The intensity of treatment is of course governed by the intensity of the symptoms. In cases of milder distress the insertion of a rectal tube or the use of warm abdominal stupes or a warm electric pad over the abdomen may prove sufficient to overcome the difficulty. In the presence of greater discomfort, the supplemental use of drugs such as Urecholine (10 to 30 mg) may be given at intervals of several hours. Prostigmin in doses of 10 to 15 mg may be used at intervals of 3 or 4 hours. In the uncommon but occasional case where a mild or moderately severe paralytic ileus is accompanied or followed by gastric dilatation, a Levine tube with or without a Wangensteen suction apparatus may be necessary. Rarely in the aged, but occasionally, 0.5 ml of pitressin may be necessary, followed by an enema.

For the most part however, paralytic ileus following fracture of the dorsolumbar spine in the aged person does not reach serious proportions and may be controlled without too much difficulty. If the patient must be confined to bed for any protracted time because of other concurrent lesions or illness, paralytic ileus may recur from time to time and must be anticipated. As in the younger adult, before treating a serious case of suspected paralytic ileus one must make certain that no real intestinal obstruction is present.

The problem of renal depression or renal shutdown is not an infrequent complication of fracture of the dorsolumbar spine, and it must be anticipated by close observation of the frequency, quantity, color, and concentration of the urine. The treatment of this complication is discussed in Chap. 2 and need not be repeated here beyond emphasizing that renal complications occurring after trauma to the vertebral column are apt to be of a more serious nature than paralytic ileus or most of the other complications.

A further serious complication in these cases among the aged is that of vertebral osteoporosis. The injury may have aggravated an existing osteoporosis or have been the apparent precipitating factor in an incipient lesion. This problem, discussed at some length in Chap. 4, must be constantly borne in mind, since secondary collapse of nearby or distant vertebrae may renew a disabling pain, invite further recumbency, and produce an invidious cycle of pain—atrophy of disuse—further vertebral collapse. The management or even the prevention of this complication will tax the therapeutic imagination of the surgeon beyond most other events during the conduct of the case. At this writing, short of the exhibition of hormones which take some time to produce their effects, no known therapy or regimen will influence this cycle unless the patient has an unusually high pain tolerance level and will keep on his feet in spite of the vertebral symptoms. In these cases the use of a spinal brace for some weeks may assist the patient in being ambulatory.

Aftercare. The aftercare of fractures of the dorsolumbar spine is a facet of the subject which is distinctive in the aged. In the "safe" fractures, that is, the simple compression fractures of the vertebral bodies, the rules of early ambulation and early mobility are paramount. Chiefly because of the associated ligamentous injuries or decompensation of the intervertebral degenerative lesions, the light belt or corset used in treatment may often be continued with comfort. The very cogent reasons for the employment of "back" exercises following fractures of the dorsolumbar vertebrae in young adults do not apply to such fractures in aged individuals. Mrs. Effie Gulatsi, C.T., who has devoted considerable expert time to trying to design a proper exercise program for elderly patients, has pointed out an anachronism in the attempt itself. Of all muscle groups that require rather strenuous work to accomplish any significant degree of strengthening, those of the lumbar and lumbosacral spine are most important. The very motions which form the basis of these exercises will stretch inelastic muscles and ligaments, will aggravate arthritic intervertebral joints, and will provoke radicular symptoms in the foramina already narrowed by the normal atrophy of the discs in the aged spine. Unless the "back" exercises attain some degree of force, one can barely perceive contractions of the lumbodorsal erector spinae. Therefore she does not attempt with the aged the usual exercises requiring trunk raising against gravity, but employs a mild set of calisthenics which involve the back muscles rather indirectly. Such exercises improve the tone of the muscles and at least impart a salubrious sense of well being to the elderly patient.

The most effective rehabilitation of the aged individual after fractures of the vertebral bodies is to encourage an early return to the usual activities of the period preceding the trauma. The principles conducive to this are further discussed by Peszczynski in Chap. 20.

The aftercare of the more threatening fracture dislocation lies in the persistent use of a protective lightweight brace until the responsible surgeon is convinced by x-ray films that a sufficiently strong paravertebral osteophytic buttress has formed to support the weakened structure. In the very unusual case where spine fusion has been found necessary, the same criteria are used in judging the length of time of support, or whether support is necessary at all, in the elderly individual as in the younger adult. Instances of unstable fractures of the vertebrae requiring fusion are so few among the aged that there is no accumulated experience of any significant validity upon which to base judgment. Responsibility must lie with the individual surgeon until such experience has been accumulated in published case reports. For the most part a period of protective support has sufficed.

Prognosis. It is the considered opinion of this writer that no elderly person who has sustained a fracture of the dorsolumbar spine ever returns to the state of comfort he or she enjoyed before the trauma occurred. As has been discussed in previous sections of this chapter, the persistence of pain in these lesions does not necessarily or indeed usually lie at the level of the fracture. More often than not in the common fractures at the dorsolumbar junction the persistent pains will be found at the lower lumbar, lumbosacral, or sacroiliac areas. The degree of discomfort varies in its intensity with (1) the degree of activity, (2) the weather, (3) the patient's subjective threshold of pain which varies from day to day, and (4) the emotional reactions to which he or she is subject. But it cannot, in any series of cases which the writer has studied, be related to the original severity of the fracture.

Fractures of the Sacrococcygeal Spine

Incidence. Fractures of the sacrum or of the coccyx are uncommon in the aged spine. The crush injury of the pelvis finds the anterior rim sufficiently fragile to give way to the stress and rarely is the sacrum involved. In the "sit down" injury, i.e., landing on the buttocks in a fall, apparently the stress is transmitted to the atrophic vertebral column through the sacrum without fracturing the latter. These are merely explanations; the fact is that fractures of the sacrococcygeal spine are quite infrequent among elderly individuals.

Common Sources of Trauma. Apparently the trauma which is apt to cause fracture of this segment of the vertebral column in the younger adult, bypasses, or its lines of stress are transmitted through, the sacrum to the pelvis or dorsolumbar vertebrae in the aged. Examples are the impact of a moving vehicle or falling heavy mass against the sacrum, the crushing of the pelvis between two heavy resistances, or a "hard" fall on the buttocks.

Clinical Diagnosis. Fractures of the sacrum or coccyx are characterized simply by pain and local tenderness in that area. (The fracture dislocation of the pelvis involving the sacroiliac joint is discussed by Garcia in Chap. 10.)

X-ray. Simple fractures of the sacrum are often difficult to discern in the aged spine. The many overlapping processes, angles, and prominences about the bone, and its position behind the rectum and genitals, make fine cracks or roaming fracture lines often barely perceptible in the broad sacral plate, the more so in the presence of an osteoporosis which in this flat bone is very apt to be irregular or spotty. It is a good practice in such cases to x-ray the part again a week or so later if the local pain persists. As in certain other parts of the skeleton, a simple fracture line, imperceptible shortly after trauma, may be more visible at the later date when necrosis makes the site more radiolucent.

Treatment. Treatment of closed fractures of the sacrum and coccyx is quite symptomatic. Relative rest for a few days until the soft-tissue reaction to the impact has subsided and the use of cushions on the chair or soft seats for a while thereafter is ordinarily sufficient. Elderly people do not tolerate firm bindings about the pelvis and hypogastrium easily. At times, if sacral pain is quite severe, the patient may prefer the relief of a sacroiliac belt with a posterior sacral pad to the primary pain of the fracture in its early period. At the patient's will, it may be left off as soon as the pain subsides to the point where it is less uncomfortable than the pelvic constriction.

Common Complications. These will be found described in Chap. 10, since complications occur in these fractures in the elderly only when the fracture is part of a more serious injury to the pelvis.

Aftercare. Aftercare in these cases is simply a protraction of the palliative treatment.

Prognosis. In simple fractures of the sacrum in the elderly, prognosis is good. Symptoms do not ordinarily persist beyond a few weeks. Prolonged pain is more apt to be due to the incidental injury of the lumbosacral junction or higher vertebrae, or to associated fractures or displacements of the pelvic ring.

PATHOLOGIC FRACTURES

Pathologic fractures of the vertebrae must be considered in two categories: the first is the spontaneous vertebral body compression of advanced bone atrophy or osteoporosis, and the second is made up of those fractures due to specific invasive lesions such as metastatic carcinoma or myeloma. In a book such as this, concerned with traumatic lesions in the aged, these fractures need only be mentioned briefly.

The spontaneous compression fracture which occurs with relative frequency in the aged osteoporotic spine may be all but asymptomatic or may cause the same pain and disability as are found in traumatic cases. In the latter instance, treatment, aftercare, and prognosis are those described in the above sections, since it will be recalled that in the broadest sense, all elderly spines are to some degree atrophic or osteoporotic.

The fractures which occur in vertebrae invaded by neoplastic disease are as varied as the traumatic variety. They do however present some noteworthy characteristics. X-ray appearances may be deceptive. Autopsy experience shows that neoplastic invasion is invariably far more widespread in the vertebrae than the x-ray film discloses. Furthermore, neoplasm may invade a vertebral body and be disablingly painful long before its presence can be detected. To find an obvious lesion on a later film and then to point a knowing finger to a questionable locus of osteolysis or increased density on an earlier film from another surgeon is an action to be performed only if the windows of one's glass house are not overly transparent. The x-ray diagnosis of early vertebral neoplasia requires careful and confident roentgenologic judgment. Later stages become self-evident. Recognition of the latter does not always justify blame for lack of earlier recognition.

Clinically, an observation which has often proved to be indicative of pathology in the experience of this writer has been the persistence of local pain when the patient is completely at rest in bed, as compared to the pain of a traumatic fracture which ordinarily is relieved by bed rest. Another characteristic of the pathologic fracture of the vertebrae is closely related to this observation. Most elderly people who have sustained traumatic fractures of the cervical or dorsolumbar vertebrae are substantially relieved by the use of some type of support during the painful period. Neoplastic fractures of the spine are not ordinarily, if ever, relieved by such body supports.

Fortunately for these elderly patients, the two most common lesions of pathologic fractures are radiosensitive. Pain may often be relieved by radiotherapy, if not altogether at least to a considerable extent. Beyond this, the therapy is that of oncology, and transcends the subject matter of this chapter and book. If the neoplasm extends to a great enough volume, paraplegia may of course occur. The treatment then becomes a matter best described in an older phraseology as "expectant," a word much used by our professional forbears, and still not superseded by a better.

BIBLIOGRAPHY

Albright, F., and E. C. Riefenstein: "The Parathyroid Glands and Metabolic Bone Disease." Baltimore, Williams & Wilkins, 1948.

Bick, E. M.: The management of fractures of the vertebrae in the elderly. *Amer. Jour. Surg.* **87**:764, 1954.

Bick, E. M.: Vertebral osteophytosis. Pathologic basis of its roentgenology. *Amer. Jour. Roentgen. and Rad. Ther.* **73**:979, 1955.

Bick, E. M.: General principles of fracture management in the aged. *Surg. Gyn. and Obst.* **106**:343, 1958.

Bick, E. M., and J. W. Copel: The senescent human vertebrae. *Jour. Bone and Joint Surg.* **34A**:110, 1952.

Davis, A. G.: Fractures of the spine. *Jour. Bone and Joint Surg.* **2**:133, 1929.

Gerston-Cohen, J., A. M. Rechtman, H. Schraer, and N. Blumberg: Asymptomatic fractures in osteoporotic spines of the aged. *Jour. Amer. Med. Ass.* **153**:625, 1953.

Grogono, B. J. S.: Injuries of the atlas and axis. *Jour. Bone and Joint Surg.* **36B**:397, 1954.

Nicoll, E. A.: Fractures of the dorso-lumbar spine. *Jour. Bone and Joint Surg.* **31B**:376, 1949.

Turner, V. C., and N. C. Mead: Compression fractures of the dorsal and lumbar spine in elderly people. *Surg. Clin., North Amer.* **29**:195, 1949.

Watson, Jones R.: "Fractures and Joint Injuries," 4th ed. Baltimore, Williams & Wilkins, 1955.

Chapter 8

Fractures of the Hip

Robert K. Lippmann

Incidence and Classification. Fractures of the hip must be sharply divided into those occurring within the hip capsule and those occurring at a lower level and involving the trochanteric area. The intracapsular fracture is most frequent in the proximal half of the femoral neck (Fig. 8-1*A*), but may also occur close to the trochanter. The trochanteric frac-

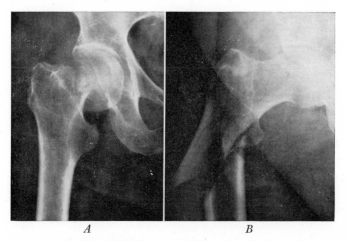

| A | B |

FIG. 8-1. The limits of the hip fracture. *A*. High subcapital fracture. *B*. Low fracture involving lesser trochanter.

ture includes those fractures below this level and involving at least one trochanter (Fig. 8-1*B*). The treatment and outlook for these groups are so different that they must be separately dealt with. Both intracapsular and trochanteric fractures are most frequent in the later decades and both are most common in women (84 per cent). As the accompanying chart of our records indicates, the trochanteric fracture is relatively more frequent in the seventh and eighth decades while the intracapsular fracture predominates during the eighth and ninth decades (Fig. 8-2).

Causes. Occasionally the intracapsular fracture results from severe trauma and may even be associated with hip dislocation and acetabular fracture, but by far most intracapsular fractures result from relatively slight trauma. A slight misstep on the floor, a dizzy spell, or a slight push by a child results in a fall from which the patient is unable to rise. In such instances, trauma represents merely the precipitating cause. On rare occasion, no trauma whatever provokes the fracture, the patient falling to the ground as a result of the hip "giving way."

The true basis of this type of fracture rests in the multiple degenerative

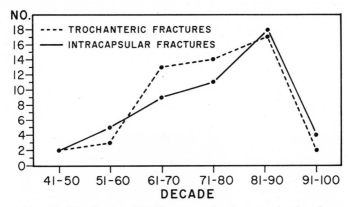

Fig. 8-2. Distribution of 100 consecutive fractures by decade.

changes of aging. Menopausal and senile osteoporosis, often augmented by brittle areas of necrotic trabeculae, play a major role in increasing the vulnerability of the femoral neck. Joint stiffness, poor coordination and balance, dizziness, retardation of protective reflexes, visual problems, etc., account for the trauma. On the basis of these circumstances, the intracapsular fracture is most commonly a pathological fracture.

Although menopausal osteoporosis appears to attack the intracapsular area of the hip selectively, the frequency with which the trochanteric fractures result from minor injuries in aged women suggests that this area may at times become at least as vulnerable. In general, the higher proportion of trochanteric fractures encountered in the sixth and seventh decades supports the general association of these fractures with greater activity and accordingly with more severe trauma. Excluding the simple avulsion fractures of the greater and lesser trochanter, there would appear to be little difference in the mechanism of the intracapsular and the trochanteric fracture. Both types of fracture are produced by direct impact in the direction of the extremity either extended or flexed (as against the automobile dashboard) by forced external rotation, by abduction, or by a combination of these forces. In the cadaver, the trochanteric fracture may be so reproduced with little difficulty. The intracapsular fracture, however, has been almost impossible to reproduce in the cadaver by any maneuver, a fact which confirms the important role of antecedent atrophic changes preceding these lesions.

Clinical Diagnosis. It is common knowledge that when an elderly person falls and is unable to rise or rises with difficulty because of hip pain, the chances are that a hip fracture has been sustained and that urgent x-ray (not fluoroscopy) is indicated. On examination, maintenance of the involved extremity in the position of external rotation and with more or less shortening is almost positive proof. In the typical fracture, the patient is unable to lift the leg or to roll it inward because of severe pain. However, this test is seldom justified in the light of the fact that hospitalization and x-ray examination are inevitably indicated on the basis of the simple history. A reliable and painless method of confirming the presence of a displaced fracture at the time of preliminary examination is the auscultatory percussion test. The principle and technique of this test are discussed by Bick in Chap. 4.

Naturally a hip fracture that is impacted may reveal only slight hip pain and tenderness and can be detected only radiologically. Hip pain following trauma, however slight, always calls for roentgen examination. An undetected, impacted fracture can separate weeks after injury, rendering therapy more difficult and far less successful.

Differential Diagnosis. In actual experience, clinical differentiation of the displaced intracapsular from the trochanteric fracture is generally most difficult and often impossible unless the patient is very thin. Moreover, the clinical differentiation is of little importance when it is appreciated that both types of lesion call for rapid hospitalization and roentgen examination which establishes the presence of the lesion as well as its localization and plane.

In the age group past 60, the younger the patient and the more severe the trauma, the greater is the probability of trochanteric fracture. The trochanteric fracture is more likely to be associated with hemorrhage and shock while the intracapsular fracture, where bleeding is confined by the joint capsule, is seldom shocking. In both types of lesion, examination of the hip may reveal the identical position of the extremity and the same degree of shortening. In a thin patient it may be possible to palpate the trochanter anteroposteriorly. The presence of swelling and ecchymosis may determine the diagnosis.

X-ray Diagnosis. It has been the practice of the present writer to limit the initial diagnostic x-ray to a single anteroposterior exposure with the extremity in the original position of deformity. Should fracture not be discernible in the film, it may be revealed if the leg is carefully rotated inward (with traction applied to the ankle) for a clearer profile of the trochanter and neck. Forcible correction of the external rotation for the roentgen exposure should be carefully avoided at this point. If the fracture consists of more than a split or impaction, the maneuver may be most painful and, in certain trochanteric fractures, may obliterate a fracture line. Moreover, forcible internal rotation can tear delicate periosteal tissues posteriorly, increase the difficulty of reduction, and injure important nutrient vessels to the head. Internal rotation should never be carried beyond the normal limits as determined by testing the well extremity.

A lateral view of the femoral neck usually serves no purpose at this point unless the above radiological views fail to demonstrate fracture. Should this be the case, a lateral "across the table" view may be added. Very rarely, this view alone can demonstrate a small split or area of impaction.

General Care of Patient and Surgical Considerations. While specific therapy of the various types of hip fracture is separately considered later, certain general principles apply to the treatment of hip fractures in the aged. Throughout the course of hospitalization it is important, especially in the older patient, that attention be focused upon the entire patient rather than upon the local lesion. In addition to the local lesion, the elderly patient entering the hospital may exhibit various stages of deterioration that are best recognized prior to the surgical attack. It is never prudent, therefore, to regard the hip fracture as a surgical emergency. If the internist so recommends, one or several days of Buck's extension or Russell traction are best allocated to him for study and preparatory therapy, and for examination by other specialists if necessary. Determination of cardiac and circulatory status is necessary for the preoperative preparation and for selection of anesthetic. Problems of avitaminosis, nutrition, and hypoproteinemia may be recognized and therapy promptly instituted. Any degree of traumatic shock must be brought into balance before the potential disturbances of anesthesia and operation are superimposed.

During the preoperative as well as the postoperative period, the fundamental thesis of care is the provision of as close an approach to the pattern of normal activity as the lesion permits. The preservation of mobility is important not only for the avoidance of surgical complications but also for the prevention of inevitable senile and cerebral arteriosclerotic changes which immobilization can precipitate. Such changes have been known to reach the degree that after healing, balance and ability to ambulate cannot be relearned although the local surgical result has been excellent. As promptly as possible a scheduled nursing and physiotherapy program commences consisting of deep breathing, rotation of the trunk from side to side to relieve sacral pressure, sitting up in bed if possible, and active and passive exercises to the trunk and well extremities. The prompt application of a Balkan frame with several hand grips helps to expedite active motion. Although traction provides only moderate relief from pain, analgesic medication must be cautiously employed because of the particularly unpredictable response of the aged to such medication and its tendency to favor immobility. The techniques of rehabilitation from traumata in general are discussed in detail in Chap. 20.

In regard to the operative approach itself, it is wisest to leave the choice of anesthesia to the anesthetist, who is best equipped to take into account the condition of the patient, the severity and duration of the contemplated procedure, and his own experience with anesthetic agents. The problem of anesthesia in the aged is sufficiently important to have merited its special discussion in Chap. 3.

In preparation for the surgical approach, it is advisable to transport the patient to the operating room in bed with traction maintained until anesthesia is complete. Transfer to the fracture table may then be accomplished without painful and tissue-disrupting spasm. The specific reduction and fixation procedures involved in the various types of hip fracture are separately considered at a later point.

The services of an experienced x-ray technician, versed in operating room technique, are imperative. Anteroposterior views of the hip joint present no special problem, but the lateral exposure calls for special planning. Either lateral films may be taken with the tube on the side of the injured hip, aiming at the injured hip from above and toward a curved cassette in the crotch, or they may be taken with the x-ray tube below, under the well extremity, with the cassette over the iliac crest of the involved hip (Fig. 8-3). In the hands of the writer, the latter procedure has been most consistently reliable. Whichever procedure is employed, a check anteroposterior and lateral film prior to draping can forestall major difficulties during the operation. Although the films are less clearly defined, it is recommended that the Lysholm grid not be used because of the greater exposure it requires, and because obliquity of the cassette with reference to the tube results in inadequate film exposure and loss of time.

The use of metal implants which serve under stress, either for the duration of fracture healing or indefinitely, is common to most of the procedures described. The surgeon should be aware of certain metallurgical limitations which apply to all such implants. Stainless Steel 18–8 SMO or Vitallium are the generally used alloys which are essentially inert and provoke no significant tissue reaction. If the instruments are mixed, however, the screws of one metal being used to fasten a plate of the other, a sustained electromotive potential results which can be destructive to neighboring bone and soft tissue. This is avoidable only by careful segregation of the Stainless Steel from the Vitallium armamentarium, or by the hospital's possession of instruments of one metal only. In the event of doubt, the manufacturer is best able to determine the nature of the metal in question.

Like all metals, Vitallium and Stainless Steel SMO are subject to flaws and fatigue fracture, the latter resulting from severe or even minute

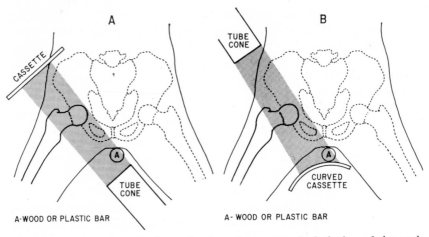

FIG. 8-3. The two methods of securing lateral roentgenological view of the neck of the femur with patient on fracture table.

bending strain repeated frequently enough. Careful manufacturers are constantly controlling their products by crystal microscopy and by roentgenography for the discovery of flaws. Instruments showing flaws or other defects are discarded, but not all flaws can be so revealed. Fatigue fracture may develop in a completely flawless instrument long after it has been weakened by bending during application. The more it is bent, the weaker the instrument becomes. After implantation to bridge a fracture, failure of a fracture to heal can result in repeated though minute bending strains and ultimate fracture of the instrument. The latter problem is amplified in the hip prosthesis which, instead of functioning merely for the duration of fracture healing, is called upon to function indefinitely. Since the strain upon these latter instruments is severe and their tenure of function unpredictable, they must be constructed as sturdily as is compatible with their purpose. It is still too early to ascertain how long the medullary stem prostheses may be trustworthy beyond the 8-year period that they have been widely employed. From a practical standpoint, the bending of metallic plates, flanges, etc., at operation should be kept at minimum, and plates, nails, or prostheses that have already given service should never be re-used though they give every superficial indication of being as strong as new.

After operation, in accordance with recognized principle, the maximal activity and mobility compatible with the lesion is resumed as promptly as possible. The preoperative routine of scheduled deep breathing, rolling from side to side, and exercise to the well extremities is reinstituted within the first 24 hours.

If the procedure has not called for plaster spica application, Buck's extension is reapplied to the extremity operated upon. This is done not so much for traction purposes but to guard against inadvertent adduction during recovery from anesthesia and while sleeping. Weight of only 2 or 3 pounds is used. After the second or third day, traction is discontinued during the daytime to be reapplied at night for a week or more depending upon the comfort of the patient. Sitting up in bed is generally possible on the first or second day, to be followed with sitting over the side of the bed or in a chair. Quadriceps and abduction exercises are added to the above activities during the first few days, the abduction group assisted by a sling suspended from the Balkan frame. In all of these activities, the active cooperation of the patient is stressed. Probably the greatest advantage of the surgical approach to the treatment of hip fracture of the aged lies in the relatively prompt relief from pain and the capacity to resume rapidly some degree of active motion and self-sufficiency.

If the operation has called for plaster, pressure erosion of the sacrum must be constantly combated by rolling the patient alternately toward the well side and to the prone position for a good part of the day and night. Within a few days a plaster window is cut over the face of the patella, and scheduled quadriceps exercises are added to the routine. From this point, the speed of progress is individual and, in the older patient, depends upon many factors. Among them are the general condition of the patient, his cooperation and agility, the quality of nursing care available, and, in cases of internal fixation, the texture of the skeleton and the security of the fixation as disclosed at operation. Although weight bearing on the injured extremity is not permitted until roentgen evidence of healing appears, the patient is instructed in ambulation with crutches as early as the above considerations permit.

THE INTRACAPSULAR FRACTURE

BACKGROUND SKETCH

Since the early era of the "sand bag" method which carried a 60 to 80 per cent mortality, the first important advance occurred in 1902 when

Whitman demonstrated bony healing after reduction and immobilization in a plaster spica. Wide adoption of Whitman's technique soon demonstrated that the method was no panacea. In most hands, the proportion of healed fractures was small; and the long period of plaster immobilization was beset with many problems of care of the severe complications of long plaster immobilization, and of high mortality. In 1938, Cleveland and Bosworth reported a failure of 61.5 per cent to heal with use of the plaster technique.

The second major advance was Smith-Peterson's demonstration of fracture healing following immobilization with the trifin nail, reported in 1931. Originally Smith-Peterson accomplished fracture reduction and nail insertion at open operation and under direct vision. In 1932, following the lead of Johansson, closed reduction and nailing under x-ray control through a small lateral incision almost universally replaced the open operation. With closed reduction, the importance of careful lateral as well as anteroposterior radiographic control became evident.

Mortality was greatly reduced by the nailing procedure. Fewer complications, painless motion of the involved hip within a short time, simplified nursing care, abbreviated hospital stay, and early ambulation (though without weight bearing) became possible. As far as the hip was concerned, however, gains were disappointing. While the proportion of nonunion was considerably improved, a new complication, aseptic necrosis, was recognized to take a toll even higher than that of nonunion.

In the hope of gaining better results through stronger fixation, a wide variety of new apparatus were developed. These included modifications of the trifin nail, multiple small nails and wires, threaded screws, and compression bolts to secure and maintain impaction of the fragments against each other. Although initial reports by the proponents of many of these instruments were optimistic, their use in general has become limited to cases with the special indications described below. Several new devices which incorporate a telescoping mechanism to keep pace with any loss of neck and maintain fracture surface apposition have been described. Time has not yet permitted adequate testing of these instruments.

In 1935, "The Unsolved Fracture," a paper by Speed, called sharp attention to the unsatisfactory status of the intracapsular fracture and pleaded for a more comprehensive basic study of the problem. Speed's pessimistic report was followed shortly by a number of statistical follow-up studies from various clinics which supported his plea. In 1941, The Fracture Committee of the American Academy of Orthopaedic Surgeons reported 30 per cent nonunion in collected reports from fracture surgeons throughout this country. In 1944, Linton reported nonunion in 16 per cent and aseptic necrosis in 39 per cent. Boyd and George, in 1947, reported 13.5 per cent nonunion and 33.6 per cent aseptic necrosis, the proportion of "good" results being 43.6 per cent. In 1954, Cleveland and Fielding reported 22.3 per cent nonunion and 25 per cent aseptic necrosis. Few comprehensive long term reports have indicated favorable local results in more than 50 per cent. The repetition of Speed's plea by Gray, in 1956, reflects the lack of significant clinical progress in the intervening period. Despite the lack of progress in therapy, much has been accomplished in bringing to light the many biomechanical complexities of the intracapsular fracture, for example, the reasons for the failure of the purely mechanical approach, and the knowledge that not only is the fracture "unsolved" but that a high proportion of fractures are, in fact, "insoluble," at least by mere modification of the methods of internal fixation.

BIOMECHANICS OF THE INTRACAPSULAR FRACTURE

A unique combination of anatomic, biological, and mechanical factors is responsible for the relatively poor outlook of the intracapsular fracture in the aged. Mechanically competent as the immobilization device may be in the younger and healthier patient, its task is greatly amplified in the aged. The brittle, osteoporotic bone of the older patient is often unable to buttress and support it with the necessary strength to resist the shearing muscle-pull force constantly operating it. In the younger patient, the supportive trochanteric trabeculae are not only stronger themselves but are assisted by the trabeculae extending well into the femoral neck. In aged osteoporotic bone, neck trabeculation has all but disappeared. The fixative device is required to bridge the hollow neck from trochanter to capital fragment (Ward's triangle) with minimal support, thus increasing the leverage stress upon the bone of the trochanter, while the slower healing time of the older patient extends this demand over a longer period. If, as is often the case, a segment of the femoral neck absorbs, the fixation may loosen; and as slipping develops and progresses, the fracture surfaces lose apposition and healing potential.

Pauwels has called attention to another mechanical factor that can operate to obstruct fracture healing, namely, the verticality of the plane of the fracture line. Pauwels has demonstrated the increased shearing stress and consequent poorer outlook in the vertical fracture as opposed to those fractures in a more horizontal plane (Fig. 8-4).

Biologically, the healing of aged tissues may be further hampered by an unpredictable amount of necrosis of the capital fragment due to avascularity. It has been demonstrated (Erdheim, Sherman) that owing to aging and peripheral circulatory insufficiency, large areas of trabecular bone may die and remain completely asymptomatic for long periods of time. Microscopically, such areas give little evidence of "creeping substitution" or repair; and they cannot be identified radiographically.

Although Trueta has been unable to detect vascular compromise due to aging in the vessels supplying the femoral head, the necrosis is not easily accounted for on other grounds. In any event, dead bone is brittle and could well explain those fractures that occur spontaneously or after minimal injury.

In the course of internal fixation of fractures in older patients, a striking disparity is sometimes noted between the x-ray appearance of density and the surprisingly poor bony resistance offered by the bone during insertion of the fixative instrument. It is possible that massive areas of trabecular necrosis, undetectable on roentgenography, are responsible for the poor texture so disclosed. When fracture occurs, further necrosis of the femoral head may develop secondary to damage to the subsynovial vessels that enter the hip laterally and course along the periosteum of the neck to supply this fragment with its main source of nutrition. If fracture repair is sufficiently impeded by adjacent areas of necrosis, laxity and slipping of the fixative device become inevitable. If areas of necrosis are mainly at the apex of the head, healing of the fracture may occur, but the invasion of soft granulation tissue will result in the ultimate collapse of the structure. Avascularity and necrosis of the greater part of the capital fragment will inevitably be followed by nonunion and by gradual absorption of the bone of the proximal fragment. The two latter developments will lead to a final outcome at least as unfortunate as that resulting from nonunion.

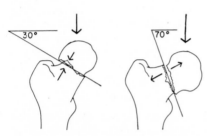

FIG. 8-4. The mechanical advantage of the horizontal over the vertical fracture plane. (*F. Pauwels*)

THERAPY

Choice of Primary Surgical Procedure. There can be little disagreement that in patients who are not moribund the intracapsular fracture presents a surgical indication to provide relief of pain and some degree of mobility. These are lifesaving measures. In more than half of the patients operated upon with the goal of fracture fixation, however, pain had been relieved only temporarily and ultimately recurred because of nonunion or because of the late femoral-head changes of aseptic necrosis. This common clinical observation, and the biological explanation underlying it, renders the continued routine application of internal fixation to all intracapsular fractures questionable. With the growth of experience with prostheses, the experimental substitution of a primary prosthetic approach is gaining favor in fractures that present a poor outlook with treatment by internal fixation.

Theoretically, primary prosthetic insertion in such cases offers essentially the opportunity for a moderately sound hip as opposed to the sizable risk of long invalidism followed by ultimate failure and a second or even a third operation. Prosthetic insertion is far simpler and less traumatic to the patient if performed promptly rather than as a secondary procedure. Acetabular reaming is practically never required. Since bony union is not anticipated, postoperative weight bearing may be commenced very early and the patient may be able to leave the hospital, walking, within 5 or 6 weeks. In the aged, when time is at a special premium, the elimination of the long non-weight-bearing period avoids the difficult late problem of relearning independent ambulation. Deformities of the femoral head due to avascularity cannot occur. Experience with prostheses over the past 8 years leaves little doubt that, properly applied, most prostheses of the stem type are capable of measuring up to the moderate need and limited tenure called for in the aged patient.

On the other hand, it cannot be too strongly emphasized that prosthetic insertion as a primary procedure has not yet achieved general acceptance. Its above described advantages must be tested in terms of statistical experience—a project that will require a long period of further study. The operative procedure is considerably more extensive than any of the internal fixation procedures and calls for a higher measure of surgical skill and experience. The difficulty in choosing the suitable prosthetic candidate arises because failure cannot as yet be predicted with certainty in the individual patient. The studies of Boyd with P^{32} may prove to be an important lead in the objective determination of the viability of the capital fragment.

At present, and on a tentative basis, clinical criteria built upon collective experiences with internal fixation failures must be relied upon. Such criteria include those patients whose physiological age is high and who appear to demonstrate inability to survive through, or learn to utilize crutches through, a long non-weight-bearing period; obese patients who might impose an excessive load upon internal fixation; and patients whose lack of balance, dexterity, or cooperation might pose the same hazard in ambulation. At the fracture site, indications include wide separation of the fragments prior to reduction, probably reflecting severe damage to the important capsular vessels supplying the femoral head; excessive osteoporosis involving the hip that could therefore not supply adequate buttress to the immobilizing device; a high subcapital fracture, especially with verticality or comminution of the line, generally known to yield poor results after internal fixation. Various combinations of these factors presenting in a patient tentatively suggest the elimination of the protracted trial period required after internal fixation and the substitution of primary prosthetic insertion. The candidate for primary prosthetic procedure must indicate capacity to withstand the more severe operation and the possible requirement of 10 days to 2 weeks of subsequent plaster spica. The fracture site must be free of Paget's disease since prostheses have been shown to be unstable and to exhibit a tendency to migrate and become painful in bone of this character. Moreover, the prosthetic procedure cannot be employed if the fracture area is the site of quiescent or latent infection.

Internal Fixation.

Choice of the Internal Fixation Device. If, as in most cases at the present time, treatment by internal fixation is elected, consideration must be given to the choice of immobilizing devices to be used. For the surgeon relatively inexperienced in the technique of internal fixation, the cannulated trifin nail of Smith-Peterson or multiple pins of the Knowles or Austin Moore type present the simpler and less potentially damaging techniques (Fig. 8-5). The results of immobilization with them are statistically comparable to those obtained from the use of more complex devices (Fig. 8-6*A*). Instruments of the compression or lag-screw type such as the corkscrew bolt have the technical advantage of securing and maintaining firm contact and compression of the fracture surfaces against each other (Fig. 8-6*B*). Charnley has pointed out the benefit of such firm apposition in speeding union of trabecular bone.

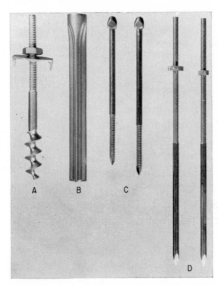

Fig. 8-5. Devices frequently employed for fixation of the intracapsular fracture: *A.* Corkscrew bolt, *B.* Smith-Peterson nail (modified and cannulated), *C.* Knowles pins, *D.* Moore pins.

The writer's experience with the corkscrew bolt in over 300 intracapsular fractures indicates confirmation of this thesis at the hip. However, the device has several limitations. It is not cannulated and must be accurately aimed without the aid of a guide wire. (Cannulation requires enlargement of the diameter of the corkscrew to such a degree that torsion of the proximal fragment may occur during insertion.) Moreover, if the fracture is too oblique in the lateral plane or if comminution of the posterior cortex is severe, the pull of the mechanism can produce angulation or even lateral displacement of the fragments instead of impaction.

Accordingly, the corkscrew bolt calls for some measure of skill and experience as well as the careful selection of cases for its application. Under these circumstances, the more rapid healing that may ensue is so dramatic that weight bearing becomes possible in 5 to 6 weeks.

A number of surgeons have turned to the use of nails with attached flanges of the type currently employed for fractures of the trochanteric area. Although these devices greatly reinforce the hold and the angle of the nail with the trochanteric bone, they possess a serious disadvantage. Following possible loss of bone substance at the fracture site, the Smith-Peterson nail can extrude and so preserve bony apposition. This is not possible if the nail is fastened and cannot slide. As a result, either it can

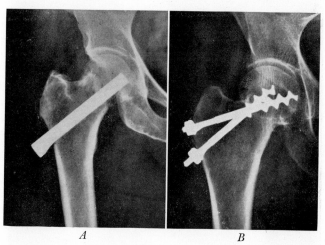

A *B*

FIG. 8-6. *A*. Fixation of varus intracapsular fracture by Smith-Peterson nail. *B*. Compression gained by use of two corkscrew bolts for fixation of varus intracapsular fracture.

permit the fracture surfaces to separate or it may intrude into the joint, making removal of the device mandatory (Fig. 8-7).

Discussion of the fixation of the intracapsular fracture thus far has been limited to the generally encountered intracapsular fracture occurring subcapitally or through the narrow neck section. Far less frequently fractures that are truly intracapsular are encountered which lie close to the trochanter in the base of the neck. Such fractures are not prone to aseptic necrosis or nonunion, but present a mechanical leverage problem far different from those occurring at a higher level. While the reduction procedure is the same for these fractures as for those at a higher level, their adequate fixation requires the use of flanged apparatus as described in the section on intertrochanteric fractures (Fig. 8-8). The operative technique employed by the writer, utilizing the Smith-Peterson nail, may be briefly reviewed.

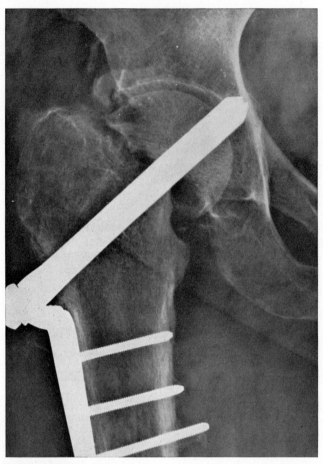

FIG. 8-7. The disadvantage of the lateral flange when femoral neck is absorbing. The nail cuts through the femoral head into and across the joint.

Reduction. The recent recognition of the hazard of even small repeated x-ray radiation has resulted in abandonment of manual leg holding during x-ray and the practically universal adoption of the fracture table. Although this hampers maneuverability, it permits the taking of appropriate roentgenograms with no significant exposure of operating room personnel.

Before attaching the foot of the well leg to the foot plate of the table, it is useful to determine and fix in mind the limit of internal rotation on that side. Reduction of the fracture is accomplished before the injured leg is included in the fixation. Under traction, the hip and knee are brought to 90° of flexion and the hip adducted about 20° to free the fracture surfaces from contact. Maintaining traction, the leg is rotated

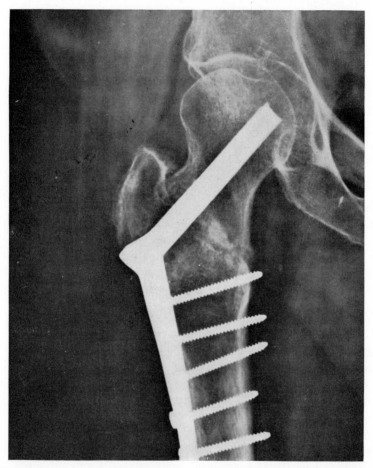

Fig. 8-8. Low intracapsular fracture. Position best maintained by device with flange. Jewett device illustrated.

inward to the limit previously observed on the opposite side and simultaneously brought down into extension and abduction of 15° while retaining the internal rotation. The foot of this side is then attached to the foot plate while the leg is carefully kept in the same degree of internal rotation, abduction, and extension. Before proceeding with preparation of the skin and draping, the approximate location of the femoral head is marked with a skin clip, anteroposterior films are taken, and any necessary adjustments are made. Accurate lateral alignment is imperative. Varus position is unacceptable.

Fixation. After satisfactory alignment is achieved in the anteroposterior and lateral planes and draping has been accomplished, a 3- to 4-inch incision is made below the greater trochanter, fascia lata split, and the ridge marking the upper attachment of the vastus lateralis noted. By subperiosteal dissection, the vastus is lifted forward exposing the lateral femur about 1½ to 2 inches below the ridge. At about 1½ inch a small drill hole is made marking the insertion point of the guide wire and nail. This low insertion point should permit the wire to pass through the lower and stronger part of the neck. Two graduated and perfectly straight guide wires of equal length are selected, one of which is laid aside and the other mounted in the drill with no more than 3 inches extending. The tip of the wire is then inserted in the drill hole, aimed toward the site of the femoral head, and drilled slightly downward toward the floor. The position of the head may be checked by inserting the forefinger anterior to the femoral shaft and palpating the neck and head through the joint capsule. The length of wire inserted can be gauged from time to time by aligning the second wire alongside the first with its point resting on the femoral cortex and applying a clamp where the inserted wire ends. The length to be inserted will approximate four-fifths of the distance measured on the film, but check radiographs are more accurate. Several attempts at wire insertion may be necessary before an acceptable and central location is attained.

After proper placing of an adequate length of wire, the cortex is reamed to prevent splitting; and the nail of proper length, with driver, is slid over the wire and hammered home. During this procedure, it is advisable to repeatedly check the length of the extruding wire to make certain that the nail is riding over it smoothly and not causing it to bend or to press into the pelvis. As the nail approaches the fracture site, its tendency to distract the fragments may be compensated for by the alternate use of the impactor until full insertion has been achieved. The ultimate acceptable position of the nail should permit at least ¼ inch clearance between its tip and the joint space laterally, and extrusion of no more than ½ inch.

If multiple nails, wires, or screws are chosen as the fixation agents, the general plan of insertion described above is followed with appropriate adjustment of technique. The number of nails or pins utilized (usually between three and five) must vary with the strength of the instruments and the porosity of the bone through which they are inserted.

Cautions. Regardless of the fixative instruments employed, certain cautions may be helpful in avoiding grief for the patient after operation. If vascularity of the femoral head has not been already impaired by the trauma or by transportation to the hospital, such damage can result from careless handling after admission, in the course of transportation to the operating room, or in draping the patient, if while under anesthesia and during draping the leg is elevated high without traction. Accordingly, it is recommended that the patient be brought to the operating room in bed with traction rather than by stretcher, and that anesthesia and preparation of the patient be accomplished while traction is maintained either by weights or manually. Equivalent circulatory damage is possible during the reduction procedure by forcible internal rotation beyond normal range. It is stressed, therefore, that prior to binding the foot to the fracture table, the limit of internal rotation of the well hip not be exceeded on the side of the fracture.

Common Complications. The major complications of internal fixation may be roughly divided into those of mechanical origin, those referable to avascular necrosis and those due to the disability resulting from late arthritic changes in the hip joint. These categories are closely related since avascular necrosis may be basically responsible for mechanical failure, or, at a later point, for arthritic changes.

Apparently of a purely mechanical nature is gradual extrusion of the nail with loss of hold on the femoral head and ultimate loss of position. The reason for this phenomenon is not clear. Reinsertion of a nail may be employed together with the addition of some flange device to fix the base of the nail to the trochanter maintaining position. In the case illustrated, McMurray osteotomy was successfully performed (Fig. 8-15). Extrusion of the nail may also follow partial absorption of the neck of the distal fragment. In the writer's opinion, this extrusion is practically always due to false motion at the fracture site. If apposition of the fragments keeps pace with such extrusion, healing may still proceed uneventfully and only the continued avoidance of weight bearing is called for. Should the nail fail to take up the slack and the fragments become increasingly widely spaced, nonunion is inevitable. Occasionally, instead of extruding from the trochanter, the nail penetrates the capital fragment and protrudes into the hip joint (Fig. 8-7). If this condition is permitted to persist for any length of time, the joint becomes progressively destroyed, causing increasing pain on motion. In such cases, prompt correction of the protrusion is essential to preserve the cartilage of the joint. Reinsertion of a shorter nail may be performed provided the capital fragment presents no evidence of avascular necrosis and alignment of the fragments has been maintained. If the femoral head presents evidence of avascularity, its removal is usually advisable and appropriate salvage procedures are added.

Nonunion. Also often of mechanical origin is loss of the position and failure to heal. As above described, this complication may be due to a vertical fracture line providing the nail with inadequate support for fixation of the proximal fragment. The bone of the distal fragment is generally the site of initial loss of support (Fig. 8-9*A*). More often, nonunion is referable to varus or incomplete reduction, to poor placement of the device at operation, to severe osteoporosis (Fig. 8-9*B*), or to delayed healing due to major avascular necrosis involving the proximal fragment (Fig. 8-9*C*). In the event of progressive evidence of nonunion, the prompt institution of salvage procedures is expedient. The latter are considered at a later point in this chapter.

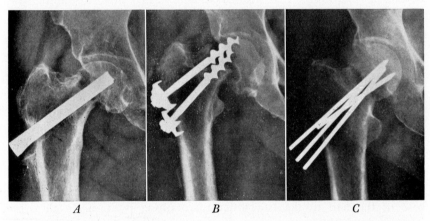

A   *B*   *C*

Fig. 8-9. Examples of nonunion after fixation with various devices. *A*. Nonunion due to slip of nail in trochanteric fragment. *B*. Nonunion due to poor purchase of corkscrew bolts in osteoporotic short capital fragment. *C*. Nonunion due to massive avascular necrosis of capital fragment (Telson threaded wires).

Avascular Necrosis. Avascular necrosis, if large in extent, is often recognizable at a month or 6 weeks after operation by the gross appearance of condensation and by the persistence of the original pattern of trabecular structure in the head. If this is confirmed in subsequent films and supported by evidence of delay in healing, slipping of the fixation, or beginning absorption of the head commencing at the site of fracture, prompt salvage would appear to be indicated. Avascular necrosis involving a smaller area of the head is almost always impossible to recognize early postoperatively. In this circumstance, healing may proceed uneventfully and no symptoms or signs of the presence of necrosis be manifest until many months or even years after the hip injury. Its advent is generally presaged by pain on weight bearing after a variable period of apparent cure. The diagnosis is established roentgenographically by disorganization of the head secondary to ingrowth of soft granulation tissue and ultimate collapse (Fig. 8-10). Still smaller areas of involvement in the apex of the head may produce symptoms of stiffness and pain as late in onset as 7 or 8 years after injury. In this event, symptoms are generally arthritic in nature and result from collapse and deformation at the apical weight-bearing area followed by secondary joint changes. Except for the latter circumstance which may be tolerable to the patient, a salvage procedure is generally indicated.

Primary Prosthesis Application.

Choice of Prostheses. In the event that primary prosthetic substitution is elected, various models of stem-type prostheses are available from which

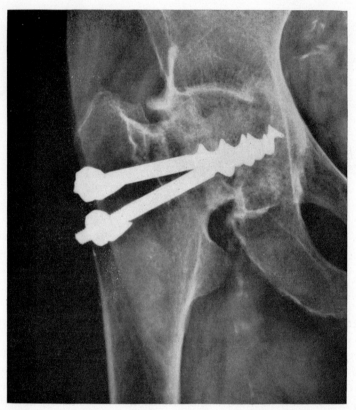

Fig. 8-10. Late collapse of femoral head 2 years after corkscrew bolt fixation with uneventful rapid healing of fracture.

a suitable one may be selected (Fig. 8-11). Sufficient data has accumulated concerning prostheses which follow the axis of the neck to indicate that they are subject to loosening and consequent pain within a few years. Medullary stem prostheses such as the Moore, Eicher, or Thompson have proved to yield considerably longer service. Each of these prostheses, however, calls for amputation of the femoral neck at its base for their insertion, a weakness which provides little resistance to gradual loosening when the leg is rolled into external rotation. For this reason, the author utilizes the transfixion prosthesis which, although somewhat more difficult to apply, utilizes and preserves the buttress of residual neck and transfixes the main stem through the outer cortex. For these reasons, a firmer initial hold upon the host femur is provided. The relative merits

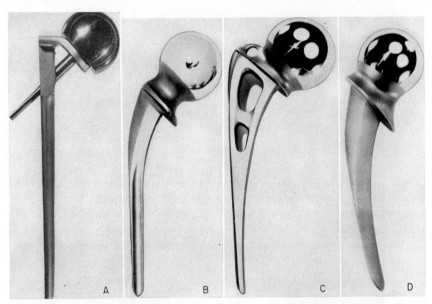

Fig. 8-11. Various prostheses in current use. *A*. Transfixion prosthesis (Lippmann). *B*. Eicher prosthesis. *C*. Moore prosthesis. *D*. F. R. Thompson prosthesis.

claimed for the various types of medullary stem prostheses will require years of further study for confirmation by statistical data.

Regardless of the type of prosthesis employed, it is important to bear in mind that the reconstructed hip is artificial. In these days of common litigation, it is important that the patient understand that a metallic hip joint is, at best, more vulnerable than a normal one, and that he give consent to the proposed substitution procedure before the operation. The insertion techniques for the devices mentioned above and the instruments required for the application of each are well set forth by their respective inventors. It is recommended that relevant literature be carefully reviewed before the performance of any prosthetic procedure.

Procedure for Insertion of Transfixion Prosthesis. The procedure employed for the introduction of the transfixion prosthesis (Fig. 8-12) with which the writer has had greatest experience may be quoted as follows:

The patient is placed on the operating room table on his well side.

The lateral approach to the hip joint as described by Gibson and modified by McFarland has proved excellent for exposure of the crest of the femoral neck and consequently for the insertion of the transfixion prosthesis. With the stem rotated so that the end plate will be in approxi-

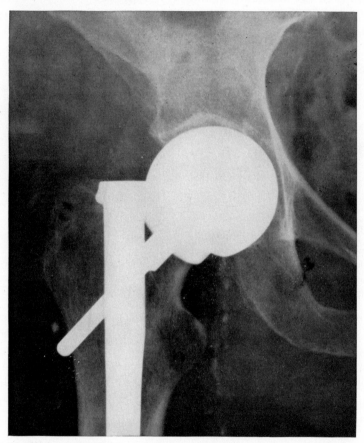

FIG. 8-12. Successful transfixion prosthetic replacement. Patient walked with cane 6 weeks after operation with minimal discomfort.

mate alignment with the femoral neck, a chosen point upon the apex of the neck is penetrated by the pointed tip (Fig. 8-13). The rod is driven down the femoral shaft. As the saddle plate approaches the stump, opportunity for precise fitting is given. Rotatory deviation is corrected with a vise grip or with a special twister. Any prominence above the neck is leveled off so that the saddle can accurately be seated. The stump is accurately trimmed to parallel the plane of the saddle plate, the plate serving as a guide. If, when the rod is hammered home, any gap exists between the stump and end plate, the nail is elevated about ½ inch and one or two collars are inserted to close the gap.

It is most important that any such gap be closed before the insertion is completed and the rod is finally hammered home. Several firm blows are delivered to break down small bone prominences that might prevent close contact. The drill guide is applied to the end plate. The drill is inserted through it and guided by it through the hole in the axial rod,

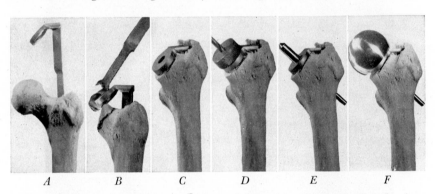

| A | B | C | D | E | F |

Fig. 8-13. Steps of the insertion procedure. *A.* Insertion of stem. *B.* Use of twister for precise fitting and trimming of stump. *C.* Main rod is hammered home, note end-plate contact with stump of femoral neck. *D.* Use of drill guide to ensure accurate direction for transfixion of shaft. *E.* Pivot rod tapped into position through above channel. *F.* Application of head of proper size.

continuing until the outer femoral cortex is penetrated. This step in the insertion procedure requires a drill of the proper size and length, and a drill guide. Without a drill guide, blind penetration of the transfixion hole is practically impossible; with it, it is impossible to miss and the procedure takes a minimum of time. When the drill and guide are removed, the pivot rod is directed through the new channel and is tapped into position.

A head of proper size is applied, the dislocation is reduced, and the wound is closed. After the operation, a plaster spica immobilization for 10 days to 2 weeks overcomes the occasional tendency of the prosthetic head to dislocate. Exercises are begun promptly and partial weight bearing is allowed at 4 to 5 weeks.

Complications of the Prosthetic Operation.

FRACTURE. During the insertion of the prosthesis into the host femur, or later during too forcible reduction of the prosthetic head, the brittle, thin bone of the trochanter or shaft may split or crack. Prevention of this accident is possible by gentleness and avoidance of force. Should fracture occur, it may be necessary to prolong the postoperative spica until x-ray evidence of healing is present.

DISLOCATION OF PROSTHETIC HEAD. During the first or second week post-operatively, the prosthetic head has been known to slip out of the acetabulum. This may occur if the reduction has been effected with great difficulty because of contracture and shortening, if the socket becomes filled with excessive fluid, or if infection and suppuration has occurred. In our experience, risk of dislocation (except for that due to infection) may be entirely eliminated by the use of a low one and one-half spica which immobilizes the leg operated upon in the position of abduction and internal rotation for 2 weeks postoperatively.

INFECTION. Operative infection is probably the most serious of all complications since antibiotic therapy alone is rarely adequate treatment. Removal of the prosthesis is almost always necessary for healing, at which operation the femoral neck or trochanter may be inserted into the acetabulum. After operation, immobilization of the hip in a plaster spica often leads to solid bony union with recovery and loss of pain. Of course, the best therapy for this complication is prevention, and consists of scrupulous attention to asepsis and atraumatic surgery with careful control of bleeding.

MIGRATION. Prosthetic migration may occur centrally into the pelvis or downward with reference to the host femur—both in association with some degree of pain. It is probably more surprising that prosthetic stability occurs in the great majority of instances than that a few should be attacked by this complication. Central migration is recognized to occur when bone has been softened by Paget's disease or by indolent infection, and it may also develop if too small a prosthetic head has been used. It is a rare complication in the absence of these conditions.

Downward migration into the host femur is somewhat more common, and a downward shift of less than $\frac{1}{8}$ inch a year is not unusual or productive of symptoms. Occasionally, in the absence of infection or overt Paget's disease, the prosthesis becomes painful and moves downward in the femur at a more rapid rate promptly after insertion. Sometimes this condition may result from poor seating of the instrument at operation, that is, seating that has failed to take full advantage of available bone buttress and distribution of pressure area. In some instances the reason for this untoward lack of bony resistance is unknown. Attention was called above to the occasional discrepancy between the roentgen appearance of normally firm bone and its actual lack of resistance as disclosed at operation—a circumstance not clearly understood and requiring further study. It is noteworthy that even the severely osteoporotic bone of the menopausal or senile variety generally offers firm resistance to prosthetic migration. Nevertheless, x-ray evidence of prosthetic sag calls for the avoidance of weight bearing for several months, and the trial of estrogenic or mixed-hormone therapy. In the event of failure of anchorage, prosthesis removal may become necessary and arthrodesis of the joint performed.

PAIN. The prosthetic hip is seldom entirely normal or completely pain-free. Postoperatively some degree of discomfort, ache, or pain is practically inevitable. The postoperative pain that develops on resumption of weight bearing or on change of position after long sitting or standing generally recedes slowly after a year or so, remaining as a mild ache after excessive activity. This may persist for years despite an excellent technical result.

Gradual increase of hip pain may be merely the result of increased function to the point of excess, for which the remedy is obvious. Occasionally such pain may reflect laxity of the prosthesis in the host femur and a tendency toward migration. A period of increased rest is indicated and, if the bone is porotic, the administration of estrogen-androgen therapy. A rapid, sharp increase in pain is suggestive of indolent infection which may be verified by x-ray and appropriate laboratory tests. In the two such instances of our experience, ultimate removal of the prosthesis was required. Occasionally pain, limp, and stiffness may result from the insidious development of myositis ossificans about the joint. Its cause remains obscure. The condition may arrest spontaneously or progress to the point where a salvage procedure becomes necessary.

LIMP. Aside from the limp that always accompanies the painful hip, limp may be due to shortening and may be relieved by a shoe lift. More often it is attributable to gluteus weakness which usually lasts for at least a good many months after operation. Gluteus medius function remains weak for a longer period than other hip motions, and some weakness can persist permanently. The prompt institution of abduction exercises, done with persistence, can do much to overcome this muscle's weakness, and the Trendelenberg limp can be greatly diminished by the use of a cane on the well side until sufficient abductor strength has returned.

The Secondary Salvage Procedure. Should the intracapsular fracture fail to heal after a fair trial of internal fixation, or should severe pain and disability develop due to slipping of the fixation or later to avascular collapse of the femoral head, a surgical attempt at salvage is justifiable if the general condition of the patient permits. A wide variety of salvage procedures are available, chief among them being the subtrochanteric angular osteotomy (Schanz and Dickson), the displacement osteotomy (McMurray), the bifurcation osteotomy (Lorenz), transplantation of the trochanter into the acetabulum (Colonna), prosthetic insertion, and arthrodesis of the hip.

The osteotomies have for their major function realignment of weight bearing, relieving the fracture site and the hip joint of some degree of weight-bearing stress (Fig. 8-14). The McMurray operation supplies direct support of the femoral head by the lower fragment which is displaced under it (Fig. 8-15). The angular osteotomy transfers some weight bearing to the lateral pelvis and converts the vertical fracture line to a more oblique plane, thus favoring compression and healing. The planes of the osteotomy and the methods by which the fragments may be fixed internally are legion. Both methods of osteotomy have been applied to nonunion as well as to aseptic necrosis where major deformity of the femoral head is absent. Only the angular osteotomy attempts to relieve the femoral head of a share of weight bearing by shunting this function to the lateral wall of the pelvis. Both must be performed with precision.

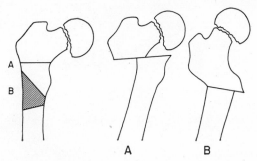

FIG. 8-14. The two major principles of osteotomy. *A.* The McMurray. *B.* The angular.

If the bone of the femur is sufficiently strong, fixation may be accomplished internally and plaster avoided. With or without plaster immobilization, osteotomy requires abstinence from weight bearing until bony healing is established, an important disadvantage to the elderly patient. Furthermore, in instances of aseptic necrosis, it provides no assurance that the deformed femoral head will not continue to respond with pain to the share of weight bearing allocated to it. Osteotomy does not attempt to relieve leg shortening which, in fact, is generally increased by operation, and finally, the distortion of the femoral shaft accomplished by these operations precludes a later trial of medullary stem prostheses should the operation fail. In the author's opinion, osteotomy offers most to younger patients and in those cases of nonunion or delayed union with slipping of the fixation in which the femoral head appears to remain intact and vascular. The reconstruction of Colonna has, for the elderly, the disadvantage of the postoperative plaster spica and ultimate shortening, though Colonna has demonstrated surprisingly good and relatively painless weight bearing after the operation.

The prosthetic operation offers numerous theoretical advantages because of its basic approach to the problems of nonunion and of head deformity, and because it makes possible a close approximation to normal architecture with preservation of mobility and leg length after relatively short periods of postoperative invalidism. It is still too early, however, to ascertain whether statistically these advantages outweigh the obstacles

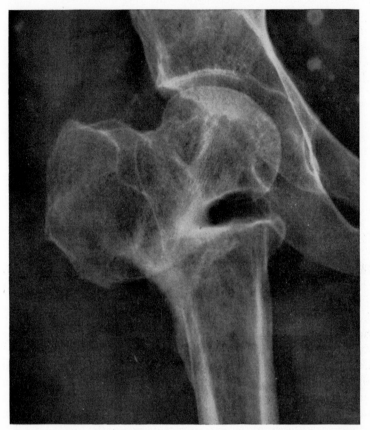

Fig. 8-15. Successful healing of nonunion after McMurray type of osteotomy. Postoperative immobilization by plaster. No internal fixation used.

posed by this demanding procedure and the frequency of its attendant complications. Although the replacement of a deforming femoral head with a lasting round one is desirable, the ultimate degree and duration of stability and relief from pain will require many more years of follow-up study. As previously described, results of the prosthetic procedure are largely dependent upon the stability and durability of the prosthesis employed, and comparative clinical evaluation of these instruments is not yet possible. As stated above, those prostheses that follow the axis of the neck have been widely discarded because of their tendency to loosen and to become painful rapidly. The medullary stem prostheses, especially the Moore, Eicher, and Thompson, have achieved wide current popularity. They may be inserted with little difficulty and their use is probably to be recommended for salvage where a large segment of femoral neck has been absorbed. If prosthetic substitution is performed relatively early and a fair segment of neck remains, however, its buttress value is of considerable importance, especially in resisting rotary laxity and favoring stability. This factor may be utilized by the transfixion prosthesis, the insertion of which has been described above. With this instrument, residual femoral neck does not wash away but remains and hypertrophies in response to the nonabrasive and nonshearing weight-bearing pressure applied to the stump surface through the prosthesis.

Arthrodesis is applicable to selected cases following nonunion or the unsuccessful trial of a prosthesis. Unfortunately, arthrodesis in an elderly patient does not present the same favorable outlook that it does in relative youth. The lack of agility and suppleness, the disc lesions and stiffness of the lumbar spine—which takes on the additional function of the fused hip—often cause irremediable pain. The older patient who spends a greater share of his time sitting finds difficulty in the postural distortion required. The healing time is slow regardless of the method of arthrodesis employed. Nevertheless, in an agile and active patient with a good range of lumbar spine motion, a totally painless hip results from arthrodesis and the lumbar spine can afterwards assume its increased burden painlessly.

Arthrodesis of the hip may be performed in many ways. In the elderly patient, the writer has employed a Smith-Peterson or a posterolateral incision. The previous fixative or prosthetic device is removed and the hip dislocated. The acetabulum is denuded of cartilage—especially superiorly—and the residual neck or trochanter, also denuded above, inserted as deeply as possible into the socket. The largest possible area of raw bone-to-bone contact is desirable. The limb is then brought into neutral position to make certain of stability, and the foot is incorporated in the foot plate of the table in as close to neutral position as possible with the hip at about 150° of flexion.

An extra plaque of bone is brought down from the iliac flare and laid across, bridging the denuded ilium and superior neck or trochanter. Available chips of autogenous bone are added. Closure of the wound is followed by application of a long single or double plaster spica making certain that the position of the limb has not been altered. Radiological examination before and after application of the spica is an indispensable precaution.

Approximately 10 days after operation, the plaster is windowed on the outer aspect of the entire thigh, and the skin is prepared for the low vertical application of a long Smith-Peterson nail designed to intrude 1½ inches or so into the acetabular roof and ilium. The additional fixation provided by the nail allows for the subsequent use of a low single spica to below the knee. Ambulation is possible generally in 4 to 5 weeks after the initial operation.

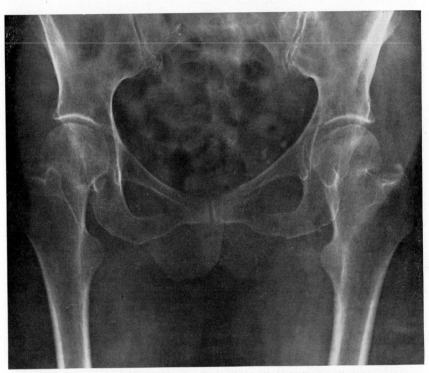

Fig. 8-16. Bilateral deformity secondary to valgus fractures occurring 7 months apart. Both treated solely by bed rest and light traction (3 pounds), for immobilization.

The Valgus or Impacted Intracapsular Fracture

The valgus or impacted intracapsular fracture poses far less of a problem than does the displaced or varus fracture. The former is invariably the consequence of forced abduction beyond the stretch limit of the inferior capsule of the hip joint. The injury itself tends to impact the fracture and the valgus position causes the impaction to be reinforced by subsequent muscle pull and spasm. Nevertheless, the stability of the fracture in an individual case is unknown. In the past 2 years, the author has had occasion to treat three such fractures that have spontaneously separated and displaced into varus position 10 days, 3 weeks, and 5 weeks, respectively, after the initial injury. When such separation occurs, the benign valgus fracture becomes converted into one possessing all the hazards that apply to the displaced varus group described above. It is probably erroneous to attribute the benignity of the impacted fracture

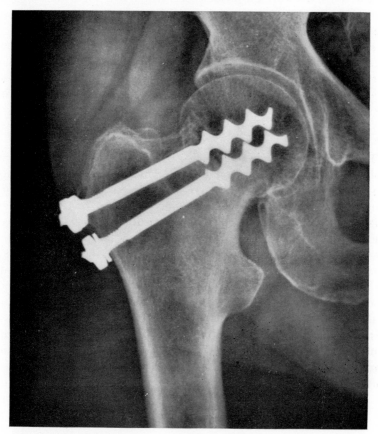

FIG. 8-17. Corkscrew bolt fixation of valgus fracture. Provides safety. However, further compression at fracture site is not the objective. Top nuts are firm but not screwed tightly.

entirely to its valgus position since displaced fractures converted into equivalent position fail to exhibit the same benign course. The explanation probably rests in the periosteal and vascular tears associated with the original displacement.

Each displacement in the author's experience has been due to either the lack of medical attention or the failure of the attending physician to recognize the injury and its hazards and hence to forbid continued weight bearing.

A younger patient may elect to avoid surgery and remain in bed until healing of the fracture has been attained (Fig. 8-16), probably a period of 7 to 8 weeks. In the older patient however, the risks of long bed rest are less desirable. For this reason, internal fixation is employed to permit ambulation early during convalescence. In the fixation of the valgus fracture, the trifin nail should not be used because of the danger of driving the impaction apart during its insertion. Multiple fixative devices, such as screws, lag screws, Knowles pins, Austin Moore pins, etc. (Fig. 8-17), are far safer for the fixation of this type of fracture. Lag screws should not be used, however, to gain further compression. Four to six weeks after fixation, ambulation with partial weight bearing may be safely permitted.

TROCHANTERIC FRACTURES

The term trochanteric fracture is generally applied to the wide range of fractures below the femoral neck in which at least one extremity of the fracture line lies between the greater and lesser trochanter. The group ranges from simple avulsion fractures of the greater or lesser trochanter (Fig. 8-18) which pose no difficult therapeutic problem to the severely comminuted fractures (Fig. 8-19) that extend for 6 inches down the femoral shaft. Most trochanteric fractures, however, have a base line that extends from the greater to the lesser trochanter; and in about half of these, the fracture does not extend materially beyond these limits. The trochanteric fracture is generally associated with more severe trauma than is the intracapsular fracture, but in elderly osteoporotic women it may be also encountered, like the intracapsular fracture, as a result of minimal trauma. Because it is not confined by the hip-joint capsule, the more severe lesion may be associated with marked bleeding into the soft tissues and shock factors which probably play a large role in the higher mortality rate associated with the fracture—almost double that of the intracapsular fracture.

BACKGROUND SKETCH

Until the late 1930s the trochanteric fracture was treated by prolonged immobilization in a plaster spica or traction, Buck's extension, or Russell traction. Internal fixation of the trochanteric fracture was not instituted on a broad scale until some 10 years of experience had accumulated with the internal fixation of the intracapsular fracture. Its introduction then brought about sharp improvement in mortality figures, in complications, in ultimate hip and knee function, and in ease of nursing care. In 1947, Cleveland, Bosworth, and Thompson reported reduction of mortality from 34 to 12.6 per cent, in senile psychosis from 11 to 2.1 per cent. The method has become almost universally accepted. For fixation, the in-

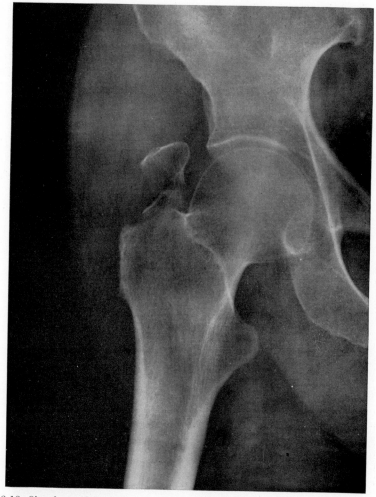

FIG. 8-18. Simple avulsion fracture of greater trochanter treated by Buck's extension for 5 weeks.

struments of Jewett, Neufeld, and McLaughlin have received widest acceptance (Fig. 8-20).

REDUCTION

Reduction of the trochanteric fracture necessarily varies with the plane and extent. If the fracture is simple and extends from greater to lesser trochanter, elements of posterior periosteum often remain intact. The fracture opens anteriorly like a book, and may be closed with perfect reduction merely by reproducing the limit of internal rotation previously determined in the opposite leg (Fig. 8-21). Internal rotation must be gently performed, however, lest the thin, remaining periosteum be torn and the fracture converted into a more difficult problem. If, after affixing

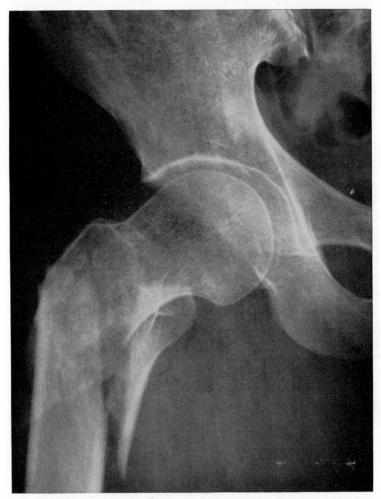

FIG. 8-19. The low-level fracture including lesser trochanter.

the foot to the foot plate of the table with minimal traction in this position, radiographs indicate satisfactory position, preparation of the operative field, draping, and fixation may be undertaken.

Should the fracture be more comminuted, satisfactory reduction of the major fragments may usually be accomplished by traction in the position of slight adduction followed by gentle abduction to 10° and inward

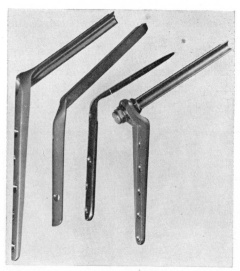

FIG. 8-20. Various flanged devices for the fixation of trochanteric fractures—in order, Jewett, Neufeld, Moore-Blount, and McLaughlin.

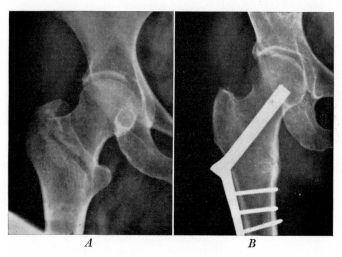

A   *B*

FIG. 8-21. *A.* Simple trochanteric fracture corrected merely by internal rotation. *B.* After internal fixation.

rotation of the leg to the above described limit. It is important to recognize that although shattering and displacement of smaller fragments often exist, the objective of the procedure is limited to the fixation of the two or possibly three major fragments in proper alignment and at proper trochanteric angle (Fig. 8-22). If, after incorporating the foot and applying sufficient traction, the above maneuver accomplishes this goal as revealed in the anteroposterior and lateral roentgenograms, preparation for fixation may be made with the surgical field limited as above to the

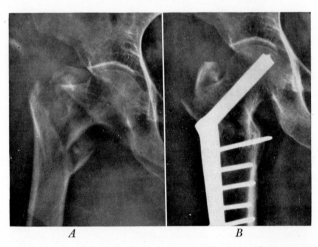

A   *B*

FIG. 8-22. *A*. Comminuted trochanteric fracture. The most frequent plane of the trochanter fracture. Internal fixation is limited to the major two or three fragments. *B*. After fixation.

lateral aspect of the upper thigh. Should satisfactory reduction be unobtainable by the maneuver, it is our practice not to attach the foot of the injured leg to the foot plate but to prepare it for the sterile field so that it may be freely maneuverable when the fracture is surgically exposed.

Three circumstances account for most cases in which closed reduction fails. First is extension of the fracture into the upper third of the femoral shaft with separation and displacement of large supportive fragments. Generally such fragments may be reduced with little difficulty and so maintained with a bone clamp until fixation is accomplished. Secondly, the proximal fragment may be locked against the shaft an inch or more below its normal position. This circumstance calls for enlargement of the exposure upward and the application of direct upward traction upon the distal portion of the proximal fragment while countertraction is applied to the leg in neutral or adducted position.

The third reason for failure of closed reduction consists of extensive disruption of posterior soft-tissue continuity resulting in the proximal fracture surface being rotated posteriorly and the peripheral trochanter segment lying forward in front of the neck. Reduction may be possible by direct lateral traction upon the trochanter segment, rolling the leg externally so that its fracture surface faces that of the proximal fragment. Fixation is then accomplished with the leg in the position of external rotation. With the incision enlarged upward, it may be necessary to pull the distal end of the proximal fragment forward, maintaining it in this position until fixation is applied to maintain it there.

Caution. Especially in the older patient, the characteristically sparse trabeculation often results in compression and telescoping of the substance of the trochanter at the time of fracture. Accordingly, reproduction of the normal trochanteric angle may leave an unfilled gap at the lower fracture site. Gaps in the approximation of the major surfaces are slow to heal and impose a severe strain upon the fixative device. Delayed healing and metallic-fatigue fracture with loss of position occasionally occur under these circumstances.

If reestablishing the normal trochanteric angle results in such a separation, it is safer to accept a lower-than-normal angle with fragments approximated, though it may entail some degree of coxa vara and shortening.

FIXATION

Fixation of the trochanteric fracture is accomplished through a lateral incision only slightly longer than the flange of the fixative instrument. The incision may be enlarged either upward or downward as may be required. Upward extension is possible through the cleft between the tensor fascia lata and the gluteus medius, exposing the anterior surface of the trochanter. For downward extension, the anterior surface of the lateral fascial plane can be followed down to bone by retracting the bulk of the vastus lateralis muscle forward, the lateral surface of the femur being exposed by subperiosteal dissection.

The fixative devices for trochanteric fractures are designed to maintain the two or possibly three major fragments in appropriate position. It is practically never advisable to attempt to gain anatomic reposition of smaller fragments unless they are supportive. For the latter, separate screws or plate fixation may be required if the screws applied through the flange are inadequate. They must avoid the area to be occupied by the flange later applied. However, the device is not excessively bulky and possesses the advantage of a single piece unit. Whatever angle device is used, the length of the nail section should be somewhat shorter than would be chosen for a corresponding intracapsular fracture. The center point of the femoral head is a useful guide to mark the upper limit of length.

Our experience has been mainly with the Jewett and McLaughlin instruments. The adjustable angle of the McLaughlin instrument renders the insertion procedure simpler, since the angle at which the trifin nail

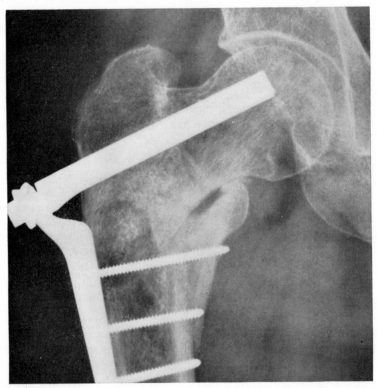

FIG. 8-23. Loosening of the McLaughlin device (older model) a few weeks after firm application.

is inserted is not critical provided its tip is properly placed. After the nail penetrates the trochanter, the lateral flange is attached to it, aligned with the plane of the femoral shaft, and screwed firmly to the nail at this angle. Objections to this device have been twofold. In the first place, the complicated variable-angle mechanism that binds the flange to the nail has become separated weeks after insertion, requiring a second operation (Fig. 8-23). Secondly, its bulk has proved persistently uncomfortable and painful to pressure, especially in thin people, a complaint often requiring removal of the instrument after healing. Recently, McLaughlin has improved the firmness of the angle mechanism of the device to hold more securely. Its bulk however remains large.

If the Jewett one-piece trifin nail and flange is employed, a large assortment of variable angles, length of nail, and flange must be available from which to choose the one appropriate for the patient. The insertion of the Jewett nail must be more precise than that of the McLaughlin mechanism. Not only must the angle of insertion correspond to the fixed angle of the mechanism, but the rotation of the instrument must also be carefully controlled in the lateral plane to ensure accurate alignment of the flange with the femoral shaft.

Cautions. 1. In the aged patient, the cortex of the trochanter is paper thin and fragile, and it is easily split during insertion of the nail. Splitting can generally be avoided by the use of a cannulated reamer inserted over the guide wire to provide a cortical channel for the nail segment. If splitting of the trochanter should occur, it may act as a source of increased postoperative pain, but it is not of great concern since the lower fragment will be adequately fixed by the flange of the instrument.

2. After insertion of the nail segment, impaction must be gentle lest the weak trabeculae at the fracture site become compressed, driving the tip of the nail into the joint. It is always useful to check the position of the tip of the nail in the head by x-ray before the lateral flange is screwed to the shaft. If required, its substitution with a shorter nail over a reinserted guide wire is easily performed at this point.

3. In healing, further absorption of the trochanteric trabeculae may occur, especially when the angle of the nail and flange used is more obtuse. Since the attachment of the flange to the shaft prevents extrusion, the nail can penetrate the femoral head and intrude into the joint, destroying it. It is important, therefore, to provide leeway for further nail intrusion during healing by making certain at the operation that the nail protrudes no further inward than the center point of the head. Also, since latitude exists in the angle of the device chosen, it is probably advisable to select the lowest angle compatible with that of the reduced fracture.

Complications. 1. In spite of the manufacturing precautions and proper insertion technique, all types of angle devices occasionally have been known to fracture during the late months of convalescence, generally with more or less loss of valgus position of the hip. Whether the fault is metallic and due to flaws, due to metal fatigue as a result of bending, the result of absorption or loss of tissue at the fracture site, due to too early weight bearing, to weakening of the flange as a result of bending at operation, to strain imposed by reduction at too great a valgus angle with poor contact below, or to too sudden excessive demand, is often difficult to determine. Should such fracture of the instrument be accompanied by marked loss of position of the fracture, there is no alternative to prompt reoperation and insertion of a new and shorter instrument. At reoperation, it is advisable to accept less valgus and accordingly to employ an instrument with less valgus than the original one. If fracture of the instrument occurs late during convalescence after some healing has developed, only slight alteration in the position of the fragments may result. Such fractures, if relieved from weight bearing, have been known to heal promptly after fracture of the instrument and present no need for urgent repair unless varus is progressive. In the event of progressive shortening, internal fixation must be reapplied in more varus position than the original fixation.

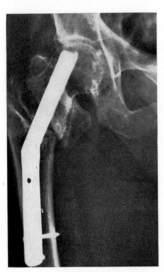

FIG. 8-24. Nonunion following use of Neufeld nail probably the result of severe osteoporosis.

2. If appliances that require bolting with screws have been used, gradual loosening of the screws is a possibility. We have observed the same screw of such a device loosen three times despite what was said to have been firm tightening. The recourse is in reoperation, preferably with a new device.

3. Protrusion of the tip of the nail into the joint may result from telescoping of osteoporotic bone during healing, especially if the femoral neck is in marked valgus so that fixation has required a steeply angled fixative device. Replacement of the device by one with a shorter nail segment is required. Urgent replacement is necessary if the projection is above and involves the acetabular roof. The ideal fixative instrument would provide for withdrawal and adjustment of the nail without the need of unfastening the instrument. In our opinion, no simple mechanism has been devised as yet to permit this.

4. Rarely, a wide gap develops at the fracture line with failure of bony union. The remedy lies in exposure of the fracture site anteriorly through an incision prolonged upward, removal of the fixative instrument, deep curettage of the fracture surfaces, reapplication of a fixative instrument with the fracture surfaces in contact, and reinforcement anteriorly by bony grafts taken from the ilium (Fig. 8-24).

Osteotomy with medial displacement of the lower fragment (McMurray) may be added to this procedure with the purpose of bridging the fracture with viable bone. Fixation of the proximal fragment to the shaft is generally possible with the Jewett appliance, the trochanteric segment being separately dealt with. The entire operation is a major procedure that should not be lightly undertaken.

THE AVULSION FRACTURE

Occasionally in the aged, simple avulsion of the greater or lesser trochanter occurs without any interruption of continuity of weight-bearing structure. In these fractures, callus appears to bridge even large intervals of separation within a surprisingly short time. Reparative surgery is never required in the case of the lesser trochanter, and for the greater trochanter only in the event of the rare occurrence of wide separation. In the latter circumstance, the fragment may be replaced and maintained by two bone screws.

BIBLIOGRAPHY

Barr, J.: Discussion of report of committee on fractures and traumatic surgery on the use of a prosthesis in treatment of fresh fractures of the neck of the femura. *Jour. Bone and Joint Surg.* **40A**:885, 1957.

Blount, W. P.: Blade plate fixation of high femoral osteotomies. *Jour. Bone and Joint Surg.* **25**:319, 1943.

Boyd, H. B., and I. J. George: "Campbell's Operative Orthopedics," vol. 1, 2d ed., p. 437. St. Louis, Mosby, 1947.

Boyd, H. B., D. B. Zilversmit, and R. A. Calandruccio: Use of radioactive phosphorus P[32] to determine the viability of head of the femur. *Jour. Bone and Joint Surg.* **37A**:260, 1955.

Campbell, W. S.: Treatment of fracture of the neck of the femur by internal fixation: report of American academy of orthopaedic surgeons' fracture committee. *Jour. Bone and Joint Surg.* **23**:386, 1941.

Charnley, J.: "Compression Arthrodesis." Edinburgh and London, E. & S. Livingstone, Ltd., 1953.

Cleveland, M., and W. L. Bailey: An end result study of intracapsular fractures of the neck of the femur. *Surg. Gyn. and Obs.* **90**:393, 1950.

Cleveland, M., and D. M. Bosworth: Fractures of the neck of the femur. *Surg. Gyn. and Obst.* **66**:646, 1938.

Cleveland, M., D. M. Bosworth, and F. Thompson: Intertrochanteric fracture of the femur. *Jour. Bone and Joint Surg.* **29**:1049, 1947.

Cleveland, M., and J. W. Fielding: Continuing end result study of intracapsular fractures of the neck of the femur. *Jour. Bone and Joint Surg.* **36A**:1020, 1954.

Colonna, P. C.: A new type of reconstruction operation for old ununited fractures of the neck of the femur. *Jour. Bone and Joint Surg.* **17**:110, 1935.

Dickson, J. A.: The "unsolved" fracture. *Jour. Bone and Joint Surg.* **35A**:805, 1953.

Erdheim, J.: Personal Studies, 1926.

Evans, E. M.: Trochanteric fractures. *Jour. Bone and Joint Surg.* **33B**:192, 1951.

Gray, C. H.: Fractures of the Neck of the Femur, in H. Platt, "Modern Trends in Orthopaedics," 2d series, p. 306. New York, Hoeber-Harper, 1956.

Jewett, E. L.: One piece angle nail for trochanteric fractures. *Jour. Bone and Joint Surg.* **23**:803, 1941.

Johansson, S.: On the operative treatment of medial fractures of the neck of the femur. *Acta Orth. Scand.* 3:362, 1932.

Knowles, F. L.: Fractures of the neck of the femur. *Wisconsin Med. Jour.* 35:106, 1936.

Linton, P.: Different types of fractures of the femoral neck. *Acta Chir. Scand.* 90:Suppl. 86, 1944.

Lippmann, R. K.: Use of auscultatory percussion for the examination of fractures. *Jour. Bone and Joint Surg.* 14:118, 1932.

Lippmann, R. K.: Experiences with the corkscrew bolt. *Jour. Bone and Joint Surg.* 21:735, 1939.

Lippmann, R. K.: The transfixion prosthesis. *Jour. Bone and Joint Surg.* 39A:759, 1958.

Lorenz, A.: Über die Behandlung der irreponiblen augenborenen Hüftluxationen und der schenkelhalspseudarthrosen Mittels Gabelung. *Wiener Klin. Wchnschr.* 32:997, 1919.

McFarland, B., and G. Osborne: Approach to the hip. *Jour. Bone and Joint Surg.* 36B:364, 1954.

McLaughlin, J.: Adjustable internal fixation element for the hip. *Amer. Jour. Surg.* 73:150, 1947.

McMurray, T. P.: Ununited fractures of the neck of the femur. *Jour. Bone and Joint Surg.* 18:319, 1936.

Moore, A. T.: Fracture of the hip joint (intracapsular): a new method of skeletal fixation. *Jour. S. Carolina Med. Ass.* 30:199, 1934.

Moore, A. T.: Blade plate internal fixation for intertrochanteric fractures. *Jour. Bone and Joint Surg.* 26:52, 1944.

Moore, A. T.: Self locking metal hip prosthesis. *Jour. Bone and Joint Surg.* 39A:811, 1957.

Neufeld, A. J., F. Jayen, and G. M. Tayler: Internal fixation for intertrochanteric fractures. *Jour. Bone and Joint Surg.* 26:707, 1944.

Pauwels, F.: Der Schenkelhalsbruch: ein mechanisches Problem. Beilagheft 2, *Ztschr. f. Orth. Chir.* 63:1935.

Reynolds, F. C.: Report of committee on fractures and traumatic surgery on the use of a prosthesis in treatment of fresh fractures of the neck of the femur. *Jour. Bone and Joint Surg.* 40A:877, 1958.

Schanz, A.: Über die nach Schenkelhalsbruchen zurückbleibenden Gestoerungen. *Deutsche Med. Wchnschr.* 51:731, 1925.

Sherman, M. S., and W. Selakovich: Bone changes in chronic circulatory insufficiency. *Jour. Bone and Joint Surg.* 39A:892, 1957.

Smith-Peterson, M. N., E. F. Cave, and G. W. Van Gorder: Intracapsular fractures of the neck of the femur. *Arch. Surg.* 23:715, 1931.

Speed, K.: The unsolved fracture. *Surg. Gyn. and Obs.* 60:341, 1935.

Taylor, M., A. J. Neufeld, and J. Jargen: Internal fixation for intertrochanteric fractures. *Jour. Bone and Joint Surg.* 26:707, 1944.

Thompson, F. R.: Two and a half years' experience with a vitallium intramedullary hip prosthesis. *Jour. Bone and Joint Surg.* 36A:489, 1954.

Thornton, L., and C. Sandison: Recognition of modern treatment of broken hips. *Southern Med. Jour.* 29:456, 1936.

Trueta, J., and M. H. Harrison: The normal vascular anatomy of the femoral head in adult man. *Jour. Bone and Joint Surg.* 35B:442, 1953.

Whitman, R.: A new method of treatment for fractures of the neck of the femur. *Ann. Surg.* 36:746, 1902.

Chapter 9

Fracture Dislocations of the Hip

Robert K. Lippmann

As friability of bone increases with age, simple dislocation at the hip becomes increasingly rare, and our hospital records disclose no single instance of simple hip dislocation beyond the sixth decade. In the aged, the traumata which in the younger person may produce hip dislocation commonly result in fracture of the femoral neck and far less frequently in fracture dislocation. Fractures about the acetabulum associated with some degree of dislocation basically fall into the grouping proposed by Armstrong.

Group 1. Central depression of the socket with central displacement of the femoral head

Group 2. Posterosuperior acetabular rim fractures with femoral head displacement in the direction of the displaced rim fragments

Group 3. Dislocation associated with major damage to the femoral head or neck

(Occasional mixed lesions and some difficult to classify in the above groups are encountered.)

FREQUENCY

In younger people, group 2 or fracture dislocations with acetabular rim lesions have been most common. Armstrong reports that of 55 fracture dislocations in the Royal Air Force, 43 were acetabular rim fractures, 7 involved the acetabular floor, and 5 involved fracture of the femoral head. In an older civilian age group, Thompson and Epstein reported 61 fracture dislocations in which 28 involved the floor of the acetabulum, 22 the acetabular rim, and 11 the femoral head. In the aged, fracture of the acetabular floor or group 1, is relatively most frequent, while fracture of the femoral head is seldom encountered. (Surgical approaches upon groups 1 and 2 disclose that the femoral head is seldom entirely uninvolved and that abrasions and minor traumata to its articular surface are the rule.) Fractures of the pubic and ischial rami are common accompaniments to these lesions. All three types of fracture dislocation

243

of the hip are far more frequent in male patients, probably because of the wider exposure of males to the severe traumata of this mechanical age and because of the greater selective rarifaction and vulnerability of the femoral neck in older women.

MECHANISM

Fracture dislocation of the hip can result from direct as well as indirect force. In the aged, fracture of the acetabular floor (group 1) can be produced by a simple fall upon the trochanter, the impact being transmitted along the femoral neck. Indirectly, the limited abduction of the hip in the aged can produce the same fracture as would be the result of any impact which forces the thigh into wide abduction or the torso in the same direction. Dislocation with fracture of the acetabular rim or of the femoral head (groups 2 and 3) results from impact in line with the femoral shaft. As pointed out by Knight and Smith, the position of the rim fracture depends upon the position of the thigh at the time of the impact. If the hip is in flexion and adduction (as when the legs are crossed) or in neutral, the impact will be sustained by the posterior acetabular wall. If the hip is extended, the superior aspect of the socket will receive the blow and the fracture. If the blow forces the leg into adduction, flexed or extended, it will tend to dislocate the hip and may fracture the femoral head as it slips across the rim of the socket.

BACKGROUND SKETCH

Until recent years, it was common practice to treat all varieties of fracture dislocation at the hip by nonoperative measures. Traction to the involved extremity in the direction opposite to the fracture displacement was the guiding principle, its application varying with the ingenuity of the surgeon. Simple Buck's extension or Russell traction was widely employed for therapy of acetabular rim fractures. For central dislocation, traction in line with the axis of the neck was utilized by adding a cuff to the thigh pulling laterally, by direct pull, upon a screw or pin inserted into or through the greater trochanter, and more recently, by leg-to-leg plaster with distraction apparatus or windlass separating them.

Although complete and stable anatomic reduction is scarcely if ever attained by these methods, acceptable and sometimes surprisingly asymptomatic results have not been infrequent—especially in the central displacement fractures. For reasons to be discussed later, there would seem to be ample justification for the continued use of certain of these methods at the present time.

Aside from occasional publications, the first significant report of a series of surgical approaches to the therapy of acetabular lip fractures was made by King and Richards in 1941. When a major portion of the acetabular roof is involved and displaced, and reduction of the hip by closed methods fails to replace the rim fragment, lasting instability of the hip may result. King and Richards reported eight cases demonstrating the feasibility of replacing and anchoring the rim fracture by means of screws through a transgluteal approach. Satisfactory results were reported and the method is widely employed at present.

In 1951, Thompson and Epstein reviewed 61 fracture dislocations of the hip treated in the Los Angeles County Hospital. The findings indicated no significant gain from operative reduction except in the event of inclusion of fragments in the acetabulum preventing adequate closed reduction. They pointed out the great frequency of late changes of arthritis and aseptic necrosis, and emphasized the importance of early reduction.

Stewart and Milford, in 1954, presented a series of 193 fracture dislocations of the hip. On the basis of these cases, the authors stressed the importance of immediate attempts at closed reduction, and if unstable, the application of traction until surgical approach becomes possible. Avascular necrosis is common after both open and closed methods.

In 1958, Knight and Smith reported upon an operative approach to central hip dislocation, reducing the displacement with the help of Knowles pins inserted into the fragments. The eight cases presented were all young patients, and the authors took pains to emphasize the problems encountered in ascertaining radiologically the areas involved by the fracture, the need for great care in selecting a suitable approach to reach them, and the difficulties of the procedure. It still remains to be demonstrated that avascular necrosis of the femoral head may be significantly reduced by the surgical attainment of better reduction, although it is plain that late arthritic changes may be so diminished. Since the procedure is most difficult and still experimental, it is scarcely applicable to older patients at this time. In most orthopedic clinics, central acetabular fracture dislocations continue to be treated by nonoperative measures.

A recent study of fracture dislocations of group 3 (involving the femoral head) was made in 1957 by Pipkin. Twenty-five cases of dislocation with damage of varying degrees to the femoral head and neck were pooled from the records of 15 orthopedic surgeons. While the outcome was short of excellent in all members of the group, best results were obtained by prompt closed reduction when this was feasible. (Primary prosthetic substitution was performed in only one instance of irreparable head damage.) While all grades of fracture dislocation in the aged continue to challenge the ingenuity of orthopedic surgeons, the basic problem of avascular necrosis and bone collapse in so strategic an area as the femoral head remains without solution. Certainly when the femoral head is fractured, and probably in central and acetabular rim fractures, this complication is established at the time of original injury.

THERAPY

GENERAL CONSIDERATIONS

The difficulties in therapy presented by fracture dislocation of the hip in the younger age group are greatly amplified in the aged. Early sitting in a chair or ambulation, as striven for in simple hip fracture, is seldom possible when the fragile iliac structure of the aged is involved by major fracture, whatever plan of therapy may be instituted. In the elderly patient, whether traction or plaster spica, with or without surgery, is carried out, early passive and active mobilization of as much of the body as possible is of greatest importance. Competent and constant nursing and physiotherapeutic care to encourage and ensure these activities assumes the importance of a lifesaving measure. Of these activities, deep-breathing exercises, active use of involved extremities, and frequent rolling and turning from side to side when possible will help to prevent bed sores, will improve circulation, and will promote a sense of well-being. The heels must be protected from excess pressure. The choice of local therapy in the aged must give primary consideration to the physical status and ambulatory capabilities of the patient prior to injury. It is dangerous and foolhardy to attempt major reconstructive procedures upon patients previously unable to get about comfortably, or in the face of rapid general deterioration or short life expectancy. On the other hand, the properly prepared older patient can generally accept a major surgical procedure more easily than a long period of incarceration in bed or in plaster. A surgical approach that may avoid or abbreviate an otherwise long period of plaster or traction is generally the procedure of choice.

LOCAL TREATMENT

Central Acetabular Displacement (Group 1). The severity of these lesions ranges from slight depression of the acetabular floor to lesions of great complexity in which fracture lines radiate widely from the socket in various planes and with various degrees of medial displacement of the femoral head. In the milder lesions, the central displacement of the socket is created by a well-rounded and grossly unimpaired femoral head. Accordingly, the soft bone of the socket in the aged, although comminuted, generally compresses and retains its general shape and conforms well with that of the intact femoral head. In such lesions, therapy is obviously conservative and directed mainly toward the preservation of general health.

Initially, mild traction may be applied for comfort, and within a few days progressive passive and active exercises to hip and knee may be instituted. Within a few weeks, sitting in a chair is usually possible; but weight bearing is delayed for 6 to 8 weeks. Practically normal return of function may be attained, the central migration of the socket being of small moment.

Late arthritic changes or avascular necrosis of the femoral head with associated increasing pain and limitation of function occur in less than one-third of the cases. The more severe lesions characterized by widespread comminution and marked penetration of the femoral head into the pelvic canal present, in the aged, a more difficult problem. Such injuries may be accompanied by considerable shock, but in older people severe hemorrhage is not often observed—probably because of the arteriosclerotic changes common to this age group. However, associated lesions of other parts of the skeleton are frequent and often delay proper local therapy. They call for careful skeletal survey to exclude them.

The variety of methods of local treatment for severe fracture dislocation of this sort gives evidence of their general inefficiency. Practically all of the nonoperative methods consist of some type of traction applied to the involved extremity in a downward and lateral plane. The two-plane traction is generally accomplished by (1) Buck's extension with lateral pull of a large cuff about the thigh, (2) direct pull upon a wire or Steinman nail transfixing the greater trochanter anteroposteriorly, (3) insertion of a large screw (of corkscrew variety) laterally into the trochanter and applying traction to the tip of the screw which is left protruding through the skin, or (4) by means of leg-to-leg plaster with intervening windlass or other adjustable mechanism to produce lateral pull upon the involved femoral head. Except for the last method, total bed rest is necessary and rotation from side to side is not possible during convalescence, a severe handicap in the older patients. Moreover, the experience of the author with these methods is, in accord with that of Knight and Smith, that anatomic reposition is seldom if ever achieved by any of them. Healing, however, is almost universal and, if the acetabular roof is in good alignment and avascular necrosis does not occur, remarkably good and enduring clinical results may be attained although some shortening, or limitation of motion with limp, persists (Fig. 9-1). Operative intervention on these lesions as reported by Knight and Smith has the objective of more accurate reposition of the displaced elements. Careful and multiple radiographic views are essential to plan the approach required for the exposure of the irregular, radiating fracture lines that may be otherwise totally inaccessible through a carelessly planned incision. Surgery of this nature, especially in the aged, is precarious and calls for considerable experience and skill.

It is important to bear in mind, moreover, that even after the accomplishment of accurate reposition, fractures as extensive as these commonly impair the circulation to the femoral head (Fig. 9-2). If the circulatory damage is established by the injury, any benefit from such precarious surgery will be short-lived. The problem calls for further statistical study. At this point, in the opinion of the author, the major operative approach upon most fractures of this nature must be considered as still experimental and certainly not to be contemplated in aged patients.

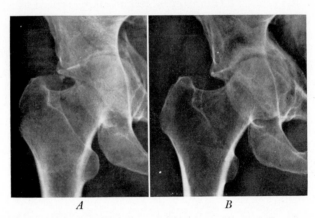

A   *B*

Fig. 9-1. Central depression fracture resulting from direct fall upon trochanter. *A*. On admission to hospital. *B*. Two years after therapy. (Leg distraction technique.) Note absence of changes of avascular necrosis and well-rounded acetabulum. Patient walks normally. Abduction limited 10°. Asymptomatic.

An exception to this rule presents itself when the roof of the acetabulum is badly tilted or displaced so that it can no longer yield adequate weight-bearing support or causes marked distortion of the acetabulum. If there is neighboring sturdy anchorage, correction of the tilt would appear justifiable (Fig. 9-3). Such correction is usually not difficult and, with some ingenuity, may often be secured through a superficial approach and maintained by a few screws. Except for these instances, where instability of the acetabular roof occurs the preference of the author in such fractures has been strongly in favor of a modification of the leg-to-leg distraction method suggested by Jahss. It has the great advantage of permitting the patient a far greater latitude of mobility and appears to be quite as effective as the various traction methods in obtaining partial reduction of displacement as well as subsequent maintenance of reduction. With this device, the patient may sit up, may be rotated from side to side, and may be prone. Later, if the help of orderlies is available to help lift the patient, the wheel chair may be used, thus providing for adequate position changes during convalescence. Unfortunately, the method does

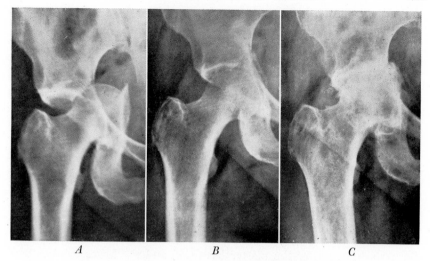

FIG. 9-2. Central depression fracture resulting from auto crash. *A*. On admission to hospital. *B*. Reduction attained and maintained by leg distraction. *C*. Result 3 years later. Note collapse of apex of femoral head secondary to avascular necrosis. Hip gradually becoming increasingly painful. Flexion blocked at 120°. Internal rotation one-third normal. Patient walks with moderate limp—up to ½ mile.

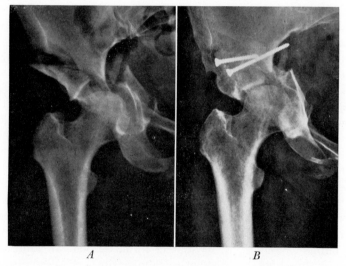

FIG. 9-3. Extensively comminuted fracture resulting from auto crash injury. *A*. On admission to hospital. *B*. Fifteen months after replacement and fixation of acetabular roof followed by traction. Flexion blocked at 100°. Abduction slightly limited. Walks without pain for time being. Ultimate arthritis is anticipated. (*Courtesy of Dr. E. S. Barash*)

not exclude the late development of avascular necrosis or arthritic changes and their attendant symptoms.

DISTRACTION PLASTER METHOD

Without anesthesia, a sturdy but well-padded plaster is applied to each lower extremity, toes to upper thigh. Special attention to reinforcement of the plaster and to padding at pressure areas is required. After adequate drying, brackets for reception of a windlass are applied to the inner aspect of the plaster at the level of both thighs above the knee joint. A hinge, or solid but slightly flexible bar about two feet in length, is then incorporated in the plaster above the ankles, maintaining separation between them with the legs in neutral rotation and abducted about 30°. The windlass of appropriate size is then applied and expanded to the tolerable limit. If the femoral head has penetrated the acetabular floor and lies deep within the pelvis, the author has found it expedient to initiate the distracting force after the plaster has dried and the lower bar has been applied. A brief anesthesia permits the initial distraction of the thigh, application of the proper size of windlass, and its expansion to proper bearable tension.

Whether or not primary anesthesia is employed, the compressibility of felt requires that the windlass be expanded every few days and its position checked at least weekly by x-ray for the first 3 weeks or so. After the first week, the plaster about the patellae is removed so that regular quadriceps exercises may be checked (Fig. 9-4).

Caution. Especially in older people, the areas subjected to the separation pressure must be well padded to avoid pressure sores, and the same applies to the heels. The complaint of pain in these areas calls for some release of windlass pressure, and if persistent, for prompt inspection by windowing the plaster and application of a softer medium. Since damage of plaster may entail loss of position, the initial plaster should be especially well reinforced and sufficiently sturdy to maintain integrity despite possible windowing.

FRACTURE DISLOCATION OF THE ACETABULAR RIM (GROUP II)

Therapy of the fracture dislocation of the acetabular rim in the aged must depend largely upon the general status of the patient as well as the local findings presented. In its simpler form, trauma can cause the hip to displace, break off a section of acetabular rim, and spontaneously return to normal position. If the hip is stable, there is no therapeutic problem.

Displacement of a small rim segment with residual subluxation of the hip usually responds well to simple traction (Fig. 9-5). If the head of the femur remains out of the socket following displacement of the acetabular

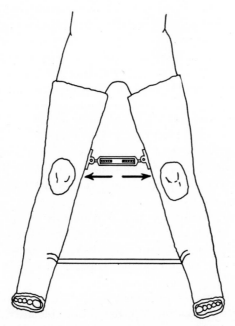

FIG. 9-4. Diagram of distraction method. (*Modified from Jahss*)

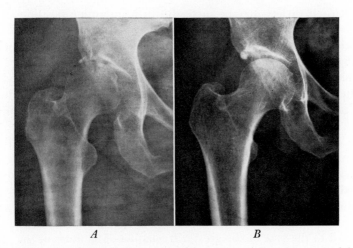

A   B

FIG. 9-5. Minor acetabular rim fracture with persistent luxation treated by skin traction. *A*. On admission to hospital. *B*. Two years later. Patient completely asymptomatic. Full range of motion and power.

lip, the indication for an attempt at closed reduction is urgent. The shorter the interval between dislocation and reduction, the better is the opportunity for success and the smaller the risk of late avascular necrosis. The reduction procedure should be gently performed lest the rim of the socket or the femoral head be further damaged during the procedure. The least traumatic method of closed reduction is probably that described by Watson-Jones, as follows: "The anesthetized patient is laid in blankets on the floor so that the surgeon stands over the hip. An assistant kneels by the patient and steadies the pelvis. The hip and knee joints are flexed to the right angle. With the patient's foot held between the operator's thighs, the knee is grasped with both hands. The limb is slowly and gently rotated from the position of deformity into neutral rotation and then lifted with firm, steady traction."

If reduction and stability are gained, it may be most confidently maintained by plaster spica despite the hazards of immobilization to the older patient. Otherwise, traction must suffice. As always, the importance of constant nursing care cannot be overemphasized when the spica is employed.

The major problems are presented by the hip that cannot be reduced by closed measures and by the hip that is unstable after reduction, tending to slip back into the position of deformity. In the latter event, several courses of procedure are possible. If associated injuries permit, traction of the Russell variety may be successful in maintaining position of both head and rim fragments. The employment of traction calls for constant vigilance and weekly radiological control. Persistent loss of position for more than 2 days renders reposition of the rim by traction almost impossible. The application of a plaster spica with the leg moderately abducted and internally rotated is preferred whenever possible. In the event that closed reduction cannot be attained because of forced delay or because of blocking by a femoral head or rim fragment, operative reduction must be considered. Persistence of dislocation, in contradistinction to the central depression type of fracture, usually implies deformity, lasting pain, and invalidism (Fig. 9-6). In suitable candidates, King and Richards have reported good results by surgical replacement (Fig. 9-7).

Operative Replacement. The patient is placed in the prone position. The incision extends from the posterior superior spine outward and downward to the base of the greater trochanter. The fibers of the gluteus maximus muscle are exposed and its aponeurosis divided. Very little bleeding is encountered, as the branches of the superior and inferior gluteal artery lie at opposite ends of the incision. The gluteus maximus muscle is retracted along the line of the incision. The sciatic nerve, the gluteus medius, piriformis, abturator internus, gemelli, and superior border of the quadratus femoris muscles are thereby exposed. The interval between the superior border of the piriformis and the inferior border of the gluteus medius is located, and the tip of a curved hemostat is inserted from above downward under the common tendon of the piriformis obturator internus and gemelli. Another hemostat is inserted under this

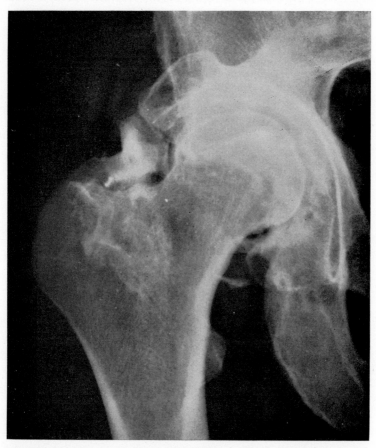

FIG. 9-6. The penalty of persistent dislocation and rim displacement 10 years after injury. Severe myositis ossificans. Progressive limitation of motion and pain and development of flexion adduction contracture. No evidence of avascular necrosis.

tendon from below, passing between the superior border of the quadratus femoris and the inferior border of the gemelli.

The tendon is then divided and the muscle belly retracted medialward. The posterior wall of the acetabulum is now exposed. The trunk of the sciatic nerve is well protected by these muscles which enclose it. A long, narrow rubber retractor is placed in the pelvis between the greater sciatic

notch and the ischial spine and against the intrapelvic surface of the acetabular floor. Subperiosteal elevation of the gluteus minimus superiorly
will provide further exposure if necessary.

In the average case, the dislocation will have already been reduced and
it will merely be necessary to derotate the hip fragment, place it in its ana-

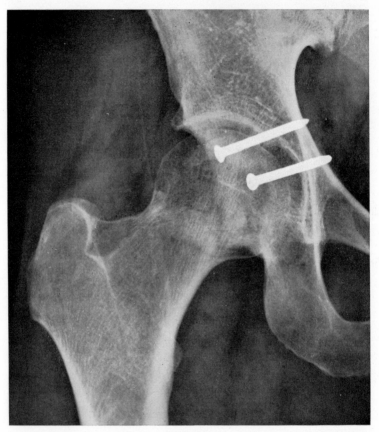

Fig. 9-7. Anchorage of posterior lip fracture with excellent result (method of
King and Richards).

tomical position, and affix it with Matthews wires, nails, or Vitallium
screws driven into the ilium. The screw must be placed at an oblique
angle upward toward the middle of the iliac crest. This will avoid penetration of the articular cartilage. Traction, a hip spica cast, or Wilkie
boots may be used. Active exercise is allowed in from 8 to 10 weeks.

Although this description of the operative procedure was presented by
King and Richards almost 20 years ago, there is little that can be added
at present. For various reasons, the large approach of the procedure may

be contraindicated in aged patients. In such instances a compromise procedure focusing attention upon the acetabular roof is sometimes possible. As in the central depression group of fracture dislocations, the superior lip may be approached, replaced, and anchored through an upper seg-

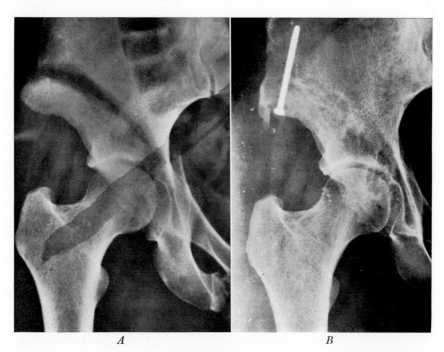

A   *B*

FIG. 9-8. Acetabular roof fracture resulting from auto crash injury. The long extension of the superior lip provided a simple method of reposition with reestablishment of contour of socket. *A.* At time of injury. *B.* Four years later. No residual signs of symptoms.

ment of the Smith-Peterson incision, and sometimes through an even more superficial approach if the hip is attached to a long fragment (Fig. 9-8).

DISLOCATION WITH MAJOR FRACTURE OF FEMORAL HEAD OR NECK (GROUP III)

The rare third type of fracture dislocation of the hip (involving fracture of the femoral head or neck) appears to be especially infrequent in the aged. Twenty-five cases collected by Pipkin from experience at various clinics contained two instances occurring as late as the seventh decade, and the author has encountered only one. Almost invariably, fractures of the femoral head and neck occur as a result of impact against the acetabular rim in the course of dislocation, or during the reduction procedure.

In the event of head fracture, therapy is locally determined by the amount of head that has broken off and by the possibility that the broken fragment or fragments may block and prevent reduction fully or partially. If the major segment of femoral head including its superior weight-bearing surface remains attached, urgent closed reduction should be attempted, preferably by the method described by Watson-Jones and quoted above in this chapter. Extremely gentle performance of the reduction is imperative since the broken femoral head is more vulnerable than one that is intact. If complete reduction is attained, the report of Pipkin indicates that the resultant hip may continue serviceable for many years.

It must be recognized, however, that ultimate arthritic changes are inevitable. Simple traction for 6 to 8 weeks is sufficient to stabilize the reduction. Should less than half of the head remain attached, or should its weight-bearing surface be broken off, there is little to be gained from even an attempt at closed reduction unless the condition of the patient precludes an open approach. In the opinion of the author, prosthetic insertion would represent the procedure of choice (Fig. 9-9).

Should reduction be partially or completely blocked by displaced head segments, an operative approach is necessary. The acetabulum may be cleared of small fragments and the residual head reduced. If the included fragments are large, however, prosthetic insertion is preferable. Relatively poor results have followed efforts to reassemble the fragments of a fractured femoral head because of the rapid development of subsequent arthritic changes (Pipkin). The prosthetic procedure is simpler, entails a shorter convalescence, and has proved compatible with the shorter life expectancy of the aged. (If the implantation of a transfixion prosthesis is under consideration, the approach to the acetabulum should be posterolateral.)

If, instead of the head of the femur, the femoral neck is fractured, it is the author's belief that any attempt at closed reduction of the dislocation is contraindicated. There is little chance of the femoral head surviving the avascularity of ligamentum teres tear plus the inevitable trauma to the nutrition of the structure from below following the reduction attempt. The condition of the patient permitting, primary prosthetic insertion represents the procedure of choice.

Essential Operative Intervention. From the preceding review, it is clear that even in the aged, there are certain clear-cut indications for operative intervention whenever the patient's general condition allows it. These may be summarized as follows:

1. Dislocation irreducible by closed measures because of forced delay, blocking bone fragment, or associated fracture of the femur rendering manipulative control of femoral head impossible

2. Reduction blocked because of inclusion of fragment or fragments of head or of acetabular rim in the acetabulum

3. Reduction entirely unstable because of displacement or torsion of acetabular roof

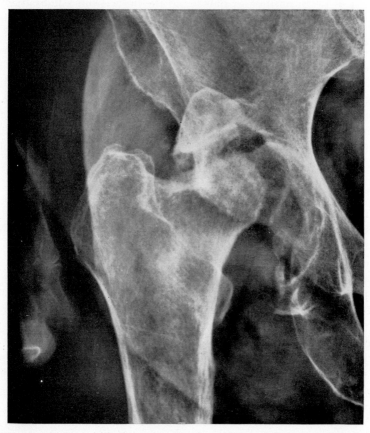

FIG. 9-9. Destruction of hip joint 3 years after auto crash injury causing fracture dislocation including major fracture of femoral head. Large fragment of head is visible in the radiogram lying against posterior wall of socket. When first seen 3 years after injury patient was unable to bear weight on injured leg and used two crutches. Prosthetic substitution resulted in relatively painless walking. Cane is still utilized.

4. Associated fracture of the femoral neck in which closed reduction, even if successful, must inevitably be followed by avascular necrosis of the head

5. Sciatic paralysis secondary to pressure of bone fragment on nerve

EARLY COMPLICATIONS OF FRACTURE DISLOCATION

Careful neurological examination of the leg and foot of the injured leg is necessary before and after the reduction procedure to exclude the possibility of sciatic nerve damage. This may occur at the time of injury as a result of pressure upon or damage to the nerve from a bony fragment, or during the reduction procedure when the nerve is caught and drawn forward in front of the femoral neck. The postreduction presence of foot drop or anesthesia about the foot and leg calls for urgent exploration of the sciatic nerve through the posterior approach as described by King and Richards and quoted above. The outcome of these lesions is favorable in about half the cases. If strong adhesive plaster traction is employed, the late discovery of foot drop is practically always the result of peroneal nerve traction rather than sciatic damage. The distinction is simplified by the preservation of active extension by the muscles of the calf. The latter lesion has a slow but benign course.

LATE COMPLICATIONS OF FRACTURE DISLOCATION

Traumatic Arthritis of the Hip—Avascular Necrosis of the Femoral Head. Since it is often difficult to differentiate these lesions clinically or radiologically, they may be considered together. According to Armstrong "traumatic arthritis" becomes apparent within 4 years in 25 per cent of acetabular rim fractures, 60 per cent of fractures of the femoral head, and 100 per cent of fractures of the acetabular floor. Thompson and Epstein's figures are even more pessimistic, while those of Stewart and Milford indicate that these complications occur in less than 30 per cent. Watson-Jones quotes the figure of 30 per cent for simple hip dislocations, the proportion rising rapidly after delayed open reduction. In all probability, the variance in the above figures is due to the varying severity of the lesions, to the use of different age groups, and to the different criteria employed.

Prophylaxis. The marked variation in the above figures renders it difficult to determine the cause of the complication or the measures that might minimize its frequency. Certainly the case for rapid reduction whenever possible is clear. The contention of Knight and Smith, that traumatic arthritis may be curtailed by accurate reduction of acetabular fracture displacement, is probably correct in part. However, the damage to the articular surface of the femoral head, incurred at the original dislocation, observed at operation, suggests that most of these lesions are determined largely at the time of the original trauma. Certainly they may be safely predicted if gross acetabular or femoral head discrepancy is permitted to remain.

Therapy. Significant pain, limitation of motion, and disability in the hip joint developing up to 6 years after fracture dislocation would suggest the use of prosthetic insertion provided the general health of the older patient permits it. It is recommended that the operation be performed before stiffness becomes marked. The procedure has been described in the section on fracture of the hip.

Although arthrodesis of the hip is seldom an operation of choice in the older patient, it is recommended in lesions that have already produced marked stiffness and pain. In the elderly patient, a very stiff but painful hip may be greatly benefited by the simple application of a long Smith-Peterson nail inserted low in the femur almost vertically, transversing the femoral neck and anchoring the head to the ilium above. A firm ankylosis develops in a fair proportion of properly selected cases. However, if the range of motion at the hip is more than a few degrees, the above procedure cannot be trusted to produce fusion. In such cases, arthrodesis must include denuding the joint of cartilage and preferably the application of a bridging bone graft. The latter procedure requires the subsequent application of a plaster cast.

BIBLIOGRAPHY

Armstrong, J. R.: Traumatic dislocation of the hip joint. *Jour. Bone and Joint Surg.* **30B**:430, 1948.

Jahss, S. A.: Injuries involving the ilium. *Jour. Bone and Joint Surg.* **17**:338, 1935.

King, D., and V. Richards: Fracture dislocations of the hip joint. *Jour. Bone and Joint Surg.* **23**:533, 1941.

Knight, R. A., and H. Smith: Central fractures of the acetabulum. *Jour. Bone and Joint Surg.* **39A**:1, 1958.

Pickett, J. C.: Injuries of the hips. *Clinical Orth.* 4:64, 1954.

Pipkin, G.: Grade IV fracture dislocations of the hips. *Jour. Bone and Joint Surg.* **39A**:1027, 1957.

Rowe, C.: Discussion of paper of Knight and Smith (Central fractures of the acetabulum). *Jour. Bone and Joint Surg.* **39A**:16, 1958.

Stewart, M. J., and L. W. Milford: Fracture dislocation of the hip. *Jour. Bone and Joint Surg.* **36A**:315, 1954.

Thompson, V. P., and H. C. Epstein: Traumatic dislocation of the hip. *Jour. Bone and Joint Surg.* **33A**:746, 1951.

Watson-Jones, Reginald: "Fractures and Joint Injuries." vol. 2, 2d ed., p. 619. Baltimore, Williams & Wilkins, 1940.

Chapter 10

Fractures of the Pelvis

Alexander Garcia, Jr.

Fracture of the pelvis is not a common trauma in the aged. In a study of over 2,000 patients above the age of 60 who sustained fractures, only 3 per cent of the fractures were classified as pelvic injuries. This is not too surprising. Serious fractures of the pelvis are usually due to severe, direct injury, or are avulsions due to a strong muscle pull. Many of the lesser fractures are unrecognized and treated with a period of rest without medical attention, hence the incidence is probably higher than that recorded. Since the older person is not employed in industry to the same extent as the younger person, he is not subjected to the mechanical violence inflicted in the course of coupling trains, loading trucks, or similar activities which cause most of these severe injuries. Furthermore, the avulsion-type injury resulting from strong muscle pull which we see in young, muscular athletes obviously does not ordinarily occur in the older person. (This chapter excludes fractures of the acetabulum which are discussed by Lippmann in Chap. 9.)

However, the elderly person does frequently slip on scatter rugs or polished floors. A minor fall may produce a fracture of the pelvis just as easily as it may break the hip in an aged individual. Fractures of the pelvis due to these minor falls are apt to be acetabular or to involve the ramus of the pubis. A certain number unquestionably make satisfactory recoveries in a short period of time spent resting at home. In other instances the symptoms may suggest a fractured hip, and the true diagnosis of minor fracture of the pelvis comes as a great relief to the admitting surgeon.

Next to falls in the home, automobile accidents are the chief producer of fractures of the pelvis in the aged. Such fractures usually occur when a pedestrian steps into the path of a moving automobile. Such cases are apt to be the more seriously disabling ones. The patient complains of pain in the region of the groin, and has great difficulty when attempting to stand or indeed cannot stand. Any attempt to make him raise the lower extremity provokes considerable discomfort at the groin. The differential diagnosis between fracture of the pelvis and an undisplaced or impacted fracture of the neck of the femur may be difficult to make clinically. Occasionally, the finding of direct tenderness over the pubic bone makes the diagnosis quite apparent.

When severe injury about the pelvis has driven the patient into shock, the probability of fracture with retroperitoneal hemorrhage must be seriously considered. Shock is not common in fractures of the hip in older patients. The presence or absence of blood in the urine should be established, by catheterization if necessary. It must be further emphasized that the type of vehicular injury which seriously damages the pelvis is most likely to cause multiple injuries, not only in the immediate neighborhood of the pelvic ring but at distant parts as well.

X-ray. X-ray of course is essential to the diagnosis. Care must be taken to include the pelvis in films of suspected hip fractures. In evaluating a suspected injury to a hip with an inadequate exposure showing only the hip joint and acetabulum, one may easily overlook a fracture of the pubic ramis or other parts of the pelvic ring. When clinical evidence is strongly suggestive of fracture and the usual anteroposterior view of the pelvis reveals no perceptible fracture, angled views, particularly those from below the ring, may disclose fracture of the pelvic appendages, sacrum, or luxations at the sacroiliac joints.

In the osteoporotic pelvis of the elderly, a torus type fracture may often be sustained at the ischiopubic junction of the inferior ramus (Fig. 10-1). This lesion is frequently misinterpreted as a normal variant since a certain bulging at this point is not infrequently seen in otherwise undamaged pubic rami. However, if there is a persistence of symptoms referable to the groin, particularly if there is pain on attempting to flex the hip with knee extended, this area should be rechecked by x-ray from several angles. A dissolution of the cortical lines not demonstrable in a direct anteroposterior view may become apparent from an angled exposure.

Treatment. Fractures of the pelvis may be classified according to their anatomical location, e.g., pubis, ischium, ilium, tuberosity, crest, etc. While of interest to record files, this classification is not as valuable in the management of such cases as one based on whether the pelvic ring remains intact or is broken.

Those fractures in which the contour of the pelvic ring is undisturbed, such as a fracture of one pubic ramus or of an appendage of the innominate, usually require only symptomatic treatment. Those in which the pelvic ring is fractured at two or more points, permitting inward or upward displacement, or in which the fracture involves the ilium adjacent to the sacroiliac isthmus, may require active reduction (Fig. 10-2). If displacement is considerable and the pelvic ring proves to be unstable, it must be held in reduced position with traction or plaster spica fixation.

Fortunately most fractures of the pelvis in older people, other than those of the acetabulum, are of the nondisplaced type, or are displaced to such a slight degree that no reduction is necessary. In this connection it is important to remember that in the elderly a considerable amount of deformity can be accepted in the pelvic girdle with assurance of a reasonably satisfactory functional result. It would be folly to attempt to secure

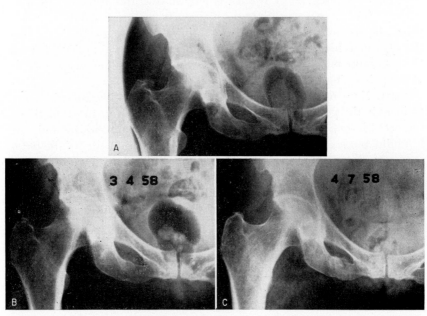

FIG. 10-1. Torus fracture of pubic ramus in osteoporotic bone. Age 75. Osteoporosis, senile. Classical clinical picture of fractured pelvis, right. *A*. X-ray read as negative. *B*. Early callus 18 days later. *C*. Obvious fracture with callus 7½ weeks later.

an anatomical reduction at the expense of prolonged traction or immobilization when the procedure would not materially advance functional recovery. This is true even in cases in which there is some displacement of the sacroiliac joint. Moderate displacements of this joint are ordinarily well tolerated by the older age groups in view of their lessened demand for extended weight bearing.

Fracture of the ischial tuberosity is most unusual in the elderly, and when it occurs is apt not to be remarkably displaced. It should require little in the way of treatment and rarely, if indeed ever, demands surgical correction. In similar fashion, fracture of the anterosuperior spine, a possible result of direct impact in an osteoporotic pelvis, requires little but rest. Neither of these latter lesions is in the axis of weight bearing, and even fibrous union would suffice for the functional demands of the elderly person. In the aged, separation of the symphysis pubis has not often been seen as a single lesion. If it occurs it should be quite rare. The pubic rami will fracture first under the impact of trauma. Treatment consists primarily of bed rest, alleviation of pain with a minimum of sedation, encouragement of motion within the limits of pain, and a watchful eye for the development of medical complications, especially signs of thromboembolic disease, urinary infection, and congestive pneumonia.

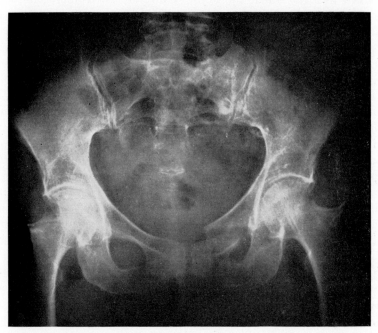

Fig. 10-2. Moderate instability of pelvic ring. Female, age 77.

Fractures of the pelvis in which the ring has been disrupted in two places, causing an inward displacement of a large section of the pelvis, are rare in the elderly, but on occasion are seen in a person who has been struck by an automobile. In these instances traction on the trochanter as well as on the tibial tubercle is indicated for as short a period of time as is necessary to stabilize the fracture. Freedom of action in bed within the limits of the traction apparatus is encouraged to the point of toleration. This relative immobilization may be necessary for 3 to 4 weeks.

A pelvic belt often adds considerable comfort in the early weeks of weight bearing. The so-called "polo belt," worn low, is easily obtained and satisfactory for the purpose. There are few if any indications for operative treatment in fractures of the pelvis, except for certain fractures involving the acetabulum. These have been discussed in some detail by Lippmann in Chap. 9.

Common Complications. The complications of fractures of the pelvis are the major concern of the surgeon looking after these patients. This is especially true of such fractures occurring in the aged. The common complications encountered are those of shock, injuries to the genitourinary tract, retroperitoneal hemorrhage, and thrombophlebitis.

Shock is not a frequent complication of fracture of the single ramus sustained in a fall about the house. However, where there has been a severe injury with a gross displacement of the pelvic ring, shock may be of serious concern. Massive retroperitoneal bleeding should be suspected in such cases, and if found, counteracted with appropriate measures, chiefly the transfusion of whole blood. A base-line blood count and hematocrit are mandatory and these should be watched along with the blood pressure and other vital signs.

Injury to the bony pelvis when the bladder is full frequently results in injury to the bladder with extravasation of urine in either the retroperitoneal or peritoneal region. This complication should always be thought of in any injury to the pelvis, particularly in those in which there is gross displacement. A specimen of urine should be examined on admission, resorting to a catheter to obtain it if necessary. Gross hematuria is all but unquestionable evidence of injury to the bladder or urethra. Immediate measures must be taken to assure an adequate flow of urine. This may be accomplished by catheter in most cases. In more severe lesions suprapubic cystotomy may be required.

In many instances the casually voided specimen shows evidence of microscopic hematuria. This in itself is of no significance but merits a repeated urine examination. Generally this type of bleeding subsides in a period of 2 or 3 days. It is most likely related to a direct impact on the bladder without penetration or rupture.

In connection with genitourinary complications, bladder infections secondary to prolonged use of a catheter remain a constant threat. One should remember that the catheter is to be removed as soon as it is possible for the patient to void comfortably, or as soon as the genitourinary tract has been reconstituted to the point where the patient can void spontaneously. It is advisable to use chemotherapy prophylactically in cases in which a catheter has to remain in place. When in spite of prophylaxis cystitis does develop, urine cultures are obtained and appropriate antibiotics used to control the infection. In general, such infections respond to treatment readily. A great deterrent to bladder infection is ambulation and the patient's use of a commode rather than a bedpan. Hence the patient is urged to be out of bed and to walk about as soon as some degree of weight bearing is tolerable.

In cases where more damaging injury to the genitourinary system has occurred, the services of a qualified specialist are called for if such are available. This aspect of complicated fractures of the pelvis is discussed by Draper in Chap. 15.

The most fearful complication of fractures of the pelvis at any age is thrombophlebitis. The lethargic elderly patient with circulatory difficulties is especially prone to this complication since he will be forced to remain at bed rest for some length of time during which almost any motion will cause pain.

Whereas in general one frequently sees the classical case of posttraumatic phlebothrombosis with calf tenderness and a positive Homans' sign, in fractures of the pelvis the first manifestation of thrombophlebitis is apt to be a pulmonary embolus. This may be massive with sudden chest pain, signs of pleurisy, perhaps cyanosis or dyspnea, bloody sputum, and the classical findings of embolization. On occassion thrombophlebitis following fracture of the pelvis may be manifested merely by cramps in the buttocks with a slight rise in temperature and pulse.

Because of the great hazard of thrombophlebitis, and especially since its manifestation may be a fatal one, prophylactic anticoagulation therapy should be considered in all serious pelvic fractures. It should not be instituted, however, until there is assurance that there is no massive retroperitoneal bleeding. In a case with a history of recent cerebral hemorrhage or a in which there are signs of fragility of the blood vessels anticoagulant therapy is also contraindicated. Frequently urinalysis must be done to detect microscopic hematuria. Although its presence does not necessarily warrant the discontinuance of anticoagulants, it is a means of knowing when the treatment is approaching the hazardous stage. Any other type of bleeding is, of course, an indication for stopping anticoagulants and administering vitamin K (Mephyton).

Anticoagulation therapy should be kept up until the patient has been up and about for some time. If the patient has a history of thromboembolic phenomona, or is obese, or has a family history of phlebitis, he is kept on the drug for a period of approximately 1 month. On the other hand, the patient who is the thin, wiry, muscular, active type will probably do just as well without anticoagulants after a week or 10 days of activity.

Once these patients are ambulatory they are encouraged to return to their normal routine as quickly as possible. At first the patient may require the use of a mechanical walker. In an undisplaced fracture or one with minimal displacement, the patient will usually tolerate some weight bearing after a period of 3 or 4 weeks of bed or chair rest. There is some variation in this time factor depending upon the degree of displacement of the fragments and, of course, on the pain threshold of the individual.

Five to six weeks would represent a normal time range for return to ordinary activity for the aged person in uncomplicated cases.

Prognosis. Nonunion of fractures of the pelvis is unusual. Despite the early use of anticoagulants, x-rays taken 3 weeks after injury almost invariably show some callus in the region of the fracture site. At times callus may be quite abundant at this stage of repair. This rapid callus formation is probably related to the cancellous nature of the bone, its excellent blood supply, and the fact that it is held fairly rigidly by the envelope of muscles that surround these bones.

The prognosis as to pain is a guarded one in all cases of fractures of the pelvis in the aged. Where there is gross displacement of the sacroiliac joints or the sacral extremity of the ilium, where fractures at that area chiefly occur, pain may remain quite persistent in elderly patients. This is due partly to the continuing strains on the lumbosacral and sacroiliac ligaments which attempt to compensate for the structural deformity. These patients may continue to complain of pain in the region of the sacroiliac, and if the displacement is marked, may retain a limp. Fortunately these fractures are quite rare in the aged. Even in lesser fractures of the pelvis in elderly persons some modicum of persistent or recurrent discomfort usually remains, although its intensity is not apt to be disabling.

Rehabilitation. Rehabilitation of these patients is a most urgent aspect of their management. Due to the inevitable involvement of important supporting ligaments, muscles, and tendons about the pelvic girdle, more or less discomfort is apt to persist even in the simple fractures of this area in the elderly for a period of time quite beyond that expected in younger people. The relative inelasticity of these soft tissues in the aged mitigates against their earlier recovery from the trauma. Walking about, even at short intervals as soon as it is tolerable, and mild exercises of the extremities, pelvic and abdominal muscles are certainly factors contributing to functional recovery. Mild analgesics should not be withheld. As has been repeatedly stated in these chapters, an early return to the accustomed activities of daily living is probably the most direct aid to the rehabilitation of the elderly.

Chapter 11

Dislocations and Other Traumatic Lesions of the Joints

Edgar M. Bick and Alexander Garcia, Jr.

Traumatic dislocation may occur in the elderly as in any age group. In actual practice, however, the shoulder, the elbow, the fingers, or the hips are the luxations most apt to appear in any extended series of skeletal trauma among elderly persons. (Dislocations of the hip joint are discussed separately by Lippmann in Chap. 9.)

These injuries in the aged often require a somewhat different approach to therapy than would be used with younger persons. This is conditioned by several facts. One has been frequently mentioned in previous chapters on skeletal injury but is particularly significant here, that is, the limited elasticity and resiliency of the connective tissues which form the capsules and ligaments of the intraarticular and periarticular structures in the aged. Furthermore, certain luxations which must almost of necessity be reduced in the younger working adult, even though reduction be late and require surgical intervention, may be left alone in the elderly with less disturbance of function or less cosmetic defect than would be acceptable in the younger group. Lastly, certain luxations which are reducible with relative ease in the younger adult require more painstaking manipulation and at times offer greater risk when attempted in the older patient.

Recovery from some of the common dislocations which may be all but complete in young adulthood is seldom as satisfactory in the aged even under the best of circumstances. The damage done to periarticular and intraarticular tissues and the inevitable disruption of the articular-vascular network, which would have been for the most part healed in the younger patient, leave irreversible cytologic and histologic disturbances in and about the aged joint. These disturbances hasten the degenerative processes which have in the nature of age already begun to destroy articular surfaces (De Palma). Synovial tissues which are apt to have become somewhat hypertrophic or fibrotic become more so after the trauma.

Subchondral atrophy or porosis is aggravated by the periarticular-vascular trauma.

Aside from these specific lesions there are other residua of joint injury unfortunately too common in the aged. They are referred to as "weather ache," and the so-called "geling phenomenon." Weather ache is a common complaint after any injury to the musculoskeletal system, but is particularly frequent after injuries to and about the articulations. It is not well understood and cannot be correlated to humidity or temperature. It has been somewhat related to the effect of barometric pressure on the peripheral circulation. However, the clinical fact remains that change in the weather will cause the injured joint to ache long after the specific lesion appears to be well healed.

By "geling phenomenon" is meant the temporary stiffness which will affect a joint after it is maintained in one position for a period of time. Aged patients frequently complain of this disability. The analogy has been drawn between aged joint capsules and shoes that have remained on the closet floor for many months. Both structures, being in the colloid state, undergo some change recognized as stiffness which clears with use.

In brief, traumatic dislocation is a more destructive and less recoverable injury in the aged than it is at other times of life. It is less tragic only because in later life the stresses imposed upon the articulations are as a rule considerably less demanding, and the cosmetic effects of an unreduced luxation are less offensive than they would be in the more active years of youth and young adulthood. Dislocations in the aged require meticulous care, gentle handling, and above all, sound judgement.

THE SHOULDER GIRDLE

Acromioclavicular Joint. Dislocation is quite uncommon in the aged since the type of injury which would ordinarily cause luxation in a younger person would be far more apt to fracture the outer third of the clavicle in the older individual. The trapezoid and conoid ligaments which bind the clavicle to the scapula become quite tough and sometimes even partly ossified in elderly individuals. They are far less apt to tear or stretch, and without this luxation is hardly possible. When luxation or subluxation at the acromioclavicular joint is noted after an injury in an elderly individual one must consider the possibility of an older lesion made temporarily more prominent by local trauma and swelling.

Dislocation or subluxation at this site in an aged person requires merely a period of rest and analgesic treatment. Even in younger persons, pressure immobilization or surgical fixation is of questionable usefulness; in the aged it is not only futile, but functionally a waste. The cosmetic element is seldom a factor. Two or three weeks of partial rest in a sling is sufficient therapy. Following this an encouraged resumption of activity, especially repeated attempts to lift the arm higher day by day, will ordinarily lead to adequate recovery even if full abduction of the shoulder is not regained. In an occasional case, the acromioclavicular joint does remain intolerably painful. In such instances, the writers prefer to resect the outer end of the clavicle in an aged individual than to attempt restoration of articular position. Recovery is not only quicker, but the functional result is considerably better (Fig. 11-1).

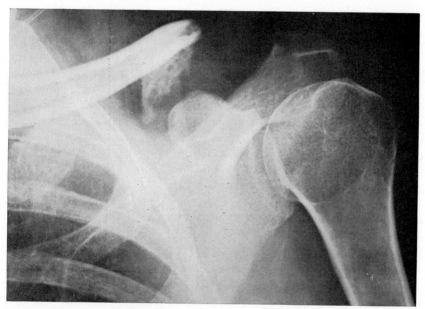

FIG. 11-1. Male, age 65. Status postdislocation acromioclavicular joint. Resection outer end of clavicle. Ossification coracoclavicular ligaments.

Sternoclavicular Joint. Dislocation or subluxation of this articulation in an aged person is a rarity. The writers have neither seen a case nor found one recorded in this age group. When it does occur it may be either anterior or posterior. The posterior dislocation may compromise the trachea and great vessels of the cervicothoracic function as it has done in younger adults. Such injuries may be fatal. Prompt reduction, with any grasping instrument at hand, should be performed. Reduction is usually simple, but it may be difficult to maintain. If necessary the medial end of the clavicle is resected.

Anterior dislocation is not in itself a serious injury. If uncomplicated by other local trauma, it requires no treatment. Even in younger people the lesion does not greatly impede function of the shoulder girdle when left unreduced; in the elderly it should present no particular problem other than the cosmetic one. Symptomatic treatment and analgesics should suffice.

Glenohumeral Joint. Dislocation of the shoulder joint is the most common luxation found at any age. In a series of 600 skeletal traumas in the aged noted in Chap. 6, this lesion occurred in 1.6 per cent. As in all ages the common type is the anterior luxation. The posterior position is quite uncommon in elderly individuals. Its etiology and diagnosis are no different in the aged than they are in younger persons. The expected deformity of the shoulder, its loss of contour as compared to the normal side, is present, and the humeral head is palpably out of its socket. The complete stiffness of the limb, or at least its very marked restriction of motion is obvious to both the patient and the examiner. Local pain is always present, but in an aged individual it may be much less acute than it would be in a younger person.

In the elderly person, however, dislocation at the shoulder joint is more serious in its potential complications. As rather fully discussed in Chap. 6, dislocation or fracture dislocation presents a serious threat to the neurovascular bundle passing down the arm from the axilla. All the complications inherent in fracture dislocation at the shoulder apply equally to simple dislocation when it occurs.

In the aged, dislocation is more often than not accompanied by at least some dissolution at the greater tubercle (Fig. 11-2). This may be either comminuted or a single fragment, and appear to be either an avulsion fracture or one caused by forcible pressure of the tubercle against the acromion process. For all therapeutic purposes these dissolutions at the greater tubercle may be ignored in the elderly. Their periosteal and fascial attachments usually prevent any great displacement; they are extraarticular, and they seldom if ever materially influence the time or extent of recovery.

Treatment of the uncomplicated dislocation of the glenohumeral joint in the aged is an emergency situation. If reduction is attempted within a few hours posttrauma it usually may be accomplished under intraarticular procaine (or Xylocaine) anesthesia or, where possible, under Pentothal or simple gas-oxygen anesthesia with less disturbance to the patient. If reduction is delayed, it may require far more forcible maneuvers since the periarticular soft tissue and capsule of the aged persons once contracted, or even inflamed, is less resilient tissue than it is at a comparable period in the younger adult. Forcible manipulation of the elderly dislocated shoulder, necessitated by delay, works only to the detriment of the joint and not infrequently is a cause of nerve injury not present before the intervention.

The maneuver of choice in reducing a dislocated shoulder in an aged individual is simple traction with the arm abducted at an angle of 30 to 60° from the body and elevated from 20 to 40°. Countertraction in an elderly person should never be applied to the axilla. To do so is a deliberate invitation to neurovascular injury. Countertraction is applied by any available helper whose hands can be placed against the upper

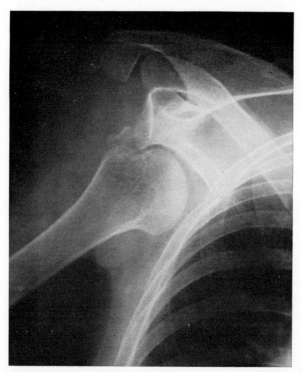

FIG. 11-2. Female, age 75. Dislocation of the shoulder; innocuous avulsion fracture at greater tubercle.

lateral side of the chest just below the axilla. One hand of the surgeon pressing outward at the upper end of the medial surface of the arm often facilitates reduction. The traction should be steady and may often have to be maintained for some time. The patience to perform this repays itself in the final ease of the reduction and the lessened trauma to the joint.

After reduction, a swathe and sling for 10 days (Fig. 6-1), followed by a sling alone for an equal period, provides enough immobilization. The patient is then urged to gradually increase the usefulness and mobility of the arm by attempts at daily purposeful activity. As noted in Chap. 6, in the aged traumatized shoulder this will probably increase the range of motion and restore general functional usefulness more quickly than would formal exercise or painful stretching.

The two serious complications of dislocation of the shoulder in the aged have been referred to above, vascular injury and nerve damage. Both of these were discussed in some detail in connection with fractures and fracture dislocation of the humeral neck in Chap. 6, and need not be repeated here. One warning must be emphasized. In undertaking the management of dislocation of the shoulder, especially in the aged, the surgeon is technically and morally obligated to examine the neurologic status of the extremity before attempting reduction. Even under the best of circumstances the nerve supply, which may have been intact following the trauma, may be injured by traction during the reduction maneuver. The damage following the original dislocation may or may not be permanent; it may or may not be a complete avulsion higher up in the brachial plexus. The neurologic lesion of a well-performed reduction, on the other hand, is seldom permanent and usually recovers in 4 to 6 weeks.

The treatment of an old unreduced dislocation of the shoulder at any age carries a surgical risk. In the aged the risk of damage to the brittle or fragile brachial artery is considerably more serious. Unless the lesion represents a severe dysfunction or causes intractable pain, the elderly person may be better off with the inconveniences and limited function of his unreduced shoulder than he would be following surgical intervention. In those occasional instances when symptoms or dysfunction demands correction, the writers far prefer simple excision of the humeral head to the risks and limitations of surgical reduction. In the older person the loss of strength following resection is far less of an inconvenience than the restriction of motion which ordinarily follows the more extensive surgery of reduction.

Elbow Joint

The elbow joint is the second in frequency of dislocations among the aged, occurring in 0.5 per cent of a series of 600 skeletal traumas in this group. It is not ordinarily complicated by serious fracture although on occasion small flecks may be avulsed from the epicondyles of the humerus or the tip of the coronoid process. When significant fractures do occur near the elbow joint, sufficient displacement takes place at the line of dissolution so that the stress which might have led to luxation of the humero-ulnar articulation is dispersed.

When dislocation occurs in the elbow of older individuals, it is most apt to be a complete luxation of the ulna and radius from the trochlear and capitular surfaces of the humerus. Simple dislocation of the head of the radius, a common lesion in childhood, either does not occur in the aged or is quite rare. The deformity is obvious and need be differentiated only from fractures of the lower end of the humerus, which occurred even less frequently in the present writers' list of cases. However, the total number of cases was not great enough to make this observation conclusive. On the other hand, no other observation on the statistics of this differentiation in the elderly has been as yet recorded.

X-ray examination is of course imperative to define the lesion. The dislocation is all but invariably posterior, with the tip of the coronoid process behind the trochlea (Fig. 11-3). Small avulsed flecks of bone may be ignored. If a larger piece of bone is visible, one is dealing with fracture dislocation. At the elbow, the free piece is apt to be intraarticular.

Simple dislocation at the elbow if seen within a short time posttrauma may be reduced with relative ease by simple traction or manipulation in traction and flexion. If reduction is performed almost immediately, topical ethyl chloride spray may sometimes afford sufficient anesthesia. If the maneuver is early but not immediate, or if ethyl chloride spray proves insufficient, a few ml of 1

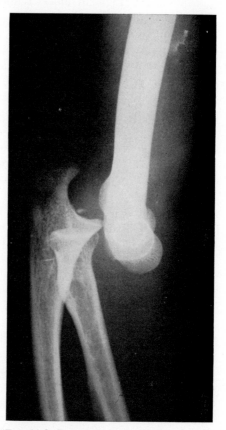

FIG. 11-3. Female, age 64. Dislocation of elbow without fracture. (Second in frequency of dislocations in the aged.)

per cent Novocain or Xylocaine into the elbow joint often proves effective. It must be emphasized, however, that about 5 minutes or more should be allowed after injection before reduction is attempted. Failure is too often due to disregard of this rule. If both these forms of local anesthesia fail, or in a case not seen for some hours after the injury, Pentothal or a light gas anesthesia will of course be required.

Reduction is ordinarily easily effected in cases not complicated by displaced intraarticular bone fragments. When such are discovered in the x-ray plate an attempt at closed reduction should still be made. Often enough reduction in the elderly, as in the younger fracture dislocations about the elbow, is quite possible, and in favorable cases the maneuver may even bring the fragment into satisfactory apposition.

When a free fragment blocks reduction, arthrotomy is required in the elderly case just as it is in the younger. Permanent dislocation of the elbow, unlike the shoulder, is quite disabling in the aged, and surgical reduction carries far less risk than it does at the axilla. Intraarticular fragments found in the elbow of an aged person are best removed. Restoration of motion will be possible earlier if no attempt is made to restore the fragment to its normal position. But for exceptional instances, loss of the fragment should not materially interfere with the function of an elbow in the elderly individual.

If a case of old, untreated, disabling dislocation of the elbow in an aged person were presented to the writers, they would advise the performance of an Ollier resection of the elbow joint. There have not been enough such cases recorded to justify the use of any one procedure as against another. Hence, such advice remains a matter of personal judgment rather than justifiable rule. In other lesions, resection of the elbow has proved to be less detrimental to function than have other procedures. In the aged, some decrease in strength and stability is far more tolerable than would be the inconveniences of fusion or fibrous ankylosis which would inevitably follow the more extensive arthroplasties. This judgment has no relation whatsoever to the writers' opinion of surgical measures advisable in similar situations among younger adults or children.

In the unusual case of dislocation of the radial head in the aged, simple closed reduction should suffice. If reduction is not accomplished or, in the presence of an old unreduced lesion, again specifically referring to the aged, the present writers would resect the head rather than attempt surgical replacement.

Following either closed reduction or surgical intervention, a simple sling holding the forearm at 45 to 60° flexion is sufficient immobilization for the elderly individual. The collar and cuff, with acute flexion at the elbow, perfectly proper at a young age, has proved intolerable about the neck of most elderly individuals. Furthermore, with the less elastic tissues about the aged joint, the more comfortable sling has proved quite adequate. On occasion a posterior molded plaster slab has been used for the first week or so, more as an added comfort than as a required splint. In this older age group, 3 to 4 weeks of wearing the sling is sufficient. After that, gradual use of the arm is permitted, with rest periods in the sling or on the lap. As in the younger cases, extension follows gravity, and no attempt to force it by weights or exercise is permitted. Flexion is encouraged by the purposeful acts of eating, ablutions, and similar daily occupations. Restoration of function about the injured elbow takes considerable time at all ages; it will not be more rapid in the aged individual and will not respect his impatience.

Dislocations of the elbow are fraught with potentially serious complications. Among these are (1) the vascular catastrophe leading to Volkmann's ischemic contractures, (2) reversible or irreversible damage to any or all of the three major nerves which pass the elbow and control the function of the hand, and (3) the as yet unpreventable formation of local traumatic myositis ossificans which may severely diminish the mobility of the elbow.

Impending vascular ischemia (Volkmann's paralysis) in the aged is an emergency at any age. If the elbow has not been reduced, this must be accomplished immediately and preparations made for opening the fascial compartment from the antecubital space distalward without too conservative a waiting period. If signs of ischemia are noted after reduction, there is no waiting period permissible. A complete exposure of the fascial compartment of the forearm is demanded, as it would be at any age.

(The signs, symptoms, and pathological physiology of Volkmann's ischemic paralysis are well known, or should be so to any surgeon dealing with trauma. It has its own interesting and controversial literature which needs no review here. There is no question at this time, however, of the indications for, or choice of, emergency surgical intervention.)

Nerve damage at the time of dislocation at the elbow is seldom altogether irreversible even if pressure is removed by immediate reduction. In the aged a fair return of function may ordinarily be anticipated, though some sensory or small motor residue of paresthesia or paresis may remain. In the occasional case of more serious interruption of the pathways, neurosurgical measures are ordinarily not of great value in the aged arm. Methods of tendon transplant or joint fusions may prove more functionally effective.

The third common complication mentioned above, local traumatic myositis ossificans (or more properly myofibrositis ossificans), is of a different order. This is true of injuries about the elbow at any age. At the present writing there is no means of influencing the local tissues in respect to the appearance or nonappearance of this pathologic lesion. Early motion has been said to stimulate its formation; withholding early motion invites fibrous contractures. When the signs of myositis ossificans appear on the x-ray film, rest of the part is indicated. In the elderly the present writers would reapply the sling and urge relative rest rather than more effective immobilization. The presence of this complication inexorably adds some further restriction to the anticipated residual disability. One hopes it will not greatly interfere with the functional demands of the elderly individual.

Early surgical intervention is of course contraindicated in the aged as it is in the young; it most likely would stimulate a larger deposit in the unsusceptible tissues. A well-ossified mass of longer standing which effectively interferes with the elderly individual's use of the arm may sometimes warrant surgical removal. When this is attempted the calculated risk of its reappearance must be fully appreciated.

For the most part, the uncomplicated dislocation of an elbow in the aged person, reduced early, will lead to a fair prognosis. Some residual limitation of motion, especially that of extension and supination, is to be anticipated. The degree of disability will of course vary with each case in terms of absolute range of motion and in relation to the functional demands made upon the individual.

WRIST—CARPUS

Dislocation at the wrist joint occurs as a displacement of elements of the carpus in relation to the lower end of the radius or in relation to other bones of the carpus. Although Watson-Jones is correct in stating that any combination of carpal bone luxations may occur, only two such lesions are met with in common practice, dislocation of the carpus on the lunate or dislocation of the lunate in relation to the radiocarpal joint. These traumas are quite unusual in the elderly where the lower end of the radius is far more susceptible to fracture than displacement. When such a lesion does occur, manual reduction is of course the immediate indication. Seldom can this be effected in an aged person without anesthesia unless one is willing to subject the patient to a considerably painful second trauma.

If closed reduction cannot be effected, or if the dislocation is an old one, open reduction may be necessary. Here there is some difference between the treatment of this lesion in the aged and its treatment in a younger individual. The mere fact of dislocation of a carpus or a lunate, does not in itself demand open reduction in an older person. If the lessened activities to which the elderly individual has become adjusted in his daily life are not impeded by the deformity of the wrist, surgical intervention is unnecessary. However, an unreduced, dislocated lunate can easily be excised for the sake of comfort. True, this procedure is not generally advocated in the younger person since the long-term results are apt to lead to arthritic changes which interfere with the ordinary use of the hand. This may not be true in the elderly individual in view of the lesser functional demands made on his hand. After reduction a short period of splint immobilization is necessary for comfort. The splint may be removed in about 10 days and gradually increased use of the hand begun.

There are several very troublesome complications which rather frequently attend or follow these traumas. The first is avascular necrosis of the displaced lunate after reduction. This cannot be influenced or prevented by any method presently known. It leads to pain at the wrist. Since late excision merely exchanges the pain of the necrotic bone for that of the inevitably occurring arthritic syndrome at the wrist, one can merely offer symptomatic treatment. It is because of the threat of this complication that early excision of the lunate has been advocated. There are too few of these cases recorded in the aged, and none with sufficient study, to permit a definitive opinion. Judgment still rests with the responsible surgeon.

A second complication following any dislocation at the wrist or carpus to which the elderly are perhaps more prone than are younger individuals is traumatic osteodystrophy. This may accompany any injury at the wrist and was fully discussed in Chap. 6. The third complication is median-nerve paralysis which was also discussed in that chapter under the complications attending fractures of the lower end of the radius.

FINGERS

Dislocations of the metacarpophalangeal or interphalangeal joints are uncommon in the aged. Self-reduced subluxations occur not infrequently, leaving sore and swollen knuckles or finger joints. Dislocation when it does occur is ordinarily easily reduced under ethyl chloride spray anesthesia if it is recent, or under Novocain if not too greatly delayed. Old dislocation is corrected simply enough by surgical exposure through a lateral incision. After reduction of a dislocation in the elderly hand, a retention bandage or a simple malleable finger splint for 10 days to 2 weeks is sufficient restraint. Immediately after removal of the bandage or splint active motion is encouraged. Flexion over a proper-sized hand sponge repeated at frequent intervals during the day is a convenient and effective method of mobilizing the fingers.

The so-called "button hole" dislocation of the interphalangeal joint which prevents closed reduction was much talked of in former years. It is still referred to in occasional essays as a complication to cause concern. In this lesion the end of a phalanx was supposed to protrude through a split in the extensor aponeurosis and so be restrained from reduction by the grip of its bands. Whatever its theoretical significance may be, the present writers have never been aware of any difficulty in reducing a dislocated finger, so that the "button-hole" description seems to be chiefly a matter of anatomic interest. The only complication of simple dislocation of these joints is the really disabling one of stiffness of the fingers. Except for quite unusual circumstances serious restriction

of range of motion in these cases is most apt to follow unnecessarily prolonged immobilization or failure to supervise active motion after the
removal of immobilization.

Open (compound) dislocation of a finger joint can be a severely disabling injury in reference to hand function. But a lesion of this nature
comes into the domain of wound healing and tendon injury (see Chaps.
4 and 12).

Even in uncomplicated dislocations of the fingers in the aged, restoration of a normal range of motion may not be anticipated. Some degree
of restriction is the inevitable result of periarticular fibrosis of the capsule and ligaments already afflicted with the relative inelasticity common
to aging connective tissues.

Pelvic Girdle and Hip Joint

(Dislocations at the acetabulofemoral joint are the subject of special
consideration by Lippmann in Chap. 9. Dislocations at the sacroiliac
joints and displacement of the pubic ramus are rare in the aged. They
are discussed by Garcia in Chap. 10.)

Knee

Dislocations at the knee joint are fortunately as uncommon in the
aged as they are in younger adults. In the aged this trauma is apt to be an
even greater catastrophe because of the increased danger of impingement
on the more friable popliteal artery. Since the popliteal nerve and its
adjacent distal major branches are bound more securely by the relatively
less elastic perineurial connective tissues, damage to these may be likewise more severe in the elderly individual.

This injury must of necessity be the result of a major force directed
in a restricted direction. The vectors of this force have never been satisfactorily analyzed. This of course is an entirely academic problem since
the accident is not under the victim's control. Those accidents that have
been described ordinarily cause severe fractures about the knee. To
permit dislocation, the cruciate ligaments and other related intraarticular
structures of the joint must be ruptured or ripped.

Diagnosis, or at least its probability, should be obvious to the examiner.
*Complete dislocation of the knee presents so urgent a threat to the vascu-
lar supply of the leg and foot that the deformity should be immediately
corrected by hand traction by the first practitioner to attend the patient.*
One need not be a specialist. X-ray study can follow later. Whether or
not fracture complicates the dislocation is of no immediate consequence,
and replacement of its fragments can await definitive treatment.

Following reduction, the limb is held in a long-leg plaster. There is
always some degree of hemarthrosis in these lesions. If the joint is mod-

erately swollen, aspiration is indicated. If swelling is not excessive, aspiration is not necessary. In either case some bleeding must of necessity recur and will be absorbed by normal physiological processes. The plaster must not include the foot in its early period since the most important and exclusive concern in the immediate postreduction period is constant testing of the dorsalis pedis and posterior tibial pulsations in order to determine the continued patency of the popliteal artery. In dislocation of the knee in the aged, one is obligated to assume some degree of damage to the popliteal vessels, since the arteries of the lower extremity are those most likely to be involved in sclerotic degeneration. Hence, even if the artery has not been torn or ruptured at the time of injury, some degree of contusion, or at least temporary compression, must be assumed. This of course is an invitation to thrombosis at that level. Traumatic vascular spasm of the popliteal vessel and its distal extensions, which in a younger patient may subside without residual effect, may not do so as easily in the aged.

In the event of demonstrable damage to the popliteal vessel, the posterior surface of the knee must be exposed, even under difficult circumstances, and the surgical measures described by Madden in Chap. 18 applied at once. At best, even in the healthy young adult, the prognosis in respect to saving the limb after rupture of the popliteal artery is poor; in the aged the prognosis is most tenuous.

In the fortunate event that the circulation is not irreversibly impaired, the plaster is worn for 5 to 6 weeks. Following this a careful regimen of rehabilitation is begun with constant appreciation of the possibility of local arterial thrombosis or of venous thrombosis. Crutch walking, light massage, graded exercises of the quadriceps and leg muscles must be carefully supervised until maximum recovery has been attained. A significant but variable degree of limitation of the range of motion at the knee joint is inevitable following dislocations at the knee. However, restitution of adequate function is still a happy outcome in the elderly individual. Dislocation of the knee in the aged is not only potentially a seriously disabling trauma; it is veritably dangerous to life and limb.

Involvement of the major nerves in dislocation at the knee is common enough but fortunately is usually a matter of temporary concern. In the aged, as in younger persons, given time and the prevention of contractions in the parts served by the nerves, neuromuscular function is apt to recover more often than not. If some residual paresis persists, it is ordinarily not severely disabling and may be controlled by proper bracing. The aged person often prefers to accept some limping rather than the inconvenience of a brace. The matter should be left to his will. In advanced years, as has been repeatedly remarked in these pages, comfort is often preferred to perfection.

Among the dislocations at the knee joint, that of the patella merits some notice. It is quite unusual and more often than not self-reduced before the surgeon appears. Nevertheless it is not a minor trauma to the older person. It either marks the beginning of clinically apparent degenerative arthrosis at the knee or aggravates seriously the arthrosis already present.

Ten days to two weeks of protection by adhesive tape, as described in Chap. 6 in connection with fractures of the patella, will prove sufficient immobilization. In the very old, if the skin will not tolerate adhesive tape, a cotton and flannel pressure bandage will prove adequate. Following this the usual gravitational exercises will recover an adequate degree of mobility in the uncomplicated case. As in the more serious trauma noted above, aspiration of the joint is required only in the event of excessive expansion of the capsule by synovial fluid or blood.

ANKLE

Dislocation does not occur at the ankle without fracture except under most unusual circumstances. The combined lesion was discussed in Chap. 6. However, a form of subluxation does occur following severe sprains when the lateral or medial ligament may have been torn. In these cases, the talus is no longer held firmly in its mortise between the tibial and fibular malleoli and with each step moves irregularly against the tibial articular cartilage. Such severe sprains do not occur in the aged with the frequency found in the younger adults. When they do occur the results are the same: persistent pain on weight bearing and eventual arthritic degeneration of parts of the joint.

The only effective treatment of posttraumatic subluxation of the ankle joint is the same at all ages, *prevention*. This lesion is ordinarily quite preventable when sprains of the ankle are properly cared for (see below). When it does occur, the treatment which has been suggested for younger individuals, surgical repair of the ligaments, is of very doubtful value in the aged. The surgical intervention itself is an invitation to further fibrosis. The necessary period of immobilization which follows would probably serve to hasten further degeneration of the joint.

Protection of the ankle by a leather or canvas cuff during periods of walking or standing has in practice afforded considerable relief to several cases of this lesion in elderly people, and is advised as the most feasible solution. Seldom if ever does the degree of discomfort warrant ankle fusion in the aged. Time is too valuable and, but for exceptional circumstances, the demands of daily life do not require excessive walking.

TARSAL AND TARSOMETATARSAL JOINTS

Dislocation of the bones of the feet have not as yet been reported among the aged as isolated lesions. When they are found it is invariably as one item of a multiple injury and treatment is but part of the general management of the complex foot trauma.

METATARSOPHALANGEAL AND INTERPHALANGEAL JOINTS

Traumatic interphalangeal-joint dislocation of the toes is rare in the aged. Self-reduced subluxations are the probable pathology of the frequently "stubbed toe" when the elderly foot strikes against household furniture. In the examining of an aged foot following such an injury, the surgeon must be aware of the common finding of hammer toes and so-called "claw toes." In the latter, it is common to find the proximal phalanx riding above the head of the adjacent metatarsal. Examiners not experienced in orthopedic matters are sometimes not aware of the fact that a single claw toe or a single hammer toe is not uncommon, and that often enough the elderly person has never particularly noticed the deformity until the toe was injured. These common deformities of the toes must not be confused with dislocations. A recent dislocation of a toe is easily reduced by traction and its snapping into place is audible or palpable, and final. The old displacements of claw toes or hammer toes are pathologic contractions of the periarticular tissues and are not manually reducible.

In the rare instance of true dislocation, the reduced toe is held in place by simple adhesive splinting to the neighboring normal toe. Ten days of protection is sufficient. After this, the minor discomfort will disappear with time and use. No further therapy is ordinarily required.

SPRAINS IN AGED JOINTS

A sprain by pathologic definition implies a tear of fibers composing some part of the periarticular or intraarticular connective tissues. A few fibers may be torn within an otherwise intact tissue, or a distinct element such as the lateral ligament of the knee joint may be ripped apart. Sprains occurring in the joints of the aged do not differ in cause, type, pathology, or symptoms from those occurring at any age. The same ecchymosis, the same inflammatory reaction of the connective tissues and adjacent synovia take place, and either excess synovial fluid or blood may appear within the joint cavity. There is one aspect of the lesion, however, which is particular to the aged. The healing time, as observed by the persistence of symptoms, is considerably prolonged. This fact to some extent modifies treatment.

In young adults, sprains may be minor transient incidents relieved by a few days of rest, perhaps ameliorated in its early stages by cold packs, and followed by a short afterperiod of moderate restraint. In more severe instances a sprain may be a major trauma destructive to ligaments, even to the point of requiring surgical repair and protracted protection. In the aged, the latter severe type seldom appears, but when it does it leaves an inevitable residue of joint degeneration, painful osteodystrophy, and fibrous adhesions with significant permanent restriction of motion. From the functional point of view, at its mildest, a sprained joint in an elderly individual is never a minor incident for precisely the same reasons, though perhaps to a lesser degree. It is here particularly that "weather ache" and the "geling phenomenon" discussed in the introduction to this chapter can be troublesome.

In the care of a sprained joint in an aged person one must remain aware of a fact often repeated in the chapters concerned with musculoskeletal injuries, that is, the decreased elasticity of aging connective tissue. The process of healing of the torn ligament or its parts is accomplished by collagen fibers without elastin. Prolonged immobilization for relief of pain in an elderly individual is an invitation to persistence of local pain and disability when activity is resumed. This of course is true of younger individuals as well, but in practice the younger adult sooner or later "stretches" the adhesions or, by some modification, loses the painful stimuli except in the most serious and perhaps neglected cases. The elderly person is quite apt not to lose his local pain even in less severe injuries.

Sprain and its often concomitant traumatic synovitis in the aged must be treated with the meticulous care one would offer to the young athlete or dancer expecting to return to activity. It is all but neglect to pass off a joint injury in an elderly person on the grounds, too often glibly offered, that the x-ray was negative. True, no life or death tragedy is involved, and an uncomplicated sprain will not lead to amputation. But neglect or undertreatment will lead to permanent discomfort at a time of life when a pleasant walk in the neighborhood or a bit of housework or visiting is among the few pleasures of the passing days.

In the treatment of sprains in the aged, rest during the early days of acute reaction is the primary treatment. In the upper extremity this means a light splint. In the lower extremity it means no weight bearing, and partial immobilization in a pillow splint if necessary for comfort. If joint fluid is excessive, its aspiration will relieve excessive pain. This should be performed under aseptic conditions through a dermal wheal of 1 per cent Novocain or Xylocaine. Aspiration will afford dramatic relief and may be repeated for several days during the acute period.

After a few days, when the acute reaction has subsided, any one of a number of methods may be used to permit early resumption of graded activity. A wristband (never elastic, the old-fashioned leather strap worn comfortably firm rather than tight), an elastic bandage, or adhesive strapping, at the knee or ankle, and the temporary use of a walking stick are all helpful. Daily hot soaks or compresses and the use of analgesic liniments or light massage are home treatments probably equally as effective as the mechanical modalities of the office or clinic. In a rather persistent case, healing seems to be hastened by a few injections of 6.5 to 25 mg of Hydrocortone or a similar steroid at 5- to 7-day intervals. It must not be forgotten that pain after a sprain means inflammatory reaction in the tissues. One is not treating pain, one is treating the persistent tissue response to the recent trauma.

On occasion it is necessary to treat the residual symptoms of an old sprain which had been either neglected or undertreated (often the patient's fault rather than the doctor's), or which had been so severe as to leave disabling periarticular adhesions. Sometimes the sprained ligament had healed well but the accompanying traumatic synovitis remained symptomatic. In either case, a short course of injections of Hydrocortone at the locally tender site (not necessarily the subjectively painful one) has proved the most effective of procedures in the present writers' experience. Ordinarily three to six injections of 12.5 to 25 mg have sufficed.

Occasionally disabling symptoms persist in spite of therapy. In the aged person some type of partial support has been found the only means of affording comfort. The wristband, the knee cage (see illustration in Chap. 6), or the ankle cuff is still a kindness to the aged individual, and one is often amazed at the difference its wearing makes in the comfort of his daily living.

Sprain has been discussed as a general lesion. In its treatment it must be emphasized that a "joint" is never sprained. The direction of treatment and its intelligent application are best served when one recalls that the damage has been done to one or more of the specific elements of the complex periarticular or intraarticular connective tissues. In the recording of these injuries, for both present and future recognition, the term *sprained wrist* is not permissible. The individual has suffered a trauma specifically to the dorsal radioulnar ligament, the ulnarcarpal ligament or other local structure, or to a multiplicity of these. The same rule applies of course to other joints. Prognosis in sprains about the joints of the aged is not as happy as it ordinarily is in the younger adult. At best symptoms last much longer; too often some degree of painful disability is permanent. A last warning is imperative in any discussion of sprains at any age: there is no acceptable diagnosis of sprain without an x-ray film!

ROTATOR-CUFF TEAR AT THE SHOULDER JOINT

This injury occurs in the aged as it may at any period of adult life. A large percentage of patients over 60 have degenerative changes in the rotator cuff. They may not present the classical syndrome described by Codman, since little old ladies as well as laborers have cuff tears. These can be diagnosed by the clinical picture. There is little defect in passive motion, and an absence of contracture, although pain may give an impression of stiffness. In experienced hands, arthrography may be of help in demonstrating the tear.

Many patients of all ages with cuff tears are able to compensate for the defect so that they regain a normal, painless range of motion. Since this is so, early operative intervention is never indicated. As long as symptoms improve with supportive treatment involving the use of heat and salicylates and an insistence upon active motion, surgery can be deferred. There is no place for the use of an abduction spica or airplane splint in managing this injury. These methods are poorly tolerated by older patients and furthermore contribute little toward the healing of the tear. When symptoms continue, or fail to improve, there is time enough to recommend surgical intervention. Repair should be carried out meticulously. Even though one hesitates to resort to surgery in the aged patient, it is sometimes unjustified to withhold surgical relief in a lesion which can become as disablingly painful as this one.

"FROZEN" SHOULDER

The stiff shoulder is one of the most common and difficult problems to deal with in elderly patients. It may appear as the result of many etiological factors—traumatic, associated with intercurrent illness, or even perhaps emotional factors. The internist must often deal with the coronary patient who will not move his arm and gets a stiff shoulder. The surgeon sees it in the postradical mastectomy or thoracoplasty patient. A common denominator seems to be disuse in the dependent position, but another important factor is the personality make up of the patient. It is very difficult to encourage the passive, dependent patient to continue active use of his upper extremities, and this type of patient frequently develops a frozen shoulder. Any injury to the upper extremity, and particularly one which prevents use of the hand, such as Colles' fracture, is a frequent cause of frozen shoulder. Diagnosis is simple enough—the shoulder will have little or no glenohumeral motion, frequently there will be pain at the extreme of motion with no specific perceptible lesion to account for it.

Treatment of the stiff shoulder is prevention. Overimmobilization after injury or related lesions, reliance on passive treatments, such as diathermy or baking, to the exclusion of active exercises, dulls the patient into disuse and subsequent restricted motion. Once the diagnosis of frozen shoulder is established, the patient should be made to understand the problem with reassurance that healing will take place, that only active use and the passage of time are necessary before normal motion is regained. Each patient must be encouraged differently, some must be threatened, others cajoled, some reasoned with. All must be supervised and instructed in the exercises. Activity should be graded, beginning with pendulum exercises, followed by the assistive exercises such as those involving the use of a pulley. The patient should be seen at regular intervals until motion is well established.

"Tennis Elbow"

We use the nonspecific term because the exact pathology is not understood. The implication inherent in the term *lateral* or *medial epicondylitis* is that there is an inflammation of the epicondyle; this is certainly not the case. In all likelihood there is a partial tearing of the insertion of the common extensor aponeurosis or its medial counterpart, with some degeneration. Occasionally a calcium deposit is noted.

The clinical picture is quite characteristic. Patients complain of being unable to lift a coffeepot or to shake hands without feeling pain in the forearm. Any motion requiring extension of the wrist or fingers may cause similar pain. There is exquisite tenderness over one or the other of the epicondyles. Resisting supination or pronation will provoke pain over the medial or lateral epicondyle, depending upon which aponeurosis is affected.

Infiltration of the point of tenderness with 1 per cent procaine followed by multiple punctures of the area with a "hypo" needle and instillation of $\frac{1}{2}$ to 1 ml of hydrocortisone offers relief to the majority of patients. It is wise to warn the patient that there may be a reaction more painful than the original pain for 24 to 48 hours. One might defer treatment until symptoms are severe enough, since many patients have only very mild complaints which may subside spontaneously. Section of the aponeurosis below the epicondyle, while indicated in some patients who fail to respond, is rarely indicated in the older patient. X-ray therapy or physiotherapy plays little if any role in managing this problem; its benefits are probably fortuitous, coinciding with the self-limited nature of the lesion. Although self-limited, the process may be of long duration, even upward of a year. Under treatment, symptoms should be relieved; but one expects several recurrences requiring relief before the lesion corrects itself.

Olecranon Bursitis

A blow on the tip of the elbow is frequently followed by an effusion into the subcutaneous olecranon bursa with a resultant large, generally painless, fluctuant mass. Occasionally this becomes red and painful as the result of inflammation or even at times infection. Rest will usually result in its absorption in one to several weeks. Aspiration may be indicated at times if there is considerable pain. This should be carried out only under the strictest conditions of asepsis, for infection in this bursa is one cell layer away from the ulna and not much more distant from the synovial cavity of the elbow joint. Iatrogenic infection here can be tragic.

If the bursal wall becomes thickened and is cosmetically objectionable or constantly being struck, it may be surgically removed. Postoperatively, the elbow is kept at rest for about a week. Normal activity is then encouraged. In the older patient surgery should be seldom necessary since the location of this bursal enlargement does not impair function.

STENOSING TENOSYNOVITIS (DE QUERVAIN)

This is a condition seen frequently in older patients. The patient complains of a painful and tender mass in the region of the radial styloid. This can be very annoying and disabling because of pain on using the thumb. Its origin may or may not be traumatic. It is common among elderly ladies who do a lot of knitting, but it also occurs frequently enough without perceptible precipitating cause.

On examination there is tenderness over the dorsal carpal ligament in the region of the abductor pollicis longus and extensor pollicis brevis tendons. Frequently a sensation as though one were pulling a knotted string through a hole can be felt. This sensation is due to the fusiform swelling that occurs in the tendon where it is pulled through the narrowed sheath. Another clinical sign is pain on forcibly putting the wrist into ulnar deviation or flexing the thumb into the palm.

There are two stages in the development of this condition. One is the acute inflammatory stage in which there is pain and tenderness with little mechanical obstruction. The second is the stage of scarring and constriction at which time the mass and the mechanical symptoms are more prominent. The latter or chronic phase is the lesion referred to in the eponym *De Quervain.*

In the inflammatory phase, injection of the abductor sheath over or distal to the radial styloid with procaine, and then instillation of Hydrocortone into the tendon sheath, is often effective. In cases which do not respond to three or four such injections, or which have been present in the second stage for a long time, it is necessary to incise to tendon sheath at its fibrotic constriction. A transverse skin incision, with care being taken to avoid the superficial radial nerve, gives the best scar. The sheath is of course incised longitudinally over the tendon.

TRIGGER FINGER

Trigger finger is seen frequently in older patients. The characteristic snapping sensation on flexing and extending the fingers is palpable in the palm over the region of the metacarpophalangeal joint. A pea-sized mass can be felt to pass over the examiner's fingers on flexion and extension. As in certain other lesions mentioned in this section, the question of trauma is disputable. It is seen sometimes after immobilization in a plaster cast for a Colles' fracture. It is seen more often among elderly osteoarthritics.

As in De Quervain's disease, this lesion can be managed by injection with Hydrocortone in the acute stage, or treated by surgical section of the sheath when chronically stenosed.

CALCIUM DEPOSITS ABOUT THE ARTICULATIONS

While these do occur in older people they are more common in the middle-aged. The most frequent location is in the shoulder cuff, with the gluteus medius tendon at the hip next in frequency and the flexor carpi ulnaris at its insertion third. Calcium deposits can occur in any tendon and, in the hand, in the capsule of its joints. These deposits do not occur in bursae primarily, although they may evacuate into a bursa.

Calcium may be deposited in any injured tissue in which cellular degeneration has occurred. The supraspinatous tendon is one of the favorite sites. Calcium accumulates probably as a calcium carbonate-oxalate salt. These salts are very irritating and the acute deposit is in reality a chemical furuncle. As long as the deposit is within the thickness of the tendon, it may remain asymptomatic or only mildly symptomatic. When this deposit enlarges so that it is under pressure, the pain increases until it may become excruciating when the surface of the tendon and the floor of the bursa are reached. Motion in these circumstances is apt to be intolerable. This accounts for the characteristic holding of the involved member with the other hand to keep it from moving and the worsening of symptoms on lying down. Lying down removes the weight of the upper extremity which pulls the humeral head down from the acromion.

As in the case of a furuncle there are two ways in which the calcific nodule may develop. It may absorb, or come to a head and evacuate itself. It never remains stationary. It is self-limited. It may subside with no treatment at all. Because it is self-limited, many types of treatment have been and are in vogue. In an acute episode needling with procaine in order to decompress the deposit seems the most logical approach. In practice this is often successful. It may fail in cases in which there are multiple deposits. X-ray therapy has been widely used for the acute stage and recently Butazolidin has been used with good results. Both of these modalities are difficult to evaluate because of the self-limited nature of the lesion.

Calcium deposits are found in the region of the hip within the gluteus medius tendon. As in other areas, this may be the result of a known strain or other trauma or may appear without apparent cause. The lesion is easily diagnosed clinically by local tenderness. Occasionally a patient presents himself with an acutely painful hip, may even have a slight temperature, elevated white-cell count and elevated sedimentation rate, with marked spasm of the hip musculature. Usually the symptoms are much milder. X-ray will show a calcium deposit in the region of the reflected head of the rectus femoris or near the insertion of muscles and tendons about the greater trochanter.

The gluteus medius deposit will respond to needling. Since the deposit in the reflected head is difficult to needle, it is best managed with bed rest and sedation.

Deposits in the wrist and hand may be acute and resemble a local cellulitis. Calcium within the flexor carpi ulnaris may cause actual lymphangitic streaking. Local tenderness at the insertion of the tendon into the pisiform and an x-ray disclosure of the calcific deposit establish the diagnosis. Treatment should consist of needling and a volar molded splint. If nothing is done the patient will recover, but will take a longer period of time to do so and may suffer considerably during the episode.

TENOSYNOVITIS OF THE FOOT

An acute tenosynovitis is not unusual in the anterior tibial tendon sheath of the aged. This may be due to an unusual strain such as an unguarded step from a curb or stair. The symptoms are localized pain and tenderness over the sheath, increased by motion. Frequently a crepitus can be felt as the tendon moves.

Treatment consists of rest, elastic bandage, and perhaps warm soaks. Occasionally a plaster boot must be applied to rest the part. Stenosing tenosynovitis of the peroneal tendons occurs just inferior to the lateral malleolus as they pass under the retinaculum. As in De Quervain's disease, a definite click may be felt at times. Treatment consists of three or more local injections of Hydrocortone (0.5 ml). In an occasional case, incision of the tendon sheath is necessary.

HALLUX RIGIDUS

Repeated injury to the metacarpophalangeal joint of the great toe will result in a traumatic arthritis which provokes severe pain and limitation of motion of this joint. While far more common in middle life it occurs not infrequently in the aged. It is occasionally found following an unrecognized fracture into the joint.

If relief cannot be obtained by three or four injections of Hydrocortone (0.5 ml), a hemiphalangectomy of the proximal phalanx of the great toe will relieve symptoms. A resection of the head of the first metatarsal gives equal relief, and some orthopedic surgeons prefer this procedure.

BIBLIOGRAPHY

Bick, E. M.: Clinical aspects of aging connective tissues. *Bull. N.Y. Acad. Med.* **35**:547, 1959.

De Palma, A. F.: "Surgery of the Shoulder." Philadelphia, Lippincott, 1950.

Horn, J. S.: The traumatic anatomy and treatment of acute acromioclavicular dislocation. *Jour. Bone and Joint Surg.* **36***B*:194, 1954.

Lernin, P.: "The Knee and Related Structures." Philadelphia, Lea & Febiger, 1952.

MacAusland, W. R.: Perilunar dislocation of the carpal bones and dislocation of the lunate bone. *Surg. Gyn. and Obst.* **79**:256, 1944.

McLoughlin, H. L.: Posterior dislocations of the shoulder. *Jour. Bone and Joint Surg.* **34***A*:584, 1952.

McLoughlin, H. L.: "Traumatic Surgery." Philadelphia, Saunders, 1959.

McLoughlin, H. L., and E. G. Asherman: Lesions of the musculo-tendinous cuff on the shoulder. *Jour. Bone and Joint Surg.* **33***A*:76, 1951.

Osmond-Clarke, H.: Dislocation of the knee joint with capsular interposition. *Proc. Roy. Soc. Med.* **35**:759, 1942.

Rank, B. K., and A. R. Wakefield: Surgery of repair as applied to hand injuries. London and Edinburgh, E. & S. Livingstone, Ltd., 1953.

Urist, M. R.: Complete dislocations of the acromio-clavicular joint. *Jour. Bone and Joint Surg.* **28**:813, 1946.

Watson-Jones, R.: "Fractures and Joint Injuries," 4th ed. Baltimore, William & Wilkins, 1955.

Chapter 12

Tendon Injuries and Hand Trauma

Bernard E. Simon

In proportion to their seemingly trivial nature, no injuries can match those of the hand in their devastating social and economic consequences. To the aged patient, such an injury may be catastrophic. The grandmother whose help about the house is her *raison d'être* and pride and the elderly independent worker who still holds down a job are no less dependent on their hands than a machinist, textile worker, or craftsman. The surgeon caring for these injuries must use all the skill and judgment at his command since both the elderly patient and his injury will require not only professional expertness but sympathy and understanding as well.

ANATOMICAL AND FUNCTIONAL CONSIDERATIONS OF CLINICAL IMPORTANCE

The structure and function of the individual components of the hand are covered in detail in the monumental "Surgery of the Hand" by the late Sterling Bunnell, and in the monographs of Rank and Wakefield, and of Furlong. Kaplan's exhaustive treatise, recently published, covers the anatomical minutiae. Without a secure knowledge of what Littler has called "Architectural Principles," the surgeon will find himself quite at sea with neither compass nor anchor.

The hand can be divided into two systems, (1) a fixed portion comprising the second and third metacarpals set solidly into the carpus, about which rotate (2) the mobile fourth and fifth metacarpals with 15 and 30° of movement respectively on the ulnar side and the even more freely movable first metacarpal on the radial aspect. The transverse arch with all its adaptability is tied together at the metacarpal heads by the strong intermetacarpal ligaments. Acting on the mobile components at either end are the thenar and hypothenar muscle masses which originate almost centrally and draw the two ends of the arch together.

Functioning at right angles to the transverse arch is a longitudinal arch. Here the carpus and the metacarpals are fixed and the phalanges form the mobile component.

Littler speaks of the thumb as "the other half of the hand" (Gr. *anticheir*). The unique arrangement of the articular surfaces, the marked laxity of the joint capsule, and the lack of reinforcing ligaments of any importance in the carpometacarpal joint of the thumb permit the latter to be swung freely to oppose the fingers. The action not only includes circumduction, permitting movement in a wide arc measuring 90°, but it includes at least 15 to 20° of axial rotation.

THE POSITION OF FUNCTION

The concepts noted in the preceding section and a knowledge of normal joint motions and their ranges lead logically to an appreciation of the importance of the so-called "position of function." Without this, place-

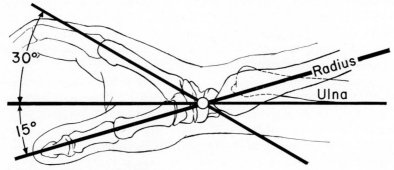

FIG. 12-1. The position of function as drawn from an x-ray. The thumb metacarpal is aligned with the radius and forms an angle of 45° with the second metacarpal. The hand is dorsiflexed 30° in relation to the forearm.

ment of the injured hand and its components becomes haphazard. With this knowledge splinting of even a badly traumatized hand becomes simple and obvious. Crippling sequelae, such as hyperextension deformities of the metacarpophalangeal joints and adduction deformity of the thumb, can be avoided.

The position is simple enough (Fig. 12-1). With the forearm in midpronation, the hand is dorsiflexed to 30° at the wrist. The thumb is in line with the radius. Because of the position of the forearm bones in midpronation it will be noted that the thumb and index metacarpals will form an angle of about 45° and that the plane of the first metacarpal will be at right angles to the plane of the palm. The metacarpophalangeal and interphalangeal joints will be semiflexed and the fingertips will be on equidistant radii from the pulp of the thumb. It will be readily appreciated that the arch of the palm is maintained in midposition and that the fingers are progressively more flexed or curled ulnarwards, this being the normal resting attitude of the hand. Prolonging the line of each finger causes it to point to the tubercle of the carpal scaphoid.

STIFFNESS OF THE HAND FOLLOWING TRAUMA IN THE AGED

The salient feature that distinguishes the response of the aged to trauma and surgery as contrasted with that of the child and younger adult is an overwhelming tendency to stiffness. This unpleasant sequela, usually associated with major trauma, infection, or extensive surgery, may follow surprisingly short periods of immobilization, often after relatively trivial injuries. This tendency has been called "the stiffening factor" by Julian Bruner and although it bears a relation to age, it does not run strictly parallel to it. It is not to be confused with rheumatism or arthritis. It would appear to be a nonspecific response in certain individuals to a variety of tissue insults, including ischemia, infection, burn, and crush injury. Rough handling of tissue by the surgeon must not be forgotten as a contributory cause equally traumatic.

The pathogenesis of stiffening is far from being completely understood. There is little doubt that edema, of either infectious or hydrostatic origin, is of prime importance. This fails, however, to explain why the tendency to stiffening increases with age, since edema occurs in younger individuals. The answer probably lies in the connective and supportive tissues themselves. Recent studies by Bick suggest that progressive degenerative changes occur in the elastic component of the aging tissues.

ROLE OF EDEMA

A clear understanding of the pathologic physiology of edema is essential to rational treatment in hand surgery. Edema fluid is not water or saline. Moberg has likened it to a kind of liquid glue. Its presence in a tissue excites a diffuse fibroblastic response which in its most extreme form (usually after massive infection) can destroy a hand, changing it from a delicate mechanism to a clawlike paperweight. The reaction to edema is universal. The intense subcutaneous fibrosis around stasis ulcer in the lower extremity, and the thick fibrous capsule seen surrounding the liver, spleen, and in the peritoneal cavity in chronic cardiac edema are merely manifestations of the same response.

Arterial blood enters the hand on the volar aspect. Venous and lymphatic outflow is collected via perforating vessels and leaves the hand from its dorsum. The pressure of the arterial inflow is not sufficient to drive blood and lymph back into the larger collecting vessels of the arm.

Two ancillary mechanisms are needed to effect return flow. The first is compression of vessels in the restricted fascial compartments of the palm and fingers, and the second is gravitational, put into use each time that the arm is raised above the level of the right heart. The first mechanism presupposes the ability to make a fist or at least partially to flex the fingers, and it is therefore dependent upon the integrity of the longitudinal arch of the hand. A freely mobile shoulder joint is essential for putting the second mechanism into play. It is apparent that prolonged immobilization in extension with consequent shortening of the collateral ligaments of the interphalangeal and metacarpophalangeal joints will seriously interfere with the normal pumping action. This leads to the vicious cycle of further edema, and organization with fibrous tissue. Contraction of the latter produces further limitation of motion and deformity causing still more edema. Eventually contraction of the diffuse fibrous network leads to a stiff, useless, rakelike member, which no longer appears grossly edematous. In this final stage, damage is irreversible.

In the aged, in addition to surgical immobilization, anything which restricts flexion of the hand will cause edema, particularly if the hand is dependent, thereby failing to make use of the second mechanism. Under these conditions, edema is seen in the pareses following cerebrovascular lesions, and in neurosurgical patients with cord disorders. Moberg has called attention to the puzzling presence of edema in the left hand in severe cardiacs who are bedridden and whose activity has been restrained. The minimal activity of the right hand is just sufficient to render it edema free in contrast to the left. Edema of the hand is seen after forearm injuries, particularly Colles' fracture, when the metacarpophalangeal joints are not actively flexed either because of insufficient instruction to the patient or because of a cast extending beyond the distal palmar crease. Overly tight dressings, causing pain with consequent immobilization, will likewise provoke edema by their tourniquet effect. Last, but not least among those in whom disastrous edema and stiffening may occur, is the uncooperative or frightened patient who holds the hand and entire arm rigidly and protectively immobile.

EXAMINATION, PREOPERATIVE ASSESSMENT, AND RECORDING OF FINDINGS

The injured hand is first examined without disturbing the dressing after the details of "how, when, and where" have been ascertained (which is particularly important in determining the elapsed interval in tendon injuries). With stabilization and control of proximal joints by the examiner, and by careful sensory testing with a sterile pin, it should ordinarily be possible to assess nerve and tendon integrity with a minimum of error. Allowance should be made for restriction of motion due to pain. Exposure of the wound may follow *only for purposes of observation by the examiner and notation of the location and direction of wounds.* In the aged patient whose mental state or general physical condition makes cooperation in the examination unsatisfactory, this will at least help the surgeon to determine which deeper structures may have been injured. Inspection of the wound in the emergency department may likewise be justified where a crush or avulsion injury exists, since it may be necessary to anticipate the preparation of a donor site for a free graft or direct pedicle. *On no account may the wound be probed, explored, or otherwise entered except under operating room conditions.*

Preoperative examination is supplemented by x-ray studies where indicated. Assessment is completed in the operating room by direct inspection of the wound under sterile precautions. At this time there is added to the previous information a three-dimensional view of the extent of the entire wound pattern and confirmation of previous impressions of tendon and nerve injury.

The importance of recording the information obtained cannot be overestimated. No wordy description can take the place of a simple hand outline with wounds and scars marked in, positions of neuromata noted, areas of abnormal skin sensation mapped out, and abnormal or restricted joint ranges recorded. Notation of age, occupation, handedness, and general condition can very well complete the record.

ANESTHESIA IN HAND INJURIES

The proper approach to hand injuries includes a precise, unhurried technique stressing accuracy and gentleness. This requires effective anesthesia. Patients with hand trauma usually come to surgery hastily evaluated, poorly premedicated, and with food and drink in the stomach. Under such conditions, and especially in the elderly, a general anesthetic can pose a threat to the patient that scarcely justifies the repair of a relatively minor injury. Skillful use of regional and local anesthesia is often the way out of the dilemma. The employment of 26 gauge needles and of 3 to 5 ml Luer-Lok syringes makes possible in the precise deposition of small amounts of anesthetic solution. For minor repairs in the fingers, block of the digital nerves, whose anatomical location is quite constant, is ideal. One ml of 2 per cent procaine or lidocaine (Xylocaine) is deposited in the palm on either side of the flexor tendon beneath the palmar aponeurosis proximal to the finger base at the level of the distal transverse flexion crease. A small additional amount is placed transversely across the dorsal surface of the metacarpal head to block the dorsal nerves. These latter nerves run superficially beneath the skin and are not to be found below the deep fascia as on the volar side. Sufficient time must be permitted to elapse if anesthesia is to be effective. Injection into the base of the finger itself is distinctly less safe, and if made necessary by circumstance, epinephrine must be completely omitted from the anesthetic solution.

Local infiltration can be used for minor lacerations and is much less painful when introduced subcutaneously directly through the wound edges. The safety of this practice has been demonstrated, despite warnings in the standard texts that it carries contamination deep into the surrounding tissues. Nerve blocks at the wrist and elbow are safe and effective. Brachial plexus block is ideal for extensive procedures in the elderly poor-risk patient. In experienced hands, failures to obtain anesthesia are few; the minimal pneumothorax which occasionally occurs does not contraindicate the procedure. In hospitals where medical anesthetists are not available, it may be necessary for the surgeon who takes care of hand injuries to learn the technique. It has been clearly outlined in a small, lucidly illustrated monograph by MacIntosh and Mushin. Recently, Burnham has described a new approach to regional nerve block which may very well supplant the latter procedure. This consists of deposition of anesthetic solutions on either side of the brachial artery high in the arm. There is no danger of pneumothorax and failures are few. It has been used successfully in 56 cases at last report. Since nerve blocks take 10 minutes to reach full effect, they can advantageously precede the cleanup.

General anesthesia is indicated in extensive cases and where application of a pneumatic tourniquet for a prolonged interval is required. It is particularly useful in elective secondary procedures where proper medical evaluation, careful preparation, and premedication can be unhurriedly accomplished. Selection of the agent should usually be left to the judgment of the anesthetist.

OPERATIVE TREATMENT

Skin Preparation

The pneumatic tourniquet is secured in place, the emergency room dressings are removed, and the wound is covered with a folded sterile pad held in place by the surgeon's left hand. With the right hand, the exposed skin is carefully washed for several minutes, using a solution of green soap, or any other detergent the surgeon may favor, on sterile 4 by 4 gauze sponges. The nails are trimmed short and cleaned with an orange stick. The cleanup must be as meticulous and prolonged as that employed for the surgeon's hands. A pitcher of sterile water is used to rinse off the soapy water and detritus. The wound region is now exposed and the scrub carried to the edges. A wash of 70 per cent alcohol follows. At this point traditionalists will paint the skin with one or another of several antiseptics. It should be emphasized that the careful and intelligent mechanical cleansing of the skin is of greater importance than the type of detergent used or the antiseptic, if any, which follows. *Antiseptics must never be used in the wound.* Again, if used, the antiseptic should be colorless since the dyes interfere with the assessment of skin viability and circulatory embarrassment.

Sterile stockinette rolled onto the arm and over the tourniquet makes an excellent basic drape. It is begun at the wrist, leaving the hand exposed. It is frustrating to attempt to work on the hand through small windows. Draping is completed, and a special hand table offering a stable working surface is slid under the hand and arm. Under no circumstances should hand work be done on the usual arm board; it is simply not stable enough. By this time the regional block should have resulted in complete anesthesia of the part and the part is ready for the operation.

Use of the Pneumatic Tourniquet in the Aged

The pneumatic tourniquet for use in extremity surgery, introduced by Cushing in 1904, afforded the hand surgeon a safe and effective method whereby to secure a bloodless field. Probably no other single advance except anesthesia has done more to make possible reparative and reconstructive work in this complex region. Bunnell has suggested that a jeweler might as well attempt to repair a watch immersed in ink as a surgeon operate on the hand without tourniquet hemostasis.

Despite its importance, little was written concerning the complications and safeguards relating to the use of the tourniquet in the half century following its introduction. In 1950, before the American Society for Hand Surgery, Bruner described in detail the syndrome which may follow use of the pneumatic tourniquet and suggested specific rules for its employment which might prevent the occurrence of the syndrome.

The *postischemic hand syndrome* is characterized by the following signs: (1) Puffiness of the hands and fingers (not a pitting edema), evidenced by a smoothing out of the normal skin creases. (2) Stiffness of the hand and finger joints to a degree not otherwise explained. (3) Color changes in the hand, which is pale in the horizontal position, more so when elevated, and congested in the dependent position. (4) Subjective sensations of numbness in the affected hand without true anesthesia. (5) Objective evidence of weakness in the muscles of the forearm and hand without real paralysis.

The inconstant appearance of this syndrome led to the concept of tourniquet or ischemic tolerance. The young possess it to a high degree.

There seems little doubt that with advancing years, tolerance to ischemia becomes lessened and that tourniquet hemostasis must be used more circumspectly in the elderly. In the presence of vascular damage or extensive scarring, even the younger patient may display the postischemic hand syndrome. As was noted earlier in this chapter, there is a stiffening factor in adults which is not exactly proportional to age and not related to rheumatic or arthritic states. Certain individuals have a greater tendency than others to develop stiffness following trauma or immobilization, and Bruner suggests that such persons may have a lower tolerance to other tissue insults such as ischemia.

Bruner's rules for tourniquet application as modified by this writer follow:

1. The only safe tourniquet is the blood pressure cuff attached to a mercury manometer. The rubber bag in the cuff and its connections must be absolutely leakproof, for a pinhole will allow the pressure to fall gradually below systolic level, resulting in congestion which, if prolonged, is more dangerous than ischemia. (The writer uses the Martin tourniquet in which the pneumatic cuff is attached to a Freon cylinder. The latter maintains pressure at the same level continually after proper setting. The aneroid manometer must be carefully checked at intervals against a mercury manometer as on occasions differences of at least 50 mm have been found.)

2. The upper arm should first be padded with several turns of sheet wadding, after which the manometer cuff is snugly and smoothly applied and held in place by wide roller bandage.

3. Before inflation of the cuff, the hand and forearm should be emptied of blood by elevation for several minutes or should be stripped of blood by means of an Esmarch or sterile elastic bandage (except in the presence of infection).

4. The pressure in the cuff must be applied very quickly to prevent blood from entering the forearm while the cuff is being inflated. (The Robbins Automatic Tourniquet with its Freon cylinder raises the pressure even more rapidly than is possible by the hand bulb. For this reason, and because it keeps pressure at a predetermined level, it has been found quite useful.)

5. Pressures of 270 to 300 mm of mercury are used for adults, including the aged; 250 mm or less are used for children.

6. Time limits are not agreed upon. One hour of ischemia is generally safe for healthy adults below middle age; in older patients, greater caution should be used. Some surgical sacrifice may be necessary because of the limitation of time.

7. Reapplication of pressure after a 10-minute period of release will be necessary in many cases to complete operative work. Time limits for

the second or third periods of ischemia are unknown. A possible summation of tissue reaction must be taken into account.

8. Before the release of tourniquet pressure, the open surgical wounds of the hands or forearm should be covered with saline compresses and snugly bandaged, and the arm should be elevated. Unless this is done, the wave of arterial blood which surges back into ischemic tissues on release of the tourniquet will result in great tissue congestion. Pressure on the open wound should be maintained for 5 to 10 minutes to allow cessation of capillary oozing, after which bleeders may be caught.

9. Colored skin antiseptics should be avoided, for they may be misleading. The ruddy tint of antiseptic paint may impart a sanguine glow to the skin when the tissues are actually in a state of suspended animation. The unpainted skin gives valuable information to the surgeon relative to ischemia, cyanosis, or congestion due to a fall in tourniquet pressure.

10. During the period of ischemia, the tissues distal to the tourniquet must be kept cool. Hot spotlights must not be used. On the basis of all experimental work, frequent irrigation of the tissues in the operative field with cool or cold saline is indicated.

The use of tourniquet hemostasis in surgery of the hand should be used sparingly and intelligently. Every tissue has its limit in regard to ischemia and the hand is no exception.

REPAIR OF FLEXOR TENDONS

In the repair of flexor tendons three zones can be distinguished (Fig. 12-2):

ZONE 1

This extends from the proximal interphalangeal joint to the insertion of the profundus tendon into the base of the terminal phalanx. Essentially it is a single tendon zone although the sublimus is still present laterally and behind the profundus as one approaches the proximal portion of the area.

The effect of division of the profundus in this zone is not dramatic and it may be occasionally overlooked by the unwary examiner. By the same token, it is not a serious or crippling injury and heroic reconstructive procedures are not indicated in the aged. Over-all stiffness of the hand is crippling. Loss of flexion of the terminal phalanx is merely annoying. The question of disability is linked to the patient's age and occupation and must be so evaluated in selecting the proper treatment. *On no account should the intact sublimus be removed or compromised.*

Primary Suture. Primary suture can be performed if the factors of time, contamination, skin cover, and general condition of the patient are

propitious. In the senile patient who has little or no need of fine movements of the hand, the deformity of a divided profundus tendon may be
electively accepted and only the skin laceration repaired. After repair
has been completed, the fibrous digital tendon sheath should be windowed, allowing soft adipose tissue to come into direct contact with the
suture line.

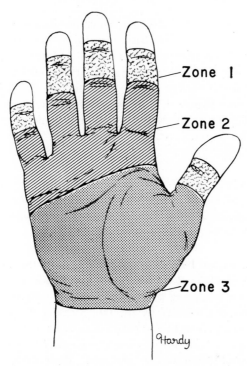

FIG. 12-2. The three zones in tendon repair.

Advancement of the proximal cut end can be carried out if the tendon
division lies within 1 inch or less of the profundus insertion. This consists of removal of the distal stump of the profundus and suture of the
proximal cut tendon end into the old insertion. The effect of this procedure is to eliminate the suture line from the gliding portion of the
sheath. In borderline injuries where the point of division is close to
zone 2 and to the pulley over the proximal portion of the middle phalanx,
the proximal end (and therefore the suture line) can easily be moved
distally about ½ inch. This is accomplished by resecting an appropriate
amount of distal stump. Advancement is most useful in the thumb and
index fingers. Here, the flexor pollicus longus and the profundus to the
index are separate muscles, not cross-connected as in the case of the

profundus to the three ulnar digits. Tendon lengthening at the wrist or Blum's "myotomy" (really an intramuscular tenotomy) can be performed to lessen the tension occasioned by the advancement.

Delayed primary suture, that is, suture performed within 3 to 4 weeks after injury, is often the method of choice. During the period of delay, the wound heals and presumably sterilizes itself. The results of this procedure are only slightly less successful than those of primary suture, and the hazards are considerably less. Since the incapacity resulting from the original injury is minimal, any impulse to perform primary suture in the presence of less than ideal conditions is foolhardy.

Failure of repair is not disastrous, since arthrodesis or tenodesis of the joint using the distal tendon stump to tether the distal joint in flexion results in adequate function. The only visible deformity is the permanently flexed distal interphalangeal joint, not a high price to pay for a completely useful finger.

Zone 2

Zone 2 extends from the proximal end of the fibrous digital sheath at the level of the distal palmar crease to the proximal interphalangeal joint where it meets zone 1. In this region there exist side by side, in the region of close tolerances, two tendons. These must move 4 to 5 cm to completely flex the fingers, and at the same time they have a differential glide of at least 1 cm one on the other. In the distal part of the region there are in effect *three* tendons as the dividing sublimus migrates to the sides of the emerging profundus tendon. This area was appropriately named "no man's land" by the late Sterling Bunnell of San Francisco, much of whose thought and effort were devoted to solving the riddle of tendon repair in this unpropitious region. The Chicago school of Koch, Mason, and Allen was at the same time studying the abysmal failures of simultaneous repair of both tendons and arriving at more or less the same logical conclusions.

Treatment. *Any attempt to repair both tendons in this region is foredoomed to failure.* Except under the most ideal circumstances, the wound should be closed, with repair of both digital nerves if they have been divided. If only one has been severed, its repair can be safely deferred until the time of definitive tendon suture since the finger will retain protective sensation.

When primary suture is performed, it will of necessity involve only one tendon, the profundus. In the course of its repair, the sublimus will have to be removed and discarded, and care will have to be taken to preserve part of the all-important pulley mechanism over the proximal phalanx, leaving about 5 mm. At the same time, as much of the rest of the fibrous sheath should be removed as can be exposed above and below the site of repair. This is a good deal of surgery. It involves extensive exposure in the finger and in the palm. Its employment should be reserved for cases that are ideal in respect to time limits, degree of contamination, and skin cover. IF IN DOUBT, THE WISEST COURSE IS SIMPLE WOUND CLOSURE.

Secondary or delayed primary repair is fruitless here and reconstruction by a free tendon graft is the procedure of choice if primary suture either was not performed or had resulted in failure.

ZONE 3

This is entirely within the palm and extends from the distal palmar crease to the base of the palm. Anatomically, this corresponds to the tendon from the proximal termination of the fibrous digital sheath to the transverse carpal ligament. Injuries in this region are often more extensive and are apt to involve several structures. The nerves in particular, due to their intimate association with the tendons passing through the area, are apt to be divided. Injuries here are more likely to be industrial in origin and to involve crushing or "untidy" types of trauma. In the home, falls with a bottle or glass in the hand or the breaking of a porcelain faucet are common causes of injury. In clean lacerations, primary suture is clearly indicated. The results, in general, are good. Both tendons can be repaired if care is taken to prevent cross union by interposition of soft tissue between the two suture lines. If laceration of the profundus is close to the lumbrical origin, the latter can frequently be wrapped around the site of repair. In general, function of the fingers will be carried out just as well by the profundus as by the combination of the two flexor tendons. If only the sublimus is divided, there is no necessity (in elderly patients in particular) for repair. The proximal end is drawn down, divided as high as possible, and permitted to retract, while the distal portion is removed through either a midlateral incision opposite the proximal interphalangeal joint or a transverse incision at the base of the finger.

If tendons to more than one finger are divided, suture of the sublimus tendons compromises the result by adding foreign body in the form of suture material, increasing the possibility of cross union and adhesion, and by prolonging the procedure. This applies particularly to multiple lacerations. It is evident that suture of all flexor tendons in the palm means eight separate repairs. This is quite unnecessary when the repair of four will achieve the same result.

Primary repair is especially desirable in the palm since this area is peculiarly liable to fibrosis and local reactions which often delay secondary surgery for many months. Such reactions occur because of the extensive synovia and other soft-part structures in this area and because of the presence of low-grade infection with irritation by blood and other products of trauma and inflammation. These stimulate massive proliferative reactions evidenced clinically by induration and tenderness. Secondary repair attempted during this phase is difficult and may end in failure. Enthusiasm for primary repair must be tempered by common sense. Blood supply, degree of soiling and contamination, condition of the skin, and length of delay should always be taken into consideration. Sepsis in the palm is disastrous, converting the hand from a precision instrument to something resembling a paperweight.

Flexor Tendon Lacerations in the Carpal Tunnel

In this area serious lacerations are unusual because of the depth of the tunnel and the protection afforded by the thick, tough, transverse carpal ligament and the high bony prominences on either side. Access to the area is gained by division of the ligament, usually along the ulnar side. The most important and vulnerable structure passing through the tunnel is the median nerve. Repair is complicated by the almost "explosive" division of the nerve into its many branches. Repair is strictly a matter of improvisation. Sublimus tendons do not require repair and should be removed.

Adjacent to the tunnel on the ulnar side is the ulnar nerve, coursing between the pisiform bone and the hamulus. It too, at this level, divides into its deep and superficial branches. The former supply all the intrinsic muscles of the hand, including the adductor pollicis and one head of the flexor pollicis brevis. Only the two radial lumbricals and the remaining intrinsics of the thumb are innervated by the median nerve. Division of the deep ulnar branch is calamitous. In lacerations of the base of the palm, its integrity must be proved preoperatively by demonstrating palpable contraction of the first dorsal interosseus. This is accomplished by requiring the patient to abduct the index finger widely while he holds the palm flat. Beware of trick movements. If division is suspected, immediate exploration and careful repair are indicated.

Lacerations at the Wrist

Complete laceration of all tendons and nerves at the wrist, though uncommon, happens frequently enough to pose a problem. To sever the 14 tendons and nerves on the flexor aspect of the wrist requires considerable force. A typical accident is a fall through a glass window or door, or a fall on a broken tumbler or bottle in the kitchen or in the tub. This is the type of accident to which the elderly are particularly prone. Repair *must* be simplified. Assuming a complete division, the following plan should be followed. Repair (1) the ulnar and median nerves, (2) the flexor pollicis longus, and (3) both wrist flexors. Then suture (4) the flexor digitorum profundus to the index finger, and (5) the flexor digitorum profundus to the middle, ring, and little fingers as a group, i.e., *one* mass repair. This results in 7 repairs as against 14, and simplifies a most formidable surgical exercise.

INJURIES TO EXTENSOR TENDONS

The extensor tendons differ in several respects from the flexors. They are flat and thin in shape, making accurate end-to-end suture difficult.

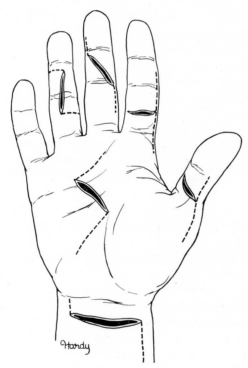

FIG. 12-3. Various wounds of fingers, palm, and wrist with suggested methods of obtaining extensile exposure. It is only necessary to extend incisions when primary repair of deeper structures is contemplated.

They lie immediately beneath the skin, with the exception of thin fascial investments. There is much less soft tissue to use as cover after suture. In the fingers, they lie in intimate association with underlying joint capsules from which they cannot be completely separated. Complete transection at the level of the distal and proximal interphalangeal articulations leads to repair over open joints with all the problems of stiffness and irritability which this entails. However, the picture is not completely black. The extensors do not lie free in synovial sheaths except where they cross the wrist. They are extensively cross-connected and do not tend to retract to nearly the same extent that is usual in the case of the flexors. The range of extensor-tendon movement necessary to move a finger through its range is distinctly less than that needed for flexion.

Specific Extensor Injuries

Mallet Finger (Baseball Finger). This is the result of traumatic avulsion or disinsertion of the terminal slip of the extensor expansion (formed by fusion of the lateral bands) from its insertion into the base of the distal phalanx. This is invariably caused by a sudden flexing force, such as that caused by being struck by a hard object while the finger is being held in active extension. In the course of its disinsertion, the extensor tendon may avulse a chip of bone, including a portion of the articular surface. (This is the "baseball finger" of youth.)

Pain and swelling are striking. The deformity, consisting of inability to extend the terminal joint, is often overlooked. The patient attributes the lack of motion to pain. Section of the extensor tendon due to an open injury produces the same deformity but usually with much less pain than that which follows a subcutaneous tear. The management and prognosis differ markedly depending on whether the tendon is transected cleanly or avulsed.

Treatment. The closed lesion is traditionally treated by a variety of splints holding the terminal joint in hyperextension and the proximal joint in 90° of flexion. However, since we are dealing with the elderly, the remarkable tendency for spontaneous improvement of this injury may lead the surgeon to abandon all treatment. To be effective, immobilization must be continued for at least 4 to 6 weeks. Such restriction may lead to stiffness, much more undesirable than the slight drop of the finger resulting from the uncorrected deformity. Furlong's amusing but hard-headed advice is most à propos: "If the patient is sufficiently intelligent and the doctor sufficiently persuasive, probably the best treatment for this injury is to ignore it." Pain and swelling of some degree will persist for several weeks. Active extension may not appear for some months.

In the case of open injury, Bunnell's fine stainless steel figure-of-eight suture supplemented by splinting has been found to be very effective by the author and is recommended for its simplicity. Removal of the suture after 2 weeks eliminates any retained foreign body from the tendon as well as the skin. Buried silk on the dorsum of the fingers and particularly over the joint is apt to excite a granulomatous reaction which produces a mass visible through the thin skin of this area.

Cut Central Slip of the Extensor Expansion. This injury occurs over the proximal interphalangeal joint and the dorsum of the proximal phalanx. It results in a characteristic flexion attitude of the proximal joint together with hyperextension of the distal joint. The deformity does not appear at the onset of the injury but is noted later when the lateral bands of the extensor expansion have migrated volarwards on either side of the joint. In the course of their forward motion, the center of rotation of the proximal finger joint is crossed. The bands, normally extensor of the proximal interphalangeal joint, have now become powerful flexors. Futile attempts to extend the proximal joint result in strong action on the normal termination of the lateral bands, resulting in hyperextension of the distal joint.

This is a difficult deformity to correct secondarily. It is, however, unlike mallet finger, a crippling deformity and an attempt should be made to bring the prolapsed lateral bands together with fine steel or catgut sutures after adequate exposure. Nichols advocates living sutures, the size of No. 1 catgut, stripped from the palmaris tendon through two very small transverse incisions.

Extensor Tendon Injuries over the Metacarpophalangeal Joint and Dorsum of the Hand. Over the metacarpophalangeal joint the extensor aponeurosis is distinctly separated from the joint capsule. Both structures, if lacerated, can and should be sutured separately. Over the dorsum of the hand, proximal to the complexities of the extensor expansions, repair is much simpler. Almost any fine suture material will do if protected by adequate splinting maintained for at least 3 weeks. The thin layer of subcutaneous tissue overlying the tendons at this point is carefully repaired as a separate layer so as to bury the site of repair as deeply as possible. Careful skin closure and a molded splint maintaining the wrist in extension and the fingers in an attitude just short of complete extension completes the repair.

THE CRUSHED OR MANGLED HAND

Because of the increasing awareness of the problem of workmen's safety, massive crushing injuries of the hands are becoming much less frequent in industry. Nevertheless, these dreadful accidents still occur in household machines, vehicular accidents, and as the result of other traumas to which the aged are exposed. Their slower protective reflexes invite such injuries in situations where a younger adult might be able to recoil in time to avoid injury. These lesions tax the skill and ingenuity of the surgeon to the utmost. Despite the almost hopeless prognosis for return of function, particularly in the elderly, much can be salvaged with care and patience.

PATHOLOGY OF THE CRUSHED HAND

This presents a diffuse picture of disorganization involving bursting and avulsing lacerations of skin and connective tissues, pulped, extruded muscle bellies (forced out of thenar and hypothenar spaces much like the contents of a burst grape), multiple open and closed fractures and dislocations, torn tendons and nerves, crushed fat cells with free fat in the tissues, and innumerable small and large hematomatas due to the disruption of many blood vessels. As time goes on, the enormous resultant edema and infiltration together with propagating thromboses of damaged vessels cut off the already minimal circulation to many areas, causing anoxia and death of additional tissue.

Preoperative care calls for prompt administration of appropriate antibiotics and antitoxins. X-rays of the hand are taken and brought to the operating room with the patient. Use of the tourniquet is contraindicated in these cases since the color of skin flaps and the ability of the tissues to bleed is important. After assessment of the damage, meticulous wound exploration is performed with removal of all unequivocally devitalized tissue. Pulped, extruded muscle is usually nonvital. Contractility may offer a guide. Fingers mangled beyond saving, particularly where skin cover and both digital neurovascular bundles are gone, are amputated directly. Occasionally, it may be possible to save the skin of a finger as a flap after filleting out the phalanges and tendons.

Deep repair of tendons and nerves is usually not attempted and is left for the reconstructive phase. The need for early restoration of joint motion absolutely contraindicates the immobilization ordinarily required after such repairs.

Badly damaged and avulsed skin must be replaced, usually by the simplest type of relatively thin "cover grafts." Elaborate pedicles have no place in the badly mangled hand, again because of the necessity for early mobilization. Damaged but still attached flaps of skin of questionable viability are best resected and replaced as they will almost certainly go on to tissue death due to propagation of existing thromboses. Occasionally, they may be defatted and set in place as free, full-thickness grafts as was suggested by Farmer.

Where multiple fractures and joint injuries are associated with crush injury, as is so often the case, treatment of the injury as a whole outweighs meticulous reduction and immobilization of the fractures. Early, active motion is all-important. Metacarpal fractures may be aligned and pinned with Kirschner wires, usually placed transversely and obliquely. Recently, fixation by intramedullary Kirschner wires introduced through the metacarpal heads, with the metacarpophalangeal joints held in flexion during the procedure, has been advocated by Furlong, Lord, and others. This has permitted very early return to light work. Phalangeal fractures are molded into the best possible position. After only a few days of immobilization over a contour splint, such as the Mason-Allen universal hand splint, active motion is begun.

In an effort to cut down the massive traumatic inflammation and edema followed by extensive infiltration of fibrous tissue which literally overwhelms the crushed hand, the use of ACTH locally and systemically has been advocated by Medl. In his cases there was little interference with healing of the wounds or fractures. The patients were given 25 mg of ACTH intramuscularly every 4 to 6 hours for 3 days. Dosage was then reduced gradually, so that by the sixth day dosage was 10 mg every 6 hours. The usual metabolic precautions were observed. Antibiotics were given in larger doses than usual. Later Medl tested the topical use of a crystalline steroid in the wound before closure.

In summary, the principles to be followed in the care of the crushed or mangled hand are: (1) convert the open wound into a healed, closed one as expeditiously as possible, (2) minimize traumatic inflammation and edema, using all means available, including hormonal means where destruction is massive, and (3) begin earliest possible motion even at the expense of some degree of deformity at the fracture sites.

AMPUTATION OF FINGERS

It has been emphasized elsewhere that in the aged elaborate reconstructive procedures are often "bad treatment." Amputation properly performed at correct levels will often lead to better rehabilitation. There are three basic rules in the primary amputation of fingers: (1) conserve every bit of length in the thumb, (2) any *single* finger can be spared without impairment of the function of the hand, and (3) in the presence of multiple finger injuries, conserve length of all injured fingers if possible. Revision or reamputation can be performed electively at a later date.

In the later stages, after the effects of the injury on the patient and his work have been evaluated, certain secondary amputations and revisions may be of value. In general, the single digit amputated much behind the distal interphalangeal joint is too short to be of much use, and ablation of the rest of the finger should be considered. Amputations leaving a small portion of phalanx distal to a joint are likewise often awkward. It is usually better to amputate through the joint and to trim the condyles of the phalangeal head to avoid unsightly bulges. In amputation of the index and little finger, an unsightly "hump" remains at the side of the hand. The metacarpal in such instances should be divided obliquely and the line of division inclined so that the side of the hand tapers into the line of the adjacent finger. This makes for a far better-looking hand. This additional procedure may be justified for an occasional elderly patient who takes considerable pride in his or her appearance. In the case of the third and fourth fingers, amputation at the metacarpophalangeal joint leaves an awkward gap and is sometimes followed by an adduction deformity of the adjacent fingers. Where the fourth finger is gone, the fifth metacarpal can be osteotomized and moved over onto the fourth, giving a much more sightly hand. No more than the distal quarter of the shaft of the third metacarpal should be removed since the important adductor of the thumb arises from the proximal three-quarters of this structure. The second metacarpal in its proximal two-thirds serves as a fulcrum over which the same muscle rides, and the line of resection should parallel the distal border of the adductor pollicis.

Resection of the metacarpal heads must be employed with caution and common sense. It does improve appearance strikingly. However, in the elderly worker still in need of an effective grasp, it may impair the strength of the metacarpal arch, formed as it is by the metacarpal heads and their strong interconnecting ligaments.

PREVENTION AND TREATMENT OF EDEMA AND THE AFTERCARE OF THE INJURED HAND

In the care of the injured hand in the elderly, prevention of edema and stiffening begins at once and is never lost sight of until the patient is discharged from the surgeon's care. Preoperatively, edema control commences with measures designed to prevent postoperative infection. At this stage it is necessary to refrain from adding to the damage and contamination by repeated exposure of the wound and particularly by needless entering into its depth to "see what's been cut." At operation, gentle, atraumatic surgery under adequate anesthesia, in a field rendered bloodless for the shortest possible period by a blood pressure cuff tourniquet, is indicated.

Postoperatively, the hand must be immobilized in the position of function (see above), whenever possible, to prevent shortening of the collateral ligaments. There are two exceptions to this rule. After repair of flexor tendons, the wrist is held flexed at about 40°; and in extensor tendon injuries, the digits are brought out into extension. However, the finger joints are not extended to the full 180°. Whenever the special features of the case permit, early active movement of even a limited extent is encouraged.

During the first few days after operation, elevation is assiduously maintained whether the patient is in or out of bed. When the patient is ambulatory, a sling is employed to prevent dependency. However, persistent use of the sling leads to a stiff shoulder and a dropped wrist, both of which throw the "pump" out of action. The shoulder joint should be put through its normal range of motion two or three times daily as soon after surgery as possible. Failure to do so may result in eventual severe limitation of motion. Thompson and Compere have reported this complication under the title of "The Iatrogenic Stiff Shoulder." The individuals who suffered from this condition were over 40 years of age and had been given no special instructions to move the shoulder.

Later in the postoperative period, active motion within pain limits is begun. Specific directions must be given as to the motions the surgeon wants the patient to perform. Vague directions to "move the fingers" are not enough. There must be purposeful attempts to flex specific joints and to "pull through" the tendons of the traumatized fingers. Performing the exercises in a basin of rather warm, soapy water is of great value, particularly if the patient is instructed to alternate several series of purposeful movements with firm stroking massage directed toward the heart and performed by the good hand. Passive movements by a therapist are excellent, provided they are not forcible enough to cause injury with consequent pain and edema and increased stiffness. The therapist, in addition, can only move the injured hand for a short period of time during the day. After the session, the patient must take over. The patient must clearly understand that he shares the responsibility for his ultimate recovery with the surgeon. It is in this later postoperative period that the surgeon dealing with older patients must be on the alert for signs of fear and discouragement. A sympathetic, understanding, and kindly attitude often will be found as important to the outcome as the surgery. If progress is overly slow, the surgeon must analyze the difficulty. Is the patient not moving because he thinks he will hurt himself? Is he contracting antagonistic muscles in his effort to accomplish motion? Patient explanation and reeducation are needed. In the aged, full restoration of motion will often be a slow, tedious process. Nature simply will not be hurried.

Splints of the functional variety, amply described by Bunnell, are useful if carefully selected, adjusted, and supervised. They have been classically described by him as splints "to mobilize," in contrast to splints "to immobilize." Of particular value are the "knuckle-bender" and the glove with elastic bands extending from finger tips to the wrist. Tension should be individually adjusted, and after a few hours' use, the appliance should be removed for periods of active motion. Pain is an indication for immediate removal since it is symptomatic of the series of events described above which lead inexorably to further stiffening. In the aftercare of an extensor tendon repair, it is well to remember that full flexion is far more important than full extension. The postoperative position of almost complete extension is distinctly not the functional position and may lead to irreparable shortening of the collateral ligaments of the metacarpophalangeal joints. Three weeks is the upper limit of such immobilization, especially in the aged, and should be followed by early active motion.

MUSCULOTENDON LESIONS

Spontaneous or stress rupture of muscles and tendons is infrequent as compared with disruption due to lacerating injuries. In a series of classic experiments, McMaster showed that the normal tendon does not rupture under stress. Disruption under these circumstances takes place at the musculotendinous junction, in the belly of the muscle, or at the tendinous insertion. Ordinary activity with even 25 per cent of the fibers severed does not result in dehiscence. When a tendon rupture occurs in a healthy young individual, some local disease or degenerative process must be assumed. Anzel and his associates recently reported from the Mayo Clinic on 1,014 disruptions of muscles and tendons of which 416 were due to causes other than laceration. They suggest that in the absence of obvious etiology, microscopic damage to portions of the vascular supply of the tendon substance plays an important role. In 87 cases in which the predisposing factors could be precisely diagnosed, the following conditions and their frequency were noted:

Factor	Cases
Tendinous calcification	28
Osteoarthritis	27
Old fracture	10
Idiopathic roughening or deformity of bone	10
Spurs and exostoses	7
Rheumatoid arthritis	2
Tuberculous tenosynovitis	2
Tumor	1
Total	87

Since this is one of the few large series in the literature, the distribution may be accepted as fairly representative. The authors point out that the figures for disruption in rheumatoid arthritis are probably low, and that with increasing awareness, the diagnosis will be made more frequently. However, Laine and Vaino, studying 1,000 cases of rheumatoid arthritis in Scandinavia, found only five spontaneous tendon ruptures. These all occurred in middle life.

Since the etiology is so often related to chronic degenerative disease, it might be expected that these injuries would be far more frequent in the aged. Surprisingly, most of the patients were in their 30s, 40s, and 50s. This suggests that a factor of stressful activity is necessary in addition to local degeneration. The elderly simply do not put enough physical strain on their aging and degenerating tendons and muscles to cause frequent disruption. With an aging population, however, an increase in the absolute number of these injuries can be expected.

DISRUPTIONS IN THE UPPER EXTREMITY

The Fingers. The most frequent disruption is disinsertion of the extensor complex from the base of the distal phalanx, so-called "baseball" or "mallet" finger. This is not characteristically an injury of the elderly. Its treatment, which has been discussed above, should be conservative in the aged, and should approach skillful neglect.

Rupture of the central slip of the extensor expansion permits the partially flexed proximal interphalangeal joint to protrude through the lateral bands. The latter press volarwards, causing the characteristic deformity of flexion at the proximal interphalangeal joint and hyperextension of the distal joint. The protrusion of the knuckle through the aponeurotic dorsal hood gives rise to the name "button-hole" or "boutonnière" deformity. Treatment is usually operative, as discussed above. In the aged, however, the activity and needs of the patient should be assessed. Conservative treatment may be employed in injuries less than 1 week old by means of a splint. The disability due to the injury must be weighed against the possible stiffness due to prolonged immobilization.

The Wrist. Rupture of the extensor pollicus longus may occur either spontaneously or following a Colles' fracture. The susceptibility of the tendon to rupture is due to the anatomical peculiarities of its course over the wrist. In this location, it is closely applied to the distal end of the radius in a bony groove capped by the annular ligament. It then angulates abruptly about Lister's tubercle. The angle becomes particularly sharp when the wrist is in dorsal and radial flexion. Repeated motion of the wrist leads to damage of the tendon by simple attrition. Rupture has been related to certain trades, such as polishing, drumming, wood carving, carpentry, and tailoring. One of the first descriptions came from the pre-1914 German army where it was described as "Drummer Boy's Palsy."

Rupture is more often seen when the bony groove is distorted by fracture of the lower end of the radius. The condition has been well described by Trevor, who reported 85 cases associated with Colles' fracture in the world literature up to 1950. Bunnell, Mason, Posch, and others have emphasized the association.

On the average, rupture occurs 3 months after fracture, but has been noted as early as 1 week and as late as 10 years. It may occur while the patient is in the primary cast or splint for immobilization of his fractured radius. The accident occurs suddenly, and is characterized by loss of extension of the distal joint of the thumb often with some partial loss of extension of the proximal joint. The tendon is frayed over its area of excursion of at least 1 to 1½ inches. Primary end-to-end suture cannot be carried out since the gap will be too large. The injury is rather crippling since the thumb cannot adequately "clear" objects to be grasped. Tendon grafting employing the palmaris longus tendon has been suggested. In the elderly, the simpler maneuver of transferring the tendon of the extensor indicis proprius into the distal segment of the thumb tendon is distinctly preferable.

Ruptures or disinsertions of flexor tendons at the wrist are usually due to violent trauma forcing the fingers or thumb into extension while active flexion is taking place. These accidents usually occur in the younger age group. Flexor tendon rupture in rheumatoid arthritis is a condition of middle life.

The Arm. Separation of the long head of the biceps brachii is the only disruption of importance in the elderly. The tendon runs upward in the bony bicipital groove across the humeral head to be inserted into the rim of the glenoid. Angular and rotatory movements subject it to attrition in the same way that movements of the wrist fray the long extensor of the thumb. It is therefore a condition apt to occur in the elderly. Because of its pathogenesis, it takes place in an appreciable number of instances with no history of injury. There is pain in the shoulder. Flexion of the elbow is weak but present. The belly of the muscle is larger and more spherical, and a gap can be felt above, where the muscle has moved distally down the arm. Ability to raise the arm is unimpaired unless there is an accompanying tear of the musculo-tendinous cuff of the shoulder.

In the aged, repair is not indicated since functional impairment is minimal and corrective surgery extensive. In elderly patients who are physiologically young and active, repair may occasionally be justified. In these instances, it should consist merely of fastening the tendon to the bicipital groove.

Disinsertion of the biceps tendon from the radial tubercle is unusual at any age. It may follow severe stress and is far more likely to occur in the younger adult.

RUPTURE OF TENDONS AND MUSCLES
IN THE LOWER EXTREMITY

Disruption of the extensor apparatus of the knee joint, and of the triceps surae and its terminal tendo achillis, occurs occasionally in the aged. It has been long known that the quadriceps femoris is not inserted into the upper border of the patella. The tendon flows over and around this sesamoid to be inserted into the tibial tubercle. Its integrity is much more dependent on the strong lateral expansions than on the patella. The latter may be fractured without loss of extension, provided that the expansions are intact.

Watson-Jones has emphasized that rupture may occur at four levels and that each of these injuries is characteristic of a different age group.

1. Rupture may occur at the upper border of the patella, the injury being known as avulsion of the quadriceps. This occurs characteristically in the elderly.

2. Rupture at the patella with fracture may occur at any age but is usually seen in middle life.

3. Rupture at the lower pole of the patella, known as avulsion of the ligamentum patellae, is usually seen in young patients.

4. In adolescence, avulsion of the extensor apparatus from the tibia occurs. The injury often includes fracture of the tibial tubercle with separation of its epiphysis, the so-called "Osgood-Schlatter's lesion."

It is evident that only rupture at the upper border of the patella, essentially a disruption at the musculotendinous junction, falls into the age group being considered here. The cause of this dramatic accident is usually an attempt to check a fall by means of a strong muscle pull. The knee is flexed by the momentum of the patient's weight as he stumbles forward, while at the same time the quadriceps opposes this stress by contracting powerfully.

The patient falls to the ground and cannot rise. On examination he is found to be unable to extend the affected knee. There is pain, tenderness, and a gap is felt just above the patella. Hematoma is usual between the torn ends of muscle and tendon. Unrepaired, the hematoma is organized, and myositis ossificans may follow.

Treatment is surgical, *even in the elderly*. The quadriceps is sutured to the upper border and sides of the patella (really to the stumps of the tendinous expansions), using material of the surgeon's choice. Active motion is begun early but weight bearing must wait 3 to 5 weeks until the integrity of the repaired tendon is beyond question. Rupture of the triceps surae occurs in much the same way. Its symptoms and repair are the same except that there is no bony structure between the torn musculotendinous junction and the tendo achillis. As might be expected, rupture of the tendon itself is an accident occurring in a younger age group in whom more violent stress is the rule.

BIBLIOGRAPHY

Anzel, S. H., K. W. Covey, A. D. Weiner, and P. R. Lipscomb: Disruption of muscles and tendons. *Surgery.* 45:406, 1959.

Bick, E. M.: Histologic observations on aging of the human connective tissue. *Jour. Mt. Sinai Hosp.* 26:501, 1959.

Bruner, J. M.: Safety factors in the use of the pneumatic tourniquet for hemostasis in surgery of the wound. *Jour. Bone and Joint Surg.* 33A:221, 1951.

Bunnell, S.: "Surgery of the Hand," 3d ed. Philadelphia, Lippincott, 1956.

Burnham, P. J.: Regional block anesthesia for surgery of the fingers and thumb. *Indust. Med.* 27:67, 1958.

Burnham, P. J.: Regional block at the wrist of the great nerves of the hand. *Jour. Amer. Med. Ass.* 167:847, 1958.

Burnham, P. J.: Simple regional nerve block for surgery of the hand and forearm. *Jour. Amer. Med. Ass.* 169:941, 1959.

Cannon, B.: Open grafting on raw surfaces of the hand. *Jour. Bone and Joint Surg.* 49A:79, 1958.

Clarkson, P.: The care of open injuries of the hand and fingers with special reference to the treatment of traumatic amputations. *Jour. Bone and Joint Surg.* 37A:521, 1955.

Furlong, R.: "Injuries of the Hand." Boston, Little, Brown, 1957.

Furlow, G. R., R. G. Pulvertaft, P. Brooks, and C. R. Berkin: Discussion and reconstruction of the hand after injury. *Proc. Roy. Soc. Med.* 48:605, 1955.

Kaplan, E. B.: "Functional and Surgical Anatomy of the Hand." Philadelphia, Lippincott, 1953.

Kelikian, H., and A. Doumanian: Some problems of hand surgery. *Surg. Clin. North Amer.* 37:3, 1957.

Laine, V. A. I., and K. J. Vaino: Spontaneous ruptures of tendons in rheumatoid arthritis: 1,000 cases, only 5 ruptures. *Acta Orth. Scand.* 24:250, 1955.

Littler, J. W.: Architectural principles of reconstructive hand surgery. *Surg. Clin. North Amer.* 463:476, 1958.

MacIntosh, R. R., and W. W. Mushin: "Local Anesthesia: Brachial Plexus," 2d ed. Oxford, Blackwell, 1947.

Mason, M. L.: Rupture of tendons of hand, with study of extensor tendon insertions in fingers. *Surg. Gyn. and Obst.* 50:611, 1930.

Mason, M. L.: Repair of tendon injuries in the hand. *Northwest Med.* 57:1287, 1958.

Mason, M. L., and J. L. Bell: The treatment of open injuries to the hand. *Surg. Clin. North Amer.* 36:1337, 1956.

McMaster, P. E.: Tendon and muscle ruptures: clinical and experimental studies on causes and location of subcutaneous ruptures. *Jour. Bone and Joint Surg.* 15:705, 1933.

Medl, W. T.: ACTH in crush injuries of the hand. *Surg. Clin. North Amer.* 34:363, 1954.

Metcalf, W., and W. Whalen: The surgical, social and economic aspects of a wrist hand injury. *Jour. Bone and Joint Surg.* 39A:317, 1957.

Nichols, H. M.: Repair of extensor-tendon insertions in the fingers. *Jour. Bone and Joint Surg.* **32A**:836, 1951.

Posch, J. L., P. J. Walker, and H. Miller: *Amer. Jour. Surg.* **91**:669, 1956.

Rank, B. K., and A. R. Wakefield: "Surgery of Repair as Applied to Hand Injuries." London and Edinburgh, E. & S. Livingstone, Ltd., 1953.

Sawyer, C. D., R. H. Kennedy, E. W. Lampe, E. Moberg, W. T. Medl, and J. W. Littler: Panel discussion—hand injuries: primary care. *N.Y. State Jour. Med.* **55**:1728, 1955.

Sponsel, K. H.: Urgent surgery for finger flexor tendon and nerve lacerations. *Jour. Amer. Med. Ass.* **166**:1567, 1958.

Stromberg, W. B., Jr., M. L. Mason, and J. L. Bell: The management of hand injuries. *Surg. Clin. North Amer.* **38**:1501, 1958.

Thompson, R. G., and E. L. Compere: Iatrogenic stiff shoulders. *Jour. Amer. Med. Ass.* **169**:945, 1959.

Trevor, D.: Rupture of extensor pollicis longus tendon after Colles' fracture. *Jour. Bone and Joint Surg.* **32B**:370, 1950.

Watson-Jones, R.: "Fractures and Joint Injuries," 4th ed. Baltimore, Williams & Wilkins, 1955.

Part III

Visceral Trauma in the Aged

Chapter 13

Wounds and
Other Trauma of the Abdomen

John E. Sullivan

Incidence. The majority of abdominal injuries occurring in aged persons are the results of automobile accidents and falls. Gunshot and stab wounds do occur, of course, but with much less frequency. Approximately 70 per cent of the injuries are to the kidney, spleen, and liver, 20 per cent to the bowel and bladder, and 10 per cent to the abdominal wall. About 30 per cent have one or more serious injuries in addition to the abdominal one.

There were 132 patients operated upon for intraabdominal injuries in St. Vincent's Hospital, New York City, during the past 10 years. Of these, only 12 patients were 60 years of age or over. The oldest patient was 80 years of age and he sustained a pancreatic injury due to a fall. Of these 12 patients, 10 were male. This is about the same percentage of intraabdominal injuries occurring in the aged as have been reported elsewhere. McGowen in 1935 analyzed 164 cases of penetrating wounds of the abdomen. Of this group there was only one gunshot wound in a patient over 60 years of age. Helsper reported three patients in the sixth decade out of 61 patients who incurred blunt trauma to the abdomen. Ficarra reported 18 cases of perforation of the small intestines caused by blunt force. Three of the patients were over 60 years of age and their injuries were caused by automobile accidents.

Traumatic rupture of the spleen in the elderly was more common in our series, as 4 of the 12 patients suffered this injury. However, in the report of Knopp and Harkins in 1954 on 28 cases of traumatic rupture of the spleen, only two were over 60 years of age. In an analysis of 177 cases of delayed splenic rupture by Zabinski and Harkins in 1943, there was only one patient over 60.

Intraabdominal injuries in aged patients who are admitted to hospitals are becoming more common. There are probably several factors responsible for this. The obvious one is that there are more older people at this time. There are also more automobile accidents. Another factor of considerable importance must not be underrated. The emergency treatment of injured patients has improved considerably, so that more patients live to be admitted to hospitals. Another source of injury not to be ignored is the increase of inadvertent operative trauma. Since more older patients are being operated upon, there is more chance for surgical accidents to occur, especially accidents involving the pancreas and spleen. These are most apt to appear during the course of operations upon the stomach and biliary tract. Occasionally the gall bladder is perforated during needle biopsy of the liver.

Ogilvie has pointed out that people with abdominal injuries die from hemorrhage, shock, or infection. *In the first few hours after injury, death is due to hemorrhage. In the first few days, death is due to shock; and after this, it is due to infection.* The aged are less able to withstand any of these pathological conditions. Resuscitation from hemorrhage and shock is more difficult in the aged because of the earlier onset of fatigue in the autonomic nervous system, the endocrine system, and the myocardium. As noted in the previous chapters, a lowered blood volume is more likely to exist prior to injury so that further blood loss becomes a very serious condition. Anemia and malnutrition occur more frequently in the aged. Blood loss that would only slightly disturb a younger person may render an older one unfit for operation, until this condition is corrected. Hypotension in the aged increases the risk of acute renal failure and of anoxia of the liver. The older patient is more susceptible to postoperative thrombosis, either coronary, cerebral, or venous. The elderly are more prone to develop postoperative pulmonary complications. Poor wound-healing is often found in this group because of the increased incidence of inadequate diet and chronic illness. Postoperative infections, whether in the wound or in the respiratory, enteric, or urinary tract, are more difficult to combat in the aged and are more frequent. Bosch and his associates reported that in operations upon 500 patients over 59 years of age, 260 had some concurrent disease other than that for which they submitted to surgery. Furthermore, twice as many of these patients died following operation as did those free of concurrent disease. Balch has emphasized that hyperglycemia and the prior use of steroid medication are apt to invite infection in surgical patients. Hyperglycemia is not an infrequent condition in the aged, and a recent history of steroid therapy is not unusual. Colp states that obesity in the aged also constitutes a major hazard.

Whatever the age, all intraabdominal trauma must be considered potentially fatal. The rapidity and the severity of the onset of symptoms depend upon the location and the intensity of the injury. The immediate symptoms that are produced are due to peritoneal irritation, either by gastric or pancreatic juices, bile or intestinal contents, or by free blood in the peritoneal cavity. The later symptoms are the result of infectious processes.

Visceral injury is more difficult to diagnose when it is caused by blunt trauma than when the injury is perforating. Following blunt trauma, solid viscera are more susceptible to injury, and it is unusual for more than one organ to be injured. While penetrating wounds are more obvious and their diagnosis less difficult, multiple injury is the rule. Following penetrating trauma, the viscera are injured in direct proportion to the amount of space occupied by each organ. Thus the spleen and liver are more frequently injured following blunt force, while bullet wounds cause more injuries to the intestinal tract.

The mortality rate of patients with intraabdominal trauma is high. It is increased in patients over 60 years of age and especially in patients over 70. The mortality rate of patients following blunt trauma is usually about twice that of patients with perforating wounds. Extraabdominal associated injuries often affect the prognosis of the patient with intraabdominal trauma. Usually these injuries are the result of a greater destructive force, and the dangers of hemorrhage and shock are increased. It is noted that patients who suffer associated injuries of the extremities rarely sustain intestinal perforation as the result of blunt force. Diagnostic problems are increased when there are extraabdominal injuries. The patient with a brain injury may not appreciate abdominal pain. Fractured ribs may cause sufficient abdominal pain and muscle spasm to mask an associated rupture of the spleen or liver.

Diagnosis. The diagnosis of intraabdominal trauma is not always evident. Clinical manifestations frequently appear slowly and may be obscured by excitement, prostration, and shock. Pain is not a constant symptom of visceral damage. This is even more apparent among elderly patients. Some authors state that 20 per cent of patients complain of no immediate abdominal pain. Vomiting is also not a constant symptom and even seems to be an unusual one. All diagnostic aids are of value when positive, but negative findings are frequent following major injury. A careful history, if it can be obtained, and thorough physical examination and frequent re-examinations are of chief value in detecting injury to any abdominal viscus.

Diffuse abdominal tenderness associated with muscle spasm is a definite indication of peritoneal irritation. The absence of peristalsis following abdominal injury is presumptive evidence of peritoneal contamination. However, bowel sounds may be decreased or absent when there is a hematoma of the abdominal wall. Shifting dullness is rarely found, but it is a classic sign of intraperitoneal effusion.

Leukocyte counts are usually above 15,000 and are helpful in making a diagnosis. As a general rule the more severe the abdominal trauma the higher the leukocyte count. Injuries, such as stab wounds, that produce less contusion to the organs usually cause less elevation in the count. The degree of leukocytic response is usually more pronounced in patients that have suffered blunt trauma than in those that have received penetrating injury. The exception to this is found in injuries to the intestinal tract where the leukocytic response is about the same regardless of the type of trauma. It is important to observe, however, that the rise in the leukocyte count is not as marked in the aged as in younger people. The hematocrit is of value, but a falling hematocrit may not be present for from 8 to 12 hours following the onset of bleeding.

X-ray of the abdomen is a valuable aid to diagnosis. Air beneath the diaphragm indicates the rupture of a viscus. As a general rule, air under the diaphragm is more likely to be present when the injury is to either the stomach, upper small intestines, or colon. Rupture of the middle and lower segments of the small intestines is less likely to produce signs of air free in the peritoneal cavity. Retroperitoneal rupture of the duodenum may cause a collection of air about the right kidney and adjacent retroperitoneal tissues. Elevation of the left diaphragm, increased density in the left upper quadrant of the abdomen, displacement of the stomach toward the right, and the presence of free fluid between loops of intestines are diagnostic of a ruptured spleen. A generally hazy film may suggest free abdominal fluid, but even large amounts of fluid may be impossible to detect. Unfortunately, flat x-ray films of the abdomen are not always helpful and may at times be misleading. At best positive findings are merely suggestive of the nature of the trauma.

Diagnostic peritoneal tap may be a valuable aid to diagnosis following blunt injury to the abdomen. An 18 gauge spinal puncture needle or a 14 gauge stylet needle with a polyethylene tube is inserted in the four lateral quadrants following the infiltration of local anesthesia. Blood, bile, intestinal contents, or pancreatic fluid may be obtained. If traumatic pancreatitis is suspected, the fluid may be measured for amylase activity, although the elevation may not occur for 48 hours after injury. Marked abdominal distention is a contraindication to the use of peritoneal tap and scarred areas of the abdominal wall should be avoided when inserting the needle.

The use of a gastric tube is also valuable as a diagnostic aid. Blood may be suctioned from the stomach in the presence of a gastric or upper intestinal injury. In rare instances the presence of blood in the stomach may be a sign of rupture of the liver.

Treatment. All patients with intraabdominal trauma should have early restoration of blood loss and early operation for the repair or removal of a ruptured organ. This is of especial importance in the aged, as prolonging the time interval between injury and operation increases the gravity of the condition. This means early exploration of the abdomen whenever there is a reasonable suspicion of intraabdominal injury. The decision to operate is usually an easy one when the trauma is of the penetrating type. Stab wounds and gunshot wounds almost always demand exploration. However, in an elderly patient who has received blunt trauma the decision may be very difficult. If the patient has extraabdominal injuries, the surgeon is hesitant to add the risk of anesthesia and operation unless he is quite certain of the diagnosis.

In preoperative preparation of the patient, emphasis is placed on restoration of blood volume. The only known way at the present time to accomplish this is to transfuse with blood or to introduce into the circulation fluids containing colloids which will remain in the circulation over a considerable period of time (see Chap. 2). In elderly patients it is preferable to administer whole blood, especially following severe hemorrhage. Ravdin has pointed out the danger of intensifying shock in severe hemorrhage by the use of plasma expanders, as they may dilute the red cells which are the oxygen carriers of the blood. Shock, whether caused by hemorrhage or by a leaking wound of the intestinal tract, is best treated in elderly patients with abdominal trauma by administering blood.

Gastric intubation and lavage is necessary prior to operation. This is done not only for diagnostic purposes, but in order to empty the stomach before anesthesia is administered. This reduces the risk of aspiration of stomach contents into the lungs.

Operation itself must be rapid, complete, and well planned. A general plan of exploration should always be followed so that no injury will be overlooked. A generous vertical right paramedian incision or a long transverse incision just above the umbilicus should be made. If a large amount of blood is found in the peritoneal cavity, first priority should be given to finding the source of the blood and controlling it. When bleeding is from the liver, temporary compression of the portal vein may be of help while the abdominal contents are examined. The intestinal tract and its mesentery should then be inspected. Any damaged portion should be wrapped in a moist pack and, if possible, left outside of the abdomen until the total injury has been assessed. The liver, spleen, kidneys, pancreas, bladder, and pelvic organs should next be examined. This necessitates incising the peritoneum of the paracolic gutters and the gastrocolic omentum. If any retroperitoneal effusion of blood or bile staining is present, the duodenum should be mobilized by division of the peritoneum lateral to the second portion of the duodenum. To examine the terminal part of the duodenum it is necessary to transect the ligament of Treitz. This gives adequate exposure so that the pancreas, superior mesenteric vessels, and the right ureter can be examined.

Very little has been written about the repair of the larger vessels of the abdominal cavity. An elderly patient cannot tolerate ligation of the superior mesenteric artery with its attendant wide intestinal resection. Suture of the superior mesenteric artery has been accomplished and should be borne in mind in case this injury is encountered. Fortunately injuries to the great vessels in the abdomen following blunt trauma are rare. Traumatic aortic aneurysms occur in the thoracic aorta but apparently not in the abdominal aorta. (Madden discusses this in Chap. 18.)

On opening the abdomen at the time of operation, attention should be directed toward the character of the gas and free fluid in the abdomen, if any is present. This may be a clue to the source of the injury. Massive bleeding is most apt to be from a lacerated liver, spleen, gastric, or mesenteric vessel. Odorless gas and colorless fluid are usually the result of a gastric tear. Brownish fluid suggests a rupture of the ileum, and fluid mixed with solid material suggests an injury to the large intestine.

Priestley states that postoperative complications account for the majority of surgical deaths. This is especially true in the elderly, and every effort should be directed toward prevention of such complications. Unfortunately, following abdominal trauma, time does not permit the taking of extended preoperative measures such as correction of a patient's nutritive status or the reduction of cough or bronchial secretions. For this reason, particular attention should be given to the reduction of pulmonary complications following the operation, as these are the most numerous in the aged. Bronchoscopy at the conclusion of the operation may be indicated. A prophylactic tracheotomy should be considered in all older individuals with intraabdominal injury, and especially in those with associated head and chest trauma. Nasotracheal aspiration should be employed as one of the postoperative measures to prevent atelectasis.

Nasogastric suction is a valuable procedure following operation, but in older patients it may cause irritation of the nose and pharynx, thereby increasing the danger of pulmonary complications. If the tube remains in place over a period of days it may cause ulceration of the esophagus. For these reasons, consideration should be given to insertion of the tube directly into the stomach through a stab wound of the abdominal wall at the time of operation. Suction may thus be maintained for as long as necessary without incurring the risks mentioned before.

Particular attention must be directed toward closure of the incision. If pulmonary complications are reduced, one factor in the production of wound dehiscence is diminished. Wound disruption is frequently a precipitating cause of some other complication, such as congestive cardiac failure. In other cases it may be the last straw in a series of complications.

Whenever an elderly patient is even suspected of having deficient coronary circulation, adequate oxygenation must be maintained and protection given against periods of hypotension. Careful attention must be directed toward prophylactic measures to prevent postoperative thromboembolic complications, as these occur more frequently in the aged.

COMPLICATIONS FOLLOWING VISCERAL TRAUMA

Priestley has mentioned possible undesirable sequelae of some aspects of postoperative treatment which especially apply to the aged. Overly long rest in bed, unnecessary intravenous administration of fluids, prolonged use of indwelling tubes and catheters, enemas, repeated use of sedatives, and excessive numbers of laboratory tests may be physiologically upsetting to the older patient.

Wound infections are common complications following operations for abdominal trauma, especially if there has been fecal spillage. If such spillage occurs it is advisable to leave the skin and subcutaneous tissues open for either delayed suture or to allow the wound to heal by second intention. Because infection is frequent, postoperative hernias in the aged are not uncommon.

As a general rule, severely injured patients have a stormy postoperative course. Intraabdominal abscesses, intestinal obstruction, duodenal fistulas, pancreatitis, pancreatic pseudocysts and fistulas, and paralytic ileus are not infrequent complications.

Paralytic or adynamic ileus occurs frequently after abdominal trauma, but it may occur in the absence of apparent injury to the abdomen or its contents. It sometimes occurs when the injury is to the extremities only, and it is a common complication of fractures of the vertebrae, especially in the aged. It is also a more common postoperative complication in older patients. Since the small intestine is innervated by the sympathetic system through the splanchnic nerves (which inhibit peristalsis) and by the parasympathetic or vagus nerves (which stimulate it), cutting of both chains results in the continuance of bowel contractions but without true peristalsis. Paralytic ileus apparently results from some abnormal stimulus of these nerves which supply the gastrointestinal tract. This stimulus may be a reflex disturbance or it may be due to a central paralysis such as has been described in metabolic disturbances with ketonemia. Acute potassium deficiency is manifested by paresis of the small and especially of the large intestine. Paresis of the vagus nerve, such as is found in basal skull fracture or fracture of the cervical spine, may cause a paralytic type of ileus.

In paralytic ileus, painless distention begins about 24 to 48 hours after operation or injury. The distention may be rapid, as in acute dilatation of the stomach, or it may be slowly progressive. The early distention is caused by gas, later by fluid and gas. The small bowel alone or the colon may be involved. Vomiting occurs and the bowel sounds are subdued or absent. There may be some tenderness present. The respirations become thoracic in type. The temperature remains near normal, but the pulse rate increases. The blood pressure may fall and the urinary output may diminish.

It is important to differentiate this condition from organic obstruction of the bowel. In organic obstruction, localized tenderness of the abdomen with a rising temperature and leukocyte count is more likely to occur. Also, pain is usually a more predominant symptom when organic obstruction exists. However, there are exceptions to these rules.

X-ray studies are of value in the differentiation of these two conditions. In paralytic ileus the early roentgenogram shows dilatation of both the small and large bowel. Following enemas, only the small bowel pattern may be seen. In organic obstruction of the small intestine, the colon may be empty from the first.

Gastric suction, maintenance of electrolytic fluid balance, restoration of blood loss, oxygen inhalation, and sedation for pain along with gentle handling of injured parts help to prevent and to treat paralytic ileus. Paravertebral procaine blocks, spinal anesthesia, intestine-stimulating and ganglionic-blocking drugs have all been advocated for treatment but are usually not successful. Enterostomy is occasionally necessary but it rarely succeeds in emptying many loops of bowel. Heat to the abdomen is comforting but not curative.

Gerber and his associates have recently reevaluated gastrointestinal suction in paralytic ileus. They believe that the disadvantages of this method outweigh its advantages. They compared 300 patients with paralytic ileus treated without suction to a control group treated with it, and found that the nonintubated patients recovered from the ileus as quickly as the intubated ones. They believe that complete withholding of oral intake is one of the most important factors in the prevention and treatment of paralytic ileus.

Another complication that follows major surgery, stress, and trauma is the development or activation of a *peptic ulcer*. This is more common in older patients and is probably caused by a hypersecretion of hydrochloric acid and pepsin without the normal buffering action of food, saliva, and duodenal contents during the postoperative or posttraumatic period. Occasionally the ulcer produces massive hemorrhage, which in the aged is a serious and often fatal complication.

Subphrenic abscess following abdominal trauma is a complication that may occur with or without perforating injury of the gastrointestinal tract. In recent medical literature the incidence of this condition following trauma is higher than in the cases reported 20 to 30 years ago. In a review by Ochsner and DeBakey in 1938, only 2.2 per cent of the cases followed abdominal trauma; while Cameron and Sykes reported in 1952 that 23 per cent were the result of injury.

The aged are more prone to develop *intraabdominal abscess* under similar circumstances. This is a condition that is frequently difficult to diagnose and still carries a high mortality rate. The abscess may occur on either the right or left side, with a higher incidence on the right side.

Patients with subphrenic abscess rarely complain of pain referable to the area of the disease. Chest symptoms are common, and this abscess is often confused with atelectasis of the lung and pneumonia. Pain in the back is occasionally a symptom. An irregular febrile course, an elevated pulse rate, and leukocytosis almost always accompany this condition. Pain on pressure over the costal margin anteriorly and over the lower ribs posteriorly is a sign that is considered diagnostic of abscess, but in practice it is unreliable. Anteroposterior chest x-rays usually show an elevated diaphragm with some evidence of pleural reaction and atelectasis above the area of the abscess when it is on the right side. Films of the abdomen may show a haze in the region of the upper quadrants or single or multiple collections of air. When the abscess is on the left side, it is more difficult to diagnose early in its course. Barium in the stomach or large bowel may show displacement of the stomach, the transverse colon, or the splenic flexure.

Fluoroscopy is an important adjunct to diagnosis. Restriction of motion of the diaphragm is always present. This may vary from slight restriction early in the course of the disease to immobility later. If bilateral abscess is present, the motion of the diaphragm may be restricted equally on both sides and the restricted motion may be construed as normal for that patient, thus presenting another diagnostic difficulty. Pleural effusion is a common occurrence with this disease and thoracentesis may be hazardous. It is therefore important to consider subphrenic abscess whenever pleural effusion occurs following abdominal trauma.

Subphrenic abscesses must be adequately drained, and preferably by an extraserous route so that neither the pleural nor peritoneal cavity is entered. The type of incision and method of drainage depend upon the location of the abscess. Abscesses may be drained posteriorly by excising the twelfth rib and entering the subphrenic space at the level of the spinous process of the first lumbar vertebra. Anterior abscesses may be drained by an incision along the costal margin and dissection of the peritoneum from the diaphragm until the abscess is found. In some instances transperitoneal drainage has been successfully performed. Drainage must not be delayed in older patients as they do not tolerate long periods of infection as well as younger ones.

Another postoperative complication that is peculiar to aged patients is *acute cholecystitis,* which develops in the early postoperative period following surgical treatment of unrelated disease. This disease is more likely to occur in males than in females, and occurs following fracture of various bones, especially hips, in the elderly patient. This condition has also been described as acute gangrenous cholecystitis secondary to trauma.

Causative factors in the pathogenesis of acute cholecystitis occurring postoperatively are probably the same as those in acute cholecystitis occurring at any other time. Systemic infection, uremia, and limited activity all seem to play a part in this process. In postoperative acute cholecystitis there seems to be a developmental relationship to the resumption of oral feedings after a variable period of fasting. Fever, dehydration, and drugs such as morphine, Demerol, and codeine which have a spasmogenic effect upon the sphincter of Oddi may have a relationship to the cause of the disease. There seems to be a higher incidence of noncalculous gall bladders in this type of postoperative acute cholecystitis.

A previous history of biliary tract disease is present in most cases and serves as an aid in diagnosis. Onset of pain in the abdomen localizing in the right upper quadrant, usually associated with nausea and vomiting and following the resumption of feeding, should lead one to suspect cholecystitis. If this is accompanied by leukocytosis and some elevation of temperature, the diagnosis may be relatively certain. Unfortunately the effects of the primary injury or operation may confuse the diagnosis. It may also be difficult to make a differential diagnosis between acute cholecystitis and coronary disease or pancreatitis.

Cholecystectomy is the therapy of choice as it relieves the patient of the pain of the condition and the hazards of continued biliary tract disease, and eradicates the danger of perforation and peritonitis. However, elderly patients who have had a severe injury may not be suitable candidates for cholecystectomy. In some patients technical difficulties may preclude such a procedure, and cholecystostomy may be preferable as it can be performed under local anesthesia. In other patients it may be possible to treat the disease conservatively without jeopardizing the life of the patient. However, minimal clinical findings may have been present prior to perforation, so that careful judgment must be exercised in determining whether or not to operate, what type of operation to employ, and when the optimal time for the procedure occurs.

Postoperative *acute pancreatitis* is another complication that is more common in the aged patient than in the younger. This usually follows a procedure in which organs operated upon are adjacent to the pancreas, but it also has been known to occur when the operation was remote from this organ and with no apparent trauma to the pancreas. Nasogastric suction, parenteral fluid and electrolytic replacement, vagal blocking agents, and antibiotic therapy are advocated in the treatment.

Duodenal fistula is a serious postoperative complication of duodenal injuries, especially in the aged. The fistula is usually of the "lateral" type as described by Bartlett and Lowell, in contradistinction to the "end" type which usually follows a partial gastrectomy. The "lateral" type carries a higher mortality rate as it apparently produces greater difficulty in maintaining nutrition.

Albright and Leonard have summarized the management of duodenal fistula as follows: (1) The prevention of maceration of the abdominal wall, (2) maintenance of fluid, electrolyte, and nutritional balance, and (3) the ultimate closure of the fistula itself. The easiest way to prevent maceration is not to allow contact between the fluid and the skin. This may be accomplished by means of a catheter inserted into the fistulous tract and by the use of a sump pump. Chemical neutralization, inactivation of enzymes, and the protection of the skin by various preparations have all been advocated but are unnecessary if proper suction is applied. Meticulous care for the correction of water and electrolyte balance is necessary, and frequent blood, plasma, or albumin transfusions help to prevent starvation, alkalosis, and dehydration. A feeding jejunostomy or a secondary gastroenterostomy may be necessary; but aged patients with duodenal fistulas are rarely good candidates for major surgery, and the mortality rate of such operations is as high as 85 per cent. However, if an adequate nutritional status can be maintained, eventual spontaneous healing of the fistula usually occurs.

Contusion and Hematoma of the Abdominal Wall

Contusions of the abdominal wall are frequently found following trauma to the abdomen. Usually the contused areas are located at the site of injury and present little difficulty in diagnosis unless considerable concealed bleeding occurs. When this happens, the symptoms and signs may suggest intraabdominal injury. Large hematomas of the abdominal wall may follow direct blows to the abdomen or exertion on coughing or straining. Sometimes they follow injury to the epigastric vessels during paracentesis. Occasionally there is no apparent cause for this occurrence. A variety of names have been used to describe this condition, such as spontaneous hematoma of the abdominal wall, rupture of the epigastric artery, rupture of the rectus abdominal muscle, and hematoma of the rectus abdominis.

Predisposing factors in the production of the hematomas are severe infections, especially typhoid fever which may cause hyaline degeneration of the rectus abdominis muscle fibers, and diseases that affect individual muscle cells, such as miliary tuberculosis and chronic alcoholism. Arteriosclerosis of the epigastric vessels is another predisposing cause. Most of the hematomas occur in elderly patients and are more frequently found in women.

Usually there is a sudden onset of sharp pain in the abdomen. This is located in one of the quadrants of the abdominal wall and may be accompanied by anorexia, nausea, and vomiting. The temperature and pulse rate show a slight to moderate rise. There is little or no change in blood pressure unless the bleeding is severe. There is usually protective muscle tightness at the site of the hematoma, and a mass is frequently found. Ecchymosis is not seen soon after injury, and it may be several days before it becomes visible. The bowel sounds are usually decreased and may be absent.

Hematomas above the semicircular line of Douglas are usually smaller than those below the line because of the absence of the posterior rectus sheath in this area. Also because of the absence of this limiting membrane, hematomas below the line of Douglas may spread into the pelvis. Unless the hemorrhage is severe, there is little change in the red blood count, hemoglobin, or hematocrit. There is usually a slight rise in the leukocyte count.

On first examination of patients with bleeding of the abdominal wall, intraabdominal injury is frequently suspected. However, on further observation, patients with slight bleeding show improvement in their symptoms and signs and should therefore be treated conservatively. When there is considerable bleeding, it is necessary to operate upon the patient in order to control the hemorrhage and evacuate the clots. The mortality rate is low following this condition and death, when it occurs, is usually due to associated pathology of the cardiovascular or pulmonary system.

Rupture of the Spleen

The most common intraabdominal injury of the aged patient following blunt trauma is rupture of the spleen. At all ages nonpenetrating injury to the spleen occurs more frequently than penetrating injury, and this is especially so in patients over 60 years of age. The most frequent causes of injury are automobile accidents and falls, and occasionally blows to the left side of the abdomen. There is no relationship of age to splenic trauma following automobile accidents, but industrial accidents and athletic injuries occur in the younger and middle age groups. Sometimes the accident may be quite trivial, such as a fall from a sofa.

Injury to the spleen may be the only abdominal injury following either penetrating or nonpenetrating trauma, but it is more likely that there will be other injuries associated with it. Parsons and Thompson reported that 73 per cent of their patients had associated injuries, and Cloutier and Zaepfel reported over 50 per cent with other injuries. The most frequent associated injuries are fractures of the ribs and injury to the left kidney.

The symptoms of rupture of the spleen may be either immediate or delayed. Approximately 15 per cent of all cases are delayed, but in the older age groups this percentage is smaller. Occasionally the spleen may rupture several months following injury, but usually secondary hemorrhage occurs before the end of the first week. The final rupture is believed to be due to the rupture of a subcapsular hematoma or to exacerbation of hemorrhage which was initially controlled by a tamponade effect. In the aged particularly the delayed rupture may be initiated by a simple exertion such as lifting, straining, or coughing, or it may occur spontaneously.

The immediate symptoms of splenic rupture are usually generalized abdominal pain, possibly more severe in the left upper quadrant, nausea, vomiting, and sometimes pain referred to the left shoulder (Kehr's sign). Shock may or may not be present. When it occurs, it is usually a reflection of the severity of the blood loss. Muscle spasm, especially over the left upper quadrant, is usually apparent. Occasionally an enlarging left-upper-quadrant mass is found. The pulse rate rises and the bowel sounds are hypoactive or absent. The patient is usually pallid, but anemia is difficult to measure early in the course as it may be masked by hemoconcentration. Leukocytosis usually occurs, with an average white-cell count of about 15,000. Abdominal paracentesis is of value in the diagnosis of hemoperitoneum from rupture of the spleen. However, a negative tap should not influence the diagnosis or course of treatment. Whenever the suspicion of rupture exists, frequent physical examinations and repeated taps may be necessary in order to establish the proper diagnosis.

X-ray examination of the abdomen is also of value. Enlargement of the splenic outline is a fairly constant early sign of rupture. Elevation of the left diaphragm with downward displacement of the gastric bubble and colon and serration of the greater curvature of the stomach have been described as x-ray signs of rupture. Conversely, it has been stated that the presence of a small, well-outlined spleen on x-ray practically rules out splenic injury.

In delayed rupture, there may be no symptoms during the latent period, or there may be some abdominal pain, varying from discomfort to moderate pain localized in the left upper quadrant. Bollinger and Fowler reported that they found a left-basal pleuritic reaction, shown by x-ray, in a high percentage of their cases with delayed rupture.

Splenectomy is the treatment for rupture of the spleen. Following the treatment of the patient's shock with replacement of blood, celiotomy should be performed. However, this is one condition where delay of operation in order to treat the shock may sometimes be contraindicated. If the patient does not respond quickly to shock treatment and a diagnosis of rupture of the spleen is made, there is more risk to the patient's life in delaying control of the hemorrhage. A left rectus, left costal, or transverse incision will give adequate exposure. A left rectus incision is more often made because it is easier to extend if exploration of other organs is deemed necessary. One point in surgical technique should be emphasized. Early in the procedure, after the abdominal cavity is opened, the splenic pedicle should be grasped by the fingers in order to stop bleeding as quickly as possible.

The most common complications following operations for rupture of the spleen are pulmonary in nature. Next in frequency are wound infections and separations. Occasionally a stubborn postoperative ileus occurs. The mortality rate in the aged patient is low where the splenic injury is an isolated one. However, when associated abdominal or chest injuries are present, the mortality rate increases and is dependent upon the nature of the associated injury. The mortality rate following operation in delayed rupture is lower than that following immediate rupture.

Injuries to the Liver

Injuries to the liver in the aged are caused most often by automobile accidents. These injuries are usually nonpenetrating in type and carry a high mortality rate. It has been estimated that following this type of trauma to the liver and biliary system, about 45 per cent of the elderly injured will die at the site of the accident, 45 per cent will die within 6 hours, and about 10 per cent will survive. The next most frequent cause of liver injury in the aged is gunshot wounds. These injuries usually occur in men and most often have been the result of hunting accidents. Stab wounds are rare in elderly people. With penetrating injuries, approximately 60 per cent will be injuries to the liver and other abdominal organs and about 40 per cent either will be thoracoabdominal or will involve both the thoracic and the abdominal cavities separately. The mortality rate is lower following penetrating trauma.

Associated injuries occur frequently with injury to the liver, whether penetrating or nonpenetrating. Rib fractures are common and may occur on either the right or the left side or bilaterally. Rupture of the spleen or other abdominal organs may be associated with hepatic injury. Fractures of bones in other parts of the body, especially pelvic fractures, are not uncommonly associated with rupture of the liver.

In the majority of cases the injury is to the right lobe of the liver. In penetrating wounds, both lobes are involved in about 5 per cent of the cases.

Surgical injury to the liver in the aged patient is most commonly caused by needle biopsy. Hemorrhage from the liver is the most frequent complication of needle biopsy and has been the chief cause of death following this procedure. Most cases of fatal hemorrhage have resulted from the perforation of distended portal or hepatic veins or aberrant arteries, and have usually been associated with impaired blood coagulation due to liver disease. Bile peritonitis resulting from liver biopsy is a serious

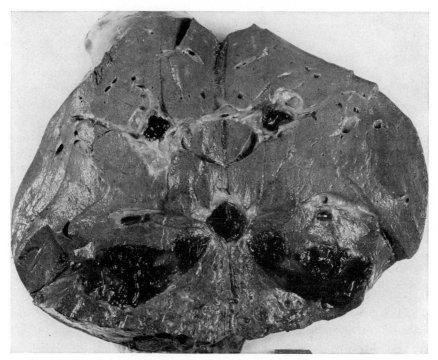

FIG. 13-1. Surgical traction trauma of liver. (Adenomyoma of the liver.) Male, 68 years old.

complication that follows bile leakage from the dilated biliary passages of patients with obstructive jaundice. For this reason needle biopsy is contraindicated in patients with known obstructive jaundice.

Injury to the liver from too vigorous retraction may occur during operation, especially upon the biliary tract. This is a greater hazard among the elderly than in younger patients. A large hematoma may result and may be unrecognized at the time of operation. An example of such an injury is shown in the photograph of the liver of a 68-year-old man (Fig. 13-1). A large hematoma of the right lobe of the liver resulted from operative injury during cholecystectomy and drainage of the common duct, and subsequently bleeding occurred through the T tube in the common duct. The patient died on the thirty-ninth post-operative day from portal vein thrombosis and septicemia.

The symptoms and signs of liver injury are dependent upon the extent of damage to the liver. The most common early symptoms and signs are those of shock, hemorrhage, and bile peritonitis. Whenever the degree of injury to the liver is sufficient to produce shock, it means that there has been considerable hemorrhage and some escape of bile into the peritoneal cavity. Pain is the most common symptom in the conscious patient. The degree of pain varies with the extent of injury. There may be slight pain following stab wounds of the liver and severe pain following macerating injuries. Pain is usually increased on movement and often more marked on deep inspiration. It is usually in the right upper quadrant of the abdomen, but may be in the left upper quadrant or generalized over the whole abdomen, depending upon the amount of blood and bile that has escaped into the peritoneal cavity. The pain usually radiates to the shoulder on the side of the injury if the superior surface of either lobe has been damaged.

Nausea and vomiting are not constant symptoms, especially soon after injury. It is possible to have melena and hematemesis following central rupture of the liver. Blood enters the bile ducts and goes to the intestine, either because of necrosis or tearing of the central hepatic vessels. When this occurs the patient presents a puzzling train of symptoms of intermittent gastrointestinal hemorrhage, biliary colic, or incomplete extra-hepatic obstruction.

The amount of blood and bile in the peritoneal cavity determines the location and degree of tenderness, both direct and rebound, and of muscle spasm. In the absence of fracture of the ribs, tenderness over the right side of the abdomen on compression of the lower portion of the rib cage, along with pain referred to the right shoulder, is diagnostic of rupture of the superior surface of the right lobe. The presence of a mass in the right upper quadrant of the abdomen, caused by hemorrhage, is evidence of serious liver damage.

There is always an increase in the pulse rate, and the rapidity of this increase is often an index of the extent of injury. There is ordinarily a rise in the body temperature. The red blood count is usually below 4,000,000 with a corresponding decrease in the amount of hemoglobin. The white blood count varies from normal to over 30,000. In the majority of cases it will be over 10,000 with a rise in the polymorphonuclear count.

Direct demonstration of laceration of the liver by means of x-ray is possible only in rare cases. Blood and blood clots may collect on the surface of the liver and consequently show a loss of normal liver outline and a local elevation or flattening of the diaphragm. If the rupture is in the lower surface of the liver, a loop of intestine lying adjacent to the organ may penetrate into the rupture. In this case the lower border of the liver shows a step-like contour corresponding to the site of rupture. However, this sign is not reliable. Indirect evidence of rupture is manifested by loss of normal liver outline due to hemorrhage, or x-ray evidence of fluid in the right flank.

Operation is almost always necessary in the treatment of injuries to the liver, whether penetrating or nonpenetrating in type. Nonoperative management has been advocated, but this type of treatment is unpredictable as neither hemorrhage nor the escape of bile into the peritoneal cavity can be controlled. The principles of treatment stated by Glenn are (1) supportive measures before, during, and after operation directed toward the control of hemorrhage and shock, (2) excision of necrotic liver tissue, (3) diversion of escaping bile, and (4) the prevention of infection.

Preoperative measures should be directed toward (1) the combatting of shock and hemorrhage by replacement of blood and electrolytes, (2) control of pain, (3) gastric decompression, and (4) evaluation of the cardiac and pulmonary status of the patient. The latter measure is particularly important in the older patient. If it can be obtained, a good past history is of great value. In controlling pain, opiates should be used in small amounts and preferably intravenously, as the capacity of the damaged liver to utilize opiates may be diminished and the release of these drugs following subcutaneous injection may be delayed.

There is no uniform method of treating the liver wound. Closure of the wound by means of sutures of any type that are effective in the control of hemorrhage and bile drainage is the procedure of choice. This may be technically difficult when the wound is inaccessibly located or when the tissues are fragmented. Oxidized cellulose or gelatin sponges may be of value in controlling the hemorrhage in these situations. The use of gauze packing should be avoided as it is frequently associated with secondary infection and with hemorrhage on its removal. However, its use is sometimes necessary. Various autografts have been advocated, such as muscle, fascia, omentum, and the round ligament, but these are usually difficult to use except as free grafts, which means adding devitalized tissue. However, hemorrhage must be controlled. Sparkman and Fogelman have pointed out that it is axiomatic that hepatic bleeding which is not controlled at the time of operation will not be controlled thereafter.

Necrotic tissue must be excised, and in some instances debridement may be feasible. In injuries limited to the left lobe this may be accomplished by amputating the lobe.

Escaping bile can be diverted from the peritoneal cavity by drainage to the exterior. Adequate drainage is an important factor in the treatment of traumatic wounds, although some surgeons do not believe it is essential in every case. In deep laceration of the liver, it is necessary to drain the liver parenchyma in order to prevent hemobilia. Wherever there is an associated injury of the pancreas, more liberal drainage should be instituted as the escape of bile increases the digestive activity of the pancreatic enzymes.

Every effort to prevent infection should be made. Careful aseptic technique should be employed, necrotic tissue or detached liver fragments removed, and antibiotic therapy should be instituted. The liver harbors bacteria which are propagated by anoxia induced by hypotension or by the local vascular insufficiency which may follow injury to the organ.

Patients with extensive liver damage suffer a high incidence of postoperative complications. When hepatic injury of any degree is associated with injury to the colon or pancreas, complications are all but inevitable.

The complications following operation usually fall into the following categories: (1) recurrent hemorrhage, (2) the complications of biliary drainage, or (3) infection. Recurrent hemorrhage may be a sequel to necrosis, infection, hemobilia, or derangement in the clotting of blood due to hepatic insufficiency. Defective coagulation secondary to hepatic damage may result in bleeding from the liver wound or from multiple sources in the body. Where hemobilia occurs with resulting progressive deterioration of the patient's condition, a desperate measure that has sometimes been successful is ligation of the right hepatic artery.

External biliary fistulas are not uncommon and may close spontaneously. Some degree of bile peritonitis is almost always present, but if there is a combined wound of the thorax, biliary pleural fistula and biliary pleuritis may occur. Intrahepatic bile cysts are unusual complications. Subphrenic or intrahepatic abscesses occasionally occur. Wound infections are not uncommon and are more difficult to control in the aged. Sequestration of avascular liver tissue and pulmonary embolism of liver tissue have been described.

In the older patient, hepatic failure after trauma is more frequent than in the younger adult. Following operation, irrationality and stupor are a poor prognostic sign. Cardiopulmonary complications, cerebrovascular accidents, and acute renal failure are common sequelae and should be anticipated, particularly in these older victims of hepatic trauma.

Gall Bladder and Bile Duct Trauma

Traumatic rupture of the gall bladder in the aged following nonpenetrating injury to the abdomen is a very rare occurrence. Such injuries are usually caused by blows on the abdomen when the muscles are relaxed. They have followed steering-wheel injury in automobile accidents. The gall bladder may be contused, lacerated, or avulsed from the liver bed. Operative injury to the bile ducts is not uncommon and many articles are written on the prevention and treatment of this condition.

The diagnosis of injury to the gall bladder is always difficult and has seldom been made prior to operation. It is even more difficult in the aged. The symptoms and signs are those of peritonitis caused by extravasation of bile into the peritoneal cavity. Usually the bile is spilled slowly and locally about the area of the gall bladder, and therefore the symptoms are delayed. However, if large amounts of concentrated bile are spilled into the general peritoneal cavity, the symptoms are immediate and the clinical picture is that of a severe peritonitis. Hematemesis has been described following traumatic hemorrhagic cholecystitis. In this type of case the blood reaches the intestines by way of the cystic and common bile ducts.

Penetrating injuries to the gall bladder caused by gunshot and knife wounds usually involve other viscera in the abdominal cavity. The symptoms and signs will again be those of peritonitis. *In the aged, injury to the gall bladder during the course of needle biopsy of the liver is probably the most common of all types of gall bladder injury.* When this occurs the bile usually spills out fairly rapidly and within a short time the patient complains of abdominal pain in the right upper quadrant. If a considerable amount of bile is extravasated, there may be generalized pain and muscle rigidity. Leukocytosis occurs, and there is a rise in temperature and pulse rate.

Whatever the type of injury to the gall bladder, cholecystectomy is the treatment of choice in the older patient. If this procedure is not warranted by the general condition of the patient or is too difficult technically, cholecystostomy may be performed.

Rupture of the extrahepatic bile ducts from nonpenetrating trauma is a rare injury, especially in the elderly patient. It is usually caused by crushing trauma to the right upper quadrant of the abdomen, where the force is applied in such a manner as to crush the duct between the liver and the bodies of the vertebrae. Usually there is a marked degree of shock immediately following the injury, which will subside and be followed by a period of relative freedom from symptoms. If operation is not performed, jaundice appears in the patient within 3 days, accompanied by bile in the urine and clay-colored stools. Fluid accumulates in the abdomen and the patient complains of increasing abdominal pain. The pulse rate rises and there is an elevation of body temperature. Paracentesis is of value in establishing the diagnosis.

Early celiotomy is of great importance in the treatment of rupture of the extrahepatic bile ducts. Once the injury is located, the type and site of the lesion will determine the subsequent operative procedure. Restoration of continuity of bile flow to the intestine is the aim of treatment.

Laceration of the choledochal wall will heal spontaneously if the duct is decompressed by means of external drainage or by cholecystostomy. Complete severance of the duct may demand cholecystenterostomy or choledochoenterostomy. End-to-end anastomosis of the severed duct with T-tube drainage above the site of injury has been performed.

The same rules of treatment apply to penetrating injury to the bile ducts.

INJURIES TO THE PANCREAS

The pancreas, being deeply seated in the abdomen, is somewhat more protected than are other viscera, especially from blunt injury. However, direct blows to the abdominal wall when the abdomen is flexed, such as steering-wheel injuries, may cause injury to this organ. Rarely, trivial accidents, such as minor blows to the abdomen suffered during falls, will cause injury and be followed by pancreatitis. Penetrating injuries to the pancreas are usually caused by gunshot wounds. Along with this, concomitant trauma to the stomach, duodenum, liver, spleen, or kidney should be anticipated and sought for.

In the aged, the most frequent cause of injury to the pancreas is operative trauma. Pancreatitis is not uncommon following operations upon the stomach, duodenum, or biliary tracts where the pancreas has been manipulated or damaged. Dunphy believes that minor interference with the blood supply to the pancreas combined with injury to the gland or partial obstruction of the ducts will cause this condition. Severe or fatal postoperative pancreatitis is more common in elderly patients than in younger adults. Fourteen out of twenty-two patients reported upon by Frieden were over 60 years old. Ferris and his associates reviewed nine cases of fatal postoperative pancreatitis and six of the patients were over 60. This pathological condition may follow operations far removed from the pancreas, such as transurethral resections.

The symptoms and signs of postoperative pancreatitis appear within 3 days following the operation. The initial features are commonly abdominal pain located in the epigastrium or midabdomen, hypotension, and occasionally shock. Fever, abdominal distention, and varying degrees of leukocytosis are frequently present. In the fatal cases, oliguria usually follows. The serum amylase levels are apt to be raised, but this is not necessarily diagnostic of severe postoperative pancreatitis. Perryman and Hoerr found a significant serum amylase rise in 32 per cent of unselected postoperative cases, especially those following gastric resections and common bile-duct explorations.

The clinical signs and symptoms of either blunt or penetrating trauma are dependent upon the type and extent of injury to the pancreas. Mild trauma to the pancreas alone causes edema and small hemorrhages which may give no signs or symptoms. However, even following mild trauma, pancreatic secretions may escape causing the digestion of small devitalized areas of the pancreas, and massive hemorrhage or extensive pancreatic necrosis may follow. The patient may complain of mild or intermittent abdominal pain for several days and then complain of sudden severe pain. Also following mild trauma, there may be few signs of abdominal injury until a gradually expanding mass in the upper abdomen is found. This may represent a hematoma or a pancreatic cyst. Pinkhorn believes that trauma is responsible for about 20 per cent of the cases of pseudocyst formation.

In more severe injuries involving penetration or fracture of the gland, severe abdominal pain and shock may appear. Shock is not usual in pancreatic injury unless complete transection occurs or major vessels are severed. The abdominal pain starts in the epigastrium and frequently spreads to the flanks. It may radiate to the back or to the shoulders. Pronounced nausea and vomiting usually accompany the pain.

The physical signs vary with the severity of the injury. In major degrees of pancreatic injury, marked abdominal tenderness and muscle spasm are usually present. Cyanosis and dyspnea may occur. Some fever and leukocytosis with a rise in the serum amylase usually follow all types of pancreatic trauma. Serial determinations of the serum amylase may be necessary to detect the serum amylase rise. Abdominal paracentesis can be of diagnostic value. This is best accomplished by aspiration of the right lower quadrant of the abdomen, with the patient in the right lateral position. The fluid obtained following pancreatic rupture is thin and blood tinged, and the amylase units are markedly increased. Scout x-ray films may reveal some degree of localized ileus, the so-called "sentinel loop."

Nonoperative management of pancreatitis following nonpenetrating trauma is preferred if associated injuries to other abdominal organs or blood vessels can be ruled out. In the elderly patient this may be quite difficult. Nasogastric suction, sedation, intravenous fluids, and parasympatholytic drugs such as atropine or Probanthine which block the vagal control of pancreatic function are used in treatment. If the patient's condition does not improve on conservative management, or if there is any question of the presence of peritonitis, surgical intervention is indicated. Since penetrating injuries are usually associated with injuries to other abdominal viscera, the need for surgery is apt to be more immediate. Following severe injuries, evacuation of hematomas, control of hemorrhage, and adequate drainage of the area are all that is necessary. Any laceration of the pancreas should be sutured, but this may not be easily accomplished in all cases. Sump drainage is an effective method of protecting the abdominal wall. In operative injuries to the duct of Wirsung, repair should be attempted. Anastomosis to either the duodenum or jejunum may be necessary. Distal duct injuries can usually be treated by ligation and drainage.

The morbidity and mortality from minor injury of the pancreas are due to its complications. These are numerous and may be severe. Hematoma, secondary hemorrhage, pancreatic fistula and abscess, pseudocyst formation, subdiaphragmatic abscess, or suppuration of the gall bladder may follow. Diabetes may also follow pancreatic injury as the islet tissue of the pancreas may be destroyed. Islet cells once destroyed apparently do not regenerate. Complete rupture of the pancreas associated with other injuries always carries a high mortality rate. In the aged the mortality rate may be all but absolute.

Complications due to injuries to the pancreatic ducts, whether penetrating, nonpenetrating, or operative, are usually serious. The accessory duct does not always communicate with the main pancreatic duct. When no communication exists, ligation or division of either duct may result in a pancreatic fistula. Pancreatic fistulas tend to heal spontaneously, but even so, they may be recurrent. Recurrent attacks of pancreatitis are also not infrequent following the healing of the fistula. The fluid and electrolyte loss from a complete pancreatic fistula can be severe. Management of these fistulas, as recommended by Warren, is directed toward (1) maintenance of fluid and electrolyte balance, (2) protection of the skin of the abdomen from pancreatic secretions, (3) supplementary support to digestion and nutrition, and (4) suppression of the external secretions of the pancreas. Sump drainage with constant suction is the best method of protecting the skin. Adequate doses of pancreatin along with enteric-coated bicarbonate tablets, which resist the action of the gastric juices in the stomach, should be given for replacement therapy. Probanthine is of value in helping to suppress external pancreatic secretion.

Injuries to pancreatic cysts are very unusual but Case has reported the course of one such patient who was admitted to St. Vincent's Hospital. The patient was 80 years of age and entered the hospital 2 days after a fall. He complained of abdominal pain, nausea, and vomiting. The abdomen was distended and tender. The blood count was 9,100 with 64 per cent neutrophiles. X-ray of the abdomen showed dilated loops of intestine. In the abdominal cavity, blood arising from the pseudocyst was found at the time of operation. Following evacuation of the hematoma, control of the hemorrhage, and drainage, the patient had an uncomplicated postoperative course for 5 days. On the sixth day he died following a coronary artery thrombosis.

INJURIES TO THE STOMACH

Of the hollow viscera in the abdomen, the stomach is the least frequently injured by external trauma. The stomach is somewhat mobile and distensible and this makes rupture due to nonpenetrating injury unlikely. However, when a patient receives a severe blow to the epigastrium, a bursting type of rupture may occur, especially if the trauma occurs shortly after the victim has eaten a full meal. The usual location of the rupture is at the most dependent portion of the greater curvature or near the cardiac end of the greater curvature. A circular perforation may be thereby produced. Contusion of the stomach is seldom diagnosed and it is doubtful if such a condition would produce symptoms. Spontaneous rupture of the stomach occurs in elderly people, but is a very rare event and is almost always fatal.

Penetrating injuries to the stomach are far more common than are those from external blows and are usually the result of bullet or stab wounds. When penetrating wounds of the stomach are present, other organs are usually involved. The pleura, lung, heart, liver, spleen, pancreas, kidney, colon, and small intestines have all been found associated with gastric injury. It is possible for the stomach to be injured by endoscopy, the perforation usually occurring at the cardia.

Whatever the cause of the perforation, a chemical peritonitis similar to that caused by a perforated peptic ulcer results. Severe abdominal pain with tenderness and muscular spasm follows. Shock may occur either as a result of the chemical peritonitis or from hemorrhage. If severe or prolonged, it should be assumed that shock is due to hemorrhage. Hematemesis may or may not be present. However if a Levine tube is inserted into the stomach, fresh blood is usually aspirated. The body temperature remains near normal and the pulse rate slowly rises. As with perforated peptic ulcer, there is a period when the pain diminishes temporarily, and it is at this time that the diagnosis may be difficult. There is an early and persistent rise in the leukocyte count. X-ray of the abdomen, especially in the erect position, may show free air under the diaphragm. In spontaneous rupture of the stomach, sudden severe epigastric pain occurs, followed by shock, marked distention of the abdomen, and subcutaneous emphysema.

The treatment of any type of injury to the stomach is surgical repair of the perforation as quickly as the patient can be prepared for operation. Wounds of the gastric wall can usually be treated by simple suture. If a penetrating wound is found in one wall of the stomach, the wound of exit in the opposite wall must be searched for and sutured. The gastrocolic omentum should be divided and the posterior wall carefully examined, since small wounds in this location can easily be overlooked.

If only the stomach is injured and operation is early, drainage of the peritoneal cavity is not necessary.

Of all the hollow viscera, the stomach appears to have the greatest ability to close a perforation spontaneously before a fatal peritonitis develops. For this reason it is possible to treat some perforated peptic ulcers successfully without operation. However, *this form of treatment has no place in the care of perforation due to penetrating injury.* Exploration is necessary to determine the presence and extent of associated injuries. The peritoneal insult in such cases is greater since gastric leakage emanates from both the anterior and posterior lacerations.

Prognosis of stomach perforation depends upon the associated injuries and the length of time elapsing between injury and repair. Operation under 4 to 6 hours offers the best prognosis, if only the stomach is injured. Bacterial contamination of the peritoneum occurs at an earlier time in perforation caused by wounds than in perforation due to peptic ulceration, as organisms are introduced by the agent that causes the injury.

Wound infection and wound dehiscence are more frequent in the aged following this type of injury than in younger patients. Some degree of paralytic ileus almost always follows. Pulmonary complications occur and subhepatic abscesses are not unusual. In the aged with postoperative peritonitis, the development of infection may be slow and atypical. Intestinal obstruction resulting from the contraction of fibrous adhesions is not a common complication, but does occur. Retroperitoneal abscesses may follow penetrating type of injury to the stomach if the retroperitoneal tissues have been contaminated.

Injuries to the Small Intestines

In general, most injuries to the small intestines are penetrating wounds such as gunshot or stab wounds. Fewer lesions occur from unexpected blows to the abdominal wall. However, the incidence of penetrating wounds decreases with advancing age, and among the elderly members of any collection of such cases a large proportion of the injuries will have been caused by blunt trauma. Blunt trauma often occurs when the driver of an automobile is thrown forward against the steering wheel as the car comes to a sudden stop. Injury to the intestine occasionally follows a fall. It is also possible to rupture the intestine by lifting heavy objects or straining against strong resistance. This is more likely to happen when the patient has an inguinal hernia. About 84 per cent of nonpenetrating intestinal injuries occur in the jejunum and ileum, 12 per cent in the duodenum, and 4 per cent in the colon.

Two cases of traumatic strangulation obstruction of the small intestine in patients 62 and 68 years of age have recently been reported by Mock.

This type of injury undoubtedly occurs in elderly people more frequently than is indicated by the case reports in medical literature.

When rupture of the intestine following muscular effort occurs, the perforation is usually found on the antimesenteric surface of either the lower jejunum or ileum. When the small intestine is injured by blunt force, the areas most frequently involved are those where there are fixed segments, such as the duodenum near the ligament of Treitz and the ileum near the ileocecal region. In patients over 60 the lower ileum is injured more often than are other areas.

Trauma may cause rupture of the mesentery and injury to the blood supply of the intestine without affecting the bowel itself. This is apt to cause gangrene and perforation of the intestine several days later if not corrected soon after injury. Chylous peritonitis may also occur secondary to mesenteric trauma.

Injuries caused by bullets and knives, in which a penetrating wound of the abdominal wall is present, usually present little difficulty in diagnosis. However, where there is no evidence of injury to the abdominal wall, the presence of intestinal or mesenteric rupture may be obscured.

Retroperitoneal injury to the duodenum still carries a high mortality rate due to the difficulty of diagnosis. When this injury occurs as an isolated one, the diagnosis can often be suspected from the history. Following injury there is a period of several hours during which the patient has no symptoms because time must elapse before sufficient duodenal contents spill into the retroperitoneal tissues to cause symptoms. When this leakage is sufficient, the pain becomes steady, progressively more intense, and may be localized in the right upper quadrant, the right lumbar region, or the right lower quadrant. Nausea and vomiting may or may not occur after the onset of pain, and if present, the vomitus may contain blood.

Testicular pain has been reported with this condition due to irritation of the retroperitoneal tissues. Shock due to the original trauma, to leakage of duodenal contents, or to blood loss secondary to the rupture may result. It is possible that the retroperitoneal escape of air may be sufficient to cause crepitation, which may be detected on rectal examination. Increase in the leukocyte count occurs and sometimes there is an increase in the serum amylase. Roentgen findings may show pneumoperitoneum, but a more diagnostic finding is a collection of air about the right kidney and adjacent retroperitoneal tissues. Estes states that in doubtful cases, a ruptured duodenum may be diagnosed by x-ray after a small amount of Lipiodol or thin barium has been swallowed.

Diagnosis of rupture of the small intestine beyond the ligament of Treitz is less difficult than with retroperitoneal injury. Pain, nausea and vomiting, abdominal tenderness, muscle spasm, and the absence of bowel sounds are usually noted, accompanied by leukocytosis and a rising pulse rate. In the aged, white blood counts may be below 10,000. However, all symptoms and signs are important, and no single one should be considered diagnostic. Neither should any symptom or sign be disregarded. Roentgenograms are valuable diagnostic aids when air is found under the diaphragm. However, when gas is not seen, the possibility of perforation of a hollow viscus is not excluded. Positive x-ray findings are more common in rupture of the upper small bowel than in the lower segment. When intestinal contents are aspirated from the peritoneal cavity by means of abdominal paracentesis, the diagnosis is obvious.

It must be remembered that associated injuries, whether intraabdominal or extraabdominal, often determine the ultimate outcome in patients with small-bowel injuries. With duodenal injury, the nearby organs are frequently involved. Attention should be drawn to the possibility of injury to the right ureter associated with injury to the duodenum, as this is easily overlooked at the time of operation. Following penetrating trauma, the lower in the intestine the injury, the more likely multiple lacerations will be.

The treatment of laceration of the small intestine, no matter what the cause, is operative repair. There may be no intraperitoneal evidence of retroperitoneal rupture of the duodenum on opening the abdominal cavity. Hematomas or bile extravasation or both, with or without fat necrosis in the ascending or transverse mesocolon or in the retroperitoneal tissues, are good evidence of a laceration of the duodenum. If the injury is massive and the blood supply of the suture line is compromised, or if stenosis is feared, a gastrojejunostomy should be performed. In older patients a gastrojejunostomy should be considered if there is any question of stenosis or compromised blood supply. Drainage of the retroperitoneal tissues must always be done.

Lacerations of the small intestine beyond the ligament of Treitz are less difficult to recognize and may be repaired with less worry about the blood supply. If there is any question of compromising the blood supply or causing stenosis of the intestine, resection of the involved area should be performed.

The most frequent complications of small-bowel injuries are abscesses, which may be subphrenic, retroperitoneal, pancreaticoduodenal, or within the abdominal wall. Duodenal fistulas, pancreatitis, paralytic ileus, and wound dehiscence are not uncommon complications. Intestinal obstruction caused by adhesive bands applied following operation may occur.

The mortality rate is higher following injury to the duodenum than when the injury is lower in the small intestine. The mortality rate is also dependent upon the associated injuries present. There is an obvious increase in this rate with advancing age of the patient.

PERFORATING INJURIES TO THE LARGE INTESTINE

Perforating injuries of the large intestine are among the most serious of all abdominal injuries. This is because of the virulent nature of the fecal stream and the danger of both intraperitoneal and retroperitoneal sepsis. Most of the injuries are caused by bullets, knives, and shotgun blasts. Injuries caused by ingested foreign bodies, impalement, and instrumentation occur but are infrequent. One injury peculiar to the elderly is perforation of the colon by an enema tube in the patient who has had a colostomy. Most of these injuries are self-inflicted and may occur at any time after the initial colostomy. Foreign bodies are occasionally inserted into the rectum by senile patients. Usually they cause little or no damage, but sometimes serious injury results either from the insertion or from the manipulation of the foreign body in the attempt to remove it. The most common instrumentation injury occurs during proctoscopy when either the proctoscope is pushed through the bowel wall or the bowel is perforated by a biopsy instrument. This injury is particularly common in aged patients.

Following perforating trauma, the transverse colon is injured somewhat more often than the right or left colon, and the rectum about one-fifth as often as the left colon. Injuries to the transverse colon are also more likely to be accompanied by injuries to other viscera. The most common associated injuries are to the small intestine, liver, stomach, kidney, extremities, chest, and spleen.

As with penetrating injury elsewhere in the abdomen, the diagnosis is usually not difficult. The symptoms and signs are those of peritoneal irritation. Shock commonly follows gunshot wounds, but it is not usual following knife or instrumentation injuries. Roentgenograms may show free air in the peritoneal cavity, and are of importance in determining the location of retained missiles. In cases of suspected rectal injury, proctoscopy is of value.

There is usually time to prepare the patient adequately for operation, although the longer the time interval between the injury and the operation, the worse the prognosis. Operation is not extremely urgent except in cases of exsanguinating hemorrhage or where massive evisceration occurs. Shock should be treated, oxygen administered, a nasogastric tube introduced, and a Foley catheter inserted into the bladder prior to operation. Tetanus antitoxin or toxoid must be injected, and there is some advocacy of the prophylactic use of gas gangrene antitoxin. However, its value is doubtful and its use is no longer generally recommended.

At the time of operation, the following principles should be observed. (1) An adequate incision should be made, giving good exposure. (2) Any source of hemorrhage in the mesentery should be controlled with great care so that the blood supply to the segment of bowel is not further endangered. (3) Fecal contamination must be controlled, and (4) contaminated retroperitoneal tissues must be drained.

Control of fecal contamination presents a problem in judgment. During World War II, the exteriorization of the damaged colon and proximal decompression of the sutured bowel by colostomy was advocated and resulted in a lower mortality rate. However, there are many reports in civilian surgery which indicate that small wounds of the large bowel may be successfully treated with primary suture alone. Such treatment makes repeated operations unnecessary, avoids additional complications, and certainly reduces the discomfort and mortality in older patients. However, large, grossly contaminated wounds are best treated by exteriorization whenever possible. In the sigmoid and rectosigmoid, this is not feasible, so that primary suture with a proximal colostomy is necessary. Exteriorization is principally used in mobile sections of the colon. However, it must be remembered that mobilization tends to be a shocking procedure. In the elderly patient this fact demands perhaps greater deliberation than in the younger adult.

Exteriorization of the colon is also difficult in an obese patient. Resection of an unprepared bowel should be avoided whenever possible but is occasionally necessary. Resection with exteriorization may have to be done in severe wounds. Resection with primary anastomosis is occasionally justifiable in large wounds of the right colon or when the blood supply of a segment of the colon is endangered. Complete destruction of a segment of bowel demands exteriorization whenever possible.

Extraperitoneal rectal wounds almost always require a proximal-loop colostomy. However, there are occasional cases of perforation, such as those caused by a sigmoidoscope or by a rubber tube during the administration of an enema, that may be primarily sutured without colostomy, provided that the operation is performed soon after injury and that there has been little fecal contamination. If a proximal sigmoid colostomy is performed, it is not always necessary to suture the wound of the rectosigmoid. In every instance the retroperitoneal space should be drained.

Where the colon is perforated following an enema after a colostomy, operation should be performed immediately. If possible, the perforated segment should be excised and a new colostomy fashioned. If this is not feasible, diversion of the fecal stream can be accomplished by a proximal transverse colostomy and drainage of the site of perforation.

Postoperative wound infection is a frequent sequel to any operation

involving fecal contamination. For this reason it is advisable to use retention sutures and to consider delayed suture of the skin and superficial
fascia. The next most common complication is wound dehiscence. Colos-
tomies or exteriorized portions of the colon should not be placed in the
primary wound as this increases the danger of wound infection and disruption. This is particularly true in the aged where tissue malnutrition is so common and the wound therefore more susceptible to dehiscence. Fecal fistulas and intraabdominal abscesses occasionally occur.
Postoperative intestinal obstruction is not infrequent. Complications
due to the course of a bullet, such as osteomyelitis of the sacrum or lumbar spine, are also possible.

The prognoses of patients with wounds of the large intestine depend
upon (1) the type and location of the wound in the colon or rectum, (2)
the associated injuries, (3) the time interval between injury and operation, and (4) the age of the patient. Injuries to the sigmoid and rectosigmoid carry a grave prognosis. Because injuries to the transverse colon
are more likely to be accompanied by injury to other abdominal viscera,
the mortality rate is higher. Injuries to the ascending and descending
colon are more often single and therefore have a better prognosis. The
mortality rate of patients with enema tube perforation of colonic stomas
is about 30 per cent, usually because of delay in seeking treatment or
in diagnosis. When the interval between injury and operation is over 6
hours, the mortality rate rises sharply following any type of perforation.
The mortality rate in patients over 60 years of age is about three times
higher than in those under that age.

NONPENETRATING INJURIES OF THE COLON

Nonpenetrating injuries of the colon are much less frequent than those
occurring to the small intestine. They comprise about 2 to 4 per cent
of all injuries to the colon. Usually the injuries are fairly severe and they
are most frequently the result of automobile accidents, falls, or heavy
blows to the abdomen. Rupture of the cecum or sigmoid may result
from violent straining, but this is quite unusual. The presence of an inguinal hernia seems to be a predisposing cause. Spontaneous rupture of
the rectosigmoid with prolapse of one or two loops of small intestine is
a rare occurrence. It usually occurs while straining at stool in women
who have preexisting rectal prolapse.

The common sites of injury are near the points of fixation, as in the
sigmoid. Fullness and coexisting pathological disorders, such as divertic-
ulitis and adhesive bands, render the colon more susceptible to injury.
If a portion of the large intestine is enclosed in a hernial sac, the chances
of bursting following injury are increased because the fluid and gas cannot escape from the relatively fixed intestinal loop. Retroperitoneal hema-

tomas involving the mesocolon have been described as the cause of later perforation of the colon, even though the intestine appeared viable at operation soon after injury.

Because the injury is usually severe there is more frequently a contusion or skin laceration on the abdominal wall. A bloody discharge from the rectum may be present and is of diagnostic significance. The severity of the symptoms and signs is dependent upon the amount of spillage of the bowel contents into the peritoneal cavity. Peritoneal irritation is a prominent sign accompanied by a decrease in peristaltic activity. Leukocytosis is usually present and there is some rise in the temperature and pulse rate. Shock is not usually an early event unless the amount of spillage is massive or the rupture has been accompanied by severe hemorrhage. On x-ray examination, the presence of free air is diagnostic of perforation, although its absence is of no significance. Paracentesis may be of value, especially if free air or fecal matter is aspirated. However, in a small number of patients, an exploratory laparotomy must be undertaken as a diagnostic procedure. At operation, damage to the colon should be repaired either by suture of the laceration, with or without proximal colostomy, or by exteriorization of the injured portion. Proper judgment at this time may prevent the later complications of stenosis of the intestines or delayed perforation if the blood supply has been impaired.

Postoperative complications are similar to those found in penetrating trauma to the colon. The mortality rate is slightly higher than that following penetrating wounds. The higher mortality may be due to a delay in the application of definitive therapy because the patient seeks treatment at a later time, or to the fact that diagnosis following blunt trauma is more confusing to the examiner. Both of these difficulties appear more often in aged patients than in the younger adult. As is the case following penetrating trauma, the greater the time interval between injury and operation the worse the prognosis. Even when proper and timely care is administered, however, the mortality rate following nonpenetrating injuries to the colon increases progressively with the age of the patient.

BIBLIOGRAPHY

Albright, H. L., and F. C. Leonard: Duodenal fistula—problems in management. *Ann. Surg.* **132**:49, 1956.

Anglem, T. J., and M. L. Bradford: Major surgery in the aged. *New Eng. Jour. Med.* **249**:1005, 1953.

Balch, H. H.: Nutrition and resistance to infection. *Ann. Surg.* **147**:423, 1958.

Bartlett, M. K., and W. H. Lowell: Acute postoperative duodenal fistula. *New Eng. Jour. Med.* **218**:587, 1938.

Bollinger, J. A., and E. F. Fowler: Traumatic rupture of the spleen with special reference to delayed splenic rupture. *Amer. Jour. Surg.* **91**:561, 1956.

Bosch, D. T., A. Islami, C. T. C. Tan, and C. A. Beling: The elderly surgical patient. *A.M.A. Arch. Surg.* **64**:269, 1952.

Bradley, R. L., and J. M. Cook: Bowel perforation due to nonpenetrating abdominal trauma. *Amer. Jour. Surg.* **88**:564, 1954.

Burnett, H. A., and C. M. O'Leary: Nonpenetrating abdominal injuries. *Surg. Gyn. & Obst.* **91**:105, 1950.

Byrne, R. V.: Diagnostic abdominal tap. *Surg. Gyn. & Obst.* **103**:362, 1956.

Cameron, D. A., and E. M. Sykes: Subphrenic abscess in trauma. *Amer. Jour. Surg.* **83**:412, 1952.

Case, T. C.: Rupture of cyst of pancreas. *Amer. Jour. Surg.* **91**:145, 1956.

Christensen, N., J. Ignatius, and C. Mathewson: Treatment of injuries of large bowel in civilian practice. *Amer. Jour. Surg.* **89**:753, 1955.

Cloutier, L. C., and F. M. Zaepfel: Traumatic rupture of the spleen. *Surg. Gyn. & Obst.* **107**:749, 1958.

Cohn, I., H. R. Hawthorne, and A. S. Frobese: Retroperitoneal rupture of duodenum due to nonpenetrating abdominal trauma. *Amer. Jour. Surg.* **84**:293, 1952.

Cooke, H. H.: Traumatic rupture of the intestines caused by automobile accidents. *Ann. Surg.* **96**:321, 1932.

Cottrell, J. C.: Nonperforative trauma to abdomen. *A.M.A. Arch. Surg.* **68**:241, 1954.

Counseller, V. S., and C. J. McCormack: Subcutaneous perforation of the jejunum. *Ann. Surg.* **102**:365, 1935.

Cutler, C. W.: Clinical patterns of peptic ulcer after sixty. *Surg. Gyn. & Obst.* **107**:23, 1958.

DeBakey, M. E., and F. A. Simeone: Battle injuries of the arteries in World War II. *Ann. Surg.* **123**:534, 1946.

Donald, J. W., and J. G. Donald: Complete severance of the common bile duct due to non-penetrating trauma. *Ann. Surg.* **148**:855, 1958.

Doubilet, H.: Physiology of the human pancreas. *Surg. Gyn. & Obst.* **107**:97, 1958.

Drye, J. E., and A. M. Schoen: Studies in the mechanisms of the activation of peptic ulcer after nonspecific trauma. *Ann. Surg.* **147**:738, 1958.

Dunphy, J. E., J. R. Brooks, and F. Achroyd: Acute postoperative pancreatitis. *New Eng. Jour. Med.* **248**:445, 1953.

Estes, W. L., T. L. Bowman, and F. F. Meilicka: Non-penetrating abdominal trauma with special reference to lesions of the duodenum and pancreas. *Amer. Jour. Surg.* **83**:434, 1952.

Farris, J. M., and G. K. Smith: An evaluation of temporary gastrostomy: a substitute for nasogastric suction. *Ann. Surg.* **144**:475, 1956.

Ferris, D. O., T. E. Lynn, J. C. Cain, and A. H. Baggenstoss: Fatal postoperative pancreatitis. *Ann. Surg.* **146**:263, 1957.

Ficarra, B. J.: Traumatic perforations of the small intestine due to non-penetrating abdominal injuries. *Surgery.* **15**:465, 1944.

Fletcher, D. G., and H. N. Harkiss: Acute peptic ulcer as a complication of major surgery, stress or trauma. *Surgery.* **36**:212, 1954.

Fomon, J. J., and J. R. Hinshaw: Rupture of the hepatic ducts due to blunt trauma. *Surgery.* **39**:322, 1956.

Frieden, J. H.: Postoperative acute pancreatitis. *Surg. Gyn. & Obst.* **102**:139, 1956.

Frimann-Dahl, J.: "Roentgen Examination in Acute Abdominal Diseases." Springfield, Ill., Charles C Thomas, 1951.

Furste, W.: Hematoma of the abdominal wall. *Amer. Jour. Surg.* **91**:540, 1956.

Gallison, D. T., Jr., and D. Skinner: Bile peritonitis complicating needle biopsy of the liver, *New Eng. Jour. Med.* **243**:47, 1950.

Gerber, A., F. A. Rogers, and L. L. Smith: The treatment of paralytic ileus without the use of gastrointestinal suction. *Surg. Gyn. & Obst.* **107**:247, 1958.

Gerendasy, J.: Foreign body in the rectum. *Amer. Jour. Surg.* **91**:126, 1956.

Glas, W. W., M. M. Musselman, and D. A. Campbell: Hepatic injuries. *Amer. Jour. Surg.* **89**:748, 1955.

Glenn, F.: Acute cholecystitis following the surgical treatment of unrelated disease. *Ann. Surg.* **126**:411, 1947.

Glenn, F.: Injuries to the liver and biliary tract. *Amer. Jour. Surg.* **91**:534, 1956.

Glenn, F., and G. E. Wantz: Acute cholecystitis following the surgical treatment of unrelated disease. *Surg. Gyn. & Obst.* **102**:145, 1956.

Grillo, H. C., and G. L. Nardi: Perforation of the colon during enema into the colonic stoma. *Surg. Gyn. & Obst.* **107**:659, 1958.

Gurd, F. N.: Management of shock and convalescence in the elderly and infirm. *Amer. Jour. Surg.* **83**:379, 1952.

Haug, C. A., and W. A. Dale: Major surgery in old people. *A.M.A. Arch. Surg.* **64**:421, 1952.

Helsper, J. T.: Nonperforating wounds of the abdomen. *Amer. Jour. Surg.* **90**:580, 1955.

Hicken, N. F., and V. L. Stevenson: Traumatic rupture of the choledochus associated with an acute hemorrhagic pancreatitis and a bile peritonitis. *Ann. Surg.* **128**:1178, 1948.

Hoffman, E.: Acute gangrenous cholecystitis secondary to trauma. *Amer. Jour. Surg.* **91**:288, 1956.

Hunt, G. H., and J. N. Bowden: Rupture of intestine caused by non-penetrating trauma of the abdominal wall: a report of cases. *Arch. Surg.* **49**:321, 1944.

Karlan, M., R. C. McPherson, and R. N. Watman: Experimental production of pseudocytes of the pancreas of the dog. *Surg. Gyn. & Obst.* **107**:221, 1958.

Kinnaird, D. W.: Pancreatic injuries due to nonpenetrating abdominal trauma. *Amer. Jour. Surg.* **91**:552, 1956.

Knopp, L. M., and H. N. Harkins: Traumatic rupture of the normal spleen: analysis of 28 cases. *Surgery.* **35**:493, 1954.

Krieg, E. G.: Hepatic trauma: analysis of 60 cases. *Arch. Surg.* **32**:907, 1936.

Larghero, Y. P., and F. Girua: Traumatic rupture of the spleen. *Surg. Gyn. & Obst.* **92**:385, 1951.

Lewis, K. M.: Traumatic rupture of the bile ducts. *Ann. Surg.* **108**:237, 1938.

McGowen, F. J.: Penetrating wounds of the abdomen. *Ann. Surg.* **102**:395, 1935.

Mansfield, R. D.: Traumatic rupture of the normal spleen. *Amer. Jour. Surg.* **89**:759, 1955.

Mason, L. B., J. B. Sidbury, and S. Guiang: Rupture of the extrahepatic bile ducts from nonpenetrating trauma. *Ann. Surg.* **140**:234, 1954.

Mathewson, C., and B. L. Halter: Traumatic pancreatitis with or without associated injuries. *Amer. Jour. Surg.* **83**:409, 1952.

Millar, T. M., J. Bruce, and J. R. S. Patterson: Spontaneous rupture of the stomach. *Brit. Jour. Surg.* **44**:513, 1957.

Miller, E. M.: Abdominal injuries due to blunt force. *Surg. Gyn. & Obst.* **106**:355, 1958.

Mock, C. J., and H. E. Mock: Strangulated internal hernia associated with trauma. *A.M.A. Arch. Surg.* **77**:881, 1958.

Morton, J. H., J. R. Hinshaw, and J. J. Morton: Blunt trauma to the abdomen. *Ann. Surg.* **145**:699, 1957.

NATO Handbook: "Emergency War Surgery." U.S. Government Printing Office. 1958.

Ochsner, A., and M. DeBakey: Subphrenic abscess. *Internat. Abstr. Surg.* **66**:426, 1938.

Ogilvie, W. H.: Abdominal wounds in the western desert. *Surg. Gyn. & Obst.* **78**:225, 1944.

Parker, W. S., and F. R. Robbins: Traumatic amputation of gall bladder without a wound on the abdominal wall. *Ann. Surg.* **138**:915, 1953.

Parsons, L., and J. E. Thompson: Traumatic rupture of the spleen from non-penetrating injuries. *Ann. Surg.* **147**:214, 1958.

Patterson, R. H., and B. Bromberg: Abdominal injuries. *Amer. Jour. Surg.* **83**:383, 1952.

Perryman, R. G., and S. O. Hoerr: Observations on postoperative pancreatitis and preoperative elevation of serum amylase. *Amer. Jour. Surg.* **88**:417, 1954.

Pinkham, R. D.: Pancreatic collections (pseudo-cysts) following pancreatitis and pancreatic necrosis. *Surg. Gyn. & Obst.* **80**:225, 1945.

Poer, D. H., and E. Woliver: Intestinal and mesenteric injury due to non-penetrating abdominal trauma. *Amer. Jour. Surg.* **84**:293, 1954.

Pontius, G. V., B. C. Kilbourne, and E. G. Paul: Nonperforative trauma to abdomen. *A.M.A. Arch. Surg.* **72**:800, 1956.

Pontius, R. G., O. Creech, Jr., and M. E. DeBakey: Management of large bowel injuries in civilian practice. *Ann. Surg.* **146**:291, 1957.

Powers, J. H.: Perforations of the pouch of Douglas. *Amer. Jour. Surg.* **83**:403, 1952.

Priestley, J. T.: Postoperative complications. *Surg. Gyn. & Obst.* **107**:375, 1958.

Rappaport, R. L., J. P. Rohm, and G. Curry: Tracheotomy—then what? *Amer. Jour. Surg.* **93**:550, 1956.

Ravdin, I. S., and M. A. Casberg: A second look at surgical care in major catastrophes. *Amer. Jour. Surg.* **89**:721, 1955.

Rousselot, L. M., and C. A. Illyne: Traumatic rupture of the spleen. *Surg. Clin. North Amer.* **21**:455, 1941.

Schaer, S. M., J. M. Dziob, and R. K. Brown: Bile duct rupture from blunt trauma. *Amer. Jour. Surg.* **89**:745, 1955.

Shallow, T. A., and F. B. Wagner: Traumatic pancreatitis. *Ann. Surg.* **125**:66, 1947.

Smith, S. W., and T. N. Hastings: Traumatic rupture of gall bladder. *Ann. Surg.* **139**:517, 1954.

Snyder, H. E.: Early recognition and management of shock. *Amer. Jour. Surg.* **83**:382, 1952.

Sparkman, R. S., and M. J. Fogelman: Wounds of the liver: review of 100 cases. *Ann. Surg.* **139**:690, 1954.

Spector, N.: Ligation of the right hepatic artery in hemobilia. *Ann. Surg.* **145**:244, 1957.

Stransky, J. J.: Retroperitoneal rupture of duodenum due to non-penetrating abdominal trauma. *Surgery.* **35**:928, 1954.

Strickler, J. H., P. D. Erwin, and C. O. Rice: Diagnostic paracentesis. *A.M.A. Arch. Surg.* **77**:859, 1958.

Strohl, E. L., and W. G. Diffenbaugh: Wounds of the diaphragm, stomach and duodenum. *Amer. Jour. Surg.* **88**:390, 1954.

Tucker, J. W., and W. P. Fey: Management of perforating injuries of colon and rectum in civilian practice. *Surgery.* **35**:213, 1954.

Ulvestad, L. E.: Repair of laceration of superior mesenteric artery acquired by non-penetrating injury to abdomen. *Ann. Surg.* **140**:752, 1954.

Warren, K. W.: Management of pancreatic injuries. *Surg. Clin. North Amer.* **31**:789, 1951.

Webb, H. W., J. M. Howard, G. L. Jordan, and K. D. J. Vowles: Surgical experiences in the treatment of duodenal injuries. *Internat. Abstr. Surg.* **106**:105, 1958.

Welch, C. E., and W. P. Giddings: Abdominal trauma: clinical study of 200 cases. *Amer. Jour. Surg.* **79**:252, 1950.

Welch, C. S., S. Propp, W. B. Scharfman, and R. A. Stoller: Indications for splenectomy. *N.Y. State Jour. Med.* **57**:2355, 1957.

Werelius, C. Y., and C. C. Guy: Problem of ileus following trauma. *Amer. Jour. Surg.* **93**:636, 1956.

Wilensky, A. O., and P. A. Kaufman: Subparietal rupture of the intestine due to muscular effort. *Ann. Surg.* **106**:373, 1937.

Woodhall, J. P., and A. Ochsner: Management of perforating injuries of colon and rectum in civilian practice. *Surgery.* **29**:305, 1951.

Zabinski, E. J., and H. N. Harkins: Delayed splenic rupture. *Arch. Surg.* **46**:186, 1943.

Zamchek, N., and O. Klausenstock: Needle biopsy of the liver: the risk of needle biopsy. *New Eng. Jour. Med.* **249**:1062, 1953.

Zeifer, H., and R. Colp: Abdominal surgery in the elderly patient. *A.M.A. Arch. Surg.* **68**:315, 1954.

Ziperman, H. H.: Acute arterial injuries in the Korean war. *Ann. Surg.* **139**:1, 1954.

Chapter 14

Trauma to the Thorax and Rib Cage

Robert H. Wylie

The effects of injury to the thorax are modified in several ways when the injured person is past 60. First there are the minor changes in the cardiorespiratory systems due solely to age. There are some limitations of pulmonary reserve due to mild fibrosis, minimal emphysema, and diminution of the expansile capacity of the chest wall. There may also be some mild limitation due to myocardial fibrosis in the reserve capacity of the heart. These minimal changes in the aged person must be considered by the physician and surgeon in the choice of treatment. Second, there are alterations which occur frequently in patients of the older group that are pathological and call for special consideration. Well-established pulmonary emphysema and limiting arteriosclerotic disease of the heart may be expected often and must be of great concern to the physician and surgeon who are called upon to treat injuries of the chest. When confronted with an injury to the thorax, the first consideration is not the external wound or fracture but rather the alterations that have occurred in the physiology of this vital part of the body as a result of the trauma. In the aged the equilibrium of the cardiorespiratory system is most delicate and therefore careful judgment and anticipation of problems are required in treating these patients successfully.

GENERAL CONSIDERATIONS

Before embarking on descriptions of specific injuries and their treatment, it is important to consider certain principles of a general nature. The recognition at the time of first examination that an injury of the thorax exists is of utmost importance. If there is obvious respiratory difficulty or external evidence of trauma, this recognition is usually easy. However, where severe multiple injuries are present, serious damage within the thorax may go unnoticed because of concentration upon a more obvious injury. There is no substitute for the immediate and complete physical examination of the severely injured patient which should include an x-ray film in the posterior, anterior, and lateral projections if injury involving the thorax is suspected. It is most important in the first examination of the aged patient to attempt to get some idea of the patient's cardiopulmonary reserve prior to injury. Is there a history of dyspnea, edema, or "heart attack" of any type? Had the patient taken digitalis? Had he a chronic cough or wheeze? How much sputum did he raise? The answers to these questions may be of enormous aid in planning the treatment of the elderly patient.

In considering the treatment of chest injuries, certain changes in respiratory physiology must be given weight even in the most minor of injuries. Thus, in a simple fracture of a rib, there will be disturbance of respiration due to painful limitation of normal ventilation. When the integrity of the chest wall has actually been destroyed, as in the open sucking wound with collapse of the underlying lung and pendulum swing of the mediastinum, ventilation becomes markedly inhibited and life is threatened. Also, in severe crush injury of the chest, the effectiveness of ventilation becomes markedly hampered where multiple fractures of the ribs cause the chest wall to lose its rigidity, and paradoxical respiration with inward motion of the chest wall in inspiration is produced.

Added to this loss of the normal bellows action of the chest wall is the contusion and laceration of the lung itself, with resulting edema and hemorrhage of pulmonary tissue, extravasation of blood into the bronchial air passages, plus pneumothorax and hemothorax. These changes in the injured lung are aggravated by the ineffectiveness of cough, the retention of mucous secretions, hemorrhage extravasation, and edema and fluid in the tracheobronchial passages. Hemorrhage itself, although rarely extensive from the lung, may be so severe from the chest wall as to fill the pleural space, compress the lung, and threaten life with exsanguination.

With these general considerations in view, certain principles of treatment are evident. These consist of the early recognition of chest injury and its extent, the reestablishment of the integrity of the chest wall and its bellows action, exhaustion of air and blood from the pleural cavity to re-expand the lung, clearance of secretions and blood from the tracheobronchial tree to facilitate expansion of all lung tissue, and treatment of shock.

In the aged patient, the adoption of proper methods to accomplish the above aims requires vigilant judgment. Review of the various degrees of chest injuries will emphasize the modifications of treatment which may be required in the elderly patient.

CHEST WALL INJURY

In most instances the simple fracture of a rib in an aged· patient requires no exceptional treatment. However, careful examination of the lungs is always indicated to detect the presence of a pneumothorax or hemothorax. In most instances, x-ray or fluoroscopic examination is indicated. It must be emphasized that there is danger that a small pneumothorax or hemothorax, undisclosed by physical examination immediately after injury, may develop with serious encroachment upon the lung during the ensuing 12 to 24 hours. The treatment of hemothorax and pneumothorax will be dealt with later.

Respiratory pain may often be minimized by adhesive strapping of the costal margin to splint chest motion on the side of fracture.

In general, a minimal injury of this type in the aged individual is tolerated well and is of no consequence except for the attendant respiratory pain. However it must be borne in mind that such a trivial injury may, in rare instances, be enough to tip the balance in a patient with far advanced emphysema with impaired respiratory reserve, or may possibly precipitate cardiac decompensation in the elderly patient already on the border of heart failure.

When such advanced pulmonary or cardiac disease is recognized in a patient with a minimal chest injury, scrupulous care is required in management, and admission to the hospital may be required. Where there is marked emphysema, it is advantageous to utilize repeated intercostal nerve block with Novocain to control the pain and allow these patients to cough and clear their secretions. In the patient who is precipitated into cardiac failure or is known to be close to decompensation, it may be wise to utilize oxygen by nasal catheter in addition to Novocain intercostal nerve blocks, and to review the need for an increase in the dose of digitalis if the heart rate is accelerated.

INTRATHORACIC INJURY ASSOCIATED WITH FRACTURE OF RIBS

In more severe injuries where fractured ribs are associated with contusion or laceration of the lung with various degrees of pneumothorax, hemopneumothorax, or hemothorax, the specific treatment varies little with the age of the casualty. A general policy of care will be outlined later indicating the modifications which may arise because of the patient's age.

Pneumothorax. Except where there is a minimal pneumothorax evidenced by a 1 to 2 cm rim of air at the periphery of the lung, it is wisest to re-expand the lung immediately by intercostal catheter drainage to a water-seal bottle. The intercostal tube for pneumothorax associated with trauma is usually most advantageously placed in the lower lateral chest. Because some degree of hemothorax is invariably present, a drainage tube at a site in the lower chest will drain both air and fluid more adequately.

If there is only a small rim of air as described above, or a minor accumulation of blood blunting the costophrenic angle by x-ray and no active therapy is decided upon, these patients must be followed by serial x-ray films or fluoroscopic examination to be certain that reabsorption is progressing and that no further leakage of air or accumulation of blood has occurred.

The presence of a tension pneumothorax should always be suspected in any patient with a chest injury who has shortness of breath. If on percussion and auscultation and palpation of the trachea the presence of a pneumothorax is confirmed, a needle should be introduced into the chest and air aspirated. This is most easily performed through the second or third interspace anteriorly in the midclavicular line. Such a maneuver is only a temporary expedient for dealing with an acute situation. The needle should be replaced as soon as possible by an intercostal catheter as described above. When the needle cannot be replaced for some time, it may be attached by tubing to an underwater trap bottle.

In the elderly patient with emphysema, even a small pneumothorax associated with fractured ribs may cause embarrassment of respiration and shortness of breath. It is safer in this instance to use intercostal catheter drainage even where the pneumothorax is minimal.

Another complication which may be encountered in an elderly patient with emphysema is the difficulty of re-expanding the lung. The laceration of the lung may have occurred through a bullous area of the lung and the resulting air leak may be large enough to require the institution of suction drainage through the intercostal catheter to overcome the air leak and allow the lung to re-expand more completely. Such a large pulmonary air leak may require suction drainage over many days and may require the insertion of catheters in more than one site. If two catheters are necessary for adequate drainage, one through the second interspace anteriorly and the other through the seventh or eighth interspace posterolaterally will most commonly give the best results.

Hemothorax. The treatment of hemothorax remains the same in the elderly patient as in the younger. There is no evidence that the tendency to hemorrhage from the lung or from the intercostal vessels is increased as the patient's age advances. The following outline of treatment holds for patients of any age group with a traumatic hemothorax.

Hemorrhage from the lung is usually self-limited except where the wound involves the large vessels at the hilus of the lung, as may occur with a penetrating wound of the chest, or, rarely, in the most violent types of crush injuries. Laceration of the large vessels is almost always fatal. Persistent hemorrhage, if it occurs, is usually a result of laceration of the intercostal or internal mammary vessels of the chest wall.

The treatment of hemothorax is by needle aspiration, except in the case of minimal hemothorax as described previously. If a massive hemothorax is present within the first hours of injury, there may be embarrassment of respiration owing to collapse of the lung and shift of the mediastinum. Various degrees of circulatory failure will accompany this and the actual blood loss. Transfusion should be started and the hemothorax aspirated. If blood for transfusion is not immediately available, the blood aspirated from the chest in the first hours following injury may be collected in a sterile manner in a bottle containing citrate and then used for transfusion. A practical method of collection is to attach the aspirating needle in the chest directly to a donor vacuum bottle.

Persistent hemorrhage as evidenced by increasing hemothorax and persistent or recurrent signs of blood loss should be treated in the same way as any other hemorrhage would be, that is, by exploratory thoracotomy and ligature of the bleeding vessels, plus transfusion. In the rare instance where a pulmonary vessel at the hilus is the cause of bleeding, ligation or even pulmonary resection may be indicated.

A hemothorax should be aspirated immediately if the hemorrhage is massive and encroaches on the respiratory reserve. If it does not encroach on the respiratory function there can be temporization of hours' but not of days' duration. The theory that early aspiration may cause recurrent hemorrhage has not been substantiated by facts. Certainly where there is a hemothorax of any size, a primary aspiration should be performed within the first 6 hours. Hemothorax cannot usually be dissipated by a single aspiration. Aspiration should be continued daily, at sites determined by physical signs or the changing x-ray appearance.

Loculation and partial thrombus formation are not uncommon. In most instances the hemothorax can be eliminated readily if aspiration is performed early and repeated daily; but in some cases, particularly if the aspiration has been delayed and chest wall damage is severe, there may be extensive thrombus formation and aspiration will not suffice to remove it. Where the remnant of hemothorax or, more accurately, clotted hemothorax after aspiration is minimal, showing up as a shadow at the base obliterating the costophrenic angle and ascending the lateral chest wall a short distance, the wisest decision is to leave it alone. The surgeon should encourage respiratory exercises of the chest wall and diaphragm. At worst, the final deformity and limitation will consist only of lateral tenting and fixation of the diaphragm.

If x-rays still show a considerable shadow at the end of a week or 10 days, denoting a moderate to large size thrombus within the pleural cavity, streptokinase should be employed to lyse the fibrin clot and allow it to be evacuated. In preparation for using the fibrinolysin material, an intercostal catheter with fenestration is introduced into the clotted hemothorax. One ampule of Varidase is then diluted with 20 ml of saline in order to give an adequate volume for injection through the catheter into the thrombus. Antihistamines and aspirin are given to minimize the febrile reaction to these enzymes. After the injection of Varidase, the tube is clamped and connected to a water-seal trap. The clamp should be left on the catheter between 8 and 12 hours and then released. This procedure may be repeated again after an interval of at least 24 hours following the release of the catheter. When drainage through the catheter stops, the catheter is withdrawn.

Varidase must not be used too early in the presence of hemorrhage, since it may start bleeding again. Furthermore, where there has been laceration of the lung tissue and bronchopleural fistula, the use of the enzyme even in a late stage of healing may open up an already sealed bronchopleural fistula.

Where there has been neglect of a clotted hemothorax for 4 or more weeks, the above methods may not be successful in eliminating the already organizing thrombus. If this thrombus is large, and particularly if it extends along the lateral chest wall, thoracotomy and decortication of the lung will be needed. If aspiration is started early and continued daily, the necessity for using Varidase will be uncommon; and where both these methods have been employed in a timely fashion, the need for thoracotomy and decortication will be extremely rare.

In addition to the instance where a large clotted hemothorax has been neglected for 4 weeks or more, there are two other situations in which decortication may be advisable at an earlier date. In the first of these a hemothorax will have become infected but without localization into empyema. Here there may be extensive low grade infection with loculation. When this occurs decortication is indicated for removal of the infected thrombus and re-expansion of the lung. Second, where there has been a massive hemothorax with thrombus formation it may sometimes be wiser to operate in the first week to evacuate the clot and re-expand the lung rather than rely on the use of enzymes.

There are no special considerations in the handling of a hemothorax in the elderly patient except for the fact that the encroachment of space-occupying blood upon the already limited pulmonary reserve may make removal of the blood more urgent so as to allow re-expansion of pulmonary tissue. The use of oxygen for inhalation support may often be required until the lung capacity is restored.

REMOVAL OF TRACHEOBRONCHIAL ACCUMULATIONS

In the aged chest casualty the problem of effective cough mechanism is of prime importance. The normal cough, with deep inspiration followed by a phase of increased intertracheal and bronchial pressure with sudden release of air outward in exhalation, is the most effective method of evacuating the contents of the bronchi. The preliminary inspiration forces air distal to the bolus which is suddenly expelled by explosive exhalation. In the aged patient this mechanism becomes less effective because of the limitations imposed by various degrees of emphysema. In advanced emphysema the chest wall is fixed, the diaphragm flattened, and the deep inspiration and forceful expiration required in an effective cough are impossible. Added to this is the fact that in trauma this mechanism is crippled to various degrees or rendered entirely ineffectual by limitations imposed by pain, abnormal mobility of the chest, or the cushioning effects of fluid and air in the pleural cavity.

It is therefore of extreme importance in the elderly patient to appraise the severity of the injury and the amount of emphysema present as these may affect the ability to cough effectively. The use of tracheostomy early in treatment is often lifesaving in the aged patient. Where there is advanced emphysema and a relatively minor chest injury, tracheostomy should be considered. On the other hand, in instances where there has been a severe crush injury in an elderly patient without obvious emphysema, tracheostomy should always be considered, and when in doubt performed.

It is of utmost importance that posttracheostomy care be diligently and intelligently applied. It is not enough merely to perform the operation. The nursing care is of even greater importance. Frequent adequate suctioning using a large, soft rubber catheter is necessary. If oxygen is used it should be humidified and introduced into the opening of the tracheostomy via a bent No. 18 needle so that a jet of high-flow oxygen is not forced into the trachea. Occasionally agents such as Alevaire or sodium lauryl sulphate 0.1 per cent solution which reduce surface tension or liquefy tenacious mucus will help considerably to raise secretions. These agents may be added to the water jar used to humidify the oxygen or may be sprayed by a nasal spray directly into the tracheostomy.

If it has been decided that tracheostomy is not necessary for the treatment of the particular aged patient with a chest injury, other methods of clearing the tracheobronchial airways must be utilized. Where pain is the chief limiting factor, encouragement to cough after injection of an opiate may be all that is necessary. In the usual case 50 to 75 mg of Demerol is sufficient. If this does not control pain sufficiently, intercostal nerve block using 5 ml of 1 per cent Novocain in each interspace covering the area of rib injury and one interspace above and below is necessary to obliterate pain and allow the patient to cough. If the patient cannot or will not cough up secretions using these methods, intratracheal catheter aspiration should be performed. This not only stimulates cough but is a useful method of removing the secretions. If this method fails, bronchoscopy should be resorted to for removal of accumulated mucus and blood to allow lung expansion.

In the elderly patient, discerning judgment and skill may be required to decide on and to carry out the proper methods of keeping the tracheobronchial airways clear. It is of greatest importance to recognize early that patient who will require a tracheostomy either because of emphysema and profuse secretions or by reason of the severity of the chest injury itself.

EMPHYSEMA AND RESPIRATORY ACIDOSIS

The elderly patient with advanced emphysema will require particular attention when chest injury has occurred. As emphasized before, these patients have a greatly diminished respiratory reserve and pose difficulties in the removal of secretions. The use of oxygen by inhalation either by nasal catheter or oxygen tent is often required for support following chest injury in these patients to relieve dyspnea and cyanosis. Oxygen, particularly in high concentrations, must be used with caution, however, because carbon dioxide retention may occur in patients with emphysema. The retention of carbon dioxide may be increased when oxygen is given and ventilation reduced. As a consequence of the reduction in ventilation less carbon dioxide is blown off and retention occurs with the onset of respiratory acidosis.

Drowsiness, mental confusion, and finally coma may ensue in these patients if respiratory acidosis is not detected and treated. In suspected cases carbon dioxide and pH determination should be made on the blood to corroborate the diagnosis. If respiratory acidosis with carbon dioxide retention is present, either a respirator must be used with a face mask or, if a tracheostomy has been performed, the respirator can be connected directly to the tracheostomy tube. By this means mechanical respiration supports and augments the normal respiration and carbon dioxide is blown off. It is therefore important, in considering the over-all treatment of the elderly patient with emphysema, to be alert to the possibility that the use of oxygen without a respirator may be hazardous. It is also pertinent to emphasize that the use of narcotics in this same group of elderly patients may be equally hazardous because narcotics may slow ventilation and allow carbon dioxide retention. The combination of highly concentrated oxygen inhalations with large doses of opiates will be particularly harmful in these patients and should be eschewed.

CARDIAC MANIFESTATIONS SECONDARY TO CHEST TRAUMA

The importance of knowing the cardiac history of the aged patient who has had a chest injury has been stressed. Where there is overt cardiac failure, appropriate measures to deal with it under the stress of injury must be observed. These measures may include an increased dose of digitalis, the use of oxygen, limitation of fluids and salt, and the use of diuretics. However, of importance also are the cardiac arrythmias which commonly follow trauma in the elderly patient who has no obvious cardiac limitations. Following chest injuries of moderate and severe degree, auricular fibrillation may and often does develop during the first week. This occurs very commonly, and the physician should be constantly vigilant because the rapid, ineffective contractions may bring decompensation with them. An electrocardiogram should be obtained to substantiate the diagnosis and the patient must be digitalized forthwith. If digitalis does not suffice to convert the fibrillation, quinidine should be employed.

When the elderly patient with chest injury does not have overt cardiac decompensation or does not develop an arrythmia, the question arises as to whether digitalis should be used prophylactically. In those instances in which the elderly patient has had a severe injury not directly affecting the heart, and particularly where there is a considerable degree of tachycardia, digitalization offers some support and should be used.

TREATMENT OF SHOCK

In the treatment of shock in severe injury of the chest, there are certain important factors that should be observed beyond those discussed by Sullivan in Chap. 1. The treatment, however, does not specifically apply to the older age group but generally applies to all patients with chest injury or suffering from shock. The usual Trendelenberg position favored in other forms of injury is usually poorly tolerated by patients with respiratory difficulty due to chest injury. These patients are more comfortable and are better treated during the period of resuscitation in a semi-sitting position.

The replacement of blood and the use of oxygen by means of a nasal catheter are procedures which should go hand in hand with the measures outlined above to restore respiratory equilibrium, to stabilize the chest wall, to remove blood and air from the pleural cavity, and to re-expand the lung by clearing the tracheobronchial airway. Blood replacement should be prompt and adequate, but particular care should be taken that the patient does not receive too much fluid or blood. Overtransfusion and/or hydration may lead to pulmonary edema and death in the serious chest casualty even more easily than in other lesions. Morphine must be used in relatively small doses in chest injury and repeated with great caution in the presence of shock. With restoration of circulation the delayed absorption of the drug, which had been given subcutaneously during the period of circulatory collapse, may result in serious respiratory depression. The use of oxygen is indicated in the emergency care of chest injury with any degree of respiratory difficulty. Where circulatory collapse is present the use of oxygen is particularly urgent.

CRUSH INJURY OF THE CHEST

These injuries are the most lethal of all in civilian life and are particularly serious in the older age group. The treatment outlined here applies to all ages. Treatment of the aged patient does not vary except that tracheostomy should be employed more frequently.

The most serious closed type of chest injury, the so-called "crush injury," is of increasing importance because of the accident rate in high-speed transportation. Here the chest wall is "stove in" so that it loses its rigidity and becomes a "flail chest." If the crushing force is from the lateral direction the pathology of the injury consists in fractures, in two places at least, of multiple adjacent ribs. As a result a central portion of chest wall will be "floating," since the ribs are fractured on both extremities of the area. This "floating" section moves in and out with respiration in a reverse or paradoxical direction to the rest of the chest wall. This paradoxical respiration markedly decreases the efficiency of ventilation and is accompanied by severe pain which renders the coughing mechanism ineffectual. Hemothorax or hemopneumothorax of considerable degree is frequently associated, together with marked contusion and often laceration of the lung. There is extravasation of blood, edema, and retention of secretions in the bronchial tree.

This type of injury requires immediate action to relieve a markedly disturbed respiratory physiology. Fixation of the chest wall, removal of blood and/or air from the pleural cavity, and clearing of retained secretions from the tracheobronchial tree are often lifesaving. When the paradoxical motion of the chest wall is marked, most often anterolaterally where the rib cage is not covered by the scapula or latissimus dorsi, fixation of a rib is imperative. A rib should be selected in the central portion of the "floating" section as the pivotal point of fixation. Under local anesthesia an incision is made into the subcutaneous tissues and a medium-sized towel clip is used to grasp the rib. If, on pulling up on this rib, the chest wall is not stabilized, another rib in the most mobile remaining portion of this section is selected and another towel clip used to secure it in a similar fashion. Traction is then applied constantly in the desired direction, using a Balkan frame and just enough weight to stabilize the chest. This does not usually have to be more than 3 to 5 pounds.

If the direction of the crushing force has been from the front to back rather than laterally there will exist a so-called "steering-wheel injury" in which the sternum may be fractured transversely, often together with bilateral fractures of multiple anterior ribs or cartilages. Such a severe anterior crushing injury with a mobile sternum requires fixation immediately. Satisfactory upward traction can be obtained using a uterine tenaculum. Small incisions are made in the skin on either side of the mobile portion of the sternum under local anesthesia. Through these incisions, the arms of a tenaculum are inserted to grasp the borders of the sternum. Upward traction is then effected using a Balkan frame with pulley and weight, just enough to overcome the severe mobility. Various other methods of procuring upward traction and fixation have been devised making use of screws, specially constructed tongs, or wire ladders for fixation on chest wall.

Open reduction of the sternum and fixation by means of wire sutures under general anesthesia are rarely indicated, since satisfactory immobilization is most often attained by the other methods outlined above.

Of greatest importance in the treatment of this most severe type of "crushing injury" is the employment of tracheostomy. This procedure has a twofold utility. In the first place these patients cannot cough effectively because of pain and mobility of the chest wall. Therefore tracheostomy affords a method by which the tracheobronchial tree may be kept clear of mucous secretions, edema fluids, and blood extravasations. It must be remembered in doing a tracheostomy that cough has been abolished, therefore strict attention must be paid to frequent catheter aspirations of the trachea. Secondly, the tracheostomy bypasses the narrowed area of the larynx and, by permitting freer entrance and egress of air, reduces the bellows action of the chest wall and paradoxical motion is minimized. Following tracheostomy, the replacement of labored, grunting respirations by quiet, even ventilation may be striking. Also, because tracheostomy bypasses the column of tidal air from the site of the tracheostomy to the mouth, less dead air must be carried back and forth and respiration becomes more efficient.

In some patients with severe, bilateral, multiple rib fractures with marked paradoxical motion, the above measures may not be enough to allow for adequate ventilation. Under these circumstances it may be necessary to use a mechanical respiratory machine. Since the performance of a tracheostomy will be one of the first steps in treating such a patient, the machine will be connected to the tracheostomy tube. If this technique is to be utilized, it is of importance to avoid the prolonged use of a cuffed endotracheal tube because of the potential danger of damage to tracheal mucosa by pressure and motion of the cuff. It is therefore desirable that a noncuffed tube be used and ventilation provided for by high flow. The air which will escape around the tube and into the mouth during inspiration will help expel the secretions which tend to puddle in the pharynx. The information gained through the use of these machines in postoperative heart patients indicates that metal or nylon tubes are better tolerated than some of the other types of tracheostomy tubes. The use of a negative phase machine is to be condemned since it increases the paradoxical motion of the chest. In order adequately to ventilate a patient with a machine, it is necessary to take over the ventilation rather than to assist it, since most patients with crush injuries will not have respiratory effort sufficient to trip the machine.

Since the crush injury is indeed a serious and often lethal trauma, the importance of the early employment of the foregoing measures in the severely crushed patient cannot be overemphasized.

OPEN WOUNDS OF THE CHEST

In this type of wound, which is associated with an open "sucking" communication with the pleural cavity, there is a marked disturbance of the respiratory physiology. The lung on the side of the injury is rapidly collapsed. The contralateral lung is seriously compromised by the respiratory inefficiency and the cardiac output is diminished by reduction of circulation through the heart.

In open sucking wounds of the chest there is a pendulum swing of the mediastinum during respiration. In inspiration the collapsed lung on the side of the open injury moves toward the good lung because of the relative negative pressure on this side. The passing of air into the contralateral lung is diminished and the lung is filled with a mixture of stagnant air from the collapsed lung and fresh tracheal air. In expiration there is a swing of the mediastinum toward the injured side with an increase in intrapleural pressure as the glottis closes in the formation of a grunt; thus the uninjured lung fails to expire efficiently and some of the outgoing air will fill the injured lung. During this phase also, with increased pressure within the thorax, circulation through the heart is diminished. These alterations in the physiology require immediate closure of the chest wall wound as the first means of resuscitation.

Thus, all open sucking wounds of the chest should be closed immediately by an occlusive dressing using, if possible, petroleum jelly gauze next to the skin and a bulkier outer gauze dressing held in place by adhesive strips. It is often best, if possible, to apply the closure dressing as the patient makes a forced expiration.

The initial and often lifesaving procedure necessary in patients with open wounds of the chest is the immediate closure of the wound in the manner described. Following this, further resuscitation should be carried out before evaluating the necessity for operation. This resuscitation may require (1) administration of oxygen by nasal catheter; (2) aspiration of blood and air from the chest, usually accomplished by the introduction of intercostal catheter water-trap drainage; (3) blood replacement by transfusion; and often (4) the reestablishment of bronchial drainage by intercostal procaine injection with the return of cough or by tracheal aspiration. As soon as resuscitation has been accomplished, the sucking wound of the chest is closed by definitive suture under endotracheal anesthesia. In choosing the proper time for surgical intervention during resuscitation, it must be remembered that the possibility of abdominal injury through the diaphragm and/or continued hemorrhage may force the issue and that operation itself under endotracheal anesthesia is a continuation of resuscitation. Control of respiration under intratracheal anesthesia, with adequate aspiration of accumulated secretions and blood from the trachea, re-expansion of the lung with removal of blood and air from the pleural cavity, and finally, control of hemorrhage and firm closure of the chest wall defect will contribute to the patient's improvement.

Chapter 15

Traumatic Lesions of

the Genitourinary Tract

John W. Draper

The general surgical principles which govern the management of serious traumatic lesions of any part of the body usually apply also to those involving the urinary tract. The first problem after injury is to determine the presence of shock, to evaluate its degree, and to treat it immediately. This is particularly true in elderly patients, who do not withstand prolonged periods of hypotension as readily as do younger people. The general measures for combating shock have been treated elsewhere in this book and will not be considered in any detail in this chapter. Patients who have massive internal bleeding reach a "point of no return" which our keenest surgical insight and our most reliable laboratory aids may fail to reveal. As a general rule, therefore, we feel that if patients are bleeding from the urinary tract and their shock cannot be reversed by the intravenous injection of 2,000 ml of blood, control of the hemorrhage must be attempted by surgical intervention.

Certain features or considerations modify the incidence and severity of urinary tract injuries in the aged. Most of these people are no longer employed in hazardous occupations. However, an increasing number of older people continue to live despite the deterioration of their mental and physical faculties, and are increasingly subject to the ordinary traumas of their daily activities. They are more likely to have associated diseases, such as cancer of the kidney, hydronephrosis, urinary retention, musculoskeletal weaknesses, and other underlying conditions which predispose these organs to injury from relatively simple trauma. Such associated ailments often serve to provoke a multiple injury or at least a multiple lesion problem.

LESIONS OF THE KIDNEY

Etiology. Injuries to the kidneys result from either external or internal trauma. External injuries may be caused by direct or indirect blows to the kidney (Fig. 15-1). Although the kidney appears to be well protected by the lower ribs and the strong muscles of the back, it is remarkable how severely it may be injured by a very mild blow. This susceptibility to injury is due to the fact that the kidney lies in such a position that it is sometimes flexed over the twelfth rib. It is also quite movable, so

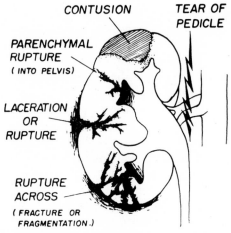

FIG. 15-1. Common lesions from external trauma to the kidney. (*From V. F. Marshall: Textbook of Urology, New York, Hoeber, 1956.*)

that when the patient falls on the buttocks or on the extended legs, it drops suddenly and pulls on its vascular pedicle, thus avulsing the blood vessels. The contralateral kidney is sometimes damaged by *contrecoup*. Contusions of the kidney, whether caused by direct or indirect trauma, result in injuries to the capsule, to the cortical tissue, to the medulla, to the renal pelvis, or to the vascular pedicle. The seriousness of the injury depends on the site and extent of the trauma. While a very minor tear in the vascular pedicle may produce severe bleeding and death in a few minutes, severe capsular lesions may not even require surgical correction. It is often surprising to see extensive damage to the soft tissues inside the capsule without any laceration of the capsule itself. Any actual disruption of the continuity of the renal collecting system which results in extravasation of the urine may be followed by infection or abscess formation, perinephric abscesses, fibrosis, or ultimately the calcification of hematomas.

Penetrating wounds involving the kidney are unusual in civilian life.

During the last war, however, 5 to 7 per cent of gunshot wounds of the abdomen involved a kidney. It is almost axiomatic that a gunshot or stab wound of either kidney will involve other important structures. The aorta and vena cava, spleen, pancreas, and large bowel lie in close proximity to the kidney, and it would be most unusual for such a wound to involve that organ alone. In the elderly patient, of course, these represent particularly grave hazards.

Diagnosis. A satisfactory history is often difficult to obtain from patients who have suffered from contusions or a penetrating wound of the kidney. If any history can be obtained, however, it may well indicate to the physician which kidney has been injured. The physical examination may show superficial skin abrasions, lacerations, or puncture wounds. If the patient is not in severe shock, blood, urine, or both may drain from these wounds. Pallor of the skin and mucosa may be prominent. Palpation often reveals a mass in the loin, and this is occasionally found to have increased in size upon repeated examinations. This observation, supported by the presence of falling blood pressure, increasing pulse rate, and other stigmata of shock, should arouse suspicion of perirenal bleeding, urinary extravasation, or both. If the bleeding is confined within Gerota's fascia, sufficient tamponade may result so that the hemorrhage will be controlled. However, if Gerota's fascia is also lacerated, the bleeding will extend through the fascia into the relatively flexible tissues of the loin, and tremendous quantities of blood may be lost without sufficient tamponade to control the hemorrhage. Bleeding within Gerota's fascia may extend across the midline into the fascial planes surrounding the opposite kidney. Since the ureter is also encased by the extension of Gerota's fascia, blood and urine find their way down along it into the bony pelvis.

A falling hemoglobin and red count, with diminished blood volume and dropping hematocrit, are ominous signs, and therefore hemograms should be performed frequently. Recently more reliance has been placed on the hematocrit and blood volume determinations than on hemoglobin and red-cell count variations, since the latter are often slow in reflecting the seriousness of gross bleeding. The determination of the amount of blood lost from wounds or passed with the urine may be useful. Urinalysis will usually show gross or microscopic hematuria. If gross, an aliquot of each voided or catheterized specimen should be saved in a test tube so that the degree of bleeding can be estimated by comparing this with subsequent samples.

Intravenous pyelography should be carried out as soon as the condition of the patient permits. If the films are not diagnostic, cystoscopy and retrograde pyelography may be necessary.

Ileus is a fairly prompt complication when the kidney is so injured

that there is retroperitoneal extravasation of blood, urine, or both. The resulting abdominal distention makes it increasingly difficult to diagnose subsequent, progressive, associated intraabdominal lesions, such as rupture of the liver, spleen, or intestines, and therefore general surgical considerations should not be delayed. The intraabdominal injuries may be of greater urgency than the renal, and transperitoneal exploration may be preferred to a loin incision.

Treatment. Patients having renal injuries fall into three categories as far as treatment is concerned. Those who appear to have a very mild

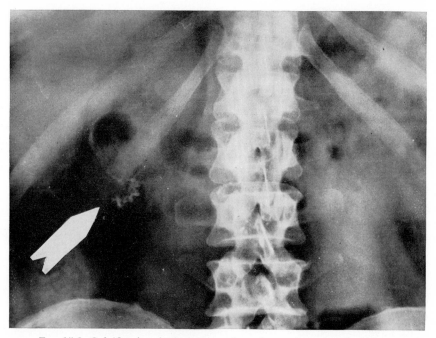

Fig. 15-2. Calcification in hematoma from laceration of right kidney.

injury are treated conservatively by all urologists. Those who have a serious injury with obvious bleeding which is uncontrollable by conservative measures are treated by prompt surgical intervention by all urologists. The third group comprises patients who fall in between these two extremes, and there is considerable divergence of opinion as to the proper method for their treatment. Many urologists feel that patients with moderately severe contusions and lacerations of the kidney should be treated conservatively and operated upon only if they develop infection or intractable hemorrhage. Others believe that these patients should be operated upon in order to prevent secondary hemorrhage, infection, stone formation, fistulas, and other complications. Arteriosclerotic vessels which cannot contract after injury tend to prolong bleeding.

Simple laceration of the renal cortex may be closed by any suitable suture. Large lacerations may be closed by mattress sutures tied over strips of ribbon catgut, fat, or fascia. Lacerations of the pelvis are easily closed.

Nephrectomy is the procedure of choice in patients with massive injuries to the cortex or large vessels, providing a normal kidney is present on the opposite side. Any patient who has had a renal injury should have periodic follow-up films, since calculi, hypertension, and other delayed complications may result (Fig. 15-2).

LESIONS OF THE URETER

Injury involving the ureter, especially in older persons, is quite rare, except where it is iatrogenic. Fortunately the ureter is a flexible and elastic tube, so that injury from external violence is unusual. A few instances of partial or complete severance of the ureter resulting from stab, gunshot, or similar wounds have been reported. When there is a history of a penetrating wound, or when such a wound is actually present, drainage of urine from it would suggest an injury to the urinary tract. The presence of an expanding mass in the flank or pelvis would also suggest the possibility of an extravasation of urine. The diagnosis may often be established by an intravenous or retrograde pyelogram demonstrating extravasation of urine through a perforation or complete severance of the ureter. Hydronephrosis and hydroureter above the site of the injury to the ureter may progress as a result of scar tissue resulting from the injury.

The majority of ureteral injuries, especially in older people, result from surgical trauma. In our enthusiasm to pass ureteral catheters beyond obstructions, the catheter itself may be pushed through the wall of the ureter. Attempts to extract stones from the ureter by various manipulations have resulted in many injuries. This damage may be simply a stripping of the mucosa where it is caught in an extraction basket, or complete avulsion of the ureter when traction is placed on the stone in an attempt to withdraw it into the bladder. The ureter may be perforated when one of the wire arms of a Johnson basket breaks off and remains in the ureteral wall above the stone in attempting its extraction. In one such case the wire and stone were removed together at open operation and no permanent damage resulted (Fig. 15-3). The prompt recognition of ureteral injury which could result in strictures or extravasation of urine is important. In the latter instance the patient generally notes the onset of pain in his side as the urine extravasates. There is a swelling which is tender to palpation, and these signs are accompanied by elevation of temperature and white count. If the extravasation is intraperitoneal, signs of peritonitis may ensue.

An intravenous pyelogram or Woodruff-type ureterogram will often locate the ureteral injury, which should be treated promptly by retroperitoneal drainage of the extravasated urine and repair of the injured

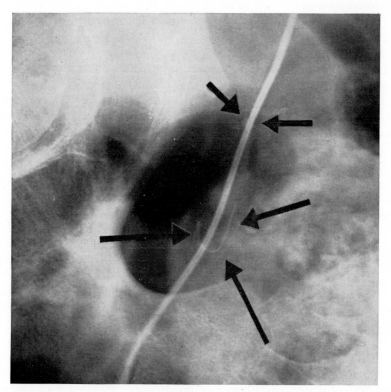

FIG. 15-3. Catheter in left ureter. Arrows show stone and wire broken from extractor. Both were removed at operation.

ureter. In instances of incomplete separation, it may be wise to place a tube to the kidney above the site of injury and a small splinting catheter down the ureter through the injured area. If there is necrosis of the wall following long-sustained pressure of a ureteral stone, it is advisable to resect the necrotic segment and to free the ureter so that an end-to-end anastomosis may be carried out over a ureteral splint. In carrying out such an anastomosis, it is advantageous to attempt to secure a careful mucosal approximation with everting sutures. Whenever possible, it is also helpful to cut the ends of the ureter to be approximated obliquely rather than at a right angle, so that a longer anastomosis may be made.

One of the most important principles of successful ureteral surgery is to make every effort to conserve as much blood supply as possible, and to avoid catheters and splints which are too tight. Even under the most favorable circumstances iatrogenic injuries of the ureter are very apt to result in stricture of the ureter with a greater or lesser degree of hydro-ureter and hydronephrosis above the point of stricture.

A very common site of injury to the ureter is the point where it passes under the uterine artery deep in the pelvis. At this site the ureter is not infrequently exposed to injury during pelvic surgery. The presence of a large tumor mass in the pelvis makes it extremely difficult for the operating surgeon to clamp the uterine arteries without occasionally clamping the ureter as well. Whenever a large mass is to be removed from the true pelvis, it is advisable to pass ureteral catheters as a preliminary procedure so that these may be easily palpated and the position of the ureters thus identified during subsequent surgery. Damage to the lower third of the ureter, the usual site of injury during pelvic surgery, may be managed without end-to-end anastomosis. If both ureters are accidentally ligated, anuria results and immediate removal of the obstruction is necessary.

Because of the high incidence of stricture following end-to-end anastomosis, it is sometimes advisable to reimplant the ureter into the bladder rather than to suture it back to the ureteral stump if the injury is in its lower 3 or 4 cm. If the ureter is reimplanted into the bladder, it can be carried down through a submucosal tunnel into the bladder wall and a cuff of ureter turned back upon itself and sutured to the mucosa of the bladder wall. This will provide a ureteral bud within the lumen of the bladder. This surgical procedure helps to prevent reflux of urine from the bladder up the ureter.

Unfortunately, many injuries of the lower ureter are so placed that reimplantation into the bladder is not feasible. In some such cases, a tube can be formed of the bladder wall and brought up to the end of the proximal portion of the ureter so that it can be anastomosed at that level. Patients who undergo this procedure almost routinely have reflux from the bladder up the ureter. In the elderly patient with a good contralateral kidney, nephrectomy may be the treatment of choice in ureteral injury because of the long morbidity often associated with corrective surgery on the ureter.

INJURIES OF THE URINARY BLADDER

Injuries of the urinary bladder are becoming increasingly frequent in all age groups. The severity of injury is usually in direct proportion to the quantity of urine in the bladder. A relatively mild degree of trauma exerted against a very distended, tense bladder may result in complete rupture. On the other hand, the empty bladder is tucked down behind the symphysis pubis in the bony pelvis and so is well protected from external violence in the case of a penetrating wound or pelvic fracture. It is obvious that a distended bladder is more prone to injury by a penetrating object than one which is empty. If the force produces a rupture

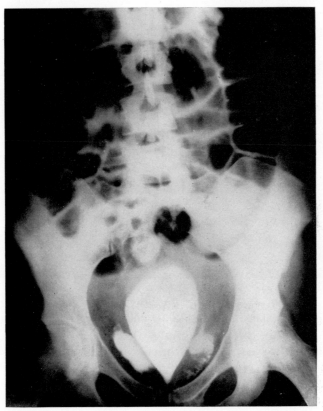

Fig. 15-4. Extraperitoneal rupture of bladder. Note "teardrop" cystogram caused by extravasated urine and blood in the pelvis.

of the bladder wall, the urine extravasates into either the peritoneum or the perivesical space (Fig. 15-4). If the pubic rami are fractured, spicules of bone sometimes perforate the bladder and may even be found within its lumen at operation.

The diagnosis of perforation or rupture of the bladder may be made from a history of injury in the region of the pelvis (Fig. 15-5, *A* and *B*). It is noteworthy that many patients with damage to the bladder are so severely injured or so intoxicated that it is difficult to obtain a history. For this reason it is extremely important to consider the possibility of a laceration or rupture of the bladder in any patient who has sustained trauma of any kind to the bladder region. The bladder is particularly subject to injury in elderly male patients, who frequently carry considerable amounts of residual urine. Physical examination may reveal no evidence of superficial injury, or there may be lacerations or perforations of the skin, large areas of ecchymosis, obvious fracture of the pelvis, and local accumulations of urine and blood in the peritoneal cavity in the patient whose peritoneum has been perforated.

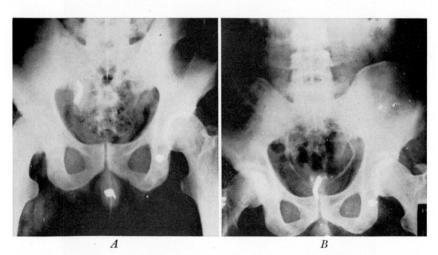

A   *B*

Fig. 15-5. *A*. Shell fragment in pelvis causing no urinary symptoms. *B*. Later film shows fragment migrated through bladder wall causing intermittent obstruction.

Whenever there is the slightest possibility of injury to the bladder, a urine specimen should be obtained immediately on admission to the hospital. If the patient is unable to void, he should be catheterized and the catheter left in place. The presence of blood in the urine should direct attention to further study of the urinary tract. If a catheter is passed successfully and bloody urine is obtained, the catheter should be left indwelling and a cystogram made. Attempts to make a diagnosis of laceration of the bladder by filling it with measured quantities of saline and measuring the return from the catheter are notoriously unreliable. There is no substitute for the cystogram at this point, and it can be made very readily with a portable x-ray machine if the patient's condition will not permit his removal to the x-ray department.

The bladder should be filled with a diluted solution of intravenous contrast medium and anteroposterior, oblique, and evacuation films secured. A scout film should, of course, be made prior to injection of the contrast medium, and this will usually demonstrate any injuries to the bony pelvis. If such injuries are present, they should in themselves arouse suspicion of bladder injury, particularly if the pubic rami are fractured. The cystogram of extraperitoneal laceration shows the extravasating material around the bladder (Fig. 15-6). In intraperitoneal rupture the contrast medium may almost disappear in the intraabdominal fluid.

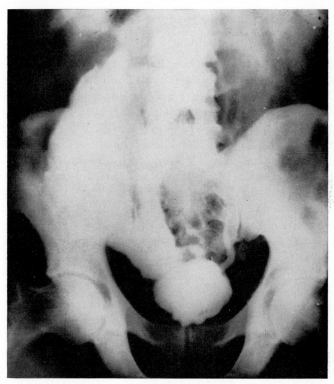

Fig. 15-6. Extraperitoneal rupture of bladder. Note marked extravasation of medium.

Treatment. When the diagnosis of ruptured bladder has been established, the patient should be operated upon as soon as his general condition will permit. Shock must be treated, of course, and fractures and other associated injuries may demand priority. If the patient has an intraperitoneal rupture of the bladder, a surgical approach is sometimes facilitated by passing a Foley catheter with a 75 cc balloon. Inflation of the balloon distends the bladder, making the point of laceration in its wall visible. Before opening the peritoneum, it is sometimes helpful to irrigate the bladder with a solution of indigo carmine or other dye. If this is seen within the peritoneal cavity, no question can exist as to the presence of intraperitoneal rupture of the bladder. The practice of placing air within the injured bladder is unsafe because of the danger of air embolism. After the laceration in the bladder wall has been closed and the adjacent opening in the peritoneum has been sutured, drains are placed in the retroperitoneal space down to the point of injury and brought out between the peritoneum and the bladder. The peritoneum should be closed completely without drains and a cystostomy tube left in the bladder to ensure adequate urinary drainage. Some surgeons prefer a urethral catheter, but since many of these patients are critically ill, it may be wiser to ensure good drainage by a large suprapubic tube. This is especially important for the elderly male with prostatic obstruction.

Iatrogenic injuries of the bladder are all too frequently the sequelae of modern surgery. The lithotrite and resectoscope have increased the surgical armamentarium of the urologist, but they have also put into his hands instruments capable of doing great damage in the bladder. Fortunately, most of these bladder injuries can be recognized as soon as they occur, and can be treated by surgical drainage. If the perforation of the bladder is not visualized during the operation and the postoperative course suggests that this has happened, a contrast cystogram will confirm the diagnosis. Only prompt intervention will reduce the morbidity and mortality of these surgical accidents.

Vesicovaginal fistula is a very distressing complication of radical hysterectomy. It follows the placing of a suture through the walls of the vagina and bladder, and the injury is unfortunately seldom apparent until several days after the surgical procedure has been carried out. The diagnosis is usually quite obvious and can be substantiated by a cystoscopic inspection of the bladder. Intravenous pyelogram should always be done to rule out injury of the ureters. If the lower ureters have not been injured at the same time, the most satisfactory way to attack this problem is by a suprapubic incision and dissection of the bladder from the peritoneum down to the site of the vesicovaginal fistula. The fistulous tract from the bladder to the vagina is then separated and divided. The vaginal side is excised and the freshened margins inverted into the vagina and closed with a continuous Connell suture of chromic catgut. The opening in the bladder is closed by a similar suture of plain catgut, inverting the mucosa into the lumen of the bladder. Reinforcing sutures of chromic catgut should be used to support the continuous plain catgut closure. This type of closure has been more successful than transvaginal or transvesical procedures. Incidentally, it is wise to catheterize the ureters before placing any sutures or doing any dissection in the neighborhood of either ureter.

Vesicorectal fistulas may be given the same treatment as has been described above for vesicovaginal types, but sometimes they are better closed by a perineal approach. Vesicovaginal fistulas or vesicorectal fistulas which result from irradiation and ulceration of the bladder wall are far more difficult to treat. The irradiated tissue has poor viability, and the results of closure are notoriously bad.

At times fistulas in these areas are so difficult to correct locally that urinary diversion to the colon, ilial segment, or skin may be necessary. Such procedures carry a high morbidity and mortality rate and are usually the "children of despair."

Injuries to the Urethra: Female

The female urethra is short and so situated that it is seldom subject to the same kind of trauma as the male urethra. It is, however, occasionally injured by external violence or by fractures involving the pubic bones. Injury to the urethra in the female is much less serious than in the male. The sphincter which retains the urine in the normal female bladder is at the bladder neck. Therefore, the female urethra can be badly traumatized distal to the bladder neck with perforations leading into the vagina, and yet the patient will have normal urinary control and will be able to void satisfactorily.

The diagnosis may be made by direct inspection, by the inability to pass a catheter into the urinary bladder, by the presence of continuous bleeding from the urethral meatus independent of urination, or by the presence of extravasated urine and blood in the anterior vaginal wall. Urethroscopic examination or retrograde urethrogram will confirm the injury, locate its site, and evaluate its severity.

Treatment. Primary repair of avulsion or severe laceration of the urethra will require adequate surgical exposure and closure of the defect with fine, plain catgut sutures. An indwelling catheter should be left in place following this repair, and the anterior vaginal wall should be closed so as to reinforce the urethral sutures. Scarification following the injury can cause strictures in the female urethra identical with those found in the male.

Injuries to the Urethra: Male

Injuries to the male urethra are considered in two separate categories, those involving the urethra above the urogenital diaphragm (triangular ligament), and those which occur below or distal to the urogenital diaphragm. Because their etiology, symptomatology, and treatment are quite different, we will consider them separately.

Injuries to the male urethra occurring posterior to the diaphragm may cause contusion, laceration, or avulsion (Fig. 15-7). The urogenital diaphragm is fixed anteriorly to the symphysis pubis and the pubic rami, and contains between its two leaves the voluntary sphincter of the urethra, a portion of the membranous urethra, and Cowper's glands. It is a very strong structure; and when the pubic rami, to which it is attached, are displaced by fracture of the pelvis, the pull on the diaphragm will often avulse the urethra completely. In this manner the prostate and prostatic urethra are separated from the remaining portion of the urethra, and because bleeding and extravasation of urine are often associated with this trauma, the prostate is pushed up into the bony

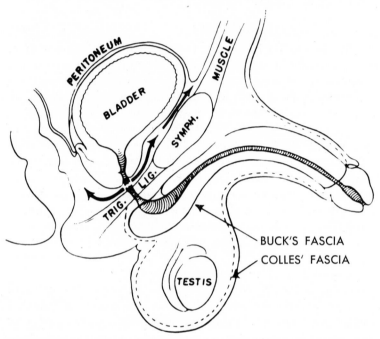

FIG. 15-7. Rupture of urethra behind the triangular ligament. (*From V. F. Marshall: Textbook of Urology, New York, Hoeber, 1956.*)

pelvis. If the diaphragm remains intact, the extravasated urine and blood are contained above the diaphragm and present a swelling in the suprapubic area. Ecchymosis of the skin may be noted. If the diaphragm is lacerated during the injury, the extravasated blood and urine may appear in the perineum, scrotum, along the shaft of the penis, or under the superficial abdominal fascia.

The diagnosis of rupture of the male urethra proximal to the urogenital diaphragm is first suggested by a history of rather severe trauma. There is also usually x-ray evidence of fracture of the pubic rami. The patient is almost always anuric or passes very small amounts of urine through the urethra. Suprapubic tenderness, swelling, and ecchymosis gradually appear. Rectal examination reveals a boggy induration in the prostatic fossa, and sometimes the prostate can be felt high in the pelvis, where it has been dislocated by the contracture of the bladder musculature and the pressure from the extraperitoneal blood and urine. Attempts to pass a catheter are almost always unsatisfactory. An intravenous contrast agent injected through the urethra or catheter extravasates at the point of laceration or rupture of the urethra. An intravenous pyelogram may reveal that the bladder is dislocated upward and has a so-called "teardrop" shape due to its compression by the surrounding extravasated urine and blood.

Treatment. As soon as the patient's condition permits, the suprapubic area should be explored. The peritoneum is opened to rule out intraperitoneal injury. The extravesical urine and blood and splinters of pubic bone are removed. The bladder should be opened and a Foley urethral catheter passed from the meatus through the severed portion of the urethra at the diaphragm, through the prostatic urethra into the bladder. When the Foley bag is distended and traction is applied to the catheter, the prostate will be reapproximated to the membranous urethra at the urogenital diaphragm. To reinforce this approximation, it is wise to suture the urethra with interrupted plain catgut. Sometimes this is impossible because of technical difficulties or because of the condition of the patient. Reapproximation of the urethra by suture whenever possible will provide a more satisfactory result than the more haphazard approximation obtained from the use of the Foley catheter. To fix the bladder in its normal position, some surgeons advocate using long needles to place mattress sutures through its base and out through the perineum where they are tied over gauze pads. The periprostatic and perivesical space should be well drained with Penrose tubes, and a cystostomy tube left in the bladder.

If the injury has caused extravasation of blood and urine through the urogenital diaphragm, perineal exposure with drainage of the collected blood and urine in the perineum and within the confines of the pelvic fascia should be carried out in addition to the suprapubic drainage. In rare instances, the blood and urine may extravasate along the subcutaneous fascia and extend as high as the clavicles and even into the axillary spaces. In one such case incision and drainage had to be carried out as high as the axilla.

Injuries to the male urethra below the urogenital diaphragm are generally the result of a straddle fall, in which the bulbous urethra is compressed against the symphysis pubis, thus causing contusion, laceration, or avulsion of the urethra (Fig. 15-8A). The diagnosis is made from the description of the injury or from the presence of blood dripping from the urethra independent of urination. There may be a painful swelling in ·the perineum, and, with continued bleeding, the scrotum and shaft of the penis become swollen, tense, painful, and ecchymotic. The extrav-

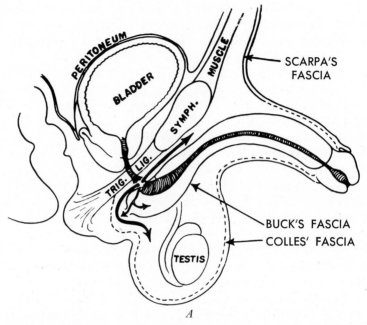

Fɪɢ. 15-8. *A*. Rupture of urethra (bulb) anterior to the triangular ligament. (*From V. F. Marshall: Textbook of Urology, New York, Hoeber, 1956.*)

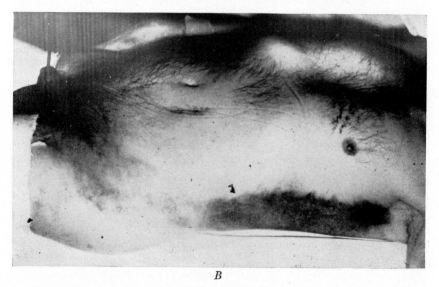

Fɪɢ. 15-8. *B*. Rupture of urethra distal to ligament with extravasation of blood into scrotum and under superficial abdominal fascia extending into left axilla.

asating fluid may extend up in the abdominal wall under the superficial abdominal fascia as far as the clavicles and into the axilla, just as it does with the urethral phlegmon (Fig. 15-8*B*). If a diagnosis cannot be made by simple palpation and inspection, a urethrogram may be required. Although urethroscopic examination can be performed, it is seldom justified. If the injury is a simple contusion or a small laceration, a urethral catheter may be passed directly into the bladder. If this is accomplished, the catheter should be left indwelling to ensure adequate urinary drainage. When the urethra has been perforated or avulsed, the catheter often will not pass beyond the point of injury.

Surgical repair of the lacerated or avulsed urethra is required as soon as the patient's condition will permit. Devitalized tissue should be removed and an end-to-end anastomosis carried out over a urethral catheter, using everting interrupted mattress sutures of 00 catgut. This operation must be accomplished with the patient in lithotomy position, and it is sometimes feasible to mobilize the urethra distal to the site of the injury in order to secure sufficient length of normal urethral tissue to accomplish the anastomosis without tension on the sutures. If, as often happens, there is difficulty in locating the proximal end of the urethra, it may be possible to find it by giving the patient an intravenous injection of indigo carmine as the operation begins, and then, when the perineum is opened, exerting pressure on the suprapubic region to force some of the blue-stained urine out through the urethral stump. If this maneuver is not successful in demonstrating the proximal end of the urethra, it may be necessary to perform a suprapubic cystostomy and pass a sound or catheter down the urethra from above, thus identifying the proximal end. If this is indicated, a small catheter is passed through the site of the anastomosis on out through the urethral meatus. The proximal end of the catheter is brought through the cystostomy incision and fastened to the anterior abdominal wall so that it will not be passed through the penis. If the catheter cannot easily be kept *in situ* in this fashion, heavy silk ligatures may be placed through the vesical end of the catheter and then brought out and fastened to sponge sticks on the abdominal wall. A cystostomy tube is placed beside the urethral catheter or along the ligatures going to the urethral catheter.

The long-term results of rupture of the urethra, either above or below the urogenital diaphragm, are usually unsatisfactory. Most of these patients develop strictures of the urethra which require periodic dilation for the rest of their lives. A considerable number of these patients are also impotent following their injury.

Injury to the male urethra in the scrotal or pendulous portion is less common, since the urethra at this site is flexible. When it does occur, the treatment is very much the same as that already described for injuries to the urethra in the bulb. These injuries are more apt to be caused by instrumentation than by direct violence. A surprising number of elderly men develop strictures in the distal urethra following transurethral surgery. The basic principles of treatment are the same whether the injury is due to trauma from within or from without the urethra. An occasional urethrocutaneous fistula complicates injury to the pendulous urethra, and these are often difficult to close.

LESIONS OF THE PENIS, SCROTUM, AND SCROTAL CONTENTS

Trauma to the shaft of the penis is unusual, but it does occur, and is sometimes a potentially serious injury. Any penetrating injury involving the shaft of the penis may cause disruption of the continuity of the corpora and so produce excessive bleeding. This bleeding is sometimes very difficult to control with ligatures, but is almost always easy to control with pressure dressings. Any injury of the shaft of the penis which involves the corpora calls for reapproximation of the fascia with sutures, and the application of pressure dressings which should start from the urethral meatus and extend in a circular fashion back to the base of the penis.

One type of traumatic injury to the shaft of the penis which is seldom seen in elderly patients, but may occasionally be found, is gangrene of the shaft of the penis resulting from the application of a band of metal, such as a wedding ring. Several such instances have been seen, and by the time the patients seek medical care there is so much edema in the tissues that it is almost impossible to get at the encircling band of metal. A jeweler's saw may be used to cut the metal when the penis cannot be decompressed, and the band so removed. In one case on the Second Urological Division at Bellevue Hospital, the patient introduced his penis through the center of a Timken bearing of the kind used in automobile wheels. These are made of the hardest kind of steel, and, of course, could not be cut with any of our surgical instruments. Since the penis had been strangulated for 3 days, it was necessary to make multiple incisions in it and to literally wring out the edema before the penis could be pushed back through the bearing. Extensive grafting was necessary to replace the skin which had become gangrenous. Fortunately for most of these patients, the corpora are not devascularized, and the skin which is lost through pressure necrosis can be replaced by split-thickness grafts. Patients are occasionally seen who have severe burns involving the penis and scrotal skin. These are treated by prompt debridement and grafting (Fig. 15-9, A and B).

Injuries of the scrotum and scrotal contents cause marked swelling and edema of the scrotum due to its elasticity. If a relatively small amount of scrotal skin is involved in the injury, it may be discarded. If a large area

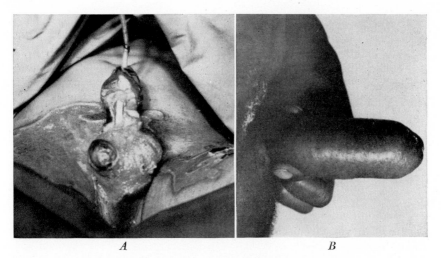

A   B

FIG. 15-9. *A.* Chemical burn of penis, corpora, urethra, scrotum, and skin of both thighs. Catheter in penis shows defect in urethra. Right testis exposed. *B.* Phallus constructed from abdominal skin flap after amputation.

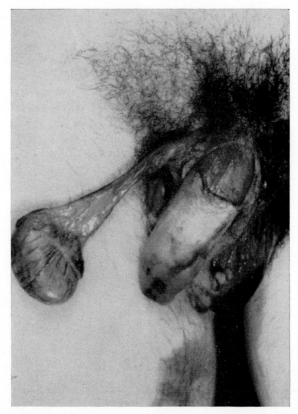

FIG. 15-10. Traumatic avulsion of skin of scrotum and penis in auto accident.

of the scrotal skin is avulsed or burned away, it must be replaced by grafting (Fig. 15-10). Hemorrhage occurring within the tunicavaginalis from direct blows or stab wounds can usually be controlled by pressure dressings. If not, incision and drainage of the hematoma may be required. The injection of proteolytic enzymes may be helpful. Testicular injuries cause severe pain owing to the relative inelasticity of the tunica propria. These may be treated by the application of pressure dressings, the use of ice bags, and occasionally, when they are gangrenous, by orchiectomy. Torsion of the testicle following trauma to the scrotum occasionally occurs, and when it does, the cord must be untwisted or gangrene of the testicle will result. In some forms of trauma, the testicle will be forced out of the scrotum and into the inguinal canal or even up into the abdomen. When this occurs, surgical intervention and orchiopexy are usually necessary.

Part IV

Injuries to the Aged Somatic Tissues

Chapter 16

Crush Syndrome

Joseph Trueta

DEFINITION

The term *crush syndrome* designates a pathologic sequence of prolonged compression injury to a limb, causing a variable amount of local damage to muscles, lymphatics, and nerves, followed by anuria and kidney failure which is frequently fatal from the seventh to ninth day.

HISTORY

This type of delayed kidney failure following compression injuries was first noted by German doctors attending the victims of the Messina earthquake of 1908, and was again studied by Minami during the First World War in Germany; but its isolation as a separate clinical entity and the coining of the name "crush syndrome" was done by Bywaters and his coworkers early in the Second World War.

ETIOLOGY

While the trauma responsible for the development of the "crush syndrome" following burial underneath the debris of air raids, earthquakes, and mining accidents is prolonged compression of any extremity, there is now some doubt as to whether the syndrome itself differs from the type of kidney failure due to a large number of other causes such as mismatched transfusion, severe wounds, blackwater fever, traumatic uremia, or sulfonamide poisoning. Many authors identify it with the large group of conditions which cause "lower neuron nephrosis" as described by Lucke, even though this view is strongly resisted by Bywaters.

PATHOGENESIS

In his early description, Bywaters attributed the kidney failure to the obstruction and damage of the convoluted tubules of the kidney by pigmented casts produced by muscle necrosis. He later called this process "myohemoglobinuric nephrosis" and considered it related to the mechanism of anuria by hemolysis in mismatched transfusion described by

Lindau in 1928. Bywaters believed it was also due to the blocking of the distal convoluted tubules by blood pigments. Both entities would constitute a group by themselves, having in common the nature of the cause, blocking pigments, the localization of the tubular damage to their distal portion, as opposed to the proximal tubular lesion of other types of kidney failure included in Lucke's "lower nephron nephrosis." In the latter lesion the damage is mainly in the proximal tubules. Morison thought that the kidney failures in myelomatosis and crush injuries were both due to the blockage of the distal tubules by pigments.

These views have been opposed by many authors who believe that anoxia by ischemia, probably due to arterial spasm, is the real cause of the tubular damage and thus of the renal failure in all these diverse conditions leading to anuria, including "crush syndrome." This was the view of the present writer when, early in 1941, he investigated experimentally the part played by arterial spasm in causing anoxia following the compression of a limb by a tourniquet. His views were that the renal failure was probably due to spasm of the renal arteries, since the clinical picture of the patients who died of renal failure was apparently similar to that of ischemia of the kidneys. In the course of experiments the author and his coworkers found that certain electrical stimulations and the use of several drugs and hormones produced constriction of some arteries and dilatation of others. They pointed out that under the influence of a thigh tourniquet and other stimuli, there was a difference in response between the renal and the mesenteric arteries, whereas the femoral and renal arteries always reacted together either constricting or dilating under the effect of the same stimuli. The similarity in response between the skin and the renal cortex appeared so striking that, for practical purposes, they considered the renal cortex as a portion of buried skin and the two kidneys with their renal arteries as two "intraabdominal" extremities.

Parallel observations have been made by several investigators, including Jardine and Teacher. As early as 1911 they believed that renal-cortical necrosis and Raynaud's disease of the fingers had much in common. Muller and Patersen, in 1929, and later Miles, Muller, and Patersen, demonstrated that chilling, which is accompanied by a definite constriction of the arterioles of the skin even when acting for a short time, caused a marked constriction of the renal vessels as judged by a definite contraction of the kidney; whereas the vascular bed of the splanchnic area dilates in response to chilling. The division of the sympathetic nerves to the kidney causes a dilatation of the renal vessels and prevents these effects of chilling; these results are very similar to those observed in the extremities after division of their sympathetic supply. The effect of chilling on the kidney had already been noticed by Bright in 1843. Recently

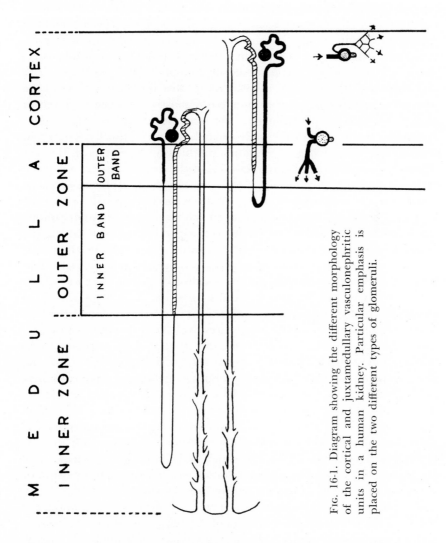

F<small>IG</small>. 16-1. Diagram showing the different morphology of the cortical and juxtamedullary vasculonephritic units in a human kidney. Particular emphasis is placed on the two different types of glomeruli.

Garai reported new data which support the correlation between the kidneys and the skin in cases suffering from the consequences of prolonged immersion.

The behavior of the renal cortical arterioles seems unique in the animal body. It has been known since Krogh that anoxia causes vasodilatation which relaxes any existing vascular contraction. This capillary and arteriolar dilatation seems to be caused by anoxia in every one of the organs investigated except in the kidney, where it produces cortical-vascular spasm, a feature which was observed by Adolph, in the frog, as early as 1934. Bick and his associates, in 1938, found that the renal arteries in the frog, which are connected with glomeruli, constricted when deprived of oxygen; whereas the remainder of the renal arterioles and the arteries of all the other organs of the body dilated. This had also been observed to occur after hemorrhage by Tamura and his coworkers. One of the first observations on the paradoxical behavior of the cortical arteries was made by David in 1925, showing that a low concentration of phenol urethane constricted the renal vessels but did not constrict the vessels of the leg. In 1937, Green and Hoff found that in monkeys and cats limb volume usually increased, whereas the kidney volume was diminished during the response to stimulation of the cerebral cortex. More recently, Hoff and his associates have found that if India ink was injected into the right common carotid artery during the pressor response caused by electrical stimulation of foci on the anterior sigmoid gyri of the cerebral cortex, there was evidence of exclusion of the ink from the renal vascular bed except in the juxtamedullary region. Similar results have been obtained by Lofgren, who has repeatedly found that the emotional upset produced in cats by confronting them with a dog may cause a total cortical ischemia, whereas the medullary vessels may remain open and sometimes extremely well injected, as has been evidenced by the beautiful sections he has obtained. All this suggests that the vessels of the kidney, or at least those arterioles connected to the cortical glomeruli, react to many types of stimuli by vasoconstriction. Considering this response together with the rest of the vascular changes elicited by shock or by postoperative disease, we can picture what Franklin calls an "order of sacrifice"—a suppression of the blood flow in the tissues caused by vascular spasm.

The purpose of this mechanism appears to be the preservation of the blood supply of the coronary arteries of the heart and brain, the two organs which cannot survive even a short interruption of the blood supply. This phenomenon was discussed by Sullivan in Chap. 1.

As a result of any severe hemodynamic change which can produce an alteration of the blood flow to the systems essential to life—brain and heart—a reduction of the superficial circulating area takes place and the skin begins to scale off. At that juncture the kidney also begins to be anemic. If the circulation of the kidney were not reduced under the conditions of shock, the essential higher centers would be deprived of circulating blood to such a degree that their integrity could be endangered. *It must be remembered that the blood destined to the kidneys is a fourth of the total blood volume, i.e., as much as is required to supply the lower limbs.* Van Slyke and his associates observed that in experimental hemorrhagic shock in dogs, there is an increased oxygen consumption in every organ which was examined except in the kidney. The dog's kidney removes from 1.5 to 3.5 volume per cent of its oxygen under normal conditions, and Van Slyke believes that the intense vasoconstriction of the kidney in conditions of shock contributes to the survival of the patient or experimental animal, placing more blood at the disposal of the higher centers. The suppression of urine formation contributes also to the maintenance of the blood volume. Meriel et al. have recently confirmed the working of a renal shunt in human shock.

Reubi and his associates found that under the action of epinephrine, the amount of oxygen in the renal veins increases, almost equalizing that of the arterial blood. That is, under the action of epinephrine the oxygen consumption of the kidney decreased. The explanation seems to be that under the circumstances of cortical arteriolar constriction, the blood which still circulates through the kidney reaches the renal vein without having been sufficiently in contact with the tubules, as if it had bypassed part or the whole of the cortex. Here we may have an example of the medullary bypass, operating in most cases without causing permanent damage to the kidney. This would suggest that the redistribution of the intrarenal blood is a mechanism of adaptation to stimuli which might vary from the light disturbance caused by cold or emotional stress to the severe disorders of shock.

The part played by renal arteriolar spasm in causing renal failure was not a new discovery. In 1925, Vollhard had already thought that acute "glomerulonephritis" was due to vascular spasm in the small renal arteries, and Kuczynski confirmed these views anatomopathologically. Hudfeldt and Bjering, in 1937, described two cases of traumatic shock which, after immediate apparent recovery, died of kidney failure at the eighth day, and suggested that the anuria was probably due to vascular spasm. Tomb, early in World War II, wrote that in "crush injury" the renal failure and associated histological changes in the tubules are caused solely by oxygen-want, the epithelial cells of the convoluted tubules being more sensitive to lack of oxygen than the endothelium of the blood capillaries. Maigraith and coworkers were of the same opinion. Many views similar to these were soon to appear after the pathology and localization of the main tubular lesions were studied. Darmady, in a series of cases with severe kidney failure following traumatic shock, found widespread necrosis of the tubular epithelium among those who died, and saw that casts occupying the tubular lumen also occurred despite the fact that only one patient had died after a crush injury. He considered renal anoxia the most likely mechanism leading to renal failure. Hicks contributed with more cases and concluded that the anuria of crush syndrome and traumatic uremia are similar in nature. Green and others also suggested that traumatic uremia by vascular spasm may show the tubules to contain casts.

The experimental evidence favoring the view that anoxia or ischemia, probably due to vascular spasm, is the general cause of kidney failure following incompatible blood transfusion, crush injuries, sulfonamide poisoning, hemorrhage, trauma, and the like, is very profuse, and only a few of these works can be mentioned here. Van Slyke and his associates caused death in dogs by renal ischemia lasting for more than 4 hours, and the histological examination showed changes in the *distal* tubules that they consider similar to those seen in "crush syndrome." Fajers, by causing ischemia to rabbits; Overman and Wang, by hemorrhage and electrical stimulation to the sciatic nerve; and Hamilton, by renal ischemia and high temperature in dogs, all caused renal failure resembling that following a crush injury. Earlier, Mason and Mann had noted the diminution of kidney volume when hemoglobin solution was injected intravenously, a diminution believed to be due to renal vasoconcentration.

It may be said in summary that a large amount of evidence now favors the view that the underlying factor causing kidney failure in "crush syndrome" and in a number of other disorders is renal ischemia, initially caused by renal spasm.

PATHOLOGY

In compression injuries, the affected extremities show local lesions mainly ischemic in nature, the muscles being the tissues which suffer most. Gross edema due to increased transudation, together with the cessation of lymphatic circulation caused by muscle inactivity, fills the affected limb. If not checked, the edema may further aggravate muscular ischemia.

Apart from a variable amount of muscle necrosis, edema, and some hemorrhage in the compressed limb, skin damage and early blistering are frequent. *The amount of muscle necrosis bears no relation to the severity of renal failure,* a number of cases having died who at autopsy showed very moderate muscle damage. But a great extent of muscle necrosis accompanies many of the severe cases, this being as much related to the "shocking" effect of a prolonged and severe compression of an extremity as to the amount of the muscle autolysis. The *liver* shows central vein necrosis and early fibrosis.

The *kidneys* appear with widespread necrosis of the tubular epithelium, most marked in the ascending and descending loops of Henle. The first convoluted tubules show currently mild degenerative changes. In the lumen of the tubule, only albuminous material may be seen, but the second convoluted tubules usually show more advanced epithelial changes and dense cast formation. The loops of Henle show a striking presence of casts. Tubular ruptures occur most commonly in the boundary zone.

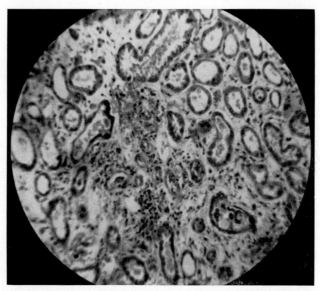

FIG. 16-2. Kidney. Hematoxylin and eosin. ($\times$ 120). Tubular necrosis in deeper part of cortex. Nuclei of cells becoming blurred or absent; lumen containing débris and desquamated cells; inflammatory cells around completely dead tubules. Mitotic figures of early regeneration visible at higher magnification.

Alteration of the glomeruli is usually minimal but frequently they appear bloodless. Renal edema is seen to be present in many cases in the early stages of the condition.

CLINICAL PICTURE

During the time the patient is pinned under the compressing debris (beams, stones or the like) the signs and symptoms of early shock appear. In air raids he is usually covered with dust, looks very pale and apathetic apart from the manifestation of pain at the compressed region. His condition changes little immediately after he is freed from the crushing rubble. During the early hours after trauma his systolic blood pressure may well be reasonably high, frequently above 110 mm Hg. If assistance is not given at once, the patient will slide downhill and develop a severe type of traumatic shock with hypothermia, collapse of blood pressure, and signs of peripheral anoxia such as bluish nails and lips and very shallow and frequent breathing.

Early oliguria, amounting in some cases to total anuria, accompanies early shock. If allowed to persist, renal tubular damage, too often irreversible, is then established. Peculiarly enough, with energetic antishock treatment, partial resumption of renal function may offer grounds for an unjustified optimism which lasts only for a short time.

The patient is thirsty and alternatively anxious or apathetic and drowsy, being well aware of the severity of his condition. If early and appropriate treatment has been given, the resumption of renal function can be maintained and the initial increase in blood urea and potassium which occurs during the early phase of "shock" is seen to diminish progressively at the time of increasing urine output. The edema of the affected and, frequently, also of the undamaged extremities tends to subside progressively and the normal condition is restored by the eighth to the tenth day. On the other hand, if there is forced delay in instituting correct treatment, or if therapy is wrongfully employed, a progressive deterioration of kidney function develops until fatal anuria with uremia and retention of potassium chloride takes place, usually between the seventh and tenth day.

The changes occurring in the compressed limb when the condition cannot be arrested are of interest. As stated before, edema is the earliest manifestation of tissue change, to which a brownish color of the skin and blisters are soon added. Skin sensation is impaired and total or partial paralysis may be present. Severe circulatory embarrassment of the entire extremity, while not exceptional, is not a frequent feature. On many occasions gangrene of the extremity or severe muscle necrosis forces one to amputate, but in those cases in which ablation of the limb was done with the aim of relieving the kidney from the damaging pigments liberated by muscle autolysis, the results have been repeatedly discouraging.

PROGNOSIS

The clinical picture and diagnosis of these patients is clear enough to prevent oversight or a misleading diagnosis, but prognosis is much more difficult. Even with the extensive experience of the war years experts were frequently unable to foresee the future of a patient suffering from this form of traumatic shock. Nevertheless, some guidance may be obtained from several sources.

Duration of Compression. The extension, number, and type of extremities affected all influence the outcome to some extent. The upper limbs cause in general less severe shock than the lower ones, and the legs less than the thighs.

Time Lag between Liberation and Treatment. In war, the fact that many of the casualties suffering from "crush syndrome" on admission appear less seriously injured than others may cause delay in treatment. This mistake could be fatal.

Age of the Patient. The work of Oldrich and his collaborators has shown that age reduces renal blood flow even in normotensive persons. In hypertensive patients, renal blood flow may be severely impaired before shock and the margin of safety may be trespassed even before collapse. Lindop has shown experimentally that anoxia by stress is increased by age. Clinical experience confirms these findings.

An indication of early severe shock is a systolic pressure below 90 mm Hg in an old patient who probably had a previous blood pressure of 160 mm Hg or more. Again, it is repeatedly found that even surgical shock affects the aged more than the young, and recovery of renal function is less prone to occur in old patients if renal anoxia has been present for some time.

Quality of Management. Prognosis depends not only on the factors mentioned above but also on the wisdom of the treatment instituted. This is particularly true during the decisive first 24 hours.

An indication of a good prognosis is the progressive reduction of the size of the affected limb. For that reason it is convenient to take circular measurements of the limb at its most prominent part. The correct recording of blood pressure and its plotting against time is also important. Thus, an *early* collapse of systolic pressure, i.e., after less than 4 hours of compression, to below 80 mm Hg is a sign of bad prognosis.

TREATMENT

Rational treatment must cover as many of the factors contributing to renal failure as possible, and for this the views expressed in the above sections on etiology and pathogenesis of renal failure must provide guidance.

During the Local Compression Lesion. First of all, pain must be controlled by morphine, 10 to 20 mg, given preferably before the victim is freed from compression. Once the patient has been relieved, the affected limb is immobilized as well as possible for transportation to the hospital. On admission, the limbs affected must be firmly bound with an elastic bandage. A Thomas splint gives satisfactory support and immobilization and allows the limb to be elevated to an angle of 45 to 50°. Rubber or plastic bottles containing ice are placed around the limb to keep it cold. Coldness reduces the metabolism of the tissues and lightens the burden on the kidneys. All these measures help to decrease fluid loss through edema. Amputation of the affected limb, even when gangrene makes it necessary, does not influence shock.

During Early Shock. The patient is almost always admitted late, frequently when peripheral vascular spasm has been causing tissue anoxia for some hours. The skin is pale white and cold but the systolic blood pressure is relatively high, not infrequently above 120 mm Hg. Immediate action must be taken if severe secondary shock is to be prevented or minimized. First the osmotic pressure of the blood must be raised by intravenous perfusion of plasma and of blood. Excessive perfusion of plasma alone may decrease the already impaired oxygen saturation of the tissues and aggravate the severity of secondary shock. This was a great mistake for which we paid dearly in the first years of the Second World War, despite the fact that the lesson had already been learned in the Governmental Army in the Spanish Civil War. Never give more than 2 pints of plasma without adding at least 1 pint of whole blood. This rule does not apply to wound shock where hemorrhage is an important part of the pathology. In such cases only blood should be given.

Large amounts of fluid made alkaline by sodium bicarbonate (1 teaspoon per pint of water) must be given per mouth. To maintain renal blood flow, sodium chloride given intravenously is of help. During the early vasoconstrictive phase of renal shock hydrates of ergot alkaloids (DHE and Hydergin) have been tried with success. Oxygen by mask or in a tent must be administered from the beginning to reduce the dangers of impending peripheral collapse.

With a view to restoring renal blood flow, transient suppression of splanchnic innervation has been done with encouraging results. The best method is that described by Hingston, using conduction anesthesia by the caudal route with an analgesic solution given for several days by means of a nylon catheter. When the level of the tenth and eleventh dorsal nerves is reached, the renal vascular spasm is abolished. This method has repeatedly succeeded in restoring renal blood flow and thus kidney function.

During the early oliguric period, a large protein breakdown occurs caused not only by muscle autolysis but particularly by the catabolism of starvation. A reduction of the protein breakdown takes place if a fat-glucose suspension is administered which provides the necessary calories (400 Gm of glucose and 100 Gm of peanut oil, mixed with acacia and 1,000 ml of water).

The administration of intravenous isotonic solutions of chloride or lactate may not achieve its purpose of causing diuresis. In this case further persistence with these perfusions may be dangerous as overloading occurs easily. Careful records must be kept of the total amount of fluid intake and of urine (and vomit) output. At regular intervals the urea concentration, alkalinity, and specific gravity of the urine must be measured and the treatment modified accordingly.

The vascular spasm and subsequent renal anoxia cause renal edema. The limited capsular elasticity may cause the edema to further increase the tubular anoxia and in some cases the only rational treatment is renal decapsulation as recommended by Peters. There is little doubt that a number of patients owe their lives to this operation. Unfortunately, this is not a minor procedure for a patient seriously ill.

During Secondary Shock. Occasionally the patient is admitted into the hospital at the beginning of collapse, that is, during the vascular paralytic phase of shock. On many occasions this state is reached while the patient is already receiving attention in a hospital bed. The blood pressure is low, the skin becomes mottled, bluish-pale, and the lips and nails cyanotic. Tachycardia and very shallow and fast breathing occurs, and hypothermia develops.

At this stage, apart from the means already mentioned to combat shock, other lifesaving procedures must be added. It must be remembered that renal embarrassment caused by tubular damage would be only transient in many cases if the patient were to live for 2 or 3 weeks, as epithelial regeneration is the rule in a high proportion of cases. Consequently, methods have been devised to bridge the dangerous period and some of these methods will now be described. They have in common the object of eliminating from the blood nitrogenous and other waste products which are responsible for causing death.

Peritoneal Irrigation. Gantner introduced peritoneal lavage in 1923 and the method was revived in 1946 by Frank and his coworkers. Odel and his associates found that, by 1948, 53 cases, of which 13 survived, had been reported in the literature.

This method attempts to use the peritoneum as a dialysing membrane, large amounts of fluid being perfused through a No. 30 mushroom catheter into the peritoneal cavity under local anaesthesia above the iliac crest. Another similar catheter is placed above the other iliac crest and both catheters are kept in position by light stitches through the peritoneum. A modified Tyrode solution with added sulfadiazine, penicillin, and heparin is dropped into one of the catheters at about 150 drops per min. The overflow is aseptically collected from the other catheter. Irrigation may go on for from 4 to 6 days at the most. This gives sufficient time for epithelial regeneration. Further evidence of the usefulness of this and similar procedures is now available.

Dialysis through the Small Intestine. Rogers and his associates experimentally in dogs, and Marquis and Schnell in the human, have tried to use the small intestine as the dialysing membrane, by placing a Miller-Abbot tube in the small intestine for gastroduodenal suction. With this method the nonprotein nitrogen of the blood has been seen to drop from 330 to 120 mg per 100 ml in 12 hours.

Modern development of the "artificial kidney" has made attempts to remove waste products from the blood by these methods less frequent. But both peritoneal irrigation and dialysis through the small intestine must be remembered in case the more elaborate methods based on complex instrumentation are not available when urgently needed.

"Artificial Kidney." Kolff and Berk introduced this method of dialysis. Successive modifications and improvements by Alwall et al. and by others have helped to popularize it and we have today a large mass of evidence on its merits as a lifesaving procedure. Survivals for more than 3 weeks after irreparable cortical necrosis have been reported. Correction of acidosis and of any electrolytic imbalance, apart from the elimination of urea, are the principal merits of the "artificial kidney." Nevertheless, the role of this apparatus should be confined to the treatment of anuria by acute nephritis, while anuria of shock should be controlled by the treatment of the responsible condition, namely, shock.

As a summary of the views expressed in this chapter it is convenient to emphasize the basic unity of the mechanism of renal failure in traumatic shock and in a number of other acute anurias with uremia. "Crush syndrome," while depending for its renal failure on the local lesions caused by the compressing object, particularly muscle ischemia with production of myohemoglobin, like the other types of shock affects the renal tubules by anoxia. Thus the whole aim in dealing with such conditions is to limit the time in which the renal tubules become damaged by oxygen lack.

In the aged patient, the natural tendency to reduced blood flow further limits the scope of success in the treatment of "renal shock." For the aged the principles of treatment set forth here are of particular importance, and immediate treatment is especially important if irreversible renal lesions are to be prevented.

BIBLIOGRAPHY

Adolph, E. F.: Asphyxia of the frog's kidneys. *Amer. Jour. Physiol.* **108**:177, 1934.

Alwall, N., L. Norvitt, and A. M. Steins: Clinical extracorporeal dialysis of blood with artificial kidney. *Lancet.* **1**:254–260, 1948.

Barnes, J. M., and J. Trueta: Arterial spasm: an experimental study. *Brit. Jour. Surg.* **30**:74, 1942.

Bick, L. V., R. T. Kempton, and A. N. Richards: *Amer. Jour. Physiol.* **122**:676, 1938.

Bloxsom, A., and N. Powell: Treatment of acute temporary dysfunction of the kidneys by peritoneal irrigation. *Pediat.* **1**:52, 1948.

Bright, R.: Reports of Medical Cases Selected with a View to Illustrating the Symptoms and Cure of Diseases by a Reference to a Morbid Anatomy. London, 1827.

Bywaters, E. G. L.: Renal anoxia. *Lancet.* **1**:254, 301, 1948.

Bywaters, E. G. L., and D. Beall: Crush injuries with impairment of renal function. *Brit. Med. Jour.* 1:427, 1941.

Cannon, W. B.: "Traumatic Shock." New York, Appleton, 1923.

Cerletti, H., R. Bircher, and E. Rothlin: *Helv. Physiol. Acta.* 7:333, 1949.

Darmady, E. M.: Renal anoxia and the traumatic uraemia syndrome. *Brit. Jour. Surg.* 34:262, 1947.

Darnadt, E. M.: "The Traumatic Uraemia Syndrome." M.D. Thesis, Cambridge University, 1946.

David, E.: *Pflugers Arch. ges. Physiol.* 208:146, 1925.

De Navasquez, S.: The excretion of haemoglobin with special reference to the "transfusion" kidney. *Jour. Path. Bact.* 51:413, 1940.

Dibbs, R. H.: Treatment of anuria following intravascular haemolysis. *Lancet.* 1:252, 360, 1947.

Dole, V. P., K. Emerson, Jr., R. A. Phillips, P. Hamilton, and D. D. Van Slyke: The renal extraction of oxygen in experimental shock. *Amer. Jour. Phys.* 145:337, 1946.

Duran-Jorda, F.: The Barcelona blood-transfusion service. *Lancet.* 1:236–773, 1939.

Fajers, C. M.: *Acta Path. Mikrobiol. Scand., Suppl.* 166, 1955.

Frank, H. A., A. M. Seligman, and J. Fine: Treatment of uremia after acute renal failure by peritoneal irrigation. *Jour. Amer. Med. Ass.* 130:703, 1946.

Franklin, K. J.: History of physiology. *Brit. Med. Jour.* 1:419, 1950.

Gantner, B.: *Münch. Med. Wchnschr.* 70:1948, 1923.

Garai, D.: *Brit. Heart Jour.* 1:260, 1945.

Green, H. D., and E. C. Hoff: Effects of faradic stimulation of the cerebral cortex on limb and renal volumes in the cat and monkey. *Amer. Jour. Physiol.* 118:641, 1937.

Green, H. N., H. B. Stoner, H. J. Whiteley, and D. Elgin: A case of traumatic uraemia. *Brit. Jour. Surg.* 39:80, 1951.

Hamilton, P. B., R. A. Phillips, and A. Hiller: Duration of renal ischemia required to produce uremia. *Amer. Jour. Physiol.* 152:517, 1948.

Hicks, J. H.: Crush syndrome and traumatic uraemia. *Lancet.* 1:254–286, 1948.

Hingston, R. A.: *Curr. Res. Anesth.* 26:117, 1947.

Hoff, E. C., J. F. Kell, N. Hastings, D. M. Sholes, and E. H. Gray: *Jour. Neurophysiol.* 14:317, 1951.

Husfeldt, E., and T. Fjering: Renal lesion from traumatic shock. *Acta Med. Scand.* 91:279, 1937.

Jardine, R., and J. H. Teacher: *Jour. Path. Bact.* 15:137, 1911.

Jasinski, Von B., and H. Brutsch: Zur Pathogenese, Prognose und Therapie traumatischer Myoglobinurien. *Schweiz. Med. Wchnschr.* 82:29, 1952.

Joekes, A. M., and G. M. Bull: Accidental haemorrhage with bilateral cortical necrosis of the kidneys treated by artificial kidney. *Proc. Roy. Soc. Med.* 41:678, 1948.

Koff, W. J., H. T. J. Berk, M. Welle, A. J. W. Van Der Ley, E. C. Van Dijk, and J. Van Noordwijk: The artificial kidney: a dialyser with a great area. *Acta. Med. Scand.* 117:121, 1944.

Krogh, A.: "The Anatomy and Physiology of Capillaries." New Haven, Conn., Yale University Press, 1929.

Kuczynski, M.: *Kran. Rheitsforsch.* 1:381, 1925.

Lindau, A.: *Acta Path. Mikrobiol. Scand.* 5:382, 1928.

Lindop, P. J.: *Gerontologia.* 12:86, 1957.

Lofgren, F.: (Personal Communication.)

Lucke, B.: *Mil. Surgeon*. **99**:371, 1946.

Lull, C. B., and R. A. Hingston: "Control of Pain in Childbirth," 3d ed. Philadelphia, Lippincott, 1948.

Maegraith, B. G.: *Trans. Roy. Soc. Trop. Med. Hyg.* **38**:1, 1944.

Maegraith, B. G., and G. M. Findlay: Oliguria in blackwater fever. *Lancet.* **2**:247, 403, 1944.

Marquis, H. H., and F. P. Schnell: The treatment of anuria by intestinal perfusion. *Amer. Jour. Med. Sci.* **215**:686, 1948.

Mason, J. B., and F. C. Mann: The effect of hemoglobin on volume of the kidney. *Amer. Jour. Physiol.* **98**:181, 1931.

Meriel, P., F. Galinier, F. M. Suc, and M. Desander: Renal shunt in shock. *Lancet.* **1**:268, 1224, 1955.

Milles, G., E. F. Muller, and W. F. Petersen: *Arch. Path.* **13**:233, 1932.

Minami, S.: Über Nierenveranderungen nach Verschüttung. *Virchows Arch. f. Path. Anat.* **245**:247, 1923.

Morison, J. E.: Obstruction of the renal tubules in myelomatosis and in crush injuries. *Jour. Path. Bact.* **53**:403, 1951.

Muller, E. F., and W. F. Petersen: *Ztschr. f. Exp. Path. u. Therap.* **66**:442, 1932.

Odel, H. M., D. O. Ferris, and M. H. Power: Clinical considerations of the problem of extrarenal excretion. *Peritoneal Lavage. Med. Clin. N. Amer.* **32**:989, 1948.

Olbrich, O.: *Rev. Med. de Liège.* **5**:647, 1950.

Olbrich, O., M. H. Ferguson, J. S. Robson, and E. P. Stenard: *Edinburgh Med. Jour.* **57**:117, 1950.

Overman, R. R., and S. C. Wang: The contributory role of the afferent nervous factor in experimental shock: sublethal hemorrhage and sciatic nerve stimulation. *Amer. Jour. Phys.* **148**:289, 1947.

Peters, J. T.: Origin and development of a new therapy for crush injury, transfusion kidney and a certain number of other diseases. *Acta. Med. Scand.* **123**:90, 1945.

Peterson, L., and M. Finland: The urinary tract in sulfanamide therapy, *Amer. Jour. Med. Sci.* **202**:757, 1941.

Reubi, F. C., H. A. Schroeder, and A. H. Williams: *Fed. Proc.* **7**:101, 1948.

Rogers, J. W., E. A., Sellers, and A. G. Gornall: Intestinal perfusion in the treatment of uremia. *Science.* **106**:108, 1947.

Tamura, K.: *Jour. Med. Sci. (Pharmacol.).* **1**:211, 1927.

Tomb, J. W.: *Med. Jour. Aust.* **2**:569, 1941.

Trueta, J.: "The Principles and Practice of War Surgery." St. Louis, Mosby, 1943.

Trueta, J., A. E. Barclay, K. J. Franklin, P. M. Daniel, and M. M. Pritchard: "Studies of the Renal Circulation." London, Oxford, 1947.

Van Slyke, D. D., R. A. Phillips, P. B. Hamilton, R. M. Archibald, V. P. Dole, and K. Emerson, Jr.: *Trans. Amer. Physiol.* 58, 119.

Von Colmers: *Arch. f. Klin. Chir.* **90**:701, 1909.

Chapter 17

Craniocerebral Injuries

William J. German

Craniocerebral injuries in the aged differ little from similar injuries among younger adults. The basic differences are related to recovery potential, diagnosis, complications, and a slight predisposition to subdural hematoma formation. The summation of all factors related to age is most evident in the high mortality rates of acute head injury to the aged. Gurdjian and Webster reported 41 deaths among 143 such injuries in patients 61 years of age and older, a mortality rate of 29 per cent. This compared with 16 per cent mortality in the age group 51 to 60 and 10 per cent in the 41 to 50 span. These data were derived from a series of 1,285 cases of various ages with 144 fatalities, an over-all mortality of 11 per cent.

RECOVERY POTENTIAL

The process of aging is frequently associated with specific structural and physiological alterations in the brain which have a bearing upon the response of that organ to injury. Structural changes in the cerebral parenchyma are of the atrophic type, affecting the neurons of both the cortical and central gray matter. The net result of such atrophy is a slight reduction in the size of the brain, the intracranial volume being maintained by an increase of cerebrospinal fluid commensurate with the degree of brain atrophy. Under these circumstances the brain becomes more movable within its hard cranial confines and thus more subject to trauma from acceleration and deceleration of the head.

Cerebral physiological alterations associated with aging, the functional counterpart of neuron atrophy, may have a causal relation to injuries by virtue of slower reactions in perceiving and avoiding danger. Similarly, minor degrees of incoordination in the aged lead to falls, industrial accidents, and various types of injuries. In brief, the aged are somewhat more prone to injury. However, it is the alterations in the vascular system, so frequently associated with aging, which influence more specifically the effects of craniocerebral trauma. Since this aspect of the problem is not generally appreciated, a brief outline of its basis will be given.

The brain derives its energy almost entirely from the oxidation of glucose, each mole of which requires six moles of oxygen and delivers about 670 calories together with six moles each of CO_2 and water.* The brain extracts about 10 per cent of the glucose from the blood passing through it. The oxygen requirement of the brain under basic conditions is 3.3 cc per 100 Gm of brain per minute. This is readily supplied by the average cerebral blood flow of 54 ml per 100 Gm of brain per minute in normal young adults, amounting to about 17 per cent of the resting cardiac output. However, the cerebral blood flow in the aged may be considerably reduced (as low as 43 ml), approaching the critical level of 30 ml. Similarly, the cerebral respiratory rate decreases with aging, having an average value of 2.4 cc O_2 per 100 Gm per minute in a series of subjects 50 to 92 years of age. Thus aging is associated with a 20 per cent reduction in cerebral blood flow and over 25 per cent reduction in cerebral oxygen consumption. The role of the vascular system in relation to these factors may be expressed in terms of cerebral vascular resistance, the mean blood pressure required to propel 1 ml of blood through 100 Gm of brain per minute. In normal young adults this amounts to 1.6 cerebrovascular resistance units. Assuming a blood pressure of 150/100 in an older subject, with a cerebral blood flow of 43 ml, the vascular resistance is increased 80 per cent to 2.9 units. The significance of all this in regard to craniocerebral trauma is that such injuries tend to increase cerebrovascular resistance and introduce a temporary increment in oxygen demand. Thus the aged patient has a considerable potential for a serious cerebrovascular deficit.

In addition to the above factors, there is a general tendency in elderly individuals toward slower and less complete recovery from all types of injuries. Psychological factors contribute to this tendency, such as enforced absence from employment or usual environment, lessened drive toward recovery, or minor psychotic effects. Finally, serious mental and emotional disturbances are not infrequent sequels to severe head injuries in the aged, especially in those with preexisting cerebrovascular disease.

DIAGNOSIS

In younger individuals the diagnosis of a head injury is usually evident *ipso facto*. The aged, however, may fall as the result of syncope or spontaneous cerebrovascular accident, and even evidence of external injury to the head may be insufficient grounds for assuming a purely traumatic incident. An accurate history of the circumstances of the fall is important under these conditions, but it may be difficult or impossible to obtain. X-ray confirmation of a fracture of the skull is at least an indication of

* About 15 per cent of the glucose is metabolized by glycolysis only, resulting chiefly in lactic acid.

the application of considerable force to the cranium, but it does not exclude the possibility of a coexisting spontaneous cerebrovascular accident. Recovery of consciousness within a day or two with a prolonged residual hemiparesis or other marked neurological deficit favors the diagnosis of spontaneous cerebrovascular accident. When an early fatality occurs, post-mortem examination of the brain may reveal the true answer to the situation, but even this is not infallible. The problem is most compelling when medicolegal aspects are involved, including the double-indemnity clause in many life insurance policies for accidental death. It may be helpful to recognize that craniocerebral trauma superimposed upon a spontaneous cerebrovascular accident is at least an aggravating factor and may make the difference between survival and fatality.

Diagnosis of head injury includes assessment of evidence indicative of increased intracranial pressure. Signs such as bradycardia, elevated blood pressure, and rhythmic respirations are highly suggestive of intracranial pressure elevation when they are found in younger patients. In the elderly subject of cranial trauma such factors as heart block, auricular fibrillation, digitalis medication, vascular hypertension, and Cheyne-Stokes respirations during sleep introduce an element of uncertainty regarding the significance of these signs. This is especially true when the medical background of the patient is unknown to the clinician responsible for the care of the craniocerebral injury.

There is no doubt that accurate diagnosis of the type and degree of intracranial injury in senescent individuals is uncommonly difficult. However, regardless of age, certain well-established diagnostic principles are usually productive of satisfactory results. These include assessment of the circumstances surrounding the injury, with special reference to the probable amount of force applied to the head, the state of consciousness immediately following the accident, and subsequent alterations of consciousness prior to examination. While complete examination at the earliest time is highly desirable, preliminary attention must be directed to such factors as inadequate respiratory function, hemorrhage, shock, splinting of long bone fractures, and the possibility of concomitant spinal injury, especially in the cervical region.

Having disposed of these matters, the state of consciousness may be estimated. This will include the response to verbal stimuli, light painful, or strong painful, or no stimuli. The state of the pupils is extremely important in the unconscious patient at this time and throughout the subsequent course. Unilateral pupillary dilatation (third cranial nerve) during the first 6 to 8 hours is highly suggestive of extradural hematoma. Bilaterally dilated and fixed pupils frequently herald an early fatality associated with a tentorial pressure cone. Similarly, extreme pupillary constriction is an omen of pontine damage, though an elderly patient with glaucoma may have medicinally constricted pupils. Evaluation of motor function in the unconscious patient depends upon observation of spontaneous movements, if any, and motor responses to "painful" stimuli, together with the normal and pathological reflexes. The optic fundi should be examined, though it is unusual to find papilledema during the first 12 hours, regardless of the degree of intracranial pressure.

Needless to say, the neurological examination should be as complete as the patient's state of consciousness and cooperation permits. With the exception of suspected compound fracture of the skull or extradural hematoma, it is probably wise to postpone x-ray examinations until the elderly patient's condition has stabilized. Subsequent observation should include recording of the vital signs (pulse, blood pressure and respirations), the state of the pupils and of consciousness, at 15 to 30 minute intervals until there is definite evidence that the patient is improving. The temperature should be checked every 1 to 2 hours at the outset.

When the initial examination is completed, the first attempt at precise diagnosis may be made. It is helpful at this time to estimate the prognosis, with special reference to the probable duration of unconsciousness, based upon all the information so far assembled. In this way it may be possible to suspect the presence of a progressive surgical lesion (hematoma), when the patient's progress becomes less favorable than the original estimate indicated. The insidious development of subdural hematoma is especially likely to occur in elderly patients.

CLASSIFICATION OF CRANIOCEREBRAL INJURIES

It is obvious from the foregoing that some form of classification is necessary. The following outline has the advantage of simplicity; most of the entities may exist alone or combined with others.

CLASSIFICATION OF CRANIOCEREBRAL INJURIES

I. Scalp
   A. Abrasion
   B. Contusion (hematoma)
   C. Laceration (surgery indicated)
   D. Avulsion (surgery indicated)
II. Cranium
   A. Fracture
     1. Simple
      a. Linear (bursting)
      b. Depressed (bending; surgery indicated)
     2. Compound
      a. External (surgery indicated)
      b. Into sinuses, nose (surgery indicated), or ear.

III. Intracranial
    A. Concussion (usually brief unconsciousness)
    B. Contusion-laceration (neurological deficit and longer unconsciousness)
    C. Swelling (edema may be progressive)
    D. Hemorrhage
        1. Extradural (immediate surgery urgent; latent interval usually less than 6 hours)
        2. Subdural (surgery indicated; latent interval usually days or weeks)
        3. Subarachnoid (frequently associated with contusion-laceration)
        4. Parenchymal (surgery indicated; high mortality if large)
        5. Ventricular (usually fatal)

Since the purpose of this book is to indicate the special problems of trauma to the aged, reference is made to general works on craniocerebral injuries for details of diagnosis and treatment not specifically pertaining to elderly patients. This is not to imply that older individuals are spared from the usual injuries, but merely that their problems are similar enough to those of younger age to exclude particular consideration here. However, chronic subdural hematoma is sufficiently pertinent to the aged to justify its special consideration at the conclusion of this chapter. Other features of treatment of special interest to the older age group will be included under complications.

SPECIAL DIAGNOSTIC PROCEDURES

Radiographic examination of the skull is indicated in most patients subjected to head trauma, regardless of age. However, as previously noted, it may be advisable to delay this procedure for hours or even days, until it is certain that the patient's condition will not be affected adversely by the disturbance and manipulation involved. In the last analysis, the information of advantage to the patient which can be obtained from radiographic examination is limited to compound or depressed fractures, an occasional fracture across the middle meningeal groove in extradural hematoma suspects, and shift of a calcified pineal body in space-occupying lesions. The condition of elderly patients may be very unstable during the first few hours after a serious head injury, and any diagnostic procedure not clearly and immediately indicated may amount to the proverbial last straw.

Electroencephalography is unlikely to supply significant information in the early posttrauma period. Toward the end of the first week it may give a hint of the presence of a subdural hematoma, on the basis of low voltage and slow waves over the involved hemisphere. A procedure without risk, it can be recommended in the elderly patient at the appropriate time. Information may also be obtained concerning a convulsive tendency as a result of brain contusion-laceration. *A word of caution may be added regarding the interpretation of minor abnormalities, especially in older individuals. Such abnormalities may be without significant relation to the head trauma.* This problem is most likely to arise in regard to the medicolegal aspects of such injuries.

Lumbar puncture raises a question upon which there is a great diversity of opinion. It is not unlikely that the intrinsic hazards of the procedure are magnified in senescent patients. *Early* lumbar puncture is clearly indicated only when the diagnosis of head injury is obscure and meningitis is suspected. During the second or third day, if the patient is still unconscious but otherwise in a reasonably satisfactory condition, cerebrospinal fluid studies, including pressure, Ayala index, amount of blood, and xanthochromia, may give information of value concerning the possibility of a subdural or intracerebral hematoma. The persistence of xanthochromia into the third week is a definite suggestion of the presence of a subdural hematoma. The Queckenstedt test is strictly contraindicated in the presence of an intracranial lesion.

Pneumoencephalography is not indicated in the acute phase of craniocerebral trauma at any age. The hazards of lumbar puncture are multiplied and the desired information can be obtained by other procedures at less risk to the patient. It is doubtful whether pneumoencephalography is ever desirable in problems of head injury in the aged. The frequent association of vascular hypotension, nausea, and vomiting while the subject is restrained in the sitting position could provoke a cerebral thrombosis.

Ventriculography is not without risk, especially in elderly patients, but at times the information obtained from it may be of sufficient advantage to the patient to justify its use. This is especially true when the clinical evidence suggests the presence of a space-occupying mass (hematoma) which has not been disclosed by preliminary exploratory burr holes. Thus it may be combined with the latter more direct procedure. It is seldom indicated in extradural hematoma suspects, where the time interval available for successful relief of intracranial pressure may be so brief that nothing short of exploration in the appropriate area (usually temporal) will suffice. However, it may be the means by which a chronic subdural hematoma is brought to light.

Arteriography has achieved a position of considerable popularity as a diagnostic tool since it was introduced in 1927. Its present relative safety, with such newer media as Hypaque, together with the high yield of useful information which may be obtained, has made it the first choice among indirect diagnostic measures of many neurologists. It is relatively safe for traumatic space-occupying lesions in most age groups, but since cerebral arterial occlusion (or spasm) is its most frequent adverse effect, it may not be recommended unequivocally in the aged subject. Before using it in the senescent group it is well to ask oneself if the problem cannot be solved by a safer method.

Trephination, a time-honored procedure, serves a dual function, being both diagnostic and therapeutic for subdural hematoma and occasionally for intracerebral hematoma. It is usually well tolerated by elderly patients and is the method of choice of this writer in those instances where the suspicion of subdural hematoma is great. Initial bilateral burr holes just above the superior attachment of the temporal muscles, about equidistant between the frontal and occipital poles, have the highest statistical probability of a positive yield for subdural hematomas. Next in the order of probability is the frontal area, followed by the occipital regions. If the pathology is not thus disclosed and the brain is found to be under increased tension, ventriculography may be done through the occipital burr holes, to confirm or exclude an intracerebral hematoma. The entire procedure is readily accomplished under local anesthesia with minimum disturbance to the patient.

COMPLICATIONS

The aged are subject to all the complications of other groups plus those intrinsic to advancing years. Some of the former are specifically related to the injury to the brain. Thus, *convulsions* in the acute phase are usually indicative of cerebral contusion-laceration or one of the varieties of hemorrhage. Delayed convulsions may represent posttraumatic epilepsy from a cortical scar, or may be due to the presence of a chronic subdural hematoma. *Decerebrate rigidity* is one of the results of severe injury to the brain stem and is an extremely grave prognostic sign, especially in older patients.

Hyperthermia, also frequently related to brain stem or hypothalamic injury, is of particularly serious import in elderly individuals. The metabolism of all tissue is increased by elevation of temperature. Fever therefore places an added burden on the vascular system already operating at a minimal margin of safety in the brains of many aged persons. The routine treatment for hyperthermia until recently has been limited to the use of such antipyretic agents as aspirin (per rectum), alcohol sponges with or without fanning to the skin, and cold rectal taps, all with the modes objective of preventing excessive elevation of body temperature. Lately, means have become available for the induction of hypothermia by controlled refrigeration. It is still too early to assess the results, but experimental evidence indicates that the nervous system is capable of tolerating both vascular deficiencies and certain types of trauma at temperatures of 30°C which are poorly accepted by the brain at or above normal body temperature. The metabolism of the brain may be considered as following van't Hoff's rule that the velocity of chemical reactions is increased twofold or more for each rise of 10°C in temperature. At present, moderate induced hypothermia appears logical in elderly patients, especially when increasing fever is threatened.

Other complications, such as pneumocephalus, cerebrospinal rhinorrhea, meningitis, brain abscess, osteomyelitis, otitis media, and mastoiditis are related to potential or actual infection, hazardous at any age but more so in elderly individuals. Their treatment is the same at any age: chemotherapy, elimination of external connections with the intracranial space, and removal of infected material. Fat embolism is an unusual complication unrelated to age and usually associated with fracture of a long bone. It may induce a clinical state which is difficult to distinguish from one of the forms of intracranial hematoma if the patient has co-existing evidence of head injury. The presence of petechiae about the lower neck and upper chest (or fat in the sputum or urine) is strong evidence of fat embolism. The interference with intracranial circulation makes this an especially serious complication in elderly individuals.

The complications more specifically related to old age are those affecting the *pulmonary, cardiovascular* and *urinary systems*. Under basal conditions, the brain utilizes about 20 per cent of the oxygen supplied by the lungs, and at any given moment there is a reserve of oxygen in the brain sufficient to support its normal metabolism for only 10 seconds. From these facts it is clear that either pulmonary or circulatory deficiency can lead rapidly to cerebral hypoxia. It is especially important that adequate pulmonary ventilation be maintained at all times in elderly subjects of head injury. If this cannot be accomplished by appropriate posturing, oral or nasal airway, and clearing of secretions by gentle suction, tracheotomy should be done without delay. *An oxygen tent is no substitute for an adequate ventilatory system.* One may see a remarkable improvement in the previously deteriorating condition of an elderly patient several hours after tracheotomy. Many patients in this age group have very limited respiratory reserves on the basis of chronic pulmonary diseases. The lessened dead space and resistance afforded by tracheotomy may be of great advantage under these circumstances.

Cerebral circulation must be maintained in spite of increased cerebrovascular resistance, common to both intracranial injury and old age. Thus, a prolongation of even a mild degree of shock cannot be tolerated. The hypertensive individual whose usual systolic blood pressure is 180 may be at a considerable circulatory disadvantage with a pressure of 120. Such cardiac problems as decompensation, fibrillation, or heart block should receive adequate treatment as soon as possible.

Urinary tract complications begin with the problem of bladder care in the unconscious patient. This is usually best handled by drainage with a three-way retention catheter of the Foley type, and mild urinary anti-sepsis. The problem may be compounded by the presence of prostatic hypertrophy, making catheterization difficult or impossible. Impaired renal function is not uncommon among elderly individuals, and the transition from a posttraumatic unconscious state to one related to uremia may be almost imperceptible. Appropriate blood chemistry deter-minations are indicated for this, as well as for the possibility of unsus-pected diabetes or electrolyte disturbances.

CHRONIC SUBDURAL HEMATOMA

When blood remains in the subdural space for 2 or 3 weeks, a menin-geal membrane forms a capsule around it, constituting a chronic sub-dural hematoma. Such lesions appear to have a slowly expansile charac-ter, permitting a considerable latent interval before the appearance of secondary symptoms. Furthermore, the initiating trauma may be of such a mild nature as to be overlooked by the subject. Although the condition occurs in all age groups, the tendency toward cerebral atrophy in the elderly gives greater opportunity for the movement of the brain within the cranium, movement which can tear a spanning vein between the cerebrum and the superior sagittal sinus. It is this type of injury which accounts for most chronic subdural hematomas. In a group of such patients personally observed by the writer, 72 per cent were over 40 years of age, 43 per cent were over 50. The insidious nature of this entity is further emphasized by the fact that 47 per cent of the 47 patients in this series gave no history of previous head trauma. Among those patients with a history of known head injury the symptomatic latent interval averaged about 1 month. The longest duration of symptoms in any pa-tient was over 2 years.

Symptoms in this series frequently failed to give a strong clue to the diagnosis. The more common ones were: headache, 78 per cent; mental changes, 74 per cent; drowsiness, 47 per cent; nausea and vomiting, 38 per cent; motor disturbances, 30 per cent. The symptomatic onset was usually vague, though in eight patients it consisted of sudden collapse with loss of consciousness. Conversely, two patients lacked any specific symptoms, the hematomas being incidental autopsy findings.

Signs of chronic subdural hematoma are notoriously difficult to inter-pret. In the series cited, papilledema was present in 28 per cent, with another 23 per cent having blurred optic discs or engorged retinal veins. Pupillary changes were present in 36 per cent, but the dilated pupil was on the side of the lesion only slightly more often than the reverse, and four of the seven patients with bilateral hematomas had unilateral pupil-lary dilatation. Motor and reflex abnormalities were present in about half the patients, but these signs were of positive localizing value in only half of this group.

Diagnostic procedures are often required to arrive at the diagnosis of chronic subdural hematoma. In the present series, lumbar puncture disclosed either increased pressure, xanthochromia, or elevated protein in 21 of 31 patients. X-ray studies of the skull revealed a lateral shift of the calcified pineal body in 20 per cent. Ventriculography demonstrated the presence and location of a space-occupying lesion in 12 of 18 patients, while the hematoma was encountered and drained during the course of the procedure in the remaining 6.

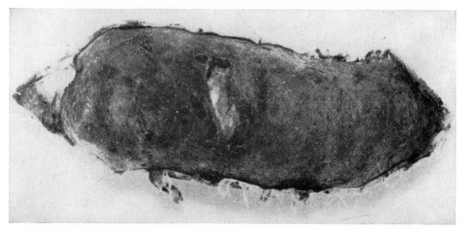

FIG. 17-1. Chronic subdural hematoma of 8 months' duration, removed intact by osteoplastic craniotomy. The symptoms began insidiously about 3 months after an apparently mild head injury and consisted of blurring vision, headache, emotional instability, impaired memory, followed by urinary incontinence, speech difficulty and finally right hemiparesis. The hematoma measured 14 by 5 by 3 cm. The previously adherent, shaggy dural aspect is shown, the reverse arachnoid aspect was smooth and glistening. The fringe about the margin marks the fusion of the two membranes.

Treatment usually consists of drainage of the hematoma through one or more burr holes in the skull. After removal of the customary redbrown fluid by saline irrigation, subsequent expansion of the brain may be facilitated by lowering the patient's head below the horizontal and leaving a soft drain in the hematoma cavity for 1 or 2 days. Recurrent symptoms usually indicate retained fluid, requiring further drainage. Rarely, an osteoplastic craniotomy may be necessary to remove a densely organized hematoma (Fig. 17-1). The operative mortality bears a striking relation to the preoperative state of consciousness. Thus, in the present series, of the nine patients treated while in coma, three died. The mortality for all other patients operated upon was 3.8 per cent. The urgency for early operation is obvious from these figures.

SPINAL CORD AND ROOT INJURIES

Elderly persons are subject to the same types of injuries to the spinal cord and its roots that occur in other age groups. However, they are usually spared that tragic result of a flexed-neck dive into shallow water, transection of the cervical spinal cord, though similar injuries occasionally result from falls among the aged. Traumas to the thoracic and lumbar cord are commonly associated with fractures of the spine. These are discussed by Bick in Chap. 7. Ruptured intervertebral discs with spinal root compression are rather uncommon in elderly individuals, but such injuries acquired earlier in life may continue to plague the patient into senescence.

CERVICAL SPONDYLOSIS

This condition has been reported in a high percentage of patients over the age of 60. Radiographic evidences of the disorder are of two general types, (1) narrowing of the spinal canal, and (2) encroachment on the neural foramina. Each of these was noted in 75 per cent of a series of patients over 50 years of age. Aside from the capabilities of cord and cervical root symptomatology inherent in these entities, they may play a significant role in response to injury to the neck of older persons. Falls and vigorous hyperextension-hyperflexion movements of the neck are the usual mechanisms involved. In the presence of cervical spondylosis, the reduced space available for the cord and roots increases the probability of their injury. Furthermore, the ligament flava tend to fold inward in a series of accordion pleats when the neck is in hyperextension, further decreasing the volume remaining for the neural structures. When evidence of cord injury follows trauma of this type in the absence of fracture or dislocation of the cervical spine, it is likely that the condition under discussion is present. The other reasonable alternative is an acute massive rupture of a cervical intervertebral disc.

The clinical syndrome in such patients may be that of the anterior cervical cord: paralysis and loss of pain and temperature sense below the level of the lesion, with relative retention of other sensory modalities. In other instances root symptoms, both motor and sensory, may predominate. In the latter case conservative treatment, such as immobilization with light head traction in a neutral or slightly flexed position of the neck, will usually suffice. When signs of severe cord dysfunction are present, laminectomy must be considered. If bladder paralysis is included, this should receive immediate attention with a retention catheter and appropriate urinary antisepsis. The question of tidal drainage of the bladder depends upon the familiarity of the nursing staff with this rather "temperamental" apparatus. Unimpeded bladder drainage is preferable to a poorly functioning tidal drainage. This and other general therapeutic problems are similar to those of the paraplegic in the younger age groups and need not be further considered here. However, it is worthy of emphasis that meticulous care of the skin to prevent wetness or pressure, leading to decubitus ulcer formation, is even more important in elderly patients. Use of a turning mechanism such as a Foster or Stryker frame or alternating pressure air mattress, is recommended.

Special surgical considerations are required for the elderly patient with cervical spondylosis who develops paraplegia after an injury to the neck, without fracture or dislocation. The prevalent neurosurgical policy in opposition to laminectomy for acute cervical spinal cord injuries does not apply unequivocally in this instance. Nor does the criterion of a spinal fluid block, as determined by a positive Queckenstedt test, serve as a clear indication in regard to operation. The spinal fluid channels are usually patent in these cases. Although myelography is thought by some to be undesirable, because of the tendency to impose hyperextension of the neck during the procedure, the writer would recommend its cautious use. The injection of 9 ml of Pantopaque into the lumbar subarachnoid space provides a sufficient bolus of opaque material to fill the anterior cervical canal through the probable area of involvement, C3 to C7. With the patient in a prone posture on the fluoroscopic tip-table, the neck is gently moved into a position of *very slight* extension, to avoid precipitous flow of the opaque medium into the cranial cavity. The head of the table is then lowered until the Pantopaque begins to flow over the dorsum rotundum, when the declivity of the table should be lessened to prevent cascading of the medium, which is to be pooled in the cervical region. These are the only recommended modifications of the usual cervical myelographic technique.

Having determined the site or sites of canal narrowing and assessed the probability of associated disc rupture by myelography, one is in a position to evaluate the advisability of laminectomy. Furthermore, the details of the operative approach can be planned in logical sequence. There are several alternatives: simple decompressive laminectomy, extradural (or transdural) removal of extruded disc, or section of denticulate ligaments. All save the latter are standard neurosurgical procedures, not especially pertinent to the elderly patient with spondylosis. Further discussion will therefore be limited to the last procedure.

The tethering effect of the denticulate ligaments upon the cervical cord in the presence of anterior encroachment upon the spinal canal by either a midline ruptured disc or spondylosis, has been neatly demonstrated in a study of stress analysis by Kahn. The loci of primary and secondary stress correspond to the locations of the pyramidal and spinothalamic tracts, thus coinciding with the anterior cervical cord syndrome. The denticulate ligaments, frail in appearance but strong in tension, bind the cord against the anterior canal encroachment, constituting the primary stress, and by traction deformation of the cord, produce secondary stress at the sites of their attachments. When these ligaments are cut, the cord migrates into the posterior aspect of the canal, ample to receive it by virtue of the laminectomy and removal of the ligamenta flava, intrinsic to the operative exposure.

While detailed operative technique is outside the scope of this book, a few highlights may be outlined. The type of anesthesia must be decided on the basis of each individual patient. If endotracheal anesthesia is used, intubation must be accomplished without hyperextension of the neck. Local anesthesia has many advantages, but it may be difficult to avoid pain when working near the roots. Certainly these structures should be blocked individually as they become available. For posturing on the operating table, the writer has come to prefer the lateral recumbent position. This avoids the hazards intrinsic to the prone and sitting postures and affords a surprisingly satisfactory exposure of the dependent aspect of the cord. After laminectomy, it is customary to explore the extradural space with regard to extruded discs before opening the dura. However, it may be safer to release the tethered cord before removing the ruptured disc. In any case, section of the denticulate ligaments is readily accomplished through a midline dural opening with evacuation of subarachnoid fluid. The ligaments are lifted individually on a nerve hook and cut near their dural attachments. If root symptoms have been present, decompression of the involved roots is indicated. Meticulous closure of the dura should prevent the possible complication of a surgical meningocele.

The anterior cervical cord syndrome discussed here may have an insidious onset without relation to specific neck injury. However, in the last analysis, it might be considered as a traumatic condition, related to daily activity involving flexion and extension of the neck causing repeated minimal stresses to the cord. The diagnosis and treatment are the same as have been described for the acute syndrome.

BIBLIOGRAPHY

Evans, J. P.: "Acute Head Injury." Springfield, Ill., Charles C Thomas, 1950.
German, W. J., W. R. Page, and L. S. Nims: Cerebral blood flow and cerebral

oxygen consumption in experimental intracranial injury. *Trans. Am. Neur. Ass.* **72**:86, 1947.

Gurdjian, E. S., and J. E. Webster: "Head Injuries." Boston, Little, Brown, 1958.

Kahn, E. A.: The role of the dentate ligaments in spinal cord compression and the syndrome of lateral sclerosis. *J. Neurosurg.* 4:191, 1947.

Kahn, E. A., R. C. Bassett, R. C. Schneider, and E. C. Crosby: "Correlative Neurosurgery." Springfield, Ill., Charles C Thomas, 1955.

McIlwain, H.: "Biochemistry and the Central Nervous System." Boston, Little, Brown, 1955.

Pallis, C., A. M. Jones, and J. D. Spillane: Cervical spondylosis. *Brain.* **77**:274, 1954.

Chapter 18

Vascular and Cardiac Trauma

John L. Madden

In peacetime, trauma to the heart and major blood vessels in the aged occurs under circumstances which are entirely similar to the occurrence of the same type of injury in the young adult. Regardless of the patient's age, the basic principles of treatment remain the same. However, admittedly in the elderly, degenerative changes in the cardiovascular system are commonly present, and accordingly the prognosis for both life and limb is in general more grave.

The common sources of cardiovascular trauma in the aged are: vehicular collisions, occupational injuries, falls from high places, blunt trauma of varying types, and occasionally knife and gunshot wounds. For the sake of clarity, the types of cardiovascular injuries will be considered under three separate headings, namely: (1) venous trauma, (2) arterial trauma, and (3) cardiac trauma.

VENOUS TRAUMA

LACERATIONS

The treatment of a lacerated vein will vary somewhat depending upon its size, location, and the type of injury that has been sustained. Generally the most rapidly effective method for hemostasis is digital compression.

In the extremities, particularly in their distal portions, elevation and the application of a firm compression dressing usually suffices to control bleeding. However, in the more proximal areas, either digital compression or clamps for hemostasis may be required.

In the cervical region, lacerations of the external and internal jugular veins may terminate rapidly in death if hemorrhage is not promptly controlled. The hazard in an aged person is considerably greater than in a younger adult. Hemostasis is most readily accomplished by digital compression overlying the site of injury. Once adequate hemostasis is obtained, the digital compression is continued until some form of de-

415

finitive surgical treatment may be substituted. In the interim, resuscitative measures to stabilize the patient's condition should be prescribed. These would include the administration of fluids, plasma, and blood, the maintenance of body heat, and the judicious use of sedatives.

The type of definitive surgical treatment employed is dependent upon the character of the laceration. In some lacerations, hemostasis may be obtained with sutures of fine silk swedged on minimum-trauma needles. In others, such as large, irregular, and jagged lacerations, it may prove necessary to clamp, sever and ligate the vein.

In some semiclosed or closed injuries of the cervical veins a rapidly expanding hematoma may enlarge with such rapidity that acute compression of the trachea and impending suffocation rather than blood loss are of prime importance. This complication should be treated by immediate incision of the overlying tissues and evacuation of the expanding hematoma. Dependent upon the response of the patient, a tracheostomy may or may not be necessary. If one doubts its necessity, this in itself may be considered a good indication to perform the operation. It is much better to err by performing a tracheostomy too early than too late, especially in the elderly where oxygenation is often in precarious balance for reasons unrelated to the trauma.

In the management of acute massive hemorrhage of venous origin, one cannot overemphasize the importance of digital compression for the immediate control of bleeding and the resuscitation and stabilization of the patient prior to any attempt to obtain definitive hemostasis.

In stab wounds and gunshot wounds of the abdomen, injury to the mesenteric veins and inferior vena cava may occur. Usually this is evidenced by the clinical manifestations of acute blood loss and the presence of shock dependent upon the severity of the hemorrhage. Fortunately, in such types of abdominal wounds, the principal indication for operation is to exclude injury to the intraperitoneal viscera. Accordingly, if a concomitant vascular injury is unsuspected clinically, the diagnosis may be made at the time of exploration.

The control of bleeding from the mesenteric veins is dependent upon the particular findings in the individual patient. In some instances, one or more veins may be lacerated with active bleeding into the peritoneal cavity. Under such circumstances, hemostasis is readily obtained by the use of clamps and ligatures. In other instances, the hemorrhage is enclosed within the "leaves" of the mesentery. Depending upon the severity of the hemorrhage, this may result in either spontaneous stoppage of bleeding or its continuance as an expanding hematoma, terminating in compromise to the circulation of a varying-sized segment of the bowel. If the circulation to the bowel is irreversibly compromised, or if in doubt, segmental resection, well beyond the area of devitalized gut, and primary end-to-end anastomosis, preferably of the "open" type, is done. Age in this vital circumstance may not in the least suggest any degree of conservatism. Contrariwise, if the bowel is viable, one may or may not elect to incise the hematoma within the mesentery, evacuate the clots, and control the source of hemorrhage. The decision in this regard would depend upon the size and character of the hematoma. In large, expanding hematomas, incision to relieve pressure and control bleeding is required, whereas in those of the nonexpanding variety, either small or moderate in size, spontaneous hemostasis usually occurs and nothing further need be done.

In lacerations of the vena cava, bleeding into the free peritoneal cavity may occur, or more commonly, retroperitoneal hematomas of varying size may form according to the severity and duration of the hemorrhage. When patients with such lesions are seen in the emergency room of a hospital, they are frequently in profound hemorrhagic shock and show all the clinical manifestations of acute blood loss: marked pallor, thirst, restlessness, cold, clammy perspiration, dyspnea, and a rapid pulse of small volume. Concomitant with the treatment of shock, preparations for immediate operation should be made. If one waits too long for a complete response to resuscitative measures, the delay may lead to irreversible shock and death. However, resuscitative treatment concomitant to early operation will give these patients the best chance for recovery. It is only by early control of the source of bleeding that the hemorrhagic shock state can be treated in a definitive manner. It is of interest to note that in Dale's report of 1958, he listed 16 cases of ligation of the vena cava. Six were over 60 years of age, and five of these were over 70!

When operation is performed, exposure of the inferior vena cava may be easily obtained if the right side of the colon is mobilized by severance of the fascia fusion layer of Toldt, the so called "white line," and reflected toward the midline (Fig. 18-1). The retroperitoneal clots are quickly evacuated and the site or sites of hemorrhage from the vena cava are controlled by firm digital compression (Fig. 18-1E). Once this is accomplished, nothing further is done until the condition of the patient is stabilized by adequate blood replacement. The retroperitoneal area is then thoroughly irrigated with copious quantities of warm saline solution which is evacuated by suction siphonage. Two long "stick sponges" are used to occlude the vena cava, cephalad and caudad respectively to the area of digital compression, and the compression is slowly released. One may then unhurriedly survey the extent and type of injury and determine the method of repair. If desired, single or multiple Babcock clamps,* modified on the Potts' principle, or a curved Potts' clamp, the type which is generally employed in doing a portacaval shunt, may be used to

* Manufactured by Edward Weck & Company, Inc., Brooklyn, N.Y.

occlude the site of laceration and the "stick sponges" may be removed (Fig. 18-1F). Digital compression of the vein between the thumb and index finger is also a useful, ever-ready, and rapid means of effective hemostasis preparatory to a suture closure of the rent. It is believed that the ordinary type of clamp used for hemostasis predisposes the vein to further damage and should not, if at all possible, be employed. The same admonition applies to the use of gauze packing, namely, to employ it only as a last resort. Subsequent to the control of bleeding from the vena cava, the wound is closed in layers, preferably without drainage, even though a concomitant intestinal resection may have been required.

Ideally, closure of lacerations of the inferior vena cava should be done with either continuous or interrupted sutures of 00000 silk swedged on a minimum-trauma needle. If the rent in the vena cava is caudad to the renal veins and the extent of the damage precludes a satisfactory closure by the suture method, double ligation in continuity on either side of the injured segment, or transection between clamps and double ligation of the severed ends, may be done. However, if the injury is cephalad to the renal veins, primary closure of the defect is mandatory. The same applies to tears of the renal veins. In this regard, if suture repair is not possible and bleeding cannot otherwise be controlled, nephrectomy must be performed. In spite of the advanced age of the patient, lacerations of the vena cava demand heroic measures as the only chance of saving life.

THROMBOPHLEBITIS

Acute traumatic thrombophlebitis is not an infrequent complication of trauma to the lower extremities. In fact, it may occur following the simplest form of trauma. It is not uncommon, particularly in the aged, to have it occur when the sitting posture is assumed for prolonged intervals, as in traveling by either plane or automobile. However, acute traumatic thrombophlebitis is more commonly associated with direct injury such as contusions, burns, and fractures of the lower extremities. Paradoxically, it is rarely a complication of either hemiplegia or paraplegia despite the presence of multiple predisposing factors.

Symptoms. The symptoms are dependent upon the system of veins that is involved, namely, the superficial or deep. Acute traumatic superficial thrombophlebitis usually occurs in patients with preexisting and usually asymptomatic varicose veins. It is a relatively common finding in the aged. The symptoms may vary from a palpable, nontender, noninflammatory segmental thrombosis to an extensive, tender, and rapidly propagating thrombotic occlusion of the whole superficial saphenous system of veins. Characteristically, despite the local severity of the symptoms, pitting edema of the extremity is absent. Furthermore, pulmonary em-

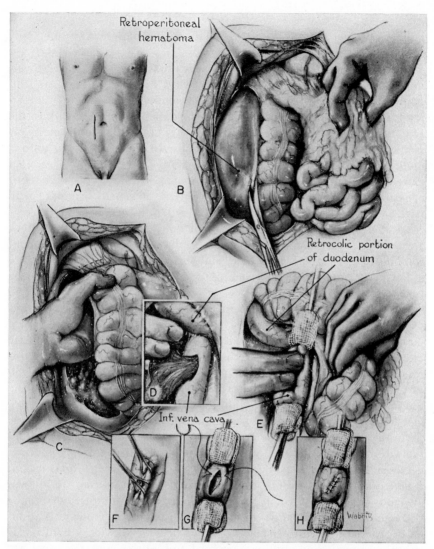

FIG. 18-1. Control of bleeding from lacerated wound of inferior vena cava. *A.* Right paramedian skin incision. *B.* The retroperitoneal hematoma is visible as scissor dissection to mobilize the right colon is commenced. *C.* The mobilization of the colon is continued by manual dissection in the retroperitoneal space. The severance of the right phrenocolic ligament is indicated by the dotted line. *D.* The mobilized colon is reflected toward the midline and the bleeding site in the vena cava is about to be controlled by digital compression. *E.* The hemorrhage is controlled and two gauze "stick sponges" are used cephalad and caudad for hemostatic compression of the vena cava prior to the release of the fingers. *F.* If desired, Babcock clamps, modified on the Potts' principle, may be used to occlude temporarily the lacerated wound. *G.* The "stick sponges" are used for hemostasis as the wound margins are approximated with interrupted sutures of fine (00000) silk. *H.* The completed closure.

bolic phenomena as associated systemic manifestations are commonly absent.

Acute traumatic deep thrombophlebitis usually occurs in a previously normal extremity. The symptoms may vary in severity from a slight, nontender swelling or heaviness of the extremity to those of a fulminating form of thrombophlebitis in which the patients are acutely ill. In the acutely ill patient, chills, fever (103 to 104°F), and a painful, massively swollen extremity are the usual symptoms. In some instances, diffuse, mottled, purplish discoloration of the skin of the massively swollen extremity (phlegmasia cerulea dolens) is present, and even gangrene of a part of the extremity may occur (gangrene of venous origin). Fortunately this is not a common occurrence in persons of advanced years.

Characteristically, in deep thrombophlebitis, systemic manifestations are usually prominent and pulmonary embolization may be a frequent complication. In fact, a pulmonary embolus may be *prima facie* evidence of an occult deep thrombophlebitis in either one or both lower extremities.

In a discussion of traumatic deep thrombophlebitis it is believed that surgical emphasis should be given to the acute fulminating form (phlegmasia cerulea dolens), because if it is unrecognized and improperly treated, the loss not only of a limb but of life itself may occur. In this condition there is an extremely rapid formation and propagation of the thrombus to involve the whole of the deep venous system. Because the venous blockade is so extensive and complete, there is no adequate passage for the outflow of arterial blood. In fact, the abnormally high venous pressure built up within the extremity may be sufficient to obstruct the arterial inflow mechanically and cause varying degrees of ischemic necrosis. The terms *pseudoembolic gangrene, gangrene of venous origin, le phlebite bleu* (Grégoire), and *phlegmasia cerulea dolens,* are all synonymous with deep thrombophlebitis of the acute fulminating form.

Diagnosis. The diagnosis of acute superficial thrombophlebitis in an elderly patient is easily made from the history, the local findings of either a segmental or diffuse superficial thrombosis, and the usual absence of edema. In deep thrombophlebitis the characteristic findings of edema with a variable discoloration of the skin, the generally more severe systemic manifestations, the occurrence of pain in the calf of the leg on both direct compression and dorsiflexion of the foot (Homans' sign), the presence of dilated superficial veins (satellite veins), and the occurrence of pulmonary emboli are all diagnostic. In the acute fulminating form with gangrene of a part of the extremity, the differential diagnosis from a primary arterial occlusion is made by the presence of extensive and massive edema. Edema is not associated with gangrene that is primarily arterial in origin.

Treatment: Acute Traumatic Superficial Thrombophlebitis. In general, ambulation is encouraged and an elastic compression-bandage support is prescribed if its use provides subjective relief. In the acute, rapidly propagating form of superficial thrombophlebitis, in addition to symptomatic care, bed rest, elevation of the extremity, and the continued application of warm, moist dressings (vascular pack) is advocated. Anticoagulants are not used. In selected instances, particularly if preexisting varicose veins are the site of the thrombophlebitis, thrombectomy and segmental vein resection are performed. When the operation is done early, immediate relief of pain is obtained and the period of disability is shortened. This is a matter of real importance to the elderly patient.

Treatment: Deep Thrombophlebitis. In the patient with mild clinical manifestations and minimal local findings, the use of an elastic compression-bandage support and active muscle exercises, particularly walking, is advised. This method of treatment is continued for a period of 4 to 6 weeks, and if there are no recurrences of symptoms, such as swelling of the extremity, nothing further is done. However, periodic examination of the patient is continued for prolonged periods to prevent, if possible, the occurrence of the late and frequently unrecognized complications, notably postphlebitic ulceration.

In the acute, rapidly propagating, and extensive deep thrombophlebitis, the patients are usually acutely ill and physically incapacitated. In such instances, general supportive and symptomatic care is prescribed. The whole of the affected extremity is encased in a massive, warm moist dressing (vascular pack) and elevated on pillow supports. Anticoagulants and antibiotics are also used, the anticoagulant of choice being heparin. This drug, in doses of 100 mg, is administered intramuscularly every 6 hours in conjunction with 200,000 units of aqueous penicillin. The combination of both has proved more effective clinically than either used alone. The antibiotic is continued for 8 to 10 days and the anticoagulant for 12 to 15 days. When the general and local condition of the patient permits, an elastic compression bandage is firmly applied to the affected extremity and active ambulation is advised. The compression-bandage support is used for 6 to 18 months longer and is discontinued only when edema does not recur in the unsupported and actively weight-bearing extremity. In some patients, an elastic compression support may be required permanently.

The chief hazard of deep thrombophlebitis is that of pulmonary infarction. Unfortunately the initial embolic episode may be rapidly fatal and in fact it may be the first indication of an occult deep venous thrombosis in the extremity. If the pulmonary embolus is nonfatal, one has the choice of either anticoagulant therapy or vein ligation. This applies to patients in any age group. The choice is dependent mainly

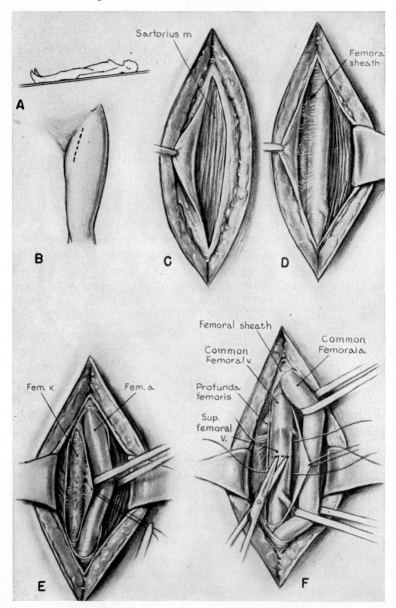

FIG. 18-2. Ligation of the superficial femoral vein. *A* and *B*. The patient is placed in a 10 to 15° semi-Fowler's position (*A*) and the site of the incision in the upper third of the thigh overlying Scarpa's triangle is indicated in dotted outline (*B*). *C* and *D*. The incision is deepened through the underlying subcutaneous fat and deep fascia (*C*) to expose the medial border of the sartorius muscle which is retracted laterally to demonstrate the proximal portion of the femoral sheath and the enclosed femoral artery and vein (*D*). The characteristic anatomic feature

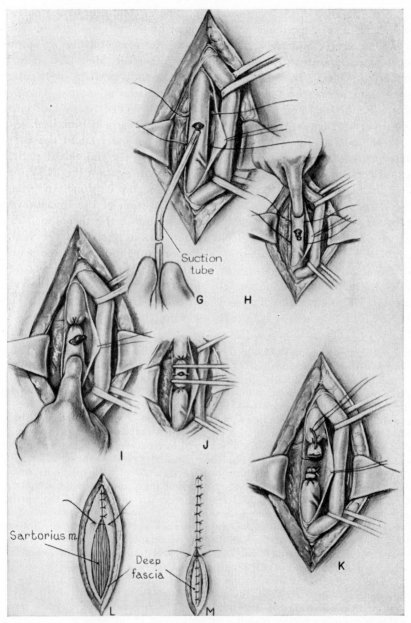

Suction tube

G   H

I

J

K

Sartorius m.

Deep fascia

L   M

of the common femoral sheath is that the encased vessels are each enclosed by their own respective sheaths which are demonstrable in the succeeding illustrations (*E, F*). *E*. The common femoral sheath is opened and the mobilized portion of the femoral artery is encircled with a cotton tape and retracted laterally. The separate sheath encasing the femoral vein is incised and the lateral cut margin is

(Caption continued on next page)

upon the severity of the symptoms, the general condition of the patient, and the clinical experience and judgment of the surgeon. If the attack is not too severe and the patient is in satisfactory condition, combined anticoagulant and antibiotic therapy as previously described may be employed. During this period increasing physical activity, particularly active muscle exercise for the lower extremities, is advocated. However if, under this regimen, a pulmonary embolus recurs, ligation of either the superficial femoral vein or the inferior vena cava is practiced.

In the acutely ill patient, early operation is preferred to the use of anticoagulants. Depending upon the findings in the individual patient, a unilateral or bilateral superficial femoral vein ligation (Fig. 18-2) or a ligation of the inferior vena cava (Fig. 18-3) may be done. In general the latter is preferred. The advantages of ligation of the inferior vena cava are (1) it is at a sufficiently high level above the thrombus, (2) it effects an abundant collateral circulation, (3) it interrupts the venous circulation from both extremities at the one operation. In three acutely ill patients (with temperatures of 103 to 104°F), one of whom was a 63-year-old man, ligation of the inferior vena cava proved a lifesaving measure. This operation has been performed in 25 patients with satisfactory follow-up results both early and late (13 years).

---

secured in a guy suture (000 silk) for traction preparatory to the mobilization of the underlying femoral vein. *F*. The femoral artery is encircled by two cotton tapes and retracted laterally. In this regard caution must be observed to avoid excessive tension and angulation of the artery because of the danger of producing arterial spasm and secondary stasis thrombosis. In fact, the traction force and angulation of the artery depicted in the illustration is unwarranted and should not be practiced. The superficial femoral vein is mobilized and partially encircled by two ligatures of silk (00). The dotted line between the ligatures indicates the site of the opening to be made in the anterior wall of the vein by scissor dissection. The clot within the lumen of the vein is depicted by the dark shadow extending cephalad to the level of entrance of the profunda femoris tributary. *G*. The incision in the superficial femoral vein is completed and the partially extruded clot is being aspirated by suction. *H, I*, and *J*. By digital retrograde "milking" more of the clot is extruded through the phlebotomy site (*H*) and when the cephalad evacuation of the clot is completed, the upper encircling ligature of silk (00) is tied (*I*). Similarly, by digital "milking," the clot, caudad in the lumen of the vessel, is evacuated (*I*) and the lower encircling ligature is tied (*J*). The superficial femoral vein is doubly clamped between the ligatures and the transection of the vein at the site of the phlebotomy is completed as indicated by the dotted line (*J*). *K*. The distal transected end of the superficial femoral vein is further occluded with a suture ligature of silk (000) and its proximal transected end is being similarly occluded. For clarity the clamp has been removed from the proximal transected end as the suture ligature is being inserted. *L* and *M*. The deep fascia (*L*) and skin (*M*) are closed with interrupted sutures of 000 silk to complete the operation. (*From J. L. Madden: Atlas of Technics in Surgery, New York, Appleton-Century-Crofts, 1958.*)

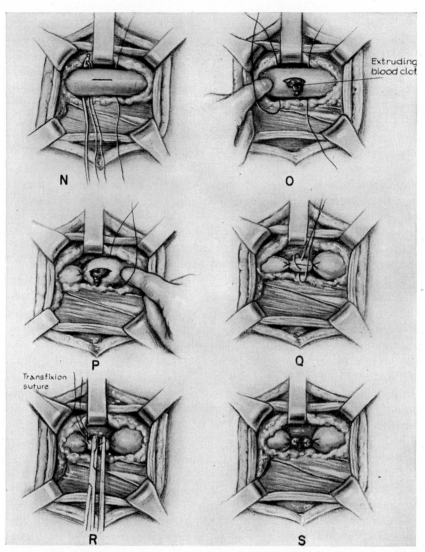

Fig. 18-3. Thrombectomy and ligation of the inferior vena cava. *N, O, P,* and *Q.* These illustrations depict the technique that is employed when a thrombotic occlusion of the lumen of the inferior vena cava, commonly associated with phlegmasia cerulea dolens, is present. The vena cava is incised between the encircling but untied ligatures of silk (No. 1) and the thrombus is evacuated *(O).* This is done by digital compression, first from above downward until free retrograde bleeding from the renal veins occurs and the proximal ligature is then tied *(P).* The thrombus is next evacuated from below upward and the distal ligature is tied *(P).* If desired an additional suture of the transfixion type may be inserted between the ligatures as indicated *(Q). R* and *S.* These illustrations depict an alternate but less preferable method of transection of the vena cava between clamps following double ligation in continuity. The severed ends are occluded with transfixion sutures of silk as the clamps are removed. *(From J. L. Madden: Atlas of Technics in Surgery, New York, Appleton-Century-Crofts, 1958.)*

The prompt and active treatment of acute fulminating deep thrombo-phlebitis, or phlegmasia cerulea dolens, is particularly important because it may terminate fatally within a short period of time. The treatment employed is based on its pathogenesis, namely, an extensive and rapidly propagating thrombotic occlusion of the whole of the deep system of veins in either one or both lower extremities. There is an old axiom in surgery: "Mechanical obstruction necessitates mechanical (operative) in-tervention." Accordingly, the ideal in treatment is the evacuation of the thrombus from the deep veins by a direct operative approach. This may be performed through the superficial femoral vein or the inferior vena cava. If operation is done early, the clinical response, both local and general, may be dramatic. The mistake in treatment is to employ nonspecific expectant methods for prolonged periods with the resulting potential loss of a part of a limb or even life itself. Early venous throm-bectomy as a specific curative therapy cannot be emphasized too strongly.

In 1948, Ochsner and De Bakey were the first to report the efficacy of removal of the thrombi from the superficial femoral vein. It may also be of interest to know that in the first five cases reported in the literature in which ligation of the inferior vena cava was performed in the treatment of this condition, thrombotic occlusion of the vena cava was present in each instance. All of the patients survived, and in each the final result was wholly satisfactory. In the case reported by Grant and Deddish, phlegmasia cerulea dolens occurred as a postoperative compli-cation following an abdominoperineal resection of the rectum and was the direct cause of death. In addition to the clinical findings of gangrene of both lower extremities, at necropsy thrombotic occlusion of the inferior vena cava and multiple pulmonary emboli were observed.

The author has employed venous thrombectomy early in the treatment of five patients with phlegmasia cerulea dolens. In three patients the surgical approach was through the inferior vena cava, which was throm-botically occluded to the level of the renal veins. Upon opening the inferior vena cava, the thrombus cephalad was first removed by digital "milking" in a retrograde manner, and after establishing a free retro-grade flow of blood, the vena cava was ligated (No. 1 silk) cephalad to the incision. Similarly the thrombi in the caudad portion of the vena cava were evacuated through the incision, distal to which the vena cava was ligated (No. 1 silk). If desired, an interposing transfixion suture may also be inserted (Fig. 18-3E), but this is not necessary.

In the remaining two patients the thrombi were evacuated through the superficial femoral vein, unilaterally in one patient and bilaterally in the other, with a 7-day interval between the operations. In each instance, extensive and sticky molasses-like thrombi were first evacuated from the superficial femoral vein distally until a free flow of blood was obtained. The vein distal to the phlebotomy site was then ligated in continuity (00 silk). A glass suction tip was next inserted through the lumen of the cephalad portion of the superficial femoral vein into the common femoral and common iliac vein, and strong suction siphonage was applied. There occurred a sudden and forceful retrograde flow of venous blood, subsequent to which the cephalad portion of the superficial femoral vein was ligated with a previously encircled and untied ligature of 00 silk. The vein was then doubly clamped between the ligatures, transected, and the clamps replaced with suture ligatures of silk (000). The general systemic and local response obtained in each of the five patients treated as described was immediate, and the recovery in each was complete. It may be of interest to note that after removal of the thrombi, an unexpected and consistent finding was the normal glistening sheen to the surface of the intima.

In terminating the discussion on phlegmasia cerulea dolens, it is believed that early diagnosis and early venous thrombectomy are prime principles in treatment, and their importance cannot be over emphasized. Early operation is considered most essential if uniformly satisfactory results are to be obtained.

ACUTE ARTERIAL INJURIES

ARTERIAL CONTUSIONS

Contusion of an artery may be caused directly by penetrating or perforating trauma of varying kinds or, more frequently in the aged, indirectly by blunt, nonpenetrating trauma to the overlying tissues.

Symptoms. The injury commonly involves the major vessels of the extremities, and the symptoms manifested are those of arterial insufficiency secondary to either traumatic arterial spasm or local traumatic thrombotic occlusion of the arterial lumen. Characteristically, the symptoms are pain, numbness, pallor, absence of peripheral arterial pulsations, and impairment or loss of function in the part affected. The underlying pathologic cause of the symptoms is a blockage of the arterial circulation.

Diagnosis. The diagnosis is based upon the history of trauma and the symptoms and signs of arterial insufficiency. However, one cannot with accuracy differentiate clinically the symptoms due to traumatic arterial spasm from those secondary to a thrombotic occlusion of the arterial lumen. Accordingly, both the correct diagnosis and the treatment are dependent upon the interval between the occurrence of the injury and the examination of the patient.

Treatment. If the patient is examined within a short interval after the trauma, interruption of the sympathetic pathways to the injured

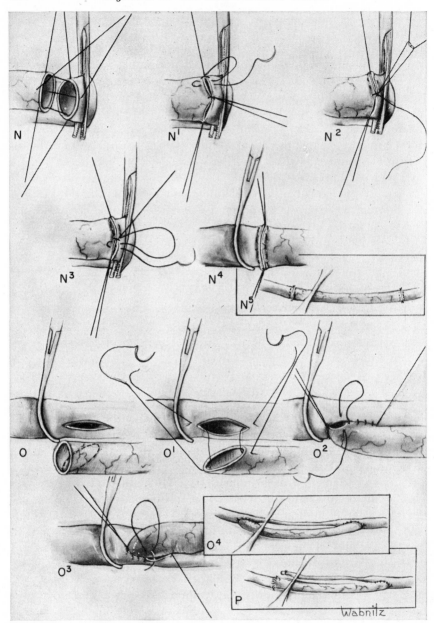

Fig. 18-4. Restoration of peripheral arterial continuity by a shunt bypass graft. N, N^1, N^2, N^3, N^4, and N^5. The technique of performing an end-to-end anasto-mosis with a continuous everting mattress rather than an over-and-over suture which is preferred. O, O^1, O^2, O^3, and O^4. These illustrations depict the technique for the performance of an end-to-side bypass of an occluded arterial segment. The artery cephalad is cross clamped and just below the clamp a lateral opening

extremity may be effected by performing a lumbar paravertebral "block" for the lower extremity and a brachial plexus "block" for the upper extremity with the use of 15 to 20 ml of procaine (1 per cent) solution. If an adequate clinical response is obtained, as indicated by improvement in the arterial circulation to the extremity, the immediate treatment is conservative. However, if the improvement in the circulation is questionable, or the interval between the injury and definitive treatment is prolonged (beyond 10 to 12 hours), surgical exploration at the site of trauma is performed. The demonstration of a contused segment of the wall of the artery in association with the absence of arterial pulsations immediately distal, is considered an indication to excise the segment and restore arterial continuity, preferably by a direct end-to-end anastomosis. Should this not be possible, the use of an autogenous vein graft, knitted cloth prosthesis, or arterial homograft, in order of preference, would be required (Fig. 18-4, N-N[5]). An alternate method of primary treatment would be the use of a bypass graft (Fig. 18-4, O-P) using autogenous vein, knitted prosthesis, or arterial homograft, depending upon the location of the injury and the preference of the surgeon.

ACUTE ARTERIAL LACERATIONS

An acute laceration of an artery may be inflicted by stab wounds, gunshot wounds, automobile accidents, self-inflicted wounds, accidental operative trauma, and miscellaneous types of trauma including, particularly in the aged, those secondary to fractures of the extremities.

Symptoms. The symptoms and signs as well as the method of treatment are dependent upon the character of the related soft-tissue injury, namely, whether the wound is open or closed. If the laceration of an artery occurs

is made into the arterial lumen (O). The end of the vein graft is cut on a bias (dotted outline) to obtain a flat approximation to the side of the artery (O). The angle guy sutures (00000 silk) are inserted but not tied (O[1]). The needle strand of the lower guy suture is inserted from below upward as an over-and-over suture toward the upper angle guy suture (O[2]) where it is tied to its free end. The needle strand of the upper angle guy suture is then inserted on the opposite side from above downward as an over-and-over suture toward its starting point at the lower angle (O[3]) where it is tied to the free strand of the lower angle guy suture. The inset (O[4]) shows the completion of the end-to-side bypass shunt utilizing an autogenous vein (long saphenous) graft. P. This inset shows a modified bypass shunt in which an end-to-end anastomosis is performed cephalad and an end-to-side anastomosis caudad. This method was used in one patient in whom a thrombus formed in the lumen of an end-to-side bypass shunt vein within 8 to 10 minutes after its insertion. The cephalad end of the anastomosis was disconnected, the thrombus evacuated, and the lumen of the vein was irrigated with heparin-saline solution. The re-anastomosis cephalad was performed end-to-end rather than end-to-side with a satisfactory result. (*From J. L. Madden: Atlas of Technics in Surgery, New York, Appleton-Century-Crofts, 1958.*)

in an open wound, frank hemorrhage is visible and the primary object of treatment is immediate hemostasis. Usually this may be readily and efficiently obtained by digital compression of the affected artery through the intact skin just proximal to the site of the soft-tissue wound. If this is not possible because of the location and/or character of the wound, digital compression of the lacerated vessel within the wound itself is done. Under such emergency circumstances, the control of hemorrhage may be essential to the preservation of life, and therefore takes precedence over the potential risk of infection. A tourniquet, because of its inherent dangers, should rarely be required for hemostasis. When employed, it should be released at 20-minute intervals to avoid the complications incumbent upon its use. If, following its release, the bleeding does not recur, the tourniquet should not be reapplied.

Treatment. Following the emergency control of hemorrhage, treatment is dependent upon the medical facilities which are immediately available, the extent of the blood loss, the character and severity of the arterial injury, and the general condition of the patient. If a hospital is close to the scene of the accident, hemostasis may be maintained by digital compression. If there is no hospital nearby, the intermittent tourniquet control of bleeding, if practical, may be required. After hospitalization, a sterile clamp or sterile gauze pressure dressing may be substituted for the digital or tourniquet control of hemorrhage. Otherwise the primary treatment is referable to the general condition of the patient.

Impending or actual shock is treated by the administration of parenteral fluids, plasma, and blood transfusions, concurrently with oxygen inhalation. When the resuscitative measures are completed, the patient is transferred to the operating room for definitive treatment of the wound. A wide circumference of the area surrounding the wound is surgically prepared and sterile drapes are applied. When necessary, an incision is made through the normal intact tissue proximal to the wound and overlying its arterial supply. The uninvolved cephalad segment of the affected artery is mobilized and encircled with a length of cotton tape. Control of the arterial flow is now established and the wound itself is then surgically prepared. Clamps or gauze packing, if previously inserted, are removed, and the wound is cleansed thoroughly with a warm solution of neutral white soap mixed with hydrogen peroxide. Subsequently the wound is irrigated with copious quantities (2 to 3 liters) of warm saline (0.9 per cent) solution while mechanical debridement is done. If at any time during this process bleeding should occur, the arterial inflow cephalad to the wound is immediately occluded and the occlusion is maintained until preparations are completed for the definitive control of bleeding.

When the wound has been prepared, the surgical team changes gloves and a second set of sterile drapes is applied. Using a new set of sterile instruments, further mechanical cleansing of the wound is done as indicated, and the type of arterial injury is carefully assessed. The ideal and simplest method of treatment of an acute arterial laceration is an arteriorrhaphy utilizing either a continuous suture or interrupted sutures of 00000 silk swedged on a minimum-trauma needle. If the artery is transected, a direct end-to-end anastomosis is preferred. In such instances, to prevent tension at the suture line, one should avoid resection of undue lengths of the severed ends of the artery. Depending upon the location of the injured artery, a defect in continuity may be satisfactorily bridged by flexion of the adjacent limb joint. However, the extent of the arterial injury may preclude a primary anastomosis regardless of the means employed, and a graft replacement for restoration of arterial continuity may be necessary. The choice of graft depends upon the location of the vessel and the experience and preference of the surgeon. In general, an autogenous vein graft is preferred.

The retrograde flow of blood from the caudad end of a severed major artery (Henle-Coenen phenomenon) is of good prognostic import relative to the salvage of a limb if the arterial blood flow is immediately restored. However, its presence should not be interpreted as an indication that the severed ends of a major artery may be ligated with impunity. In fact, the ligation of an essential artery to a limb should be done only under dire, extenuating circumstances which would make its performance a lifesaving measure.

Anticoagulants are not used upon completion of the repair of an arterial defect, either by arteriorrhaphy, direct anastomosis, or graft replacement, because of the untoward complications, particularly hemorrhage, that may occur. Admittedly, this is a personal preference with which many may rightly disagree. The reasoning for not using them is based on the assumption that if the operation is performed early, they are not necessary, and if it is performed late, they are of no value.

When, in addition to the arterial injury, there is an accompanying fracture, either open (compound) or closed (simple), the treatment of the arterial injury should take precedence. Furthermore, either concomitant or subsequent treatment of the fracture should not entail the use of plaster encasements or fixation devices which might possibly interfere with the circulation to the extremity.

In the management of a lacerated artery in a closed wound, the immediate treatment is supportive and expectant. The affected extremity is carefully observed at frequent and regular intervals for any evidence of compromise of the circulation. Commonly, the increasing pressure secondary to an expanding hematoma encased within the subfascial compartment is sufficient to effect spontaneous control of bleeding from the site of arterial injury. Although the posttraumatic convalescence may prove uneventful, such patients should be examined periodically during the ensuing 3 to 6 months for the possible occurrence of a "pulsating hematoma," or traumatic ("false") aneurysm, the treatment of which is later discussed.

In some instances the expanding pressure within the subfascial compartment may exceed the local systemic arterial pressure and cause a stoppage of the arterial circulation. Under such circumstances the release of the pressure within the extremity is mandatory. Preliminary to this operation, a separate incision is made cephalad to the hematoma to isolate and control the arterial inflow to the part. A linear incision is next made overlying the tense and distended portion of the injured limb and deepened through the underlying fascial layers. This in itself, or else multiple linear fasciotomies, may release the arterial compression enough to restore an adequate circulation. If not, it then becomes necessary to evacuate the subfascial hematoma and at the same time have control of the arterial inflow cephalad in the event of sudden and forceful arterial hemorrhage. If this occurs, the arterial inflow is temporarily occluded and the source of bleeding is identified. According to the type and severity of the arterial injury, it is treated as previously described. Contrariwise, if active arterial bleeding does not occur, the skin incision is loosely closed and the extremity is examined at frequent intervals during the succeeding 7 to 10 days. In cases of this sort, particularly in the less resilient arterial walls of the aged, the imminent danger is secondary hemorrhage.

It is *àpropos* at this time to consider also the emergency control of accidental hemorrhage occurring during the performance of a surgical operation. Even though in such instances the trauma has occurred under ideal circumstances, life may be lost if the acute emergency is improperly handled. One cannot overemphasize the importance of utmost calm and deliberate action. Regardless of the region of the body in which the operation is being performed, one should avoid the "blind" application of clamps into an operative field obscured with blood. One should always remember that the fingers are readily available for immediate, efficient, and atraumatic hemostasis. Accordingly, hemorrhage may be controlled with "dynamic immediacy." The use of this method for the control of hemorrhage from either the cystic or hepatic artery is stressed because of the frequency with which operations on the biliary tract are performed, particularly in the older age groups. If arterial bleeding should occur suddenly during the removal of a gall bladder, the surgeon, or better, the first assistant, should immediately compress the hepatic artery between the index finger within the foramen of Winslow and the thumb overlying (Pringle maneuver). The operative field is toiletted, and with the structures clearly visualized, the compression of the hepatic artery is slowly released and then immediately compressed. The spurt of blood from the severed cystic artery may be seen and the artery is clamped and ligated under direct vision. Occasionally the source of bleeding is an opening in the convex arch formed by the hepatic artery and caused by an avulsion of the cystic artery from its site of origin. The emergency control of bleeding remains the same, but definitive hemostasis is obtained by sutures (00000 silk) rather than a clamp and ligature. If the right hepatic artery is severed, arterial continuity should be restored, preferably by a direct end-to-end anastomosis. Otherwise, a fatal complication may ensue because of the interruption of the arterial circulation to the segment of the liver so supplied.

In operations performed in the neck, sudden massive hemorrhage may occur following injury to the subclavian artery. As previously mentioned, digital compression is a most efficient method of hemostasis, particularly for bleeding in the depths of a wound. When the condition of the patient is stabilized, definitive control of the source of bleeding is undertaken. Because of the location and type of trauma, this may be best accomplished by a separate anterior thoracic incision in the second interspace through which the subclavian artery is either temporarily clamped or definitively ligated at its origin from the arch of the aorta.

Acute Traumatic ("False") Aneurysm

A traumatic aneurysm is a delayed complication of an acute arterial injury associated with a closed type (stab wounds, puncture and perforating wounds) of soft-tissue trauma.

Symptoms. The symptoms depend upon the location and the size of the aneurysm. In some patients there are no symptoms, whereas in others the aneurysm may be manifest by interference with joint motion, pain due to pressure on the surrounding structures, actual leakage of the aneurysm, or a combination of one or more of these symptoms.

Diagnosis. The diagnosis may be readily made from the history of trauma, the subjective complaints, and commonly the local finding of an expansile, pulsating tumor mass. Traumatic aneurysms of the thoracic aorta, though they may be asymptomatic, are commonly discernible on chest roentgenograms.

Treatment. Traumatic arterial aneurysms are treated by operation. Once an aneurysm is formed, it increases progressively in size with varying degrees of rapidity and with an ever-increasing propensity for rupture. In fact, the first symptoms manifest may be those of a fatal rupture. Recently Steinberg made a plea for the conservative treatment of traumatic aneurysms of the thoracic aorta. This is believed to be an un-

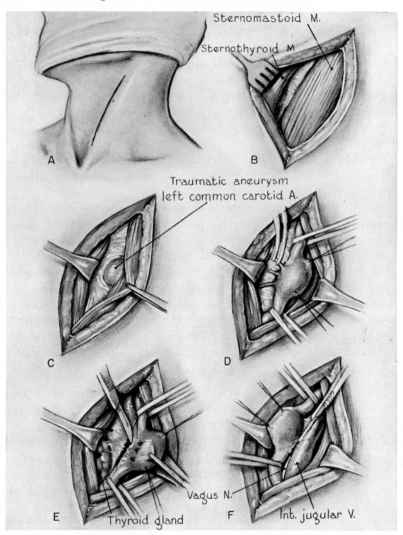

FIG. 18-5. Excision of aneurysm of the common carotid artery and the insertion of an autogenous vein graft. *A.* The oblique cervical incision paralleling the anterior border of the left sternomastoid muscle is indicated by the solid line. *B.* The incision is deepened through the subcutaneous fatty tissue, the platysma muscle, and the anterior layer of the deep cervical fascia to expose portions of the sternothyroid and sternomastoid muscles. *C.* The muscles are retracted and the summit of the traumatic aneurysm of the left common carotid artery is visible beneath the retracted margin of the sternomastoid muscle. *D.* The aneurysm and its collateral arterial branches are mobilized from the surrounding tissues by a combination of sharp and blunt dissection. The common carotid artery, both cephalad and caudad to the aneurysm, is encircled by cotton tapes for traction, and if necessary, for temporary mechanical occlusion of the arterial lumen.

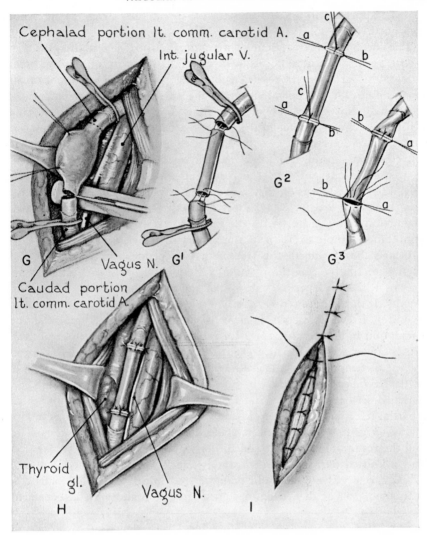

Guy sutures of silk (000) for traction are also inserted in the wall of the aneurysm. *E* and *F*. The collateral arterial branches are ligated and severed and mobilization of the aneurysm is continued by scalpel dissection. The adherence of the aneurysm to the internal jugular vein is visible. *G*. The mobilization of the aneurysm and portions of the common carotid artery both cephalad and caudad is completed. The common carotid artery is occluded by Potts' serrafine or "bulldog" clamps on either side of the aneurysm preparatory to its excision. A cuff of the adventitious layer of the artery is removed at each site of election for its transection. This maneuver is more readily accomplished with the artery in continuity as depicted. The carotid artery caudad is being transected with a scalpel over an underlying sterile tongue depressor. The site of arterial transec-

(*Caption continued on next page*)

realistic approach to an ever-present, life-threatening danger, and is not condoned.

The ideal in the treatment of a traumatic aneurysm is the resection of the aneurysm and restoration of arterial continuity either by direct anastomosis or by graft replacement. The particular method of treatment applicable is dependent upon the size of the aneurysm and its location. In some of the smaller peripheral types, such as those of the carotid, brachial, and femoral arteries, excision and direct anastomosis may be done. However, two patients with traumatic aneurysms of the left common carotid artery were each treated by resection of the aneurysm and the interposition of an autogenous vein (saphena magna) graft (Fig. 18-5) for restoration of the arterial circulation. These two patients have been followed for 8 and 6 years respectively, and in each the graft is functioning satisfactorily. In the smaller arteries which are not of vital importance, simple excision of the aneurysm is performed.

In the thoracic aorta the treatment is dependent upon the type of aneurysm. In those of the saccular variety a well-defined neck may be present which will permit excision of the aneurysm and lateral aortorrhaphy. If this is not feasible, excision and graft replacement is necessary. However, irreversible cord damage may occur after interruption of the circulation in the thoracic aorta for relatively short periods. Accordingly, provisions must be made to prevent this complication. Hypothermia and the use of temporary bypass grafts, utilizing either homografts or heterografts, have been employed with success. However, the preferred method is that described by Cooley and his associates and by Gerbode in which a partial left sided bypass, employing an extracorporeal circulatory pump, is used (Fig. 18-6). This permits an unhurried excision of the aneurysm and the restoration of aortic continuity with a graft replacement, preferably a knitted dacron, cloth prosthesis (De Bakey). In Gerbode's list of 17 cases, one was a 66-year-old male injured in an automobile accident.

In aneurysms of the abdominal aorta, resection and graft replacement

---

tion cephalad is indicated by the dotted line. G^1, G^2, and G^3. The excision of the aneurysm is completed and the free graft of saphenous vein which is reversed (cephalad portion is caudad) is aligned between the transected ends of the common carotid artery by three equidistantly placed cardinal guy sutures (00000 silk) which are inserted but not tied (G^1). The guy sutures are tied (G^2), and the long strands are used for traction to facilitate the rotation of both the graft and the transected ends of the carotid artery for the insertion of the silk (00000) sutures posteriorly (G^3). *H.* The excision of the traumatic aneurysm of the left common carotid artery and the insertion of the reversed free graft of the great saphenous vein is completed. The relation of the graft to the surrounding structures is visible. *I.* The anterior layer of the deep cervical fascia and then the skin are closed with interrupted sutures of 000 silk. (*From J. L. Madden: Atlas of Technics in Surgery, New York, Appleton-Century-Crofts, 1958.*)

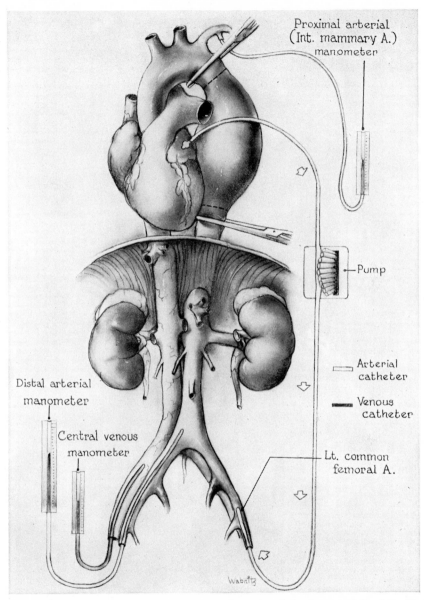

Fig. 18-6. Artist's illustration of the method employed for bypass of the left side of the heart in the treatment of aneurysms of the thoracic aorta.

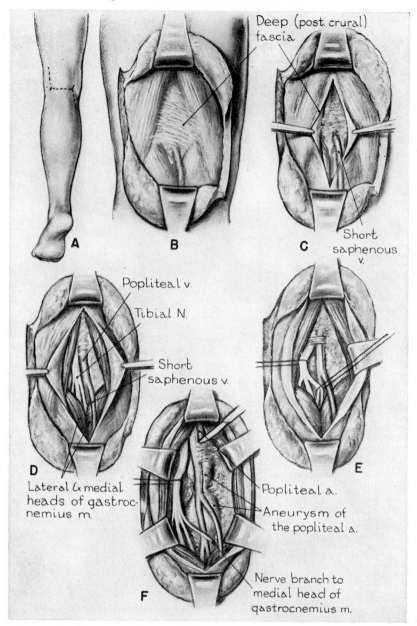

Fig. 18-7. Excision of dumbbell aneurysm of the popliteal artery and replacement by homologous arterial graft. *A.* The incision employed, depicted in dotted outline, is preferred to the use of one of the midline longitudinal type. *B.* The mobilized flaps of skin and subcutaneous fatty tissue are retracted to expose the posterior crural fascia and the underlying muscles. The perforation of the

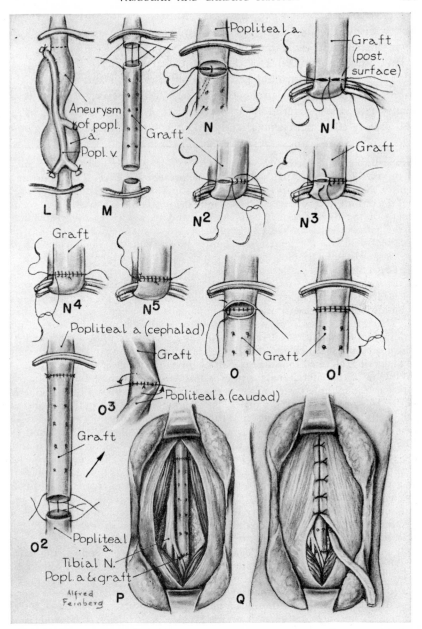

crural fascia by the short saphenous vein (saphena parva) is visible. *C, D,* and *E.*
The incised margins of the linear incision in the posterior crural fascia are
retracted in clamps (*C*), and by scissor dissection in the underlying tissue the
popliteal vein and the entrance of its tributary, the short saphenous vein, are

(*Caption continued on next page*)

are practiced. Similarly, as above, the knitted dacron prosthesis of De Bakey, either the single tube or bifurcation type, is preferred, depending upon the site and the extent of the aneurysm.

In traumatic aneurysms of the popliteal artery in which there is an adequate peripheral arterial bed ("run off"), excision and graft (knitted dacron) replacement is preferred (Fig. 18-7). However, if there is an inadequate distal arterial "run off," ablation of the aneurysm by an obliterative endoaneurysmorrhaphy (Matas) is recommended. This oper-

---

demonstrable. A portion of the tibial nerve and its branches, as well as portions of the surrounding musculature, are also delineated (D, E). F. The dissection is continued within the deeper tissue and the superior pole of the popliteal artery and the outline of its dumbbell aneurysm immediately distal are visible. A greater length of the tibial nerve is now exposed and its branch to the medial head of the gastrocnemius muscle may be seen arched across the lower portion of the popliteal vein. L. The superior and inferior poles of the dumbbell aneurysm are clamped (Potts' clamps) prior to transection (dotted lines) and removal of the aneurysm with the attached popliteal vein. M. In this patient the diameters of the lower portion of the femoral artery and the distal segment of the popliteal artery were extremely large and required the use of the thoracic segment of an alcohol (70 per cent) preserved homologous aortic graft to obtain a proper fit. The three cardinal guy sutures (00000 arterial silk) are inserted, one posteriorly and one at either lateral angle, but not tied. N, N^1, N^2, N^3, N^4, and N^5. The guy sutures are tied and the suture strands are left long (N). The lower end of the graft is elevated to show the start of the posterior layer of the anastomosis (N^1). One of the lateral angle sutures is inserted as a continuous over-and-over suture to the midline posteriorly where it is tied to the free end of the posterior cardinal guy suture (N^2). The needle attached strand of the posterior cardinal guy suture is similarly continued as an over-and-over suture (N^3) and tied to the free end of the remaining lateral angle cardinal guy suture (N^4, N^5). O and O^1. The aortic (thoracic) graft segment is turned downward to show the insertion of the sutures forming the anterior layer of the anastomosis. The needle attached strand of one of the lateral angle cardinal guy sutures (N^5) is continued anteriorly as a continuous over-and-over suture (O) and tied to the free end of the opposing lateral angle guy suture (O^1). The needle is inserted from the "inside-out" on the host popliteal artery to impinge the calcific plaques which are frequently present in the intima against the underlying coats of the vessel. O^2. The proximal anastomosis is completed and the three cardinal guy sutures are similarly inserted distally but not tied. O^3. The use of the free ends of the lateral angle cardinal guy sutures to rotate the graft and arterial segments for the insertion of the posterior layer of sutures as previously depicted is shown. P. The insertion of the thoracic segment of the alcohol (70 per cent) preserved homologous graft to restore continuity of the popliteal artery is completed and its relation to the surrounding structures is visible. Q. A rubber tissue drain is inserted into the popliteal fossa and the incision in the posterior crural fascia is closed with interrupted sutures of 000 silk. The closure of the skin incision and the application of a sterile gauze compression dressing completes the operation. (From J. L. Madden: Atlas of Technics in Surgery, New York, Appleton-Century-Crofts, 1958.)

ation, originally described and subsequently developed by Matas, was performed for the first time in 1888 in the treatment of a traumatic aneurysm of the brachial artery which had been operated upon twice previously without success. Despite the later advances made in vascular surgery, this operation may, in selected cases, still prove the one of choice. Accordingly, it is not only of historical but also of practical importance, and one should be thoroughly familiar with its use.

Traumatic Arteriovenous Fistula

Traumatic arteriovenous fistulas are commonly caused by stab or gunshot wounds. This of course is quite uncommon among the elderly. However, traumatic arteriovenous fistulas may also occur as a complication of automobile accidents and other varied types of trauma which increasingly do involve the aged.

Symptoms. The characteristic initial symptom of an arteriovenous fistula is the occurrence of sudden and severe hemorrhage which is controlled with surprising ease by the application of firm compression over the wound site. Depending upon the severity of the blood loss, varying degrees of shock may be present. When a fistula is established between an artery and vein, the objective symptoms are (1) a continuous thrill with systolic accentuation, (2) an audible bruit, and (3) an increase in both the pulse pressure and the pulse rate. In a fistula of long standing, venous stasis, edema, and ulceration of the extremity may occur and cause continued disability even after the surgical correction of the fistula.

An arteriovenous fistula may also produce systemic effects in the cardiovascular system, consisting of cardiac enlargement and congestive heart failure. This is even more to be feared in the aged where a certain degree of heart failure may be present before the appearance of the arteriovenous fistula. Not infrequently, on the other hand, the occurrence of congestive heart failure may be the first indication of an occult arteriovenous fistula. There are four main factors which determine the effect of an arteriovenous fistula upon the heart. These are (1) the size of the fistula, (2) its duration, (3) the proximity of the fistula to the heart, and (4) the cardiac reserve of the patient.

An arteriovenous fistula may form with surprising rapidity. Mason reported the death of a patient from cardiac failure 4 days following a traumatic left subclavian arteriovenous fistula secondary to a stab wound. The author has observed symptoms 6 hours after a stab wound over the femoral region. However, symptoms may be delayed 4 to 6 weeks and observed only after the absorption of a primary expanding hematoma. In fact, in any patient with a stab wound overlying the major vessels which is associated with severe hemorrhage that is relatively easily controlled by simple compression, the possibility of an arteriovenous fistula should always be considered. Accordingly, such patients should be examined at frequent intervals over a period of 2 to 3 weeks before negating the presence of a fistula.

Diagnosis. When an arteriovenous fistula is closed by digital compression, there may be observed an elevation in the diastolic and, to a lesser degree, in the systolic pressure in conjunction with a decrease in both the pulse pressure and the pulse rate. The occurrence of a decrease in the pulse rate is frequently referred to as Branham's bradycardia phenomenon.

In the less readily accessible regions such as the thorax and the abdomen, the presence of an arteriovenous fistula may be first manifested by general systemic rather than local symptoms. This was dramatically demonstrated in a 63-year-old man who was admitted to the emergency room in shock following a gunshot wound of the abdomen. The wound of entrance was in the right upper quadrant of the abdomen, and the bullet, subsequently shown to be a .38 caliber, was palpable just beneath the skin in the left paravertebral area overlying the eleventh rib. On exploratory celiotomy, a perforated wound of the right lobe of the liver and a hemoperitoneum were observed. Sutures of silk (0) were used for hemostasis in the liver and the abdominal incision was closed without drainage. Two months after operation the patient was readmitted to the hospital in congestive heart failure. The blood pressure was 200 mm Hg systolic and 80 mm Hg diastolic. On examination of the abdomen, a palpable thrill and audible bruit in the left paraumbilical area were present. At operation there was a fistula between the superior mesenteric artery and the left renal vein. The fistula was disconnected and the openings in the artery and vein were closed. Postoperatively the blood pressure was 130 mm Hg systolic and 90 mm Hg diastolic and there were no symptoms of congestive heart failure. To the knowledge of the author this is the first time that an arteriovenous fistula involving these vessels has been reported.

Treatment. The treatment of a traumatic arteriovenous fistula is dependent upon its size, location, and duration. The immediate treatment of a freshly established fistula is conservative. This is done to permit the development of an adequate collateral circulation, to allow the adjacent tissues to return to relatively normal status which facilitates surgical dissection, to lessen the likelihood of infection when operation is subsequently performed, and, finally, to allow for a possible spontaneous closure of the fistula.

Until comparatively recently, the operation most commonly performed and championed by Reid was quadruple ligation and excision of the fistula. Prior to its performance it was necessary to establish the competency of the collateral circulation to the affected part. This was readily done through the use of the Matas test. In performing the Matas test, applicable to the extremities, the limb is elevated and emptied completely of blood by the application of an Esmarch bandage from the tip of the digits to the level of the fistula. The artery cephalad to the fistula is completely occluded by either firm digital compression or a Matas arterial compressor. While the occlusion of the artery is maintained, the Esmarch bandage is quickly removed. If within 3 minutes following its removal a hyperemic "blush" to the whole of the extremity is observed, the collateral circulation is considered adequate.

Although this operation proved curative and without loss of the limb, the postoperative follow-up studies demonstrated certain functional inadequacies. It was observed that the patients postoperatively showed a variable intolerance to exercise which was characterized by intermittent claudication, early fatigue, and a sensation of heaviness in the affected extremity. Accordingly, although the limb was viable, the patient oftentimes was functionally incapacitated.

The ideal in the treatment of an arteriovenous fistula, both anatomic and physiologic, is the restoration of the normal arterial continuity. This may be accomplished in a variety of ways, one of the simplest and yet practical methods being the transvenous closure of the fistula and concomitant ligation of the vein as suggested by Bickham. If this operation should not prove feasible, one may excise the fistula and restore arterial continuity by either direct end-to-end anastomosis or graft replacement as previously described.

It is believed pertinent at this time to comment on the pathologic changes which occur in the vessels which are united by a fistula. These changes were emphasized by Reid and characterized as arterification of the vein and venification of the artery. The artery proximal to the fistula becomes thin and dilated as a consequence of the decrease in the peripheral vascular resistance. Contrariwise, the vein at the site of and caudad to the fistula becomes thickened because of the increased work load. These changes assume surgical significance in that particular care must be observed in the dissection of the thin-walled artery to avoid its rupture.

The discussion of the treatment of arteriovenous fistulas should not be terminated without emphasis upon an operation which should not be done, namely, ligation of the artery alone proximal to the fistula. Blood flow always follows the path of least resistance. Accordingly, if the forceful, pulsating arterial flow is occluded proximal to the fistula, the collateral arterial flow will bypass the peripheral resistance within the capillary bed and return to the heart through the pathway provided by the fistula. Consequently the part caudad to the fistula will "bleed to death" from within and frequently cause irreversible compromise of the circulation to the limb.

CARDIAC TRAUMA

Injury to the heart may occur in a variety of ways by direct or indirect trauma. Direct trauma is manifested by contusions, lacerations, puncture wounds, penetrating and perforating wounds, and cardiac rupture. Indirect trauma to the heart generally occurs in the patient who has suffered multiple injuries, and the cardiac injury is frequently not diagnosed nor even suspected. Therefore, in every patient with multiple injuries, and particularly in those who have suffered blast injuries, the possibility of concomitant cardiac trauma should always be considered.

CONTUSIONS OF THE HEART

Cardiac contusions are usually caused by direct trauma to that portion of the sternum which overlies the heart, and characteristically occur in automobile accidents when the sternum is forcibly compressed against the steering wheel. However, cardiac contusions may also occur following indirect trauma, such as that caused by a fall from a height or any other accident productive of multiple injuries.

Symptoms. The symptoms are dependent upon the severity of the injury. The main subjective complaint is precordial pain which varies in intensity according to the nature of the trauma. In cases of severe trauma, tachycardia, cardiac arrhythmias, hypotension, vertigo, dyspnea, cyanosis, distention of the cervical veins, and peripheral vascular collapse —all manifestations of cardiogenic shock—may occur. In fact, the injury may actually produce a traumatic thrombosis of the coronary artery. In other instances, the symptoms may be so minor that the possibility of cardiac trauma is not even considered.

Diagnosis. The diagnosis of myocardial contusion is unfortunately not made frequently enough. This is believed mainly owing to the lack of awareness on the part of the examining physician. The possibility of the presence of myocardial contusion must be considered before the correct diagnosis can be established. The electrocardiographic tracing is the best means of diagnosis. Characteristically, changes in the RST complex with depression of the S-T segments are present. Cardiac arrhythmias of varying types, none of which are specific, may also occur. Commonly the heart tracing may be identical with the changes that are observed in a myocardial infarction secondary to primary coronary artery disease. As stated previously, the trauma itself may actually cause a coronary arterial occlusion, or, particularly in the aged, aggravate a preexisting one. The previous history of the patient relative to the cardiovascular system is often an aid in the differential diagnosis.

Treatment. The treatment of contusions of the heart is supportive, symptomatic, and expectant. The same regimen is followed as one would outline in the treatment of a fresh myocardial infarction. This would include bed rest for 2 to 4 weeks, the exact period depending upon the clinical response of the patient, the serial ECG findings, and the judgment of the physician.

In instances of traumatic rupture of the heart, the diagnosis is usually made at necropsy and the rupture is frequently one of many extensive injuries in a severely traumatized patient. Accordingly, the patient does not usually survive long enough for a consideration of either diagnosis or treatment. In the aged, with the usual decrease in cardiac reserve, the chance of survival is minimal. Rarely, a localized rupture of the heart may occur as the result of direct blunt trauma. The signs and symptoms would be those of cardiac tamponade, the diagnosis and treatment of which are next considered.

CARDIAC TAMPONADE

Under this heading direct trauma to the heart, such as that caused by stab, ice pick, and gunshot wounds, as well as the puncture wounds secondary to osseous trauma, is considered. Of the 81 cases discussed by Maynard and his associates in 1952, the oldest was 61 years of age. Of 20 cases reported by Drye and his associates in 1956, one received his wounds at 60 years of age, a second at 66. Both survived. Gunshot wounds of the heart usually are of the through and through perforative type, and as a consequence the patient generally expires within minutes from massive hemorrhage. In the remaining types of open wounds of the heart, the patients may survive for prolonged periods which permit their transportation to a hospital for definitive surgical treatment.

Symptoms. The symptoms of cardiac tamponade must be known before one can make the diagnosis. In the excitement of the emergency room, the underlying cause of the shock state may be misdiagnosed and an avoidable death may occur. It is axiomatic that any physician responsible for the care of the acutely traumatized patient should be thoroughly familiar with the signs and symptoms of cardiac tamponade if it is to be diagnosed promptly and properly treated.

The symptoms and signs of acute cardiac tamponade are secondary to a mechanical interference with the flow of blood entering the right side of the heart. It is also noteworthy that the volume of blood within the pericardial cavity that is required to obstruct the venous filling of the heart may be surprisingly small. In some instances complete relief of symptoms may be obtained by the withdrawal of 12 to 15 ml of blood from the pericardial cavity.

One of the first manifestations of an increase in the intrapericardial pressure is an elevation of the systemic venous pressure, which may be indicated clinically by distention of the cervical veins. The normal venous pressure varies between 7 and 10 centimeters of water. In acute cardiac tamponade the body economy may adjust to a venous pressure level of approximately 18 centimeters of water, beyond which death occurs. Contrariwise, in chronic tamponade, during which the intrapericardial pressure is elevated slowly over an extended time interval, the body may satisfactorily adjust to venous pressures of 40 to 42 centimeters of water.

In cardiac tamponade, the decrease in the venous filling of the right side of the heart causes a progressive diminution in both the stroke and minute-volume outputs of the heart, despite the compensatory tachycardia which is effected. Consequently there is a concomitant decrease in both the systemic arterial and pulse pressures. A paradoxical pulse is commonly present, which is characterized by a diminution in the pulse volume or even complete absence of the pulse on inspiration. The diminution in the cardiac output and the encasement of the heart in a fluid medium combine to produce muffled or distant heart sounds on auscultation. Furthermore, on fluoroscopic examination of the heart, the cardiac pulsations are markedly diminished or absent. Finally, the mechanical interference to the flow of blood into the lungs and the venous stasis peripherally cause a deficiency in the volume of oxygenated blood to the tissues. This results in a pronounced increase in the amount of reduced hemoglobin in the systemic venous bed with concomitant dyspnea and cyanosis.

Diagnosis. A prime factor in the diagnosis of cardiac tamponade is a consideration of its possible presence. When a patient is admitted to the emergency room in shock and has a wound of the chest in proximity to the heart, one should first and always consider acute cardiac tamponade as a possible diagnosis. This diagnosis is substantiated by the additional findings of distended cervical veins, distant or muffled heart sounds, low pulse pressure, paradoxical pulse, and finally the aspiration of blood from the pericardial sac.

Treatment. In the treatment of acute cardiac tamponade, the first requisite is the removal of the causative factor which, in the acutely traumatized patient, is invariably blood within the pericardial cavity. The manner in which this is accomplished is still a matter of some controversy. Although Riolomus, in 1649, advocated aspiration in the treatment of heart wounds, it was attempted for the first time in 1829 by Larrey. Singleton, in 1933, effected a cure of a patient with a stab wound of the heart and cardiac tamponade by the aspiration of 250 ml of blood from the pericardial cavity. However, prior to 1943, the generally accepted treatment for acute cardiac tamponade caused by penetrating wounds of the heart was immediate exploratory thoracotomy and pericardiotomy with definitive treatment of the heart wound. In 1943, Blalock and Ravitch recommended simple aspiration of the blood from the pericardial cavity as the method of choice in the treatment of acute cardiac tamponade and reported complete recovery in three of four patients so treated. In 1949, the same authors reported a series of eight patients with stab wounds of the heart and acute cardiac tamponade, all of whom were treated successfully by aspiration. This brought the number of patients treated by aspiration to 11, with complete recovery in 10 (91 per cent).

In a comparative clinical study, Elkins, in 1951, reported upon the treatment employed in three groups of patients with stab wounds of the heart. The first group, prior to 1941, comprised 38 patients, in each of whom exploratory thoracotomy, pericardiotomy, and suture repair of the heart wound were done. The mortality rate was 42 per cent. The second group included 23 patients who were treated during the period 1941 to 1944. Each patient was treated by simple aspiration with a mortality rate of 22 per cent. In the third group, subsequent to 1944, there were 18 patients; of the 17 who were treated by aspiration, one died (5.9 per cent). The remaining patient failed to respond to aspiration and died following operation.

Maynard and his associates, in general, prefer operation as the primary method of treatment. In an experience totaling 81 patients with penetrating wounds of the heart, 20 (24.2 per cent) died before operation could be performed. In the remaining 61 patients operated upon, 26 (42.7 per cent) died. Twelve of this group were operated upon during the last 3-year period of this study (1948 to 1951), and 10 (83.3 per cent) recovered. This high recovery rate was believed an expression of better organization in the treatment of these emergencies.

The type of treatment prescribed, operative or nonoperative (aspiration), is dependent upon the particular findings in the individual patient. In general, the immediate treatment is by aspiration, although preparations are concomitantly made for operation, should this be warranted. If the symptoms are relieved following aspiration and the patient remains asymptomatic, nothing further is done. However, if the symptoms recur, the aspiration is repeated, and depending upon the experience and the judgment of the surgeon, the patient is either observed further or operated upon forthwith. Although complete recoveries have been reported following three and even four aspirations, the necessity for repeated aspirations is generally a sign of continued bleeding and is considered a good indication for operation. Prior to or concomitant with either aspiration or operation, Stead and his associates have demonstrated the value of the intravenous administration of saline solution in the restoration of an effective blood volume in the presence of acute cardiac tamponade. Plasma and blood for the same purpose are also administered as indicated.

When operation is performed, the heart may be exposed through either a standard right or left anterolateral thoracotomy incision, depending upon the site of trauma. More recently preference has been given to the median sternotomy (Duval-Barasty) incision. Regardless of the choice of incision, the immediate concern is the release of the tamponade and the control of the source of bleeding. The pericardium is widely incised, and the contained blood is evacuated. In some instances, it will be observed that active bleeding is stopped. If so, the operative field is cleansed by irrigation with adequate quantities of warm, normal (0.85 per cent) saline solution and the heart is inspected for the site of injury. If a lacerated wound is readily visible, one may or may not elect to suture the wound although it is not actively bleeding, depending upon its appearance and the likelihood of secondary hemorrhage. On the contrary, when the heart is actively bleeding, hemostasis is believed best obtained by immediate digital compression with the use of a gauze sponge overlying the bleeding site. This is maintained while the operative field is cleansed and the condition of the patient is being stabilized. Hemorrhage from a wound of the atrium is best controlled by either a Potts'-type of curved portacaval clamp or a series of Babcock clamps, modified on the Potts' principle.

Once the condition of the patient is stabilized, the digital compression of the ventricle is replaced by sutures of silk (0) swedged on minimum-trauma needles. Similarly, clamps on the atrium are replaced by either continuous or interrupted sutures of 0 silk. Bleeding that may occur from the insertion of these sutures may be controlled by momentary pressure with a dry sterile gauze sponge. An "anchoring" suture in the apex of the heart is believed more of a danger than an aid and is not used. Similarly, sutures on either side of the heart wound for "cross-traction" control of bleeding are not employed.

Upon completion of the control of hemorrhage, the incised margins of the pericardium are loosely approximated, water-seal drainage of the pleural cavity or cavities is effected, and the wound is closed in layers.

TRAUMATIC CHRONIC CONSTRICTIVE PERICARDITIS

Chronic constrictive pericarditis, or chronic compression of the heart, may occur as a complication of acute cardiac tamponade. In Dalton's series, one case aged 63 and another aged 78 appear.

Symptoms. The symptoms of this condition may occur within 6 to 12 months following the original trauma, or they may be delayed for several years. Characteristically they are similar to those previously described for acute compression of the heart with the exception of the chronicity of symptoms and the presence of hepatomegaly and ascites.

Beck listed a triad of symptoms for both the acute and chronically compressed heart. In the acute form the triad consists of (1) a small quiet heart, (2) a falling arterial pressure, and (3) a rising venous pressure. In the chronic form it consists of (1) a small quiet heart, (2) elevated venous pressure (above 20 ml of water), and (3) hepatomegaly and ascites.

Diagnosis. The diagnosis of chronic traumatic constrictive pericarditis, like other forms of cardiac trauma previously discussed, is dependent principally upon an awareness of its possible presence. In the differential diagnosis one must consider congestive heart failure and cirrhosis of the liver. In chronic congestive heart failure, the history of prior heart disease, the absence of a history of cardiac trauma, and the characteristic clinical, fluoroscopic, and roentgenographic findings should suggest the correct diagnosis. Similarly, in cirrhosis of the liver, the previous clinical history, again the absence of cardiac trauma, the normal cardiac findings, the normal venous pressure, the usual absence of dyspnea, orthopnea, and hepatomegaly, and the evidence of abnormal liver function studies should aid in making the correct diagnosis. In those instances in which disseminated calcific deposits are demonstrable on roentgenograms of the chest, the diagnosis of chronic constrictive pericarditis is simplified (Figs. 18-8A and B).

Treatment. The treatment of chronic traumatic constrictive pericarditis is surgical, based on the axiom that "mechanical obstruction necessitates mechanical intervention." The operation, decortication or pericardiectomy, consists in excision of the fibrous and/or calcific scar which compresses or constricts the movements of the heart. This operation was first suggested in 1897 by Délorme of France, and was performed for the first time in 1913 by Rehn of Germany. Subsequently, the recorded experiences of the German surgeons, Sauerbruch and Schmieden, substantiated the soundness and the practicality of the operation. However, pericardiectomy was not performed in the United States until 1928 at which time it was completed successfully by Churchill of Boston and reported upon the following year (1929).

In the performance of a pericardiectomy the matter of first importance is an adequate exposure of the operative field. Many different types of surgical exposures have been advocated, but the choice of the author is the Duval-Barasty median sternotomy incision (Fig. 18-8D). Through this incision the whole of the precordial area is exposed without the necessity of opening either pleural cavity.

The pathologic findings may vary from a generalized encasement of the heart to a localized scar contracture about the inflow tracts. In

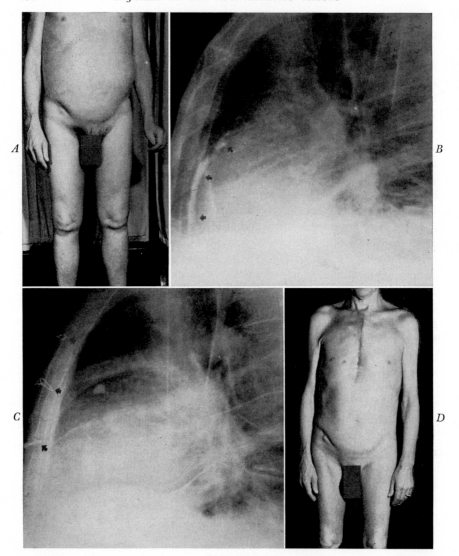

FIG. 18-8. *A.* Preoperative photograph to depict the prominence of the abdomen (ascites) and the stasis edema and pigmentation of the lower extremities. Male, 63 years of age. *B.* Preoperative roentgenogram, lateral view, showing the thick rim of calcium (arrows) deposited within the pericardium. *C.* Postoperative roentgenogram, lateral view, showing the absence of the calcific rim and the presence of the sutures (3) of interrupted No. 28 stainless steel wire (arrows) used to approximate the cut margins of the sternum. *D.* Postoperative (3 weeks) photograph showing the well-healed median sternotomy incision (Duval-Barasty) and the complete disappearance of the ascites and the stasis edema of the lower extremities.

removing the scar tissue, the dissection in the tissue plane between the scar and the myocardial surface of the heart is commenced over the left ventricle. Decompression of the left ventricle first is preferred because its wall is much thicker than that of the right ventricle, and accordingly is less apt to rupture if its chamber is suddenly distended with blood. The decortication of the heart is continued until both ventricles, the encased portions of the auricles, the diaphragmatic surface of the heart, and the areas about the entrance of the superior and inferior vena cava are freed. In the presence of calcification, some calcific deposits may be so intimately adherent to the myocardium that it is best to leave such "islands" *in situ* rather than risk the complication of hemorrhage during the attempt to remove them.

During the operation, one or both pleural cavities may be entered either electively or unintentionally. If so, postoperative water seal-tube drainage of the pleural cavity or cavities is performed. The longitudinal cut margins of the sternum are approximated with interrupted sutures of No. 28 stainless steel wire (Fig. 18-8C), and the overlying soft tissues and skin are closed in layers using interrupted sutures of 000 silk.

Postoperatively, the general measures routinely employed in any thoracic operation are carefully followed. The use of digitalis preparations or quinidine is dependent upon the specific indications in each patient. The improvement following operation may be most dramatic. In the patient illustrated, a weight loss of 42 pounds occurred within the first 3 postoperative weeks (Fig. 18-8). In other instances gradual but progressive improvement may occur and continue for periods of months. This variation in the rapidity of improvement does not of necessity bear any relation to the duration of symptoms preoperatively. In fact, the patient first mentioned was physically incapacitated for 3 years prior to operation. It may also be of interest to note that during this period the patient was in the hospital on six different occasions before the correct diagnosis was established.

BIBLIOGRAPHY

Venous Trauma

Crane, C.: Deep venous thrombosis and pulmonary embolism: experience with 391 patients treated with heparin and 126 patients treated by venous division, with review of the literature. *New Eng. Jour. Med.* **257**:147, 1957.

Dale, W. A.: Ligation of the inferior vena cava for thromboembolism. *Surgery*. **43**:24, 1958.

DeBakey, M. E.: A critical evaluation of the problem of thromboembolism. *Internat. Abst. Surg.* **98**:1, 1954.

DeBakey, M. E., and A. Ochsner: Phlegmasis cerulea dolens, and gangrene associated with thrombophlebitis: case reports and review of the literature. *Surgery*. **26**:16, 1949.

Ellis, S. T., and S. W. Windham: Acute massive venous occlusion in the lower extremity. *Ann. Surg.* **135**:262, 1952.

Grant, R. R., and M. R. Deddish: Phlegmasia cerulea dolens and gangrene. *N.Y. State Jour. Med.* **52**:584, 1952.

Gregoire, R.: La phlébite bleue (plegmatia caerulea dolens.) *Presse Med.* **46**:1313, 1938.

Haimovici, H.: Gangrene of the extremities of venous origin: review of the literature with case reports. *Circulation.* **1**:225, 1950.

Haimovici, H., and G. Suffness: Gangrene of the extremities of venous origin: report of a case. *Amer. Jour. Med. Sci.* **215**:278, 1948.

Homans, J.: Venous thrombosis. *Surgery.* **26**:8, 1949.

Madden, J. L.: Ligation of the inferior vena cava. *Ann. Surg.* **140**:200, 1954.

Madden, J. L.: Venous thrombosis and thromboembolism. *Amer. Jour. Surg.* **87**:909, 1954.

Mahorner, H.: New method of management for thrombosis of deep veins of extremities: thrombectomy, restoration of lumen and heparinization. *Amer. Surgeon.* **20**:487, 1954.

Miles, R. M.: Phlegmasia cerulea dolens: successful treatment by vena cava ligation. *Surgery.* **30**:718, 1951.

Oaks, W. W., and H. R. Hawthorne: Pseudoembolic phlebitis with ligation of the inferior vena cava: case report. *Ann. Surg.* **127**:1247, 1948.

Ochsner, A., and M. E. DeBakey: Thrombophlebitis and phlebothrombosis. *South. Surgeon.* **8**:269, 1939.

Osius, E. A.: Acute massive venous occlusion. *A.M.A. Arch. Surg.* **65**:19, 1952.

Starzl, T. E., R. K. Broadway, R. C. Dever, and G. B. Reams: Management of penetrating wounds of inferior vena cava. *Amer. Surgeon.* **23**:455, 1957.

Veal, J. R., T. J. Dugan, W. L. Jamison, and R. S. Bauersfeld: Acute massive venous occlusion of the lower extremities. *Surgery.* **29**:355, 1951.

Arterial Trauma

Bickham, W. S.: Arteriovenous aneurisms. *Ann. Surg.* **39**:767, 1904.

Brooks, B., G. S. Johnson, and J. A. Kirtley, Jr.: Simultaneous vein ligation: an experimental study of the effect of ligation of concomitant vein on the incidence of gangrene following arterial obstructions. *Surg. Gyn. and Obst.* **59**:496, 1934.

Cooley, D. A., M. E. DeBakey, and G. C. Morris, Jr.: Controlled extracorporeal circulation in surgical treatment of aortic aneurysm. *Ann. Surg.* **146**:473, 1957.

DeBakey, M. E., and F. A. Someone: Battle injuries of the arteries in World War II. *Ann. Surg.* **123**:534, 1946.

Edwards, W. S., and C. Lyons: Traumatic arterial spasm and thrombosis. *Ann. Surg.* **140**:318, 1954.

Elkin, D. C.: Traumatic aneurysm: Matas operation—57 years after. *Surg. Gyn. and Obst.* **82**:1, 1946.

Foley, P. J., E. V. Allen, and J. M. James: Surgical treatment of acquired arteriovenous fistulas. *Amer. Jour. Surg.* **91**:611, 1956.

Gage, M.: Traumatic arterial aneurysm of the peripheral arteries. *Amer. Jour. Surg.* **59**:210, 1943.

Gerbode, F., M. Brainbridge, J. J. Osborn, M. Hood, and S. French: Traumatic thoracic aneurysm: treatment by resection and grafting with use of extracorporeal bypass. *Surgery.* **42**:975, 1957.

Gerbode, F., E. Holman, E. H. Dickenson, and F. C. Spencer: Arteriovenous fistulas and arterial aneurysms: the repair of major arteries injured in warfare, and the treatment of an arterial aneurysm with a vein graft inlay. *Surgery.* **32**:259, 1952.

Holman, E.: Arteriovenous aneurysm: clinical evidence correlating size of fistula with changes in the heart and proximal vessels. *Ann. Surg.* **80**:801, 1924.

Holman, E.: "Arteriovenous Aneurysm." London, Macmillan, 1937.

Holman, E.: War injuries to arteries and their treatment. *Surg. Gyn. and Obst.* **75**:183, 1942.

Hughes, C. W.: The primary repair of wounds of major arteries: an analysis of experience in Korea in 1953. *Ann. Surg.* **141**:297, 1955.

Jahnke, E. J., Jr.: Late structural and functional results of arterial injuries primarily repaired: study of 115 cases. *Surgery.* **43**:175, 1958.

Jahnke, E. J., Jr., and S. F. Seeley: Acute vascular injuries in the Korean War. *Ann. Surg.* **138**:158, 1953.

Lloyd, J. T.: Traumatic peripheral aneurysms. *Amer. Jour. Surg.* **93**:755, 1957.

Lord, J. W., Jr., and P. W. Stone: Use of autologous venous grafts in peripheral arterial system. *A.M.A. Arch. Surg.* **74**:71, 1957.

Makins, G. H.: "On Gunshot Injuries to the Blood Vessels." Baltimore, Wood, 1919.

Mason, J. M.: Traumatic arteriovenous aneurysms of the great vessels of the neck. *Ann. Surg.* **109**:735, 1939.

Mason, J. M., G. S. Graham, and J. D. Bush: Early cardiac decompensation in traumatic arteriovenous aneurysm. *Ann. Surg.* **107**:1029, 1938.

Matas, R.: Traumatic aneurism of the left brachial artery. *Med. News,* Philadelphia, **53**:462, Oct. 27, 1888.

Matas, R.: Radical cure of aneurism: present status of the method of intrasaccular suture or endo-aneurysmorrhaphy. *Jour. Amer. Med. Ass.* **47**:990, 1906.

Matas, R.: Endo-aneurysmorrhaphy: I. Statistics of the operation. *Trans. South. Surg. Ass.* **32**:447. II. Personal experiences and observations on the treatment of arteriovenous aneurisms by the intrasaccular method of suture. *Ibid.* **32**:451, 1919.

Matas, R.: On the systemic or cardiovascular effects of arteriovenous fistulae: A general discussion based upon the authors surgical experience. *Trans. South. Surg. Ass.* **24**:623, 1923.

Morris, G. C., Jr., O. Creech, Jr., and M. E. DeBakey: Acute arterial injuries in civilian practice. *Amer. Jour. Surg.* **93**:565, 1957.

Seeley, S. F., C. W. Hughes, F. N. Cook, and D. C. Elkin: Traumatic arteriovenous fistulas and aneurysms in war wounded: A study of 101 cases. *Amer. Jour. Surg.* **83**:471, 1952.

Shumacker, H. B., Jr.: Emergency management of wounds of large blood vessels. *Surg. Clin. North Amer.* **36**:1329, 1956.

Spencer, F. C., and R. V. Grewe: Management of arterial injuries in battle casualties. *Ann. Surg.* **141**:304, 1955.

Steinberg, I.: Chronic traumatic aneurysm of thoracic aorta: report of 5 cases with plea for conservative treatment. *New Eng. Jour. Med.* **257**:913, 1957.

Storey, C. S., G. L. Hardi, and W. H. Sewell: Traumatic aneurysms of the thoracic aorta. *Ann. Surg.* **144**:69, 1956.

Strassman, G.: Traumatic rupture of the aorta. *Amer. Heart Jour.* **33**:508, 1947.

Swan, H., H. T. Robertson, and M. E. Johnson: Arterial homografts: the fate of preserved aortic grafts in the dog. *Surg. Gyn. and Obst.* **90**:568, 1950.

Ziperman, H. A.: Acute arterial injuries in the Korean War. *Ann. Surg.* **139:**1, 1954.

Cardiac Trauma

Beck, C. S.: Contusions of the heart. *Jour. Amer. Med. Ass.* **104:**109, 1935.

Blalock, A., and M. M. Ravitch: Consideration on non-operative treatment of cardiac tamponade resulting from wounds of the heart. *Surgery.* **14:**157, 1943.

Brockman, H. C., D. A. Cooley, and M. E. DeBakey: Factors influencing survival in experimental heart wounds. *Surg. Forum* (1953). 108, 1954.

Churchill, E. D.: Decortication of the heart (De Lorme) for adhesive pericarditis. *Arch. Surg.* **19:**1457, 1929.

Churchill, E. D.: Pericardial resection in chronic constrictive pericarditis. *Ann. Surg.* **104:**516, 1936.

Cooper, F. W., E. A. Stead, and J. V. Warren: Beneficial effect of intravenous infusions in acute pericardial tamponade. *Ann. Surg.* **120:**822, 1944.

Dalton, J. C., R. J. Pearson, Jr., and P. D. White: Constrictive pericarditis: review and long term follow-up of 78 cases. *Ann. Int. Med.* **45:**445, 1956.

De Vernejoul, R., P. Buisson, R. Courbier, and R. Tricot: Post-traumatic constrictive pericarditis. *Presse Med.* **65:**241, 1957.

Drye, J. C., W. S. Coe, and J. P. Stamer: Heart wounds: a long term follow-up of twenty cases. *Amer. Jour. Surg.* **91:**597, 1956.

Ehrenhaft, J. C., and R. E. Taber: Hemopericardium and constrictive pericarditis. *Jour. Thoracic Surg.* **24:**355, 1952.

Elkin, D. C.: Suturing wounds of the heart. *Ann. Surg.* **95:**573, 1932.

Elkin, D. C.: The diagnosis and treatment of cardiac trauma. *Ann. Surg.* **114:**169, 1941.

Elkin, D. C., and R. E. Campbell: Cardiac tamponade: treatment by aspiration. *Ann. Surg.* **133:**623, 1951.

Farringer, J. L., Jr., and Duane Carr: Cardiac tamponade. *Ann. Surg.* **141:**437, 1955.

Griswold, R. A., and J. C. Drye: Cardiac wounds. *Ann. Surg.* **139:**783, 1954.

Hale, H. W., Jr., and J. W. Martin: Myocardial contusion. *Amer. Jour. Surg.* **93:**558, 1957.

Holman, E.: The recognition and correction of constrictive pericarditis. *Jour. Thoracic Surg.* **18:**643, 1949.

Kissane, R. W.: Traumatic heart disease: nonpenetrating injuries. *Circulation.* **6:**421, 1952.

Maynard, A. De L., N. W. V. Cordice, and E. A. Naclerio: Penetrating wounds of the heart: A report of 81 cases. *Surg. Gyn. and Obst.* **94:**605, 1952.

Ravitch, M. M., and A. Blalock: Aspiration of blood from pericardium in treatment of acute cardiac tamponade after injury: further experience with report of cases. *Ann. Surg.* **58:**463, 1949.

Rehn, L.: Zur experimentellen Pathologie des Herzbeutels. *Arch. f. klin. Chir.* **102:**1, 1913.

Rehn, L.: Über perikardiale Verwachsungen. *Med. Klin.* **16:**999, 1920.

Volhard, F., and Schmieden, V.: Über Erkennung und Behandlung der Umklammerung des Herzens durch schwillige Perikarditis. *Klin. Wchnschr.* **2:**5, 1923.

Wilkinson, A. H., Jr., T. L. Buttram, W. A. Reid, and J. M. Howard: Cardiac injuries: evaluation of immediate and long-range results of treatment. *Ann. Surg.* **147:**347, 1958.

Chapter 19

Injuries of the Face and Neck

John F. Daly and Walter A. Petryshyn

Injuries which result from falls and industrial accidents frequently involve the region of the head and neck. Almost all victims of automobile accidents sustain some injury to the face or neck because they tend to be thrown forward, head first. With an aging population and greater dependence on the automobile, the number of head and neck injuries in the older group has increased. In reviewing automobile accidents, Kulowski found that 11 per cent of the injured were people over 60 years of age.

In the older patient, it is essential to establish function as soon as possible following the injury. This can only be done by giving the patient definitive therapy as soon as this is medically feasible. Since many of these injuries occur in areas which are remote from the larger medical centers, the treatment will frequently be the responsibility of the general surgeon or otolaryngologist, who may not always have the facilities to produce intricate dental appliances. The therapeutic techniques should therefore be simple and widely available.

The management of the face and neck injury can be divided into three phases:

1. Emergency care
2. Examination and planning of therapy
3. Specific problems

EMERGENCY CARE

The patient with an injury to the face or neck frequently suffers from an acute respiratory obstruction. He may be unconscious, lying on his back, and having difficulty breathing. This situation may arise when the relaxed tongue falls posteriorly or when the soft tissues from a fractured jaw are displaced. Blood and mucus may have accumulated in the pharynx and larynx while the patient is lying in the supine position. It is vitally important to relieve this obstruction as quickly as possible by aspirating secretions from the pharynx and larynx, by elevating the tongue with an oral airway or nasopharyngeal tube, and, if possible, by placing the patient in a prone position so that the soft tissues of the tongue will fall forward and help to reestablish an open airway. If respiratory obstruction continues after these preliminary procedures, the pharynx and laryngopharynx should be thoroughly examined for an obstructing denture or other foreign object. Dentures should be carefully inspected to see if a small section has been broken off, since such a fragment may have become lodged in the larynx or trachea. If respiratory difficulties persist despite all these procedures, the neck should be examined for a compression type of injury in the region of the laryngeal cartilages or trachea. Indirect or direct laryngoscopy may be necessary at this time to determine the condition of the intrinsic larynx. If all the possibilities of an upper airway obstruction have been ruled out, then the chest wall and the lungs should be examined. Fractured ribs producing a penetration into lung tissue with a resulting pneumothorax must be diagnosed quickly, and corrective measures must be taken immediately. A 16 gauge needle attached to a 50-ml syringe may be used to aspirate the air from the pleural cavity, and then underwater drainage should be instituted as soon as possible. A mediastinal emphysema may sometimes be revealed by the presence of a subcutaneous emphysema found while palpating the neck. Oxygen must be given to the patient without unnecessary delay. Frequently, severe injuries in the region of the nose and the mouth preclude the use of a mask, and oxygen should then be administered by either a nasal or oral catheter at the rate of 5 liters per minute. The pulmonary situation may be further complicated by the fact that the patient has vomited and aspirated food and other foreign material into his trachea and bronchi. This in turn may progress to atelectasis, pneumonia, or lung abscess. Therefore obstruction in the tracheobronchial tree must be recognized quickly and immediately relieved by bronchoscopy or by aspiration. After the patient's status has been rapidly evaluated and any necessary emergency procedures have been carried out, consideration must be given to the need of a tracheotomy for the continued maintenance of the airway. In the aged patient, the pulmonary reserve is frequently lowered owing to emphysema, fibrosis, or cardiac decompensation. Therefore, even after the hurdle of acute obstruction has been passed, it is vitally important to assure the continuance of the airway.

The tracheotomy, once used only when a patient was on the threshold of death from suffocation, has now been shown to be valuable in a large number of situations. In discussing its use in bulbar poliomyelitis, Galloway stimulated interest in this procedure for removing pharyngeal and pulmonary secretions. Workers in other fields, such as Carter and Giuseffi in thoracic surgery, Echols, Taylor, and Austin in neurosurgery, Atkins in postoperative and debilitated patients, and Johnson with the aged, have evaluated tracheotomy from many aspects and have established its value.

The indications for tracheotomy may be classified into three large groups, mechanical obstruction, aspiration of secretions, and elective.

Mechanical obstruction may be due to inflammation, edema, neoplasm, trauma, or foreign body. Occasionally the obstruction may be temporarily relieved by the use of the endotracheal tube or bronchoscope. However, these methods provide only temporary benefit, and at the time of their use, a decision must be made as to whether tracheotomy is indicated for more permanent therapy.

Aspiration of secretions occurs when a patient is unconscious, paralyzed, in pain, or debilitated. Many of the problems of the aged fall into this category. Among these are the elderly individuals who develop hypostatic pneumonia while they are bedridden, those with chest injuries who cannot cough up their own aspirated secretions, and those with pulmonary emphysema and secretions who must struggle against 150 cc of dead air in the respiratory tract before they can get oxygen into their alveoli. Such cases are benefited by tracheotomy. In some patients, pulmonary complications result from a combination of mechanical obstruction and aspiration of secretions.

Elective tracheotomy for reasons of prophylaxis or surgical expediency is now more frequently used than it had been in the past. Within this group fall many problems associated with fracture of the mandible and maxilla. The procedure may be carried out immediately preceding surgery in order to facilitate the administration of general inhalation anesthesia, or soon after the operation to prevent complications from possible vomiting and aspiration.

The technique used in performing the tracheotomy will vary with the experience of the surgeon. The general surgeon familiar with thyroid surgery may prefer to use a transverse or collar-type incision. We have found, however, that a vertical incision provides a direct, midline, anatomically simple approach, which partially eliminates the danger of working too far laterally in the neck. The soft tissues in the midline of the neck from the cricoid cartilage to the suprasternal notch are infiltrated with 2 per cent Novocain. A vertical incision is made extending from the cricoid cartilage to one finger's width above the superior edge of the sternum, through skin and subcutaneous tissue (Fig. 19-1, step 1). The superficial layer of the deep cervical fascia, identified as a glistening white sheet, is then incised in the midline. The sternohyoid and sternothyroid muscles are then separated in the midline and the isthmus of the thyroid is exposed (Fig. 19-1, step 2). If the isthmus is narrow, it may be retracted superiorly or inferiorly; if wide, it must be incised between clamps and the cut ends inverted (Fig. 19-1, steps 3 and 4). The trachea is now exposed and a window is made in the anterior tracheal wall through the second or third tracheal ring (Fig. 19-1, step 5). A tracheotomy tube of the appropriate size is inserted into the opening in the

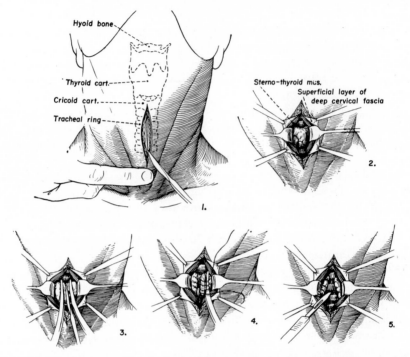

FIG. 19-1. Tracheotomy. *Step 1:* An incision is made in the midline through skin, subcutaneous fat, and the superficial layer of the deep cervical fascia from the level of the cricoid cartilage to one finger's width above the suprasternal notch. *Step 2:* The sternothyroid and sternohyoid muscles are separated in the midline and retracted laterally, exposing the isthmus of the thyroid gland. *Step 3:* The thyroid isthmus is elevated from the trachea and incised in the midline between tightened hemostats. *Step 4:* The cut ends of the thyroid isthmus are closed, using the thyroid capsule and an inverting suture. *Step 5:* A window is made in the second or third tracheal ring with a scalpel and the appropriate-sized tracheotomy tube is inserted.

trachea and tied securely around the neck. A 6-inch strip of ½-inch-wide iodoform packing is then placed lightly around the tube to keep the incision slightly open. The superior and inferior ends of the incision may be closed with a 3/0 black silk suture. The wound must not be closed tightly around the tracheotomy tube because this invariably causes subcutaneous emphysema. The emphysema may come on rapidly, spread over the entire body, and add to the patient's morbidity. Oxygen may be delivered directly into the tracheotomy tube through a catheter placed in it to a depth of 2 inches. The oxygen, which is first moistened by passing it through water or by nebulization, should flow at the rate of 5 liters per minute. At other times a moist gauze apron is placed over the tube to prevent drying of the tracheal secretions and also to trap the secretions which are coughed up.

Postoperatively, the inserted trachea should be suctioned frequently to remove residual secretions. The inner cannula should be removed, cleaned, and replaced at least 3 times a day. The entire tracheotomy tube should be changed on the third postoperative day and periodically thereafter. The iodoform packing is removed permanently on the first changing. Good postoperative handling of the tracheotomized patient depends on the skill and knowledge of the nurses assigned to him. The operating physician should demonstrate the required techniques so that there is no misunderstanding of duties and responsibilities.

Bleeding is an emergency which must be handled immediately. Bleeding which is visible on the face or neck should be controlled with pressure dressings, or if the bleeding is arterial, the vessel should be isolated in the wound, clamped with a hemostat, and ligated. It is unlikely that a patient suffering from a laceration of any of the major neck vessels would survive the injury unless first aid were given immediately after the accident. Bleeding into the nasal chambers, oropharynx, or laryngopharynx may not be recognized and thus may cause considerable harm before it is detected. Blood clots forming in the region of the larynx may block the airway, and if bleeding into the tracheobronchial tree continues, the patient may literally drown in his own blood. A specific search for active bleeding should be made when the patient's mouth and pharynx are examined, and blood should be aspirated from this area. Bleeding from the ear canal is rarely brisk, and it is better not to pack the canal unless an emergency arises.

EXAMINATION AND PLANNING OF THERAPY

When a patient's airway has been established, bleeding controlled, and shock treated, the extent of injuries should be thoroughly assayed and therapy planned.

Superficial lacerations on the head and neck present no difficulty in diagnosis, but deeper injuries, particularly those of the bony framework, may require several modalities of examination before complete evaluation can be made.

Though x-rays are important, the palpating finger and the examiner's clinical ability provide invaluable information about the severity of the injuries. Gentle palpation to determine crepitus and abnormal motion may reveal fractures of the bony framework of the face and jaw which can later be confirmed by x-ray. In examining the soft tissues, careful palpation is more revealing than x-ray examination. The mouth should be examined for loose teeth and injuries of the buccal mucosa. These may not be detected on the preliminary examination unless specifically sought. The tongue should also be carefully examined to determine if there has been any laceration. The eyes should be examined to see if there are any lacerations of the lids, abrasions of the cornea or sclera, or perforating wounds of the eyeballs. A 2 per cent fluorescein solution may be used to stain a possible corneal abrasion. The eye should be carefully searched for any foreign material which can be removed by gentle irrigation with warm, normal saline solution, and the eye patched with a sterile dressing until the opthalmologist can take over the management.

The external ear as well as the auditory canals should be examined to determine the presence of free blood or cerebrospinal fluid. A laceration of the ear canal may be an early indication of a basilar skull fracture through the temporal bone. Red or blue discoloration of the drum or hemotympanum may also indicate the possibility of a deeply located basilar fracture and actual fracture lines can be seen and palpated. If the patient is conscious, his hearing can be grossly tested by whispering or speaking to him, but careful audiometric evaluation should follow as soon as possible.

The external nose should be palpated for any abnormalities in contour of the nasal bones or cartilages. A depressed type of fracture is readily detected by palpation as well as by x-ray. The nasal chambers should also be inspected for lacerations causing hemorrhage and for the presence of cerebrospinal fluid resulting from a fracture through the cribiform plate. Any displacement of the nasal septum should be noted. Starting in the region of the infraorbital rim, the facial bones should be palpated for separations, buckling, or crepitus. The anterior face of the maxilla should be examined for possible depression of the anterior wall of the maxillary sinus, and the malar prominence and the zygomatic arch for abnormality of position or motility. In addition to inspection of the teeth, examination of the mouth should include palpation of the gingival arches to detect an alveolar type of fracture of both the maxilla and mandible.

The temporomandibular joint should also be examined for motility. Palpation of the neck, particularly of the hyoid bone and laryngeal cartilages, may reveal abnormal motion, crepitus, or tenderness, which should then be further investigated. Indirect laryngoscopy with a laryngeal mirror should be attempted if there is any suggestion of injury to this area, and also to determine the airway status. Occasionally ecchymotic areas will be seen in the posterior pharyngeal wall and in the regions of the laryngopharynx and of the larynx.

A complete examination requires x-ray studies. Injuries to the cervical spine can be adequately demonstrated only by x-ray. The usual views are the forehead-nose (Caldwell) position, nose-chin (Waters) position, and right and left lateral views. If injuries to the mandible are suspected, oblique views are helpful. Other views may be suggested by the roentgenologist if additional information is necessary. A soft-tissue x-ray of the neck may sometimes be valuable, particularly if there is a possibility of a foreign body in the neck. The x-ray may occasionally demonstrate a fracture which has been overlooked because it caused no displacement and minimal symptoms. Since x-rays may become important records in legal action, they should be procured even if physical signs and symptoms appear to be minimal.

After the patient's injuries have been examined, and given emergency care, attention should be turned to his general condition. Such factors as the patient's age, nutrition, and general medical status are especially important in determining the future care of older people.

The proper anesthetic must be carefully selected for the aged patient. All too frequently these cases are complicated by brain injury and intercranial or subdural hemorrhage, and the patient may be unconscious or semicomatose. With the airway under control, definitive surgery must be postponed until the patient's general condition has improved and a general anesthetic can be administered safely. The injuries may involve other regions in addition to the face and neck, and when feasible, the surgical procedures should be so arranged that they may be carried out at one time, to avoid repeated anesthesia. Consultation should involve the anesthesiologist, as well as any general or special surgeons whose services may be required, and should attempt to determine whether all the necessary procedures can be performed during one operative session.

Whenever possible, local anesthesia should be used, in the form either of local infiltration or of nerve block. Where several or multiple injuries to the face and jaws require prolonged procedures, surgery around the mouth may be facilitated if a preliminary tracheotomy under local anesthesia is done first and the general anesthetic is administered through an endotracheal tube inserted through the opening. Although the method of anesthesia is usually determined by the anesthesiologist, the one most commonly used is intravenous Pentothal sodium and succinylcholine plus nitrous oxide and oxygen. If at all possible, the patient should be adequately prepared with atropine sulfate and if necessary, a barbiturate. Narcotics such as morphine should not be used if the head has been injured. When severe trauma to the neck makes subsequent edema probable, or when the jaws have been wired in the occlusal position, a tracheotomy is done at the conclusion of the procedure and left until the patient has adequately recovered from the surgery and anesthesia. The tracheotomy may then be left in place for a period of several days or until all danger of obstruction is past.

Along with the special attention demanded in the aftercare of the local injuries, the patient's general physiology, nutrition, and early release from bed care are managed as described by Wade and Braunstein in Chap. 2.

SPECIFIC PROBLEMS

Soft-Tissue Injuries. Injuries to the soft tissues of the region of the face and neck range from small, simple lacerations to extensive avulsions and losses of tissue. Because of their exposed location, resulting deformities are likely to prove disfiguring, if not actually disabling. The aged patient is as acutely aware of an unsightly scar as the adolescent. The antibiotics now provide great flexibility in the attempt to preserve tissue, but they do not eliminate the need for the most thorough cleansing of the lacerations and wounds. In the region of the head and neck, every effort should be made to preserve the maximum amount of healthy, viable tissue. Large pieces of tissue should not be removed indiscriminantly, and debridement should be meticulous and conservative. Elderly victims of automobile accidents are frequently thrown onto a road where many small particles of dirt may become embedded in the soft tissues of the face and neck. A painstaking cleansing of the tissues will prevent pigmented and tattooed scars. An eye spud or a stiff bristle or wire brush may be useful in removing foreign particles.

The skin edges of the lacerations should be trimmed conservatively to produce a smooth line of approximation. Subcutaneous retaining sutures should be so placed that a minimum of tension is exerted on the skin sutures. In this manner more delicate suture material such as 4-0 silk and 5-0 Dermalon may be used to approximate the skin edges. The stitches should be small and should be removed as early as possible to prevent stitch scars. The retaining suture should be of absorbable material such as chromic catgut. In extensive avulsions, the suturing of the tissues should follow such anatomical landmarks as the vermilion border of the lip, the folds of the alae nasi, and the inner and outer canthus of the eye. The eyebrows should be repaired without shaving since they grow back very slowly.

If a structure such as the external ear, nose, or scalp is totally avulsed, an attempt should be made to replace it if it is available, although this is only rarely successful. Where large areas of skin are denuded, early grafting is essential to prevent contraction of scarring. Lacerations of the oral mucosa should be closed loosely, leaving small openings for drainage. Suture materials may be of either silk or chromic catgut. Lacerations through the tongue are most conveniently repaired with heavier chromic catgut such as 00. Minor skin abrasions may be dressed with petroleum jelly gauze. Tight, circular bandages around the neck should be avoided, since posttraumatic edema may cause them to produce either respiratory or circulatory obstruction.

Tetanus antitoxin or toxoid should always be administered in this type of injury. The patient should first be tested, and if he is not sensitive to horse serum, 3,000 units of tetanus antitoxin should be given. If he is sensitive to horse serum, cow serum may be used.

When penicillin is used prophylactically in a case of severe facial

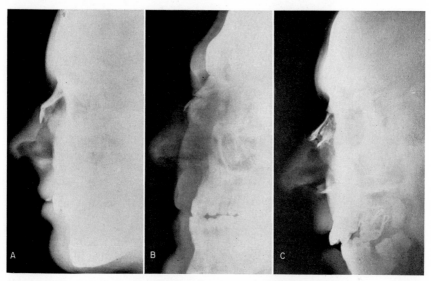

Fig. 19-2. *A, B,* and *C.* Illustrating fractures of the distal, middle, and proximal third of the nasal bones. These fractures can be adequately handled by elevating the nasal bones as illustrated in Fig. 19-6. If necessary the reduced position of the nasal bones can be maintained by packing the nasal chambers with ½ inch petroleum jelly gauze.

lacerations, patients have fewer postoperative complications. In all cases of compounded fracture of the facial skeleton, appropriate antibiotics are administered until the soft tissues are completely healed.

Nose. The external nose is made up of both a bony and a cartilaginous framework which is covered by skin and lined by mucous membrane. The simplest type of injury to the nose is usually a laceration which may also involve the periostium or perichondrium. It is best managed by cleansing, controlling the bleeding vessels with ligatures, and then suturing in layers. The skin is closed with 5-0 interrupted Dermalon sutures. In repairs around the alae nasi, careful approximation of facial landmarks is important. Careful comparison of one side with the other will assist in diminishing deformities.

The bony framework, consisting of the nasal bones and the frontal process of the maxilla, may be injured by a blow from the front or the

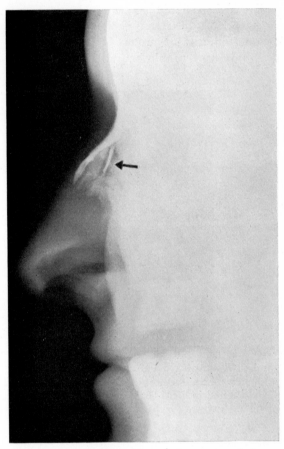

Fig. 19-3. Overriding of the depressed lateral fragments of the nasal bones may be visible as a density in the x-ray. Unless this fragment is elevated, the patient will have a deformity of the nose.

side. The simplest type of injury to the nasal bone is usually a slight depression or angulation of the tip, which may sometimes become overriding owing to displacement (Fig. 19-2A). It may also be injured in its middle portion or in the region of the nasal frontal bone junction (Fig. 19-2B and C). A lateral blow may depress the nasal bones so that they will lie under the frontal process of the maxilla, and this may show up on the lateral nasal x-ray (Fig. 19-3). Severe fractures may show marked comminution, with or without compounding to the external surface of the face or into the nasal cavity (Fig. 19-4). However, nasal bleeding frequently indicates compounding into the chamber. Severe frontal

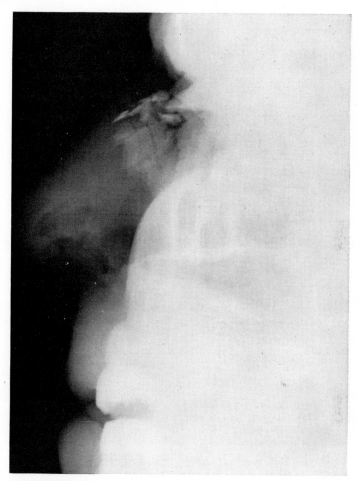

Fig. 19-4. A nasal bone fracture with marked comminution will need to be reduced and maintained in proper alignment by the technique described in Fig. 19-7.

blows, such as those inflicted by the steering wheel, may produce a saddle-nose type of deformity as well as depression of the glabella of the frontal bone, and these injuries are usually complicated by the fact that the frontal sinuses are involved (Fig. 19-5).

In addition to the injuries of the bony structures, the cartilages may be torn loose from their bony attachments and displaced. The nasal

septum may be displaced from its attachment to the upper and lower
nasal cartilages as well as from the palate and vomer. Examination of the
nasal chamber reveals this displacement, but x-rays, especially a good
occlusal film, will give additional information.

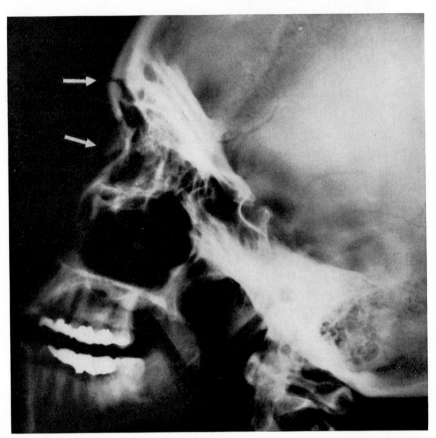

FIG. 19-5. Multiple fractures of the nasal bone, glabella, and frontal sinus usually
require an open reduction for the replacement of the fragments. Special effort
should be made to retain the natural ostium of the frontal sinus.

The external nose should be thoroughly cleansed. Many injuries to
the nose can be adequately treated under local anesthesia produced by
infiltrating the nasal dorsum and adjacent areas with 2 per cent Novocain
and applying 1 per cent Xylocaine or 10 per cent cocaine on cotton
tampons within the nasal chambers. The nasal septum should be replaced
into its normal position in the midline. When this structure is severely
impacted it may be necessary to resort to manipulation with the Asch
nasal forceps. Using the fingers externally as a guide for the proper mold-

ing of the nasal bones, a thin, narrow elevator, its end covered with rubber tubing, is inserted into the chamber underneath the nasal bones and the fragments are then manipulated into position (Fig. 19-6). Frequently the nasal bone fracture is reduced with an audible click, and the bones are aligned into their normal position. If the reduction main-

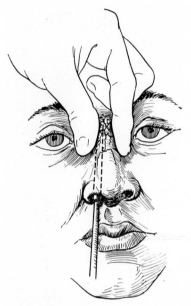

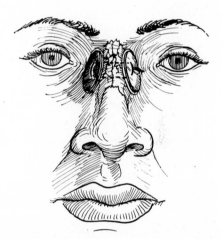

Fig. 19-6. A narrow elevator, covered with a thin piece of rubber tubing, is used to elevate the depressed nasal bones. If the fragments do not retain their position on withdrawal petroleum jelly gauze packing is placed in the nasal chamber against the bones to support them.

Fig. 19-7. Lead plates, brought together by a stainless steel wire which passes through the skin, nasal bone fragments, and nasal septum, will create a nasal dorsum in the severely crushed nose. A piece of felt should be used under the lead plate to avoid a direct skin and metal contact.

tains itself in the original position when the elevator is withdrawn, nothing further need be done, except to control bleeding. However, if the nasal bones appear to become displaced as soon as the elevator is withdrawn, an attempt to maintain them in proper position may be made by packing both nasal chambers with ½-inch petroleum jelly gauze. It may also be necessary to use an external splint made from dental stent material.

When the fractured bones are markedly comminuted and depressed, the approach described by Erick may be required. Soft lead plates are placed on both lateral aspects of the crushed nose, and a transfixion wire is passed through the crushed nasal bones and through both lead plates and then knotted over one of the metal plates (Fig. 19-7). This maneuver will give height to the nasal bones and restore a satisfactory profile without the use of involved intranasal splints and headcaps. Severe fractures

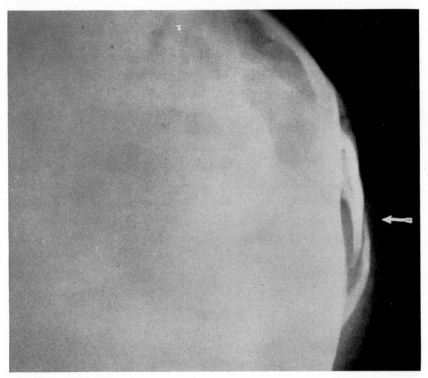

Fig. 19-8. A fracture of the zygomatic arch with minimal displacement or depression does not require surgical intervention.

involving the glabella and frontal sinus will usually require open reduction and interosseous wiring of the individual fragments.

Zygoma. Because of the overlying soft-tissue edema, fractures of the zygoma may be missed when the patient is seen soon after the injury unless there is interference with motion of the mandible. When the soft-tissue swelling subsides, the facial deformity becomes prominent. Therefore, the zygomatic arch should always be specifically investigated in all injuries to the side of the head and face. Palpation may reveal crepitus on pressure and depression of the bony zygomatic arch, which can later be confirmed by a superior x-ray view of the skull. The fracture of the zygomatic arch may be slightly or markedly displaced. If there is no

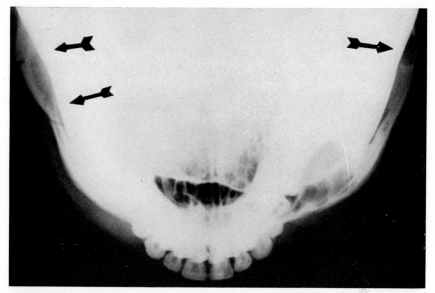

FIG. 19-9. The depressed fracture of the left zygomatic arch will need to be elevated. This can be done with the Gillies' procedure as illustrated in Fig. 19-10. The right zygomatic arch reveals an asymptomatic bone cyst.

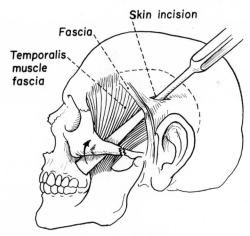

Skin incision

Fascia

Temporalis muscle fascia

FIG. 19-10. The Gillies' procedure, done through an incision in the hair-covered area, can be used successfully to elevate a depressed zygomatic arch fracture. The elevator must lie on the temporal muscle fascia and under the zygomatic arch to be in the right plane for the elevation.

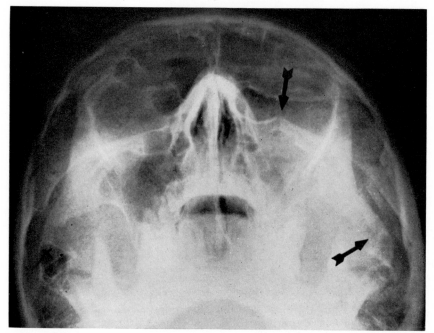

Fig. 19-11. Fractures of the zygomatic tripod with slight displacement can be reduced by the Gillies' procedure and may not require further fixation.

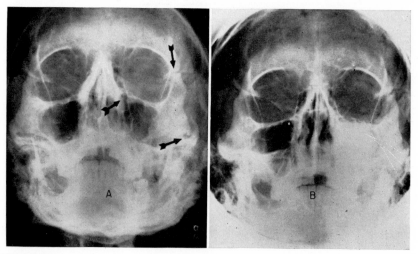

Fig. 19-12. Fractures of the zygomatic tripod with moderate displacement can be reduced and maintained in position by packing the antrum with iodoform gauze through the Caldwell-Luc incision.

displacement, nothing further need be done (Fig. 19-8). When the arch is depressed, the approach in the temple area described by Gillies is often successful in effecting reduction, which then maintains itself without further maneuvers (Figs. 19-9 and 19-10).

The more complicated fractures of the zygoma involve its articulations with the frontal, temporal, and maxillary bones. Displacement may be

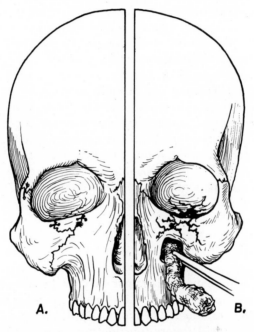

FIG. 19-13. *A*. A fractured and movable zygomatic bone can be immobilized in the correct position by interosseous wiring, through small drilled holes. *B*. Fractures of the lower orbital rim, the floor of the orbit, and the anterior face of the maxillary antrum can be immobilized by packing the antrum with iodoform gauze through the Caldwell-Luc incision.

diagnosed by palpating the floor of the orbit for any interruptions or buckling (Fig. 19-11). There may be a displacement of the lateral aspect of the orbital rim at its union with the frontal bone. If the displacement is marked, the patient will complain of diplopia.

The fracture of the zygomatic bone may be treated by several approaches: first the temporal approach through the Gillies' incision (Fig. 19-10), second the maxillary sinus approach (Figs. 19-12 and 19-13*B*), third the buccal approach, fourth the intranasal approach, and fifth by direct interosseous wiring (Fig. 19-13*A*). It may sometimes be necessary to try more than one approach for satisfactory permanent reduction.

Fractures of the zygoma which are not markedly displaced may at times be satisfactorily reduced by the Gillies' approach (Fig. 19-10). If depression of the floor of the orbit produces diplopia, the approach through the maxillary antrum with visualization of the floor of the orbit is valuable, and the reduction may be maintained by packing the maxillary antrum with iodoform gauze until the bones unite (Figs. 19-13B and 19-14). The packing is allowed to emerge through the Caldwell-Luc incision or through an intranasal antrotomy. If the zygomatic bone is markedly fragmented so that the position of the bones cannot be adequately maintained by either of the two previously described techniques, an open reduction with interosseous wiring of fragments should be used, as illustrated by Adams (Fig. 19-13A). This direct approach results in minimal postoperative complications and eliminates the need for cumbersome and uncomfortable headdresses with appliances. The intranasal approach can also give satisfactory results in skilled hands, but the maneuver is done by touch and without complete visualization.

Techniques for Immobilization. The principle of restoring function of the injured part as soon as possible is never more applicable than in the case of the aged patient. *The physician should choose the method of treatment which will activate the patient most quickly even if the end result is less than perfect.* This truism, emphasized in most chapters of this book, is as applicable to face and neck injury as to other injuries of the elderly victim of trauma. The aged patient does not have sufficient resiliency to respond to the repeated surgery and anesthetics which may be needed to achieve perfection, nor may he be able to tolerate the physical and emotional difficulties involved in wearing appliances over prolonged periods of time. When properly used, the following recommended techniques will restore function quickly and will give an excellent result without the necessity of deferring definitive treatment because of the lack of specialized facilities.

Fractures of the maxilla and mandible may be reduced and immobilized by using one or more of the following methods.

Intradental wiring is the technique of wiring together adjacent teeth either across the line of fracture or in occlusion. No. 26 stainless steel wire is looped securely around the neck of the tooth and tightened. The wires are fastened together across the line of fracture, and then the upper and lower jaws are wired together in normal occlusion.

Arch-bar wiring utilizes either the Jelenko or Winter prefabricated splint or the stainless steel arch bar. This technique is useful in a large variety of maxillary and mandibular fractures. The fractured fragments of teeth are realigned and then anchored to the dental arch bar which is bent to conform to the patient's gingival arch. This method is not

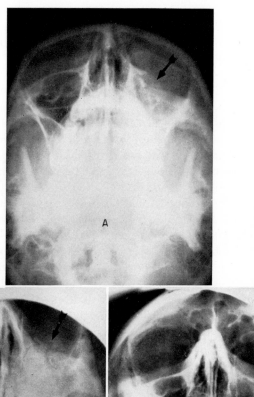

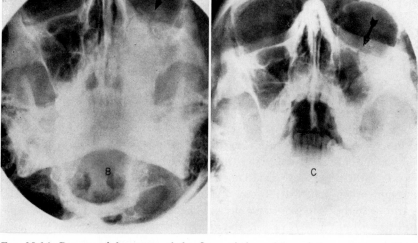

FIG. 19-14. Depressed fractures of the floor of the orbit and the anterior wall of the maxillary antrum are treated by reducing the fracture and packing the antrum with iodoform gauze. *A.* Displaced fracture of the floor of the orbit and anterior antral wall. *B.* The antrum is packed with iodoform gauze reducing the fracture. *C.* Six months postoperative revealing good alignment of the floor of the orbit and a normal left antrum.

serviceable when the patient does not have enough teeth to anchor the arch bar securely. However, only a few teeth are needed.

Both of these methods require a minimum of equipment and do not involve the complicated technique associated with dental casts and cemented splints.

If the patient is edentulous and wears a complete denture on one arch, this should be used to maintain the proper spacing between upper and lower jaw. It can be wired directly to the alveolar arch, and then inter-dental wiring is used on the opposing teeth. If the patient's own denture is not available, most dentists can easily fabricate a temporary one, or a prefabricated Gunning-type splint may be used. If both jaws are edentulous, upper and lower dentures are wired to the appropriate jaws and then wired together in apposition. Edentulous jaws should never be wired together in apposition unless proper spacing is left for the teeth. A set of temporary dentures can be made for this purpose. If the mandible needs to be immobilized firmly against an edentulous upper jaw, the nasal pyriform crest may be used for fixation, as described by Thoma and Fordyce.

Interosseous wiring of bone fragments is effective when the patient is edentulous or when the fracture is already exposed by a laceration. This method is also useful where comminution has occurred. This technique is preferable to others in the older patient, where rapid restoration of function is necessary. Where there has been marked comminution with loss of bone, function is rapidly restored by primary insertion of a Vitallium splint directly to the osseous fragments, as described by Freeman and Conley. Bone grafts can be used in conjunction with the Vitallium splint. The crest of the ilium is particularly suitable as a donor site since it has two cortical surfaces and is of the same thickness as most of the mandible.

Fractures of the Maxilla. Fractures of the maxilla may range from simple ones of the alveolar arch to the most complicated types of cranial facial disjunction. Since maxillary fractures are frequently associated with those of other bones, a surgical approach should be selected which will facilitate reduction in several areas. The maxillary bone forms part of three cavities, the oral, nasal, and ocular. Fractures in the maxilla have a tendency to occur along certain lines of structural weakness as described by LeFort. However, since no powerful muscles are attached to the maxilla, displacement is not as marked as that seen in fractures of the mandible. In the examination of the patient whose face is injured and who is suspected of having a maxillary fracture, several areas must be carefully observed. The floor of the orbit should be palpated for any separation or displacement. The alveolar ridges should be examined for displacement and loss of teeth, and the dental occlusion should be checked for proper articulation with the lower jaw. Fractures of the anterior face of the maxilla can be detected by palpating this area through the mouth.

Definition of the floor of the orbit through sinus x-rays taken in the usual positions (frontonasal, mentonasal, and lateral view) will aid in the diagnosis. If the maxillary antrum on one side is opaque in contrast to the opposite side, a fracture through the antrum should be suspected even if the bone does not reveal displacement (Fig. 19-15).

Fractures of the maxilla with no displacement or interference with the normal occlusion of the teeth may be treated conservatively with

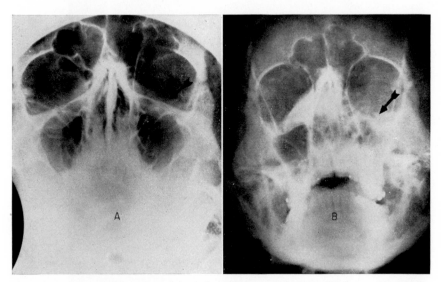

FIG. 19-15. Fractures of the floor of the inferior orbital rim with a minimal displacement requiring no surgical reduction. *A.* The left maxillary antrum is normal. *B.* Blood in the left maxillary antrum makes it appear opaque on x-ray.

antibiotic therapy and observation. The more severe injuries which require specific and definitive therapy include depression of the anterior face of the maxilla, depression and displacement of the floor of the orbit, and any involvement of the occlusion of the teeth. Depressions of the anterior face of the maxilla are best approached with the Caldwell-Luc incision, through which the anterior face of the maxillary antrum can be visualized and the extent of damage determined. The maxillary sinus is opened and blood aspirated from it. An attempt should be made to replace the fragments so as to restore the anterior face to its normal contour, which can then be maintained by packing the antrum with iodoform gauze (Figs. 19-13*B* and 19-16). The end of the packing can be brought out through the incision in the mouth or through a nasal antrotomy in the inferior meatus of the nose.

A displaced fracture of the floor of the orbit may also be treated through the Caldwell-Luc incision, cleaning out the blood clot, and packing the maxillary antrum. If this is not totally satisfactory in maintaining the normal contour of the floor of the orbit, open reduction with

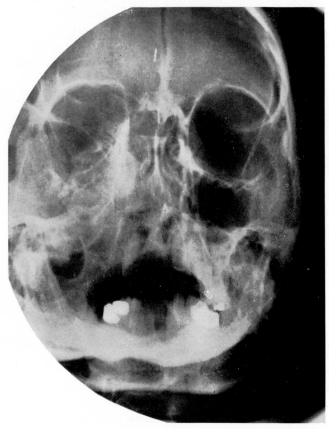

FIG. 19-16. A severe injury, crushing the floor of the orbit and the anterior wall of the maxilla. This injury is treated by packing the maxillary antrum with iodoform gauze packing through a Caldwell-Luc incision.

an interosseous wiring of the floor of the orbit is necessary (Fig 19-13A). Fractures of the alveolar arch or of the maxilla transversely through the alveolar arch are best reduced with an arch bar wired to the dental arch. In fractures of the alveolar processes, it is important to determine whether any dental roots have been devitalized or fractured. Fragments of teeth are best removed and an alveolectomy done to remove all sharp edges of bone. If the teeth are attached to the fractured fragment and are still in reasonably satisfactory condition, the entire fragment should be restored to its normal position and maintained by wiring to a dental arch bar. Wiring the maxilla and mandible in proper occlusion will provide additional support.

Where sections of the maxilla which have been broken loose from the surrounding bone contain teeth, they can be replaced and maintained in position by wiring to a dental arch bar and interdental wiring between the upper and lower jaws. Large fragments that do not contain teeth may be immobilized by interosseous wiring.

Displaced transverse fractures through the maxilla should be restored to their normal position of occlusion with the lower dental arch and maintained there by interdental wiring. The mandible should then be supported by a Barton type of bandage. To restore occlusal relationship in a patient with an edentulous maxilla, it may be necessary to develop this procedure further by wiring the denture to the upper jaw and then by wiring the denture, in turn, to the mandible. Again, a supporting bandage is used to restrict mobility of the lower jaw to a minimum. Cumbersome head apparatus with wires should be avoided if possible.

A fundamental principle in the handling of maxillary fractures which involve displacement of the dental occlusion is the restoration of the patient's normal bite, and surgeons who may be called upon to treat such injuries should acquaint themselves with its normal variations. A full complement of teeth is not absolutely necessary for good functional reduction. However, many aged people are edentulous, and in these cases the open reduction wiring technique is extremely useful in restoring the normal occlusion. The patient's future dentures can then be made with any necessary corrections.

Fractures of the Mandible. The proper reduction of the fractured mandible also aims to restore the patient's normal dental occlusion. Matching the opposing articulation surfaces of the teeth will correct any displacement, and then the bones must be immobilized in that position. This is frequently accomplished with interdental or arch-bar wiring. However, the aged patient may be edentulous, and in a way this simplifies the problem, since the dental requirement is minimized and the surgeon can then directly approach the realignment of the bone. The edentulous state may be corrected later with dentures. Because of the importance of rapid restoration of function, open reduction with interosseous wiring or plating is valuable in the edentulous patient. The fractured mandible may require one or more methods of therapy, depending on the type and location of the injury.

The condyle is frequently fractured either alone or with another bone. The fracture may be a slight crack without displacement, greenstick, or a complete and displaced break. If the condyle is fractured alone and the patient has enough teeth to permit the procedure, interdental wiring

of the mandible to maxilla is used (Fig. 19-17). The mandible is immobilized in the occlusal position for 3 to 6 weeks. No special attempt is
made to reduce the fractured condyle to the anatomical alignment. Even
if the fracture heals with anatomical displacement, the patient will usually have a good functional result. Open surgery upon the condyle is
unnecessary in most cases. If both condyles are fractured, it may be
desirable to do an open interosseous fixation of one condyle as described
by Shapiro. If the patient subsequently develops pain, a condylectomy
may be needed.

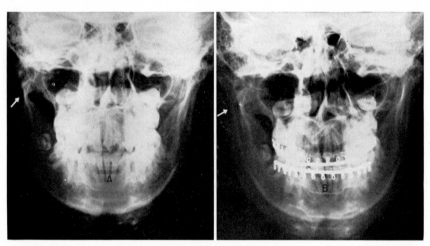

FIG. 19-17. A greenstick fracture of the right mandibular condyle is treated with
wiring to dental arch bars and interdental rubber band fixation for 6 weeks.

Fractures of the coronoid process are uncommon and produce minimal
displacement. If the patient has pain, interdental wiring is used for
immobilization.

In fractures of the ramus, displacement is unusual because of the elevator muscle attachment, and immobilization with interdental wiring
usually suffices.

The body of the mandible is thicker than the ramus and the fracture
occurs along the weak line of junction between these two parts, at the
angle. If there is pain, motion, or displacement and the patient has good
teeth, interdental wiring with immobilization is used. If the mandible
is edentulous, or if the fracture cannot be satisfactorily reduced and
maintained because of the pull of the elevator muscles, open reduction
with interosseous wiring of the fractured ends is the best method of
handling this problem.

A crack of the body with no displacement, motion, or pain may be adequately handled by rest and a liquid diet. A unilateral fracture would be managed by wiring the remaining teeth to the arch bar and immobilizing the mandible and maxilla with interdental wiring. If the condyle is also fractured, this procedure will correct it at the same time. If the mandible is edentulous, interosseous wiring is easily done, bilaterally if necessary, following the technique described by Gibson.

Fractures in the midline through the symphysis usually show minimal displacement and are usually treated by interdental wiring across the midline. If the condyle is involved, the mandible is wired to the maxilla, and if the patient is edentulous, open reduction and interosseous wiring are used.

If the fracture of the alveolar ridge shows moderate displacement, an attempt can be made to immobilize the fragment on an arch bar. If the fragment is floating loose and periosteum is torn, a primary alveolectomy with removal of the fragments is advised.

Postoperatively the patient is advised to maintain good oral hygiene by the frequent use of normal warm saline mouthwash after and between meals.

Ear. Injuries to the ear can be divided into two major groups. Those to the external ear involving the pinna and the external canal have been discussed in the section on soft-tissue injuries. Those involving the middle and inner ear and the facial nerve are related to fractures of the temporal bone which occur in conjunction with skull injuries (Fig. 19-18).

Fractures of the temporal bone are of two basic types, longitudinal and transverse. The longitudinal type is the more common, and may occur as the result of a blow on the vertex or side of the skull. Fracture of the temporoparietal area will extend into the external bony canal, along the roof of the middle ear, and will then follow along the roof of the eustachian tube and carotid canal (Fig. 19-1, step 1). The transverse type is more serious and occurs most frequently from an occipital blow and occasionally from an anterior fossa fracture. The fractures may stem from the foramen magnum, laterally transecting the petrous bone. Transverse fractures of the petrous bone are almost always extensions of posterior fossa fractures (Fig. 19-19). Pure transverse or longitudinal fractures are uncommon. In most cases there is some comminution, and in the more severe injuries there may be a combination of both types.

Fractures of the temporal bone may produce injury to hearing, to balance, or to the facial nerve, individually or in combination. Examination of the patient who has sustained a fracture of the temporal bone may reveal blood in the ear canal as well as laceration of the lining skin. The bleeding in the ear canal is usually minimal, but if severe, it should arouse suspicion of injury to the lateral sinus, jugular bulb, tympanic plexus, middle meningeal artery, or carotid artery. The tympanic membrane may be torn. Laceration of the external auditory canal lining in conjunction with a deformity in the bony canal wall indicates a longitudinal type of fracture. An apparently uninjured bony external canal wall and a tympanic membrane that is intact but bulging because of a hemotympanum or clear fluid is more suggestive of a transverse type of

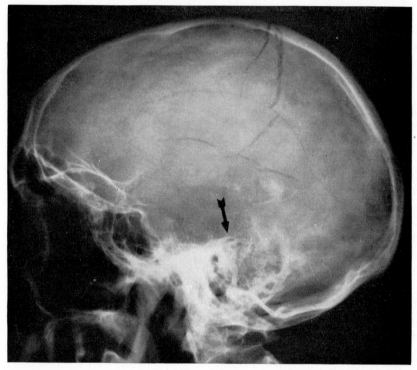

FIG. 19-18. A blow to the vertex or the parietal area of the skull will produce a longitudinal fracture of the temporal bone with bleeding into the external auditory canal.

fracture. In transverse fractures, bleeding from the external auditory canal is unusual, but a cerebrospinal otorrhea is more common. If the temporal bone fracture is 4 or 5 days old, there may be ecchymosis over the mastoid area, which is called Battle's sign.

Hearing loss may occur without a temporal bone fracture. This is called a concussion deafness, and is characterized by a high-tone perceptive hearing loss which is believed to arise as a result of distortion and injury to the basilar membrane from the blow. This type of hearing loss has been produced experimentally in cats by Schuknecht. In the longitudinal type of temporal bone fracture, there may be a conductive element in the hearing loss, owing to injury to the drum and possibly to blood in the middle ear. Further causes of hearing loss are dislocation of the incus or fracture of the neck of the stapes. The conductive deafness frequently tends to resolve. However, conduction deafness alone is not most common in fractured temporal bones. More frequently, a perceptive element is also involved, and this has a smaller degree of recovery. Trans-

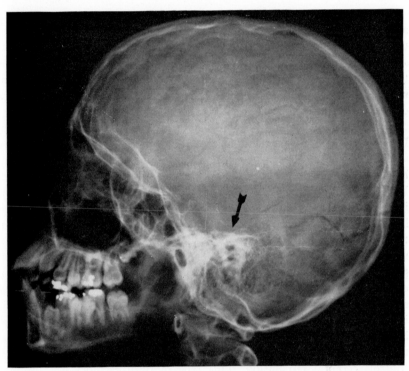

Fig. 19-19. An occipital blow will occasionally produce a transverse fracture of the petrous bone. A hemotympanum may not be present.

verse fractures almost always produce an immediate and total loss of hearing of a perceptive type on the homolateral side. This type of hearing loss is frequently permanent or recovers only partially. A large number of patients suffer hearing loss in the contralateral nonfractured ear, which is probably due to labyrinthian concussion.

Hearing loss should not be tested until the patient's sensorium is clear. The whispered-voice and tuning-fork tests may be used, but they do not produce any reliable quantitative records. Audiogram studies are a necessity, and should be repeated on several occasions if malingering is suspected. The most severe hearing losses usually occur in the range of 3,000 to 8,000 cycles. The deafness or loss of hearing is usually noticed immediately after the injury, but it may develop over a period of 4 to 6 months

as degenerative changes take place. Testing for the recruitment phenomenon seems to indicate that the trauma damages the organ of Corti.
In the older patient the perceptive hearing loss may be further complicated by the presence of presbycusis. Grove has stated that in longitudinal
fractures the function of hearing is more severely damaged with increases
in age.

Tinnitus, the subjective symptom of noise in the ears, occurs commonly
as a result of injury to the temporal bone and may not be related directly
to the severity of trauma. Tinnitus is also found in many older patients
simply as part of the aging process. It is, therefore, sometimes difficult
to evaluate the effect of injury on the appearance of tinnitus. When tinnitus occurs as a result of trauma, it frequently is the most persistent
of the residual symptoms.

Disturbances of equilibrium will occur with injury to the labyrinth.
In the longitudinal type of fracture, the labyrinthian capsule is frequently
spared. In the transverse type, there may be some tearing of the membranous labyrinth as the result of a fracture of the labyrinthian capsule.
If the labyrinthian capsule is fractured, the cochlear vestibular function
is usually lost completely. Vertigo and dizziness are common sequelae of
head injuries. If there is injury to the peripheral vestibular end organ,
the patient is usually subject to attacks of vertigo. On clinical examination he may show spontaneous nystagmus, disturbance of balance, and
past pointing. He may also have nausea and vomiting associated with
cold sweats, but this symptom usually subsides in several weeks, and
subsequently the patient may have an abnormal caloric response. This
injury to the end organ is usually associated with tinnitus and some
hearing loss. There may also be a central type of equilibrium dysfunction which is believed due to injury of the vasomotor apparatus which
controls cerebral circulation. This type of disorder does not produce
vertigo, but instead the patient may have attacks of loss of equilibrium
which are brought on by bending over and moving quickly.

Such drugs as Dramamine and Bonamine have been extremely valuable
in relieving the symptoms of labyrinthian irritation until the process
has subsided. The permanent loss of vestibular function may be recorded
by using the Atkinson modification of the Kobrak test. Two ml of ice
water are instilled into the ear canal, and the onset and duration of
nystagmus are recorded. Normally the nystagmus starts in 30 seconds and
lasts about 1 minute. This test should be limited to intact tympanic
membranes unless sterile water is used.

The facial nerve may be injured within the temporal bone or externally on the face. Most surgeons agree that facial paralysis occurs more
frequently in the transverse fracture (50 per cent) than in the longitudinal
(10 to 18 per cent). If the facial canal is involved in the longitudinal frac-

ture, the region of the genu is usually damaged. In the transverse fracture, the facial nerve may be torn or transected in the internal auditory meatus, frequently at the geniculate ganglion. In this event, paralysis may be permanent. The symptoms of facial paralysis may start immediately after the injury or after a lapse of 4 or 5 days. When symptoms begin later there is usually satisfactory and sometimes spontaneous recovery. There are two types of facial nerve paralysis, peripheral and central. In the peripheral type, the patient loses the ability to contract all of the facial muscles on the involved side. He cannot whistle, or wrinkle his forehead on the paralyzed side, and in addition he loses the corneal reflex. In the central type, there is usually activity of the forehead and eye while the other facial muscles are paralyzed.

Authors differ on how the facial paralysis should be handled. Ninety per cent of the cases will recover spontaneously. Kettle believes that 2 months after injury is adequate time for spontaneous recovery and that after this period, surgical exploration is indicated. Maxwell and Magielski feel that the patient should be observed for a period of 3 months. Others feel that a period of at least 18 months should pass before surgery is tried. This is still a controversial question, but in all probability, if a facial paralysis has lasted longer than 3 months, its recovery will be only partial, and therefore the facial nerve should be explored at the end of that time. During the period of waiting prior to surgical intervention, physiotherapy should include massage, heat, and exercise to the involved side of the face.

The paralyzed facial nerve may be handled by decompression, nerve grafting, or nerve suturing. In doing a decompression, the entire length of the facial canal is opened until the area of injury and its type are determined. This procedure may occasionally reveal that a spicule of bone has compressed the facial nerve, and its removal may reestablish the physiologic continuity of the nerve. However, more frequently decompression is a mere preliminary to either nerve grafting or nerve suturing. Either the ilioinguinal or great auricular nerve is used. This technique was described by Ballance and Duel. Nerve suture is rarely done directly in the fallopian canal, but the nerve is first lifted out of it and the two ends sutured together in the region of the promontory. This has been described by Bunnell. Both nerve graft and nerve suture have produced satisfactory results. The surgeon undertaking these procedures must be thoroughly familiar with the anatomy of the temporal bone.

The facial nerve may be injured peripheral to the stylomastoid foramen as a result of deep lacerations of the face. The injury should be diagnosed at the initial examination and treated at the time of the primary repair of the laceration. Delayed repair of the facial nerve will not reestablish the pathway but will produce instead a fibrosis and muscle atrophy that may make future reestablishment of continuity extremely difficult if not impossible. It may be necessary to insert a nerve graft if there has been an extensive loss of facial nerve tissue. In a clean laceration, such as may occur from a cut by a piece of glass, nerve suture may be sufficient.

X-ray visualization of many of the temporal bone fractures may be unsuccessful. However, if a fracture line is seen to extend from the vertex to the petrous bone, and examination shows that the patient is bleeding in the ear canal, it is safe to assume that the temporal bone is fractured. The Stenvers and Mayer x-ray views may be of value to demonstrate the fracture line.

Emergency treatment for the temporal bone fracture consists mainly of rest, control of bleeding in the ear canal, and antibiotics to prevent intracranial complications. As soon as the patient's general condition has become stabilized and he is well enough to tolerate an audiometric evaluation, his hearing should be tested. If the hearing loss is of a conductive type, return of function may be expected. If it is perceptive, the prospects for good functional return are poorer. If conductive hearing loss persists, the ossicular chain and middle ear can be explored at a future date using a transtympanic approach. If the loss in such cases is due to disarticulation of the ossicular chain, this surgical approach may make it possible to reestablish the ossicular chain and so to improve the patient's hearing. In some cases, a tympanoplasty may be valuable. The vertigo and dizziness may gradually subside. Nevertheless, many of the symptoms can be minimized with medications like Dramamine and Bonamine. Tinnitus may be permanent, although it may diminish in volume. Antibiotics should be administered to prevent intracranial complications such as meningitis or brain abscess. Any blood that seeps from the ear canal should be collected with a pledget of sterile cotton at the external canal, and this should be changed as often as necessary until the discharge ceases. Persistent cerebrospinal otorrhea may require intracranial surgery to close the dural defect.

Parotid Gland. The parotid gland is injured at the time of open injury to the face, when there may also be damage to the facial nerve requiring suture. Injury to the parenchyma of the gland is usually best handled by controlling the bleeding and suturing the capsule over the gland. If Stenson's duct is severed, an attempt should be made to restore continuity by an end-to-end anastomosis. This can be most conveniently accomplished by threading both cut ends of the duct over a narrow polyethylene tube, one end of which is allowed to protrude into the oral cavity through the papilla of the duct, and then approximating them with fine dermalon or silk sutures. Injury to Stenson's duct may be associated with damage to the nearby buccal branch of the facial nerve. Such damage should be sought and repaired. If Stenson's duct cannot be repaired, the severed ends should be ligated and the parotid parenchyma allowed to remain *in situ.* It will eventually undergo atrophy and fibrosis, and salivary fistulas will rarely occur.

Neck. Neck injuries of any consequence may involve either the large vessels or the air or food passages. If the external or internal jugular veins are lacerated, the patient will be exsanguinated within a few minutes unless the bleeding is controlled instantly. Pressure over the bleeding area will usually retard the flow of blood. In addition, it is important to compress the distal end of the severed vein to prevent air from entering the circulation from negative pressure and thus producing an embolus. Injury to the common carotid also will lead to rapid death unless the bleeding is stopped. If pressure controls this bleeding, every attempt should be made to repair the injury rather than to tie the common carotid off completely. Furthermore, because of circulatory changes, the older individual is in a much less favorable position than the younger person if the common carotid must be ligated. In some cases a temporary repair may enable the surgeon to ligate the vessel gradually, and so to minimize some of the dangers of sudden occlusion in the aged.

Hyoid Bone. Fractures of the hyoid bone are infrequent, and unless there is concomitant laceration, therapy is usually unnecessary. If discomfort or distress upon swallowing persists for more than 6 weeks, the situation should be further investigated, and if necessary the hyoid bone should be excised.

If the thyrohyoid membrane is lacerated, it should be closed in the usual manner with interrupted silk or catgut sutures. The hyoid bone and the superior edge of the thyroid cartilage should be placed in their normal position and held with a number 26 stainless steel wire suture. The muscles acting on both the hyoid bone and thyroid cartilage tend to pull them apart in the event of injury to the thyrohyoid membrane. It is necessary to keep both structures in their normal relationship with the wire suture.

Larynx and Trachea. Injuries to the larynx may cause acute laryngeal obstruction, and this must be investigated and remedied as soon as possible. If palpation of the thyroid cartilage shows that it has not been fractured, the interior of the larynx must be investigated to determine injury in that area. Frequently, a blow to the neck will produce a hematoma within the lumen of the larynx, and unless this is evacuated, it will continue to increase, ultimately producing a respiratory obstruction. Where a marked crushing blow to the thyroid cartilage has caused comminution, the lumen of the larynx must be reestablished as soon as possible. Otherwise fibrosis will occur within 2 weeks and may result in stenosis of the larynx. This type of injury is best handled with an emergency tracheotomy, and as soon as the patient's general condition permits, the lumen of the larynx should be reestablished and maintained with an acrylic stent or mold held in place with wire retaining sutures until the cartilages are healed. The common mistake of making the tracheotomy too high in the trachea will further complicate the situation. If possible, the tracheotomy should be made in the region of the third or fourth tracheal ring (Fig. 19-1, steps 1 to 5). Acute injuries to the trachea produce a respiratory obstruction which may be relieved by tracheotomy and the insertion of a long tracheotomy tube or an endotracheal tube. If any tracheal cartilage is lost, an attempt can be made to fill the defect with a plastic mesh tubing or skin graft over an acrylic obturator, as described by Work. Autogenous cartilage grafts have not been consistently successful.

Thyroid. Injuries low in the neck and in the midline may cause a laceration of the thyroid gland with profuse bleeding. If this cannot be adequately controlled with pressure, it may be necessary to ligate the vessels. Injuries low in the neck may also open up the superior mediastinum, permitting air to enter and causing an emphysema. This type of situation can best be controlled by applying pressure to the area of the opening.

BIBLIOGRAPHY

Adams, W. M.: Internal wiring fixation of facial fractures. *Surgery.* **12**:523, 1942.

Adams, W. M., and L. H. Adams: Internal wire fixation of facial fractures: a 15 year follow up report. *Amer. Jour. Surg.* **92**:12, 1956.

Atkins, J. P.: Tracheotomy for prevention of pulmonary complications in postoperative and severely debilitated patients. *Jour. Amer. Med. Ass.* **146**:241, 1951.

Ballance, C. O., and A. B. Duel: The operative treatment of facial palsy. *Arch. Otolaryng.* **15**:1, 1932.

Bauer, F.: Dislocation of the incus due to head injury. *Jour. Laryng. and Otolaryng.* **72**:676, 1958.

Bunnell, S.: Suture of the facial nerve within the temporal bone. *Surg. Gyn. and Obst.* **45**:7, 1927.

Caparosa, R. J., and A. R. Zaratsky: The occlussal film: an adjunct to the roentgen diagnosis of nasal fractures. *A.M.A. Arch. Otolaryng.* **66**:503, 1957.

Cardwell, E. P.: Fracture of the zygomatic tripod. *Plastic and Reconstructive Surg.* **4**:235, 1949.

Carter, G. N., and J. Guiseffi: Tracheotomy: useful procedure in thoracic surgery. *Jour. Thoracic Surg.* **21**:495, 1951.

Conley, J. J.: Use of Vitallium prosthesis and implants in reconstruction of mandibular arch. *Plastic and Reconstructive Surg.* **8**:150, 1951.

Echols, D. H., R. Llewellyn, H. D. Kirgis, R. C. Rehfeldt, and F. Garcia-Bengochea: Tracheotomy in the management of severe head injuries. *Surgery.* **28**:801, 1950.

Erich, J. B.: Management of fractures and soft tissue injuries about the face. *A.M.A. Arch. Otolaryng.* **65**:20, 1957.

Feinmesser, M.: Facial paralysis following fracture of the skull. *Jour. Laryng. and Otolaryng.* **71**:838, 1957.

Fomon, S., J. Bell, A. Schattner, and V. Syracuse: The facial wound problem. *A.M.A. Arch. Otolaryng.* **65**:20, 1957.

Fomon, S., A. Schattner, J. W. Bell, L. Kleinfeld, and R. Lewy: Management of recent nasal fractures. *A.M.A. Arch. Otolaryng.* **55**:321, 1952.

Fordyce, G. L.: Pyriform operature wiring in the treatment of mandibular fractures. *Brit. Jour. Plastic Surg.* **9**:304, 1957.

Freeman, B. S.: Use of Vitallium plates to maintain function following resection of mandible. *Plastic and Reconstructive Surg.* **3**:73, 1948.

Galloway, T. C.: Tracheotomy in bulbar poliomyelitis. *Jour. Amer. Med. Ass.* **123**:1096, 1943.

Gibson, Thomas, and Ian MacD. Allan: A removable wire suture for internal fixation of mandibular fractures. *Brit. Jour. Plastic Surg.* **9**:117, 1956–57.

Gillies, H. D., et al.: Fractures of the malar-zygomatic compound. *Brit. Jour. Surg.* **14**:651, 1927.

Gisselsson, L.: Bilateral fixation of the incudo-stapedial joint. *Jour. Laryng. and Otolaryng.* **72**:329, 1958.

Grove, W. E.: Skull fractures involving the ear: a clinical study of 211 cases. *Laryngoscope.* **49**:678, 1939.

Grove, W. E.: Skull fractures involving the ear: a clinical study of 211 cases. *Laryngoscope.* **49**:833, 1939.

Johnston, K. C., R. J. McMahon, and P. H. Holinger: Broadening indications for tracheotomy in the aged. *Jour. Amer. Geriatrics Soc.* **1**:47, 1953.

Kazanjian, V. H., and J. M. Converse: "The Surgical Treatment of Facial Injuries." Baltimore, Williams & Wilkins, 1949.

Kennedy, R. H.: Management of injuries in the aged. *Bull. N.Y. Acad. Med.* **32**:487, 1956.

Kettel, K.: Peripheral facial paralysis in fractures of the temporal bone. *A.M.A. Arch. Otolaryng.* **51**:25, 1950.

Kettel, K.: Repair of the facial nerve in traumatic facial palsies. *A.M.A. Arch. Otolaryng.* **66**:634, 1957.

Kulowski, J.: Motorist injuries among persons over sixty. *Geriatrics.* **10**:425, 1955.

MacLennan, W. D.: Mandi fracture: review of 180 cases of fracture of the condylar neck. *Brit. Jour. Plastic Surg.* **5**:122, 1952.

Martin, B. C., J. C. Trahue, and T. R. Leech: An analysis of the etiology, treatment and complications of the malar compound and zygomatic arch. *Amer. Jour. Surg.* **92**:920, 1956.

Maxwell, J. H., and J. E. Magielski: The management of facial paralysis associated with fractures of the temporal bone. *Laryngoscope.* **66**:599, 1956.

Naftzger, J. B.: Fractures of the facial bones involving the nasal accessory sinuses. *Ann. Otol. Rhin. and Laryng.* **37**:486, 1928.

Olmstead, E. G.: Fractures of hyoid bone: presentation of two cases with review of literature. *Arch. Otolaryng.* **49**:266, 1946.

Poppel, M. H., and R. O. Christman: Fracture of the hyoid bone. *Amer. Jour. Roent., Rad. and Nuclear Med.* **76**:1144, 1956.

Proctor, D. F.: "Anaesthesia and Otolaryngology." Baltimore, Williams & Wilkins, 1957.

Proctor, B., E. S. Gurdjian, and J. E. Webster: The ear in head trauma. *Laryngoscope.* **66**:16, 1956.

Robinson, D. W.: Management of facial injuries. *Surg. Clin. North Amer.* **36**:1309, 1956.

Rowe, N. L., and H. C. Killey: "Fractures of the Facial Skeleton." London and Edinburgh, E. & S. Livingstone, Ltd., 1955.

Schuknecht, H. F., and R. C. Davidson: Deafness and vertigo from head injury. *A.M.A. Arch. Otolaryng.* **63:**513, 1956.

Schuknecht, H. F., W. D. Neff, and H. B. Perlman: Experimental study of auditory damage following blows to the head. *Ann. Otol. Rhin. and Laryng.* **60:**273, 1951.

Shapiro, R. N., G. R. O'Brien, and C. Wilkie: Treatment of jaw fracture. *A.M.A. Arch. Otolaryng.* **60:**548, 1954.

Shea, J. J.: Management of fractures involving the paranasal sinuses. *Jour. Amer. Med. Ass.* **96:**418, 1931.

Straith, C. L.: Management of facial injuries caused by motor accidents. *Jour. Amer. Med. Ass.* **108:**101, 1937.

Suraci, A. J.: A method of reduction of the zygoma. *Amer. Jour. Surg.* **88:**843, 1954.

Taylor, G. W., and G. M. Austin: Treatment of pulmonary complications in neurosurgical patients by tracheotomy. *A.M.A. Arch. Otolaryng.* **53:**386, 1951.

Thoma, K. H.: Use of pyriform aperture wiring to immobilize mandible when jaw is edentulous: original description. *Amer. Jour. Orthodont.* **29:**433, 1943.

Thoma, K. H.: New methods for immobilization of mandible. *Oral Surgery.* **1:**98, 1948.

Walden, R. H., P. R. Wohlgemuth, and J. H. Fitz-Gibbon: Fractures of the facial bones. *Amer. Jour. Surg.* **92:**915, 1956.

Williams, R. A.: Head injury with fracture of stapes. *Jour. Laryng. and Otolaryng.* **72:**606, 1958.

Work, W. P., and E. G. McCoy: Surgical repair of the cervical trachea following trauma. *Ann. Otol. Rhin. and Laryng.* **65:**573, 1956.

Part V

Rehabilitation of the Aged

Chapter 20

Posttraumatic Rehabilitation

Mieczyslaw Peszczynski

Permanently impaired function may frequently be the aftermath of trauma. The purposes of rehabilitation are to prevent disability, or to minimize its development during the recovery period, and to teach a disabled person to live as independently as possible within the limits of his remaining capabilities.

In dealing with the adjustments to disability in the aged, little or no space will be devoted to those methods of treatment which are also used in the management of the adult disabled. This chapter will be concerned with problems typical of advanced biological age and the complications caused by its commonly superimposed diseases. Many rehabilitation methods used for the aged are based on clinical experience rather than on scientifically established data. The reader is expected to consider the subjects covered in this chapter as only an introduction to the complex and diversified aspects of posttraumatic rehabilitation of the aged.

WHY DO OLD PEOPLE FALL?

Trauma may result from external force or may be a consequence of the individual's diminished ability to cope with his physical surroundings, such as polished floors and scatter rugs, or to maintain his body in an upright position in space.

Falling accidents remain the primary cause of trauma in the older age group. Our understanding of the reasons elderly people fall is inadequate. Many of the abnormal findings in the aged are generally considered to be at the periphery of pathology, and therefore do not commonly find their way into the physician's notes. However, thorough knowledge of the patient's mental, physical, and social status will enable us to improve through therapy some of his daily life activities, as for example walking, grooming, and bathroom needs; may help us to define his limitations more exactly; and will direct our suggestions for manipulation of his physical surroundings by such methods as installing an elevated toilet seat (Fig. 20-1), use of a walker or a cane, supervised ambulation, or, in some cases, wheelchair existence.

Within recent years considerable information about falling accidents in the aged has been collected, screened, and correlated. Sheldon surveyed the subject by interviewing a sample of old people. He concluded that whether we are dealing with complaints of vertigo, difficulty in the dark, or liability to fall, we are probably concerned with different clinical aspects of one underlying condition, that being a decline in the ability to maintain the upright position. He found that in the younger half of

Fig. 20-1. Elevated toilet seat and grab bars.

the older age group attacks of vertigo are more often behind the tendency to fall, while older subjects (beyond 75 years old) are more liable to trip over trivial objects and have difficulty regaining their balance once they start to fall. Complaints of sudden collapse of either the legs or the whole body are also found in this advanced age group. Almost 50 per cent of those interviewed had difficulty in the dark.

Howell recently published the results of his evaluation of the status of the central and peripheral nervous system in 200 healthy pensioners, and suggested that most of the falls of older people are due to damage of proprioception.

The symptomatology and etiology of attacks of dizziness in the aged have been investigated by Orma and Koskenoja who found that about 50 per cent of the complaints of dizziness had their origin in damage to the central nervous system, 18 per cent had an otologic origin, 11 per cent a cardiac origin, and 11 per cent a post-infectious pathology.

Bruell and Peszczynski studied some aspects of visual space perception as related to age and to brain damage. Older people have a diminished ability to evaluate the objective upright within their visual field. The subjective position of the objective upright changes, especially with quick movements of an object on one side of the visual field or when the person suddenly changes the position of his head. The abnormalities in visual space perception are extremely accentuated in hemiplegic patients. Visual stimuli dominate other organs involved in our maintenance of an upright position. Correction of the position of the body to follow the false subjective upright position may produce a fall. Interestingly, people who have fallen and fractured their hips often have abnormally marked disturbances of visual space perception similar to those which only hemiplegic patients experience.

Psychological changes often found in elderly people who have recently suffered trauma not only are probably an expression of their reactive depression, but also can be explained on an organic basis as clinical effects of major or minor cerebrovascular accidents. The fact that many falling accidents are the immediate result of strokes, especially minor strokes, is more commonly accepted today. Peszczynski reviewed 28 cases of fractured hips in hemiplegic patients and found that in five cases the fall and resultant fracture occurred at the same time the patient suffered the cerebrovascular accident. Some of these cases were suspected of originally being minor strokes which developed into full hemiplegia, either on the operating table or during the immediate postoperative period.

In teaching an old person who recently suffered trauma to be up and about again safely, we must remember that all movements involving changes of the position of his head should be done very slowly. The patient should be taught to stand still for a moment after he stands up and before he starts walking. The patient who is inclined to have falls should stand still and wait when another person passes him. When turning, the patient should walk slowly in an imaginary circle instead of pivoting on his heel. These precautions are also valid when such a person enters a doorway at an angle, as when entering a bedroom door from the corridor. It is essential to eliminate the necessity of the patient's reaching for objects on high shelves at home to obviate the dangerous hyperextension of the neck.

An evaluation of the patient's home, either indirectly by an interview or preferably by a direct exploration of the patient's living quarters by a trained paramedical worker, is essential to eliminate hazards which might cause further falling accidents.

COMPREHENSIVE CARE

The prognosis for satisfactory rehabilitation of the aged after trauma is much better than is customarily realized. The key to success is a thorough medical workup which will give a basis for intensive treatment of associated disorders, especially if they influence the patient's locomotor abilities. Many old people have been living a marginal existence, and the addition of trauma or its consequences may produce a breakdown of some previously well compensated pathology. For instance, an osteoarthritic knee which did not bother the patient much before the trauma may, as a result of a few days of imposed bed rest, be painful on ambulation because of the quickly diminished power of the muscles stabilizing this knee. A patient who might have been able to control his urinary functions fairly well may lose this ability posttraumatically, and treatment of his genitourinary tract involvement may be necessary to enable him to overcome the urinary incontinence. It is known from research with primates that experimentally produced hemiparesis which seemed fully recovered clinically may show up again in instances of such unrelated diseases as acute gastrointestinal disorders. A mild anemia, which probably was not a problem before the trauma, may require treatment as an essential factor in enabling the patient to be ambulatory again. The patient's cardiopulmonary system might have been adequate for his daily life needs, but may show signs of decompensation when major stress is placed on it, such as asking the patient to do crutch walking or to perform muscle-power-building exercises.

Although the therapeutic advantages and disadvantages of rest versus movement have been debated as far back as the nineteenth century, we do not even yet have a satisfactory answer to the question. But we are today impressed by the clinical value of early ambulation and/or its substitutes, especially in the aged. Knowledge of the physiology of posttraumatic convalescence is very limited in general, and especially in reference to the aged. Significant osteoporosis has been almost four times as frequent among bedridden aged patients as among ambulatory ones. However, we do not have exact information on how bed rest, different degrees of partial rest, or mobilization biochemically influences the period of recovery. We do know that even young adults have a marked deterioration of the cardiovascular response to posture following prolonged bed rest. We also know that the ability of the aged to maintain an upright posture is basically impaired after being bedfast for several weeks. When asked to stand with the aid of a rail such an individual will often keep leaning backwards. A gentle push forward so that he can stand without the supportive pull on the rail will produce quick movements of the lower extremities to assume the original backward inclined position, which although incorrect seems subjectively "safe" to him.

There is good reason to believe that in some instances being bedfast, with its monotonous sensory environment, may be one of the factors contributing to disorganization of brain function. Sleeplessness, restlessness, emotional liability, and hallucinations have been produced in otherwise healthy young adults as a result of prolonged perceptual isolation.

Prevention of social and psychological deterioration is a basic principle of rehabilitation, and has as strong a priority as the fight with locomotor disuse. The physician makes a direct contribution in these fields by including both eye and ear examinations for many elderly persons.

Only in selected cases can presbycusis be helped with a hearing aid, but often the hard-of-hearing person and his family can profit from instructions in lip reading and other professional help. It is not always realized that after a hard-of-hearing person has been provided with an adequate hearing aid he still needs training and guidance into the new world of sounds.

Remembering that the visual information we receive supersedes any other sensory contact with our surroundings, and remembering further that visual perception deteriorates with age, we realize that an elderly patient's visual problems may not be simply determining the need for glasses or other ophthalmological treatment, but that the average older person, whether in a hospital or at home, needs good illumination, especially at night.

The physician should personally show interest in the patient's performance in the gym. Often additional pathology becomes apparent only by observing the patient when he is out of bed. Signs and symptoms which were not seen or were not suspected during the original medical workup of the patient can then be detected. The author would like to mention here subclinical forms of combined degeneration that are difficult to assess nowadays because of the common practice of multivitamin treatment of the geriatric individual at home. Initial stages of progressive muscular atrophy or polymyositis sometimes come to our attention only after we notice a locomotor performance different from the one we would, from our experience with elderly people, expect to see. Regrettably, sometimes a peroneal palsy is noticed only after the plaster cast has been removed.

There is much misunderstanding concerning the concept of the elderly patient's motivation and cooperation. In dealing with the geriatric patient we are inclined to use these terms to cover our own lack of experience in handling this type of patient. Once we learn to see and define better the patient's disease or disability problems and once we become more interested in the rational methodology of some facets of physical treatment, most of our complaints of the patient's lack of motivation disappear. With the exception of the unconscious, the semiconscious, or the evidently psychotic, the average old person will be fairly well motivated if we are able to convince him through time and especially through demonstrable results from treatment that our aims in physical medicine are realistic as well as acceptable to him. Psychologists claim that the unitary concept of motivation prevailing today is not very helpful in explaining the patient's behavioral patterns, some of which operate to facilitate the rehabilitation process while others impede it.

For all practical purposes we should not forget that rational graduation of exercises, simplicity of instruction, concentration on one aspect of the treatment program at a time, everyday practicality, and *the presentation of immediate goals for "tomorrow" and not those for the more distant future* are all basic principles in treating the geriatric patient.

Early Management

Sometimes it is difficult to ascertain during the first few weeks following trauma the degree to which the general deterioration the patient has suffered will influence his candidacy for rehabilitation. In many instances a few weeks of patience and trial of exercises are indicated. Many deeply confused patients clear satisfactorily after infection, dehydration, and malnutrition have been successfully treated. Some elderly arteriosclerotic patients show signs of transitional confusion resulting from their transfer from familiar surroundings to the new physical atmosphere of a hospital with its constantly changing personnel. Bowel incontinence continuing for more than 3 to 4 weeks is in most instances a sign of poor prognosis. However, urinary incontinence should be viewed more optimistically, because it is sometimes iatrogenic as a result of failure to remove the indwelling catheter early enough or it may be a consequence of an inadequately trained and/or limited nursing staff.

Today rehabilitation nursing is a widely accepted extension of conventional nursing practices. It deals with attitudes and techniques essential for the management of patients with long-term diseases or disabilities. The nursing staff's active cooperation with physical, occupational, speech, and hearing therapy creates on the ward an atmosphere which encourages the patient to take over, as the progress of posttraumatic recovery permits, such self-care as dressing, grooming, and toilet activities. Today the nurse should be well acquainted with the techniques for assisting a patient in safe transfer from bed to chair (Fig. 20-2), especially if he suffered trauma to a leg and is not allowed to bear weight on it. She gradually increases the patient's wheelchair-sitting tolerance, and she will organize supervision of the patient's ambulation with crutches, cane, or a walker

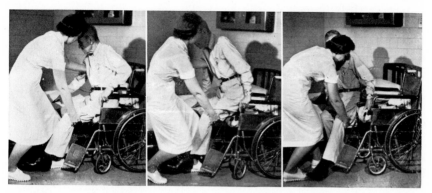

FIG. 20-2. Learning transfer techniques. Patient with healing fracture of left hip.

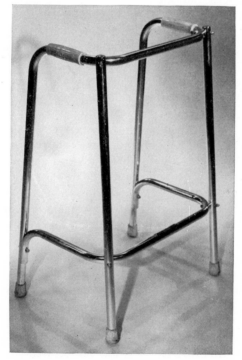

FIG. 20-3. Type of "walker."

(Fig. 20-3) on the ward when he has progressed to the point at which this can be carried through on the ward. The nurse will be aware of the patient's progress in speech and hearing therapy, and she will know what is expected from the patient in all of these areas. When nursing care no longer requires that the patient be in a high bed, the nurse will have the patient moved from the high bed to a low, more homelike bed.

The nurse's observation of the patient's behavior on the ward is valuable to social service and the family in making plans for him after his discharge from the hospital.

Much of the experience in the area of bowel and bladder training gained from spinal cord injured patients can be applied to the geriatric patient. An incontinent patient, particularly if an indwelling catheter has been kept in place for several weeks or months postoperatively, will in most instances have a small bladder with resultant frequency of urination. If the patient has recovered generally to a stage where a trial at bladder training is indicated, the bladder is gradually distended by clamping the catheter for very slowly increased periods of time. A bladder capacity of $2\frac{1}{2}$ to 3 hours can be attained within 10 to 30 days. In a very cooperative patient, a bladder training program is sometimes successful if the catheter is removed immediately and if bathroom facilities or a bedpan are secured at half-hour periods in the beginning with a gradual increase to 3 hours. Such a bladder training program requires a good deal of time from the nursing staff, but it definitely pays off in the long run. Contrary to the routine of bladder training for spinal cord injury patients, the geriatric patient should not have limited fluid intake during the evening and at night. Finally, it is only too obvious that a patient who has a bladder infection is not a candidate for bladder training.

The prevention of contractures and pressure sores has high priority during the early postaccident and postsurgery management. More nursing personnel should learn and use the techniques for turning a patient over in bed with a draw sheet to prevent sheet burns.

In discussing rehabilitation of the aged after trauma, we are especially concerned with pressure sores at the heel and external malleolus because they are one of the main reasons knee flexion contractures develop. The three main types of patients who develop pressure sores at the heel are (1) the decrepit or semiconscious individual in whom the sores were not anticipated and not prevented, (2) the conscientious patient with a fracture of the femur who after surgery was not assured that he is allowed or shown how to move his leg actively while in bed, and (3) the patient with flexor spasticity in the lower extremities where often even the best care cannot prevent pressure sores because of the heel rubbing on the sheet. In the last instance, an extensive motor denervation procedure to the lower extremity, such as an anterior rhizotomy, must occasionally be considered. Sometimes this is done only to permit satisfactory nursing care.

Pressure sores at the heel usually do not markedly involve the weight-bearing surface of the foot and, like pressure sores at the outer malleolus, should not be considered a contraindication to ambulation. On the contrary, many such sores heal best if the patient is allowed to walk as much as possible. When the patient is not ambulating, the leg is kept elevated.

Physical and occupational therapy after trauma should be individually prescribed in detail, but some basic outlines of minimal care can be mentioned here.

The semiconscious, confused, or paralyzed patient needs range-of-motion exercises to the main joints of the uninvolved extremities twice daily. In most instances these can be done during normal nursing care by properly trained nursing personnel, but sometimes they should be performed by physical therapists. It is imperative to evaluate the degree to which the involved extremities should be included in range-of-motion exercises. For example, a patient who recently had plastic surgery repair of a sacral decubitus should not have flexion movements of the hips if they produce undesirable tension on the site of the graft. However, the same patient can have knee-flexion and calf-muscle-stretching exercises while in a prone position.

A conscious, bedfast patient, such as one in a hip spica, should have power-building exercises for the other three extremities and, if possible, muscle-setting exercises for the quadriceps of the encased extremity. Power-building exercises for the flexors and extensors of the toes of the encased extremity should not be neglected. The value and purpose of muscle-setting exercises are presently being theoretically reappraised in the light of recent advances in muscle physiology. However, until well-founded applications of the new information are available, muscle-setting exercises should be continued in the traditional manner. The patient is instructed to perform isometric contractions of the particular muscle groups several times every 15 or 20 minutes.

CONTRACTURES: PREVENTION AND MANAGEMENT

The fact that our knowledge of the etiology of contractures is extremely poor is not sufficiently appreciated. Perhaps recent advances in the field of neuromuscular functioning, such as new information about the role of the small-fiber motor system, will be steppingstones toward a better understanding of contracture. A long time ago Frölich and Meyer demonstrated that the production of some contractures in the extremities of healthy animals following encasement in plaster casts was dependent upon intact innervation to that extremity. The reason for the frequent development of contractures in advanced age is probably less likely to be found in studies of the fibrous tissue than through a better understanding of senile changes in the nervous system. The contribution of the nervous system, especially the motor reaction to pain in the production of contractures, may be second only to the influence of positioning (gravity).

Pain from a pressure sore at the heel or a very small skin lesion at the external malleolus may produce marked flexor spasm and gradually a fibrous contracture of the lower extremity, probably because of the dominance of very active withdrawal reflexes. A painful shoulder resulting from trauma to that area may, in an old person, develop within a few days into a frozen shoulder as a result of the so-called "protective spasm."

Because of their very disturbing influence on the eventual result of treatment of trauma in the aged, the most common contractures will be discussed in some detail.

The hip-flexion contracture is the most frequent limitation on the range of motion of joints in the aged, but it is the one least often exposed during the physical examination. In addition to the etiological factor of pressure sores at the heel and/or external malleolus mentioned above, contractures of the hip and the knee will be found often in patients with peripheral circulatory insufficiency, especially if this insufficiency is accompanied by pain. In instances where there exists otherwise justifiable hesitation in the choice between conservative treatment and amputation, and the patient is a good candidate for training with an artificial limb, these contractures may best be prevented by a very early above-knee or below-knee amputation. Contractures which will make successful use of an artificial limb impossible may be the price paid for prolonged conservative treatment.

There is no doubt that gravity, through improper positioning, has an enormous influence upon the production of hip- and knee-flexion contractures. Some examples are excessive sitting in a chair or wheelchair without the compensation of frequent ambulation, pillows placed under the patient's knee to make him comfortable, and often footboards used to prevent a plantar-flexion contracture of the foot but instead inducing forced knee flexion in a patient who has a tendency to slide down in bed. If at all possible, such patients should lie flat in bed with a very small pillow under their heads.

Mild hip-flexion contractures are compatible with ambulation, but such a gait is clumsy and the patient becomes exhausted easily. A permanent knee-flexion contracture may be an unsurmountable obstacle to the aged patient's learning to walk again.

If flexion contractures in the lower extremities are caught in the early stage of formation, very active countermeasures should be instituted. Mild stretching should be done very carefully several times daily, preceded by the application of heat. Soft-tissue injury inflicted during too forceful stretching may only aggravate the reflexes responsible for flexor spasms. The nursing staff should be alerted to position the patient's lower extremity in straight alignment as often as possible while he is in bed.

Assisted ambulation, if at all possible, is the best treatment of flexion contractures at this stage. A temporary knee cage may be helpful. If the patient can tolerate it, he should be walked for a few minutes every 15 or 20 minutes during half or the whole working day. To walk such a patient once or twice daily for 15 minutes at a time is in most instances useless. It is also preferable that such a patient spend his time either lying or walking. Sitting in a chair or wheelchair should be avoided as much as possible.

Power-building exercises for the extensors of the knee and hip can be considered. Lying prone twice daily for half an hour to treat hip- and knee-flexion contractures *in statu nascendi* by the action of gravity is more possible in the aged than is realized. The key to success is not to expect too much at once, to place the patient comfortably on pillows so that the action of gravity stretches only a small part of the contractures at one time, and not to try at the same time to fight any degree of flexion fixation of the patient's spine. If such conservative treatment, especially ambulation, is not feasible for medical reasons, then surgical traction may have to be applied. An elderly patient whose knee-flexion contracture has progressed to the stage where a long leg brace must be considered is probably a very poor candidate for independent ambulation. However, he might still do well with a walker or crutches.

Knee-extension contractures are fairly common after long treatment in a hip spica, and the most widely accepted practice is to rely on the results of active knee-flexion exercises with the addition of gravity as a "passive" force on the lower extremity. The patient is asked to sit with his leg hanging over the edge of the bed and to let the weight of his lower leg gradually bend the knee. Occasionally a supracondylar fracture of the femur or a fracture of the distal part of the shaft of the femur may heal with adhesions of the quadriceps to the fracture site. In almost all such instances the passive range of motion of the knee is greater than it is when the knee is in active motion. Management depends upon the degree of lateral instability of the knee.

Because frequent ambulation is the best prevention and treatment for all mild and recent contractures of the lower extremities, everything possible should be done at the time of surgical intervention to enable the patient to engage in weight bearing at the earliest possible postoperative time.

The prevention and treatment of the most common contractures of the upper extremity will be best demonstrated by discussing two fractures typically found in the aged.

In most instances of impacted fractures of the surgical neck of the humerus in old people, the surgeon is less concerned with an ideal alignment of the fracture fragments than he is about eventually achieving a functional range of motion of the shoulder joint. During the first few days, the upper extremity is protected with a suspension sling or occasionally it is even bound to the thorax. A mild analgesic is given as required. During daily exercises at that early period, the physician removes the sling and manually supports the upper extremity as he assists the patient in performing a limited range of motion of the shoulder. This exercise is preceded by measures designed to control the patient's pain on movement, such as spraying (but not freezing) the skin over the fracture site with ethyl chloride. The purpose of this practice is to eliminate gradually the pain on movement and to encourage the patient by demonstrating to him that controlled movement of the shoulder joint is feasible and desirable. After 10 to 14 days, the protective suspension sling can in most cases be removed and the patient may be encouraged to move the upper extremity within the already gained range of motion as often as possible. Once daily, the physical therapist or trained nurse gives mild assistance while the patient gradually increases the active range of motion of his shoulder joint. In another few days the patient is permitted to use the upper extremity for the routine activities of daily life except those where power or extremes of motion are necessary. Six weeks after the original trauma, mildly graduated power-building exercises to the arm abductors are added. At that time, for instance, the patient may be allowed to use the upper extremity for crutch walking if multiple injuries demand it, but will not yet be allowed to do push-ups.

A rather common although unintentional extension contracture of the metacarpophalangeal joints is caused by improper application of a plaster cast to treat the Colles' fracture which so frequently occurs in the aged. Often the cast is too long on the palmar side. The correct application of such a cast will allow the patient to close his fist fully. While wearing the cast the patient should be not only advised but also trained to resume his previous activities to a great extent. He is not only taught to use his hand but he is also instructed to use the entire upper extremity. Such patients are inclined to "baby" their fracture by holding the cast close to the trunk, and they thereby fail to perform the very essential full range of motion of the shoulder several times daily. In the aged, it is rather unrewarding to treat frozen shoulders and extension contractures of the fingers after the cast has been removed.

Wheelchairs and Braces

Any department dealing with a large number of geriatric posttraumatic patients should have its own stock of various up-to-date wheelchairs. Whether the patient needs a wheelchair only temporarily while awaiting the final results of posttraumatic recovery or whether he will need one permanently, the physician should prescribe the type of wheelchair to be used. The selection of a wheelchair cannot be left to the discretion of a salesman. In many instances the choice of a wheelchair is determined not only by our knowledge of the patient's abilities and limitations but also by a supervised trial of the particular type of wheelchair.

A wheelchair should be safe for the patient, should provide him with optimum comfort, and should allow him maximum independence in the activities of daily living. Brakes are recommended on all wheelchairs. They must be locked whenever the patient does any assisted or unassisted transfer activities. The universal model, with the large wheels in the rear, is preferable in most cases, because a wheelchair with the large wheels in front would obstruct transfer from bed and toilet seat to wheelchair. Eight-inch casters are preferred routinely because of their maneuverability. The size of the wheelchair (adult, junior, or heavy duty) should be suitable to the patient and to the width of the doorways in his home. If the patient wears braces, seat measurements should be taken with the braces on. Detachable arms, suspension slings, solid back inserts, and swinging, detachable, elevating leg-rests may be prescribed in some instances. Three- to six-inch foam rubber cushions are often indicated.

A heavy elderly paraplegic may not be able to do adequate push-ups and may need a "quadriplegic" wheelchair with a fully reclining back in which he can obtain the needed relief from pressure on the ischial tuberosities by being fully reclined in the wheelchair for half-hour periods several times daily. The site of pressure is changed when the patient reclines in the chair, and thus several daily transfers from wheelchair to bed are avoided. However, we must also make sure that the rooms in the patient's home are wide enough to allow the propelling and turning of a quadriplegic wheelchair.

The amputee, particularly if he does not use a prosthesis (as so often happens in the aged), needs a special wheelchair with the axle set two and one-half inches farther back than it is on the standard wheelchair to compensate for the lost weight, particularly in the case of bilateral lower extremity amputation (Fig. 20-4). The danger of the wheelchair tipping over is thus eliminated. In the case of a unilateral amputee where the possibility of amputation of the remaining limb exists, a wheelchair with a swinging, detachable, elevating leg-rest should be prescribed.

Although one-arm-drive wheelchairs may seem perfect for hemiplegic patients or patients with one functionless upper extremity, we do not generally recommend them because they are expensive and their greater over-all width makes them unsuitable for many doorways, but primarily because mildly confused patients do not learn to handle them. Most hemiplegic patients manage a standard wheelchair quite well, using their good hand and leg to propel and guide the chair.

A few remarks concerning bracing of the geriatric patient are in order.

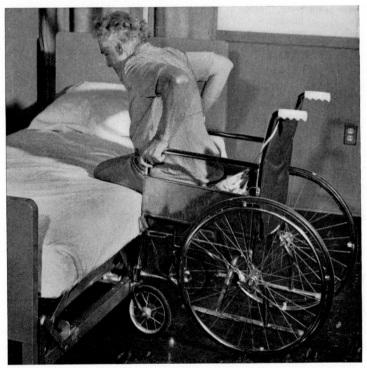

Fig. 20-4. Transfer technique. Bilateral above-knee amputee transfers from amputee wheelchair to low bed.

Upper-extremity bracing for the permanently disabled is presently going through a period of promising research and improved application. The geriatric patient is probably the least suitable candidate for upper-extremity bracing, though feeders or suspension slings may occasionally be used.

Trunk bracing is sometimes prescribed for traumatic or pathological fractures of the spine. Patients with the very common geriatric disorder of osteoporosis of the lumbar spine may have increased complaints following a fall or other trauma. In addition to medical treatment, such patients profit from a well-fitted corset with semirigid stays. Unfortunately an elderly person whose abdomen protrudes anteriorly and laterally, partly because of the shortening and flexion of the lumbar spine, often cannot be fitted to his complete satisfaction (see Chap. 7).

Some physicians almost routinely provide a fractured-hip patient with an ischial weight-bearing caliper. Elderly people do not do well with such braces and in the majority of instances they really are not needed. Weight bearing through the fractured femur will be eliminated satisfactorily only if there is adequate space between the sole of the patient's heel and the insole of his shoe to compensate on actual weight bearing for the "give" of the soft tissues near the ischial weight-bearing ring. Such an ideally fitted ischial weight-bearing caliper usually is not tolerated by old people, and compromises will defeat their purpose. The reader will have noted that such braces were not even suggested by Lippmann in Chap. 8, on the treatment of hip fractures.

In prescribing long leg braces we should keep in mind that the average geriatric patient does not do well with them. On the other hand, it is not realized often enough that in many instances what is really needed is the lateral stability given by the long leg brace, and that the patient should be allowed to walk with the knee lock of the long leg brace unlocked. Such is the case during some stages of severe disability due to osteoarthritis of the knee.

The Amputee

There is no doubt that many more aged amputees should be provided with artificial limbs than is customary in present day practice. However, we should be careful not to show an unjustifiable optimism which in the long run may be as harmful as the traditional neglect. In selecting above-knee amputees to use a prosthesis we must consider the following:

1. The status of the circulation in the other leg. It is a common occurrence for elderly lower-extremity amputees to lose their other leg within 6 to 12 months following the provision of an artificial limb. It can be assumed that this occurs because both lower extremities initially had poor peripheral circulation, and the original trauma was probably only the last straw decompensating one of the limbs. That the added strain of gait training with a prosthesis might contribute to the eventual loss of the remaining leg cannot be easily disregarded. Bilateral amputees in this age group seldom learn to use artificial limbs.

2. The degree of hip-flexion contracture on the side of the amputation. The range of the extension of the hip is measured by having the patient bend his other leg until his knee is close to his chest. In this way the movements of the lumbar spine are eliminated and the degree of limitation of extension at the hip on the amputated side can be measured. If there is a mild hip-flexion contracture of 10 to 20°, we can forecast

that even though the patient is provided with a prosthesis he will always have to use crutches or, in exceptional patients whose upper extremities are very strong, two canes. The fact that elderly above-knee amputees who are provided with and successfully taught to use prostheses often have to use crutches permanently is less known and anticipated than it should be.

3. The patient's general locomotor performance. The patient should be able to do a swing-through type of crutch walking comparatively easily and without assistance within 3 weeks from the beginning of crutch training. He must be able to swing both crutches simultaneously while bearing his weight on the remaining leg, and he should also be able to climb stairs unassisted.

An amputee who fails in these tests or shows borderline results may, after a very prolonged period of gait training, master ambulation with an artificial limb, but he will not generally use his prosthesis for normal activities outside the gym area.

Following World War II, extensive research on gait training and the structure of artificial limbs has been done almost exclusively on young adults. We do not know much about the ideal prosthesis for an aged amputee. Clinical experience has taught us to provide him with a more stable knee which will not collapse easily under weight bearing. An example is the recent acceptance of the Boch type of knee joint for elderly patients' prostheses. However, the older concept of putting the foot of the artificial limb in slight plantar flexion and making dorsiflexion more difficult in order to give knee stability on the artificial limb is still used.

The common mild hip-flexion contracture sometimes is corrected by aligning the artificial thigh with the plumb line from the patient's center of gravity. Then the socket within the artificial thigh is made at an angle to the longitudinal axis of the prosthesis. Such an arrangement may enable the patient to walk more easily, but may also result in more skin problems on the stump because of rubbing on areas of the skin that were not meant to sustain much weight. In heroic cases the problem of the hip-flexion contracture may be solved by reversing the foot on the prosthesis so that the toes fall within the weight-bearing plumb line of the patient.

There has been a great deal of discussion about the advisability of using pylons with the elderly amputee, either during the training period or permanently. This type of patient, especially if his locomotor performance is of the borderline level, will probably do better using the less expensive and more stable pylon during the trial period. The results of gait training in this age group are not ideal at best, so that the disadvantages of training someone to walk with a pylon should not be too important. The author does not favor using pylons with young adults except during the very early part of ambulation training when the patient is only balancing and not actually walking.

A patient who is to use an above-knee prosthesis must receive the conventional preliminary stump care, including power-building exercises designed especially for the hip adductors and extensors. Gait-training routines take several months for the geriatric patient, and in most instances must be done on an inpatient basis to be successful. The fact that some physicians still refer patients to a limb maker for gait training is deplorable.

The majority of elderly below-knee amputees can easily learn to use a prosthesis provided they do not have a knee-flexion contracture.

The author has had a great deal of personal experience in teaching elderly bilateral above-knee amputees to walk with short stubbies (Fig. 20-5). His feeling is that although these patients are eventually able to ambulate around the house, they are not really better off than they would be if they had been provided with a proper wheelchair immediately and ambulation training with stubbies had never been started. The double above-knee amputee needs intensive power-building exercises for the

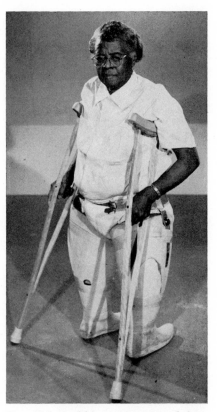

FIG. 20-5. Stubbies with reversed feet.

upper extremities so that he can be fully independent in transferring from his bed to his wheelchair and especially from his wheelchair to the toilet seat. Ideally, the patient's home should be all on one floor; and if the patient is agile enough to use one, a ramp may be constructed at the entrance nearest ground level. An appropriately experienced member of the staff should visit the patient's home in order to evaluate it and to suggest inexpensive but practical changes within it, especially if the double above-the-knee amputee is the main homemaker in the family. Some such changes are elevating the toilet seat to equal the height of the seat of the wheelchair, stabilizing the patient's bed by applying rubber suction cups under each of the four legs, rearranging the kitchen to facilitate work from the level of the wheelchair, and wherever feasible establishing light switches and electrical outlets within the reach of the wheelchair-bound patient.

The Fractured-hip Patient

Many of the problems encountered in rehabilitating the aged after trauma can best be discussed by following a fractured-hip patient through his management, particularly his gait training.

In those instances where a solid internal fixation device has been used the patient should be encouraged to move his involved lower extremity while in bed the day after the operation. Sometimes the physician has

to support the lower extremity manually, gently assisting the patient in flexing and extending his hip during the postoperative period. Passive flexion and extension of the hip should be avoided. Other movements of the hip such as abduction and rotation can be omitted in most instances. Occasionally the patient may be very cooperative about trying to move his involved leg but is not able to overcome the resistance of the bedcovers. His movement in bed should be made easier by inserting a cradle or by dressing the patient so that he may lie on top of the bedcovers. At an early time the patient is allowed to sit in a wheelchair for short periods (see Chap. 8). He is taught to assist himself in his transfer from the high bed to the wheelchair without putting weight on the involved leg.

Exercises which must precede crutch walking are introduced within 1 or 2 more days, and are graduated as the case permits. Push-ups are the easiest and best power-building exercises for the upper extremities. They are essential if the patient is to be able eventually to transfer independently, and will be needed for proper control of the crutches when he is walking. Within a week or two after the operation, the patient starts standing-up exercises between the parallel bars with limited or no weight bearing on the involved lower extremity.

Fig. 20-6. Limited weight bearing on right lower extremity.

When using the phrase "limited weight bearing," we mean that the patient is allowed to tiptoe on the involved leg while his weight is supported by the arms and shoulder depressors and the uninvolved leg. Touching the tip of the toe on the floor allows the patient to balance more easily, which is particularly essential in the aged (Fig. 20-6). It must be emphasized that there is very careful graduation of the phases eventually leading to crutch walking with limited weight bearing. Crutch training progresses from assisted and later independent standing up to walking training between the parallel bars. Later a three-point crutch gait with limited weight bearing on the involved leg is begun. The full cooperation of the patient in so far as exact limitation of weight bearing is concerned is most important, particularly in cases of (1) a markedly comminuted intertrochanteric fracture, (2) those fractures of the neck of the femur that allow shearing of the proximal fragment on the distal fragment of the fractured bone under weight bearing, (3) a high subcapitular fracture, and (4) a subtrochanteric fracture. If true limited weight bearing cannot be expected from patients with the above types of fractures, they are trained to stand up and to walk between the parallel bars with no weight bearing on the involved leg until the time when healing at the fracture site permits adequate weight bearing and therefore crutch walking outside the parallel bars.

In many instances the patient needs the help of two people to stand up between the parallel bars. If such help is required longer than a few days, a program of progressive standing-up exercises is used (Fig. 20-7). The patient begins these exercises by sitting in a chair with a special high seat or on pillows so that the knee of the uninvolved leg is almost straight. At first he may be assisted in pulling himself up at a rail in front of him, and later the assistance may be limited to the assurance of proper balance and safety. Support is placed in front of the patient's foot to prevent its slipping forward on the floor when the patient stands up. As the standing-up training progresses, the knee is gradually more flexed at the starting position by lowering the height of the seat and by moving the chair closer to the rail. At the end of this program the patient is expected to be able to stand up from a chair of normal height.

The above program automatically gives power-building exercises to all antigravity muscles and adjusts the patient's cardiovascular and neuromuscular systems to the upright position. In selected cases where graduated standing-up exercises are contraindicated, power-building exercises to the quadriceps of the uninvolved lower extremity are necessary. The tilt-table routine may be used to adjust passively the patient's postural reflexes and his cardiovascular system to an upright position. This is accomplished by gradually increasing the angle of tilt and by building up his endurance during the process.

We may start training a patient to do a three-point gait with limited or no weight bearing on the involved lower extremity between the

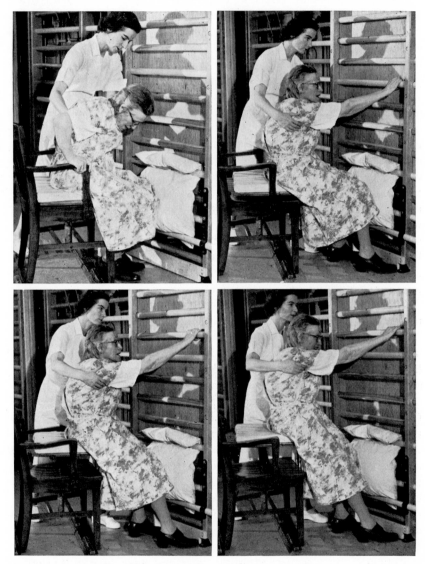

Fig. 20-7. Progressive standing-up exercises.

parallel bars even before he has learned to stand up unassisted. Walking is usually easier than standing up. Often the transition from walking between the parallel bars to walking with crutches is uncomplicated. If the patient is fearful, he can practice using crutches by leaning back against a wall, putting weight forward on the crutches, and then returning to the wall for safety and support the moment he wishes.

Conventional wooden crutches are preferred for elderly patients. Some metal crutches, especially the Lofstrand ones, may be somewhat confusing to the older patient. In general the crutches should be shorter than would be required for a young adult of the same height. It is customary to put wide suction cups on the tips of the crutches.

Contrary to the basic principle that a person bears all his weight on the handrests of the crutches, old people should be allowed to bear part of their weight through the axilla on the armrests. These are padded with foam rubber cushions and if the patient has been graduated through preliminary power-building exercises for the upper extremities weight bearing should present no difficulty. If introductory training has been adequate, crutch paralysis should not develop.

Old people generally use a modified three-point crutch gait in which they do not move both crutches forward simultaneously while bearing weight on their uninvolved leg. They feel safer in advancing each crutch separately. Some patients automatically stop after every second step to regain their balance and then continue walking. All these variations of the classical three-point crutch gait are justified for old people and should not be opposed.

The above described program of teaching an elderly person with a fractured hip to walk with crutches is based on the concept that early, limited weight bearing is feasible and safe in most instances. Full weight bearing should not be allowed until a very late date (see Chap. 8). Some elderly patients use crutches, or at least a cane, permanently after fracture of the hip.

If a patient graduates to walking with canes, they should be thick wooden ones and the handle should be especially thick and comfortable. We can assure this by padding the handle. The patient can get the most strength from his grip on a thick handle. The weight and thickness of the cane are important in enabling the patient to obtain enough information about his relationship to the floor when the proprioception of his lower extremities is diminished. Theoretically, one cane is used in the hand opposite of the fractured hip if its main purpose is to assist in balancing. It may be used in the hand on the same side as the fractured hip if its main purpose is support for weight bearing. It is the duty of the physical therapist and the supervising physician to give the patient several trials to decide in which hand the single cane should be carried.

A large percentage of geriatric patients do not progress in ambulation satisfactorily or at all if training is limited to 1 or 2 half-hour periods daily. They should be given an opportunity to participate in a "total push program," in which they stay in the gym for a half or a full day and at approximately 15-minute intervals are ambulated for 2 or 3 minutes.

Many fractured-hip patients never learn to walk with crutches. But they should be given ample opportunity to learn to walk with a walker, either with or without assistance. When ambulation by any means is not feasible, an appropriate wheelchair should be selected so that the patient will have a comfortable wheelchair existence.

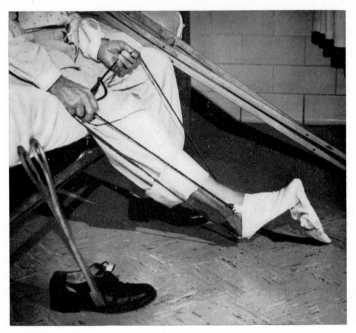

Fig. 20-8. Adapted devices to enable a patient with extension contractures of hip and knee to dress himself independently.

Some elderly people have adequate range of motion of the fractured hip after healing and do not need to learn special techniques for putting on shoes and stockings. If limitation of the range of motion of the fractured hip is present after healing, he is trained to use "gadgets" such as long handled shoe horns for putting on his shoes, elastic shoe laces to eliminate bending down to tie his shoes, and one of the simpler methods for pulling up stockings (Fig. 20-8).

If limitation of motion at the hip makes sitting in a conventional armchair uncomfortable, the patient may use the type of cushion employed successfully by many patients with a fused hip (Fig. 20-9). Frequently old people, particularly after a fracture of the hip, need an elevated toilet seat and a grab bar at home so that they can go to the bathroom without assistance. Hospitalization should not be considered completed in the case of the average patient until he has learned to climb stairs with crutches.

Occasionally an intertrochanteric fracture heals in a position of coxa vara severe enough to impede walking without crutches. If such a person refuses a corrective osteotomy, experience has shown that he can still be

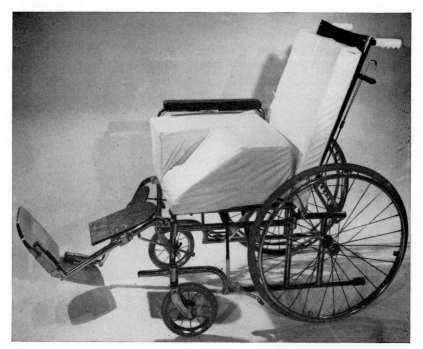

Fig. 20-9. Special cushion shaped for a fused left hip or for a hip with limited range of motion.

helped by providing him with a shoe lift overcompensating by 1 or 1½ inches the apparent shortening of the involved leg. Then with his pelvis higher on the involved side, some bending of his trunk towards the involved side, and holding a cane in the opposite hand, he usually is able to learn to walk adequately.

Many patients with ununited fractures of the hip who are not or cannot be helped operatively can learn to walk with the intermittent double-step gait. They must be willing to accept some pain at the side of the ununited fracture during the initial 2 weeks of ambulation between the parallel bars. The shaft of the femur telescopes up and down between the stance and swing phases of the gait. Usually these patients tolerate the early pain, and during the 2-week period the pain becomes only discomfort. The intermittent double step occurs because the patient tends to lose his balance while bearing weight on the involved limb and stops to regain his balance after the opposite heel strikes. After a few weeks, many of these patients learn to walk with this gait fairly comfortably using crutches or a walker. The more agile patients graduate to a cane held in the opposite hand.

The severely involved hemiplegic patient with a fractured hip, having a functionless upper extremity, cannot perform limited weight-bearing ambulation. Consequently, for 4 to 6 months, he is restrained to standing-up exercises with no weight bearing on the involved leg but with pendulum swinging or whatever other active motor function is available in the hemiplegic lower extremity. It would be exceptional to find a patient and a family that could carry out this program at home. Such patients should be hospitalized until weight bearing and proper walking are achieved.

SOCIAL REHABILITATION

Anyone working with the disabled geriatric patient is impressed by the quick deterioration of family and other social bonds during periods of prolonged hospitalization. Such a patient is by far better off in his home and in his family circle. The patient's family should be encouraged to keep themselves informed as to his progress in rehabilitation and to visit the patient frequently during physical and occupational therapy. They can then become acquainted with the simple techniques which assist the patient in the activities of daily living. The family that might have a tendency to be overprotective can be guided so that their attitude will not hamper our efforts to make the disabled person as independent as possible.

Week-end home visits are most helpful whenever they are feasible. From them the rehabilitation personnel can learn whether there are any aspects of the training for independence in which they failed and how to correct them. The family also has an opportunity to learn through experience that the older person may not be the burden they expected. Trial discharges are encouraged, with every reasonable assistance given to make home care by the family possible. Occasionally short follow-up training at home in the form of physical or occupational therapy is indicated. For instance, a senile person may have done very well in stair climbing in the hospital gym but will fail at home unless he is actually trained in using the particular home staircase. Whether the old person will be accepted back into the home will be determined to some extent by the degree to which we are able to bring some elements of the home into the hospital.

BIBLIOGRAPHY

Blashy, M. R. C., and H. V. Morelewicz: Lower extremity prostheses for patients past fifty. *Arch. Phys. Med. Rehab.* **39**:497, 1958.

Blount, W. P.: Don't throw away the cane. *Jour. Bone and Joint Surg.* **38A**:695, 1956.

Brocklehurst, J. C.: "Incontinence in Old People." Baltimore, Williams & Wilkins, 1951.

Bruell, J. H., and M. Peszczynski: Perception of verticality in hemiplegic patients in relation to rehabilitation. *Clin. Orth.* **12**:124, 1958.

Deaver, G. G., and A. L. Brittis: Braces, crutches, wheelchairs. Rehabilitation Monograph V, New York, Institute of Physical Medicine and Rehabilitation New York University–Bellevue Medical Center, 1953.

Gitman, L., T. Kamholz, and J. Levine: Osteoporosis in the aged. *Jour. Geront.* **13**:43, 1958.

Heron, W., B. K. Doane, and T. Scott: Visual disturbances after prolonged perceptual isolation. *Canad. Jour. Psychol.* **10**:13, 1956.

Howell, T. H.: The causes of falls in the aged. *Jour. Amer. Ger. Soc.* **6**:522, 1958.

Kaplan, O. J.: "Mental Disorders in Later Life," 2d ed. Stanford, Calif., Stanford University Press, 1956.

Orma, E. J., and M. Koskenoja: Dizziness attacks and continuous dizziness in the aged. *Geriatrics.* **12**:92, 1957.

Peszczynski, M.: Rehabilitation of the elderly patient with a pinned fracture of the hip. *Jour. Chron. Dis.* **2**:311, 1956.

Peszczynski, M.: The fractured hip in hemiplegic patients. *Geriatrics.* **12**:417, 1957.

Peszczynski, M.: Use and abuse of rest in physical medicine and rehabilitation. *Postgrad. Med.* **21**:626, 1957.

Peszczynski, M.: Contractures of the involved extremities of the hemiplegic adult. *Jour. Geront.* **13**:177, 1958.

Peszczynski, M.: The intermittent double step gait. *Arch. Phys. Med. Rehab.* **39**:494, 1958.

Peszczynski, M.: Exercises for Hemiplegia, in S. Licht, "Therapeutic Exercise," vol. III of Physical Medicine Library, New Haven, Elizabeth Licht, 1958.

Peszczynski, M., and B. H. Fowles: "Home Evaluations." Cleveland, Highland View Hospital Publication, 1957.

Sheldon, J. H.: "The Social Medicine of Old Age." London, Oxford University Press, 1948.

Shontz, F. C.: Concept of motivation in physical medicine. *Arch. Phys. Med. Rehab.* **38**:635, 1957.

Taylor, L. H.: The Physiological Effects of Bedrest and Immobilization, in F. H. Krusen, "Physical Medicine and Rehabilitation for the Clinician." Philadelphia, Saunders, 1951.

Index